Project Management for Engineering, Business and Technology

There is an ever-growing need for better project management within the disciplines of engineering, business, and technology and this new edition is a direct response to that need. By emphasizing practical applications, this book targets the ultimate purpose of project management: to unify and integrate the interests, resources, and work efforts of many stakeholders to accomplish the overall project goal.

The book encompasses the essential background material required, from philosophy to methodology, before presenting concepts and techniques for practical application on topics including:

- Project initiation and proposals
- Scope and task definition
- Scheduling
- Budgeting
- Risk analysis

The new edition has been updated to provide closer alignment with PMBOK terms and definitions for more ease of use alongside PMI qualifications and covers the latest developments in project management methodologies.

Supplemented by brand new case studies from engineering and technology projects, as well as improved instructor support materials, this text is an ideal resource and reference for anyone studying or practicing project management within business or engineering environments.

John M. Nicholas is Professor of Operations and Project Management and former Associate Dean of the Graduate School of Business at Loyola University, Chicago, USA. He is an active teacher, writer, and researcher in project management and manufacturing management, conducting executive seminars and consults on project management and process improvement. He has authored numerous academic and technical publications and led or worked on projects for companies such as Lockheed-Martin Corporation, Bank America, and Argonne National Laboratory.

Herman Steyn is Professor at the Graduate School of Technology Management, University of Pretoria, South Africa where he specializes in project management, initiating currently the only master's program in Project Management on the African continent that is accredited by the PMI (USA). He has been involved in project management in industry since 1975 and has managed a variety of engineering projects (system, product, and process development) in the minerals, defence, and nuclear industries. He has also managed product portfolios.

Project Management for Engineering, Business and Technology

FOURTH EDITION

John M. Nicholas
Loyola University Chicago

Herman Steyn
University of Pretoria

Routledge
Taylor & Francis Group

LONDON AND NEW YORK

Third Indian Reprint, 2015

Fourth edition published 2012
by Routledge
2 Park Square, Milton Park, Abingdon, Oxon OX14 4RN

Simultaneously published in the USA and Canada
by Routledge
711 Third Avenue, New York, NY 10017

Routledge is an imprint of the Taylor & Francis Group, an informa business

Third edition published by Elsevier Inc. 2008

British Library Cataloguing in Publication Data
A catalogue record for this book is available from the British Library

Library of Congress Cataloging in Publication Data
Nicholas, John M., 1945-
   Project management for engineering, business and technology /
John M. Nicholas and Herman Steyn. -- 4th ed.
   p. cm.
   Rev. ed. of: Project management for business, engineering, and technology :
principles and practice. 3rd ed. c2008.
   Includes bibliographical references and index.
   1. Project management. I. Steyn, Herman. II. Nicholas, John M., 1945–
Project management for business, engineering, and technology. III. Title.
HD69.P75N53 2012
658.4′04—dc23

7 3 8 6 3 0 1 1 0 2

ISBN: 978–0–08–096704–2

Typeset in Palatino by Swales & Willis Ltd, Exeter, Devon

Printed and bound in India by Nutech Print Services

For sale in India, Pakistan, Nepal, Bhutan, Bangladesh and Sri Lanka only.

Brief Contents

CONTENTS

Contents

PART V: PROJECT MANAGEMENT IN THE CORPORATE CONTEXT   551

PREFACE

When people see something impressive—a bridge arching high over a canyon, a space probe touching down on a distant planet, a curlicue ramp on a freeway, a motion picture so realistic you think you're there, or a nifty computer the size of your hand—they sometimes wonder, "How did they do that?" By *they*, of course, they are referring to the creators, designers, and builders, the people who thought up and actually made those things. Seldom do they wonder about the *managers*, the people who organized and led the efforts that brought those astounding things from a concept or idea to reality, and without whose talent, skills, and hard work most neat ideas would never amount to anything. This book is about the managers—project managers, the mostly unsung heroes of engineering, business, and technology who stand outside the public eye but are behind practically every collective effort to create, develop, or produce something.

Although the project manager is but one of many people involved in the creation of each of society's products, systems, and artifacts, he or she is usually the one who gets all of the others involved and then organizes and directs their efforts so everything will come out right. Sometimes, though rarely, the manager and the creator happen to be the same: Burt Rutan, Woody Allen, and Gutzon Borglum are examples; their life work—in aerospace, motion pictures, and monumental sculptures, respectively—represents not only creative or technological genius, but leadership and managerial talent as well.

The past few decades have seen businesses expand from domestic, nationalistic enterprises and markets into multinational, global enterprises and markets. As a result, no matter what your perspective, there is more of everything to contend with—more ideas, competitors, resources, constraints, and, certainly, more people doing and wanting things. The rate of technological change is accelerating, and products and processes are evolving at a more rapid pace; as a result, the life cycles of most things society desires or relies upon are getting shorter. This "more of everything" has had a direct impact on the conduct of projects—including projects to develop products, systems, or processes that compete in local, domestic, and international markets; projects to create and implement new ways of meeting demand for energy, recreation, housing, communication, transportation, and food; and projects to answer basic questions in science and resolve problems such as hunger, disease, pollution, and the consequences of natural disasters. All of this project activity has spurred a growing interest in project management and ways to plan, organize, and control projects to better meet the needs of customers, markets, and society within the bounds of limited time and resources.

Associated with this interest is the growing need to educate and train project managers. In the past, project managers were chosen for some demonstrated exceptional capability, although not necessarily managerial—and this is still the case today. If you were a good engineer, systems analyst, researcher, architect, or accountant, eventually you would become a project manager. Somewhere along the way, presumably, you would pick up the "other" necessary skills. The flaw in this reasoning is that project management encompasses a broad range of skills—managerial, leadership, interpersonal—that are much different than and independent of skills associated with technological competency. And there is no reason to presume that the project environment alone will provide the opportunity for someone to "pick up" these other necessary skills.

As a text and handbook, this book is about the "right" way to manage projects. It is intended for advanced undergraduate and graduate university students, and for practicing managers in engineering, business, and technology. As the title says, it is a book about principles *and* practice, meaning that the topics in it are practical and meant to be applied. It covers the big picture of project management—origins, applications, and philosophy—as well as the nitty-gritty, how-to steps. It describes the usual project management topics of schedules, budgets, and controls, but also the human side of project management, including leadership and conflict.

Why a book on project management in engineering, business, *and* technology? In our experience, technical specialists such as engineers, programmers, architects, chemists, and so on, often have little or no management training. This book, which includes many engineering and technology project examples, provides somewhat broad exposure to relevant business concepts and management specifics to help these specialists get started as managers.

What about those people involved in product development, marketing, process improvement, and related projects commonly thought of as "business projects"? Just as students of engineering and technology seldom receive formal management training, business students are rarely exposed to common practices in technology projects. This book reveals not only how "business" projects are conducted, but also concepts and necessary steps in the conception and execution of engineering, product development, construction, and other "technology" projects. Of course, engineering and technology projects are *also* business projects; they are conducted in a business context, and involve business issues such as customer satisfaction, resource utilization, deadlines, costs, profits, and so on.

Virtually all projects—engineering, technology, and business—are originated and conducted in similar ways, conceptualized in this book using a methodology called the Systems Development Cycle (SDC). The SDC serves as a general framework for discussing the principles and practices of project management, and illustrating commonalities and differences among a wide variety of projects.

This book is an outgrowth of our combined several decades of experience teaching project management at Loyola University Chicago and the University of Pretoria to business and engineering students, preceded by several years working in business and technology projects, including aircraft design and flight-test projects, large-scale process facility construction projects, and software applications development and process improvement projects. From our practical experience, we developed an appreciation not only for the business management side of project management but also for the human and organizational side. We have seen the benefits of good communication, trust, and teamwork, as well as the costs of poor leadership, emotional stress, and group conflict. In our experience, the most successful projects are those where leadership, trust, communication, and teamwork flourish, regardless of the formal planning and control systems in place; this book largely reflects these personal experiences. Of course, comprehensive coverage of the project management field required that we look much beyond our own experience and draw upon the published works of many other authors and the suggestions of colleagues and reviewers.

In this fourth edition we have revised and added material to incorporate new topics of interest, current examples, and the growing body of literature in project management. To ensure compatibility with modern software, the activity-on-node method is used in all scheduling examples, though the activity-on-arrow method is discussed in an appendix to Chapter 6. New material includes additional coverage of procurement management and the topic of agile project management, as well as 13 new end-of-chapter case studies. Books tend to grow in size with each new edition; to combat that, every chapter has been rewritten to make everything more readable and more concise. Despite the inclusion of new material, this book has fewer pages than the previous edition.

Our goal in writing this book is to provide students and practicing managers with the most practical, current, and interesting text possible. We appreciate hearing your comments and suggestions. Please send them to us at jnichol@luc.edu and herman. steyn@up.ac.za.

ACKNOWLEDGEMENTS

Writing a book is a project and, like most projects, reflects the contributions of many people. We want to acknowledge and give special thanks to those who contributed the most. First, thanks to our research assistants. Research assistants in general do a lot of work—academic as well as gofer work—and without their toiling efforts, most professors would accomplish far less. We have been fortunate to have had the assistance of several bright and capable people, particularly Elisa Denney, Hollyce James, Diane Petrozzo, Miguel Velasco, Gaurav Monga, Cary Morgan, Louis Schwartzman, and Brian Whelan.

Special thanks to current and former colleagues at Loyola University Chicago and the University of Pretoria. In Chicago, thanks to Dr Gezinus Hidding for his enthusiasm, interest, and contributions to the field of project management; and to Drs Enrique Venta, Harold Dyck, Samuel Ramenofsky, and Donald Meyer, and to Elaine Strnad, Paul Flugel, John Edison, Sharon Tylus, and Debbie Gillespie for their suggestions and support for this and earlier editions. In Pretoria, thanks to Drs Roelf Sandenbergh, Antonie de Klerk, and Tinus Pretorius for encouraging education and research in project management at the Graduate School of Technology Management. I (Herman) also want to express appreciation to Dr Giel Bekker, Philip Viljoen, Dr Pieter Pretorius, Dr Krige Visser, Corro van Waveren, Dr Siebert Benade, Ad Sparrius, Michael Carruthers, and Drs Andre Buys, Leon Pretorius, and Les Labuschagne for their direct and indirect contributions to this book, and for all that I have learned from them. I (John) want to acknowledge the influence of three of my professors, Charles Thompson and Gustave Rath at Northwestern University, and Dick Evans at the University of Illinois, whose philosophies and teachings helped shape this book.

Our wives Sharry and Karen also get special thanks. Sharry provided numerous suggestions to the first edition, and helped reduce the amount of "techno-jargon" in the book; she managed the home front, was a steadfast source of support, and freed up time so that I (John) could pursue and complete this project. Karen provided wifely support and encouragement; as in the case of so many other projects I (Herman) have been involved in, had not it been for her support my contribution to this project would not have materialized.

Thanks to the folks at Butterworth-Heinemann, especially to Hayley Salter, Lisa Jones, Fiona Geraghty, Joe Hayton, and Mike Joyce, and the folks associated with Taylor & Francis, Jackie Day, Richard Willis, Amy Laurens, and Caroline Watson.

There are other colleagues, students, and friends, some mentioned in the endnotes elsewhere throughout the book, that provided support, encouragement, and reference materials; to them also we say thank you. Despite the assistance of so many people and our own best efforts, there are still likely to be omissions or errors. We had final say, and accept responsibility for them.

John M. Nicholas
Herman Steyn

About the Authors

JOHN NICHOLAS is Professor of Operations Management and Project Management and former Associate Dean of the Graduate School of Business at Loyola University Chicago. He is an active teacher, writer, and researcher in project management and manufacturing management, and conducts executive seminars and has been a consultant on project management and process improvement. John is the author of numerous academic and technical publications, and five books including *Lean Production for Competitive Advantage* (2011) and *The Portal to Lean Production* (2006). He has held the positions of engineer and team leader on aircraft development projects at Lockheed-Martin Corporation, business analyst on operations projects at Bank America, and research associate on energy-environmental research projects at Argonne National Laboratory. He has a BS in aeronautical and astronautical engineering and an MBA in operations research from the University of Illinois, Urbana-Champaign, and a PhD in industrial engineering and applied behavioral science from Northwestern University.

HERMAN STEYN is Professor of Project Management in the Graduate School of Technology Management, University of Pretoria, South Africa. He has been involved in project management in industry since 1975, has managed a variety of large and small engineering projects (system, product, and process development) in the minerals, defense, and nuclear industries, and has also managed project portfolios. In 1996 he was appointed to his current position at the University of Pretoria, where he initiated a master's program in project management and a comprehensive continuing-education program in project management. Besides teaching graduate courses, consulting, and conducting and supervising research in project management, over the past decade Herman has conducted more than 100 seminars and workshops on project management. He has a bachelor's degree and graduate diploma in metallurgical engineering, an MBA, and a PhD in engineering management.

Introduction

I.1   IN THE BEGINNING . . .

Sometime during the third millennium BC, workers on the Great Pyramid of Cheops set the last stone in place. They must have felt jubilant, for this event represented a milestone of sorts in one of humanity's grandest undertakings. Although much of the ancient Egyptians' technology is still a mystery, the enormity and quality of the finished product remains a marvel. Despite the lack of sophisticated machinery, they were able to raise and fit some 2,300,000 stone blocks, weighing 2 to 70 tons apiece, into a structure the height of a modern 40-story building. Each facing stone was set against the next with an accuracy of 0.04 inch, and the base, which covers 13 acres, deviates less than 1 inch from level (Figure I.1).[1]

Equally as staggering was the number of workers involved. To quarry the stones and transport them down the Nile, about 100,000 laborers were levied. In addition, 40,000 skilled masons and attendants were employed in preparing and laying the blocks, and erecting or dismantling the ramps. Public works were essential to keep the working population employed and fed,

1

Figure I.1
The Great Pyramid of Cheops, an early (circa 2500 BC) large-scale project.
Photograph courtesy of Arab Information Center.

and it is estimated that no less than 150,000 women and children also had to be housed and fed.[2]

Just as mind-boggling was the managerial ability of the Egyptians—the planning, organizing, and controlling that were exercised throughout the 20-year duration of the pyramid construction. Francis Barber, a nineteenth-century American naval attaché and pyramid scholar, concluded that:

> it must have taken the organizational capacity of a genius to plan all the work, to lay it out, to provide for emergencies and accidents, to see that the men in the quarries, on the boats and sleds, and in the mason's and smithies shops were all continuously and usefully employed, that the means of transportation was ample, . . . that the water supply was ample, . . . and that the sick reliefs were on hand.[3]

Building the Great Pyramid was what we today would call a large-scale project. It stands among numerous projects from early recorded history that required massive human works and managerial competency. The Bible provides accounts of many projects that required orchestration of thousands of people, and the transport and utilization of enormous quantities of materials. Worthy of note are the managerial and leadership accomplishments of Moses. The scriptural account of the exodus of the Hebrews from the bondage of the Egyptians gives some perspective on the preparation, organization, and execution of this tremendous undertaking. Supposedly, Moses did a magnificent job of personnel selection, training, organization, and delegation of authority.[4] The famed ruler Solomon, among other accomplishments, was the "manager" of numerous great construction projects. He transformed the battered ruins of many ancient cities and crude shantytowns into powerful fortifications. With his wealth and the help of Phoenician artisans, Solomon built the Temple in Jerusalem. Seven years went into the construction of the Temple, after which Solomon took 13 years more to build a palace for himself. He employed a workforce of 30,000

Israelites to fell trees and import timber from the forests of Lebanon.[5] That was almost 3,000 years ago. About 600 years later, Nehemiah completely rebuilt the wall around Jerusalem—in just 52 days.

With later civilizations, notably the Greeks and Romans, projects requiring extensive planning and organizing escalated. To facilitate their military campaigns and commercial interests, the Romans constructed networks of highways and roads throughout Europe, Asia Minor, Palestine, and northern Africa, so that all roads would "lead to Rome." The civilizations of Renaissance Europe and the Middle and Far East undertook river engineering, and construction of aqueducts, canals, dams, locks, and port and harbor facilities. With the spread of modern religions, construction of temples, monasteries, mosques, and massive urban cathedrals was added to the list of projects. The remains of these structures throughout the Mediterranean, Asia Minor, and China testify to the ancients' occupation with large-scale projects.

With the advent of industrialization and electricity, the projects of humankind took on increasing complexity. Projects for the construction of railroads, electrical and hydroelectric power facilities and infrastructures, subways, and factories became commonplace. In recent times, development of large systems for communications, defense, transportation, research, and information technology have spurred different, more complex kinds of project activity.

As long as humankind does things, there will be projects. Many projects of the future will be similar to those in the past. Others will be different in terms of either increased scale of effort or more advanced technology. Representative of the latter are three recent projects: the English Channel tunnel (Chunnel), the International Space Station, and SpaceShipOne. The Chunnel required tremendous resources, and took a decade to complete. The International Space Station (Figure I.2) required development of new technologies, and the efforts of the US, Russian, European, Canadian, and Japanese space agencies. SpaceShipOne is the venture of a small company in California aimed at developing a vehicle and launch system for future space tourism.

Figure I.2
The International Space Station, a modern large-scale project.
Photograph courtesy of NASA/Johnson Space Center.

From these examples, it is clear that humankind has been involved in project activities for a long time. But why are these considered "projects" while other human activities, such as planting and harvesting a crop, stocking a warehouse, issuing payroll checks, or manufacturing a product, are not?

What *is* a project? This is a question we will cover in much detail later. As an introduction, though, below are listed some characteristics that warrant classifying an activity as a project.[6]

1. A project has a *definable goal or purpose*, and *well-defined end-items, deliverables, or results,* usually specified in terms of cost, schedule, and performance requirements.
2. Every project is *unique*; it requires doing something different than was done previously. It is a one-time activity, never to be exactly repeated again. Even in a "routine" project such as home construction, variables such as geography, labor market, and public services make it unique.
3. Projects are *temporary* activities. They are *ad hoc* organizations of personnel, material, and facilities organized to accomplish a goal within a scheduled time frame; once the goal is achieved, the *ad hoc* organization is disbanded.
4. Projects *cut across organizational and functional lines* because they need skills and talents from different functions, professions, and organizations.
5. Involvement in anything new or different always carries some uncertainty about the outcome. Given that a project is unique, it also involves *unfamiliarity* and *risk*.
6. The organization doing the project usually has something *at stake*. The work calls for special scrutiny or effort, because failure would jeopardize the organization or its goals.
7. A project is the *process* of working to achieve a goal; during the process the project passes through several distinct phases in the *project life cycle*. Often, the tasks, people, organizations, and resources change as the project moves from one phase to the next.

The examples described earlier are for familiar kinds of projects, such as construction (pyramids), development (transportation and information technology), or a combination of both (space station). In general, the list of activities that qualify as projects is long and includes many that are commonplace. Weddings, remodeling a home, and moving to another house are certainly projects for the families involved. Company audits, major litigations, corporate relocations, and mergers are also projects, as are new product development and system implementations. Military campaigns also meet the criteria of projects; they are temporary, unique efforts directed toward a specific goal. The Normandy Invasion in WWII on June 6, 1944 is a good example:

> The technical ingenuity and organizational skill that made the landings possible was staggering. The invasion armada included nearly 5,000 ships of all descriptions protected by another 900 warships. The plan called for landing 150,000 troops and 1500 tanks on the Normandy coast *in the first 48 hours.*[7]

Most artistic endeavors are projects, too. Composing a song or symphony, writing a novel, or making a sculpture is a one-person project. The unusual (and somewhat controversial) works of the artist Christo—draping portions of the Grand

Canyon, several islands in Biscayne Bay, and 1,000,000 square feet of Australian coastline with colored plastic—are artistic projects also, but on a larger scale. So is the making of motion pictures, whether independently made or the releases of major production studios. Some artistic projects also require the skills of engineers and builders; for example, Mount Rushmore, the Statue of Liberty, and the Eiffel Tower.

Many efforts at saving human life and recovering from man-made or natural disasters become projects. Examples include the massive clean-up following the Soviet nuclear accident at Chernobyl; rescue and recovery operations following disastrous earthquakes in Chile, Haiti, China, Mexico City, Turkey, and elsewhere; and the Indian Ocean tsunami of December 2004 and the Japan tsunami in 2011.

Figure I.3 shows generalized project endeavors, and examples of well-known projects. Notice the diversity in the kinds of efforts. The figure shows approximately where projects fall with respect to complexity and uncertainty. Complexity is measured by magnitude of the effort, number of groups and organizations that need to be coordinated, and diversity in the skills or expertise needed to accomplish the work. Time and resource commitments tend to increase with complexity.

Uncertainty is measured roughly by the difficulty in predicting the final outcome in terms of the dimensions of *time, cost,* and *technical performance*. In most projects there is some uncertainty in one or two dimensions, at least in the initial stages of planning (e.g., weddings and world fairs). The most complex projects have uncertainty in all three dimensions (e.g., the International Space Station).

Generally, the more often something is done, the less the uncertainty in doing it. This is simply because people learn by doing and so improve their efforts—the "learning curve" concept. Projects that are very similar to previous ones and about which there is abundant knowledge have lower uncertainty. These are found in the lower portion of Figure I.3 (e.g., weddings, highways, dams, system implementation). Projects with high uncertainty are in the upper portion of the figure. As manned missions to Mars become frequent, they too will move down the uncertainty scale.

The cost curve indicates that the expense of projects increases roughly in proportion to both complexity and uncertainty. Cost, represented in terms of time or economic value, is at the level of tens or hundreds of labor hours for projects with low complexity and uncertainty, but increases to millions and billions of hours for projects with the greatest complexity and uncertainty.

When the uncertainty of a project drops to nearly zero, and when the project effort is repeated a large number of times, then the work is usually no longer considered a project. For example, building a skyscraper is definitely a project, but mass construction of prefabricated homes more closely resembles a scheduled, repetitive operation than a project. Admiral Byrd's exploratory flight to the South Pole was a project, but modern daily supply flights to Antarctic bases are not. When in the future tourists begin taking chartered excursions to Mars, trips there will not be considered projects either. They will just be ordinary scheduled operations.

In all cases, projects are conducted by organizations that, after the project is completed, go on to do something else (construction companies) or are disbanded (Admiral Byrd's crew, the Mars exploration team). In contrast, repetitive, high certainty activities (prefabricated housing, supply flights, and tourist trips to Antarctica or Mars) are (or will be) performed by permanent organizations that do the same thing over and over, with few changes in operations other than scheduling. It is because projects are not repetitive efforts that they must be managed differently.

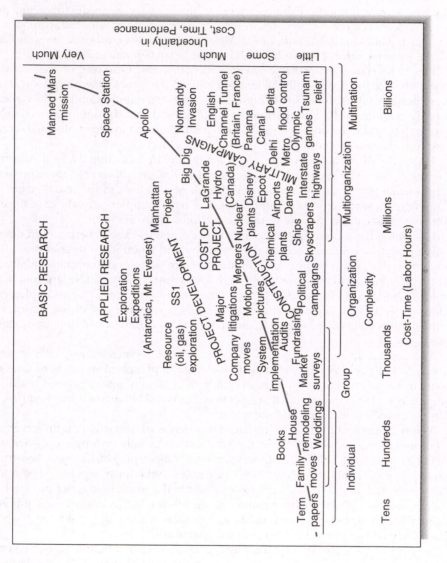

Figure I.3
A typology of projects.

6

1.3 PROJECT MANAGEMENT: THE NEED

Although humankind has been involved in projects since the beginning of recorded history, obviously the nature of projects and the environment have changed. Many modern projects involve great technical complexity, and require a wide diversity of skills. Managers are faced with the problem of putting together and directing large temporary organizations while being subjected to constrained resources, limited time, and environmental uncertainty. To cope with complexity and uncertainty, new forms of project organization and management have evolved.

Two examples of activities that required project organization and management are the Manhattan Project to develop the first atomic bomb, and the Pathfinder Mission to land and operate a rover vehicle on the surface of Mars. Projects such as these are unparalleled not only in terms of technical difficulty and organizational complexity, but also in terms of the requirements circumscribing them. In ancient times, project requirements were more flexible. If the Pharaohs needed more workers, then more slaves or more of the general population were conscripted. If builders ran out of funding during construction of a Renaissance cathedral, the work was stopped until more funds could be raised (one reason why some cathedrals took decades or centuries to complete). If a king ran out of money while building a palace, he simply raised taxes. In other cases where additional money could not be raised, more workers could not be found, or the project could not be delayed, then the scale of effort or the quality of workmanship was simply reduced to accommodate the constraints.

In the Manhattan and Pathfinder projects, the requirements were not so flexible. First, both projects were subject to severe time constraints. Manhattan, undertaken during World War II, required developing the atomic bomb in the shortest time possible to end the war. For Pathfinder, the mission team was challenged with developing and landing a vehicle on Mars in less than 3 years' time and on a $150 million budget. This was less than half the time and one-twentieth the cost of the previous probe NASA had landed on Mars. Both projects involved advanced research and development, and explored new areas of science and engineering. In neither case could technical performance requirements be compromised to compensate for limitations in time, funding, or other resources; to do so would increase the risk to undertakings that were already very risky. But constraints and uncertainty in project work are not restricted to large-scale government science programs. They are common in everyday business and technology where organizations continually strive to develop and implement new products, processes, and systems, and to adapt to changing requirements in a changing world.

Consider Dalian Company's development of "Product J," a product development project that exemplifies what companies everywhere must do to remain competitive—indeed, to survive. In the past, Dalian Company had relied upon trial and error to come up with new products: in essence, whatever worked was used again; whatever failed was discarded. In recent years the company had begun to lose market. Although it had had many innovative concepts on the drawing board, all had failed because it had been too slow to move them into the marketplace. Dalian was now considering development of Product J, a promising but radically new idea. To move the idea from concept to product would require the involvement of engineers and technicians from several Dalian divisions and suppliers. Before approving the budget, the Dalian management wanted assurances that Product J could be introduced early enough to put it well ahead of the competition. The project would need a new product development process guided by project management.

Another example is Shah Alam Hospital's installation of a new employee benefits plan to better suit employee needs, add flexibility and value to the benefits package, and reduce costs. The project would be big—it would involve developing new policies, training staff workers, familiarizing 10,000 employees with the plan, and installing a new computer network and database, and require active participation from personnel in human resources, financial services, and information systems, as well as experts from two consulting firms. This project typifies "change" projects everywhere—projects initiated in response to changing needs and with the goal of transforming the organization's way of doing things. The project would be different from anything the hospital had done before.

As a final example, consider that virtually every company in the world has or will have a website. Behind each site are multiple projects to develop or enhance the website and to integrate electronic business technology into the company's mainstream marketing and supply-chain operations. Such projects are also examples of organizations' need to change—in this case, to keep pace with advances in information technology and business processes.

Activities such as the three examples defy traditional management approaches for planning, organization, and control. They are representative of activities that require modern methods of project management to fulfill difficult technological or market-related performance goals in spite of limitations on time and resources.

As a distinct area of management practice, project management is still a new idea, and its methods are still unknown to many experienced managers. Only 50 years ago, its usage was restricted largely to the defense, aerospace, and construction industries. Today, however, project management is being applied in a wide variety of industries and organizations. Originally applied only in large-scale, complex technological projects such as the Apollo Program to land men on the moon, today project management techniques have expanded and are applicable to any project-type activity, regardless of size or technology. Methods of modern project management would have been as useful to early Egyptian and Renaissance builders as they are to present-day contractors, engineers, systems specialists, and managers.

1.4 RESPONSE TO MODERN SOCIETY

Project management has grown in response to the need for a managerial approach that deals with the problems and opportunities of modern society. It is a departure from the management of simpler ongoing, repetitive operations where the market and technology tend to be predictable, anticipated outcomes are more certain, and only one or a few parties or organizations are involved. In stable and predictable situations like these, traditional organizational forms and management procedures—forms that rely on centralized decision-making and adherence to hierarchical authority—work well. When, however, situations require adaptability and rapid response to change—change spurred, for example, by changing technologies or markets—then the project management form of organization and management works much better. Project management provides the diversified technical and managerial competency and decentralized communication and decision-making necessary to meet the challenges of complex, unfamiliar, high-stakes activities.

I.5 SYSTEMS APPROACH TO MANAGEMENT

A system is a collection of interrelated components or elements that in combination do something. The systems approach to management regards a goal or solution to a problem as the end result or outcome of a system. The focus of the approach is to optimize the performance of the overall *system* (not of its individual components) so as to achieve the goal. The approach starts by defining the goal, identifying components or elements of the system that contribute to or detract from meeting the goal, and then managing the elements to best achieve the goal.

Project management is a systems approach to management. A project is a system of interrelated components—work tasks, resources, stakeholders, as well as schedules, budgets, and plans. The purpose of project management is to integrate the components to accomplish the project goal.

I.6 PROJECT GOAL: TIME, COST, AND REQUIREMENTS

For virtually every project, the goal can be conceptualized in terms of hitting a target that floats in the three dimensions of *cost*, *time*, and *requirements* (Figure I.4). Cost is the specified or budgeted cost for the project. Time is the scheduled period over which the work is to be done. Performance is what the project end-item, deliverables, or final result must do; it includes whatever the project customer or end-user considers necessary or important. The target represents a goal to deliver a certain something, by a certain date, for a certain cost. The purpose of project management is to hit the target.[8]

Unfortunately, technological complexity, changing markets, and an uncontrollable environment make it easy to miss the target. Time, cost, and technical performance are interrelated, and exclusive emphasis on any one will likely undermine the others. In trying to meet schedules and performance requirements, costs increase; conversely, in trying to contain costs, work performance erodes and schedules slip. In earlier times, one or two aspects of the goal were simply allowed to slide so that

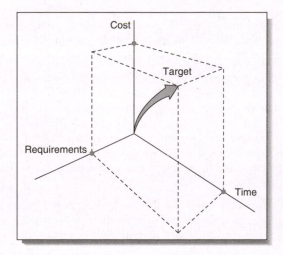

Figure I.4
Three-dimensional project goal. Adapted from Milton Rosenau, *Successful Project Management.* Belmont, CA: Lifetime Learning Publications; 1981. p. 16.

the "most fixed" could be met. Most projects, as the Pathfinder, Dalian Company, and Shah Alam Hospital examples show, do not have this luxury. To an extent, time, cost, and performance must receive equal emphasis.

Project management offers a way to maintain focus on all three dimensions and to control the trade-offs among them. As a systems approach, it integrates resources and enables simultaneous emphasis on the "whole" project goal—time, cost, and performance requirements.

I.7 PROJECT MANAGEMENT: THE PERSON, THE TEAM, THE METHODOLOGY

Three key features distinguish project management from traditional forms of management: the person, the team, and the methodology.

The Person

The most important feature regarding project management is the role of the project manager—the individual who has overall responsibility to *plan*, *direct*, and *integrate* the efforts of all project stakeholders to achieve the project goal. In the role of project manager, one person is held accountable for the project and is totally dedicated to achieving its goals. The project manager coordinates the efforts across all of the involved functional areas and organizations, and oversees the planning and control of costs, schedules, and work tasks.[9]

The Team

A project is a team effort, and project management is bringing together individuals and groups to form the team and to direct them toward a common goal. Often, the team consists of people and groups from different functional areas and organizations. Depending on project requirements, the size and composition of the team may fluctuate, and the team may disband after the project is completed.

The Methodology

The project manager and project team typically perform work in phases according to a "project management methodology." This methodology provides for *integrative planning and control* of projects, which according to Archibald refers to

the pulling together of all important elements of information related to (1) the products or results of the project, (2) the time, and (3) the cost, in funds, manpower, or other key resources. Further, this information must be pulled together for all (or as many as practical) phases of the project. Finally, integrated planning and control requires continual revision of future plans, comparison of actual results with plans, and projection of total time and cost at *completion* through interrelated evaluation of all elements of information.[10]

As a project proceeds from one phase to the next, the project management methodology helps the project manager to (1) identify the required project tasks, (2) identify the required resources and the costs, (3) establish priorities, (4) plan and update schedules, (5) monitor and control end-item quality and performance, and (6) measure project performance.[11]

I.8 ABOUT THIS BOOK

Philosophy and Objectives

As a philosophy and an approach, project management is broader and more sophisticated than traditional management of repetitive activities. The history of the theory and practice of project management reveals its roots in many disciplines, including management science, systems theory, accounting, operations management, organizational design, law, and applied behavioral science. What has evolved, and will continue to evolve, is a philosophy, approach, and set of practices, the *sum total* of which comprises project management. Some managers fail to understand this, believing that application of techniques alone, such as "Gantt charts," "PERT," or "matrix management" (all explained later) make for successful project management. Project management is much more than these.

C.P. Snow wrote an essay, entitled "Two Cultures," about the cultural gap that separates scientists from the rest of society. He wrote of the conflict of ideas, the problems of communication, and the lack of understanding between scientists and other intellectuals.[12] Managers and management scholars also tend to see the world from either of two perspectives: some see the world in "hard," quantitative terms; others see it in "soft" or behavioral terms. The "quantitativists" tend to view projects in terms of costs, dates, and economic variables; their approach is to structure problems mathematically and to follow some prescribed set of procedures to arrive at a solution. The "behaviorists" view problems in terms of people's behavior, skills, and attitudes, and systems of organization; their approach is try to motivate attitudinal and behavioral change, and to alter the processes and structure of teams, groups, and organizations.

The intent of this book is to give a comprehensive, balanced view that emphasizes both the behavioral and quantitative sides of project management. The philosophy of his book is that for managers to "do" project management, they must gain familiarity with four topical areas: system methodology; systems development process; management methods, procedures, and systems; and organization and human behavior. Correspondingly, the objectives of this book are to cover in depth:

1. The principles and philosophy that guide project management practice
2. The logical sequence of stages in the life of a project
3. The methods, procedures, and systems for defining, planning, scheduling, controlling, and organizing project activities
4. The organizational, managerial, and human behavioral issues in project management.

In recent years the scope of project management has grown to encompass more than the management of individual projects, recognizing that project success involves more than the skills and talent of a good project manager; hence, the fifth objective of this book is to describe responsibilities of the *organization* for effective project management and successful projects.

The Study Project

The best way to learn about project management is actually to participate in it or, failing that, to witness it. At the end of every chapter in this book are two kinds of questions: the first are the usual chapter review questions, while the second are "Questions About the Study Project." The latter are intended to be applied to a particular project of the reader's choosing. This will be called the "study project." The purpose of these questions and the study project is to help the reader relate concepts from each chapter to real-life situations.

The questions about the study project can be used in two ways:

1. For readers who are currently working in projects as managers or project team members, the questions can be related to their current work. The questions serve to increase the reader's awareness of key issues surrounding the project, and to guide managers in the conduct of project management.
2. For readers who are currently full or part-time students, the questions can be applied to "real life" projects they are permitted to observe and research. Many business firms and government agencies are happy to allow student groups to interview managers and collect information about their projects. Though secondhand, this is nonetheless an excellent way to learn about project management practice (and mismanagement).

Organization of This Book

Beyond this introductory chapter, the book is divided into five main parts. Part I is devoted to the basic concepts of project management. This part describes project management principles, systems methodologies, and the systems approach—the philosophy that underlies project management. Also covered are the origins and concepts of project management, situations where it is needed, and examples of applications. Part II describes the logical process in the creation and life of a system. Called the Systems Development Cycle, it is the sequence of phases through which all human-made systems move from birth to death. The cycle is described in terms of its relation to projects and project management. Part III is devoted to methods and procedures for planning, scheduling, cost-estimating, budgeting, resource-allocating, controlling, and terminating a project. The topics of resource planning, computer and web-based project management, and project evaluation are also covered. Part IV is devoted to project organizations, teams, and the people in projects. It covers forms of project organization; roles and responsibilities of project managers and team members; styles of leadership; and methods for managing teamwork, conflict, and emotional stress. Part V covers topics that lie beyond the project manager but are crucial for project success and, more broadly, the success of the organizations and communities that sponsor and undertake projects. It also covers a topic that spans most other topics in this book but requires special attention: managing projects in different countries.

The five stated objectives of this book are roughly divided among chapters in the book's five parts:

1. Basic concepts and systems philosophy: Chapters 1 and 2.
2. Systems development and project life cycle: Chapters 3 and 4.
3. Methods, procedures, and systems for planning and control: Chapters 5 through 12.
4. Organization, management, and human behavior: Chapters 13 through 15.
5. Project management maturity, the PMO, project selection and portfolio management, and international project management: Chapters 16 through 18.

The Appendices provide examples of three topics mentioned throughout the book: request for proposal (Appendix A), project proposal (Appendix B), and project master plan (Appendix C).

I.9 PMBOK

Several project management professional organizations have sprouted around the world. These organizations have served to improve the practice of project management by establishing standards, guidelines, and certifications, and have advanced project management from being a simple title or role to a recognized, respected profession. Among the more well-known among these organizations are the IPMA (International Project Management Association), the UK's APM Group (Association for Project Management), and the PMI (Project Management Institute). Starting in 1985, the PMI—the largest of these organizations—gathered up all the known, accepted best practices in the profession, and has since published them in a series of documents called *A Guide to the Project Management Body of Knowledge* (PMBOK).[13] The APM and IPMA have also published their own versions of the PMBOK. Although none of the PMBOKs cover everything about project management (and couldn't do so even if they tried), they have become the recognized standards about what, minimally, a project manager should know in practice and for attaining professional certification. The PMI calls its popular project management certification PMP—Project Management Professional.

The PMI's *Guide* to PMBOK divides project management knowledge into nine areas:

- Project integration management
- Project scope management
- Project time management
- Project cost management
- Project quality management
- Project human resource management
- Project communications management
- Project risk management
- Project procurement management

For readers interested in the PMI's PMBOK, or seeking PMP certification, Table I.1 shows the correspondence between PMBOK knowledge areas as published in the PMI's *Guide*, and the chapters in this book that address them.

I.10 STUDY PROJECT ASSIGNMENT

Select a project to investigate. It should be a "real" project; that is, a project that has a real purpose and is not contrived just so you can investigate it. It can be a current project or one already completed; whichever, it must be a project for which you can readily get information.

If you are not currently involved in a project as a team member, then you must find one for which you have permission to study (collect data and interview people) as an "outsider." The project should include a project team (a minimum of five people) with a project leader and be at least 2–3 months in duration. It should also have a specific goal in terms of a target completion date, a budget limit, and a specified end-item result or product. In general, larger projects afford better opportunity to observe the concepts of project management than smaller ones.

Table I.1 Book Chapter versus the PMI's PMBOK Knowledge Areas

BOOK CHAPTERS Key: P = PMBOK Knowledge Area is a major focus of this chapter * = PMBOK Knowledge Area is addressed in this chapter	Introduction	Project Life Cycle and Organization	Project Management Process	Project Integration Management	Project Scope Management	Project Time Management	Project Cost Management	Project Quality Management	Project Human Resource Management	Project Communications Management	Project Risk Management	Project Procurement Management
Introduction	P	*	*									
Chapter 1: What Is Project Management?	P		*									
Chapter 2: Systems Approach and Systems Engineering			*	*	*							
Chapter 3: Systems Development Cycle and Project Conception (and Appendix)		P	*	*							*	P
Chapter 4: Project and System Definition		*	*	*	P							
Chapter 5: Planning Fundamentals		*	*	*	P					*		P
Chapter 6: Project Time Planning and Networks	*		*			P						
Chapter 7: Advanced Project Network Analyses and Scheduling			*			P					*	
Chapter 8: Cost Estimating and Budgeting			*				P					*
Chapter 9: Project Quality Management			*	*				P				
Chapter 10: Managing Risks in Projects			*								P	
Chapter 11: Project Execution and Control			*	*	*	*	*			P		*
Chapter 12: Project Evaluation, Communication, Implementation, and Closeout	*		*							P		*

Table I.1 *Continued*

Chapter											
Chapter 13: Project Organization Structure and Integration	*		P								
Chapter 14: Project Roles, Responsibility, and Authority		*						*			
Chapter 15: Managing Participation, Teamwork, and Conflict		*						P			
Chapter 16: The Management of Project Management	*	*		*							
Chapter 17: Project Selection and Portfolio Management	*							*		*	
Chapter 18: International Project Management	*			*	*	*	*	*	*	*	*

If you are studying a project as an outsider, it is also a good idea to do it in a team with three to six people and an appointed team leader (i.e., perform the study using a team). This, in essence, becomes your *project team*—a team organized for the purpose of studying a project. You can then readily apply many of the planning, organizing, team-building, and other procedures discussed throughout the book as practice and to see how they work. This "hands-on" experience with your own team, combined with what you learn from the project you are studying, will give you a fairly accurate picture about problems encountered and management techniques used in real-life project management.

REVIEW QUESTIONS AND PROBLEMS

1. Look at websites, newspapers, magazines, or television for examples of projects. Surprisingly, a great number of newsworthy topics relate to current and future projects, or to the outcome of past projects. Prepare a list of these topics.
2. Prepare a list of activities that are not projects. What distinguishes them from project activities? Which activities are difficult to classify as projects or non-projects?
3. Because this is an introductory chapter, not very much has been said about why projects must be managed differently, and what constitutes project management—the subject of this book. Now is a good time to speculate about these: Why do you think projects and non-projects need to be managed differently? What do you think are some additional or special considerations necessary for managing projects?

NOTES

1. Tompkins P. *Secrets of the Great Pyramids.* New York, NY: Harper & Row; 1976, pp. 233–234; Poirier R. *The Fifteen Wonders of the World.* New York, NY: Random House; 1961, pp. 54–67.
2. *Ibid.*, pp. 227–228.
3. Barber F. In: *The Mechanical Triumphs of the Ancient Egyptians.* London, UK: Tribner; 1900, p. 233.
4. George CS. *The History of Management Thought.* Upper Saddle River, NJ: Prentice Hall; 1968, p. 11.
5. Potok C. *Wanderings.* New York, NY: Fawcett Crest; 1978, pp. 154–162.
6. Archibald RD. *Managing High-Technology Projects.* New York, NY: Wiley; 1976, p. 19; Meredith JR, Mantel S. *Project Management: A Managerial Approach*, 6th edn. New York, NY: Wiley; 2006, pp. 8–10; Roman DD. *Managing Projects: A Systems Approach.* New York, NY: Elsevier; 1986, pp. 2–10; Stewart JM. Making project management work. *Business Horizons* 1965; 8(3): 54–68.
7. Terraine J. *The Mighty Continent.* London, UK: BBC; 1974, pp. 241–242.
8. Rosenau MD. *Successful Project Management.* Belmont, CA: Lifetime Learning; 1981, pp. 15–19.
9. Kerzner H. *Project Management: A Systems Approach to Planning, Organizing, and Controlling*, 10th edn. Hoboken, NJ: John Wiley & Sons; 2009, pp. 14–16.
10. Archibald RD. *Managing High-Technology Projects.* New York, NY: Wiley; 1976, pp. 6–7.
11. Kerzner H. *Project Management: A Systems Approach to Planning, Organizing, and Controlling*, p. 19–20.
12. Snow CP. *The Two Cultures and a Second Look.* Cambridge, UK: Cambridge University Press; 1969.
13. *A Guide to the Project Management Body of Knowledge* (PMBOK Guide), 4th edn. Project Management Institute, November 2008.

Part I

Philosophy and Concepts

*T*he two chapters in this section describe the philosophy and concepts that differentiate project management from traditional, non-project management. Project management is an application of what has been called the systems approach to management. This section introduces features associated with project management, and describes the principles, terminology, and methodology of the systems approach. It sets the stage for more detailed coverage in later sections.

Chapter 1

What Is Project Management?

> *Making a film is a lot like carrying out a space mission. Both are big-ticket items produced by teams, which come into existence with budgetary and schedule constraints. The technical skills necessary to land a spacecraft on a planet are close to the ones required to create the illusion of that landing.*

—M.G Lord,
Astro Turf[1]

The projects mentioned in the Introduction—the Great Pyramid of Egypt, the International Space Station, the Chunnel, and the development of Product J—all have something in common with each other and with every other undertaking of human organizations: they all require, in a word, *management*. Certainly the resources, work tasks, and goals of these projects vary greatly, yet without management none of them could happen. This chapter contrasts project management and non-project management, and looks at the variety of ways and places where project management is used.

1.1 FUNCTIONS AND VIEWPOINTS OF MANAGEMENT[2]

The role of management is to plan, organize, and integrate resources and tasks to achieve the organization's goals. Although the specific responsibilities

19

of managers vary greatly, all managers—whether they are corporate presidents, agency directors, line managers, school administrators, movie producers, or project managers—have this same role.

Management Functions

The activities of a manager can be classified into the five functions identified in Figure 1.1. First, the manager decides what has to be done and how it will be done. This is the *planning* function, which involves setting a purpose or goal and establishing the means for achieving it consistent with higher-level organizational goals, resources, and constraints in the environment.

Second, and related to planning, is arranging for the work to be done; this is the *organizing* function. The manager must (1) hire, train, and gather people into a team with specified authority, responsibility, and accountability relationships; (2) acquire and allocate facilities, materials, capital, and other resources; and (3) create an organization structure that includes policies, procedures, reporting patterns, and communication channels.

Third, the manager directs and motivates people to attain the goal. This is the leadership function. The manager tries to influence the work performance and behavior of workers and groups.

Fourth, the manager monitors work performance with respect to the goal and takes necessary action whenever work begins to deviate from the goal; this is the *control* function. For effective control, the manager tracks information about performance with respect to costs, schedules, and goal criteria.

All four functions are aimed at the goal, which implies a fifth function: assessing the four functions to determine how well they, the functions, are doing and where *change* is needed, either to the goal or to the functions themselves.

On a day-by-day basis, rarely do managers perform the functions in Figure 1.1 in strict sequence. Although planning should precede the others, there is always a need to organize activities, direct people, and evaluate work, regardless of sequence. Managers constantly face change, which means that plans, activities, performance standards, and leadership styles must also change. Managers oversee a variety of work tasks simultaneously, and for each one they must be able to exercise any of these functions as needed.

Different managers' jobs carry different responsibilities depending on the functional area and managerial level of the job. Some managers devote most of their time to planning and organizing, others to controlling, and others to directing and motivating. No process or set of management functions applies equally in all cases. Managers must be adaptable to the situation. This is the *contingency viewpoint* of management.

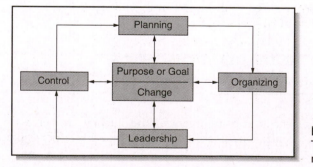

Figure 1.1
The functions of management.

Viewpoints of Management

The contingency viewpoint is but the latest in an evolving series of management propositions and methodologies. The earliest, called the *classical* viewpoint, originated at the start of the twentieth century. This held that there was one *best way* to manage with a corresponding set of universal bureaucratic and scientific management principles that could be applied to all situations. The classical viewpoint established formal principles for planning, organizing, leading, and controlling. In theory, the principles outline all the kinds of things managers should do. The drawback is that they ignore much of the reality of what actually happens in organizations, and therefore provide poor guidance about what managers should do in different situations.

The 1930s brought the *behavioral* viewpoint, in which the emphasis shifted from work principles to the human and social aspects of organizations. One of the early proponents of this viewpoint, Elton Mayo, introduced the concept of "social man"—the worker who is motivated by social needs and relationships with others, and is responsive to work group norms and pressures.[3] The contribution of this viewpoint is that it highlighted the importance of leadership style, group dynamics, and social environment—concepts not considered by the classical theorists. But the behaviorists, like their classical counterparts, tended to look at management rather narrowly. Human and organization behavior are more complex than they presumed, and many behaviorist theories concerning satisfaction, morale, and productivity are too simplistic to be of practical use.

During World War II, a third viewpoint, called the *systems approach*, was introduced. Whereas the first two viewpoints sought to simplify management through concepts that would fit all situations, the systems viewpoint acknowledges complexity and causal relationships. Simply stated, before managers can prescribe action, they must first understand the system and its relationship with the environment. Rather than give a set of rote prescriptions about how to manage, the approach suggested ways to understand the elements and dynamics of a situation, and models to help clarify problems and identify courses of action. But even this approach could not be relied upon always to tell the manager what to do.

All three viewpoints represent different perspectives, all make valuable contributions to management theory and practice, and all have limitations. The current *contingency* viewpoint recognizes that none of them alone can guide a manager in all aspects of the job in every situation. This viewpoint, which includes ideas like situational leadership[4] and the contingency approach to management,[5] stresses that all three views can be applied independently or in some combination, *depending upon the situation*. Simply, the contingency viewpoint suggests that for management practice to be effective it must be consistent with the requirements of the environment, the tasks being performed, and the motivation and skills of the people performing them.

1.2 PROJECT VIEWPOINT VERSUS TRADITIONAL MANAGEMENT

The purpose of project management is to manage a system of tasks, resources, people and organizations to accomplish the project goal; this is what makes it a systems approach to management. Nonetheless, project management also relies upon elements of the classical and behavioral viewpoints, so it is, in fact, a good example of the contingency approach because it is a management philosophy and methodology oriented toward one type of undertaking—projects.

Characteristics of Projects

A project was defined in the Introduction as:[6]

1. Having a single, definable goal or purpose and well-defined end-items or deliverables
2. Being unique
3. Being somewhat or largely unfamiliar and risky
4. Utilizing skills and talents from different professions and organizations
5. Being a temporary activity
6. Having something at stake
7. Being the *process* of working toward a goal.

Perhaps the more significant distinguishing characteristics are the second, third, and fourth: every project is unique and unfamiliar in some sense, and requires multifunctional or multi-organizational involvement. This creates uncertainty and risk, and decreases the chances of achieving the desired result. In non-project, repetitive activities like mass production or delivery of services, which involve procedures that seldom change and are performed by the same people, day-in, day-out, the results are more certain and the risks low.

Projects need a different kind of management.

Characteristics of Project Management

Looking at the characteristics of a project, the question from a management perspective is: How do you manage such a thing? The answer: use project management.

The key features of project management are as follows.[7]

1. A single person, the project manager, heads the project organization and works independently of the normal chain of command. The project organization reflects the cross-functional, goal-oriented, temporary nature of the project.
2. The project manager is *the* person who brings together all efforts to meet project objectives.
3. Because each project requires a variety of skills and resources, project work might be performed by people from different functional areas or by outside contractors.
4. The project manager is responsible for integrating people from the different functional areas or outside contractors.
5. The project manager negotiates directly with functional managers or contractors who might be responsible for the individual work tasks and personnel within the project.
6. While the project manager focuses on delivering a particular product or service at a certain time and cost, functional managers are responsible for the pool of workers and resources in their areas. As a result, conflict may arise between project and functional managers over the people and resources allotted to a project.
7. A project might have two chains of command—one functional and one project—and people working in a project report to both a project manager and a functional manager.
8. Decision-making, accountability, outcomes, and rewards are shared between the project team and supporting functional units and outside contractors.
9. Although the project organization is temporary, the functional or subcontracting units from which it is formed are permanent. When a project ends, the project

organization is disbanded and people return to their functional or subcontracting units.

Because projects involve the coordinated efforts of different units from within and outside the organization, managers and workers in different units and at different levels need to associate directly with each other. Formal lines of communication and authority are frequently bypassed and a *horizontal hierarchy* is created. This horizontal hierarchy enables members of the project organization from different functional areas and outside organizations to communicate and work directly with each other as needed.

In non-project organizations, managers tend to be specialized and responsible for a single functional unit or department. A project, however, needs the support of many departments; hence, someone from outside these departments must take responsibility for meeting the project's goals. That person is the project manager. This emphasis on project goals versus the performance of each functional unit is one feature that distinguishes project managers from functional managers.

Project managers often direct people who are not "under" them but who are "assigned" to them from different areas of the organization as needed. Thus, the tasks of project managers are more complicated than those for departmental managers. Project managers must know how to use diplomacy, resolve conflicts, and be effective leaders, and be able to function without the convenience of always having the same team reporting to them.

Example 1.1: Project Management in Construction

Large construction projects are often in the news—sometimes because of problems owing to cost overruns or schedule slippages. Although many factors are cited (labor union problems, materials shortages, weather, inflation), the real cause is frequently poor management and lack of control. Often, the manager of the project is either the architect or the contractor. This works on small, less complex construction jobs, but on big jobs it is a bad arrangement because architects and contractors each represent the interests of a separate "functional area." When things go wrong and arguments arise, both tend to be self-serving; there is no one who is impartial and can reconcile differences in the best interests of the customer—the building owner or developer.

A better arrangement is when the owner or developer appoints an independent construction project manager. The project manager represents the owner's interests during the entire design and construction process. As shown in Figure 1.2, the project manager's central position within the project organization enables him or her to monitor and coordinate all design and building tasks in accordance with the owner's or developer's goals. The project manager's role ensures that the architect's designs are within the developer's cost allowances and building

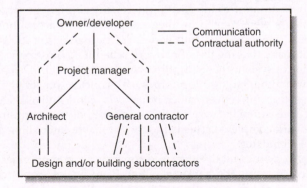

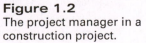

Figure 1.2
The project manager in a construction project.

requirements, and that the contractor's work is executed according to contract specifications and at a fair price. The project manager is involved throughout the project life cycle, overseeing preliminary architectural design, doing the subcontracting, and controlling site work according to design specifications, time, cost, and worker safety.

Other examples of project managers are described later in the chapter.

1.3 EVOLUTION OF PROJECT MANAGEMENT

No single individual or industry can be credited with the idea of project management. It is often associated with the early missile and space programs of the 1960s, but clearly its origins go back much earlier. Techniques of project management probably first appeared during the major construction works of antiquity, such as the Pyramids, the Roman aqueducts, the Qutab Minar mosque in Delhi, and the Great Wall of China. Later these techniques were improved and modified for usage on other forms of construction projects, such as shipbuilding.

Starting in the early twentieth century, industrial managers found that techniques used to manage construction could also be used for large-scale non-construction jobs, such as designing and testing new products, and building and installing specialized machinery. Around the same time, during World War I, improved techniques for planning non-standard, project-type work were being developed, and a new production scheduling and tracking tool called the *Gantt chart* was introduced (see examples in Chapter 5). About 30 years later, the first network-type display for describing industrial processes, called a *process flow diagram*, was developed. This would become the basis for *project network diagrams*.

By the 1950s, the size and complexity of many projects had increased so much that existing management techniques proved inadequate. In particular, large-scale projects—development of aircraft, missiles, communication systems, and naval vessels—were becoming so complex that they defied all existing methods to plan and control them. Repeatedly, these projects suffered enormous cost and schedule overruns. To grapple with the problem, two new network-based planning and control methods were developed, one by the Navy in 1958, called *PERT*, and the other by DuPont Corporation in 1957, called *CPM*. Both methods (described in Chapter 7) were created exclusively for planning, scheduling, and controlling large projects with numerous interrelated work activities. A decade later, these methods were combined with computer simulation methods to permit more realistic analysis of schedules.

By the mid-1950s, wide-scale usage of computers provided increased capability for handling the immense amount of information necessary to manage large-scale projects. Network methods were refined to integrate project cost accounting with project scheduling. These methods came into widespread usage in the 1960s when the federal government mandated the use of network scheduling/costing methods, called cost schedule control systems (C/SCS), first with Department of Defense and NASA contracts, then with other large-scale efforts such as nuclear power plants.

In the 1970s, a project tracking concept called *earned value* came into use. This concept led to performance measurement systems that track not only expenditures, but also the percentage of work completed. This led to more reliable forecasting of final project costs and completion dates.

The past 40 years have witnessed the increased computerization of project management. Initially, project planning and tracking systems were available only for large mainframe computers, and cost $10,000 to $100,000. Today, relatively low-cost software—between $200 and $2000—makes it possible to apply a variety of techniques for scheduling, costing, resource planning, performance analysis, and forecasting to virtually any size project.

Associated with the development of methods for project planning and control were the evolution of forms of project organization and the role of project manager. Not until World War II was the project recognized as a distinct organizational form. In the urgency to develop sophisticated weaponry and organize massive task forces of troops and material, pure project forms of organization evolved. In 1961, IBM became one of the first companies in industry to formally use the role of project manager; there, project managers (called "systems managers") were given broad responsibility across functional lines to oversee development and installation of mainframe computers.

In 1962, in one of the first discussions of the evolution of project management, Davis identified four types of project management organization,[8] noting that project organizations tend to evolve from one type to the next as their problems become more complex and organizations become more sophisticated in dealing with them. Davis's classification can be used to introduce four types of project managers:

- *Project expeditors*, whose purpose is to try to speed up work. They are the communication link between senior managers and the project. Their purpose is to achieve *unity of communications*. They are not really managers, but are go-betweens who translate technical concepts into business concepts such as costs, schedules, and markets. The role is limited to funneling information from technical workers to executives, and making suggestions; thus, it tends to be restricted to small projects with low risk and little at stake.

- *Project coordinators*, whose purpose is to achieve *unity of control* over project activities. They have authority to control project matters and disburse funds from the budget, but no actual line authority over workers. Their authority derives solely from their association with upper-level managers. The construction project manager in Figure 1.2, for example, would be in this position if she coordinated the work but needed approval from the developer for major decisions such as contracting or allocation of funds.

- *Matrix managers*, whose purpose is to achieve *unity of direction*. Although they serve the same purposes as the first two, they additionally have authority to plan, direct, and control project work. Matrix managers direct people located administratively in different functional departments, and the resulting crisscross pattern of vertical–functional and horizontal–project reporting relationships create what is called a *matrix organization*. In Figure 1.3, for example, the manager of Project One oversees project tasks 1–3, which are performed by people assigned from the functional areas of accounting, contracts, etc. Another example is the manager of a construction project that involves both designing and constructing a building. Managers from the architectural and construction departments assign personnel to the project, who then report to the project manager for as long as needed. The same personnel may also work on other projects and report to other matrix managers.

- *Pure project managers*, whose purpose is to achieve *unity of command* over the people in *pure project* organizations that report directly to them. They are primarily integrators and generalists rather than technical specialists. They must balance technical factors of the project with schedules, costs, resources, and human factors. In the course of a project, they deal with top management, functional managers, vendors, customers, and subcontractors. The manager of a large construction

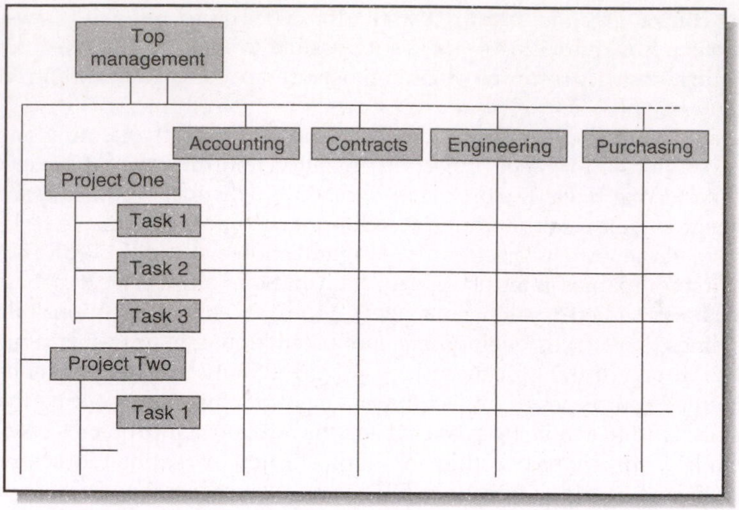

Figure 1.3
Vertical and horizontal elements of a matrix project organization.

project who is hired by the developer and delegated the authority to make major decisions (such as selecting and contracting with the architect and the contractor) has such a role.

The latter two types are most in keeping with the concept of the project manager, although the other two are also widely found.

1.4 WHERE IS PROJECT MANAGEMENT APPROPRIATE?[9]

The fact is, project management is applied almost everywhere, and there are relatively few industries or situations where project management is not applied at least some of the time. This section identifies conditions and situations where a project-type organization is applicable or essential.

Project management can be applied to any *ad hoc* undertaking. As shown in the Introduction (Figure I.3), an "*ad hoc* undertaking" includes activities that range from writing a term paper or remodeling a kitchen, to fundraising and constructing theme parks such as Walt Disney World. Generally, the more unfamiliar or unique the undertaking, the greater the need for project management to ensure nothing gets overlooked; the more numerous, interdisciplinary, and interdependent the activities in the undertaking, the greater the need for project management to ensure everything is coordinated, integrated, and completed.

Customers such as major corporations or the US government frequently request or mandate formal project management because they believe it offers better cost, schedule, and quality control, and they prefer having a single point of contact—the project manager—with whom to deal.

Criteria

Cleland and King list five general criteria for determining when to use project management techniques and organization.[10]

1. Unfamiliarity

By definition, a project is something different from the ordinary and routine. A project always requires that different things be done, that the same things be done differently, or both. For example, continuous minor changes in products such as small improvements in automobile parts can usually be accomplished without project management; however, modernizing an automotive plant, which calls for non-routine efforts such as upgrading facilities, replacing equipment, retraining employees, and altering work procedures, would certainly require project management.

2. Magnitude of the Effort

When a job requires substantially more resources (people, capital, equipment, etc.) than are normally employed by a department or organization, project management may be necessary. Examples include relocating a facility, merging two corporations, or developing or substantially redesigning a product and placing it on the market. Even when the job lies primarily within the realm of one functional area, the task of coordinating the work with other functional areas might be large. For example, a corporate software installation project might *seem* to fall entirely within the functional area of information technology, yet in reality it will require a seamless meshing of the procedures and resources of all departments affected by the installation and involve hundreds of people.

3. Changing Environment

Industries such as computers, electronics, pharmaceuticals, and communications face continual change driven by an environment characterized by high innovation, intense competition, and shifting markets and consumer demands. Other industries, such as chemicals, biotechnology, and aerospace, also exist in environments that, though less volatile, are highly competitive and dynamic. Project management provides the necessary flexibility to deal with emerging threats and opportunities in such environments.

4. Interrelatedness

Functional areas tend to be self-serving and work independently. When a multifunctional effort is required, project management is necessary to build lateral relationships between the areas to expedite work and reconcile conflicts. The project manager coordinates the efforts of internal functional areas and interactions with outside subcontractors and vendors.

5. Reputation of the Organization

If failure to complete the project satisfactorily will result in financial ruin, loss of market share, damaged reputation, or loss of future contracts, there is a strong case for project management. Although project management is no guarantee for success, it does improve the odds. It can do much to reduce the inherent risks in large, complex undertakings.

Example 1.2: Renovating the Statue of Liberty[11]

By the early 1980s, 95 years after the Statue of Liberty was presented to the American people, its surface and interior structure had become so badly corroded that it was judged structurally unsound. To oversee restoration of the statue and other buildings on nearby Ellis Island, the US Department of the Interior established a foundation.

Very little of the restoration work qualified as "standard." It involved highly specialized skills such as erection of scaffolding, construction of a new torch, building of windows for the crown, and replacement of the interior framework—expertise that tends to be found in smaller firms. As a result, the work was accomplished by a legion of over 50 small businesses, many of whose workers were immigrants or descendants of immigrants whom the statue had welcomed to America.

There were myriad notable features about the job. The scaffolding surrounding the statue never touched it at any point. Constructed of hundreds of thousands of pieces of aluminum, it qualified for the *Guinness Book of World Records* as the largest free-standing scaffolding ever built. To renovate the statue's interior, 1,699 five-foot bars were painstakingly fashioned from 35,000 pounds of stainless steel, and then individually installed. Around the crown, 25 windows were replaced. Each was handcrafted and had to be treated as a project unto itself. To fashion an entirely new torch, French artisans practiced an ancient copper-shaping technique. The project was truly a marriage of art and engineering.

The 30-month, $31 million renovation effort involved thousands of tasks performed by hundreds of people. Most of the tasks were non-routine and interrelated, and all had to be completed within a tight budget and schedule; such a situation calls for project management. (See Chapter 15 for a discussion of the company responsible for managing the renovation.)

Where Project Management Is Not Appropriate

The obverse of all of this is that the more familiar and routine the undertaking, the more stable the environment, the less unique and more standardized the end-item, and the lower the stake in the result, the less the need for project management. Production of standardized industrial and agricultural outputs, for example, is generally more efficiently managed by tried and true operations planning and control procedures than by project management. This is because for standardized, repetitive operations, there is much certainty in the process and outcome; for such operations, standardized routine procedures for production planning, scheduling, and budgeting are well-suited, while project management is not.

1.5 MANAGEMENT BY PROJECT: A COMMON APPROACH

Though not appropriate for managing every situation, project management does apply to a great many situations—not only large-scale, infrequent undertakings, but also all kinds of smaller, more frequent activities. Whenever an undertaking involves activities that are somewhat unique or unfamiliar, and that require cooperation from several parties, project management applies.

For example, consultants in every industry perform work on a project-by-project basis. Whenever this work calls for coordinated participation of several individuals or groups, project management applies. The larger the number of people or groups involved and the greater the need to coordinate them, the more project management applies.

Similarly, groups that work on developing or implementing new products, systems, or services also work on a project-by-project basis. The larger, riskier, more complex, costly, innovative, or different the thing being developed or implemented is, the more applicable is project management.

Further, any group that performs unique work on a *client-by-client basis* (so-called made-to-order, or made-to-engineer) is also performing project work. If the work requires coordinated efforts from different parties, project management usually applies.

Think about these situations for a moment, and you start to realize the many cases where projects happen and project management applies.

Managing any kind of work as a discrete project is referred to as "managing by project," or MBP.[12] With MBP, an undertaking or set of activities is planned and managed as if it were a project. In particular, MBP implies that the undertaking will have well-defined objectives and scope, firm requirements for the end-results, a plan of work, a completion date, and a budget for the required resources. A team is formed for the sole purpose of performing the work, and a project manager or team leader is assigned to guide and coordinate the work.

At some time, all organizations use project approaches. Even in stable, repetitive industries, small projects involving a few individuals are always in progress: new machines are installed or old ones are repaired; the office is remodeled; the cafeteria is relocated. It is when larger or more special undertakings arise, such as the development of a totally new product, installation of major equipment, or the move to a new location, that a more formalized project group must be formed.

Example 1.3: Relocation of Goman Publishing Company

Many companies, regardless of size (whether headquarters for a multi-billion dollar corporation or a storefront family restaurant), at some point face the decision to relocate. Relocation requires planning and coordination of numerous tasks involving many individuals, departments, and outside contractors. It is an important event that if done properly can be an exciting and profitable experience, but if done poorly can lead to financial loss or ruin. It is also representative of a situation wherein a company must do something it does not ordinarily do.

Consider Goman Publishing, a company experiencing rapid growth and which was soon to exceed the capacity of its current facility. The initial task in relocating the company was to decide between two options: buying land and constructing a new building, or leasing or buying an existing structure. After deciding to build, the next task was to select a site. The main selection criteria were purchase expense, distance from current location, prestige and size of the new location, and access to major highways. Next was the relocation planning, which had two major phases: design and construction of the new facility, and the physical move, each involving numerous considerations. For example, Goman wanted to retain its current employees, and to maximize the new facility's appeal it chose to build an indoor employee parking area and a large, well-appointed cafeteria. Among the many move-related considerations were furniture procurement, special handling of computer equipment, hiring movers, distributing information to employees and clients about the move, and maintaining corporate security. Further, the relocation would have to be scheduled to minimize downtime and interruption of operations.

To oversee the project and ensure that construction and the physical move went according to plan, Goman appointed a project manager and support staff. The project manager worked with architects and building contractors during the design and construction phases, and with representatives from functional departments and moving contractors during the move phase. Despite the scope and unfamiliarity of the project, Goman was able to complete the construction and physical move on time and according to budget.

1.6 DIFFERENT FORMS OF PROJECT MANAGEMENT

Project management has different forms with different names, including systems management, task force management, team management, *ad hoc* management, matrix management, and program management. Regardless, all these forms share two features: (1) a *project team* or project organization created uniquely for the purpose of achieving a specific goal; and (2) a single person—a *project manager*—assigned responsibility for seeing that the goal is accomplished. Beyond these, features of the forms differ somewhat.

The first section below covers "basic" project management, the most commonly understood concept of project management. The other sections cover variants of or management forms similar to project management.

Basic Project Management

The most common project approach places the project manager and functional managers on the same organizational level so that both report to the same senior-level person. The project manager is given formal authority to plan, direct, organize, and control the project from start to finish. The project manager may work directly with any level and functional area of the organization to accomplish project goals. She reports to the general manager or owner, and keeps him apprised of project status. Sometimes the project manager has authority to hire personnel and procure facilities, although more often she negotiates with functional managers to "borrow" them.

Basic project management is implemented in two widely used forms—pure project and matrix. In pure project management, a complete, self-contained organization is created. The needed resources belong to the project, and do not have to be borrowed. In matrix management, the project organization is created from resources allotted (borrowed) from the functional units. The project must share these resources with other concurrent projects, and with the functional areas from which they are borrowed. These two project management forms will be described further in Chapter 13.

Although often found in construction and technology industries, basic project management can be readily applied to small, non-technical activities as well, including in the arts and social sciences. Adams, Barndt, and Martin cite examples where basic project management could be applied:[13]

- Health, Education, and Welfare (HEW) performs social work largely on the basis of grants allocated through state and local agencies. Associated with each grant are time, cost, and performance requirements for the funding agencies. In essence, each grant results in a project to which the concepts of project management can be applied.

- When an advertising firm conducts a promotional campaign, it utilizes the support of marketing research, accounting, graphics, sales, and other units. Several projects are usually underway at any given time, each in a different stage of its life cycle. These campaigns are similar to the projects in other industries that commonly practice project management.

- A good deal of work performed in education development can be considered project work. Like HEW, much of this work is funded by grants with target goals, and cost and time constraints. Also, the work requires coordination among many educators and researchers—a task for which project management is ideally suited.

Program Management[14]

The term "program management" is often used interchangeably with project management due to the similarities of programs and projects: both (1) are defined in terms of goals or objectives about what must be accomplished; (2) emphasize the time period over which goals or objectives are to be pursued; and (3) require plans, budgets, and schedules for accomplishing the goals. That is, projects and programs both work toward goals specified in terms of a desired product or service output, a target date, and a budget.

However, for definitional purposes in this book, programs and projects are different—the main distinction being that a program extends over a *longer time horizon* and consists of *several parallel or sequential work efforts or projects* that are coordinated to meet a program goal. The projects within a program share common goals and resources, and often they are interdependent. As examples, an urban development program may include several projects, such as housing rehab, job and skill training, and small business consulting assistance; a Mars exploration program may include several projects for unmanned probes to Mars and its moons, Phobos and Diemos, followed by a manned mission to Mars. Sometimes individual projects in a program grow to become so large that they themselves become full-fledged programs, as was the case with the Apollo Lunar Program. The Manhattan Project was really a "program."

Another distinction is that projects are oriented to producing and delivering a product or service, after which the project organization is dissolved. The project organization develops and delivers the end-item, but the operation and service of the end-item is someone else's responsibility. In a program, however, once the end-item product or service has been delivered, it is up to program management to ensure that it is integrated with other systems, and operational for as long as needed. For example, several contractors might produce and deliver a satellite and its booster rocket, but afterwards someone else is responsible for launching the rocket and satellite, and after that someone else again deals with monitoring and operating the orbiting satellite. Program management would oversee everything—the development of the satellite and rocket, launch support, ongoing satellite monitoring, and so on—whatever is needed to achieve the overall satellite program goal.

Most concepts in project management apply also to the management of programs, though with modification to deal with the larger scope and magnitude of programs. A program manager oversees and coordinates the projects within the program, but because a program is composed of teams from various projects, a program structure must be created to coordinate them. This structure is similar to (and overlays) the project structure. Contrast the structure of the typical aircraft development program shown in Figure 1.4 with the project management structure shown in Figure 1.3. Since

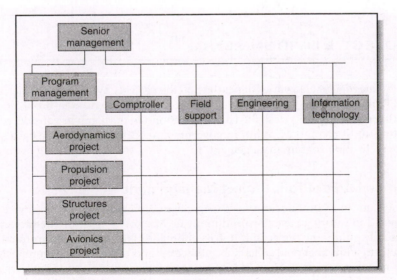

Figure 1.4
Typical aircraft development program.

many programs last too long for any one person to be in charge from start to finish, different people might occupy the role of program manager during a program's life.

New Venture Management

Project management resembles *new venture management*, a type of management used in consumer-oriented firms for generating new products or markets. In new venture management, a team is created to find new products or markets that fit an organization's specialized skills, capabilities, and resources. Once it has defined the product, the team may go on to design and develop it, then determine the means to produce, market, and distribute it.

Similarities between project management and venture management include:[15]

- The focus on a single unifying goal
- Their multidisciplinary nature, with experts and managers from various functional areas working together under a single head
- Being action-oriented and dedicated to change
- Their temporary character—once a new venture team has completed its assignment, members go back to their original departments or another venture group, or to a new division or a new company that splits off from the parent organization with the purpose of producing the newly developed product.

Product Management

The term *product management* refers to a single person responsible for overseeing all aspects of a product's production scheduling, inventory, distribution, and sales. The product manager coordinates and expedites the product's launch, manufacture, distribution, and support. Like the project manager, the product manager communicates directly with functions inside and outside the organization, and coordinates efforts directed at product goals. The product manager is active in managing conflicts and resolving problems that would degrade manufacturing capability, forestall distribution, alter price, harm sales, or in any way affect financing, production, and marketing of the product. For products with long life cycles, the product manager role is filled on a rotating basis.

1.7   PROJECT ENVIRONMENTS[16]

Project management also varies depending on the project environment, which author Daniel Roman classifies as commercial/for profit, government/non-profit, and military. All the project forms described above are found in the commercial environment. The forms most commonly found in government and the military are basic project management and program management.

Commercial/For-Profit Project Management

The end-item in a commercial project is a clearly defined product or service, often customized to satisfy a customer, and motivated by profit criteria. The project manager usually guides the project through its entire life cycle, coordinating efforts of the project team with functional areas, subcontractors, and vendors, and keeping the customer and top management informed of progress toward project and profit objectives.

Once the project is completed, the project team is dissolved and the project manager is potentially out of a job. Thus, some project managers are continually working to "perpetuate their existence" through preparing proposals and seeking out new projects, which may surface as extensions to existing projects or as upgrades to applications from former projects.

Government and Non-Profit Project Management

Government and non-profit projects differ from commercial activities in several ways. First, there is no profit incentive in government and non-profit work, and economic factors may be of lesser importance in project management. Project managers are frequently reassigned during their projects, which is problematic for administrative continuity. In government work particularly, project continuity depends heavily upon political considerations because funding is legislatively appropriated.

Second, most of these projects focus on evaluation or testing of products or services procured from commercial contractors or vendors. Because design and development work in government projects is usually done by contractors, the project manager's role is largely administrative. Though she is responsible for checking on the contractors' progress, the project manager has little control over technical matters. Project managers may oversee and coordinate multiple, related projects—in other words, they are program managers.

Military Project Management

Similar to government projects, most military projects involve testing and evaluating hardware developed by contractors. Evaluation is often based on the "weapons systems" approach, whereby each project is part of a larger systems program and hardware is evaluated for its contribution to the mission of the overall system. The major criteria for evaluating projects are technical and political; costs are of lesser importance and profit is not a consideration. Project managers are military officers. Because their tour of duty is limited, officers typically do not oversee a project for its full life cycle. The military must train or promote people with the administrative and technical competency to carry on the job.

Civilians are often employed to provide technical support and managerial continuity. This arrangement is a source of strife, because civilians are not subject to the same rotation of assignments and are often paid more, despite their formal "subordinate" status to military project managers.

1.8 PROJECT MANAGEMENT IN INDUSTRIAL SETTINGS

The following cases show typical applications of project management in a variety of industrial settings. They portray the diversity of situations in which project management is applied.

SpaceShipOne and the X-Prize Competition[17]

In April of 2003, SpaceShipOne (SS1) and its mothership White Knight were rolled out to the public. Simultaneously, it was announced that SS1 was entering the $10 million X-Prize competition, against 23 other teams from 7 countries, to be the first

Figure 1.5
SpaceShipOne beneath its mothership, White Knight.
Photograph courtesy of John Nicholas.

manned vehicle to successfully make two trips into space in less than 2 weeks (Figure 1.5). Space is internationally recognized as beginning at 100 km (or about 62 miles) up (commercial jets fly at about 8 km). The brainchild of celebrated aerospace engineer and visionary Burt Rutan and the culmination of almost 8 years of design and development work, it was but the first step in Rutan's broader dream to build vehicles to carry paying passengers into space. Rutan's major challenge was not just winning of the prize, but also designing and building a *complete space launch system*—spacecraft, aerial launch vehicle, rocket motor, and all support subsystems—without having many hundreds of engineers to do it and many millions of dollars in government support. Rutan would try to do it with his own company of 130 people, a small handful of subcontractors, and the $25 million backing of billionaire Paul Allen, cofounder of Microsoft.

Besides Rutan and Allen, the principal stakeholders in the program included the Ansari Foundation, Sir Richard Branson, and the FAA. The Ansari Foundation is the sponsor of the X-Prize competition. Its long-term goal is to spur innovations that will make space travel safe, affordable, and accessible to everyone, and its X-Prize requirements were for "a non-government-funded program to put three people safely into space twice within two weeks with a reusable spacecraft." Sir Richard Branson, founder of the Virgin Group, is the program's customer; his plan is to buy spaceships and the associated technology for his fledgling space airline, Virgin Galactic. Branson has estimated that Virgin will be able to turn a profit if it can carry 3,000 customers into sub-orbit over a 5-year period at about $190,000 a ticket—to include medical checks, 3 days of preflight training, custom-molded seats, and 5 minutes of floating weightless while in space. (By comparison, a trip aboard the Russian Soyuz costs about $20 million.) Paying passengers are another stakeholder group. Although none would be aboard SS1, the vehicle was designed with them in mind. For instance, SS1's cabin is designed to provide a "shirtsleeve" environment so passengers would not have to wear spacesuits. The FAA is also a stakeholder; it imposes a long list of requirements necessary for the spaceship to be "certified" and commercially viable.

As in most technical projects, a project engineer as well as a project manager oversees the project. The project engineer is responsible for identifying technical requirements and overseeing design work, system integration, and testing. All this, and what is left for the project manager to do, will become clearer in later chapters.

The Development of Product J at Dalian Company[18]

The future of Dalian Company depends on its ability to continuously develop and market new products. Dalian specializes in food and drink additives, but it is representative of firms in industries such as pharmaceuticals, food products, biotechnology, home and commercial appliances, computer and entertainment electronics, and communications that must continuously generate new products to survive in a competitive environment.

Dalian Company was concerned about maintaining market share for "Product H," a mainstay that accounted for the majority of its profits. It was known that competitors were developing substitutes for Product H that might be less expensive. To beat the competition, Dalian had to develop its own improved substitute, "Product J."

The product development process is facilitated by the New Product Development Department. The department is a "project office" responsible for ongoing management and coordination of all internal and externally contracted development projects so that good ideas can be developed and quickly brought to market. The department has three directors of product development who are the project managers. Each director is responsible for a certain kind of project—exploration and development, technology-related new business, and new product commercialization—and typically manages several projects at a time. The directors facilitate, coordinate, and monitor the project efforts of the various departments—research and development, engineering, marketing, manufacturing, and legal.

For each new product concept, a team is created with representatives from functional departments. A director works with the team on a weekly or daily basis to assess the project's progress and requirements. Functional managers decide what is to be done and how, but the directors have the final say over project direction. Each director always knows the status of the project and reports problems or delays to upper management, which manages the projects as a "portfolio." Projects with big problems or signs of failure are cancelled so resources can be allocated to more promising projects.

Development of Product J required many tasks: R&D needed to develop a product prototype and prepare specifications; engineering needed to define where and in what ways the product would be used; marketing needed to define the commercial market and determine how to position the product; manufacturing needed to develop a new process for making the product that would be difficult for competitors to copy; finance needed to determine the initial product costing and perform profit/loss forecasts; and legal needed to obtain regulatory approval and perform patent research.

The director for Product J was involved from project conception. She worked with R&D scientists and marketing experts to determine the feasibility of the project, and was active in convincing upper management to approve it. She worked with scientists and managers to prepare project plans and schedules. When additional labor, equipment, instruments, or raw materials were needed, she wrote requests for funds. When additional personnel were needed, she wrote personnel requests to upper management. During the project she issued monthly and quarterly progress reports, and scheduled and chaired all project review meetings.

This project was similar to many development projects. Every development project is unique, and therefore has to be estimated, planned, and organized from scratch.

Small Projects at Delamir Roofing Company

Delamir Roofing Company installs and repairs roofs for factories and businesses throughout the US. Like other businesses associated with the construction industry, Delamir considers each job a project, and assigns a project manager to oversee it.

Involvement of the project manager begins when a request for work is received from a potential customer. The project manager examines the blueprints to determine how much material and labor time will be needed (called "prepping the job"), and then prepares a budget and a short proposal. After a contract is acquired, the project manager goes to the site ahead of the crew to make arrangements and accommodations for work to begin. The project manager has discretion in work crew selection, which depends on how many workers are needed and who is available. After work begins, he is responsible not only for supervision of work and delivery of supplies, but also for maintaining budget records and reporting progress to the home office. The project manager performs the final inspection with the customer and signs off when the job is completed.

In this example, the project manager ensures that the size and skills of the crew fit the requirements of the job, and that, overall, the job is done well.

1.9 PROJECT MANAGEMENT IN THE SERVICE SECTOR

Project management is also employed in a broad range of services, including banking, consulting, and accounting. In the next example, project management is used to plan and control auditing and management consultation projects in a large accounting firm called CPAone. A second example shows project management applied to a non-profit fundraising campaign.

Improving Auditing Efficiency at CPAone[19]

The auditing division at CPAone generates financial statements to meet generally accepted accounting principles. In large audits, the size of the task requires the involvement of many people. In the audit of a national corporation, for example, numerous auditors with diverse specialties are required to investigate all aspects of operations in various geographic areas. Given the number of people and the variety of skills, expertise, and personalities involved, a project manager is needed to oversee the audit. Every audit begins by assigning the client to a partner who is familiar with the client's business. The partner becomes the audit's "project director," responsible for the project's initiation, staffing, scheduling, and budgeting.

The project director begins by studying the client's income statement, balance sheet, and other financial statements. If the client has a bad financial reputation, the project director can make the decision for CPAone to refuse the audit. If the client is accepted, the director prepares a proposal that explains the general approach for conducting the audit and designates the completion date and the cost estimate.

In determining the general approach for conducting the audit, the project director considers the company's size and number of departments. Auditors are then assigned on a department-by-department basis. The audit team is a pure project team, created anew for every audit, composed of people who have the skills best suited to the needs of the audit. Generally, each audit team has one or two staff accountants and one or two senior accountants. The project cost estimate is based on estimated labor hours multiplied by employees' hourly wages.

During the audit, the director monitors all work to ensure that it adheres to the Book of Auditing Standards and is completed on schedule. Each week, the client and project director meet to review progress. When problems cannot be solved immediately, the director may call in people for CPAone's tax or consulting divisions. If the IRS requests an examination after the audit is completed, the project director sees to it that the client is represented.

Non-Profit Fundraising Campaign Project: Archdiocese of Boston[20]

American Services Company, a fund-raising consulting firm for non-profit organizations, contracted with the Archdiocese of Boston to manage a 3-year campaign to raise $30 million for education, social and healthcare services, building renovations, and a clergy retirement fund. American Services appointed a project manager to prepare the campaign strategy and to organize and direct the campaign staff. The project manager had to deal with issues concerning three groups: donors, the Archdiocese Board of Directors, and campaign volunteers. Potential target donors had to be identified and provided with evidence to show how their financial commitments would benefit the community and the Archdiocese; the board and church leadership had to be involved in and kept apprised of campaign planning and progress; and volunteers had to be identified, organized, and motivated.

One of the project manager's first tasks was to conduct a feasibility study to determine whether there was sufficient leadership capability, volunteer willingness, and "donor depth" within the Archdiocese community to achieve the $30 million goal. Following the study, which indicated that the goal was achievable, pastors were invited to a kick-off luncheon at which time the Cardinal of the Archdiocese introduced the campaign. During the meeting, influential church personnel were signed up and the process of identifying potential donors and volunteers started.

The project manager provided guidance for establishing a campaign leadership team and project office, enlisting volunteers, forming campaign committees, and recruiting and training volunteers. In addition to organizational matters, he convened several "reality sessions" with chairpersons to remind them of the importance of the campaign and renew their commitment to the campaign goal, and organized frequent meetings with the volunteers to instill a sense of pride and involvement in the campaign.

1.10 PROJECT AND PROGRAM MANAGEMENT IN THE PUBLIC SECTOR AND GOVERNMENT

The following two illustrations about disaster recovery and the NASA organization illustrate how project management and program management is performed in large public sector and joint government/commercial undertakings.

Disaster Recovery

The aid assistance, clean-up, rebuilding, and return-to-normalcy efforts following a disaster involve the labors of numerous organizations. A large disaster such the December 2004 tsunami in the Indian Ocean impacts many countries, and requires the support and coordinated efforts of host governments; non-governmental agencies (NGOs); local business, religious, and community organizations; and international aid, charitable, and funding organizations.

Almost by definition, post-disaster recovery is a program or several programs—a host of efforts devoted to the goals of rescuing and providing immediate relief to victims and, ultimately, to returning the lives of people in the areas affected back to normal. Each program involves many projects to address the multiple aspects of a recovery effort, including projects to provide:[21]

- Immediate rescue of victims
- Food and medical care
- Temporary shelter and housing
- Clothing, blankets, and other immediate physical needs
- Social, moral, and spiritual assistance.

Ideally, disaster recovery is treated as an organized, coordinated effort—a managed program with numerous projects that enable quick assessment of the scope of the situation, identification and organization of needed and available resources, and effective deployment of those resources. For all of that to happen effectively requires leadership, usually in the person of someone with exceptionally strong organization and leadership abilities—in effect, a *program leader*. In the chaos and frenzy immediately following a disaster, however, it is often not clear who is in charge. Indeed, the poor immediate response and confused rescue and recovery efforts in New Orleans and the surrounding US Gulf coastal region following Hurricane Katrina has been blamed on a lack of leadership and coordinated management at all levels of government—federal, state, and local.

In the months and years following a disaster, the focus turns to obtaining and allocating aid funding; reconstruction, redevelopment, and rebuilding (infrastructure, organizations, facilities); permanently situating (returning home or relocating) victims; dealing with waste and debris; and providing opportunities, jobs and ongoing support. To accomplish this requires numerous projects—for instance, projects to obtain and allocate financial assistance to individuals, businesses, and local government, and to provide subsidized housing and building materials. Often, the goal is to employ the victims in many small-scale, labor-intensive projects to provide jobs and income.

For example, the December 2004 tsunami caused severe damage to coastal areas in Sri Lanka, Thailand, Indonesia, the Maldives, and other countries around the Indian Ocean; in India alone it affected an estimated 2.7 million already-poor people, 80 percent of whose livelihoods depended on fishing while 15 percent depended on agriculture. The government of India launched the Emergency Tsunami Reconstruction Project, estimated to cost US$682.8 million, to help repair or reconstruct about 140,000 damaged houses in two coastal regions and assist with the reconstruction of public buildings and the revival of livelihoods in fisheries and agriculture.[22] It is a project that in fact will consist of many hundreds of projects, take many years, and continue for as long as the funding holds out.

NASA Organization and Project Management[23]

NASA was created in 1958 from what had been the National Advisory Committee on Aeronautics (NACA). NACA had had a long, successful history of working intimately with researchers in universities, industry, and the military, and at NASA there remained a determination to continue that partnership-style of operation. NASA and industry would work closely together on technical problems, but technical initiative and technical decisions would be left to NASA field installations.

NASA organization includes: (1) top management, (2) functional support for top management, (3) program offices for developing and controlling major programs, and (4) field installations, which conduct the programs and their projects on-site or at universities or contractors. NASA is divided into four mission directorates or offices: Exploration Systems, Space Operations, Science, and Aeronautics Research (see Figure 1.6).

Each directorate is responsible for the development, justification, and management of *programs* that support broad NASA goals. Directorates are assigned field

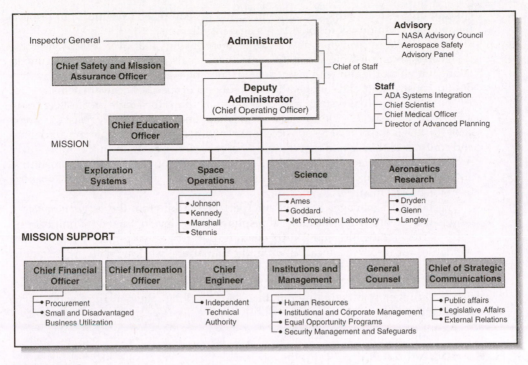

Figure 1.6
NASA program and organization chart.

installations to carry out permanent activities for the directorate, but also carry out projects or tasks under the direction of other directorates. For example, though Ames reports to Science, it also contributes to projects in Space Operations.

All four kinds of project managers described earlier—expeditor, coordinator, matrix, and pure project—are found at NASA, but the latter two are more common. The matrix is preferred for its flexibility and efficient use of talent. Employees from field centers and contractors are assigned to a project, but remain on the payrolls of their parent organization and subject to its merit reviews and promotions. Most stay in the offices of the parent organization. For the largest projects, however, the pure project form is used because it permits better control, quicker reaction from the project team, and simpler communication patterns.

In a typical (non-NASA) government project, the agency prepares specifications for a program, lets a contract, and then relies on the contractor for results. NASA uses a different approach; it feels that no single company has all of the capability to execute a large project. Although NASA relies upon industry to build, integrate, and test-fly hardware, it relies upon its own considerable in-house management and technical competence to monitor and work with contractors. Because NASA projects call for a diversity of technical and managerial competency, project managers practice the philosophy of "participative responsibility"—an integration of technical and managerial competency across industry, academia, and NASA laboratories. Regardless of location, NASA brings in experts from its own field installations, universities, and other government laboratories to assist contractors in tackling difficult problems. This participative team approach avoids the usual delays caused by working across boundaries which separate government, commercial, and military organizations. The concept utilizes teamwork, central control, and decentralized execution, but respects the semi-autonomous status of NASA's field installations.

NASA defines a *program* as a series of undertakings that over several years are designed to accomplish broad scientific or technical goals. It defines a *project* as an undertaking within a program with a scheduled beginning and end, and normally involves design, construction, and/or operation and support of specific hardware items.

NASA uses a dual system of responsibility. Perhaps the single greatest contributor to a project's success is the person upon whom final responsibility rests: the *project manager*. She is the official responsible for executing the project within the guidelines and controls of NASA, and for day-to-day supervision, execution, and completion of projects. Although most of the workers on a project are outside of the administrative authority of the project manager, nonetheless they take directions *on project matters* from the project manager.

Each project manager has a counterpart in Washington, the *program manager*, who is the senior NASA staff official responsible for developing and administering headquarter's guidelines and controls with respect to a given project. He must fight the battles for resource allocation within headquarters, work with all organizations participating in the project, relate the project to NASA's broader goals, and testify to or justify authorizations from Congress or the president. The success of a project depends on the project and program managers working together, and the quality of their relationship.

1.11 SUMMARY

Project management is a systems-contingency approach to organization and management; it applies elements of classical and behavioral management and uses organizational forms and management roles best suited to the unique environment of projects.

The most important aspect of project management is the project manager—the person who functions to unify project-related planning, communications, control, and direction to achieve project goals. The project manager is the integrator who ties together the efforts of functional areas, suppliers, and contractors, and keeps top management and the customer apprised of project progress. Project management includes many things, but in particular the organization, systems, and procedures to enable the project manager to plan, organize, direct, and integrate everything necessary to achieve project goals.

Project management can be applied to any temporary, goal-oriented activity, but it becomes more essential as the magnitude, unfamiliarity, and stake of the undertaking increase. Organizations in rapidly changing business and technology environments especially need project management.

Project management takes on a variety of forms: larger efforts typically utilize pure project, matrix, and program management forms; smaller efforts are handled by project expeditors and coordinators. Consumer-oriented firms use new-venture and product-management forms that are similar to basic project management. Project management is applied in much the same way in commercial, non-profit, government, and military projects, with variations to account for differences in the environments.

Project management is a "systems approach" to management. The next chapter describes what that means, and discusses the systems philosophy and methodologies that underlie much of project management theory and practice.

REVIEW QUESTIONS AND PROBLEMS

1. Describe five functions of management. Are any of these not performed by managers? How do you think each of these functions comes into play in the course of a project?

2. Describe the classical and behavioral viewpoints of management and how they differ from the systems approach. The classical and behavioral viewpoints originated decades ago. Are they still of use today? (For a better idea of how the viewpoints differ, refer to current popular management references or texts.)

3. Explain what distinguishes the contingency approach to management from the other three viewpoints.

4. List the main characteristics of "projects." How do these features distinguish projects from other, non-project activities?

5. What are the characteristics of "project management?" Contrast these with functional and other types of non-project management.

6. What makes project management more suitable to project environments than traditional management and organization?

7. Where did project management methods and organization originate? What happened during the twentieth century that made project management necessary?

8. What are the four types of project management roles? Describe the responsibilities of managers in each role. Are all four roles ever used in the same organization?

9. What are the five criteria that Cleland and King suggest for determining when to use project management? From these, describe briefly how a manager should know when project management is appropriate for the task.

10. When is project management clearly not appropriate? List some "project-type" activities where you think project management should *not* be used. Describe organizations or kinds of work where both project and non-project types of management are appropriate.

11. Briefly compare and contrast the following forms of project management: pure project, matrix, program, new venture, product, and *ad hoc* committee/task force. For each form, give at least one example of an organization where it is used.

12. What are some of the problems of being a project leader in commercial, government, and military projects? Where do organizations in these environments get project leaders from?

13. In the industry, service sector, and government examples in this chapter, what common characteristics of the environment, the project goals, and the project tasks make project management appropriate (or necessary)? Also, what seem to be the common characteristics of the roles and responsibilities of the project managers in these examples? What are the differences?

14. Now that you know a little about projects and project management, list some government and private organizations where you think project management might be useful. You might want to check to see if, in fact, they *are* using project management.

QUESTIONS ABOUT THE STUDY PROJECT

1. In the project you are studying, what characteristics of the company, project goals, tasks, or necessary expertise make the use of project management appropriate or inappropriate? Consider the project size, complexity, risk, and other criteria in answering this question.

2. How does the project you are studying fit the definition of a project?
3. What kind of project management is used—program, product, matrix, pure, or other? Explain. Is it called "project management," or something else?
4. What kind of role does the project manager have—expeditor, coordinator, pure project, or matrix manager? Explain. What is his or her title?

Case 1.1   Disaster Recovery at Marshall Field's[24]

Early one morning, basements in Chicago's downtown central business district began to flood. A hole the size of an automobile had developed between the river and an adjacent abandoned tunnel. The tunnel, built in the early 1900s for transporting coal, runs throughout the downtown area. When the tunnel flooded, so did the basements of buildings connected to it—some 272 in all, including that of major retailer Marshall Field's.

The problem was first noted at 5.30 am, when a member of the Marshall Field's trouble desk saw water pouring into the basement. The manager of maintenance was notified and immediately took charge. His first actions were to contact the Chicago Fire and Water Departments, and Marshall Field's parent company, Dayton Hudson in Minneapolis. Electricity—and with it all elevator, computer, communication, and security services for the 15-story building—would soon be lost. The building was evacuated, and elevators were moved above basement levels. A command post was set up and a team formed from various departments, such as facilities, security, human resources, public relations, and financial, legal, insurance, and support services. Later that day, members of Dayton Hudson's risk management group arrived from Minneapolis to take over coordinating the team's efforts. The team's goal was to ensure the safety of employees and customers, minimize flood damage, and resume normal operations as soon as possible. The team hoped to open the store to customers 1 week after the flood began.

An attempt was made to pump the water out; however, as long as the tunnel hole remained unrepaired, the Chicago River continued to pour back into the basements. Thus, the basements remained flooded until the tunnel was sealed and the Army Corps of Engineers gave approval to start pumping. Everything in the second-level basement was a loss, including equipment for security, heating, ventilation, air-conditioning, fire sprinkling, and mechanical services. Most merchandise in the first-level basement stockrooms was also lost.

Electricians worked around the clock to install emergency generators and restore lighting and elevator service. Additional security officers were hired. An emergency pumping system and new piping to the water-sprinkling tank were installed so the sprinkler system could be reactivated. Measures were taken to monitor ventilation and air quality, and dehumidifiers and fans were installed to improve air quality. Within the week, inspectors from the City of Chicago and OSHA gave approval to reopen the store.

After water was drained from Marshall Field's basements, damaged merchandise was removed and sold to a salvager. The second basement had to be gutted to assure removal of contaminants. Salvageable machinery had to be disassembled and sanitized.

The extent of the damage was assessed and insurance claims filed. A construction company was hired to manage restoration of the damaged areas. Throughout the ordeal, the public relations department dealt with the media, being candid yet showing confidence in the recovery effort. Customers had to be assured that the store was safe. The team overseeing the recovery initially met twice a week to evaluate progress and make decisions, then slowly disbanded as the store recovered.

This case illustrates crisis management, an important element of which is having a team that can move fast to minimize losses and quickly recover damages. At the beginning of a disaster there is little time to plan, though companies and public agencies often have crisis guidelines for responding to emergency situations. When an emergency occurs they then develop more specific, detailed plans to guide short- and long-term recovery efforts.

QUESTIONS

1. In what ways was the Marshall Field's flood disaster recovery effort a project? Why are large-scale disaster response and recovery efforts projects?
2. In what ways do the characteristics of crisis management as described in this case correspond to those of project management?
3. Who was (were) the project manager(s), and what was his (their) responsibility? Who was assigned to the project team, and why were they on the team?
4. Comment on the appropriateness of using project management for managing disaster recovery efforts such as this.
5. What form of project management (basic, program, and so on) does this case most closely resemble?

Case 1.2 Flexible Benefits System Implementation at Shah Alam Medical Center[25]

The senior management of Shah Alam Medical Center decided to procure and implement a new system that would reduce the cost and improve the value and service of its employee benefits coverage. The new system would have to meet four goals: improved responsiveness to employee needs, added benefits flexibility, better cost management, and greater coordination of human resource objectives with business strategies. A multifunctional team of 13 members was formed with representatives from the departments that would rely most on the new system—Human Resources (HR), Financial Systems (FS), and Information Services (IS). This team would ensure that the departments' needs would be met. The team also included six technical experts from the consulting firm of Hun and Bar Software (HBS).

Early in the project a workshop was held with participants from Shah Alam and HBS to clarify and finalize project objectives and develop a project plan, milestones, and schedule. Project completion was set at 10 months. In that time, HBS had to develop and supply all hardware and software for the new system; the system had to be brought on-line, tested, and approved; HR workers had to be trained how to operate the system and load existing employee data; all Shah Alam employees had to be educated about and enrolled in the new benefits process; and the enrollment data had to be entered in the system.

The director of FS was chosen to oversee the project. She had the technical background, and had previously worked in the IS group in implementing Shah Alam's patient care information system; everyone on the team approved of her appointment as project leader. She selected two team leaders to assist her, one each from HR and IS. The HR leader's task was to ensure that the new system met HR requirements and the needs of Shah Alam employees. The IS leader's task was to ensure that the new software interfaced with other Shah Alam systems.

Members of the Shah Alam team worked on the project on a part-time basis, spending roughly half the time on the project and the other half on their normal daily duties. The project manager and team leaders also worked part-time on the project, although each gave the project priority. Shah Alam's senior management had made it clear that meeting project requirements and time deadlines was imperative. The project manager was given authority over functional managers and project team members for all project-related decisions.

QUESTIONS

1. What form of project management (basic, program, etc.) does this case most closely resemble?
2. The project manager is also the director of FS, one of several departments that will be affected by the new benefits system. Does this seem like a good idea? What are the pros and cons of her being selected?
3. Comment on the team members' part-time assignment to the project, and the expectation that they give the project top priority.
4. Much of the success of this project depends on the performance of team members who are not employed by Shah Alam, namely the HBS consultants. They must develop the entire hardware/software benefits system. Why was an outside firm likely chosen for such an important part of the project? What difficulties might this pose to the project manager in meeting project goals?

NOTES

1. Lord MG. *Astro Turf*. New York, NY: Walker & Co.; 2005, p. 166.
2. Adapted from Szilagyi A. *Management and Performance*, 2nd edn. Glenview, IL: Scott, Foresman; 1984, pp. 7–10, 16–20, 29–32.
3. One of the earliest discussions of this viewpoint appeared in Roethlisberger FJ and Dickson WJ. *Management and the Worker*. Boston, MA: Harvard University Press; 1939.
4. See, for example, Hersey P, Blanchard K, and Johnson D. *Management of Organizational Behavior: Utilizing Human Resources*, 9th edn. Upper Saddle River, NJ: Prentice Hall; 2008. This volume presents the "situational leadership" theory and applications.
5. See Hellriegel D and Slocum J. Organizational design: a contingency approach. *Business Horizons* 16(2); 1973: 59–68.
6. Archibald R. *Managing High-Technology Projects*. New York, NY: Wiley; 1976, p. 19; Meredith J and Mantel S. *Project Management: A Managerial Approach*, 3rd edn. New York, NY: Wiley; 1995, pp. 7–9; Roman D. *Managing Projects: A Systems Approach*. New York, NY: Elsevier; 1986, pp. 2–10; Stewart J. Making project management work. *Business Horizons* 8(3); 1965: 54–68.
7. Cleland D and King W. *Systems Analysis and Project Management*, 3rd edn. New York, NY: McGraw-Hill; 1983, pp. 191–192.
8. Davis K. The role of project management in scientific manufacturing. *IEEE Transactions of Engineering Management* 9(3); 1962: 109–113.
9. Portions of this section are adapted from Johnson R, Kast F, and Rosenzweig J. *The Theory and Management of Systems*, 3rd edn. New York, NY: McGraw-Hill; 1973, pp. 395–397.
10. Cleland and King, *Systems Analysis and Project Management*, p. 259.
11. Based upon Hofer W. Lady Liberty's business army. *Nation's Business* July; 1983: 18–28.
12. Sharad S. Management by projects, and ideological breakthrough. *Project Management Journal* March; 1986: 61–63.
13. Adams J, Barndt S, and Martin M. *Managing by Project Management*. Dayton, OH: Universal Technology; 1979, pp. 12–13.
14. For more detail, see Reiss G. *Programme Management Demystified: Managing Multiple Projects Successfully*. London: E&FN Spon Chapman & Hall; 1996.
15. Szilagyi, *Management and Performance*, pp. 489–490.
16. This section is adapted from Roman D. *Managing Projects: A Systems Approach*. New York, NY: Elsevier; 1986, pp. 426–429, with the permission of the publisher.
17. This and examples in later chapters of SpaceShipOne illustrate concepts. While much factual information about the project and the systems is available from published sources, information about the design and development of the systems is confidential. SpaceShipOne, the X-Prize, and the stakeholders described are all true-life; however, for lack of information, portions of this and subsequent examples are hypothetical.
18. Based upon information compiled by Jenny Harrison from interviews with managers in Dalian Company (fictitious name).
19. Based upon information compiled by Darlene Capodice from interviews with managers in two accounting firms.
20. Information about this project contributed by Daniel Molson, Mike Billish, May Cumba,

Jesper Larson, Anne Lanagan, Madeleine Pember, and Diane Petrozzo.

21. *Disaster Response. Lesson 7: Emergency Operations Support*. University of Wisconsin, Disaster Management Center, http://dmc.engr.wisc.edu/courses/response/BB08-07.html.

22. *India: Emergency Tsunami Reconstruction Project*. The World Bank Group May 3; 2005, Press Release No: 453/SAR/2005, ReliefWeb, http://www.reliefweb.int/rw/RWB.NSF/ db900SID/ VBOL-6C3CF8?OpenDocument&rc=3&cc=ind

23. Portions of this section are adapted from Chapman R. *Project Management in NASA: The System and The Men*. Washington, DC: NASA SP-324, NTIS No. N75-15692; 1973.

24. Information about this case contributed by Jennifer Koziol, Sussan Arias, Linda Clausen, Gilbert Rogers, and Nidia Sakac.

25. Information about this case contributed by Debbie Tomczak, Bill Baginski, Terry Bradley, Brad Carlson, and Tom Delaney. Organizational names are fictitious but the case is factual.

Chapter  2

Systems Approach and Systems Engineering

> *There is so much talk about the system.*
> *And so little understanding.*

> —ROBERT M. PIRSIG,
> *Zen and the Art of Motorcycle Maintenance*

A project is a *system* of people, equipment, materials, and facilities organized and managed to achieve a goal. Much of the established theory and practice about what it takes to put together and coordinate a project comes from a perspective called the "systems approach." At the same time, work done in projects is often done for the purpose of *creating* systems, and in these projects methodologies such as "systems analysis," "systems engineering," and "systems management" are commonplace. This chapter introduces concepts that form the basis for project management and the systems methodologies commonly used in technical projects.

2.1 SYSTEMS THINKING

Systems thinking is a way of viewing the world. The key feature of systems thinking is focus on the "whole system or organism" rather than just the parts. It is the opposite of analytical thinking, which breaks things into smaller parts to better understand them. Systems thinkers look at the parts, too, and try to understand the relationships among them, but they *always* step back to see how the parts fit into the whole.[1]

Systems thinking means being able to perceive the "system" in a situation, to take a seemingly confused, chaotic situation and perceive some degree of order or harmony in it. As such, it is a useful way for dealing with complex phenomena, especially human-created systems and endeavors such as large projects.

Project managers must be familiar with and able to coordinate the individual parts of the project, but responsibility for each of those parts is largely delegated to the managers and technicians who specialize in them. Project managers are concerned with the "big picture"—the whole project, with its goals, stakeholders, and environment; they must be systems thinkers.

2.2 DEFINITION OF SYSTEM

To some people the term "system" means computer; to others it means bureaucracy. But the term is so commonly used that it could probably refer to almost everything. By definition, a system is "an organized or complex whole; *an assemblage of things or parts interacting in a coordinated way."* The parts could be players in a football team, keys on a keyboard, or components in a machine. The parts can be physical entities or they can be abstract or conceptual, such as words in a language or steps in a procedure. The word is associated every day with such disparate things as river systems, planetary systems, transportation and communication systems, nervous and circulatory systems, production and inventory systems, ecosystems, urban systems, social systems, economic systems, *ad infinitum*. Thus, a system *can* be just about anything, but besides being an "assemblage of parts" it has three other features:[2]

1. Parts of the system *affect the system* and *are affected* by it
2. The assemblage of parts *does* something; it serves a purpose or goal
3. The assemblage is of particular interest.

The first feature means that, in systems, the whole is more than the sum of the parts. The human body, for example, can be analyzed in terms of separate components—the liver, brain, heart, nerve fibers, and so on—yet if any of these are removed from the body, both they and the body will change. Parts of the body cannot live outside the body, and without the parts, the body cannot live either. The name given to the whole being more than the sum of the parts is *holism*. Holism is the opposite of *reductionism*, the philosophy that things can be understood by simply breaking them down into pieces and understanding the pieces. Certainly, many things cannot be understood by looking at the pieces. Knowing that hydrogen and oxygen are gases would never lead you to know that when combined, they form a liquid. The idea of the parts affecting the whole and *vice versa* is central to systems thinking.

The second feature of systems is that they are dynamic—they exhibit some kind of *behavior*; they *do* something. The kind of behavior they exhibit depends upon the particular kind of system at hand, but can usually be observed in the outputs of the system or the way the system converts inputs to outputs (although sometimes that conversion process may be quite obscure). In a system, the parts interact. In human-made systems, they are designed to interact to achieve some purpose or goal.

Third, systems are conceived by the people looking at them, which means they exist in the eye (or mind) of the beholder.[3] This is not to say that they do not exist unless someone is there to see them, but rather that the conception of a system can be altered to suit one's purpose. For example, in diagnosing the illness in a patient, a doctor may see the entire human body as "the system." The doctor may send the patient to a specialist, who sees only the digestive tract as "the system." If the diagnosis is food poisoning and the patient files suit, her attorney might expand the view of "the system" to include the restaurant where the victim last ate.

Systems can be classified as either *natural* or *human-made*. Natural systems came into being by natural processes (e.g., animal organisms and planetary systems). Human-made systems are designed and operated by people (e.g., communication systems and human organizations). Projects exist for the purpose of creating human-made systems.

Natural systems can be altered by or become intertwined with human-made systems. An example is the alteration of a river system and formation of a lake by building a dam; another is the alteration of the composition of atmosphere and ecosystem through CO_2 and pollutants introduced by human-made machines.

Human-made systems are embedded in and utilize inputs from natural systems, and both systems interact in important and significant ways. In recent years the appearance of large-scale human-made systems has had a significant, mostly undesirable, impact on the natural world. Examples abound, such as global warming, acid rain, and toxic contamination of water systems. Such consequences, referred to as "side effects," arise largely because system designers and users fail to consider (or chose to ignore) the impacts of human-made systems on the natural environment.

2.3 SYSTEMS CONCEPTS AND PRINCIPLES

The following concepts and principles apply to all systems.

Goals and Objectives

Human-made systems are designed to *do* something; they have goals and objectives that are conceived by people. For the intentions of this book, a *goal* is defined as a broad, all-encompassing statement of the purpose of a system, and an *objective* as a more detailed, usually quantifiable statement of purpose pertaining to some aspect of the system. The system goal is met by achieving a group of system objectives. Hence, in designing a human-made system, the place to start is with a definition of the goal of the system, and then with a hierarchy of objectives that relate to aspects of the system.

A project can be conceptualized as a system that exists for the purpose of creating a human-made system. The goal of the project may be defined as, for example, "build a space station for \$15 billion in 10 years." Starting with the goal, the project can then be defined in terms of a hierarchy of many objectives, such as "select overall design for the station," "select prime contractors," "train crew," "launch components into orbit," "assemble components," "cost \$15 billion," and so on. The objectives can be broken down into more detailed, specific objectives called *requirements*. Requirements are the specific criteria to which the system and its parts must conform for the system to meet its overall goals and objectives.

Elements and Subsystems

Any system can be broken down into smaller parts. These parts in combination form "the assemblage of parts" that constitutes the system. The smallest part of a system is an *element*. A system also can be broken down into parts which are themselves systems, called *subsystems*. A subsystem is a system that functions as a component of a larger system. When it is not necessary to understand its inner workings, a subsystem can simply be thought of as an element. Figure 2.1, a common organization chart, illustrates that the production subsystem may be viewed as an "element" in the company; if we choose to delve into it, however, production becomes a subsystem with elements of scheduling, manufacturing, and inventory. Each of these elements could in turn be viewed as a subsystem containing elements. For example, the manufacturing element can be viewed as a subsystem with the elements of team A and team B. In a project, an element could be a unit of work, a person or group doing the work, or a component of the end-item being produced by the project.

Attributes

Systems, subsystems, and elements all have distinguishing characteristics called *attributes*; these describe the condition of systems, subsystems, and elements in qualitative or quantitative terms. In human-made systems, attributes are often designed into the system because they are necessary for the system to perform as required. Often, the attributes of a system and its components are monitored to keep track of the system's behavior and performance. Time and cost are universal attributes of most elements in a project, and are tracked to assess the project's performance.

Figure 2.1
A company portrayed in terms of systems, subsystems, and elements.

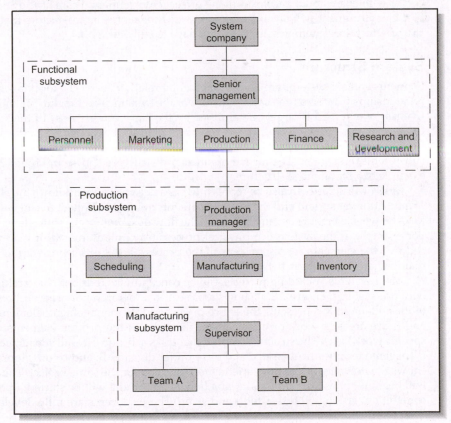

Environment and Boundary

The term *environment* refers to anything outside the system that influences the behavior or outcome of the system. In human-made systems, it usually refers to things over which system designers and managers have no control. The environment can include, for example, the community or society we live in, the air we breathe, or the people with whom we associate—although it is not necessarily any of these. A system is separated from its environment by a *boundary*. In many systems the boundary is somewhat obscure, and it is difficult to separate the system from its environment. To determine what the environment is, ask the questions "Can I do anything about it?" and "Is it relevant to the system and its objectives?" If the answer is "no" to the first question but "yes" to the second, then "it" is part of the environment. The following table shows how to distinguish a system from its environment:

		Is it relevant to the system?	
		Yes	No
Can system designers or managers control it?	Yes	System	Irrelevant Environment
	No	Environment	

Irrelevant environment includes all things that do not influence the system and that do not matter. To a project manager, the planet Jupiter is in the irrelevant environment—unless his project is to send a space probe there, in which case Jupiter is certainly relevant and, hence, part of the project environment. From here on, mention of the environment will always refer to the *relevant environment*—factors that matter to and affect the system in some way, but have to be lived with.

System Structure

Elements and subsystems are linked together by relationships. The form taken by the relationships is referred to as the structure of the system. The functioning and effectiveness of a system is largely determined by the "appropriateness" of the structure to the system's objective or purpose. Most complex systems have hierarchical structures consisting of organized levels of sub-elements within elements, elements within subsystems, and so on. The formal organization structure shown in Figure 2.1 is an example of a hierarchical structure.

System structure can also be represented as a network, which shows the elements of a functioning system and the way they are interrelated or linked. In a network, the links between elements usually represent the flow of something, or interdependency. For example, if the system is a physical process (say an automated or manual procedure), the elements represent steps in the process, and links represent the flow of material and information between them.

Most systems, including projects, can be conceptualized as both hierarchical and network systems. Figure 2.2(a) shows a project as a hierarchy of tasks and responsibilities. Element X represents the entire project and its management; elements A, B, and C are areas of work or management divisions in the project; elements a–g are specific work tasks. The structure implies that tasks a, b, and c are all subsumed under management division A, tasks d and e are under division B, and so on. Figure 2.2(b) shows the flow of work in time-oriented progression for the same project. The project will begin with task d; upon d's completion, tasks e and a will be started; upon their completion, task b will be started—and so on. These concepts are fully developed in Chapters 5 and 6.

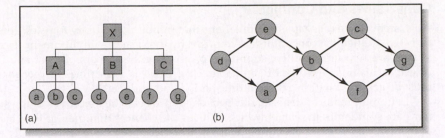

Figure 2.2

Ways of conceptualizing project systems.

(a) Project as a hierarchy of tasks and responsibilities. Element X represents the entire project and its management; elements A, B, and C are areas of work or management divisions in the project; elements a–g are specific work tasks. (b) Flow of work in time-oriented progression for the same project.

Inputs, Process, Outputs

Systems accomplish goals and objectives by converting *inputs* into *outputs* through a defined *process*. This is illustrated in Figure 2.3. Outputs represent the end-result of a system and, generally, the purpose for which the system exists. All systems have multiple outputs, including desirable ones that contribute to system objectives, neutral ones, and undesirable or wasteful ones that detract from system objectives and/or negatively impact the environment. Subsystems and most elements have inputs and outputs too.

Inputs are the raw materials, resources, or prerequisite steps necessary for the system to function and produce outputs. They include controllable factors such as labor, materials, information, capital, energy, and facilities, as well as uncontrollable factors such as weather and natural phenomena (the environment). Inputs that originate from the system itself are called feedback. For example, all systems produce information; usage of that information for guiding system behavior is called feedback input.

Process is the means by which the system physically converts or transforms inputs into outputs. An important aspect of system design is to create a process that effectively produces the desired outputs and meets system objectives, yet minimizes consumption of inputs and production of wasteful outputs.

In a hierarchical structure where systems are divided into subsystems, the subsystems each have their own inputs, process, and outputs that are interconnected in some way. In Figure 2.2(b), the output of element d becomes the input for elements e and a; the outputs of elements e and a become the inputs for element b, and so on.

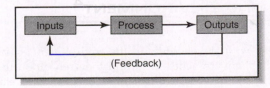

(Feedback)

Figure 2.3
Input–process–output relationship.

Constraints and Conflicts

All systems have *constraints* or limitations that inhibit their ability to reach goals and objectives. Often the constraints are imposed by the system's environment. Time and money are two universal constraints in projects; without them, almost any project objective imaginable would be attainable. The trouble is, most times project objectives must be achieved within a limited time period and budget.

In human-made systems, and especially in projects, the objectives of the subsystems are sometimes in *conflict*, which reduces the chances that they or the objectives of the overall system will ever be realized. Conflict in objectives is especially prevalent between different levels and functions in project systems. Removing the conflict between the objectives of subsystems to enable the objectives of the overall system to be met is called *integration*.

Integration

For any system to perform effectively and achieve its goals, all of its elements, the "assemblage of parts," must work in unison. Designing, implementing, and operating a system that achieves its pre-specified objectives and requirements through the coordinated (so-called "seamless") functioning of its elements and subsystems is called *system integration*. Project management seeks to integrate tasks and resources to achieve project goals. In technological projects, project management also addresses the integration of the physical components and modules that compose the project end-item. The subject of systems integration is covered in Chapter 13.

Open Systems and Closed Systems

Systems can be classified as *closed* or *open*. A closed system is one that is viewed as self-contained, and "closed-systems thinking" means to focus on the internal operation, structure, and processes of a system without regard to the environment. For some kinds of systems, closed-system thinking applies: to understand how a machine functions, you need only study the machine and its components, and not anything else. This does not mean that the environment does not affect the system, but only that the person looking at the system has chosen to ignore the environment. In fact, for analyzing or improving the design of many kinds of mechanical systems, closed-system thinking works fairly well.

But what about human organizations and social systems that interact with and are adaptive to the environment? These are open systems. To understand their behavior and functioning, you cannot ignore the environment. Any system that must be adaptable to its environment must be treated (analyzed, described, or designed) as an open system. Since mechanical systems rely upon resources from the environment and inject byproducts (e.g., pollutants) into it, in many cases they too should be treated as open systems. In fact, any system that must be adaptable to the environment must be treated as an open system.

2.4 ORGANIZATIONS AND ENVIRONMENT[4]

Human organizations interact with stakeholders in the environment (customers, suppliers, unions, stockholders, governments, etc.), and they rely upon the environment for inputs of energy, information, and material. In turn, they export to

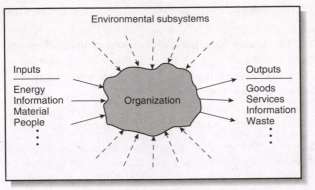

Figure 2.4
Organization as an input–output system.

the environment outputs of goods, services, and waste (represented in Figure 2.4). The point is, in establishing goals and methods of operation, organizations have to account for and deal with the environment. Sometimes, however, managers function as if the organization were isolated from the environment—as if the organization were a closed system. They do not learn from the environment, or they ignore what they have learned.

As an open system, any organization must choose goals and conduct its operations so as to respect opportunities presented and limitations imposed by the environment. Cleland and King call this the "environmental problem," meaning that a manager must[5]

1. Appreciate the need to assess forces in the environment,
2. Understand the forces that significantly affect the organization, and
3. Integrate these forces into the organization's goals, objectives, and operations.

Every project is influenced by outside forces. The project manager must understand the forces influencing the project, but, having done that, be able to guide the project to its goal. A project that is predominantly influenced by divergent forces in the environment will be difficult to control and likely to fail.

2.5 SYSTEMS APPROACH

Systems thinking is a way to visualize and analyze physical and conceptual systems, but more than that it is an *approach* for *doing* things—a framework for conceptualizing problems, solving problems, and making decisions.

Systems Approach Framework

The systems approach framework utilizes systems concepts such as goals and objectives, subsystems, elements, relationships, integration, and environment. It formally acknowledges that the behavior of any one element may affect other elements, and no single element can perform effectively without help from the others. This recognition of *interdependency* and *cause–effect* among elements is what most distinguishes the systems approach.[6]

For example, as an element of the "world system" the internal combustion engine used in automobiles can be viewed in terms of the multiple effects it has triggered in other elements and subsystems of the world system:

- Development of rich economies based largely on the production and distribution of petroleum
- Industrialization of previously nomadic societies, and redistribution of political power among world nations
- Development of new modes of transportation that have altered patterns of world travel, commerce, markets, and population distribution
- Alteration of the chemical composition of the atmosphere, causing ecological consequences such as altered weather patterns, global warming, and smog.

Managers who practice the systems approach recognize the multitude of "elements" in the systems they manage and the problems they wish to solve, the relationships among the elements, and reciprocal influences between human-made systems and the environment. As a result, they are better able to grasp the full magnitude of a problem and anticipate consequences of their actions. This reduces the chances that important elements in a situation or consequences of actions will be overlooked.

The systems approach keeps attention on the big picture and the ultimate goal; it allows focus on the parts, but only in regard to the contribution of the parts to the whole. For instance, a university system can be viewed as separate elements of students, faculty, administrators, and alumni, and it is possible to take action regarding any one of them while ignoring impacts on the others and the environment. But actions that focus exclusively on parts of the system are likely not optimal for the total system, because they disregard negative repercussions on other parts of the system. For example, although curtailing the hiring of faculty reduces costs, it can also lead to larger class sizes and classroom overcrowding, less faculty time for research, fewer research grants, lower prestige for the university, and, ultimately, reduced enrollments and less revenue. Similarly, enacting laws is one way to reduce air pollution, but laws that restrict industry can damage local economies. Every problem is inextricably linked to the environment, and attempts to solve one problem may cause others. Churchman calls this the "environmental fallacy."[7]

Examples abound of situations where solutions for part of the system have led to worse problems for the whole. These include trying to reduce traffic congestion by building more highways, trying to eliminate drug abuse by outlawing drug sale and consumption, and trying to increase the appeal of wilderness areas by building resorts in national parks. The negative consequences of these problem-solving attempts are well known. The systems approach tries to avoid the environmental fallacy.

Orderly Way of Appraisal[8]

The systems approach is a *methodology* for solving problems and managing systems. By its holistic nature, it avoids tackling problems narrowly, head-on. It says, "Let's stand back and look at this situation from all angles." The problem-solver does this by thinking about the overall system, keeping in mind:

1. The *objectives* and the *performance criteria* of the whole system
2. The *environment* and *constraints* of the system
3. The *resources* of the system
4. The *elements* of the system, their functions, attributes, and performance measures
5. The *interaction* among the elements
6. The *management* of the system.

The place to start planning for a human-made system is with the overall *objectives* of the system. Costly mistakes can be made if the true objectives of the system are vague or misconstrued. The systems approach mandates hardheaded thinking about the *real* objectives of the system, and real ways to measure them. Project management uses this kind of thinking: it begins with the mission or objectives of the system, and thereafter organizes and directs all subsequent work to achieve those objectives. The stated objective must be precise and measurable in terms of specific performance criteria (the system requirements). Criteria are the measures that enable determination of the extent to which objectives are being achieved. They are also the basis for ranking alternative solutions or courses of action to a problem. In a project, criteria for the end-item are referred to as *user requirements* and *specifications*, explained later. No matter how intangible the objectives of the system—goodwill, quality of life, happiness, or even beauty—measurement criteria must be set. They should reflect the many relevant consequences of the system, unintended or negative as well as intended and purposeful.

The *environment* of the system (other systems, groups, or persons and natural systems that affect or are affected by the system) must also be identified—no easy matter, because external forces are sometimes hidden and work in insidious ways. Looking to the future, questions must be raised about likely changes or innovations in the environment and how they will affect the system.

The *resources* to be used in accomplishing system goals must also be identified. These are assets, or the means that the system utilizes and influences to its advantage; they include capital, labor, materials, facilities, and equipment. Most system resources are exhaustible. The system is free to utilize them only for as long as they are available. When resources are depleted, they become *constraints*. The systems approach considers the availability of resources and what happens when resources are depleted.

The systems approach identifies the key *elements* of the system. In a project there are actually *two* systems, the one *being produced* by the project (the project end-result or end-item) and the one *producing* the end-item (the project itself). Defining these involves defining the subsystems, components, and parts of the hardware or software end-item system being produced, as well as the work tasks, resources, organization, and procedures of the project. Carefully defining the functions and subfunctions of the end-item system assures that the system will be designed and built to meet its objectives and requirements; carefully defining the work elements or tasks of the project assures that the project will be planned and managed to meet project objectives.

The output of a system is the result not only of the individual elements, but also of the way the elements interact. Designing a new system or resolving problems in human-made or natural systems requires not only knowing the elements of the system, but also understanding *the way they interact*. Designers use "models" of the system to help understand how the elements interact, and how altering the elements and their relationships impact system behavior and outputs.

Finally, the systems approach pays explicit attention to the *management* of the system—that is, to its planning and control—taking into consideration its objectives, environment and constraints, resources, and so on. This is precisely the role of project management.

The ordering of the six preceding concepts does not mean that they are addressed in sequence. In actuality, each concept might need to be dealt with several times before it is completely described and clearly defined. More importantly, each concept serves to suggest numerous open-ended questions that aid in investigating the system:[9] What are the objectives and criteria? What are the elements? What cause-and-effect relationships exist among them? What functions need to be performed by each? What are the resources? What are the trade-offs among resources?

Systems Models

Systems thinkers use "models" to help understand systems and assess alternative plans and solutions against objectives. A model is a simplified representation of the world; it abstracts the essential features of the system under study. It may be a physical model, mathematical formulation, computer simulation, or simple checklist. An example of a *physical model* is a model airplane. It is a scaled-down abstraction of the real system. It includes some aspects of the system (configuration and shape of exterior components) and excludes others (interior components and crew). Another kind of model is a *conceptual model*; it depicts the elements, structure, and flows in a system. The conceptual model in Figure 2.5, for example, helps demographers to understand relationships among the elements contributing to population size and to make predictions.[10]

Models are used to conduct experimentation and tests. Many human-made systems are too expensive or risky to do "real-life" experiments on. The model permits assessment of various alternatives and their consequences before committing to a decision. Engineers use model airplanes in wind tunnel tests, for instance, to try out design alternatives and measure the effect of different design parameters on airplane performance. A good model allows designers and analysts to ask "what if?" questions and explore the effects of altering the various inputs. This exploration is called *sensitivity analysis*. A good model takes into account the requirements, relevant elements, resources, and constraints, and allows the consequences of different alternatives to be compared in terms of costs and benefits. Models employed for quality assurance are discussed in Chapter 9.

Systems Life Cycle

Natural and human-made systems change over time in a way that tends to be systematic and evolutionary, and similar kinds of systems follow similar cycles of evolution. One basic cycle, that of all organisms, is the pattern of conception, birth, growth, maturity, senescence, and death. Historically, even civilizations and societies have followed this pattern. Another cycle, that of all non-living, electromechanical systems, is that of design, fabrication, installation, burn-in, normal operation, and deterioration or obsolescence. Similarly, all products follow a similar pattern—the "product life cycle." They are conceived, designed and developed, produced, launched into the market, capture market share, then decline and are discontinued. Some products, such as home computers, have life cycles of only months; others (Kool-Aid and Levi's jeans) have decades-long cycles.[11]

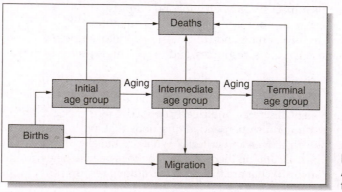

Figure 2.5
A generalized population sector model.

The creation or *development* of a system is also a cycle. A key feature of the systems approach is recognition of the logical order of thought and action that goes into developing systems, whether commercial home products, public works, or military weapons systems. The general development of a system according to a prescribed series of logical, structured steps is called the *systems development cycle*. This cycle is similar to those of organisms and products, and includes the phases of conception, definition, design and development, fabrication and testing, installation or launch, production, operation, and, finally, enhancement, replacement, or cancellation. The prescribed process within this cycle for the development of large-scale systems is called *systems engineering*. Most human-made systems start out as projects, and the early and mid-phases of the systems development life cycle constitute the phases of the *project life cycle*.[12] The systems development and project life cycles are discussed in Chapter 3.

2.6 SYSTEMS ENGINEERING

Systems engineering has been defined as "the science of designing complex systems in their totality to insure that the component subsystems making up the system are designed, fitted together, checked and operated in the most efficient way."[13] It refers to the conception, design, and development of complex systems where the *components themselves* must be designed, developed, and integrated together to fulfill the system objectives. Systems engineering is a way to *bring a whole system into being* and to *account for its whole life cycle*—including operation and phase-out—during its early conception and design.

All Systems Go

A good example of systems engineering can be seen in the design and operation of a space vehicle. The expression "all systems go," popularized during the early US space flights, means that the overall system of millions of components that make up the vehicle and its support systems, and the hundreds of people in its technical and management teams, is ready to "go" to achieve the objectives of the mission.

To get to the point of "all systems go," planners must first have defined the overall system and its objectives. Designers must have analyzed the requirements of the system and broken them down into more detailed, focused requirements, and designed the components and subsystems that meet the requirements. They must then have combined the components into subsystems, and the subsystem into the total system of space vehicle, rocket boosters, launch facilities, ground support, crew selection and training, and technical and management capability. In the end, every component and person must be assigned a role and be *integrated* into a subsystem that has been integrated into the overall system.

Systems engineering applies to any system (hardware or software) that must be developed (perhaps from scratch), implemented, and operated to fulfill some immediate or ongoing future purpose. Examples can readily be found in the design and implementation of local, national, and global systems for communication, transportation, water purification and supply, power generation and transmission, research, and defense.

Overview[14]

Systems engineering can be described in terms of the three dimensions illustrated in Figure 2.6.

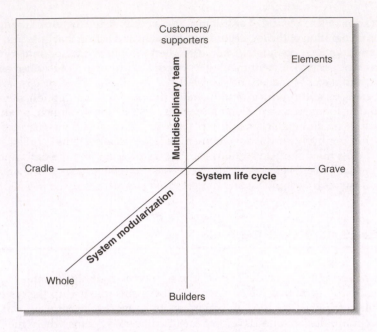

Figure 2.6
Dimensions of systems engineering.
Adapted from Auyang S. *Engineering—An Endless Frontier*. Cambridge, MA:
Harvard University Press; 2004, p. 178.

First, it is a multidisciplinary effort. Systems engineers (parties responsible for oversight of designing and building the system) work with the system's stakeholders to determine their needs and what the system must do to fulfill them. A stakeholder is any individual or group that affects or is affected by the system, positively or negatively; the primary stakeholders are customers, end users, and builders. Customers finance and own the system; users operate and maintain it; builders design and create it. Stakeholders' objectives and needs become the basis for determining the system requirements that specify *what* the system will do. The practice of involving the stakeholders in the early phases of the conception and development of a system to anticipate issues in its manufacture and operation is called "concurrent engineering," and is discussed in Chapters 4 and 13. A design methodology for converting customer needs into the requirements for a product and the processes to produce the product, called "quality function deployment," is discussed in Chapter 4.

Second, systems engineering addresses all aspects of the system, starting with whole system and ending with its individual elements. System elements, modules, and subsystems are designed to perform the functions necessary to satisfy the objectives and requirements of the whole system. This aspect of systems engineering focuses on *how* the system must function to meet the requirements.

Finally, although systems engineers are involved with the system for only a short time compared to the system's full life cycle, they take into account how the system will be produced, operated, maintained, and finally disposed of—the entire system life cycle. This helps insure that the system will be economical to develop, build, operate, and maintain, and friendly to users and the environment. The multidisciplinary team approach, which involves all the systems stakeholders, promotes this life-cycle kind of thinking.

Once systems engineers have learned what stakeholders want and defined the objectives and requirements of the system, they then look for alternative ways to meet the requirements. This involves research, analysis, and studies of alternative approaches to the system design, and the estimated costs, schedules, risks, and benefits of each. If the resources are inadequate or the technology or time is constrained, the requirements are modified. Says Brooks:

> The hardest part of building a [system] is deciding precisely what to build. No other part of the conceptual work is so difficult as establishing the detailed technical requirements [and] no other part of the work so cripples the resulting system if done wrong. No other part is more difficult to rectify later.[15]

Example 2.1: Advanced Automation System[16]

The centerpiece of the Federal Aviation Administration's (FAA) program to modernize the air traffic control system was the Advanced Automation System (AAS), which would provide controllers with new displays and computer equipment for processing radar and flight data. The FAA awarded the contract for AAS to IBM following a 4-year design competition. Requirements from the FAA initially filled a thick book, but as the program progressed they kept increasing and eventually grew to a stack 20 feet high. As the number of requirements grew, so did program delays, costs, and tensions between the FAA and IBM. Congress balked, and after 10 years and an estimated $1.5 billion it cancelled the program.

Eliciting the expectations and needs of operators and users, then translating them into measurable requirements, can be difficult for engineers, which is why the multidisciplinary teams include behaviorists and psychologists. Developing the flight deck for a commercial aircraft, for example, would include the suggestions of pilots, the airlines, pilot associations, and human factors experts. A common way to elicit responses to or suggestions about a proposed design is for users to try out a mock-up or simulator of the system.

Modularization: Iterative Analysis–Synthesis–Evaluation Cycle[17]

The process of creating a system concept is a series of steps to define the subsystems and elements that will comprise the system. The process involves an iterative cycle of (1) *top-down analysis* of details (i.e., decomposing the system into smaller parts), (2) *bottom-up synthesis* (building up and integrating the parts into successively larger parts), and (3) *evaluation* (checking to see that results meet requirements). This is illustrated by Forsberg and Mooz's "V-model" in Figure 2.7.[18]

Systems are designed and assembled from subsystems that themselves are systems designed and assembled from subsystems, and so on. The practice, called *modularization*, is what makes the design, assembly, and operation of complex systems feasible and practical. Herbert Simon gives the example of a watchmaker who assembles a watch of 100 parts. The process requires concentration, and is time-consuming and expensive. If the watch should need repair, finding and fixing the problem might be difficult. If instead the watch were made of 10 modules, each with 10 parts, assembly would be simple. If the watch were to develop a problem, the repair would be simple: just identify the module with the malfunction and replace it.[19]

The downstroke of the V represents subdividing the functions of the system into subfunctions and requirements. At each lower level the process of working

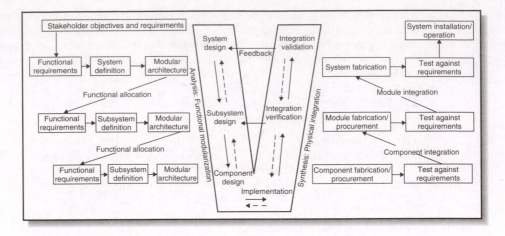

Figure 2.7
Forsberg and Mooz's "V-model."
Adapted from Forsberg K and Mooz H. In Taylor R, Dorfman M, and Davis A (eds), *Software Requirements Engineering*, 2nd edn. Los Alamitos, CA: IEEE Computer Society Press; 1997, pp. 44–77.

with customers to define requirements repeats, except the "customer" becomes the function at the next higher level and the question becomes: What must the lower-level functions do to meet the requirements of the higher level function? In this way, requirements are defined for functions at all levels.

Systems are designed by designing subsystems or modules that each perform a necessary function of the system. Functions are attributes of the system; they are the means by which a system meets its objectives and requirements. In everyday systems it is easy to identify the modules and the functions they perform. A desktop computer is almost completely modularized: it has a processor and controllers, drives, and peripheral devices that each perform a specialized function, such as data processing, data storage, and input/output processing.

The way in which system functions are grouped into modules is called the *system architecture*. The architecture of an airplane is an example. An airplane must perform several major functions, including propulsion, lift, and payload stowage; the visibly familiar modules of engines, wings, and fuselage, respectively, serve these functions. But each function is itself a composite of several subfunctions, hence each module is comprised of several submodules. A wing, for example, is subdivided into ailerons, flaps, spoilers, etc., each one performing a specific aerodynamic function.

The upstroke of the V represents assessing "design alternatives" to satisfy requirements, implementing design decisions, converting designs into physical parts, integrating the parts, and verifying that the integrated parts meet the requirements. Design alternatives are the potential solutions to problems; they are the courses of action for meeting requirements, and ultimately they show up in the final system as pieces of hardware and software. The chosen alternatives result in procuring or designing and building component parts. Components are checked individually and then assembled into modules; modules are tested, then combined with others and tested again.

If tests reveal that parts or modules are not meeting requirements, then the process returns to the downstroke of the V to determine why, and the analysis–synthesis–evaluation cycle repeats. The process is anything but smooth-flowing, as illustrated by the many feedback arrows in Figure 2.7. Within each down- and upstroke, the process moves back and forth; at times during the upstroke it loops back and over to the downstroke.

One rule of the systems approach is: *Don't rush to solutions! Look for alternatives*. Ideally, a range of alternative solutions is considered—innovative and creative, as well as familiar and available. Multidisciplinary teams are good at doing this; they combine knowledge from experts in disparate areas, and can generate alternatives that transcend any one person's or field's area of expertise.

The design and development of a complex technical system can be vexing, but the systems approach offers a method. Readers interested in systems engineering should see the Appendix to this chapter: Stages of Systems Engineering.

2.7 RELEVANCY OF THE SYSTEMS APPROACH TO PROJECT MANAGEMENT

Systems Management[20]

Project management is a form of "systems management," which is the management and operation of organizations *as* systems. Systems management draws from the major features of the systems approach. First, it is total-system oriented, and emphasizes achievement of the *overall system* mission and objectives. Second, it emphasizes decisions that optimize the *overall system* rather than the subsystems. Third, it recognizes interaction and synergy among systems and subsystems—that outputs from one system or subsystem provide inputs to other systems and subsystems. Systems management works to ensure that organizations, responsibilities, knowledge, and data are integrated toward achieving overall objectives. The systems manager recognizes interactions and interdependencies between subsystems and with the environment, and tries to account for them in making plans and taking action. This contrasts with the more typical management view, which is to focus narrowly on individual functions and tasks and on the performance of individual departments, even if at the expense of the total organization.

Project Managers Are Systems Managers

In *Winning at Project Management*, author Robert Gilbreath[21] describes the "right" way to visualize a project. From an outsider's perspective, he says, a project may look like a "continuum," something with no separate discernable parts, like a barrel containing thousands of earthworms. Obviously, if you have to manage the project such a perspective is not very useful, and you need another perspective—one that involves subdividing the continuum into a collection of elements and defining the characteristics of each.[22] Good project managers, says Gilbreath, conceptually subdivide the project into pieces and make sure each piece is well managed. The project manager knows all the pieces of the project, and the impact that each has on the others and overall project objectives.

Gilbreath discusses another feature of project management: the ability to "change focus," to zoom in on the performance of discrete elements, then zoom out and check the direction and performance of the overall project. The zoom-out view is essential, for it enables the project manager to direct the project toward global optima and not get hung up with the pieces.[23] This aspect of effective project managers has been stated before many times. In a 1969 *Harvard Business Review* article, Ivars Avots wrote: "While . . . the [project] manager must be a good technician and thoroughly familiar with the field in which the project belongs, his emphasis must be on the overall view and not technical details."[24]

In their own ways, what Avots and Gilbreath say is the same: the project manager needs to be a big-picture person who knows how to balance focus between technical elements of the project and the administrative aspects of schedules, budgets, and human relations. He needs all-round good understanding of the project tasks and the agenda of project stakeholders—the workers, customers, users, champions, executives, and outsiders who have vested interests. The ability to zoom in and zoom out, to see and know what is important to the big picture—*that* is the essence of the systems approach. Whether or not you call it the "systems approach," the point is, in managing a project it helps to look at the project as a system.

2.8   SUMMARY

A system is an assembly of parts where (1) the parts are affected by being in the system, (2) the assembly does something, and (3) the assembly is of particular interest. What is called "the system" depends upon one's point of view and purpose. Projects are systems created for the purpose of making systems.

Systems thinking is a way to deal with complex phenomena. It imparts the ability to discern a degree of order and structure in a seemingly confused or chaotic situation. Systems thinking includes the "systems approach," which is a way of conceptualizing physical entities and addressing problems. The principle components of the systems approach are: (1) the *objectives* and the *performance criteria* of the system; (2) the system *environment* and *constraints*; (3) the *resources* of the system; (4) the *elements* of the system, their functions, attributes, and performance measures; (5) the *interaction* among the elements; and (6) the *management* of the system. For development and operation of large technical systems, the systems approach is implemented through the systems engineering methodology.

Systems engineering deals with the total system and its complete life cycle. To accomplish overall system objectives, systems engineering approaches the design, testing, operation, and support of the system as a complete entity. The "system" includes not only prime mission equipment—hardware and software—but also everything needed to make it work—support information, personnel, equipment, and facilities for production, control, training, as well as management policies and programs to implement, operate, and support it. Systems engineering may involve people from different companies and organizations, spread over a wide geographic area and with no common background. The difficult task, largely undertaken by the project manager, is to get them all to work together toward a common purpose.

Systems management is the process of monitoring and controlling a system to achieve overall system objectives. The manager's role is to ensure that all necessary disciplines and functional areas are involved and integrated to meet system requirements. Project management is a form of system management; it emphasizes integration of project activities to achieve overall goals.

Part I of this book has given you an overview of project management. Projects are of finite duration—they have a beginning and an ending. What happens in between—

the stages of tasks and activities—tends to be remarkably similar, regardless of the kind of project. These stages are analogous to stages in the system life cycle, and were alluded to in the examples in Chapter 1. Part II discusses these stages and describes a framework for conducting projects: the systems development cycle.

For interested readers, the following Appendix covers systems engineering in more detail and provides examples.

APPENDIX: STAGES OF SYSTEMS ENGINEERING[25]

Systems engineering has a much wider role than ordinary "engineering," and, in fact, is not even "engineering" in the same context as other engineering disciplines. Rather, it is a logical *process* employed in the evolution of a system from the point when a need is first identified, through the system's planning, design, construction, and to the system's ultimate deployment and operation by a user. The process, outlined in Figure 2.8, has two parts; one associated with the *development and production* of the system (Stages 1 through 4, which coincide with the project life cycle), the other with the *utilization* of the system (Stage 5).

Stage 1: Needs Identification and Conceptual Design[26]

The main tasks of this stage are to define stakeholder needs and requirements, perform feasibility analysis, and perform high-level requirements analysis, system-level synthesis, and a system design review. As shown in Figure 2.7, the process moves top-down to identify the needs and objectives of stakeholders, and the requirements and functions of the system; it then moves bottom-up to assess the functions and synthesize them into groups. The result is a "functional baseline" design or list of all high-level requirements and high-level functions of the system.

Stakeholders and Needs Identification

Systems engineering deals with poorly defined problems. The customer may feel that something is wrong or something new is required, but be unclear about the source of

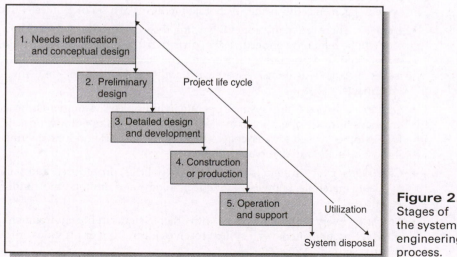

Figure 2.8 Stages of the systems engineering process.

the problem or need, or how the system should look or what it should do. Sometimes it is not even clear *who* has the problem or need. The first step in systems engineering is *identification*—identifying the stakeholders and translating fuzzy ideas into clear definitions of the needs, problems, and objectives. Needs are addressed not only for the client or customer (the party paying to develop the system and its future owner and operator), but also for others who are affected by or able to impact (contribute to, support, or block) the system. Even identifying the "customer" is not trivial; the customer might be an organization, but within the organization only certain parties have the authority to make decisions relating to the system, or will use, operate, or be impacted by it. These parties must be singled out and their needs identified.

Developing a clear conception of the need or problem begins by asking basic questions:[27]

1. How did the problem or need arise?
2. Who believes it to be a problem or feels the need?
3. Is this the root problem or need, or is it a manifestation of a deeper problem?
4. Why is a solution important? How much money (or time, etc.) will it save? What is the value of the system that will solve the problem?
5. How important is the need? Would resources be better applied to another need?

The systems engineer (system developer, contractor) works with the customer to answer these questions and prepares a preliminary description of a system that addresses the need or problem, including its expected performance, cost, and schedule. The customer reviews the description and perhaps redefines the need, in which case the contractor must redefine the system description. The process continues back and forth until the need definition and system description are set.

Requirements Definition

Requirements specify what the system must do, and what targets the system designers must seek to hit. High-level requirements should incorporate everything important about the system—its objectives, life cycle, operational modes, constraints, and interfaces with other systems.

- *Objectives:* Objectives elaborate on stakeholder needs and define the overarching aim of the system. Usually several objectives are necessary to fully specify the system. Each objective is then elaborated in terms of a set of requirements.

- *Life cycle:* There are many issues regarding the system's life cycle and how the system will be built or produced, tested, distributed, marketed, financed, operated, maintained, and ultimately disposed of. This leads to consideration of ancillary issues such as "side items"—spare parts and training of users—and environmental impacts.

- *Operational modes:* Many systems operate in multiple environments and in different ways termed "operational modes" or "scenarios of operation." An airplane, for example, is used for passengers and cargo transport and for crew training; and it must be maintained, repaired, and tested.

- *Constraints:* Every system is constrained by policies, procedures, and standards; available materials, knowledge, and technology; and limited time, funding, and resources.

- *Interfaces:* Every system interfaces with other systems in the environment. An interface occurs whenever a system receives input from or provides output to other systems.

The requirements should address the needs of all the stakeholders—producers, suppliers, operators, and others who will ultimately use, benefit from, manage, maintain, and otherwise impact or be impacted by the system. They reflect the different interests and perspectives of the different stakeholders: corporate customers who are interested in the system's market, capacity, and operating and capital costs; operators who are interested in its performance, durability, reliability, parts availability, etc.; and users who care about its comfort, safety, and usability.

The initial requirements, stated in the language of the stakeholders, are compiled in a list called the *stakeholder requirements document* (SRD). Anyone reading the SRD should be able to readily understand the mission and application of the intended system. The project should not be started until the principle stakeholders have reviewed and endorsed the SRD.

Example A2.1: SRD for the Spaceship[28]

As an example, let's revisit the X-Prize competition and SpaceShipOne described in Chapter 1. The criteria of the competition were to send a reusable vehicle capable of carrying three people into space twice within 2 weeks. Besides winning the competition, a goal of developer Burt Rutan and customer Sir Richard Branson was to develop technology that would enable low-cost space tourism. Among the constraints were a relatively small budget and a small development company with limited resources. Hence, the SRD would likely include the following:

1. Develop a spaceship that can minimally attain 100 km altitude
2. Develop a spaceship that carries three people
3. Develop a spaceship that provides comfortable flight
4. Develop a spaceship that is relatively inexpensive to design, build, and launch
5. Develop a spaceship that can be turned around in 2 weeks or less
6. Develop a spaceship that is inherently safe to operate.

Feasibility

Given the defined needs, objectives, constraints, and requirements, the question arises: What are the alternatives to satisfy them, and are the alternatives feasible? Thus, the next step is to identify high-level (system-level) alternative ways to meet the needs and requirements. The alternatives are evaluated in terms of costs, risks, effectiveness, and benefits using studies and models; the most feasible solutions are recommended to customers and supporters.

System Requirements Analysis

With approval of the project and system-level alternatives, the next step is to specify what *the system must do* to be able to meet the requirements in the SRD; this is the purpose of *system requirements*. For example, the stakeholder requirement that the spaceship would "provide comfortable flight" implies a system requirement that the spaceship's cabin temperature, humidity, and pressure all remain at "comfy" levels throughout the flight. This implies that the spaceship will be equipped to perform the necessary functions to make this happen. Whereas the SRD specifies the system in terms of stakeholder wants or needs, the system requirements tell the designer the *functions* the system must perform and the physical characteristics it must possess to meet the SRD. The process of defining requirements is called *requirements analysis*; the result of this analysis is a document called the *system specification*, described later. Requirements analysis addresses three kinds of requirements: functional, performance, and verification.

Functional Requirements

Functional requirements specify the functions that the new system must perform to meet all the requirements in the SRD, including those to support, operate, and maintain the system. A popular tool for analyzing and defining functional requirements is the functional flow block diagram (FFBD), illustrated in Figure 2.9. Each block represents a function that the system must perform to satisfy objectives or requirements. As illustrated, each function is defined in greater detail by decomposing it into subfunctions; for example, as shown, function 3 is logically comprised of five subfunctions, 3.1 through 3.5. In the conceptual design stage the decomposition of functions into smaller, better-defined subfunctions proceeds only to the next level (e.g., subdivides function 3 into 3.1–3.5). Later, in the preliminary design stage, the decomposition will resume and continue to whatever level necessary to arrive at the best possible requirements definition. In the figure, this is shown by decomposing function 3.5 into functions 3.5.1–3.5.4.

Notice the numbering scheme used in Figure 2.9: each and every function has a unique identifier that enables it to be traced to the original system-level function—e.g., function 3.5.4 contributes to function 3.5, which contributes to function 3. This "traceability" of functions is essential because throughout the system life cycle numerous changes will be made to components and functions. For each change it is necessary to know the impact on higher-level and lower-level functions. This helps prevent mistakes that could lead to later problems. In the Apollo 13 spacecraft, the cryogenic tanks were originally designed to operate at 28 volts. Later on, the Apollo's design required that certain controls be changed to 65 volts. This involved changes to numerous components including the cryogenic tanks, but somehow the required changes were not traced back to the tanks, and were never made. During the mission this oversight caused a thermostat to malfunction and a tank to explode, which ruined the mission and nearly cost the lives of the three astronauts.

Figure 2.9
FFBD for decomposing system-level functions into lower-level functions.

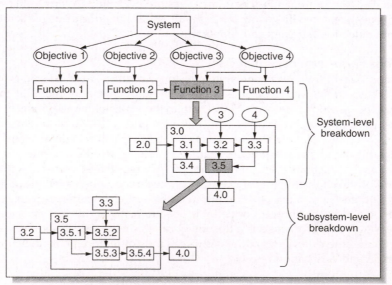

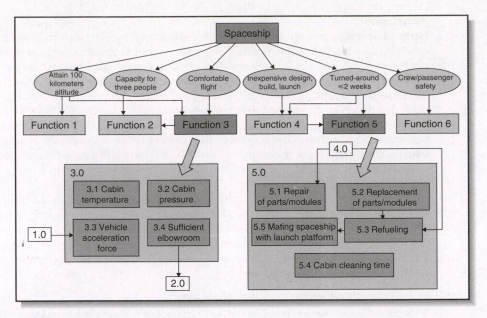

Figure 2.10
System-level breakdown of functions for spaceship.

Example A2.2: Functional Requirements Breakdown for the Spaceship

Figure 2.10 shows a portion of the FFBD for the spaceship, and decomposition of the system-level functions that address stakeholder requirements 3 and 5. The other system-level functions would be decomposed as well.

Performance and Verification Requirements

Associated with each functional requirement are several performance requirements and verification requirements. Whereas a functional requirement states *what* the system must do, a performance requirement states *how well* it must do it. Performance requirements are usually specified in physical parameters such as speed, acceleration, weight, accuracy, power, force, or time. They are the targets on which designers set their sights. For example, the stakeholder requirement "provide comfortable flight" has many functional requirements, including some for cabin temperature and pressure. The associated performance requirements for these are:

1. Cabin temperature: 75–85°F
2. Cabin pressure: 4.2–3.2 psi.

Accompanying each performance requirement is a set of verification requirements; these are the procedures, measures, and tests to verify that the performance requirement has been met. In the example, verification requirements specify the kinds of tests necessary to prove that cabin temperature and pressure will remain at the required levels during spaceflight.

Throughout the conception stage, reviews are conducted to verify and approve the system-level requirements. Requirements are categorized as mandatory, important, desirable, or optional. This tells designers later on, when faced with constraints, which requirements must be met and which can be modified or ignored.

Synthesis

Up until now the systems engineering process has been focused on top-down analysis, resulting in a big list of functional, performance, and verification requirements. The next step, synthesis, looks at relationships among the system-level requirements and alternative ways of satisfying the requirements. One question is, can these requirements be satisfied using existing, "off the shelf" (OTS) designs and products, or must new and different designs or technologies be employed? An OTS item is one that can be readily purchased or built; if it meets the requirements, an OTS item is often preferable to one that must be newly designed because it is readily available and usually less costly. Sometimes there is no OTS and to create a new design that meets the requirements would be very costly, risky, or time-consuming; in such cases, the requirements must be revised.

The result of synthesis is called the "system specification," which is a comprehensive list of all the functions the new system must satisfy, as well as a firm or tentative solution (to be developed or bought) for each function. The system specification serves as a guide for designers in the stages of preliminary and detailed system design. Often these designers are subcontractors or suppliers; the subsystem specification defines the requirements they must meet.

Example A2.3: System Specification for Spaceship Motor

A decision must be made about the kind of rocket motor the spaceship will have. Among the functional requirements for the motor are:

1.1 Must provide thrust of x
4.1 Cost of fuel and fuel handling must be economical
5.3 Refueling procedure must be simple
6.1 Fuel, fuel system, and the fuel itself must be inherently safe.

A check of existing OTS rocket motors used to launch satellites shows that none fit the requirements; all are too costly to fuel and operate, and somewhat dangerous. Hence, a new rocket motor must be developed—one that will be simple and inexpensive to fuel and operate, safe, and provide the necessary thrust. Experiments reveal a promising solution: a motor that uses ordinary rubber as the fuel and nitrous oxide (laughing gas) as the oxidant; both materials are stable, safe, inexpensive, and easy to handle. The decision is made to adopt the technology and design and build a completely new motor. Thus, one system specification for the spaceship (of many hundreds) is that the rocket motor burns nitrous oxide and rubber.

The system specification is reviewed and checked against the functional requirements at a formal meeting. When approved, it becomes the *"functional baseline"* or template for all subsequent design work.

Stage 2: Preliminary Design[29]

In the preliminary design stage, the system-level functional requirements are translated into design requirements for the subsystems. Trade-off studies are performed of the high-level elements comprising the system, and the system-level requirements are *allocated* among the subsystems.

Functions of Subsystems

The FFBD process, as illustrated in Figure 2.10, is now repeated to decompose the system-level functions into subsystem-level functions and, as before, to define functional, performance, and testing requirements for each functional block. The degree of detail of the FFBDs is whatever is necessary to completely define each subsystem and permit decisions about whether each function can be met with an OTS design or product, or must be designed and built from scratch.

In this stage of the design process, there is a subtle shift in focus away from *what* the system will do to *how* it will do it. The shift is from the *functional* design to the *physical* design.

Example A2.4: Decomposing Functions into Subfunctions

Figure 2.11 shows the FFBD for function 5.5, mating the spaceship with the launch platform. This requirement is derived from the system-level requirement of "turnaround in 2 weeks or less." Suppose the performance requirement for mating (attaching) the spaceship to the underbelly of the mothership is set at 10 hours. Having decomposed the function into all of the subfunctions in the procedure, planners are able to set time requirements for the subfunctions so that the mating procedure will not exceed the allotted 10 hours.

Grouping of Functions: Architecture and Configuration Items (CIs)

The next step is to group the identified functions and requirements according to the *physical architecture* of the system. In general, the term "architecture" refers to the major components in a system and how they are configured or arranged to satisfy the functions of the system. As an example, the architecture most people have in mind for a bicycle is:

Figure 2.11
FFBD for mating SpaceShipOne and White Knight.

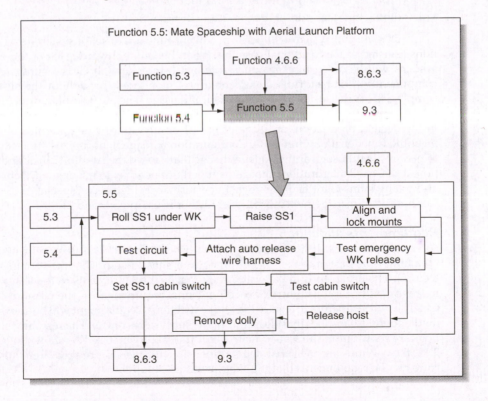

Major components: two wheels, frame, seat, pedals and chain, handlebars.
Configuration: wheel attached at each end of frame; front wheel pivots on frame; seat mounted on frame; pedals attached to frame, linked by chain to rear wheel; etc.

Sometimes the architecture "looks right," sometimes not. Often, in order to satisfy unique requirements, designers are forced to stray from the commonplace architecture, the result being a "funny looking" architecture.

Example A2.5: Architecture of the Spaceship

The spaceship will have airplane features of a fuselage and wings, although it will also have spacecraft features—namely, a rocket motor, and the ability to maneuver in space. Unlike an airplane, where the cabin and fuselage walls are the same, the cabin in a spaceship is a separate "pressure vessel" fitted inside the fuselage. The spaceship architecture will include the following subsystems:

- Fuselage: structure in which other subsystems are contained (hydraulics, avionics, motor, fuel, cabin, landing gear, etc.) or to which they are attached (wing, flight control surfaces, etc.).
- Cabin: location for pilot and passengers; includes seats, storage space, instruments and flight controls, and environmental control system.
- Rocket motor: main propulsion system, fuel system, attachments to fuselage and fuel system, and motor controls.
- Avionics: aviation electronics; computers and subsystems for communication, navigation, automatic flight controls, in-flight and auxiliary power systems.
- Wing/aerodynamic surfaces: main wing, tail, ailerons, flaps, spoilers, rudders, stabilizers, and hydraulic/electronic actuators.
- Controls for spaceflight: thrusters or reaction jets.
- Landing gear: gear doors, braces, skids or tires, brakes.

Each major subsystem will perform a major function or set of system-level functions as listed in the functional baseline. From this point onward, each of these subsystems will be called a *configuration item* or CI. In general, a CI is a subsystem or component whose history is documented and monitored throughout the system's complete life cycle—its design, production, and usage. The purpose of this documenting and tracking, referred to as *configuration management*, is to ensure that any changes in the design, production, or usage of the CI do not alter or degrade its ability to meet the functional requirements. Configuration management utilizes "traceability" to prevent snafus, such as the voltage change that caused the Apollo 13 incident mentioned earlier. Configuration management pertains not only to major subsystems, but also to any items identified as critical to performance, high risk, "special," or costly. Configuration management is discussed further in Chapters 9 and 11.

Requirements Allocation

As of this point, the design consists of (1) a list of the functional requirements, and (2) a high-level design of the system—the major subsystem or CIs (the system architecture). The next step is to "allocate" the functional requirements to the CIs, which means to *assign* responsibility for each functional requirement to one or more of the CIs. The purpose here is to ensure that every functional requirement will be addressed (and hopefully satisfied) by at least one of the subsystems or CIs. The resulting allocations are shown in an "allocation matrix" or "traceability matrix." As shown in Figure 2.12, the columns are the subsystems responsible for meeting the requirements; the rows are the requirements that the subsystems must fulfill.

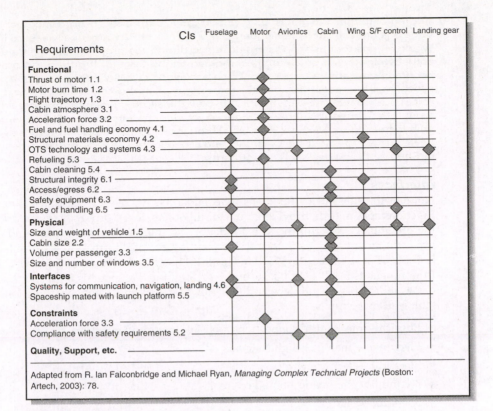

Figure 2.12
Allocation or traceability matrix.
Adapted from Falconbridge RI and Ryan M. *Managing Complex Technical Projects.*
Boston, MA: Artech; 2003, p. 78.

With this allocation, the transition from functions to physical items accelerates. Since each of the CIs represents something that will ultimately be a physical item—a piece of hardware, software, or both—the assignment of functional requirements to CIs represents a transition in thinking from *what* must be done (e.g., travel 100 km above the Earth) to *how* the system will do it (in a spacecraft that has a fuselage, cabin, wings, and engine, configured in a certain way).

Notice in Figure 2.12 that some of the functional requirements are the shared responsibility of more than one CI. For example, the weight of the system (requirement 1.5) is shared by all the CIs. That is to say, the spacecraft weight is the sum of the weights of all the CIs, and if the weight of any one is changed, so is the weight of the spacecraft. If the maximum loaded weight of the spacecraft is set at 3,600 kg, each CI must be designed so that all of the CIs combined will not exceed that requirement.

Example A2.6: Allocation of Weight among CIs

Question: How do you design and develop all of the CIs such that in the end the total weight (shared requirement) does not exceed 3,600 kg? Answer: estimate the percentage of the total spaceship weight that each CI should account for, and set that as the "target" design weight for the CI. For example, allocate, say, 30 percent of the total system weight to the fuselage and contents, 20 percent to the motor, 20 percent to the wings, 10 percent to avionics, and 10 percent for everything else. Hence, the fuselage target weight would be $0.30 \times 3,600 \, \text{kg} = 1,080 \, \text{kg}$, the motor target weight is $0.20 \times 3,600 \, kg = 720 \, kg$, and so on. Since achieving targets is critical, each is designated as a Technical Performance Measure (TPM), which means that as the CIs are designed during the project their estimated and actual weights will be carefully compared to the targets. If during the project it becomes clear that a target cannot be achieved (as will surely happen), then the allocations are readjusted. If, say, the weight of the motor cannot be held to its target but must be increased by 30 kg, then the allotted weights for other subsystems must correspondingly be reduced, or else the target weight for the spaceship increased by 30 kg to 3,630 kg. Throughout the development process it will be necessary to adjust the CI targets and allocations. The TPM process, described in Chapter 11, guides such adjustments.

Interfaces

None of the subsystems functions independently. All rely on the outputs of other functions and, in turn, provide inputs to still others; in a word, they *interface*. Part of the preliminary design process is to identify all interfaces in the system and establish requirements for the interfaces. A main source of information about interfaces is FFBDs. For example, the FFBD in Figure 2.11 shows that function 5.5 *receives* input from functions 5.3, 5.4, and 4.6.6, and *provides* input to functions 8.6.3 and 9.3. Each arrow represents an interface and the "flow" of something between functions. The "thing" flowing can be:

- Physical—mechanical connections, physical joints and supports, pipes
- Electronic—analog or digital signals
- Electrical—electric energy
- Hydraulic/pneumatic—liquid or gas
- Software—data
- Environment—temperature, pressure, humidity, radiation, magnetism
- Procedural—completion of a procedural step so another next step can begin.

Identifying the interfaces is necessary for setting requirements on the inputs and outputs of every subsystem and element. For example, since the fuselage of the spacecraft contains the motor and also supports the wings, neither wings nor motor can be designed without also considering the design of the fuselage, and *vice versa*. The requirements for each interface (e.g., allowable maximum or minimum flow or physical strength) are set by a design team that includes representatives from the subsystems at both sides of the interface.

Synthesis and Evaluation

Designing each of the CIs and its subsystems and elements involves choosing among design alternatives and, again, deciding whether to buy or modify an OTS design or product, or to develop a new design from scratch. An OTS design or product that meets all or most of the requirements for a CI and is not too costly will be purchased; otherwise the CI must be designed and built from scratch.

The selection of alternatives in the preliminary design stage must consider the synthesis of components—the impacts of each design decision on other components and the overall system. The following is an example.

Example A2.7: Trade-Offs in Designing Cabin Size

The weight requirement for a spacecraft is a big deal because the greater the weight, the more thrust required of the rocket motor to propel the vehicle into space and the greater the load-carrying capacity of the mothership to carry it aloft. At some point early in the conceptual design the maximum weight will be

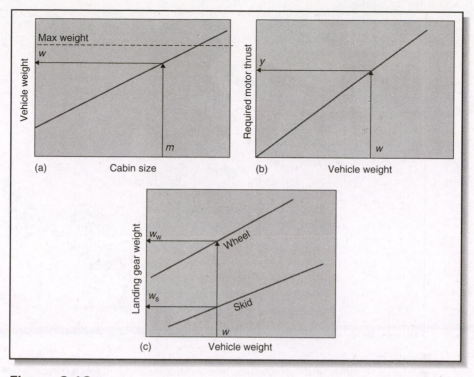

Figure 2.13
Impact of cabin size on (a) vehicle weight, (b) rocket thrust, and (c) landing gear.

set, although as the design progresses every effort will be made to find ways to reduce it. Consider below some trade-off decisions that designers face:

How big should the cabin be? In general, the cabin should be roomy enough to hold three people, instruments and controls, and stowage; a bigger cabin would be more comfortable for the occupants but would also weigh more. Suppose a cabin of volume m is chosen, which will result in an estimated weight of w for the spaceship. Suppose also that to propel a vehicle of weight w into space will require a rocket motor with thrust of y (Figure 2.13, top diagrams). Note that if the cabin size is increased, then the thrust of the rocket motor must also be increased—unless weight somewhere else in the spaceship can be reduced.

Now consider the impact of vehicle weight on another decision: landing gear. The more the vehicle weighs, the stronger the required gear—but, all else being equal, the stronger the gear, the heavier the gear. If the weight of a typical wheeled landing gear strong enough to support the vehicle is deemed too high, then an alternative must be considered, such as a skid (Figure 2.13, bottom). The skid has no wheels, and weighs less than a wheeled gear. If the skid meets other functional requirements, then it will be chosen over a wheeled landing gear.

Such trade-off decisions will be necessary for all the CIs and other components. As decisions are made, a design evolves that meets the requirements. The form and configuration of the CIs starts to evolve, and the physical appearance of the system begins to take shape. By the end of the preliminary design stage, the system architecture will have been established and all system-level requirements allocated among the major subsystems (CIs). Combined, the architecture and allocated requirements form the "allocated baseline" design (see, for example, Figure 2.14).

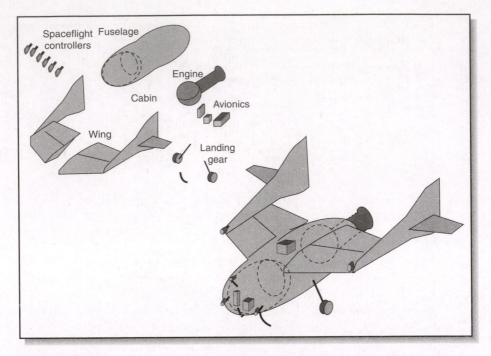

Figure 2.14
Pictorial representation of major subsystems (CIs) and allocated baseline design. (The "funny-looking" architecture comes from the spaceship having to meet many difficult requirements. On re-entry, the wings rotate and tilt back, making the spacecraft one big airbrake that floats to Earth like a shuttlecock, thus avoiding high speed and high temperature. Nearer to the ground, the wings tilt forward and the ship glides to a landing.)

Stage 3: Detailed Design and System Development

The detailed design stage involves further description of subsystems, assemblies, components, and parts of the main system and support items. Everything up to this point has been analytical in nature. With detailed design, the development process moves from "concepts on paper"—the SRD and system specifications—to a design that is ready to be built. Decisions are made about whether subsystems and components will function manually or automatically, whether components will be electronic, mechanical, or hydraulic, whether input–output will be manual, mechanical, electronic, and so on. Available, OTS components are selected on the basis of surveys or comparison tests in a laboratory, and newly developed components are tested experimentally using "breadboards" (i.e., test models that enable designs to be verified by trial and error). Breadboards are used to develop individual pieces of equipment that will subsequently be mated and integrated into the overall system. A "prototype" system—a nearly complete system assembled for purposes of developmental testing—may then be used to evaluate the overall system in terms of satisfying requirements. Much of the development work, even with the use of breadboards and prototypes, is done on computers. Prototypes and other models are described in Chapters 4 and 9.

System development and design, testing, and evaluation includes:[30]

1. Checking the operation of subsystems when combined in the complete system
2. Evaluating the validity of design assumptions
3. Paying close attention to the interfaces:
   a. "cross talk" among subsystems
   b. feedback among subsystems
   c. adjustments and calibrations
   d. serviceability and maintenance.

The system is checked under a variety of conditions and operational modes. Notable problems previously overlooked in the design process often come to light during these tests. Modifications are often necessary to correct for oversights, eliminate deficiencies, and simply improve the system.

Example A2.8: Testing SpaceShipOne

Numerous ground and flight test of SpaceShipOne resulted in many changes; among them:

- In one test flight SS1 began to pitch wildly, and only with great difficulty was the pilot able to regain control. Engineers diagnosed the cause as being a too-small tail, which they quickly redesigned. (Problem was, the small company did not have a wind tunnel in which to test it. Undeterred, they mounted the tail assembly on a Ford pick-up truck and checked it by racing up and down the runway.)

- A three-man crew was sealed in the cockpit for 3 hours, and to test cabin pressure sensitive ultrasound equipment scanned the cabin for the "hissing" sound of leaks.

- The nose skid showed excessive wear after tests, and was replaced with a stronger material.

When there is not enough time or money to build a prototype, the first few manufactured models are subjected to developmental testing and design evaluation. Gradually, after modifications have been made and the design approved, full-scale production begins. Design and development testing is phased out; quality control is phased in to ensure the end-item system as produced conforms to design specifications.

The design of the capability (facilities and related resources) to produce the system (the "process design") also begins during this phase, so that as soon as the system is fully developed it can be produced (Stage 4). Process design includes the design of new (or redesign of old) facilities and manufacturing processes, selection of specific materials and pieces of equipment, and preparations for production control, quality testing, manufacturing tooling, product transportation, personnel hiring and training, and data collection and processing.

Stage 4: System Fabrication, Construction, and/or Production

During Stage 4, the system is (1) mass produced, (2) produced in limited quantities with different features, or (3) built as a single item. This stage begins as soon as the design is approved and "frozen." The stage involves acquiring materials, managing inventory, and controlling production/construction operations to uphold performance, quality, reliability, safety, and other requirements.

Stage 5: System Operation and Support

Stage 5 completes the systems engineering process. Here, the customer operates the system until it wears out or becomes obsolete. The system developer might provide support in the following ways: assistance in deploying, installing, and checking out the system; assistance in day-to-day operation or field service and maintenance support; modification and enhancement of the system to ensure continued satisfaction; and support in closing, phasing out, and disposing of the system at the end of its life cycle. The latter, close-out and disposal of the system, is often a major consideration in the design and operation of the system—especially so for systems that have potential to degrade the surrounding environment. One example is nuclear reactors, the design of which must take into account the way each reactor will be shut down and the facility closed out. Another is mines for metals and coal, which scar the land, leave hazardous deposits, and pollute ground water and watersheds. Their closeout must include measures to restore the land, clean up wastes, and remove toxins from soil and water, which can be expensive, time-consuming, and extend the system life cycle by years or even decades.

Example A2.9: Life Cycle of SpaceShipOne

Preliminary development of SS1 and its support systems—White Knight, navigation system, flight simulator, etc.—began in 1999, and full development began in April 2001, albeit in total secrecy. Exactly 2 years later, Dick Rutan announced the intention to capture the X-Prize and flight-testing began (Figure 2.15).

Figure 2.15
SS1 beneath mothership White Knight.
Photograph courtesy John Nicholas.

In May 2004, Mike Melville piloted the craft on a test above 100 km, making him the world's first civilian astronaut. On October 29 he again flew SS1 into space, and less than 2 weeks later so did pilot Brian Binney, winning the $10 million X-Prize for the SS1 team (Figure 2.16). Today, SS1 hangs on display at the Smithsonian Air & Space Museum in Washington DC. A bigger spaceship, SS2, and a bigger mothership, WK2, have since been developed for use by Sir Richard Branson's commercial "spaceline," Virgin Galactic, which will operate a fleet of them from a site located near the town of Truth or Consequences, New Mexico.

Figure 2.16
Designer Burt Rutan
(center), and pilots Mike
Melville (left) and Brian
Binney.
Photograph courtesy
John Nicholas.

REVIEW QUESTIONS AND PROBLEMS

1. What distinguishes systems thinking from analytical thinking? Is systems thinking something new, or is it just another perspective? Explain.
2. Define "system". What notable features enable you to see something as a system? Describe briefly the American legal or education system in terms of these features.
3. How can several people looking at the same thing see the "system" in it differently?
4. Define the following concepts and explain how they fit into systems thinking: objectives, elements, subsystems, attributes, environment, boundary, structure, inputs, outputs, process, and constraints.
5. Describe the difference between open and closed systems, and between human-made and natural systems. Are all natural systems open systems?
6. Is a space vehicle an open system? Is an organization an open system? Explain.
7. Describe the systems approach. Where does the systems approach apply? Explain in a sentence what a manager does in the systems approach that he or she might not do otherwise.
8. What is the "environmental fallacy?"
9. What things does the problem-solver keep in mind when applying the systems approach?
10. Describe how the following elements of the systems approach apply to projects and project management: objectives, environment, resources, subsystems, and management.
11. Give some examples of physical models, of graphical models, and of mathematical models.
12. What is the systems life cycle? What is the systems development cycle?
13. Discuss the dimension of systems engineering in Figure 2.6.
14. What is modularization? What are its benefits in system design and operation?
15. In systems engineering, the first stage is identification. Identification of what?
16. Who are the stakeholders in systems engineering?
17. What are requirements? What aspects of the system or stakeholder needs should the requirements incorporate?

18. Distinguish stakeholder requirements and system requirements.
19. Describe the stages of systems engineering in Figure 2.8. Think of some projects, and describe the stages of systems engineering in these projects.
20. Distinguish the following: functional requirements, performance requirements, and verification requirements. Give an example of a functional requirement and its associated performance and verification requirements.
21. What is meant by the term "traceability?"
22. Think of a simple system like a mousetrap, tape dispenser, or can opener. Draw a simple high-level functional flow block diagram for it. If possible, decompose each of the functions into subfunctions.
23. What is the emphasis in systems management? How does it differ from just management?
24. What is the relevancy of the systems approach to project management?

QUESTIONS ABOUT THE STUDY PROJECT

1. Conceptualize the project organization (the project team and the parent organization of the team) you are studying as a system. What are the elements, attributes, environment, and so on? What are its internal subsystems—functional breakdown and management hierarchy subsystems? What is the relevant environment? Who are the decision-makers?
2. Describe the role of the project manager with respect to these subsystems, both internal and external. What is the nature of his or her responsibilities in these subsystems? How aware is the project manager of the project "environment," and what does he or she do that reflects this awareness?
3. Now, conceptualize the output or end-item of the project as a system. Again, focus on the elements, relationships, attributes, subsystems, environment, and so on. All projects, whether directed at making a physical product (e.g., computer, space station, skyscraper, research report) or a service (e.g., giving consultation and advice), are devoted to producing systems. This exercise will help you better understand what the project is doing. It is also good preparation for topics in the next chapter.
4. If the study project involves engineering or integration of many components, was the systems engineering process used? Is there a section, department, or task in the project called systems engineering? If so, elaborate. Are there functions or phases of the project that seem to resemble the systems engineering process?
5. As described in this chapter, besides the main end-item or operating system (i.e., the output objective of the project), systems engineering also addresses the support system—that system which supports installation, operation, maintenance, evaluation, and enhancement of the operating system. Describe the support system in the study project and its development.
6. Were the stakeholder requirements clearly defined at the start of the project? Were system requirements clearly defined? What are the requirements? In your opinion, were stakeholders identified and involved early in the project? Were their needs identified and addressed? Did the project deliver a system that met their needs?
7. What aspects of the project or parent organization appear to use systems management? What aspects do not use systems management? Describe the appropriateness or inappropriateness of systems management in the project you are studying.

Case 2.1   Glades County Sanitary District

Glades County is a region on the Gulf Coast with a population of 600,000. About 90 percent of the population is located in and near the city of Sitkus. The main attractions of the area are its clean, sandy beaches and nearby fishing. Resorts, restaurants, hotels, retailers, and the Sitkus/Glades County economy in general rely on these attractions for tourist dollars.

In the past decade, Glades County has experienced a near doubling of population and industry. One result has been the noticeable increase in the level of water pollution along the coast due primarily to the increased raw sewage dumped by Glades County into the Gulf. Ordinarily, the Glades County sewer system directs effluent waste through filtration plants before pumping it into the Gulf. Although the Glades County Sanitary District (GCSD) usually is able to handle the county's sewage, during heavy rains the runoff from paved surfaces exceeds sewer capacity and must be diverted past filtration plants and directly into the Gulf. Following heavy rains, the beaches are cluttered with dead fish and debris. The Gulf fishing trade is also affected, since pollution drives away desirable fish. Recently, the water pollution level has become high enough to damage both the tourist and fishing trades. Besides coastal pollution, there is concern that as the population continues to increase, the county's primary fresh water source, Glades River, will also become polluted.

The GCSD has been mandated to prepare a comprehensive water waste management program that will reverse the trend in pollution along the Gulf Coast as well as handle the expected increase in effluent wastes over the next 20 years. Although not yet specified, it is known that the program will include new sewers, filtration plants, and stricter anti-pollution laws. As a first step, GCSD must establish the overall direction and mission of the program.

QUESTIONS

Answer the following questions (given the limited information, it is okay to advance some logical guesses; if you are not able to answer a question for lack of information, indicate how and where, as a systems engineer, you would get it):

1. What is the system? What are its key elements and subsystems? What are the boundaries and how are they determined? What is the environment?
2. Who are the decision-makers?
3. What is the problem? Carefully formulate it.
4. Define the overall objective of the water waste management program. Because the program is wide-ranging in scope, you should break this down into several sub-objectives.
5. Define the criteria or measures of performance to be used to determine whether the objectives of the program are being met. Specify several criteria for each sub-objective. As much as possible, the criteria should be quantitative, although some qualitative measures should also be included. How will you know if the criteria that you define are the appropriate ones to use?
6. What are the resources and constraints?
7. Elaborate on the kinds of alternatives and range of solutions to solving the problem.
8. Discuss some techniques that could be used to help evaluate which alternatives are best.

Case 2.2   Life and Death of an Aircraft Development Project

Law and Callon[31] described the history of a large British aerospace project in terms of two entities: the global system and the project itself. The *global* system comprised parties and organizations *outside* the project that had a stake in the project; the *project* comprised everything *within* the project, including all work and the organizations contracted to do it.

THE GLOBAL SYSTEM

The principal stakeholders in the global system were:

1. The Royal Air Force (RAF), which initiated the project with a request for a new supersonic aircraft with short take-off capability. The aircraft would be a "tactical strike and reconnaissance fighter" called TSR.
2. The Ministry of Defence (MOD), which wanted an aircraft that would best fit the nation's current overall defense needs.
3. The Treasury, which wanted an inexpensive aircraft that would have market appeal for sale outside the UK, such as to the Royal Australian Air Force (RAAF).
4. The Royal Navy (RN), which wanted to buy *a different* aircraft but was under pressure by MOD to buy the TSR.
5. The Ministry of Supply (MOS), which wanted an aircraft that would be produced by a consortium of several UK airframe and engine manufacturers.

As is typical of most projects, each stakeholder in the global system conceptualized the project differently: to the RAF and MOD it would yield an aircraft for a specific mission; to the Treasury it would fit the defense budget and generate revenue; to the RN it was a competitive threat to the aircraft they really wanted; and to the MOS it was an instrument of industrial policy. The parties had different reasons for contributing resources and support: some were economic (in return for funds, an aircraft would be built); some political (in return for a demonstrated need, objections of the RN would be overruled); some technical (in return for engineering and technical effort, the aircraft would meet RAF performance requirements); and some industrial (in exchange for contracts, the aircraft industry would be consolidated).

THE PROJECT

The Treasury would not approve project funding until the aircraft's basic design, manufacturer, cost, and delivery date were defined. The RAF and MOD sent requests to the aircraft industry for design ideas, and selected two manufacturers: Vickers Corp. and English Electric (EE). They favored Vickers for its integration capability (combining aircraft, engine, armaments, and support equipment into a single weapons package), but they also liked EE for its design experience with supersonic aircraft. So they decided to contract with both companies and adopt a design that would utilize features from both. The idea was approved by all other parties in the global system, and funding for the project was released.

The project grew as Vickers and EE hired subcontractors and expanded their teams for design, production, and management. The two companies and several other contractors merged to form a single new organization called the British Aircraft Corporation (BAC).

RELATIONSHIPS BETWEEN THE GLOBAL SYSTEM AND THE PROJECT

As the project grew, so did the problems between it and the global system. The MOS wanted centralized control over all aspects of the project, and all transactions between the project and stakeholders in the global system. Although BAC was the prime contractor and ostensibly responsible for managing the project, the MOS would not confer upon it the necessary management authority. Rather, the MOS formed a series of committees with members from the global system and gave them primary responsibility to manage the project. This led to serious problems:

1. The committees were allowed to make or veto important project-related decisions. They, not BAC, awarded important contracts; when the RAF wanted to change its requirements, it consulted with the committees, not with BAC.
2. The committees often lacked sufficient information or knowledge. Technical committees made decisions without regard to costs; cost committees made decisions without regard to technical realities. Decisions focused on particular aspects of the project; seldom did they account for impacts on other parts of the project, or the project as a whole.

Distrust grew between BAC and the MOS; neither was able to effectively integrate the resources, information, and decisions flowing between parties in the project and the global system. Subcontractors became difficult to control. Many ignored

BAC and worked only with the MOS and RAF to get favorable treatment.

GLOBAL SYSTEM RESHAPED

Everyone knew the project was in trouble. Project costs doubled. One of the test engines exploded, and the RAF recognized it might take years to understand the cause. In addition, the RAAF announced that it would not order the TSR but was instead buying the US-built F-111. Opposition to the project grew, and in the upcoming general election the Labour Party promised that if elected it would review the project. When the Labour Party won, it immediately began an assessment of the project, which included comparing the TSR to the F-111—considered by now an alternative to the TSR. As cost overruns and schedule delays continued, the MOS slowly withdrew support. The RAF then withdrew its support, when it discovered that the F-111, which was already in production, would meet all of its requirements. The project was canceled.

QUESTIONS

1. In this case history, what is the "system" and what are its elements? What is the "environment," and what are the elements of the environment?
2. Describe the interaction between the system and its environment.
3. Do you feel that important decisions made in this project represent "system thinking"? Explain.
4. Comment on the concept of "integration" in the project. How were aspects of the project integrated or not integrated?
5. What are the main factors that contributed to cancellation of the project? Which of these factors would you characterize as project management?

NOTES

1. Schoderbek P, Kefalas A, and Schoderbek C. *Management Systems: Conceptual Considerations*. Dallas, TX: Business Publications; 1975. pp. 7–8.
2. Naughton J and Peters G. *Systems Performance: Human Factors and Systems Failures*. Milton Keynes, UK: The Open University; 1976. pp. 8–12.
3. *Ibid.*, p. 11. Innumerable systems can be perceived from any one entity. K Boulding, in *The World as a Total System* (Beverly Hills, CA: Sage; 1985) describes the world as physical, biological, social, economic, political, communication, and evaluative systems.
4. Kast F and Rosenzweig J. The modern view: a systems approach. In Beishon J and Peters G (eds), *Systems Behavior*, 2nd edn. London, UK: Harper & Row; 1976. pp. 19–25.
5. Cleland D and King W. *Management: A Systems Approach*. New York, NY: McGraw-Hill; 1972. p. 89.
6. Churchman CW. *The Systems Approach and Its Enemies*. New York, NY: Basic Books; 1979.
7. *Ibid.*, pp. 4–5.
8. Much of the discussion in this section is based on Churchman CW. *The Systems Approach*. New York, NY: Dell; 1968. pp. 30–39.
9. Thome P and Willard R. The systems approach: a unified concept of planning. In Optner S (ed.), *Systems Analysis*. Harmondsworth, UK: Penguin Books; 1973. p. 212.
10. Hamilton H. *Systems Simulation for Regional Analysis*. Cambridge, MA: MIT Press; 1972.
11. The life cycle of technological products and their impact on competition is eloquently described by Foster R, in *Innovation: The Attacker's Advantage*. New York, NY: Summit Books; 1986.
12. As common parlance, the term *project life cycle* is recognition that all projects tend to follow a similar sequence of activities, start to finish. Since every project, however, has a start and finish, when referring to a particular project the more precise term is *project life span*.
13. Jenkins G. The systems approach. In Beishon J and Peters G (eds), *Systems Behavior*, 2nd edn. London, UK: Harper & Row; 1976. p. 82.
14. Auyang S. *Engineering—An Endless Frontier*. Cambridge, MA: Harvard University Press; 2004. pp. 175–189.
15. Brooks F. *The Mythical Man Month*. Reading, MA: Addison Wesley; 1995. p. 199.
16. Auyang, *Engineering—An Endless Frontier*, p. 183.

17. *Ibid.*, pp. 192–197.
18. Forsberg K and Mooz H. In Taylor R, Dorfman M and Davis A (eds), *Software Requirements Engineering*, 2nd edn. Los Alamitos, CA: IEEE Computer Society Press; 1997. pp. 44–77. V-model adapted from reprint in Auyang, *Engineering—An Endless Frontier*, p. 197.
19. Herbert Simon, quoted in Auyang, *Engineering—An Endless Frontier*, p. 194.
20. Cleland and King, *Management: A Systems Approach*, pp. 171–173; Johnson R, Kast F and Rosenzweig J. *The Theory and Management of Systems*, 3rd edn. New York, NY: McGraw-Hill; 1973. pp. 135–136.
21. Gilbreath R. *Winning at Project Management*. New York, NY: John Wiley & Sons; 1986.
22. *Ibid.*, pp. 95–96.
23. *Ibid.*, pp. 98–102.
24. Avots I. Why does project management fail? *Harvard Business Review* 1969; XII(1): 77–82.
25. This section is derived from five sources: (1) Falconbridge RI and Ryan M. *Managing Complex Technical Projects: A Systems Engineering Approach*. Boston, MA: Artech House; 2003. pp. 9–93. (2) Blanchard B and Fabrycky W. *Systems Engineering and Analysis*. Upper Saddle River, NJ: Prentice Hall; 1981. pp. 18–52. (3) Boguslaw R. *The New Utopians: A Study of System Design and Social Change*. Upper Saddle River, NJ: Prentice Hall; 1965. pp. 99–112. (4) Chestnut H. *Systems Engineering Methods*. New York, NY: John Wiley & Sons; 1967. pp. 1–41. (5) Jenkins G. The systems approach. In Beishon J and Peters G (eds), *Systems Behavior*, 2nd edn. London, UK: Harper & Row; 1976. pp. 78–101.
26. Falconbridge and Ryan, *Managing Complex Technical Projects*, pp. 29–65.
27. Jenkins, The systems approach, p. 88.
28. The SpaceShipOne (SS1) examples in this book illustrate concepts. While there is much factual information about the project available from published sources, information about the actual design and development of the spaceship is confidential. SS1, the X-Prize, and the stakeholders described are all true-life; however, for lack of information, portions of this and subsequent examples are hypothetical. Information for this and other examples of SS1 are drawn from news articles, and the SS1 website at Scaled Composites (www. scaled. com/projects/tierone/index.htm).
29. Adapted from Falconbridge and Ryan, *Managing Complex Technical Projects*, pp. 67–96.
30. Chestnut, *Systems Engineering Methods*, p. 33.
31. From Law J and Callon M. The life and death of an aircraft: a network analysis of technical change. In Bijker W and Law J (eds), *Shaping Society/Building Technology*. Cambridge, MA: MIT Press; 1992.

Part II

Systems Development Cycle

Most systems move inexorably through a process or series of developmental stages. In planned human systems, development occurs through an intentional, logical sequence of prescribed activities called the systems development cycle. Project management takes place within the context of this cycle, and is the function responsible for planning development activities and organizing and guiding their execution. The two chapters in this section introduce the systems development cycle, and describe the first two phases, conception and definition. They cover the PMBOK topics of *procurement management* and *scope management*.

Chapter

Systems Development Cycle and Project Conception

> *There is . . . a time to be born, and a time to die; a time to plant, and a time to reap; a time to kill, and a time to heal; a time to break down, and a time to build up . . .*

> —*Ecclesiastes 3:1*

One feature of the systems approach is the concept of "life cycle"—the basic pattern of change that occurs throughout the life of a system. Two ways the systems approach accounts for this are (1) to recognize the natural process that occurs in all dynamic systems—that of birth, growth, maturity, and death, and (2) to incorporate that process into the planning and management of systems. The practice of project management does both.

For any human-made system, the process of developing, implementing, and operating it happens through a logical sequence of phases called the *systems development cycle*. Projects also follow a progression of phases from beginning to end called the *project life cycle*. This chapter describes the system development cycle and covers the first phase of the cycle, conception. The next chapter covers the second phase; subsequent chapters cover the others.

85

Systems are dynamic—they change over time. The change tends to follow a distinct pattern that is repeated again and again. Mentioned in Chapter 2 was the obvious life cycle of organisms—birth, growth, maturity, senescence, and death—and its similarity to cycles in human-made products and systems. Projects also follow such a cycle.

Project Life Cycle

Projects are done for the purpose of developing systems—either to create new ones or to improve existing ones. The natural life cycle of systems gives rise to a similar cycle in projects called the *project life cycle*. Each project has a starting point and progresses toward a predetermined conclusion. Starting with project conceptualization, projects experience a build-up in "effort" that eventually peaks and then declines—the pattern shown in the lower curve in Figure 3.1 (the upper "S-curve," shows cumulative activity). This activity can be measured in various ways, such as the amount of money spent on the project, the number of people working on it, or the amount of materials being used.

Besides changes in the level of effort, the nature and emphasis of the activity change too. For example, consider the mix of project personnel: customers and planners dominate the early stages of the project; designers, builders, and implementers take charge in the middle stages; users and operators take over at the end. Over the project life cycle, the composition of the project organization also changes.

No matter the project phase or kind of work activity, every project can be measured in three ways at any point in its life cycle: *time*, *cost*, and *performance*. Time refers to the temporal progress of activities and extent to which schedules and deadlines are being met. Cost refers to the rate of resource expenditure as compared to budgeted resources. Performance refers to outputs of the project as compared to objectives, specifications, and requirements; meeting performance requirements is a measure of the *quality* of the project output. The project manager attempts to achieve time, cost, and performance requirements as the project advances through the life cycle.

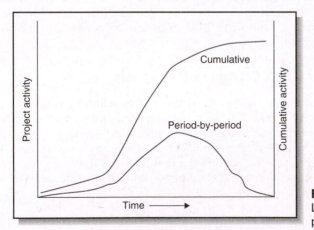

Figure 3.1
Level of activity during the project life cycle.

Managing the Project Life Cycle

Managing the project life cycle requires special treatment. Unlike non-project, repetitive operations, where everything tends to be somewhat familiar and stable, things in projects—resources, schedules, work tasks, etc.—are often unfamiliar and in a constant state of change. Little is done in a project that can be considered repetitive or even routine. Work schedules, budgets, and tasks must be tailored to fit each phase and stage of the project life cycle.

All projects contain an element of uncertainty. Unforeseen obstacles can cause missed deadlines, cost overruns, and poor project performance. Management must try to anticipate the problems, plan for them, and adjust activities and shift resources to mitigate or overcome them.

Organizations often undertake several projects at once. At a given time the projects are at different stages of their life cycles: some are just being started, others are underway, and still others are being closed out. Management must be able to continuously balance resources so each project gets what it needs, yet all their needs combined do not exceed the resources available.

3.2 SYSTEMS DEVELOPMENT CYCLE

The life cycle of a human-made system can be segmented into a logical series of phases and stages. Figure 3.2 shows the life cycle divided into four phases, collectively called the *systems development cycle*:

1. Conception phase (Phase A)
2. Definition phase (Phase B)
3. Execution phase (Phase C)
4. Operation phase (Phase D).

Virtually all of the projects described in Chapter 1 can be fitted into this four-phase cycle.

Figure 3.2
Four-phase model and detailed stages of the systems development cycle.
Project life cycle is Phases A, B, and C.

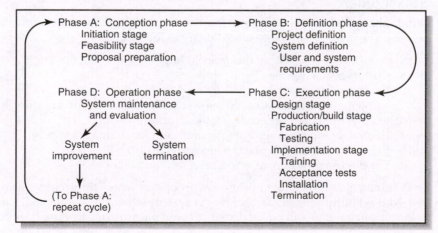

The Phases

The four-phase cycle encompasses the total developmental and operational life cycle of all human-made systems. The phases overlap and interact, yet are clearly differentiable. They reflect the order of thought and action in the development and use of all human-made systems, whether consumer products, space vehicles, information systems, or company relocations.

For some systems, the development cycle overlaps identically with the project life cycle. A project typically spans Phases A through C—the conception, definition, and execution phases of the cycle. Hence, the first three phases of the systems development cycle overlap with the project life cycle. When Phase C ends upon implementation of the system, so does the project. At that point, the system transits from being the end-result of a project to being an operational entity.

Virtually all projects progress through Phases A, B, and C, though not necessarily through the stages as shown in Figure 3.2. The actual stages in the life cycle depend on the system or end-item being developed. For some projects, some of the stages might receive little emphasis or be entirely skipped; most projects, however, *do* pass through the stages shown in Figure 3.2, even if informally. For instance, although many projects do not involve formal proposal preparation, every project starts with a proposal from *someone*. Similarly, while many projects do not require design, manufacturing, or construction, every project does require conceptualization and bringing together the pieces of something (even if only information) to produce a final result.

Sometimes, between the phases of the life cycle there are points at which decisions are made concerning the preceding phase and whether the project should be continued to the next phase or be terminated. Referred to as "gating," the project is assessed at the end of each phase and a go/no-go decision is made.

In some large-scale endeavors where the development cycle spans years—such as urban renewal, product development, and space exploration, the cycle is treated as a *program* and the phases within it as separate *projects*—sometimes each conducted by a different contracting organization. For example, Phase A would be treated as a project and conducted by one organization, Phase B as another project conducted by another organization, and so on, each phase with its own project manager. The bonds holding them together and keeping them all moving forward are common program goals, and the program manager.

Stakeholders

Within the systems development cycle are many stakeholders (actors and interested parties). The main groups of stakeholders are as follows.

1. System *customers*, *buyers*, or *clients*, including:
   a. Customer management
   b. Users and operators.
2. The system *contractor*, also called the systems development organization (SDO), developer, promoter, or consultant; these include:
   a. Contractor top management (corporate and functional managers)
   b. Project management (project manager and staff)
   c. The doers—professional, trade, assembly, and other workers.

Customers (buyers) are the persons or groups for whom the project is being done and who will acquire and/or operate the system when it is completed. Customer management pays for and makes decisions about the project; users and operators will utilize, maintain, or in other ways be the recipients of the end-item at the end of the project. It is important to identify the actual users since, ultimately, it is for them the system is being created. From here on we use the terms customer and user somewhat interchangeably, keeping in mind this distinction:

- The customer (or buyer) *pays* for the system
- The users *use* it.

The contractor or developer is the party that studies, designs, develops, builds, and installs the system. The contractor is usually external to the user organization, although of course it might well reside within the same organization as the user, as is the case of internal consulting/support groups. Since the contractor is usually an *organization*, it sometimes is referred to as the systems development organization (SDO). Because in most cases the customer *pays* the contractor to perform the project, you can think of the customer as the *buyer* and the contractor as the *seller*. Use of these terms makes sense when you think of a project in the context of being a contract between two parties wherein one (the contractor-seller) agrees to provide services in return for payment from another (the user-buyer). The project manager usually works for the contractor, although the customer might also have a project manager.

Besides these, the life cycle involves other key parties—individuals, groups, and organizations with vested interests and/or influence on the conduct of the project. Anyone who is affected by the project or potentially can alter its outcome is a *stakeholder*. Customers and contractors are considered internal stakeholders; parties outside the project (in the environment) are external stakeholders. All are important, and their needs, interests, and influences must be accounted for in the project plan and project end-items. When a project manager is assigned to a project, nobody gives him a list of all the key stakeholders; thus, as mentioned in the Appendix to Chapter 2, one of all his first tasks is to identify the stakeholders, their needs, expectation, and interests, and to develop strategies to accommodate them.

Phase A: Conception

Every project is an attempt to solve a problem. The first step in solving a problem is recognition and acceptance that the problem exists. After that, the individual facing the problem—the customer and users—seeks out someone who can help. The steps they take—soliciting people who can do the work, evaluating their proposals, and reaching an agreement—all are part of the *procurement management* process.

If the customer organization has an internal group capable of doing the work, it turns to this. If not, it will look to outside contractors, possibly by sending them a formal request for help called a *request for proposal*, or *RFP*. Each contractor examines the customer's problem, objectives, and requirements as stated in the RFP, and determines the technical and economic feasibility of undertaking the project. If the contractor decides to respond to the request, it presents the customer with a proposed solution (system concept) in a *proposal* or *letter of interest.* The customer then examines the proposal—or, when multiple contractors have responded, all the proposals—and makes a choice. The result is a formal agreement between the chosen contractor and the customer. Most ideas or proposals never get beyond Phase A; the problems the proposals address are judged as insignificant, or the proposal as impractical, infeasible, or lacking benefits to justify funding and resources. The few that are approved and reach a contract agreement move on to Phase B.

Phase B: Definition

Having reached a commitment from the customer, the contractor begins a detailed analysis of the system concept, during which it defines the requirements the system must fulfill to meet the customer's needs, and the system's functions and elements necessary to meet those requirements. This definition results in a preliminary design for the system. As the process continues, the major subsystems, components, and support systems of the proposed system are determined, as are the resources, costs, and schedules necessary to create the system. Meantime, project management assembles a comprehensive project plan that defines the activities, schedules, budgets, and resources to design, build, and implement the system. Contractor top management reviews the plan for acceptability and then forwards it to the customer, who also reviews it for acceptability.

Phase C: Execution

The execution phase is when the work specified in the project plan is put to action; it is sometimes referred to as the "acquisition" phase, because the user acquires the system at the end of the phase and most system resources are acquired then. The execution phase often includes the stages of "design," "production," and "implementation," referring to the progression through which a system moves from being an idea to a finished, physical end-item. All systems are comprised of elements arranged in some pattern, configuration, or structure, and it is in the *design* stage that the elements and pattern necessary for the system to fulfill requirements are defined. Following design the system goes into *production*, where it is built as either a single-item or a mass-produced item. Near the end of the execution phase, the system is *implemented*; it is installed in and becomes a part of the user's environment.

Phase D: Operation

In the operation phase the system is deployed; the customer takes over to operate the system and maintain it.

For systems such as products and equipment that people use and rely upon daily, Phase D may last for years or decades, in which case the phase includes not only operation and maintenance of the system, but also improvement and enhancement to keep the system viable and useful. All systems eventually outlive their purpose or simply wear out. When that happens, there are two choices: to scrap the system, or to modify it so it remains useful. In the latter case the "modification" becomes a new system concept, the beginning of a new systems development cycle, and the start of a new project.

For some systems Phase D is short or non-existent: examples are a political campaign, rock concert, and gala ceremony (the project ends on Election Day, or upon completion of the performance or ceremony).[1]

Phased Project Planning and Fast-Tracking

Within the systems development cycle, projects are sometimes undertaken in a stepwise fashion called *phased project planning* or project *gating*. At the end of each phase the project objectives, costs, and outcomes are re-evaluated, and a decision is made to continue, suspend, or cancel the project. Resources are committed only after a management review of performance to date.

The phases of the cycle as described are not always performed in discrete sequence, but can be overlapped in a practice called *fast tracking*. Before Phase B is completed, elements of Phase C are started; before Phase C is completed, portions of Phase D are started. Fast-tracking compresses the time for systems development and implementation, though it poses the risk of overlooking or misdefining tasks and having to repeat or undo them.

Project Methodologies

The first three phases of the systems development cycle shown in Figure 3.2 represent a prescribed sequence of steps in performing projects; in common parlance, it is a *project methodology*. In general, while the phases and stages comprise the project life cycle, whenever someone *prescribes or mandates* conformance to the set of phases or stages, the life cycle becomes a methodology.

Most project-oriented companies undertake projects in ways best suited for them and their projects, and they prescribe or mandate ways that management and technical tasks should be performed in their projects—i.e., they create their own homegrown project methodologies. Throughout this book, the methodology we will repeatedly refer to encompasses Phases A thorough C in Figure 3.2. We use this methodology not because it is always the best, but because it conveys a pattern very common in projects and similar to methodologies we have seen in many companies. Other methodologies are discussed in Chapter 16.

Systems Development Cycle, Systems Engineering, and Project Management

You might have noticed a similarity between the systems development cycle (Figure 3.2) and the systems engineering process (Figure 2.8). They are indeed similar, the only difference between them being one of scope. Systems engineering focuses on the technical aspects of systems, and on making sure that the elements of the system and the environment interrelate to satisfy functional requirements. Although it covers the full systems development cycle, systems engineering is mainly concerned with the conception and definition phases—formulating functional requirements, performing trade-off analysis, and designing systems.

In contrast, the systems development cycle is broader in scope than systems engineering, and encompasses virtually all considerations in systems development—not just configuration and integration, but planning, scheduling, budgeting, control, organization, communication, negotiation, documentation, and resource acquisition and allocation as well. In short, it includes considerations of project management.

The remainder of this chapter will focus on the first phase of the systems development cycle, and how projects are conceived and started. Most of what happens in this phase is part of what is called the *procurement management* process.

3.3 PHASE A: CONCEPTION[2]

The conception phase nominally comprises two separate stages. The first stage, project initiation, establishes that a "need" or problem exists, and that it is worthy of investigation. The second, project feasibility, is a detailed investigation of the need or problem, a formulation of possible alternative solutions, and the selection of one. The phase ends with an agreement that a chosen contractor will provide a specified solution to the customer.

Project Initiation

The systems development process begins when the customer or user perceives a *need*, which is recognition of a problem or opportunity and possible ways to deal with it.[3] Sometimes the need is expressed as a vision.

Example 3.1: Vision Statement at Microsoft[4]

New product development projects are often initiated with a document that outlines a "vision" about a proposed product. At Microsoft each product development project starts with a short definition of the product and its goals, called a vision statement. For a recent version of Excel, it was just five pages long.

The purpose of the vision statement is to communicate the concept and requirements of the product to the development team, other product groups, and management. At Microsoft this includes an executive summary with a one-sentence objective, a list specifying what the product will and will not do, and definitions of the typical customer and competition. The statement might describe product features and priorities in enough detail to begin preparing schedules for development, testing, user education, and preparation of English and non-English product versions. It might also list requirements for the operating system, memory, disk space, processor speed, graphics, and dependencies on printer drivers and components, although usually such details evolve later. The statement informs everyone about what they will and will not do, and gives them a common overview.

Beyond perceiving the need, project initiation requires proving that the need is significant and can be fulfilled at practical cost. It is easy to identify problems and muse about solutions, but most ideas are ephemeral and not worth much. If a customer decides to take an idea beyond speculation, he might take the "quick and dirty" route and simply implement the first solution that comes along, or he might undertake a more protracted albeit systematic and thorough approach: this would be the systems development approach. In systems development, only ideas with a reasonably high likelihood of success or return on investment are permitted to develop. To cull the few good ideas, the customer organization undertakes a brief initial investigation.

Initial Investigation

Many users know a problem exists, but do not know what it is or how to explain it. Before committing resources to a full-fledged study, the user undertakes a short internal investigation to clarify the problem and evaluate possible solutions. The investigation starts with fact-finding—interviewing managers and users, gathering data, and reviewing existing documentation. A clear statement of the problem is formulated, objectives are defined, and a list of alternative, potential solutions is compiled. The investigation focuses on the elements of the problem, including:

- The environment
- The needs, symptoms, problem definition, and objectives
- Preliminary solutions, and the estimated costs, benefits, strengths, and weaknesses of each
- Affected individuals and organizations.

Based on the investigation, the customer decides whether or not to proceed with the idea. Most ideas never get farther than this, and it is obvious why: there are endless ideas about needs and potential solutions, but resources are scarce and organizations can commit only to those comparative few that provide the most benefits and have the best chances of success.

To approve the concept for further study, the customer must be convinced that:

- The need is real and funding is available to support it
- The idea has sufficient priority in relation to other ideas
- The idea has particular value in terms of, for example, applying new technology, enhancing reputation, increasing market share, or raising profits
- The idea is consistent with the organization's goals and resources.

Pertaining to the last bullet, some organizations *prescreen* proposed projects, and only those that align with organizational goals and available resources are considered for further analysis. This prescreening, the first of several steps in "qualifying" a project for funding, is an aspect of *project portfolio management*, discussed in Chapter 17.

The initial investigation is usually conducted by the customer and is brief, requiring a few days or weeks at most. Sometimes called the *Idea Stage* or *Pre-Feasibility Stage*, its purpose is to determine whether the idea deserves further study; if it does, it then becomes a "potential project" and is approved for the next stage—feasibility.

3.4 PROJECT FEASIBILITY

Feasibility is the process of studying a need, problem, and solutions in sufficient detail to determine if the idea is economically viable and worth developing. The initial investigation is a form of feasibility study, a *pre-feasibility* study, which itself is usually rather cursory, and hence insufficient to commit to a project. A *feasibility study* is a more protracted, rigorous study that considers alternative solutions (system concepts) and the benefits and costs of each. The customer typically performs the feasibility study, but usually hires outsiders (contractors) to do it if the study requires special expertise. Deciding to build a new airport, power plant, highway, or tunnel are examples where the feasibility studies are themselves big, expensive projects undertaken by outside contractors. In such cases, a pre-feasibility study is normally undertaken.

If the feasibility study indicates that the concept is viable, one of two things happens (Figure 3.3):

1. Theme A: if the concept is something the customer can handle itself, it is passed along to an internal group for development and execution
2. Theme B: if the concept cannot be executed internally, it is given to outside contractors (SDOs).

Companies like Boeing, Microsoft, and Toyota routinely do feasibility studies for new products and then hand off the approved concepts to their own teams for the design, development, and production of the new products. However, companies like Ritz-Carlton and Swisshotel, after deciding to build a hotel of particular size at a specific location, hire outside contractors to execute the project. In the latter case, the customer solicits ideas and bids from multiple contractors with a document called an RFP (described in the next section), and chooses the best.

Competing contractors must each perform their own feasibility study to assess the merits of the project, their capability for obtaining a contract, and whether or not they want to participate. If a contractor decides to go forward, it will investigate alternative possible approaches (system concepts) to the customer's problem, choose one, and offer this in the proposal. This is called the "proposal preparation process." Upon receiving the proposals, the customer reviews them and selects the one that best fits the selection criteria—i.e., is the "most feasible."

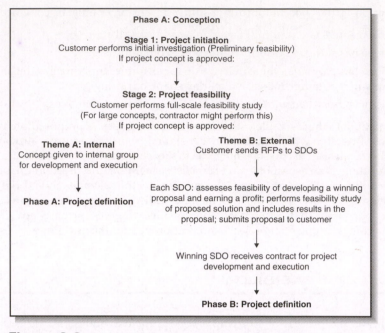

Figure 3.3
Different paths in the project feasibility stage.

In summary, project feasibility involves multiple studies and decisions—the customer assessing the "feasibility" of funding the project; the contractor determining the "feasibility" of winning the contract; the contractor conceiving alternative solutions and picking the "most feasible" one to propose; and the customer assessing the proposals and choosing the "most feasible" one to buy. When the customer reaches an agreement with a contractor, the project moves forward to Phase B.

Sometimes contractors decide *not* to prepare proposals because they don't have solutions that will be profitable or fit the customer's request. Sometimes customers conclude that *none* of the proposals meets the requirements. Either way, the concept is judged as "not feasible!" and the process ends there.

Request for Proposal

The RFP—request for proposal (or *request for bid*, *request for quotation*, *invitation for bid* (*IFB*), or similar term)[5] is a document the customer sends to potential contractors telling them the customer has a problem or need, and wants to hire someone. In the RFP, the customer describes his problems, objectives, and requirements (Figure 3.4).

The dual purpose of the RFP is to outline the user's need (problem, idea, etc.) and to solicit suggestions (proposals) for solutions—usually with the intent of awarding a contract. The customer sends RFPs to contractors on its own *bidders list*. Contractors not on the bidders list can learn about RFPs and upcoming jobs in newsletters and bulletins, and request RFPs from customers. For example, *Commerce Business Daily* is a publication that gives a synopsis of all federal jobs over $10,000. Businesses scan the jobs and request RFPs for those they might be interested in bidding on.

Often the customer will precede the RFP with a *Request for Qualifications*, which is

Statement of work

- Description of problem, need, or general type of solutions to be investigated.
- Scope of work to be performed by contractor, work to be included, work excluded, and work restrictions; criteria of acceptance for results or end-items.
- Requirements for the solution, results, or end-item, including specifications and standards; description of how work will be measured; expected relationship between user and contractor; expected completion date; constraints on cost of work to be performed.

Proposal requirements

Conditions placed on the proposal such as proposal contents and format, data requirements, sample forms to include, and submission location and deadline.

Contractual provisions

Type of contract to be awarded, sample contract, and nondisclosure provisions.

Technical information or data

Any additional data, or name of a contact person for requesting additional data, necessary to develop a solution and prepare the proposal or price quote.

Figure 3.4
Contents of a Request for Proposal.

a request for contractors to describe their qualifications. Only if a contractor is deemed qualified for the work will the customer send an RFP.

Usually the customer gets just what he asks for, and project foul-ups later can be traced to a poor RFP. The RFP must be clear, concise, and complete: when it is, the customer can expect contractors to respond with proposals that are clear, concise, and complete; when it is not, the customer can expect proposals in kind. Ultimately, the ability of contractors to *develop* solutions that uniquely fit the customer's needs will depend in part on their understanding of the requirements as specified in the RFP. Similarly, the ability of the customer to *select* a contractor that is qualified and has the best proposal will depend on information requested in the RFP. Appendix A at the end of the book is an example RFP.

Each competing contractor must carefully consider its capability of preparing a winning proposal and, should it win the contract, of performing the proposed work. Among the factors it considers are:

- Whether competitors have gotten a head start
- Whether the contractor has sufficient money, facilities, and resources to invest in the project
- Whether performance on the project could enhance (or damage) the contractor's reputation
- Other factors similar to the criteria employed by the customer in the initial investigation.

Sometimes a contractor will submit a proposal knowing full well it cannot possibly win the project, doing so to maintain its relationship with the customer, remain on the customer's bidders list, or keep the field competitive. Sometimes a customer sends out an RFP with no intention of ever signing with a contractor, doing so simply to gather ideas—obviously a situation of which respondent contractors must be wary.

Contractors can also submit proposals to potential customers without an RFP. Whenever a developer believes it has a system or solution that satisfies a need or solves a problem, the project manager works with his marketing department to identify prospective customers to which they might send *unsolicited proposals* describing the merits of the new system. Unsolicited proposals are also sent to current customers for potential follow-up work on current projects.

The Feasibility Study[6]

As mentioned, a feasibility study can be performed at multiple times and with different parties in a project: minimally, the customer performs a study to determine whether the project is worth supporting; if the project work is to be done externally, the contractor also performs one to determine whether the job is worth pursuing. In this section we consider the latter, although the same steps described apply equally to the customer or anybody doing a feasibility study.

The statement of the problem as defined in the RFP is frequently incomplete, vague, or even incorrect. If an RFP has been received it will likely contain such a statement. Thus, one of the contractor's first steps in responding to an RFP is to develop a definition of the problem that is more concise, accurate, and complete than the one in the RFP.

The prime source of information about the problem is interviews and documented information provided by the customer and user. It is thus important that the contractor identifies who the real *user* really is. Surprisingly, this is not always obvious. The "real" user, the party that will operate, maintain, or be the main beneficiary of the system, is often confused with persons who only represent the user. If the customer is an organization, the contractor must determine the individuals whose needs are to be met. The contractor should be working closely with the user throughout the feasibility study, so it is important to find users who are familiar with both the problem and the workings of the organization. Sometimes, however, the RFP specifies that in order to make the competition "fair" the customer will maintain an "arm's length" relationship with competing contractors. Even then, however, contractors are usually permitted to make inquiries to or seek additional information from a customer contact person.

The feasibility study delivers a document/report that is often called a "business case." When the document is suitable to obtain financing, it is called a "bankable business case."

Needs Definition

Problems originate from needs (definition: a problem is an unsatisfied need), and so do solutions (definition: a solution is a way to satisfy a need), so it is important that the solution adopted for the project addresses the right needs. Hence, conducting a feasibility study and preparing a proposal should begin with defining user needs. J. Davidson Frame,[7] one of the best authors on defining needs in the project context, suggests the following steps:

1. *Ask the user to state the needs as clearly as possible.*
2. *Ask the user a complete set of questions to further elicit the needs.* For example:
   Are these real needs, or are there other, more fundamental ones?
   Are the needs important enough to pursue?
   Are we capable of fulfilling these needs, or is someone else better suited?
   If the needs are fulfilled, will they give rise to other needs?
   Will satisfying these needs also satisfy other needs too?
   What effect do the unmet needs have on the organization and the user?
   What other parties are affected by these needs, and how will they react to our efforts?

3. *Conduct research to better understand the needs.* "Research" means probing to gather whatever information necessary to better understand needs, define problems, and propose solutions. Information sources include interviews, reports, memos, observation, and models, and analysis of technical data and empirical test results.
4. *Based on information from Steps 2 and 3, restate and document the needs.*
5. *Give the restated needs to the user.* The previous steps are repeated as often as necessary, concluding with a statement of needs that the user accepts and that best represents the user's interests (rather than the interests of the contractor or other parties).

Since every project is an effort to fulfill needs, a clear, well-stated, and correct needs statement is necessary to avoid a project that is meandering or irrelevant. But attaining such a needs statement is not easy. Frame describes the following troublesome aspects.[8]

- *Some needs are ever-changing.* They represent a moving target. Thus, for each need the question must be asked: "Is this likely to change?" If the answer is yes, the solutions and project plans that address the need should be flexible and easy to change.

- *Solutions are confused with needs.* Rather than stating a need, the user or contractor states a *solution*. For example, the statement "We need a new building" gives a solution, not the need. True, maybe a new building will be required, but a building is only one of perhaps many ways of satisfying the need to, for example, overcome a space shortage. By confusing solutions with needs, a solution is selected prematurely and potentially better solutions are precluded from consideration.

- *The needs identified are for the wrong user.* Who is the user? Is it the party that actually *feels* the need and is most affected by it, or is it the party who *pays* to resolve it? These are usually different. The needs statement should reflect the opinion of the party to which the solution will be directed—the user. Do not be content with what one party tells you is the need of another; talk to the other party, too.

- *There is more than one user, and their needs differ.* The user embodies several parties, all with valid needs. The question is: "Can *all* of their needs be addressed?" When multiple users exist, an attempt must be made to organize and classify all their needs into a needs hierarchy, as suggested by Frame.[9] For example, suppose the need for "more space" stems from the needs of three departments: one department needs "more space for employees," another needs "more space for technology," and the third needs "more space for inventory." These needs might all be handled by constructing a new building, but an alternative approach is to restate and prioritize the needs, and look at other solutions. For example, "more space for inventory" can be restated as "reduce inventory." Fulfilling that need would free up space to contribute toward "more space for employees." Restating the need "more space for technology" to "eliminate obsolete equipment" changes the context of the problem and potentially removes space as an issue.

- *User's needs are distorted by the "experts."* Inadvertently or intentionally, the contractor leads the user to define a distorted statement of needs. For example:
  The contractor suggests that the list of needs is much broader than the user thought. This increases the size of both the problem, and, no surprise, the contractor's billable work.
  The contractor reframes the needs in terms of what he, the contractor, is best suited to do. The contractor readily fulfills the stated needs, but the user's needs remain unaddressed.

The contractor doesn't ask but rather *states* what the user needs (because, after all, the contractor *is* the expert).

Sometimes users are resistant to clarifying needs, and expect the contractor to do it for them. The contractor should ensure that the user is involved, and the two of them work together until an agreed-upon statement of user needs is reached. The process helps both parties to better understand the needs and problems, and to ensure that the adopted solution is the right one.

User Requirements Definition

Conversation between a user and contractor:

> USER: "You installed my computer. Why didn't you install the network router, too?"
>
> CONTRACTOR: "You said you wanted the computer installed."
>
> USER: "But the computer won't be of much use around here without a router. Aren't they usually installed together?"
>
> CONTRACTOR: "You said you wanted the *computer* installed. I did just what you requested."

Another exchange:

> CONTRACTOR: "The lighting for the office addition is finished. As we agreed, I wired 20 ceiling lights."
>
> USER: "But the room seems kind of dark."
>
> CONTRACTOR: "You said you wanted 20 lights."
>
> USER: "Yes, but you said the room would be bright. It isn't."

Both cases illustrate user–contractor disagreements about the end-results. Misunderstandings like these delay project completion, drive up costs, and sometimes become legal disputes that put the outcome in the hands of the courts. The problem is lack of clear *user requirements*. User requirements describe in clear, unambiguous terms what the user wants in the finished solution. Derived from user needs, the requirements are the measure by which the user will determine whether or not the end-result or solution is acceptable. Formally documented, they are the quality measures for the project. In the above examples, they would include the *functions* that the installed computer system and overhead lighting must serve.

Ideally, user requirements address the needs not only of users but also of builders, suppliers, and other stakeholders that will benefit from, manage, maintain, or otherwise be impacted by the system. Perhaps obviously, user requirements are stated in the *language* of the users and other stakeholders. The project should not begin until the requirements have been combined into a *user's requirements* list (portion of the stakeholder's requirements document) and the customer and contractor agree that the list is complete.

Despite the necessity for good requirements, users often do not understand their importance; thus, one responsibility of the project manager is to make sure the requirements are complete, clear, and accurate. When the project is completed and the contractor says "Here's the system you ordered," the user should be able to say "Yes, it satisfies all my requirements."

There are many kinds of user requirements. Some account for the system's objectives, life cycle, and operational modes; others for constraints and interfaces with other systems.

Requirements for Objectives and Life Cycle

Every project and the end-item system to which it is directed starts with a statement of objectives that elaborate on the needs and provide the basis for defining requirements. Returning to the spaceship example from previous chapters, the need for "a reusable three-person vehicle that can be launched into space twice within a 2-week period" can be defined by the following set of objectives:

> Develop a spaceship that:
> 1. can minimally attain 100km altitude (space)
> 2. can be reused (turned around) in 2 weeks
> 3. carries three people.

Each objective is then elaborated in terms of a set of requirements. The requirements must account for whatever the users and other stakeholders think will be significant throughout the expected life cycle of the system, cradle to grave, which means they should incorporate issues regarding the system's design, development, building, testing, distribution, marketing, financing, support, upkeep, environmental impacts, and disposal.

Requirements for Operational Modes

Included in this life-cycle thinking are the different ways and kinds of environments in which the system will be used or operated; these are referred to as *operational modes*. For example, the modes for a reusable spacecraft include:

- Flight mode

    Launch and boost into space
    In-space
    Return from space
    Landing
- Turn-around between flights mode
- Crew training mode
- Ground transport mode
- Maintenance and testing mode.

The system will be expected to perform different functions and satisfy different conditions in each of the modes, and these functions and conditions must be specified in the requirements.

Requirements for Constraints and Interfaces

Every system is subject to limitations imposed by the environment and other systems it must interface with. These include mandated policies, procedures, and standards, and limits on resources, time, funding, technology, and knowledge. In addition it faces environmental constraints, including technological requirements, laws, and even social norms and customs. For instance, among the numerous constraints and interfacing systems to which the spaceship must conform are FAA regulations, technical standards of the aerospace industry, and local noise and pollution laws. The spaceship must be able to interface with existing systems for air traffic control and radio communication.

The Current System

Conceptually, a need arises because of inadequacies within the *current system*; a gap exists between the capability of the current system and a desired capability. A

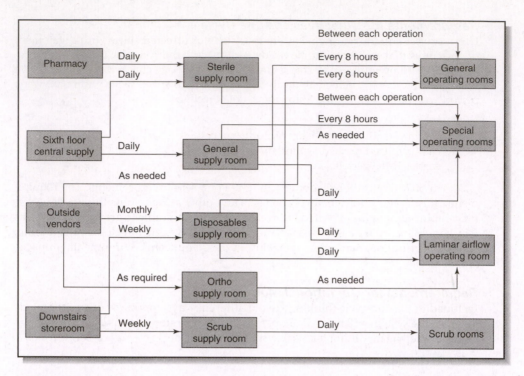

Figure 3.5
System schematic: flow of supplies to the operating room.

purpose of the feasibility study is to *fully understand* and *document* the current system, including its inputs, outputs, functions, flows, subsystems, components, relationships, attributes, resources, and constraints. The system schematic in Figure 3.5, for example, shows the elements and flows of a hospital system; it was developed in a project to reduce the cost of supplies in the operating room.

Alternative Solutions

Through the process of defining and documenting needs, requirements, and the current system, the contractor develops a good understanding of the problem, and is able to delimit the scope of alternative ways to solve it.

The contractor begins to develop alternative high-level (system-level) solutions to the problem from studies and models that take into account what the system must do (user requirements), how it can be done (technical considerations), and what it will cost (economic considerations). The solutions may include *new* systems developed from scratch, or modifications of *off-the-shelf systems* and existing technology. A good project manager encourages creativity and free flow of ideas in the search for solutions.

Analysis

Alternative solutions are analyzed for the ability to satisfy objectives and user requirements within the available resources and other constraints. The best solution is chosen and proposed to the customer. The following example provides an illustration.

Example 3.2: User Requirements and Feasible Solution for the X-Prize Project

The X-Prize competition described in Chapter 1 required developing a complete system that would meet numerous requirements relating to everything necessary to design, build, and operate a spaceship, including hardware, software, and people. To keep it simple, we will focus only on the spaceship; among its numerous user requirements are:

- Climb to an altitude of at least 100 km
- Carry three people
- Provide safe and comfortable flight
- Be relatively inexpensive to design, build, and launch
- Have a maximum "turn-around" time for reuse of at most 2 weeks.

Associated with these requirements are many issues and problems, and alternative solutions for each. One fundamental issue that impacts all of the requirements is the basic question of how, exactly, do you get people into space and then back home safely? The basic alternatives are:

1. Getting into space
   a. Launch spaceship from atop a booster rocket
   b. Launch spaceship from a high-flying airplane
2. Being in space
   a. Enter Earth's orbit
   b. Do not enter Earth's orbit
3. Getting back to Earth
   a. Follow a wide parabolic arc
   b. Follow a narrow arc almost straight up; float almost straight down
4. Landing
   a. Land in a "zone" using a parachute
   b. Land at an airport like an airplane.

After considering the requirements and constraints, designer Burt Rutan chose the combination of alternatives 1b, 2b, 3b, 4b: launch the spaceship from a high-flying airplane, do not enter orbit, follow a narrow parabolic trajectory up and down, and land airplane-like. Choosing these alternatives involved analysis of cost, risk, technology, time, and ability to meet the requirements.

The result of the feasibility study is a statement of the problem, a list of needs and user requirements, a description of the current situation, and a preferred solution and reasons for its selection. The feasibility study, when combined with the project plan, bid price, and contractor qualifications, forms the project proposal.

Environmental Impact

Part of project feasibility is determining the project's or end-item system's impact on the natural environment. In 1969, the US enacted legislation mandating that all projects receiving federal funding or licensing must assess and report on the project's environmental impacts in an Environmental Impact Statement (EIS). Since then, Canada, Australia, New Zealand, Japan, countries of the European Union, and others have ratified laws requiring environmental impact assessments (EIAs).

The contents of the EIS vary by state, country, and region, but typically include:

1. A summary of proposed development and/or management plans
2. Alternative sites and technologies for the proposed project
3. A description of the project's existing site and surrounding area

4. Potential project impacts, such as on

- Quality of air, soil, watersheds, wetlands, flood plains
- Fisheries; sensitive plants; sensitive, endangered, or threatened species
- Scenic resources; societal and aesthetic experiences
- Heritage resources (sites, structures, buildings, districts, objects)
- Historical resources (logging, ranching, grazing, mining, recreation).

5. Adverse impacts that cannot be avoided
6. Long-term impacts on resources
7. Ways to prevent, minimize or offset impacts; ways to monitor actual impacts.

The EIS is followed by a series of public reviews and hearings to discuss the findings and determine follow-up actions, especially concerning the last point above. Since the results of the EIS often affect the project plan and the system's design, the project's managers and supporters should try to develop a positive working relationship with the environmental assessment team.

3.5 THE PROJECT PROPOSAL

Proposal Preparation[10]

The proposal tells the customer what a contractor intends to do; it is the basis for selecting the project contractor. The effort to prepare the proposal is itself a project, and thus it should be managed like one. Since preparing a proposal sometimes involves significant time and money, it usually requires top management authorization. Upon authorization, management identifies a technically competent person to oversee preparation of the proposal; often, this person becomes the project manager if the contract is won. She might be entirely responsible for managing the proposal preparation effort, or, alternatively, work with another manager who is very experienced in conducting proposal-related activities. The project manager selects the project team, or part of it, to help prepare the proposal; usually the bulk of the project team is not specified until after the contract is won.

The project manager reviews the requirements of the RFP and prepares a detailed summary of the to-be proposed project. This summary guides the effort and prevents the focus from shifting to irrelevant technical or managerial considerations.

The project team outlines the work to be done for the solution identified in the feasibility study, and prepares a *statement of work* (SOW). The SOW will include the system and project objectives, technical solution, high-level requirements, and major areas of work required to deliver the solution. If a SOW appeared in the RFP (e.g., Figure 3.4), then the SOW in the proposal might repeat it but should also include new information culled during the feasibility study, and particulars about the chosen solution. In cases where the contractor believes the SOW in the RFP is inaccurate or incorrect, the contractor should state that in the proposal.

During proposal preparation, the project team must think through the entire project and prepare a rudimentary project plan that will address project time, cost, and performance issues. It uses a *work breakdown structure* (WBS) to determine the tasks necessary to achieve the requirements, and to prepare a schedule and cost estimate (topics discussed in later chapters). The proposal sometimes includes the WBS, schedule, and a cost breakdown showing how the project price was derived. When multiple solutions are proposed, a rough plan for each one is included.

The proposal is both a sales device and, if accepted, a form of contract. A good proposal not only gives the price, schedule, and other details, but also convinces the customer that the contractor is competent and capable of doing the work.

All functional departments in the contractor organization able to provide relevant information are called upon to assist with the proposal. This increases the accuracy of proposal estimates, and builds commitment from groups that will later work on the project.

As the proposal is being prepared, the contractor should establish a dialogue with the customer to determine which solutions the customer prefers, and which requirements are dominant among time, cost, and performance. Even when the RFP is clear, this will help ensure that the proposal will conform to the RFP specifications and satisfy the user's requirements. Proposal preparation can be iterative: acceptance of one proposal leads to preparation of another, more detailed proposal, as illustrated next.

Example 3.3: Writing Proposals for Real Estate Projects at Wutzrite Company

Customers come to the real estate department at Wutzrite Company for help in choosing among real-estate investment alternatives. A meeting is set up with the client to define the client's investment "problem" and goals; the client and several Wutzrite employees brainstorm to get the clearest, most accurate definition of the problem. Afterward, a project director prepares a proposal for the client that includes the problem statement, a proposed solution, and the price. Proposals that involve site development or the design and constructing of a building include a feasibility study. In proposals that only address evaluating, improving, or determining the value of a site, no feasibility study is needed. If the client likes the proposal, the director prepares a second, more detailed proposal that includes a WBS and updated schedule. If the client approves it, the second proposal becomes the high-level project plan. It specifies tasks to be done and target dates, and is the basis for assigning personnel to the project.

Approval of the second proposal usually calls for a feasibility study, demographic study, and analysis of financing, tax, accounting, or other ramifications of the recommended solution; the results of these are combined and submitted to the client in a third proposal that suggests particular courses of action regarding the solution.

The feasibility study and proposal preparation may take weeks or months to complete. Although enough time must be spent to produce a good proposal, not so much time should be spent that it becomes time-consuming or overly expensive. A good rule of thumb is: Do not try to do the entire project while preparing the proposal! In some technical projects this may be unavoidable, since the proposal includes a full-scale demonstration of the proposed solution. Developing the system to demonstrate to the customer may itself be tantamount to a good-sized project.

To assure nothing is overlooked in the proposal preparation, project managers typically employ checklists that, over the years, grow to accumulate all the important items on a proposal, including, for example, key considerations for design, assembly, test, shipment, documentation, facilities, subcontractors, supplies, travel, labor rates, training, and payment. Before the proposal can be submitted to the customer, contractor top management must be briefed about the project's scope, resources needed, price, etc., and approve it.

Proposals range in length from a few pages to many hundreds. The content varies depending on, for example, the format favored by the customer, the relationship between the customer and contractor, the technical complexity of the work, and whether it was solicited or unsolicited. Figure 3.6 shows the main ingredients of a typical proposal.[11] If the proposal is prepared in response to an RFP, the content and

Executive summary

Perhaps the most important part of the proposal, this section must convince the customer that the remainder of the proposal is worth reading. It should be more personal than the proposal, briefly state the qualifications, experience, and interests of the contractor and draw attention to the unique or outstanding features of the proposal, the price and the contractor's ability to do the project. In case the customer has questions, the contractor "contact" person is identified here. From reading this section the customer decides whether or not to examine the rest of the proposal.

Technical section (SOW)

(a) Indicates the scope of the work—the planned approach. It must be specific enough to avoid misunderstandings and demonstrate the method and appropriateness of the approach, yet not so specific as to "give away" the solution. It should also discuss any problems or limitations inherent to the approach.

(b) Describes realistic benefits in sufficient detail to demonstrate that user needs will be fulfilled, but not so specific or enthusiastic as to promise benefits that might be difficult to deliver.

(c) Contains a schedule of when end-items will be delivered. It should be based upon a work breakdown structure and include the major project phases and key tasks, milestones, and reviews. In developmental projects, portions of this section might have to be negotiated.

Cost and payment section

Breaks down projected hours for direct, indirect, and special activities and associated labor charges, materials expenses, and price of project. The preferred or required contractual arrangement and method of payment are also included.

Legal section

Contains anticipated, possible, or likely problems, and provisions for contingencies; e.g., appropriate procedures for handling changes to the scope of the project and for terminating the project.

Management/qualifications section

Describes the background of the contractor, related experience and achievements, and financial responsibility. Also includes organization of management, and resumes of project manager and key project personnel.

Figure 3.6
Contents of a proposal.

format of the proposal should conform *exactly* to the requirements or guidelines stated in the RFP. Appendix B at the end of the book is the proposal for the LOGON project prepared by the Iron Butterfly Company.

The amount a contractor spends on preparing proposals and the proportion of contracts it wins significantly affect its company overhead, since expenses for proposal preparation must be charged to overhead. Only in rare cases such as major defense contracts are the winning contractors reimbursed for proposal expenses.

Selecting the Winning Proposal[12]

Upon receiving proposals from multiple contractors, the customer evaluates and compares them. Selecting the best proposal, reaching an agreement with the contractor, and committing funds are all part of the "project selection" process. Most companies follow a prescribed procedure for evaluating and comparing proposals. When the selection involves assessing each proposed project for its contribution to a *portfolio* of projects the procedure is more involved, and includes appraising the project's contribution to company strategic goals, the resources it will entail, and its comparative benefits (expected financial return or cost–benefit ratio). These topics are covered in depth in Chapter 17. Here, we give a brief overview of proposal evaluation and project selection.

In general, selection of projects is based upon consideration of the following factors:

- Project price
- Solution's ability to satisfy stated needs (solution or technical approach)
- Return on investment
- Project plan and management
- Qualifications and reputation of contractor
- Likelihood of success or failure (risks)
- Fit to contractor resources and technological capability.

The customer may assume that a competent contractor with a good plan will do a good job, and thus select the contractor with the best project plan rather than the proposed solution or technical approach. Thus, each proposal should include a rudimentary project plan showing key activities, and start and end dates and deliverables for each. Contents of the plan and methods for preparing it are discussed in Chapters 5 through 10.

Selecting the best proposal often begins with prescreening the proposals and rejecting the ones that fail to meet certain cut-off requirements, such as too high a price tag, too low a rate of return, or insufficient experience of the contractor.

Proposals that survive prescreening are subjected to closer scrutiny. A common evaluation method, called *simple rating*, employs rating proposals according to several evaluation criteria on a checklist. Each proposal is given a score s_j for each criterion j. The overall score for the proposal is the sum of the scores for all criteria,

$$S = \Sigma s_{j'}, \text{ where } j = 1, 2, \ldots, n$$

The proposal receiving the highest overall score wins.

One limitation of the method is that all evaluation criteria are treated as being equally important. When some criteria are clearly more important than others, a method called *weighted rating* is used instead, wherein the relative importance of each criterion j is indicated with an assigned weight w_j. After a given criterion has been scored, the score is multiplied by the weight of the criterion, $s_j \cdot w_j$. The overall score for the proposal is the sum of the $s_j \cdot w_j$ for all criteria,

$$S = \Sigma s_j w_j, \text{ where } j = 1, 2, \ldots, n$$

$$\Sigma w_j = 1, \text{ and } 0 \leq w_j \leq 1.0$$

The procedures for the two methods are illustrated in Example 3.4.

Example 3.4: Evaluating the Proposals at MPD Company

In response to its RFP for the LOGON project (Appendix A, end of book), MPD Company received proposals from three contractors: Iron Butterfly Contractors, Inc.; Lowball Company; and Modicum Associates. Each proposal was reviewed and rated by a group of operations managers at MPD on five criteria using the following four-point scale:

Criteria	1	2	3	4
Technical solution approach	Poor	Adequate	Good	Excellent
Price of contract	>1.8	1.6–1.8	1.4–1.6	<1.4
Project organization and management	Poor	Adequate	Good	Excellent
Likelihood of meeting cost/schedule targets	Poor	Adequate	Good	Excellent
Reputation of contractor	Poor	Adequate	Good	Excellent

Simple Rating

The results of the assessments for the three proposals were as follows:

Criteria	Scores		
	Iron Butterfly	Lowball	Modicum
Technical solution approach	3	1	4
Price of contract	4	4	1
Project organization/management	4	2	3
Likelihood of meeting cost/schedule targets	3	2	4
Reputation of contractor	3	3	4
Sum	17	12	16

Based on the sum of simple ratings, Iron Butterfly was rated the best.

Weighted Rating

Using the simple rating, Lowball was clearly the worst, but Iron Butterfly and Modicum were considered too close to differentiate. The rating group then decided to look at the criteria more closely and to assign weights to the criteria based on their relative importance:

Criteria	Weight
Technical solution approach	0.25
Price of contract	0.25
Project organization and management	0.20
Likelihood of meeting cost/schedule targets	0.15
Reputation of contractor	0.15
	1.00

Taking the weights into account, the proposals scored as follows:

Criterion	Weight (w)	Iron Butterfly		Modicum	
		S	$(s)(w)$	s	$(s)(w)$
Technical solution approach	0.25	3	0.75	4	1.0
Price of contract	0.25	4	1.0	1	0.25
Project organization/management	0.20	4	0.8	3	0.6
Risks of solution	0.15	3	0.45	4	0.6
Reputation of contractor	0.15	3	0.45	4	0.6
	Sum		3.45		3.05

Using the sum of the weighted ratings, Iron Butterfly is clearly the superior proposal.

Assessment of proposals might also include evaluation of project risk, especially when the proposed solutions and associated levels of risk differ significantly between proposals. Methods for identifying and assessing risks are discussed in Chapter 10.

Sometimes the contract award depends more on the contractor's qualifications than on the proposed solution. Among factors the customer might consider are the following:[13]

Is the contractor big enough to do the project?
Is it adequately financed to do the project?
Does it have a good track record with this kind of project?
Does it have a good reputation in the industry?
Has it been involved in litigations and arbitrations?
Will its management be accessible?
Does it have ISO 9000, ISO 14000, or other certification?
Will the relationship with the contractor likely be amicable or touchy?

Proposal finalists are notified, and might be requested to provide more data or give presentations or live demonstrations of their proposed solution or system. The preferred contractor is recommended to top management and, if approved, awarded the contract. If several contractors receive close marks or some aspects of their proposals are unspecified or questionable, then the parties must negotiate to settle upon the final terms. If none of the proposals are acceptable or the feasibility studies show the project would be too costly, risky, or time-consuming, or not provide adequate benefits, the process ends and nobody gets a contract.

Project Initiation: Variations on a Theme

Projects are always initiated in response to a need, but they do not always involve an RFP or even a proposal. The RFP/proposal process as described largely applies to projects where the work is *contracted out*; i.e., where the customer and the contractor are not in the same organization. For internal projects—projects where the organization has the capability to perform the work on its own—initiation is with a *business case study*. Common examples of this are projects in product development (PD) and IT—two areas where companies often exhibit significant internal prowess. In PD, the "need" is manifest as the desire or mandate to fill a perceived market niche or respond to a competitive threat. The business case study, similar to a feasibility study, analyzes the market, competition, product alternatives, risk, cost, and returns, and argues in favor of launching a new PD effort. If the business case is approved and funded, the project is turned over to the PD department to begin work. The business case study serves as feasibility study and project proposal combined. Business case studies are similarly used to initiate IT projects.

The department that would do the project if it were approved (PD or IT) oversees preparation of the case study and argues for the proffered end-item or solution. Approval or denial of the project involves rating the case against other competing cases in terms of the resources required, benefits compared to goals, and priority of needs—the process described in Chapter 17. If the project is approved a project charter is created, as described in Chapter 4.

The RFP/proposal process as described represents projects with relatively few stakeholders or a single, clearly identified customer and its potential contractors. In large technical projects that touch many stakeholders, the process is more complex and protracted. Examples include projects for infrastructure and transportation systems (Boston Big Dig, Delhi Metro, telecommunication systems, Chunnel), technical systems where the subsystems and even components must be developed from scratch (commercial aircraft, SpaceShipOne, and medical devices), and large-scale property developments (resorts and planned communities).

In such cases, where it is more difficult to define the stakeholders and meet their multiple and sometimes conflicting needs, the RFP/proposal process includes a "front-end" component to identify the important stakeholders and incorporate their needs into a list of stakeholder requirements. The organization gathering the stakeholder requirements might be another contractor hired solely for that purpose, and not the same contractor that would perform the project work. After the stakeholders and needs have been identified, other contractors will be asked to review the requirements and suggest solutions, possibly through the RFP/proposal process. The process of identifying stakeholders and their requirements is a systems engineering effort that takes into account the system's far-reaching effects and the many stakeholders that will touch (or be touched by) the resulting system throughout its life cycle.

3.6 PROJECT CONTRACTING

Contracting Environment and Process[14]

Contracting is ubiquitous in project management, since all work is done in accordance with formal or informal contracts. Even in internal projects where there is no contract, an agreement exists between user and developer groups about the work to be performed to meet prespecified objectives and requirements.

Most projects, even internal ones, involve some degree of external, legal contracting because the customer often must hire someone externally to perform at least some of the work. In many projects, *everything* in the project is done or provided by external organizations. As Figure 3.7 illustrates, these "external organizations" might be linked by numerous contractual agreements. The customer might contract with a principle party (prime contractor or SDO) to oversee the entire project; in turn, this party might contract with other parties—subcontractors, consultants, material suppliers, and contract labor (union trade professionals)—to be responsible for portions of the project; these parties might then contract with still others.

The *RFP/proposal* process addresses the question of *who will do the work*, not only for the customer but also for any party seeking to hire another to do work. Whether the customer, the prime contractor, or another company down the line, each follows a process identical or analogous to the RFP/proposal process to document its

Figure 3.7
Contracting parties in a project.

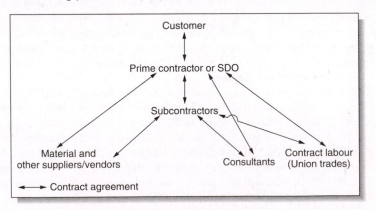

needs, solicit ideas, and choose between potential contractors. Thus, any contractor farming out portions of work to subcontractors or acquiring material or services from suppliers will follow the RFP/proposal process to identify and choose the most qualified subcontractors and suppliers. Just as the customer follows the process to hire a contractor, so the contractor follows it to hire subcontractors—and so on down the line.

The effort required to review and hire qualified subcontractors can be quite time-consuming, especially in international projects, so extra time should be allotted for it in the project schedule. If not, the process to select subcontractors can delay the start of portions of the project and cause the entire project to slip behind schedule.

The customer should seek to retain some measure of control over any contracted work. To that end, the contract should clearly specify the areas of the project over which the customer has ultimate authority for supervision and decisions, and the customer's role in tracking project progress. From the time when the contract is signed until when the project is closed out or terminated, the contractual agreement must be *managed*, which means keeping the agreement up-to-date with respect to ongoing changes in the project, the customer's needs, and the contractor's capability, and checking that all work conforms with the agreement. This process, called *contract administration*, is discussed in Chapter 11.[15]

Subcontracting[16]

Each party in Figure 3.7 must decide what portions of the project it will do itself and what portions it will contract to others. Some contractors do all the work, while some hire others to do it—i.e., they subcontract. For example, a customer hires a general or prime contractor to manage a construction project and, perhaps, to fabricate and assemble the building structure, but then the contractor hires other companies for specialized work such as wiring, plumbing, ventilation, and interior details.

Even a contractor that is capable of doing all the work itself may choose to subcontract because it has limited capacity or facilities, or believes a subcontractor could do the work for lower cost. For development projects of large-scale systems, the prime contractor will usually design the overall system and major subsystems, and will produce some elements of the system itself but subcontract the production of all others. In projects where significant portions of project work are to be subcontracted, the customer will often mandate the scope of the subcontracted work and the criteria for selection of suitable contractors or suppliers.

Usually, obligations in subcontracts exist solely between a contractor and subcontractor. This means, for example, that the contractor (not the customer) is responsible for ensuring that a subcontractor performs work according to the requirements, and the contractor (not the customer) is obligated to pay for the subcontracted work. The contractor is also responsible for the quality of delivered materials, equipment, or components, and inspection of subcontractor offsite facilities. Similarly, any communication about customer changes to the requirements is channeled through the contractor to the subcontractor. (If, however, you are a subcontractor and are having trouble getting paid, you might appeal directly to the customer to pressure the contractor into paying you.)

Like everything else in projects, work that is contracted, subcontracted, or procured from suppliers must be planned, scheduled, budgeted, and controlled. All of this is referred to as "procured" goods, work, and services, and managing it falls under the umbrella topic of *procurement management*, described in Chapter 5.

Contract Negotiation[17]

The purpose of contract negotiation is to clarify technical or other terms in the contract and to reach agreement on time, schedule, and performance obligations. Negotiation is not necessary for standardized projects for which the terms are simple and costs are fairly well known, but for complex systems that require development work or are somewhat risky it is. In fact, where an IFB (invitation for bid) for a standard or well-defined item is sent out and price is the only criterion, negotiation would be unethical and is not allowed. Different contractual agreements offer advantages to the customer and contractor, depending on the nature of the project. These agreements are discussed in the Appendix to this chapter; they are, briefly:

- *Fixed Price Contract:* The price paid by the customer for the project is fixed, regardless of the costs incurred by the contractor. The customer knows what the project will cost.

- *Cost-Plus Contract:* The price paid is based on the costs incurred in the project plus the contractor's fee. The contractor is assured that its costs will be covered.

- *Incentive Contract:* The amount paid depends on the contractor's performance in comparison to the target price, schedule, or technical specification: the contractor either receives a *bonus* for exceeding the target or must pay a *penalty* for not meeting it.

The specific type of contract agreement between the customer and the prime contractor determines the type of agreement negotiated with subcontractors. If the prime contract agreement is fixed price (FP), then subcontract agreements should also be FP otherwise the prime contractor risks being charged more by subcontractors than it will receive from the customer. If the prime contract is cost-plus or incentive, there is latitude to use any type of agreement for subcontracts.

Although negotiation is the last activity before a contract agreement is reached, the negotiation *process* often begins early during proposal preparation because the terms in the proposal must be consistent with terms in the contract and acceptable to both customer and contractor. During negotiation, terms in the proposal related to specifications, schedules, and price are converted into a legal, contractual agreement. Performance, schedule, and cost are interrelated, and a "package" agreement must be reached wherein all three parameters are acceptable to both parties. Final negotiation is the last formal opportunity to correct misperceptions that might have slipped through the RFP/proposal process. (Customers are *always* negotiating—informally—to get a better deal, even after the project is underway. The contractor must be wary of saying and writing anything that might be construed as a promise to deliver more than is specified in the contract.) In highly competitive situations, the customer will try to play one contractor against the other, seeking to raise performance specifications while shortening the schedule and decreasing the price.

Throughout negotiation, the project manager takes on the role of salesperson and pushes the merits of his proposal. His goal is to obtain the best possible agreement for his company. In countering customer objections to the proposal, the project manager's best defense is a well thought-out project plan that shows what can or must be done to achieve the desired end-results. Details of the project plan are used to define which parts of the schedule, work, or price are relatively "fixed," and which are somewhat flexible and can be negotiated.

To be able to negotiate from a knowledgeable and competitive position, the project manager must learn as much as possible about the customer and the competition. She should determine if the customer is under pressure to make a particular decision, faces an impending fiscal deadline, or historically has shown preference for one particular approach or contractor over others. The project manager should also learn about the competition—their likely approach to the problem, costs, and competitive advantages and disadvantages. She learns this from historical information, published material, or employees who once worked for competitors. (Relying on the last source is ethically questionable and, of course, works against the contractor whenever competitors hire its employees.)

To be able to negotiate trade-offs, the project manager must be intimately familiar with the technical details of system design and related costs. Sometimes the contract will include incentive or penalty clauses as inducements to complete the project before a certain date or below a certain cost. To competently negotiate such clauses the project manager must be familiar with the project schedule and time–cost trade-offs.

The signed contract becomes the binding agreement for the project. Any changes thereafter should follow formal change mechanisms, including change notices, reviews, customer approvals, and, sometimes, contract renegotiation—topics discussed in Chapter 11.

Contract Statement of Work and Work Requisitions

The contract contains a SOW that is similar to the SOW in the original RFP or the winning proposal, or is a restatement of either to reflect the negotiated agreement. This so-called *contract statement of work* (CSOW) defines the expected performance of the project in terms of scope of work, requirements, end-results, schedules, costs, and so on. The CSOW clearly specifies the conditions under which the deliverables or end-results will be accepted by the customer. Failure to clearly state these conditions can lead to later disputes and delays in completing the project.

Contracts with suppliers and subcontractors also include a CSOW, plus for each party the responsibilities and liabilities, and for each procured item specifications, quantities, delivery schedules, costs, payment schedules, indemnities, and method for handling changes or variations.

When the customer and the contractor both agree on the CSOW, the project is considered "approved" and ready to go. Before work can actually begin, however, it must be divided among the involved departments and subcontractors of the SDO, and the requirements specified in the CSOW must be translated into terminology that is understandable to personnel in these groups. The translations, aimed at the groups that will perform the work, must be identical interpretations of the requirements and scope of work specified in the CSOW. The document containing the SOW for each work group is called a *work requisition* or *work order*. Its purpose is to describe to each party the work expected of it and to authorize the work to begin. This topic is discussed further in Chapter 11.

Signing of the contract marks completion of Phase A and approval to proceed to Phase B. The steps in Phase A are summarized in Figure 3.8.

The process of initiating projects, preparing proposals, and negotiating and finalizing contracts often involves convolutions and exceptions that cannot possibly be covered in a chapter. Example 3.5 illustrates this.

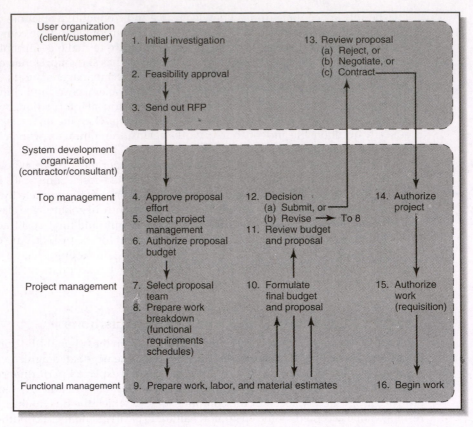

Figure 3.8
Project initiation, proposal preparation, and project authorization process.

Example 3.5: Proposal for the Apollo Spacecraft[18]

The US space program to land human beings on the moon involved thousands of contracts, all awarded by NASA in separate competitions. The biggest contracts were for the biggest components; namely, the Apollo spacecraft, the lunar lander, and the first, second, and third stages of the rocket that would propel the spacecraft and lander to the moon. Harrison Storms was vice president of North American Aviation's Space Division (NA) in Los Angeles when NASA opened bidding for the Apollo spacecraft. His division had already been working feverishly to solve difficult technical problems for a proposal to build the second stage. The technical requirements were so demanding that only a handful of contractors had stayed in the competition. Most managers in the middle of such a big effort would have considered themselves already overextended, but not Storms: he wanted to go after the *big prize* too—the Apollo contract. The Apollo spacecraft would contain systems for life-support, guidance, and navigation (ultimately comprising over 2 million parts), and would take three men to the moon and back. Problem was, NA had never built a spacecraft before, and it would be expensive to learn how. Storms gathered up his best people and put together a presentation for the company chairman and founder, old "Dutch" Kindleburger, arguing that NA should prepare a proposal for Apollo. Dutch was skeptical, but he pledged $1 million support. Storms knew that wouldn't be nearly enough, but took it anyhow. Now NA would bid on *both* the second stage *and* Apollo (Figure 3.9).

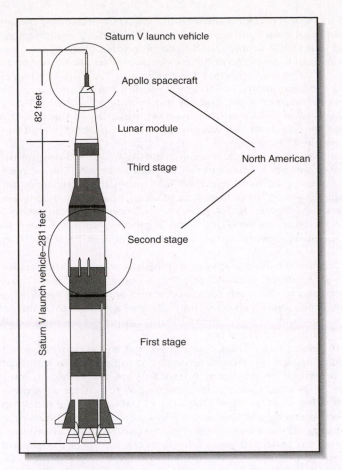

Figure 3.9
Apollo/Saturn moon rocket and North American components.
Picture courtesy NASA.

The RFP for Apollo allowed competing contractors 10 weeks to submit their proposals. Three competitors had already done Apollo studies and had a 12-month head start; one had already assigned 300 people to work on the concept, spent $3 million, and prepared a 900-page report. In large bids like this companies partner up to add muscle to the proposal, but all of the big aerospace contractors had already teamed up and NA was left to go it alone. Nobody believed Storms' proposal team had a chance, including the company president.

Storm's team labored feverishly, 7am to 11pm. Feeding them information were scores of engineers in shops, offices, laboratories, and wind tunnels throughout the company; to oversee them Storms picked the best leaders at NA he could find—smart, practical people, with solid experience, that others looked up to.

Good news arrived: NASA announced that NA had been chosen prime contractor for the second stage. But jubilation settled into gloom over prospects of also winning Apollo; nobody felt that NASA would award two major contracts for the lunar program to the same company—nobody except for Storms.

The allotted $1 million had long since been exceeded—maybe by three times—but no one knew. Back then cost statements ran 30–60 days behind billings, and Storms gambled that NASA would receive the proposal before his boss saw the final bill. With less than 6 weeks to go he picked John Paup to be Apollo program manager, someone he thought perfect for the role, a "witty, engaging person" who understood the technology. For the next month, Paup listened to presentations 18 hours a day, slept on a cot, and ate from vending machines. Every morning he gathered his team for a stand-up meeting; anyone not there by 7:45 was locked out. No coffee, no seats; he wanted to hear the problems, and how each would be fixed within 24 hours.

The proposal was encyclopedic in size, and NASA wanted dozens of copies submitted no later than 5pm 2 days before the presentation. The whole bundle, weighing 100 pounds, was hand-delivered just under the wire. Next day, Paup and his team, looking like zombies from lack of sleep, boarded the company plane for the presentation in Virginia. NASA gave each company 60 minutes to present its proposal to an evaluation team of 75 top engineers, some of them legends. Undaunted, Paup hit all the presentation high points and finished 10 minutes early.

Days later, Storms received a telegram: NASA wanted to know how, given NA's second-stage contract, it could possibly handle Apollo too. The written response was too long to telegraph back, so Storms and Paup jumped on a plane to hand-deliver it. This violated an unwritten rule that a contractor does not meet with the customer evaluating the proposal. But Storms had little regard for such rules, especially with so much at stake.

Meantime NA headquarters had determined that the proposal had cost five times the allotted $1 million, and it was fuming. But to say the overrun was worth it would be an understatement. North American won the contract, although it would take another year to formalize the details: in return for a target cost of $884 million and a fee of $50 million, NA was to deliver several mock-ups, test versions, and flight-ready Apollo spacecraft (Figure 3.10). Since the risks of sending humans to the moon were overwhelming, the contract was cost-plus. By the time the lunar program ended 10 years later with the return of the seventh crew from the moon, NA as prime contractor had earned $4.4 billion—about $23 billion in 2010 dollars.

Figure 3.10
Apollo spacecraft.
Photograph courtesy
John Nicholas.

3.7 SUMMARY

The systems development cycle can be divided into four phases: conception, definition, execution, and operation. The first three of these phases constitute the project life cycle.

The initial phase, conception, includes formulating the problem, defining needs and user requirements, evaluating alternative solutions, and preparing a proposal to conduct the project. At the start of this phase, most activities are in the hands of the customer; by the end of the phase, the activities have been taken over by the contractor or system developer. The relationship between the customer and the contractor is initiated and cemented through the RFP/proposal process and contract negotiation.

Phase A is the "foundation" part of the systems development cycle; it establishes the needs, objectives, requirements, constraints, agreements, and patterns of communication upon which the remaining phases are built. It is a crucial phase, and the place where, often, the seeds of project success or failure are planted.

APPENDIX: KINDS OF CONTRACTS

A contract is an agreement between two parties wherein one party (the seller—in a project the contractor) promises to perform a service for another (the buyer—the client or customer), typically in return for payment. Requirements about the service and the payment are clearly spelled out in the contract.

The typical contract includes the following:

- Scope of work to be done or items to be sold, including support and ancillary (side) items such as manuals, documentation, and training. Any specifications and standards referenced are considered as part of the contract.
- Duties of the contractor in providing the work or items.
- Time schedule allowed.
- Duties of the client regarding payments (including a schedule for milestones).
- How changes to the contract will be handled.
- How disputes will be handled.
- The way risks will be handled, including warranties, penalties, or bonuses/incentives.

Different kinds of contracts provide different advantages to the client and the contractor, depending on the risk of the project and the degree of difficulty in estimating costs. Each party tries to negotiate the kind of contract and the terms that best serve its own interests.

The two fundamental kinds of contacts are *fixed price* and *cost-plus* contracts. In the fixed price contract, the price is agreed upon and remains fixed as long as there are no changes to the project scope or provisions of the agreement. In the cost-plus contract, the contractor is reimbursed for all or some of the expenses incurred during the project, and, as a result, the final price is unknown until the project is completed. Within these two types are several variations, including some with incentives for the contractor to meet cost, time, or performance targets.[19]

Variables

The variables specified in a contract may include the following:

C_{ex} and C_{ac} Target (expected) cost and actual cost of the project under normal circumstances. "Cost" represents monies expended by the contractor in performing the work.

Fee   Amount paid to the contractor in addition to reimbursable costs.

Price   The price the client pays for the project. Price includes reimbursable costs (or a percentage thereof) incurred by the contractor, plus the contractor's fee.

CSR   The cost sharing ratio. When costs are to be shared by the client and the customer, this is the percentage of the cost that each agrees to share (the sum is 100%).

Fixed Price Contract

Fixed Price Contract

Under a fixed price (FP) or "lump sum" agreement, the contractor agrees to perform all work at a fixed price. The contractor must be very careful in estimating the target cost because, once agreed upon, the price will not be adjusted. If the contractor in the bidding stage estimates the target cost too low, he might win the job but make no profit; if he overestimates, he may lose the job to a lower priced bidder.

Example A3.1: Fixed Price Contract

Contract agreement:

$$\text{Cost estimate, } C_{ex} = \$100,000$$
$$\text{Fee} = \$10,000$$
$$\text{Price} = \$110,000.$$

No matter what the project actually ends up costing (C_{ac}), the price to the client remains $110,000.

    When project work is straightforward and can be specified in detail, both client and contractor prefer this kind of contract. Clients like it because they are less concerned about project costs. Contractors like it because clients tend to request fewer changes to the contract.

    The disadvantage of an FP contract is that it can be more difficult and costly to prepare. The contractor risks underestimating the cost and losing money on the project, which during the project might motivate the contractor to cut corners (use cheaper quality materials, perform marginal workmanship, or extend the completion date) to reduce costs. To counteract this, the client can set rigid end-item specifications and completion dates on the contract, and closely supervise the work. If, however, the project gets into serious trouble, bankrupts the contractor, and leaves the project incomplete, the client may be subject to litigation from other stakeholders.

Fixed Price with Redetermination[20]

Projects with long lead times, such as construction or production, have contract *escalation provisions* that protect the contractor against increases in materials, labor rates, or overhead costs. For example, the contract price may be tied to an inflation index and be adjusted in the advent of inflation, or it may be *redetermined* as actual costs become known. In the latter case, the initial price is negotiated with the stipulation that it will be redetermined later to accurately reflect actual cost data. There is a variety of redetermination contracts: some establish a ceiling price for the contract and permit only downward adjustments, others permit upward and downward adjustments; some establish one readjustment at the end of the project, others allow multiple, periodic readjustments. Redetermination contracts are appropriate where design efforts are difficult to specify or wherever the final price cannot be estimated for lack of accurate cost data. The redetermined price may apply to future items and to items already produced.

Because the only requirement to renegotiate the price is substantiating cost data, redetermined contracts tend to induce inefficiencies. After negotiating a low initial price, the contractor may produce a few items and then "discover" that the costs are much higher than expected. The contract can thus become a "cost-plus" kind of contract, and be subject to abuse.

Cost-Plus Contract

In complex, uncertain, or risky projects where it is difficult to accurately estimate all the project costs, a cost-plus contract allows work to begin before the costs are fully determined.

Cost Plus Fixed Fee (CPFF)

Under a CPFF contract, the contractor is reimbursed for all direct allowable costs plus an additional, fixed amount to cover overhead and profit. This contract is justified when costs cannot be accurately estimated or rise due to changes in the project scope or factors beyond anyone's control. Regardless of the actual cost the contractor's fee remains the same, usually computed as a percentage of the target or estimated cost, C_{ex}.

Example A3.2: Cost Plus Fixed Fee Contract

Contract agreement:

$$\text{Cost estimate, } C_{ex} = \$100{,}000$$
$$\text{Fee} = \$10{,}000$$
$$\text{Target Price} = \$110{,}000.$$

In addition to the fee, the client will pay for all allowable costs (perhaps "all" costs, C_{ac}). Thus, if the project ends up costing $C_{ac} = \$200{,}000$, the price to the client is $210,000.

In contrast to FP contracts, CPFF agreements put the burden of risk on the client. The client does not know the project price until the end of the project, and the contractor has little incentive to control costs, finish on time, or do anything beyond minimum requirements, since he gets paid the same fee regardless. A major factor motivating the contractor to control costs and schedules is the negative effect of overruns on his reputation. Another is that as long as the contractor's workforce and facilities are tied up, he cannot work on other projects.

Since a CPFF agreement can be risky in terms of price, the client must do whatever possible to ensure the contractor works efficiently and meets technical, time, and cost targets. She may specify who is to be the project manager, or have her own project manager on-site to work with the contractor's project manager.

Despite the risks, the client might have to resort to a CPFF contract just to attract contractors. CPFF is the contract of choice whenever the project involves much risk or the costs are difficult to estimate.

Time and Materials Contract (TM)

A TM contract is a simple agreement that reimburses the contractor for labor costs and materials incurred in the project. It provides for payment of direct labor hours at an hourly rate that includes direct labor costs, indirect costs, and profit. Sometimes a ceiling price is established that may be exceeded, depending on the agreement. Charges for private consultants and the services of electricians, carpenters, mechanics, etc., are usually based on TM.

Incentive Contract

When the contractor is unwilling to enter into an FP agreement and the client does not want a CPFF contract, an alternative is an incentive arrangement. This has features of both kinds of contracts: it is similar to CPFF in that costs are reimbursed, but the amount reimbursed is based on an incentive formula called a *cost sharing ratio* (CSR). A CSR of 80/20, for example, means that the client and the contractor split the costs 80/20. This encourages the contractor to keep costs low because he *pays* 20 cents on every dollar spent above C_{ex} but *earns* 20 cents more on every dollar saved below C_{ex}. As further incentive to reduce costs, the ratio might be changed for costs above C_{ex} such that the contractor must pay a higher percentage.

Cost Plus Incentive Fee Contract (CPIF)

The *project price* in a CPIF contract is based on a percentage of the actual cost, C_{ac}, using a CSR. The contract specifies the target cost, C_{ex}, and the CSR, which specifies how any cost savings or overruns will be proportionally shared between the client and the contractor.

Example A3.3: Cost Plus Incentive Fee Contract

Contract agreement:

$$
\begin{aligned}
\text{Cost estimate, } C_{ex} &= \$100{,}000 \\
\text{Fee} &= \$10{,}000 \\
\text{Target Price} &= \$110{,}000.
\end{aligned}
$$

Cost sharing: CSR=50/50, therefore

- if $C_{ac} < \$100{,}000$, client will reimburse C_{ac} plus 50 percent of amount below $100,000
- if $C_{ac} > \$100{,}000$, client will reimburse $100,000 plus 50 percent of amount above $100,000.

The incentive is for the contractor to keep costs low and to not exceed $100,000. Suppose C_{ac} is only $80,000 ($20,000 under C_{ex}). The contractor gets paid $80,000 plus $10,000 (50 percent of the savings) plus the $10,000 fee. Total price to client: $100,000. The client saves $10,000 on the price and the contractor earns a $10,000 bonus. The client must be vigilant to ensure that the incentive doesn't lead the contractor to "cut corners" on work and materials.

Now suppose C_{ac} is $200,000 ($100,000 over C_{ex}). The contractor gets paid $100,000 ($C_{ex}$) plus $50,000 (50 percent of the overrun) plus the $10,000 fee. Total price to client: $160,000. The contractor is $200,000 − $160,000=$40,000 in the red.

Fixed Price Incentive Fee Contract (FPIF)

An FPIF contract is similar to a CPIF contract but has a ceiling on both price and profit. The contractor negotiates to perform the work for a target price based upon a target cost (C_{ex}) plus a fee, and for a maximum price at a maximum profit. If the project cost ends up being less than the target cost, the contractor can earn a higher profit but only up to the maximum. If there is a cost overrun, the contractor will have to absorb some or much of it.

Example A3.4: Fixed Price Incentive Fee Contract

Contract agreement:

$$
\begin{aligned}
\text{Cost estimate, } C_{ex} &= \$100,000 \\
\text{Fee} &= \$10,000 \\
\text{Target Price} &= \$110,000 \\
\text{Maximum Price} &= \$125,000 \text{ (fee+reimbursement),} \\
&\quad \text{client will pay no more than this} \\
\text{Maximum Profit} &= \$15,000, \text{ contractor profit cannot exceed this.}
\end{aligned}
$$

Cost sharing: CSR=50/50, therefore

- if $C_{ac}<\$100,000$, client will reimburse C_{ac} plus an additional 50 percent of amount below $100,000, as long as the additional amount does not exceed $5,000

- If $C_{ac}>\$100,000$, client will reimburse $100,000 plus an additional 50 percent of amount above $100,000, but the total reimbursement cannot exceed $115,000.

Again, the incentive is for the contractor to keep costs low and not exceed $100,000. However, because the contractor cannot earn a profit of more than $15,000, there is little incentive for the contractor to cut corners to increase profit. Suppose C_{ac} is only $80,000 ($20,000 under C_{ex}). The contractor gets paid $80,000 plus the $10,000 fee, but only an additional $5,000 for the cost savings (50 percent of the $20,000 savings is $10,000, but only $5,000 is allowed because that amount plus the fee equals $15,000, the maximum allowable profit). Total price to client: $95,000, a $15,000 saving from the target price.

Suppose C_{ac} is $200,000 ($100,000 over C_{ex}): 50 percent of the overrun is $50,000, so that plus the fee plus $100,000 is $160,000. But the specified maximum price is $125,000, which is all the client pays. The contractor suffers a $200,000–$125,000 = $75,000 loss.

FPIF contracts are not true fixed price contracts. They invite contractors to negotiate unrealistically high C_{ex}s so that extra profits can be made through the incentive features. However, unlike cost-plus contracts, they provide some assurance about a maximum price and some protection against the contractor cutting corners to gain a hefty profit. FPIF contracts apply to long-duration or large-production projects. They do not apply to R&D or other projects where the target cost is difficult or impossible to estimate.

Multiple Incentives Contract[21]

Multiple incentives contracts attempt to reward contractors for meeting targets associated with achieving multiple criteria, such as time, cost, and performance. Fee weights assigned to the criteria are used to determine the amount of "fee swing" allocated to each criterion. Consider the example shown below, where the fee structure is similar to the previous CPIF example. Here the "fee swing" (F_{min} to F_{max}) is between 2 percent and 14 percent, or 12 percent.[22]

$$
\begin{aligned}
C_{ex} &= \$100,000 \\
F_{ex} &= \$8 \text{ (8\%)} \\
F_{max} &= \$14 \text{ (14\%)} \\
F_{min} &= \$2 \text{ (2\%).}
\end{aligned}
$$

The 12 percent fee swing is then divided among the criteria; for example:

CRITERION	WEIGHT	FEE SWING
Performance (x)	0.5	6%
Cost (y)	0.25	3%
Time (z)	0.25	3%
Total	1.00	12%

In engineering contracts, typically the largest weight is given to performance, followed by time and cost. To assess performance, several measures might be used at once, such as accuracy, range, reliability, and speed; an index is devised so all measures can be represented by a single performance factor.

In this example, the performance factor is given a weight of 0.5, which yields a profit swing of 6 percent; time and cost are given weights of 0.25, so each have a profit swing of 3 percent. The profit percentage is computed as a function of the three criteria according to the formula

$$P = (8 + x + y + z)\% \ (C_{ex}).$$

Values for x, y, and z, determined at the end of the project, would be based on the curves in Figure 3.11.

Since the multiple criteria in this kind of contract tend to be interrelated (e.g., performance targets can be met, but for greater time and cost), the terminology and computations involved in structuring the contract tend to be tricky; hence, this type of contract is rarely used.[23]

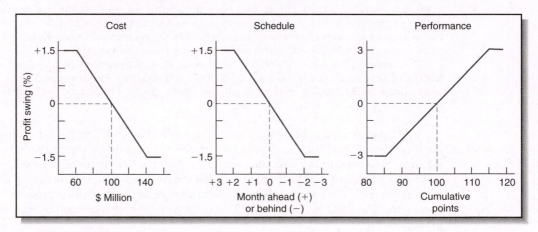

Figure 3.11
Multiple incentive contract.

REVIEW QUESTIONS AND PROBLEMS

1. How are projects initiated? Describe the process.
2. What factors determine whether or not an idea should be investigated?
3. Who is the user in the systems development process? Who is the contractor?
4. Besides the user and the contractor, what other parties are involved in the systems development cycle? Give examples for particular projects.

5. What does the term "fast-tracking" imply?
6. How does the contractor (SDO) become involved in a project?
7. What is the role of an RFP? Describe the contents of an RFP.
8. What is a feasibility study? Describe its contents and purpose.
9. What are user needs? Describe the process of defining user needs and the problems encountered.
10. What are user requirements? How do they differ from user needs?
11. Who prepares the proposal? Describe the proposal preparation process.
12. What is the statement of work (SOW)? In what documents does the SOW appear?
13. Describe the contents of the proposal.
14. How is the best proposal selected? Describe the process and the criteria used.
15. Three proposals (W, X, and Y) have been rated on six criteria as follows: 1 = poor, 2 = average, 3 = good. Choose between the three proposals using (a) the simple rating method and (b) the weighted rating method.

Criteria	Weight	W	X	Y
Attention to quality	0.25	2	1	3
Cost	0.20	3	3	1
Project plan	0.20	2	2	1
Project organization	0.15	3	2	3
Likelihood of success	0.10	2	3	3
Contractor's credentials	0.10	2	2	3

16. What contractor qualifications might the customer look for in a proposal? What else about the contractor might the customer look for?
17. What parties are considered subcontractors in a project?
18. Discuss the purpose of a business case study for internal projects. What does the study include, and who prepares it?
19. How is the RFP/proposal process adapted to large projects that potentially have numerous stakeholders although initially only a few have been identified?
20. In contracting out work, does the customer relinquish all control over the project to the contractor? Explain.
21. How can a contractor be both the sender and receiver of RFPs—i.e., how can it both prepare and submit proposals, and receive and review proposals?
22. When a contractor hires a subcontractor, to whom is the subcontractor obligated—the end-user customer or the contractor?
23. What must the project manager know to be able to effectively negotiate a contract? Consider aspects of the customer, competition, and technical content of the proposal.
24. Discuss the difference between the SOW, CSOW, and work requisition or work order.
25. Describe the different kinds of contracts (refer to the Appendix to this chapter). What are the relative advantages and disadvantages of each to the customer and the contractor?

QUESTIONS ABOUT THE STUDY PROJECT

As appropriate, answer questions 1–13 above regarding your project. Also answer the following questions: How are contracts negotiated and who is involved in the negotiation? What kinds of contracts are used in the project?

Case 3.1 West Coast University Medical Center

West Coast University Medical Center (WCMC) is a large teaching and research hospital with a national reputation for excellence in healthcare practice, education, and research. Seeking to sustain that reputation, the senior executive board decided to install a comprehensive medical diagnostic system. The system would be linked to WCMC's servers, and be available to physicians from their homes and offices via the Internet. By clicking icons to access a medical specialty area, then keying answers to queries about a patient's medical symptoms and history, a physician could receive a list of diagnostics with associated statistics.

The senior board sent a questionnaire to every department, asking managers about the needs of their areas and how they felt the system might improve doctor's performance. Most managers replied that the system would save doctors' time and improve performances. The hospital information technology (IT) group was assigned to assess the cost and feasibility of implementing the system. They interviewed managers at WCMC, and several vendors of diagnostic software. The study showed high enthusiasm among the managers, and a long list of potential benefits. Based on the feasibility study, the board approved the system.

The IT manager invited three well-known consulting firms that specialized in medical diagnostic systems to give presentations, and then hired one to assist his group in selecting and integrating several software packages into a single, complete diagnostic system.

One year and millions of dollars later the project was completed, but 6 months later it was clear the system was a failure. Although it did everything the consultants and software vendors had promised, few doctors used it; of those that did, many complained that the "benefits" were irrelevant, and that features of the system they would have liked were lacking.

QUESTIONS

1. Why was the system a failure?
2. What was the likely cause of its lack of use?
3. What steps or procedures were poorly handled in the project conception phase?

Case 3.2 X-philes Data Management Corporation: RFP Matters

X-philes Data Management Corporation (XDM) is preparing to contract out work for two large projects: Scully and Mulder. The projects are comparable in terms of size, technical requirements, and estimated completion time, but are independent and will be performed by separate project teams.

Two managers at XDM, one each assigned to Scully and Mulder, prepare RFPs for the projects and send them to several contractors. The RFP for Scully includes the following: a SOW that specifies system performance and quality requirements, a maximum price, a completion deadline, and contract conditions; incentives clause stating the contractor will receive a bonus for exceeding minimal quality requirements and finishing the project early, or will be penalized for poor quality and late completion; requirement that the contractor submits detailed monthly status reports showing progress on key quality measures. The RFP for Mulder includes a brief SOW, a maximum budget, and the desired completion date.

Based on proposals received in response to the RFPs, the managers responsible for Scully and Mulder each select a contractor. Unknown to either manager, they select the same contractor, Yrisket Systems. The Scully manager selects Yrisket because its bid price is somewhat below the budget limit and its reputation in the business is good. The Mulder manager selects Yrisket for similar reasons—good price and reputation. In preparing the Mulder proposal, Yrisket managers had to work hard to meet the maximum price specified on the RFP, but they felt that by doing quality work they could make a tidy profit from the incentive offered.

A few months after the projects have started, some of Yrisket's employees quit. To meet their commitments to both projects, Yrisket workers have to work long hours and weekends. It is apparent, however, that these extra efforts might not be enough, especially because Yrisket has a contract with another customer and must begin work soon.

QUESTIONS

1. What do you think will happen?
2. How do you think the crisis facing Yrisket will affect the Mulder and Scully projects? The two projects are very similar, yet do you expect Yrisket to treat them the same?

Case 3.3   Proposal Evaluation for Apollo Spacecraft[24]

Five proposals were submitted to NASA to design and build the Apollo spacecraft. An evaluation board of more than 100 specialists reviewed the proposals and ranked them as follows (maximum = 10):

	Technical approach (30%)	Technical qualification (30%)	Business strength (40%)	Weighted total
Martin Company	5.58	6.63	8.09	6.90
General Dynamics Astronautics	5.27	5.35	8.52	6.59
North American Aviation	5.09	6.66	7.59	6.56
General Electric Company	5.16	5.60	7.99	6.42
McDonnell Aircraft Corporation	5.53	5.67	7.62	6.41

The board unequivocally recommended to NASA senior management that Martin be awarded the contract but suggested North American as the next-best alternative, based upon NA's experience in developing high-performance military and research aircraft. This experience (technical qualification) sufficiently impressed the board that it put NA ahead of General Dynamics, despite NA's lower ratings on technical approach

(design of the space capsule) and business strength (organization and management). The board mentioned that any shortcomings in NA's technical approach could be corrected through additional design effort. Seeing the board's recommendations, and aware of NA's long, close association with NACA (NASA's predecessor agency), NASA senior management immediately selected North American.

QUESTIONS

1. How were the points in the "Weighted Total" column determined? Show the computations.
2. North American rated third out of five contractors in the Weighted Total column, yet was awarded the contract. How did that happen? What are the lessons from this example?

1. It could be argued that Phase D in an election campaign project will be extended *if* the candidate is elected, whereupon the "operation" phase represents the elected official's full political term—but that would be stretching the analogy.

2. The conception phase is thoroughly covered in Biggs C, Birks E, and Atkins W. *Managing the Systems Development Process*. Upper Saddle River, NJ: Prentice Hall; 1980. pp. 51–59; and Allen J and Lientz B. *Systems in Action*. Santa Monica, CA: Goodyear; 1978. pp. 41–63.

3. A need is a value judgment that a problem exists. However, different parties in an identical situation will perceive the situation differently; as a consequence, a need is always identified with respect to a particular party—e.g., the user. See McKillip J. *Need Analysis: Tools for the Human Services and Education*. Newbury Park, CA: Sage Publications; 1987.

4. Cusumano M and Selby R. *Microsoft Secrets*. New York, NY: Free Press; 1995. p. 210.

5. In the USA, a request for quotation (RFQ) or invitation for bid (IFB) commonly suggests that selection of a contractor will be based primarily on price; in a request for proposal (RFP), the nature of the solution and competency of the contractor are as or more important than price. Elsewhere in the world, the terms *proposal* and *bid* often are used interchangeably, a bid being the equivalent of a full-fledged proposal.

6. Other aspects of the feasibility study are discussed in Biggs, Birks, and Atkins, *Managing the Systems Development Process*, pp. 59–80; and Allen and Lientz, *Systems in Action*, pp. 65–89.

7. Adapted from Frame JD. *Managing Projects in Organizations*. San Francisco, CA: Jossey-Bass; 1987. pp. 109–110.

8. *Ibid.*, pp. 111–126.

9. *Ibid.*, pp. 120–122.

10. A thorough description of proposal preparation is provided by Hajek VG. *Management of Engineering Projects*, 3rd edn. New York, NY: McGraw-Hill; 1984. pp. 39–57. A good, succinct overview is given by Rosenau MD. *Successful Project Management*. Belmont, CA: Lifetime Learning; 1981. pp. 21–32.

11. For details of proposal contents and the proposal preparation process, see Roman D. *Managing Projects: A Systems Approach*. New York, NY: Elsevier; 1986. pp. 67–72; and Stewart R and Stewart A. *Proposal Preparations*. New York, NY: John Wiley & Sons; 1984.

12. Models for project analysis and selection are discussed in Bussey L. *The Economic Analysis of Industrial Projects*. Upper Saddle River, NJ: Prentice Hall; 1978; Baker N. R&D project selection models: an assessment. *IEEE Transactions on Engineering Management* EM-21(4); 1974: 165–171; Souder W. *Project Selection and Economic Appraisal*. New York, NY: Van Nostrand Reinhold; 1984; Souder W and Mandakovic T. R&D project selection models. *Research Management* 29(4); 1986: 36–42; see also issues of *IEEE Transactions on Engineering Management*, *Management Science*, and *Research Management* for titles regarding project evaluation and selection.

13. Murphy O. *International Project Management*. Mason, OH: Thompson; 2005. pp. 159–161.

14. This section gives an overview of the important contracting issues. It is not intended to provide legal advice about contracts; for that, you need an attorney or contracts specialist.

15. Management of the complete project contracting process, including what and where to contract, soliciting and assessing proposals, reaching a contract agreement, and administering the contract, is called "contract monitoring." See Hirsch W. *The Contracts Management Deskbook*, revised edn. New York, NY: American Management Association; 1986. Chapter 6.

16. *Ibid.*, pp. 290–315.

17. See Hajek, *Management of Engineering Projects*, Chs 8 and 9; and Rosenau, *Successful Project Management*, pp. 34–41.

18. The primary source of material for this example is Gray M. *Angle of Attack: Harrison Storms and the Race to the Moon*. New York, NY: W.W. Norton; 1992. pp. 87–116; the other source is Brooks C, Grimwood J and Swenson L Jr. *Chariots for Apollo: A History of Manned Lunar Spacecraft*. Washington, DC: NASA Scientific and Technical Information Office, SP-4205; 1979, sections 2.5 and 4.2.

19. A complete description of contracts is given in Hirsch W. *The Contracts Management Deskbook*, revised edn. New York, NY: Amocom; 1986. pp. 43–75. For construction contracts, see Furst S and Ramsey V. (eds), *Keating on Construction Contracts*, 8th edn. London, UK: Sweet & Maxwell; 2006.

20. Hajek, *Management of Engineering Projects*, pp. 82–83.
21. Miller R. *Schedule, Cost, and Profit Control with PERT*. New York, NY: McGraw-Hill; 1963. pp. 173–184.
22. Example from Miller, *Schedule, Cost, and Profit Control with PERT*, pp. 174–175.
23. See *ibid.*, pp. 183–196, for discussion of multiple incentive contracts, their usage in project network systems, and their development and application to program control.
24. Brooks, Grimwood, and Swenson, *Chariots for Apollo*, Chs 2–5.

Chapter

Project and System Definition

> *When one door is shut, another opens.*

—CERVANTES,
Don Quixote

*T*he result of Phase A is a formalized systems concept. It includes: (1) a clear problem formulation and list of user requirements; (2) a rudimentary but well-conceptualized systems solution; (3) an elemental plan for the project in the proposal; and (4) an agreement between the customer and the contractor about all of these. The project is now ready to move on to the "middle" and "later" phases of systems development and to bring the systems concept to fruition.

4.1 PHASE B: DEFINITION

As Figure 4.1 shows, given approval of the project in Phase A, the thrust of the effort now moves to definition, design, production, and implementation of the solution. In Phase A, most of the effort was devoted to investigating the *problem*—what is it, is it significant, should it be resolved, and can it be resolved in an acceptable fashion? The initial investigation and feasibility studies were largely centered on the problem. Now, in Phase B, definition, it is the solution that receives scrutiny. The solution is analyzed and defined in sufficient detail such that designers and builders will be able to produce a system that meets

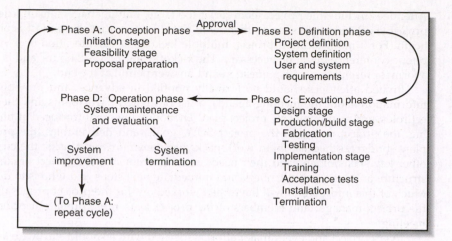

Figure 4.1
Four-phase model of the systems development cycle.

the customer's needs. The definition phase has two main purposes: determining the system requirements, and preparing the project plan.

Project Definition vs System Definition

There are two ways to look at a project: one is to see the end-item or *result* of the project, the other to see the *effort* directed at achieving that result. Looking at both is necessary: if you focus too much on the end-item and too little on the effort, the project will run into problems for lack of preparation, coordination, and control over resources, costs, and schedules. But if you focus primarily on the effort and less so on the end-item, the project will still run into problems—this time for not meeting user requirements. System definition and project definition are equally important. System definition aims at achieving a good understanding of what the end-item must do to satisfy user requirements; project definition aims at specifying what must happen in the project to produce the end-item. The two are inextricably linked. While it is not surprising that much of the literature on project management is preoccupied with project definition, it is surprising how little attention is given to system definition.

System definition begins with defining user needs and requirements; project definition begins with addressing those requirements in a proposed solution—the project proposal. Hence, some of the definition work necessary for a project is initiated in Phase A. Phase B continues this definition work and concludes with a set of system specifications and a project plan—a full suite of everything necessary to execute the project in Phase C.

Project Kickoff

The project formally begins with a kickoff meeting, which is the first formal meeting of the project team members and key stakeholders. The purpose of the meeting is to announce that the project is about to commence, communicate what the project is about, develop common expectations, and generate enthusiasm and commitment to project goals and deliverables. The project manager plans and runs the meeting.

Attendees include the project team (or, if too large, only managers, team leads, and project staff), supporters, and others who should know that the project is about to begin. For a multi-location project, multiple kickoffs at each location or a video or phone conference might be necessary. The kickoff runs for 1.5–2 hours, and is mostly a formal presentation with a question-and-answer period at the end.

Invited attendees should be formally notified in advance, and provided with information about the meeting agenda, a list of invited participants and their project roles, and a rudimentary project plan. The following are introduced at the meeting: the project manager; the project SOW, goals, and deliverables; the proposed plan—budget, schedule, main work packages; constraints and risks; the customer, other key stakeholders, and their needs and requirements; the project organization structure and key team members; and immediate next steps and who is to do what. Much of this information will have been worked out for the project proposal; if not, the project manager and members of the project team must prepare it prior to the meeting.

Every project and every major effort associated with it should start with a kickoff meeting. For a large project, preparing the proposal will itself be a project, preceded by a kickoff meeting; similarly, each large work package should be initiated with a kickoff.

Important to note is that the purpose of the kickoff is to inform and provide information, not to reach consensus of opinion, develop working relationships, or establish guidelines so team members can work together. The latter is the purpose of team-building, for which subsequent meetings should be held shortly after the kickoff. Teambuilding is discussed in Chapter 15.

Project Name

The project name is important because it is the first thing that people hear about the project—often with no accompanying explanation.[1] The name will appear again and again in virtually all communication, and persist for as long as the project—and perhaps longer. A carelessly chosen name can cause misunderstanding or a blank stare about what the project is supposed to do; it can cause people to confuse the project with other projects; and it can influence the way they react to the project. Unless the intention is to obfuscate the project's purpose ("Manhattan Engineering District"— the atomic bomb project; "Have Blue"—the F-117 stealth fighter project), the name should clearly suggest what the project is about.

Clever or cute names or acronyms should be avoided; they tend to be ambiguous and, sometimes, annoying to all but the namers. All projects are apt to acquire nicknames; these tend to indicate how people *feel* about the project ("Project from Hell") but not much else. If, however, the nickname gains widespread usage, then sometimes the sensible thing is to formally adopt it. (Boston's Central Artery/Tunnel became the "Big Dig"—not to be confused with Canada's "Big Dig," the Wascana Lake Urban Revitalization Project in Saskatchewan. The 1960s geological research project to drill through the Earth's crust to the Mohorovicic discontinuity was aptly named Project Mohole; as political and technical problems mounted, it became known as "Project *No*hole.") A project is often named for a place, person, or the end-item it creates (Petronas Towers; Bandra-Worli Sea Link Bridge), and for long-named end-items it is okay to adopt an acronym (BWSL)—though it's always a good idea to first check the acronym before keeping the name; a serious project should not make people chuckle whenever they see its acronym (*A*utomated *N*etwork for *U*niform *S*ecurity).

4.2 PROJECT CHARTER

The project charter is a proclamation that management has approved a project and given the project manager its backing. Organizations use it to announce and formally authorize the starting of *internal* projects. The charter is created upon project approval, based upon a feasibility study or acceptance of a proposal.

The purpose of the charter is to describe the project to stakeholders in the organization, and establish the project manager's authority to gather and make use of resources. It includes whatever information is necessary to give the reader a good overview of the project; for example, it can describe the project objectives, scope, stakeholders and their stakes, estimated budget and schedule, risk, assumptions and constraints, resources, and key roles, and the people responsible for filling them. Often the charter contains sections similar to the project plan. Sometimes the charter is used as *the* project plan, although commonly it is somewhat brief, several pages at most, and provides only an overview of a more comprehensive project plan.

4.3 PROJECT DEFINITION

Project definition addresses the question: What must the project do to deliver the system concept and satisfy the user and system requirements? Actually, the question is comprised of several subquestions, such as: What work must be done? Who will do it? How long will it take? How much money will it take? What resources will be needed? These questions are largely addressed in one place: the project plan.

Project definition and system definition happen concurrently and cyclically. The work to be done in the project plan must meet the system specifications, but the system specifications must conform to the constraints, work methods, technological capabilities, and acceptable risks as specified in the project plan.

Detailed Project Planning

Prior to Phase B a portion of the project definition will already have been done: at minimum, some amount of project definition was necessary in Phase A to prepare a rudimentary plan and system requirements for inclusion in the proposal. But that definition effort will have resulted at best in a detailed outline of what is to come. During Phase B, that outline must be expanded and elaborated in detail. The renewed definition effort will involve identifying the work tasks and necessary resources, creating schedules, budgets, and cost control systems, and identifying the project team and its leaders, supervisors, subcontractors, and support staff.

The project team begins to evolve from the skeletal group that worked on the proposal, sometimes in a cascading manner: the project manager selects team leaders, who in turn fill in team positions under them. The project manager negotiates with functional managers to get specific individuals or the requisite expertise assigned to the project. Sometimes she seeks the customer's approval in adding members to the project team; this is advisable whenever the customer must work closely with the team, or when the customer might have an objection. Good customer–project team rapport is crucial to maintaining a healthy customer–contractor relationship.

Project Master Plan

As key members of the project team are assembled, they begin preparing the detailed project plan or project "master plan." The plan includes:

- A scope statement or SOW that includes high-level user requirements and system requirements
- Work breakdown structure and work packages or tasks
- Project organization and responsibility assignments
- Assignment of key personnel to work packages
- Project schedules showing events, milestones, or points of critical action
- Budget and allocation to work packages
- Quality plan for monitoring and accepting project deliverables, including testing plan
- Risk plan and contingency or mitigation measures
- Procurement plan
- Work review plan
- Change control plan
- Documentation policy/plan
- Implementation plan to guide conversion to or adoption of deliverables.

Ultimately all of the elements of the plan must be integrated, meaning that each is tied to, compatible with, and supportive of the others. Details of these elements are discussed in Part III, starting with the next chapter. A sample project plan is in Appendix C at the end of the book.

In large projects, most of the planning is delegated to subordinate members of the project team. The project manager coordinates and oversees their efforts to ensure that all subplans are thorough and tie together. The final plan is reviewed for approval by contractor top management and the customer. Contractor top management makes sure that the plan fits into existing and upcoming organizational projects and capabilities, and the customer checks the plan for conformity with user requirements and conditions as stated in the contract.

Anxious to get the project underway, many contractors avoid reviewing the project plan with the customer. This is shortsighted, because the plan might contain elements to which the customer objects. Often the project is conducted and implemented within the customer's organization. Everything in the plan must fit: the project schedule must fit the customer's schedule; project cash flow requirements must meet the customer's payment schedule; the contractor's personnel and procedures must complement those of the customer; and materials and work methods must be acceptable to the customer. For all these reasons, the customer and users should be allowed to review the plan before starting work.

Once the project plan and system specifications have been approved by management and the customer, the project team turns its attention to the detailed design and building of the system, which happen in Phase C (covered in Chapters 11 and 12). As will be explained later, however, project planning never stops; it continues throughout the project life cycle.

Phased (Rolling Wave) Project Planning

A major thrust of Phase B is to develop the project plan, but seldom does it produce a comprehensive, detailed plan for the entire project. The fact is, despite all the effort devoted to planning in Phase B, the plan is developed in phases, not all at once. There are too many unknowns at the start of a project, and at that time it is impossible to specify exactly what will happen or should be done for the whole project. Only as the project progresses and the unknowns decrease can details in the plan be filled in. The situation is analogous to planning the route to some ultimate destination, but without the benefit of knowing the obstacles ahead. Since you can only see the landscape directly ahead, you can only plan the first part of the route in detail; beyond that, the route is vague. This is represented by Phase I in Figure 4.2a. As you move through Phase I you start to see more of the obstacles ahead, which enables you to plan the next part of the route, Phase II (b). The process continues, filling in details of the route, phase by phase, until you reach the destination (c and d).

At the onset of a project the customer wants to know the project cost and completion date, which can be estimated by preparing a rough plan. Although a big part of the initial plan is somewhat vague (analogous to the shaded blob in Figure 4.2), the plan is usually adequate for managers to estimate project resources, time, and cost, and to show all these to the customer. But as the project progresses, other, more detailed plans are created, but for *the most immediate phase* of the project only (dotted lines, Figure 4.2). Whereas the rough plan is based upon information from similar projects, estimates, and forecasts, the detailed plan is based upon facts about upcoming work—facts identified as the approaching work gets closer.

Figure 4.2
Phased project planning.

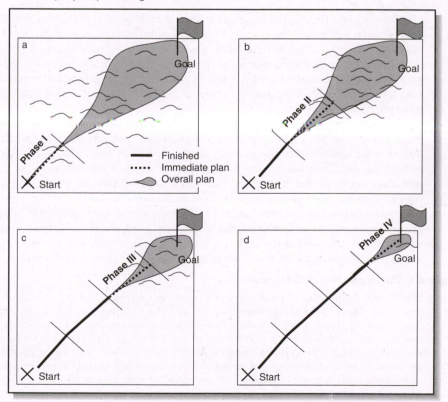

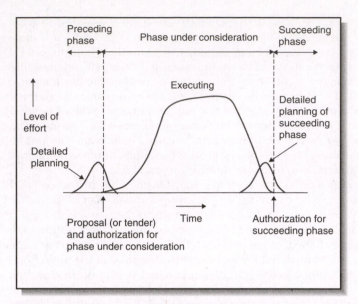

Figure 4.3
Detailed planning for each project phase.
From Steyn H (ed.). *Project Management—A Multi-Disciplinary Approach.* Pretoria: FPM Publishing; 2003. p. 27.

For unique projects, the rough plan should be seen as just that—a rough indication of project deliverables, cost, and delivery date, but not a commitment. The plan is first prepared during the feasibility study or business case study. As the project progresses through the successive phases, detailed plans are prepared, with more specific work tasks and schedules. Only for the most immediate phase where the "terrain" is clearly visible is it possible to create a detailed plan and to make commitments to work, dates, and costs.

In some projects each phase concludes with a *milestone* where the customer or management reviews the deliverables and project performance; if satisfied, they approve the deliverables and pay for work done thus far. At the same time, they review the detailed plan for the next phase and assess the costs, risks, etc.; if satisfied, they authorize the next phase. That is, the detailed plan for each phase is largely prepared in the *prior* phase, as illustrated in Figure 4.3. Authorization to begin the next phase represents a commitment by the customer or management to support the phase, and permission for the project team to proceed. If the project has to be terminated, it is terminated at the end of a phase; termination before the end of a phase should happen only as the result of unforeseen events external to the project.

Example 4.1: Mary's and Peter's New House

Mary and Peter buy a piece of land upon which to build a new house. They approach NewHome Construction and describe to Paul, the owner, what they have in mind. Among other things, they want to know what it would cost. Having been in the business for a number of years, Paul has an idea of the costs but is wary of quoting a fixed price since he doesn't know Mary and Peter very well, and whether their tastes are cheap or expensive. Also, he knows there might be hidden costs arising from, for example, poor soil conditions of the site. He therefore gives Mary and Peter a range of possible prices based upon the estimated square footage of the house, as well as a rough estimate of when the house would be completed. Nobody has yet made any commitments. To the question "Where do we go from here?" Paul answers that the first phase is to do a concept design, after which he will deliver sketches of the house. He also describes to them the other phases of the project he foresees, and the deliverables, approximate schedule, and approximate cost for each.

Mary and Peter sign a contract for Paul to provide a preliminary design and sketches. The contract specifies when they will see the preliminary design, when they will see the sketches, what the sketches will include and exclude, as well as the price for the sketches. Within a month, they receive and approve the design and sketch plans.

Paul now presents them with a second contract, this time for the detailed design to include drawings that the construction team will use to build the house. Just like the first phase, the contract specifies the deliverable (drawings), the delivery date, and the price. A few months later, Mary and Peter approve the drawings and construction begins.

Paul notes that the construction work will also be done in phases, although now, he says, there is sufficient information about the project and its costs that only one contract is needed. He shows them the contract, which lists the remaining phases of the project, including a guarantee period (occupation after completion of construction) during which NewHome Construction will fix any defects free of charge. The contract indicates milestones and deliverables for each of the phases, and specifies that a payment will be due upon reaching each milestone. Before each payment, Mary and Peter will have the opportunity to inspect the work and verify that it has been completed and meets workmanship standards as specified in the contract.

This example illustrates the benefits of phased project planning: at the start, NewHome does not have to commit to the cost of building an as yet undefined structure. During the project, Mary and Peter do not have to commit to work beyond any one phase (in fact, at the conclusion of any contracted phase they can walk away from the project). The milestone payments improve NewHome's cash flow and reduce interest payments on money borrowed from the bank for construction, and provide NewHome with some protection against bad debt: should Mary and Peter miss a milestone payment, NewHome simply stops work.

Project phases form the basis of project methodologies and project gating schemes, discussed in Chapter 16. In organizations that have project methodologies, project managers follow the prescribed sequence of standard phases for planning and executing projects. In organizations that do not have methodologies, project managers are free to develop their own.

4.4 SYSTEM DEFINITION

Systems are defined by their requirements. Requirements are therefore the starting point for all systems development projects, and the foundation for project planning. Each requirement impacts end-item scope and complexity, which in turn impact project work effort, time, cost, and risk. The requirements must be carefully defined and agreed upon, otherwise it will be impossible to fully conceptualize the end-item and create a viable project plan.

With the contract signed and the project about to get underway, earlier-defined user requirements should be reviewed and any gaps and ambiguities eliminated. The following sections describe various issues and methods related to requirements definition. The Appendix to the chapter describes quality function deployment (QFD), a methodology for ensuring user needs and requirements remain in focus throughout the systems development life cycle.

User Requirements Revisited

For products and systems in competitive markets, user requirements are initially framed in general terms—for example, outperform the F-16, taste better than Joe's beef jerky, obtain at least a 20 percent rate of return, or upgrade to the latest software release. General requirements such as these must be expanded before serious development work and project planning can be started. As shown in the next example, poor requirements definition is a source of project failure.

Example 4.2: User Requirements for Product Development

The marketing group for a kitchen appliance manufacturer wrote the requirements for a new food processor. The requirements specified the general size, weight, usage, price, and sales volume of the proposed product, but nothing about product performance, which the engineering design group set by studying competitors' products. The food processor as developed met all the requirements set by marketing and engineering, yet it was obsolete before it was even launched. Competitors had released products that better suited customer needs. In defining the product, both the marketing and engineering groups had ignored the user requirements for the food processor—i.e., the requirements of user groups in the market necessary for the product to be successful.

Defining complete, accurate requirements is not easy. Among the problems:

- Requirements must incorporate information not only from the user but also from functional areas such as marketing, engineering, manufacturing, and outside stakeholders
- The information needed to define requirements is not always available when definition occurs, so it is easy to overlook necessary requirements or include unnecessary ones
- The requirements include vague terms that cannot be accurately measured (e.g., "modern" or "low cost")
- The user or contractor is unable to adequately describe the requirements because the end-result is complex, abstract, or artistic
- The customer or contractor intentionally defines requirements in ambiguous terms to allow latitude in results later in the project.

Problems like these result in confused project planning and, later, disputes between the customer and contractor over whether the end-result met the requirements. The following are steps to reduce such problems.[2]

- Convince both the user and contractor groups of the importance of clear, comprehensive definition of requirements. Users and contractors often are reluctant to devote the time necessary to define clear and complete requirements.
- Check for ambiguities and redefine the requirements so none remain.
- Augment written requirements with non-verbal aids such as pictures, schematics, graphics, and visual or functional models.
- Avoid rigid specification of requirements that are likely to be changed because of uncertainty or changing environment.

- Treat each requirement as a commitment. Both the user and the contractor must agree to and sign off on each one.
- After the project begins, monitor the requirements and resist attempts to change them. Use a change control system to distinguish desired versus necessary changes, assess the impacts of changes, and decide whether to approve or deny them.

Detailed user requirements come from one source: the user. The project manager, however, should not be accepting of just any requirements provided by the user, but should offer to assist the user in defining them. Just as users sometimes require help in understanding the problem or need, they sometimes also need help in specifying their requirements. They may not be aware of the cost, schedule, or other ramifications of requirements, nor understand what will be necessary to fulfill them.

For most projects, the list of high-level user requirements (summary or bullet points) should fit on one page for easy reference. The contractor will refer to the list early in the project when preparing the project's scope statement, and the customer will refer to it at the end of the project to determine the acceptability of project results and end-items.

Preliminary definition of user requirements happens during the feasibility study and proposal preparation, and a summary of user requirements is included in the contract. In simple systems, user requirements rarely exceed a few lines or a page. In big systems, however, they might fill volumes of text. An example of the former is user requirements for a contract to perform a 1-day management seminar; an example of the latter is user requirements for the 9-year, multibillion dollar Delta Project to prevent the North Sea from flooding the Netherlands.

System Requirements

A major thrust of Phase B is translating user requirements into *system requirements*. System requirements are oriented toward the solution; they specify the contractor's approach and objectives for satisfying the needs and wants spelled out in the user requirements. Beyond fulfilling user requirements, a project must also fulfill contractor needs. For example, besides being profitable the contractor might specify requirements to keep skilled workers and costly production facilities occupied.

System requirements provide an overview of the system or solution approach—the principle functions, system architecture, and resulting end-item (system, solution, or product)—and a common understanding among the project team as to what must be done in the project. Whereas user requirements come from the user's perspective, system requirements derive from the contractor's perspective. They state what the system must *do* to satisfy the user requirements. Table 4.1 provides examples contrasting user requirements and system requirements.

System requirements specify what designers and builders must address in designing and building the end-item. The following illustrates this for the spaceship project.

Example 4.3: High-Level System Requirements for Spaceship

Below are five user requirements for the spaceship, each followed by one or more system requirements. The former specify what the customer requires, the latter what the spaceship and its subsystems and components must do to satisfy those requirements.

Table 4.1 Examples contrasting user requirements and system requirements

User Requirements	System Requirements Will Address:
1. Vehicle must accelerate from 0 to 60 mph in 10 seconds and accommodate six people	Vehicle size and weight, engine horsepower, kind of transmission
2. House must accommodate a family of four	Number and size of rooms
3. House must be luxurious	Quality of materials; number, quality, and expense of decorative features
4. Space station must operate life support, manufacturing, and experimental equipment	Type and kilowatt capacity of power generating equipment; technology for primary system operation; technology for back-up operation
5. Aircraft must be "stealthy"	Design of overall configuration and external surfaces; types of materials; usage of existing versus newly developed components
6. Spaceflight must be comfortable	Spaceship cabin temperature, humidity, and pressure

1. Attain altitude of at least 100 km (for this requirement, the system requirements are):
   1.1 Motor must have enough thrust
   1.2 Motor must burn long enough
   1.3 Vehicle must be lightweight.
2. Capacity for three people
   2.1 Cabin must be large enough.
3. Comfortable flight
   3.1 Cabin temperature must remain at comfortable level
   3.2 Cabin pressure must remain at comfortable level
   3.3 Vehicle acceleration force must not exceed certain level
   3.4 Cabin must have sufficient elbowroom.
4. Relatively inexpensive to design, build, and launch
   4.1 Fuel and fuel handling procedure must be economical
   4.2 Structural materials of vehicle must be economical
   4.3 Whenever possible, usage of current, off-the-shelf technology and systems
   4.4 Few people required to maintain vehicle.
5. Capable of being "turned-around" in at most 2 weeks
   5.1 Minimum repair of parts/modules between flights
   5.2 Minimum replacement of parts/modules between flight
   5.3 Minimum refueling time
   5.4 Minimum cabin cleaning time.

Notice, the system requirements specify "what" the system must do, not "how" it will do it. They say, for example, "the motor must generate enough thrust to propel the spaceship to 100 km before it runs out of fuel," but not how. Addressing the "how" comes later.

Defining requirements sufficiently so that designers will know what they are striving for is called *requirements analysis*. To make the "jump" from user requirements to system requirements so the latter are comprehensive, complete, and yet do not distort the former is not easy; a good way to do that is the quality function deployment method (QFD), described at the end of the chapter. The result of the requirements analysis is a comprehensive list of functional requirements.

Functional Requirements

Functional requirements specify the functions that the new system must be able to perform to meet the user requirements. For example, the functions of the spaceship include propulsion, handling and maneuverability, human habitability, safety, and support and maintenance. The common tool for identifying functional requirements is the functional flow block diagram, FFBD, described in the Appendix to Chapter 2. All significant functions for the system, its subsystems, components, and interfaces, including for support and maintenance, must be identified. Most systems perform several basic functions, and each function has numerous subfunctions.

Associated with each functional requirement are targets or *performance requirements*. These specify in technical terms—e.g., physical dimensions, miles per hour, turning radius, decibels of sound, acceleration, percent efficiency, operating temperature, BTUs, operating cost—the target requirements that the function must satisfy, as well as the tests, procedures, and measures to be used to prove that the targets have been met. The project team refers to these performance requirements in the design or purchase of components for the system.

In addition to these requirements, others might be imposed on the overall system or on specific subsystems and components. The following are typical:[3]

1. *Compatibility*—ability of subsystems to be integrated into the whole system or environment and to contribute to objectives of the whole system.
2. *Commonality*—ability of a component to be used interchangeably with an existing but different type of component. A "high commonality" system contains many available (OTS) components; a "low commonality" one contains many components that must be newly developed.
3. *Cost-effectiveness*—total cost of the system to achieve a given level of benefit. This includes the cost of the design as well as the cost for implementing and operating the design.
4. *Reliability*—ability of the system or component to function at a given level or for a given period of time before failing.
5. *Maintainability*—ability of the system to be repaired within a certain period of time (i.e., the *ease* with which it can be repaired).
6. *Testability*—degree to which the system can be systematically tested and measured for its performance capabilities.
7. *Availability*—degree to which the system can be expected to operate when it is needed.
8. *Usability*—amount of physical effort or strain, technical skill, training, or ability required for operating and maintaining the system.
9. *Robustness*—ability of the system to survive in a harsh environment.
10. *Expandability*—ability of the system to be easily expanded to include new functions or be adapted to new conditions.

These requirements are sometimes called "non-functional" requirements(!) because they are not tied to particular functions and are desired of the entire system and its components.

Requirements Priority and Margin

Two properties of each requirement are its priority and margin. The *priority* of a requirement is, simply, the relative importance of the requirement. When multiple requirements conflict so that not all of them can be met, priority determines which can be met and which not. Suppose a product is specified to perform in a certain way and be of a particular height, but performance has priority. Knowing this will be useful to the design team if later they determine that to achieve the specified performance the height requirement must be exceeded.

Related to priority is the *margin* on a requirement—the amount by which the requirement can vary. For example, the requirement "maximum height of 4 feet; margin of 2 inches" tells designers that in case they must exceed the height requirement, they have at most 2 more inches.

Requirements Breakdown Structure

During requirements analysis, system functions are sorted and assigned to logical groups. The requirements breakdown structure (RBS) in Figure 4.4 is a simplified example showing some ways of grouping requirements. The RBS should include every identified functional requirement; in large systems these can number in the hundreds or even thousands.

The purpose of the RBS is to provide a common reference for everyone working on the project. Often a requirement will pertain to multiple system components, which means that multiple project teams will be working to meet that requirement. The RBS enables these teams to coordinate efforts and avoid omissions or duplication.

System requirements provide general direction for the project, but they are high-level requirements and not detailed enough to tell the project team what it must design, build, or purchase to create the end-item system. Stipulations must be placed on each of the requirements; these are called *system specifications*.

Figure 4.4
Requirements breakdown structure.

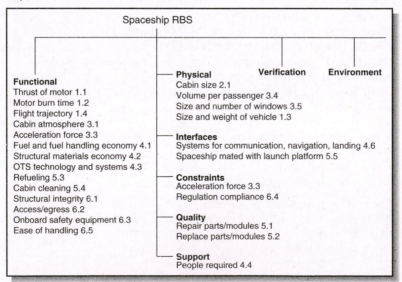

System Specifications

System specifications are derived from system requirements. They define the end-item and its subsystems, components, and processes in sufficient depth that the project team will be able to design, build, and/or procure (OTS) those subsystems and components.

System specifications are the basis for specifications of lower-level subsystems, which are the basis for specifications of even lower-level subsystems. From the system specification for a new automobile, for example, specifications are derived for the auto's drive train, suspension, steering system, brake system, etc. The specifications for these lower-level components normally take the form of a drawing or, for an OTS item, a catalog number.

Example 4.4: System Specifications for Spaceship

The progression from user requirements to system requirements and from system requirements to system specifications for the spaceship is illustrated in Figure 4.5. At the top, the system requirement "Motor must provide enough thrust" is derived from the user requirement "Spaceship must reach 100 km"; in turn, the system specification "Motor must be ≥88 kN thrust" is derived from the system requirement "Motor must provide enough thrust." System specifications tell the project team what it must do. For example, besides the motor having a specific thrust, another specification, 4.1.1, says the motor will burn nitric oxide and rubber. Since there are no commercially available (OTS) motors that do this, this tells the team it will have to design and build one from scratch. The multiple arrows to each specification in the last column mean that each specification must satisfy multiple requirements. Developing the system specifications requires analysis, modeling, and testing of design alternatives.

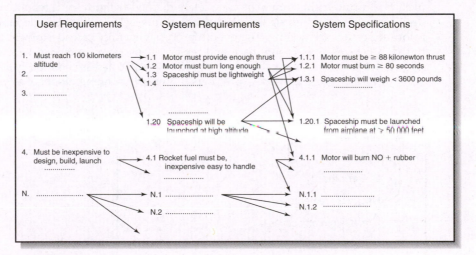

Figure 4.5
Relationships between user, system requirements, and system specifications for spaceship.

Traceability

Developing clear specifications is important, but so is keeping track of their relationships to each other and to system requirements. Throughout the systems development cycle, numerous changes and trade-offs will be made to the requirements that will each impact multiple specifications.

For example, altering the spaceship weight (Figure 4.5, system requirement 1.3) will impact the spaceship's required launch altitude (specification 1.20.1) and the motor's required thrust and burn time (1.1.1 and 1.2.1). Because weight impacts so many of the specifications, a designer cannot be cavalier about doing anything that might alter it. Any decision affecting weight must be assessed for the impact it will have on the specifications for launch and rocket motor. The ability to trace the effects of changes in some specification and requirements to others is called "traceability." The process of managing all of this—identifying specifications, tying them to physical components, tracing the impacts of changes, and *controlling* changes so requirements are met and do not conflict is called *configuration management* and *change control*, discussed in Chapters 9 and 11.

System specifications are the criteria that will guide actual project work; they are written by and for project specialists (systems analysts, programmers, engineers, product and process designers, consultants, etc.), and they address all areas of the project (design, fabrication, installation, operation, and maintenance). Besides these are *customer baseline specifications*; these are also derived from user and system requirements, but are for the customer—i.e., they are high-level and easy to understand. System specifications should be set so as to meet *but not exceed* the customer's baseline specifications. This is one way to prevent "scope creep"—i.e., the burdensome growth of project requirements that causes project budgets and schedules to increase.

Iterative Design-Testing and Rapid Prototyping

The definition of requirements and specifications, and the design and testing of the system usually happens iteratively, particularly when the project end-item is complex. The requirements cannot be completely defined without some amount of prior design work, and the design work cannot be completed without some amount of prior fabrication and testing. The overall process generally cascades down, as illustrated in Figure 4.6, but loops back and repeats steps; because the work flows from stage to stage like this, it is called the *waterfall process*. To assess and modify specifications, often a *prototype* is used. A prototype is an early running model of a system or

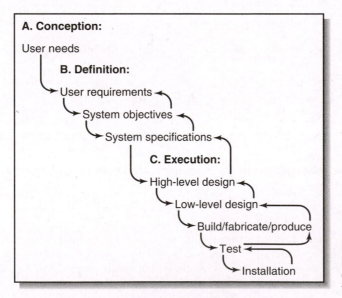

Figure 4.6
Iterative development cycle (waterfall process) for complex systems.

component built for purposes of demonstrating performance, functionality, or proving feasibility. It is built according to initial specifications, and then tested; if, based upon tests, the specifications are changed, then the prototype is modified and tested again. This process ensures that the basic system design supports the system specifications.

When no physical system exists like the one to be developed, conceptualizing the system can be difficult and confusing. The system the customer "sees" might be very different from the one the developer envisions, but without a physical or working model that difference might not be apparent. Requiring the customer to specify and sign-off on requirements early in the project only intensifies the problem. It forces the customer and developer to commit to decisions before they have reached a mutual understanding about the requirements.

In a process called *rapid prototyping*, a rudimentary, intentionally incomplete model of the product is made that is initially somewhat simple and inexpensive to produce.[4] The rapid prototype (RP) model represents *key parts* of the system but *not* the complete system, and is somewhat easy to create and modify. The customer experiments with the RP to assess the system's functionality and determine any necessary modifications or additions. After a few iterations of experimenting and modifying requirements, the final requirements and design concept are firmed up. In software development, the RP might be a series of screens or windows with queries to allow a user to "feel" what the system would be like. Architects use physical scale models of buildings for the same purpose. They know that a physical model is always better than a drawing, schematic, or list of requirements for conveying the look, feel, and functionality of a design. Drawings, schematics, and requirements tell the development project team what is expected, but the RP process ensures that drawings and requirements are finalized only after the customer has accepted them as represented by the RP model.

Ordinarily, the RP process will not speed up the definition phase; instead, it might lengthen it. The first RP model will likely be incorrect, though through experimentation it will enable the customer and developer to learn and eventually select optimum requirements. RP models and mock-ups are used, for example, to demonstrate the form and functionality of the shapes and sizes of control panels used in plants and equipment, and to design the interior layouts of automobiles and aircraft cabins.

Agile Project Management

The traditional waterfall approach in Figure 4.6 applies to projects that are somewhat lengthy, and where the customer requirements can readily be defined early in the project and will not change afterward. (Indeed, the same can be said for the project life cycle as bounded by Phases A, B, and C, shown in Figure 4.1.) Such situations are common, and include all of the projects described below, in section 4.6. But in many situations the requirements cannot be completely defined at the start of the project or might significantly change later—an example being software development where the requirements emerge or evolve due to competition and changing technology. A project like this cannot wait for all the requirements to be known because they might never be fully known. The traditional waterfall model can accommodate additions or changes to requirements, but only through a series of time-consuming and costly backward loops and iterations (shown in Figure 4.6).

In what is known as *agile project management*, the project is divided into a sequence of small efforts, each conducted by a tight-knit team dedicated to meeting a *limited set of requirements* and delivering results in a series of "releases". Take, for example, a project to develop a word processor. The team would first create a product that meets a limited set of customer requirements—say, a tablet upon which to display text and the means to store it. Later the team would address other requirements for, say, a spell checker and thesaurus. Subsequent efforts would focus on still other features.

In agile project management, the end-item system is developed in modules released in a series of quick iterations; in effect, the waterfall cycle of design, development, and testing is repeated *within each iteration*. Each iteration (called a "sprint" because it is very short—a month or less) delivers a module that is fully functional. If the project is terminated, the customer still has usable results—whatever modules were released. In contrast, a terminated waterfall-approach project often has nothing to show but a bill. Although the agile and the traditional approaches to project management differ, in fact with minor adjustment the project management principles described in this book can be applied equally well to both.[5]

The most popular agile method is called SCRUM. Drawing from a list of features desired by the customer, the SCRUM team selects the ones it will address in the upcoming sprint cycle, which allows the team no more than 30 days to design, code, and test the features. The team monitors its own progress, and meets briefly each day to assess work done and determine next steps. The sprint concludes with the release of a product or module. When the list of features or requirements is long, the requirements are prioritized and the most important ones are attacked first. The system becomes partly operational in a short time, and any limitations in its capability are eliminated in later releases.

Team Involvement in Definition

As requirements and the project plan are being developed, the questions arise: "How do you keep everyone in the project focused on those requirements?" and "How do you develop a project plan that will account for those requirements?" The problem is especially tricky when the project involves numerous people and teams, and spans months or years. Part of the answer is: make the system and project definition a *team effort* incorporating the perspectives of everyone who has or will have a significant stake in the project—customers, suppliers, functional areas such as engineering, marketing, manufacturing, customer service, and purchasing, and users and operators. The more these individuals and groups have a hand in defining requirements and the project plan, the better the project plan will account for the requirements, and the better the requirements will account for their needs throughout the system life cycle. Everyone in the project should be working to the same set of requirements—a master requirements document, RBS, or equivalent. Any additional, necessary requirements should be derived from and compatible with this master document.

In product development projects, a good way to generate product requirements is at an off-site workshop for all the key project stakeholders, including functional groups, users, and suppliers. Beginning with a list of customer needs or requirements, the team develops the system requirements (or, lacking adequate user requirements, develops them too). A facilitator who has no vested interest in the project, which means not the project manager or any involved functional managers, leads the workshop.

Among the foremost practices for actively involving key project stakeholders in requirements definition and project planning are concurrent engineering and quality function deployment. Quality function deployment is covered in the Appendix to this chapter.

4.5   Concurrent Engineering

For any product or system there are many stakeholders, and all want something different from it. The designer wants it to work; the salesperson wants it to sell; the finance person wants it to be profitable; the manufacturing person wants it to be producible; and the customer wants it to meet his needs and not cost too much. The term *concurrent engineering* refers to the *combined* efforts of all these stakeholders to address these wants to the satisfaction of everyone.

The term is somewhat misleading, because concurrent engineering attends not just to engineering but also to marketing, purchasing, finance, quality, and more. It is a team approach to involving engineers, planners, buyers, marketers, customers, and suppliers so that requirements that address all their interests are identified early in the project. It focuses on understanding the requirements and priorities so the end-item can be designed and delivered to meet customer needs, yet is realistic in terms of the capabilities of the producer and its suppliers.

Concurrent engineering teams are sometimes called *design-build teams* because they combine the interests and involvement of designers and builders into a single effort.

Example 4.5: Design-Build Teams at Boeing[6]

At one time in the Boeing factory the production plant was located on the main floor and the engineering group was upstairs. Whenever a problem occurred in the plant, engineers just walked down to take a look. Today, Boeing employs many thousands of people at several locations, and such easy interaction isn't possible. Similar to other large corporations, as Boeing grew, its finance, engineering, manufacturing, and planning units evolved into semiautonomous enclaves, each having strong self-interest and little interaction with one another. In the development of the 777 commercial aircraft, Boeing wanted to change that and implemented the "design-build team" concept, or DBT. Each DBT includes representatives from all involved functional units, customer airlines, and major suppliers. The concept emerged from one question: "How do we make a better airplane?" The answer required not simply a good understanding of aircraft design and manufacture, but also knowledge of aircraft operations and maintenance. To capture such knowledge, customers, manufacturers, and designers joined together early in the project to discuss ways of incorporating all their objectives into the aircraft design.

The formation of DBTs mirrored the physical breakdown of the major subsystems and subcomponents of the airplane. For example, the wing was divided into major subsystems such as wing leading edge and trailing edge, and then further broken down into components such as inboard flap, outboard flap, and ailerons; responsibility for each subsystem and component was handled by a DBT.

The project required 250 DBTs, each with 10–20 members and run like a little company. The teams each met twice weekly for a few hours, following a preset agenda coordinated by a team leader. The concept of having so many people at design meetings—people from airlines, finance, production, and quality—was totally new, but despite so many people representing so many interests there were actually few conflicts.

Since most components in an airplane interact with numerous others, most participants in the program had to be assigned to multiple DBTs (to insure their components would work with other DBT's components). The manufacturing representative, for instance, belonged to 27. He had the duty of telling engineers what would happen when their elegant designs met with the realities of metal, manufacturing processes, and assembly line and maintenance workers, and he made suggestions that would improve maintenance of the airplane. One of his suggestions concerned the cover on the strut-faring that holds the engine to the wing. The faring would contain a lot of electrical and hydraulic components that maintenance personnel would need to access, but engineers had failed to notice that repairing the components would require removal of the entire faring. The manufacturing rep noticed it, however, and suggested that the design include two big doors, one on each side of the faring. This would improve access to the components inside and greatly simplify their repair.

Organizational aspects of concurrent engineering teams are discussed in Chapter 13.

4.6 SYSTEMS DEVELOPMENT IN INDUSTRY AND GOVERNMENT

Most systems and projects follow a pattern similar to the four-phase systems development cycle in Figure 4.1. The following five cases illustrate this.

New Product Development[7]

Jamal Industries is a medium-sized manufacturing firm that produces products for major retailers under their own labels, such as Sears and True Value. Jamal's product development and production is done in the phases of *initiation, feasibility, analysis, design,* and *manufacturing*. The research director is the project manager for Jamal's development projects. Most projects are initiated and implemented internally, though sometimes development and manufacturing work is contracted out. In such cases, Jamal assumes the role of the customer. The following example illustrates such a case.

A competitor had just introduced a computerized timer that would have a major impact on Jamal's market share; in essence, the project was initiated by the competition. To examine project feasibility, Jamal engineers analyzed samples of the competitor's device to see whether they could develop their own version quickly enough to maintain market share. The analysis focused on whether a device as good or better could be made and sold under the retailers' private labels for 20 percent less than the competitor's price. As an alternative, Jamal could seek other distribution channels and try to sell the product under its own label. The feasibility study indicated that Jamal could not design and produce a product in-house for 20 percent below the competitor's price, although channels existed for it to sell the product profitably under its own label.

An in-depth analysis was done to determine how Jamal could contract out the design and production of the product, hence avoiding a capital investment that it could not afford. The research director and his engineering staff analyzed alternatives for contracting out the work, and decided to hire a general contractor to handle all tasks related to the design and manufacture of the product. A foreign contractor was identified that could make a superior timer that Jamal could market at a price $12 lower than the competition. Much of the planning, scheduling, and budgeting associated with the project was delegated to the contractor. Within a year, the product was designed, manufactured, distributed, and on store shelves.

As long as Jamal markets the device, the contractor will produce it. The research director will continue to monitor the contractor to ensure high quality standards are maintained. The rest of Jamal's design team was transferred to other projects.

Software Product Development[8]

In many companies, the typical product development project follows the three phases of planning, development, and stabilization; at Microsoft, however, the process is not strictly sequential, and within phases the steps may go through a series of iterations.

The *planning phase* produces a vision statement, specification document, and plans for marketing, integrating components from other products, testing, and documentation. The phase runs from 3 to 12 months, depending on whether the product is an upgrade or new application. The vision statement guides the entire project; it is a short statement about the goals, focus, and priorities of the product. The specification document is a preliminary definition outline of the product's features and packaging; an ordinary user could describe it in a single sentence. The document starts out small, but expands by as much as 30 percent before the project ends. This document, along with time estimates from developers and the plans for testing, documentation, and customer support, is used to create the project schedule. The planning phase concludes with management approval of the plans and schedule.

The *development phase* is nominally subdivided into four subphases with three internal product-release milestones. Each subphase is scheduled to last between 2 and 3 months. The schedule includes time buffers to accommodate unanticipated problems and to enable the subphase to be completed by the milestone date. The first three subphases are devoted to the development (coding), testing for bugs and functionality, and documentation of a set of major product features. The goal of each subphase is to meet the requirements for a set of product features that would be fully ready to "ship," even though shipping at that point isn't possible because the features have yet to be integrated into the product. In the event that a competitor threatens to release a similar product, the third, or even second, subphase can be bypassed to cut between 4 and 6 weeks from the development process. The product would have fewer features, but would beat the competition to launch. During the fourth subphase, product features are further tested and debugged and a freeze imposed, which means no major changes can be introduced thereafter. This enables the education group to write product documentation that will accurately correspond to the product when released.

The last phase, *stabilization*, consists of internal and external (beta) testing of a product that combines all the features developed in the previous phase. "Zero bug release" occurs when no more bugs remain. Either all bugs are fixed, or features with remaining bugs are removed from the product (to be fixed later and included in subsequent product releases). This phase concludes with the release of a "golden master" disk from which manufacturing will make copies. The project concludes with a project team meeting and postmortem report that outlines what was learned from the project.

Relocation of a Company Division[9]

In recent years the IT division of a large corporation had grown such that it was necessary to relocate to a larger work area. The main activities of the relocation closely parallel the phases of the systems development cycle: Phase I, *concept* (recognize the necessity to relocate); Phase II, *definition* (find a new location, define facility and equipment needs, and obtain designs and construction drawings); Phase III, *acquisition* (build or renovate a facility and purchase equipment); and Phase IV, *implementation* (relocate the division). All phases would be managed by a corporate project team.

Phase I happened by mandate: the division would either relocate or it would "suffocate" out of business. Phase II started with a needs analysis to determine the requirements for the new site, including space for 100 employees and a new computer room. After preliminary budget figures were prepared for the required space of 300,000 square feet for both lease and purchase options, it was decided the space should be leased. Three sites were considered, and a real estate broker and legal consultant were hired to help select the site and conduct contract negotiations. A preliminary design was prepared for each site, showing the location of workstations and work flow. A detailed budget was prepared for leasing arrangements; renovation expenses; furniture, fixture, and telecommunication costs; moving expenses; and plant and office costs. Based upon the budget and design, a site was selected.

Later in Phase II, detailed design and construction drawings were obtained for offices and computer rooms. For the computer rooms, requirements for power, air-conditioning, and data inputs were defined. Bids were secured from and contracts signed with a general contractor, distributors, installation groups, and a furniture manufacturer.

Phase III involved construction work, equipment needs analysis and purchase, and employee training. Vendors performed the electrical, sheet metal, dry wall, painting, HVAC, plumbing, plastering, and carpentry work—supervised by a team from the general contractor.

Meanwhile, bids from several moving companies were reviewed, a company was selected, and a moving schedule was prepared. At the same time, bids were received and contracts signed for procurement and installation of computer workstations, photocopy machines, vending machines, and security systems.

Phase IV, relocation to the new site and equipment installation, was supervised by the corporate project management team. Before and during the move, division employees attended an orientation program. After the move, the team conducted a final check-out to ensure that everything had been completed and all equipment worked properly. The team also met with officials from and established amicable relationships with the local city hall, community college, fire department, and utilities companies.

Overhaul of Human Services Administration[10]

Human Services Administration (HSA) is a city welfare agency that provides financial assistance in the form of money, medical care, and drug rehabilitation treatment to eligible recipients. In administering these services, HSA became plagued by a number of bureaucratic problems:

- Inefficient control measures that allowed for mismanagement and errors in payments
- High increases in the annual cost of the system
- Inadequate control in applicant approvals leading to fraudulent client abuse
- Employee productivity below 40 percent
- Excessive tardiness and absenteeism among employees.

The city's mayor allotted $10 million annually for the implementation and maintenance of a new administrative system to resolve the problems. A group of outside professionals would be hired as a project team to overhaul the system. After the team had resolved the problems, it would become a permanent part of HSA.

The project was to be conducted in four phases: *initiation and problem definition, analysis of solutions, implementation,* and *operation.* During *initiation,* HSA would define overhaul objectives and hire the professionals who would form the project team. In the *analysis* phase, the project team would identify problems and related objectives, and recommend solutions. In the *implementation* phase, the solutions would be executed, giving priority to the most severe problems. And in the *operation* phase, the project team would be interweaved with the existing organization and become an ongoing staff function.

In the initiation phase, project objectives were set:

1. Create a project management team with clear-cut responsibilities and authority
2. Eliminate opposition among members of the existing organization to the overhaul
3. Produce solutions to smaller problems so confidence could be gained and talent identified for working on larger problems
4. Gain taxpayer confidence through media attention to the overhaul project.

In the second phase, the project management team identified specific problem areas and divided them into five categories: new applications, photo identification, addicts, eligibility, and fraud. It then reorganized HSA to create a task force for each category. Each task force was to define problems, document the system, and suggest long-range recommendations and alternatives to the current system. Problems needing immediate attention were singled out and worked on first.

The second and third phases overlapped as solutions to some problems were implemented while other, longer-range problems were still being analyzed. Among the changes introduced was a photo identification system for clients, a more efficient system for processing clients, tighter controls on client eligibility, a computer system for processing and validating payments, tighter auditing controls, greater accountability of personnel, and tighter management controls.

In the final phase HSA was reorganized again, this time to create functional departments that roughly mirrored the structure of the original task forces. Most of the project management team stayed with HSA to assume management and staff positions.

Planetary Exploration Program

The NASA system for organizing and managing projects varies from project to project, but common to all are the phases of (A) *conceptualization*, (B) *study*, (C) *design and development*, and (D) *operations*. Throughout a typical scientific spacecraft program, the project manager has responsibility for all phases of the project. An example of such a project is the hypothetical "Cosmic" project, which included a series of spacecraft for the collection and analysis of geophysical measurements of the planet Mercury.[11]

Phase A, conceptualization, is initiated when, at the urging of scientists, the director for Lunar and Planetary Programs (LPP) at NASA headquarters asks the director of Goddard Space Flight Center to begin preliminary analysis of how NASA might send either a probe or a satellite to Mercury to conduct geophysical experiments. The purpose of Phase A is to determine if the mission is feasible and should be pursued. This involves looking at alternative project approaches, identifying the best ones, defining project elements such as facilities and operational and logistics support, and identifying necessary research or technology development. Phase A is conducted at NASA installations by a study team of NASA scientists and engineers appointed by the director of Goddard. The person chosen as study team leader is someone capable of becoming *project manager* if the concept proves favorable. The person selected is currently the spacecraft manager of a satellite project that is winding down.

At the same time, the director of LPP in Washington assigns a liaison with the Goddard team. If the project is approved, the liaison officer will become the *program manager*. (The distinction between project and program managers was discussed in Chapter 1.)

The preliminary analysis is favorable; the study team's recommendation to prepare a proposal and proceed to Phase B is approved by Goddard management. Phase B, study, involves comparative analysis, detailed study, and preliminary systems design. The study team leader and the liaison officer draft the project proposal and project approval document. The approval document outlines resources, specifies project constraints, defines the number of spacecraft and type of launch vehicle, and allocates funds and labor. Approval, however, is for Phase B only.

The liaison officer coordinates the approval with any necessary approvals from other involved program divisions and offices at NASA headquarters. The approval document is then sent to the top NASA administrator for a decision. With this approval, project "Cosmic" is authorized to begin.

Management formally names the liaison officer as the program manager and the study team leader as the project manager. The project manager assembles a skeleton team to develop specifications for study contracts that will provide data to determine whether or not to proceed further. Estimated schedules and resource requirements for the project are developed. The project team works with functional groups such as launch vehicle, reliability, data acquisition, and launch operations. Relationships are established to provide the necessary lead time for equipment manufacture, testing, and operations. A detailed project plan is prepared outlining technical specifications, manpower, funds, management plans, schedules, milestones, and launch and tracking requirements to meet project objectives.

The project plan is approved by management at Goddard and NASA headquarters, and becomes a contract between them. Headquarters sets up a formal information and control system and makes available the necessary financial resources. The project manager sends monthly (later weekly) reports to the program manager. This is important because, should the project run into difficulties, the program manager can work quickly to obtain or reallocate funds to support it.

The original approval document is updated throughout Phase B, and becomes the authorization document for Phase C or for both Phase C and Phase D. During Phase B, the appropriate experiments are selected and the number of Cosmic flights is put at three. At the completion of Phase B, project Cosmic appears on NASA information and control systems that permit review of financial, schedule, and technical progress. At this point, less than 10 percent of total project costs have been incurred.

During Phase C, contractors become involved in detailed engineering design, development of mock-ups, and completion of detailed specifications on all major subsystems of the Cosmic spacecraft. When the project team completes design and supporting studies, it then develops requests for proposals, reviews proposals, and selects contractors for design, development, fabrication, and testing of final hardware and project operations.

The project manager has two associates: one facilitates coordination between the project and the experimenters, another coordinates activities for modification of the launch vehicle to meet requirements for the three flights. Members of the project team are also working at Cape Kennedy in preparation for the launch, and at the Jet Propulsion Laboratory in California, which handles data acquisition from deep space probes.

When spacecraft fabrication begins, the project manager travels to the contractor's plants, where he spends considerable time in conferences for design and test reviews, quality assurance, components testing, and system integration. Meanwhile, the program manager keeps tabs on the project and keeps it "sold" at NASA. Both managers participate in formal reviews to catch errors at critical points in the project.

Phase D nominally begins with final preparation and launch of the first spacecraft, Cosmic I. The project manager oversees all the teams working in this phase;

these include the NASA launch team, NASA project management and program management, scientists whose experiments are on the spacecraft, contractors and subcontractors that built the spacecraft and launch vehicle, and the Air Force team that controls the missile range. During countdown before launch, only the project manager has authority to make the final irrevocable "go" decision.

Data are recorded between rocket lift-off and successful placement of the spacecraft in trajectory to Mercury. Problems are analyzed so as to avoid repetition with the next spacecraft. Once the spacecraft is on its way and communication and instrumentation are verifiably working and returning usable data, the project manager turns his attention to Cosmic II—now in the Phase C stage. He continues to monitor the Cosmic I operation because lessons from it will be applied to improve the design of Cosmic III, which is, by then, in Phase B.

4.7 SUMMARY

There are good reasons why the systems development cycle appears in so many kinds of projects. First, it emphasizes continuous planning, review, and authorization. At each stage, results are examined and used as the basis for decisions and planning for the next stage. Second, the process is goal oriented—it strives to maintain focus on user requirements and system objectives. Mistakes and problems are caught early and corrected before they get out of control; if the environment changes, timely action can be taken to modify the system or terminate the project. Third, user requirements and system requirements are always in sight and activities are done so they are coordinated and occur at the right time and in the right sequence.

The systems development cycle described in this chapter and Chapter 3 outlines the nominal phases, stages, and activities for projects. It is just an outline, however, and does not describe what does or should happen in all projects. As the above examples show, it can be altered or simplified so that some phases receive more emphasis, some less.

The front-end phases of a project—conceptualization and definition—are important to the viability and success of the project. Surprising is the short-shrift given to user and systems requirements definition in so many projects, and the impetus to begin preparing a plan, without even knowing what the end result of the project is supposed to be. Project definition and system definition go hand in hand; only in cases where there is much latitude in terms of what the customer wants, when he wants it, and how much he is willing to pay can a project succeed in the absence of good requirements. In the more usual case (the customer is more demanding and the schedule and budget are constrained), success is predicated on a well-defined description of what the end-result must be and do—the user requirements and the system requirements.

APPENDIX: QUALITY FUNCTION DEPLOYMENT[12]

QFD is a methodology for defining requirements and, specifically, for translating customer needs into system or product characteristics, and specifying the processes and tasks needed to produce the system or product. As demonstrated in numerous applications, QFD not only yields end-item results that meet customer needs, it also does so in less time and at a lower cost than traditional development methodologies. QFD was developed by Mitsubishi's Kobe Shipyards in 1972, adopted by Toyota in 1978, and has since been implemented by companies throughout the world.

House of Quality[13]

QFD mandates that the project team articulates the means by which the product or system being designed will achieve customer requirements. The process starts with market needs or customer requirements, then uses a planning matrix called the *House of Quality* to translate the needs or requirements into technical requirements. The structure of the house is shown in Figure 4.7.

- The left side of the matrix lists "what" the customer needs or requires
- The top of the matrix lists the design attributes or technical requirements of the product; these are "how" the product can meet customer requirements
- Additional sections on the top, right, and bottom sides show correlations among the requirements, comparisons to competitors, technical assessments, and target values.

Features of the house of quality are illustrated in Example A4.1.

Example A4.1: House of Quality for a TV Remote-Control Switch

Figure 4.8 is a portion of the house of quality matrix for the design of a television remote-control (RC) switch. The house is interpreted as follows:

- Rows (Customer requirements): these are what customers think is important about the product. They are the product "whats."
- Importance to customer: the requirements have been rank ordered 1–6 by customer preference; "multifunction buttons" is rated the highest, "RC easy to see/find" the lowest.
- Columns (technical requirements): these are the *requirements* or *attributes* of the product, the ways that the product meets customer requirements. They are the product "hows."

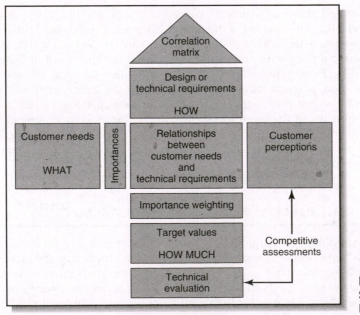

Figure 4.7
Structure of the house of quality.

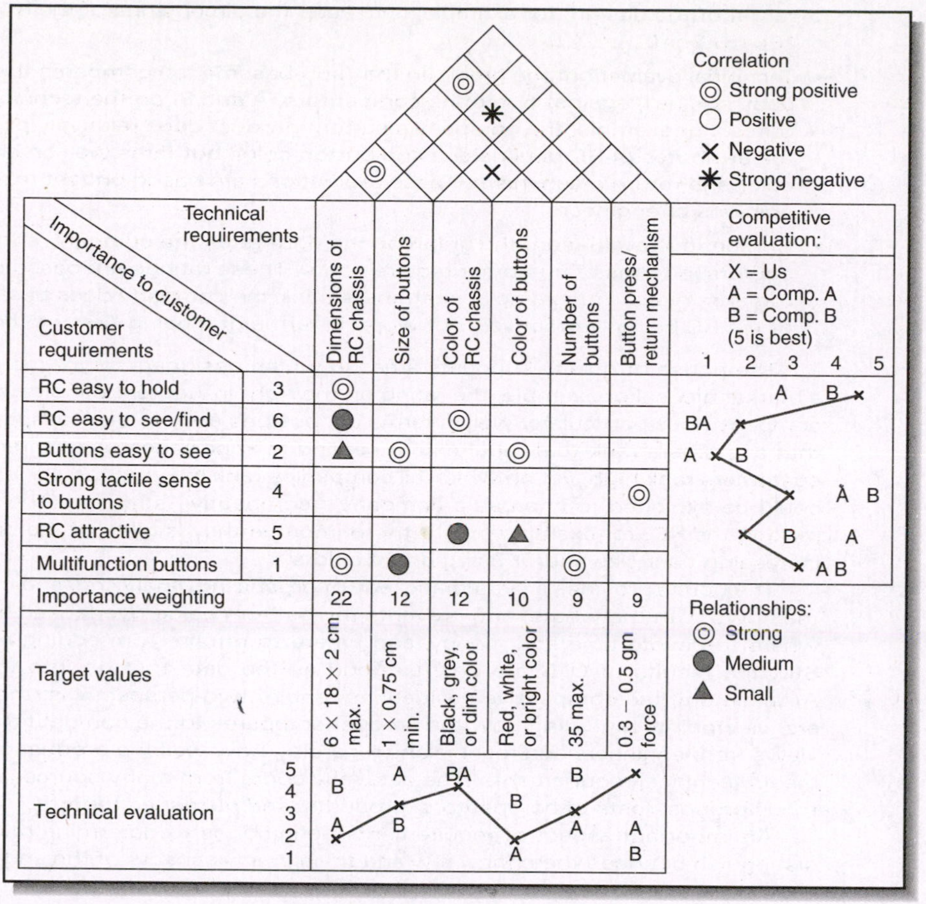

House of quality diagram (Figure 4.8):

Correlation
- ◎ Strong positive
- ○ Positive
- ✕ Negative
- ✳ Strong negative

Competitive evaluation:
X = Us
A = Comp. A
B = Comp. B
(5 is best)

Relationships:
- ◎ Strong
- ● Medium
- ▲ Small

Customer requirements	Importance to customer	Dimensions of RC chassis	Size of buttons	Color of RC chassis	Color of buttons	Number of buttons	Button press/ return mechanism
RC easy to hold	3	◎					
RC easy to see/find	6	●		◎			
Buttons easy to see	2	▲	◎		◎		
Strong tactile sense to buttons	4						◎
RC attractive	5			●	▲		
Multifunction buttons	1	◎	●			◎	
Importance weighting		22	12	12	10	9	9
Target values		6 × 18 × 2 cm max.	1 × 0.75 cm min.	Black, grey, or dim color	Red, white, or bright color	35 max.	0.3 – 0.5 gm force

Technical evaluation (scale 1–5) and Competitive evaluation charts shown to the right and bottom of the matrix.

Figure 4.8
House of quality for television remote-control switch.

- **Central matrix:** this contains symbols that show the strength of the relationship between the whats and the hows (strong positive, positive, negative, strong negative). For example, "buttons easy to see" has a strong positive relationship to the size and color of the buttons, and a positive relationship to the size of the remote-control chassis. Note that each relationship has a numerical weighting (small=1, medium=3, strong=9).

- **Importance weighting:** the weights of the symbols in each column are summed to determine the relative importance of the technical attributes. Thus, the most important technical attribute is "dimensions of the RC" (weight=9+3+1+9= 22), followed by "size of buttons" and "color of RC chassis" (9+3=12 each).

- **Gabled roof:** this contains the correlations among the technical attributes. For example, "dimensions of the RC chassis" has a strong positive correlation with "size of buttons" and "number of buttons"; "size of buttons" has a strong negative correlation with "number of buttons" (smaller buttons allow more buttons; larger buttons allow fewer).

- **Target values:** the numerical or qualitative descriptions (in the "basement" of the house) are design targets set for the technical attributes. One target of the design, for example, is to keep the dimensions of the RC within "6×18×2 cm."

- Technical evaluation: the graph (in the "sub-basement") compares the company (x="us") against two of its competitors, A and B, on the technical attributes. For example, the company's current product does relatively poorly on the attributes of RC dimensions and button color, but fares well on chassis color and return mechanism. These evaluations are based on test results and opinions of engineers.

- Competitive evaluation: the graph on the right rates the company and its competitors in terms of customer requirements. These ratings are based on customer surveys. For example, customers think the company does best in terms of the RC being "attractive," but worst in terms of it being "easy to hold."

The house of quality suggests areas in which designers might focus to gain a market niche. For example, the rating on the right in Figure 4.8 indicates that no company does particularly well in terms of "buttons easy to see" despite the fact that customers rank that requirement second in importance. A requirement that customers rank high, yet on which all companies rank low suggests a feature that could be exploited to improve a company's competitive standing. The company making the RC, for example, might try to improve the visibility of the buttons by increasing their size and/or using bright colors.

The house provides a systematic way of organizing, analyzing, and comparing the hows with the whats, and prevents things from being overlooked. It justifies where to devote time and money, and where to refrain from adding resources. Still, the results of QFD are only as good as the data that go into the house. At minimum, the competitive evaluations require two perspectives: the customers' viewpoints regarding how the product compares to the competition, and the views from engineers and technicians regarding how well the product objectively meets technical requirements. The data may come from many sources, including focus groups, tests of competitors' products, and published reports.

An important aspect of requirements definition is to determine priorities—to distinguish between the *critical few* and *trivial many* aspects of the end-item system so as to ensure that the critical ones are done correctly. As an example, a computer printer might have as many as 30 different design features that affect print quality, but the most important feature is the fusion process of melting toner on the page, which is a function of the right combination of temperature, pressure, and time. Focusing on temperature, pressure, and time narrows the design emphasis to the relatively few technical parameters of greatest importance to performance.[14] These parameters become the ones for which designers seek the "optimum" values. Once the optimum values have been set, the analysis moves on to identify important factors in the manufacturing process necessary to achieve the design requirements. The house of quality is just the first of several steps in the QFD process that leads to a project plan.

QFD Process[15]

The QFD process employs a series of matrices in a multi-phased approach to project planning. For example, the process shown in Figure 4.9 utilizes four matrices that correspond to four phases of a project: project planning, product design, process planning, and process control planning. The phases (circled numbers) are as follows.

1. Create the first matrix, the "house of quality" (A). This converts customer needs or requirements into technical requirements.
2. Develop an initial version of the project plan based upon requirements from the house of quality. The house of quality does not have to be completed to begin preparing the project plan. Start with a rudimentary plan using information

available from the house, then expand the plan as new requirements emerge in the updated matrix.

3. Create the next matrix, the design matrix (B). This matrix converts technical requirements from the house matrix into product design features and requirements.
4. Create the process matrix (C). This matrix converts design features and requirements from the design matrix into process steps or production requirements.
5. Create the control matrix (D). This matrix converts process steps or production requirements from the process matrix into process tracking and control procedures.
6. Refine the project plan to incorporate aspects of the design, process, and control matrices.

The matrices highlight the information needed to make decisions about product definition, design, production, and delivery, and they link the work requirements in the four phases so that customer needs and technical requirements as defined early in the process are translated undistorted into design features and production requirements. As shown in Figure 4.9, the link is achieved by taking the requirements or activities from the top of one matrix and putting them on the left side of the matrix in the next phase.

This linking of matrices ensures traceability (that word again)—that any project activity can be traced to the customer need or requirement that it fulfills, and, conversely, that every customer need and requirement can be traced to the necessary project activities. Put another way, QFD ensures that every activity serves a

Figure 4.9
QFD multiphase, multimatrix approach to project planning.

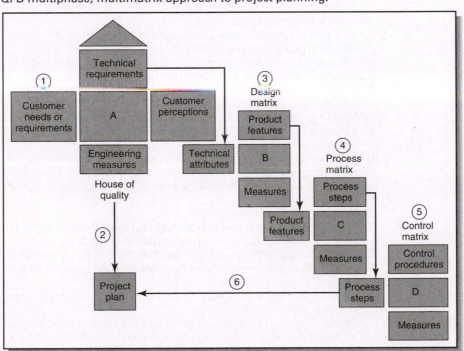

requirement, and every requirement is served by at least one activity. The result is a plan where every task throughout the project life cycle is integrated with the technical requirements listed in the original house of quality. The next chapter describes further aspects of an integrated project plan.

Although the QFD process takes longer to produce a project plan and an initial product design, it reduces the time to produce the *final* design because less redesign and fewer engineering changes are needed after the product goes into production and to the customer.

Example A4.2: Chrysler Development of the LH Car Line[16]

Chrysler first applied QFD in the design and development of its LH-platform cars (Chrysler Concorde and Dodge Intrepid). Early in the product concept stage, a program team was formed to establish overall design guidelines. The program team allocated responsibility for the different major automobile systems to different design groups (as did Boeing in its teams), and each group set up a QFD team to determine system-level requirements. Once requirements were set, smaller groups were formed to focus on designing the components within the system.

The QFD methodology was part of a broader concurrent engineering effort that yielded impressive results: the total LH design cycle took 36 months versus the historical 54–62 months; prototype cars were ready 95 weeks before production launch versus the traditional 60 weeks; and the program required 740 people compared to the usual 1,600 people. The cars received numerous awards and magazine citations for design excellence.

REVIEW QUESTIONS AND PROBLEMS

1. When does the project manager become involved in the project?
2. What is the purpose of the Kickoff meeting? When is the meeting held, and who runs it?
3. How is the project team created?
4. Describe briefly the contents of a project master plan.
5. Describe phased project planning.
6. What are user requirements, system requirements, and system specifications? Give examples. How are they related?
7. What are functional requirements? What are performance requirements? Give examples.
8. What are "non-functional requirements"? Give examples.
9. Describe the process of developing user requirements and system specifications.
10. What problems are associated with requirements definition? What are ways to minimize these problems?
11. What is the purpose of specifying priorities and margins in defining requirements?
12. Describe concurrent engineering.
13. How are the various functional areas and subcontractors involved in the requirements definition and project planning process?
14. Briefly define the purpose of quality function deployment (QFD).
15. What is the source of customer needs or requirements that appear in the house of quality?
16. How do you think the QFD process can be used as part of concurrent engineering?
17. Think about the following, or use whatever consumer research material is available to you, to define customer needs or requirements for the following:

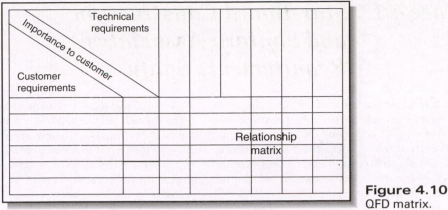

Figure 4.10
QFD matrix.

a. A "good" college course
b. Toaster (or other home appliance of your choosing)
c. Cellular telephone
d. Coffee mug for your car.

For each, define a corresponding set of physical or technical characteristics. Using the format of Figure 4.10, construct a house of quality matrix and show the relationship between the technical characteristics and customer requirements. Use the matrix in each case to "design" or suggest what the ideal product or service would be like or look like.

18. What is the purpose of the project charter? What is included in the charter?
19. To what situations does agile project management apply? How does it differ from the traditional "waterfall" model?

Questions About the Study Project

1. Did the project have a Kickoff meeting? What happened there?
2. How did the project manager become involved in the project? Was she selected as project manager before or after the proposal was completed?
3. How was the project team formed?
4. Were there user requirements? How were they defined? Were they "well-defined" requirements?
5. Were there any system requirements? Were they clear and utilized by the project team?
6. Were there any system specifications and performance requirements? If not, how did the project team know what was required of the end-item?
7. Did the project have a master plan? If so, describe the contents. If not, how did the team know what they were supposed to do (tasks, schedules, responsibilities, etc.)?
8. Describe the process to create the project plan.
9. Did different stakeholders participate in defining the requirements and creating the project plan?
10. Was QFD or a similar process used to define requirements and/or create the project plan?
11. What is your overall impression about how well the definition phase was conducted in the project, and of the quality of the system requirements and project plan?

Case 4.1 Star-Board Construction and Santaro Associates: Requirements Snafu

Star-Board Construction (SBC) is the prime contractor for a large skyscraper project in downtown Manhattan. SBC is working directly from drawings received from the architect, Santaro Associates (SA). Robert Santaro, owner and chief architect of SA, viewed this building as similar to others he had designed. However, one difference between this building and the others he overlooked was the building's facing, which was to consist of large granite slabs—slabs much larger than anything with which either he or SBC had prior experience.

Halfway into the project, Kent Star, project manager for SBC, starts to receive reports from his site superintendent about recurring problems with window installation. The windows are factory units, premanufactured according to SA's specifications. The granite facing on the building has been installed according to specifications that allow for dimensional variations in the window units. The architect provided the specification that the tolerance for each window space should be 1/2-inch (that is, the window space between granite slabs could vary as much as 1/4 inch larger or smaller than the specified value). This created a problem for the construction crew, which found the granite slabs too big to install with such precision. As a result, the spacing between slabs is often too small, making it difficult or impossible to install window units. Most of the 2,000 window units for the building have already been manufactured, so it is too late to change their specifications, and most of the granite slabs have been hung on the building. The only recourse for fitting window units into tight spaces is to grind away the granite. It is going to be very expensive, and will certainly delay completion of the building.

QUESTION

What steps or actions should the architect and contractor have taken, before committing to the specifications on the window units and spacing between granite slabs, that would have prevented this problem?

Case 4.2 Revcon Products and Welbar, Inc.: Client–Contractor Communication

Revcon Products manufactures valves for controlling the water level in industrial tanks. It had concentrated on products for the construction industry (valves for newly-installed tanks), but now wanted to move into the much larger and more lucrative replacement market. Whereas annual demand for new valves is about 100,000, it is about 1 million for replacement valves. The company envisioned a new valve, the Millennium Valve, as a way to gain a share in the tank-valve replacement market. Revcon's objective was to design and produce the Millennium Valve to be of superior quality and lower cost than the competition.

Revcon decided to outsource the development and design of the new valve. It prepared an RFP with the following objectives and requirements.

1. Product objectives:
   - Innovative design to distinguish the Millennium Valve from competitors' valves
   - Price competitive, but offer greater value.
2. Market (user) requirements:
   - Ease of installation
   - Non-clogging
   - Quiet operation
   - Ease in setting water level
   - Adjustable height.

Revcon sent the RFP to four design companies and selected Welbar, Inc., primarily based on it being the lowest bidder. Welbar's proposal was written by its sales and marketing departments and revised by senior management, but had no input from industrial designers, engineers, or anyone else who would work on the project. Welbar had no prior experience with industrial water valves, but its sales team saw Millennium as an opportunity to earn profits and align with a major equipment manufacturer. The marketing department prepared time and cost estimates using standard tasks and work packages from proposals for old projects.

The Welbar design team for the Millennium project was headed by Karl Fitch, a seasoned engineer, and included two industrial designers and two engineers. His first task was to research the valve market and talk to contractors, plumbers, and retailers. Karl reviewed the proposal, and divided the project into small work packages and prepared a Gantt chart. He concluded that the proposal had omitted several critical steps, and that its cost was substantially underestimated.

Throughout the project, the design concept, work tasks, and schedules had to be changed many times. Welbar engineers were frustrated at Revcon's constant harping about the need for both low cost and functional superiority. It could be done, but Revcon also wanted a speedy, low-cost development effort. During the project, Welbar engineers learned that to design such a valve required more resources than had been budgeted. Because of all the changes, Welbar exceeded the budget and had to request additional funds from Revcon four times. A major problem occurred when Welbar delivered a prototype to Revcon. Because the description of the prototype in the proposal was vague, Revcon expected the prototype to be a virtually finished product, whereas Welbar understood it to be a simple working model to demonstrate functionality. Extra time and money had to be spent to bring the prototype up to Revcon's expectation. To compensate, Welbar crammed project stages together. When the design stage fell behind because of the prototype, Welbar went ahead and prepared production-ready models. The finished prototype later demonstrated that the production models could not be produced.

Eventually, Welbar did design a truly innovative valve; however, the design would require substantial retooling of the factory and cost 50 percent more to produce than expected. In the end, Revcon spent twice as much time and money on development as expected. Because of that, the product could not be priced low enough to be competitive.

QUESTION

What happened to this project? What are the factors that contributed to Revcon's failure to get the product it wanted? For each factor, discuss what might have been done differently.

Case 4.3 Lavasoft.com: Interpreting Customer Requirements

Lavasoft Company is developing new website software for one of its corporate clients. The project starts out when a few Lavasoft staffers meet with the client to document a list of user needs and requirements. When they finish, they turn the list over to the Lavasoft design team.

The project manager, Lakshmi Singh, feels that the kind of system best suited to the user's needs is more or less obvious, and she creates some bullet points and flowcharts to address them. She then presents these to the design team and asks if anyone has questions. Some people are concerned that the approach as stated by the bullets and charts is too vague, but Lakshmi assures them that the vagueness will subside as details of the system are defined.

To speed up decision-making and reduce outside interference, the team works in relative isolation from other development teams in the company. Daily, the team is forced to interpret the bullet points and high-level charts and to make design decisions. Whenever there is disagreement about interpretation, Lakshmi makes the decision. The team creates a list of detailed system specifications, and the project is considered on schedule. Upon working to the specifications, however, issues arise concerning the system's compatibility with the client's existing site. Further, some of the specifications call for technical expertise that the team lacks. The design team goes back to the original user needs and discovers that some of the specifications are unrelated to the needs, and for some of the needs there are no specifications.

The team drops some of the specifications and adds new ones. This requires eliminating some of the existing code, writing new code, and retesting the system, which puts the project behind schedule. Resistance grows to changing the specifications further, since that would require even more recoding and delay the project further. Lakshmi adds people to the project to get it back on schedule. Eventually the system is ready for installation, although it is 2 months late. Because more people were needed to staff the project, Lavasoft does not make a profit. Because the specifications were incorrect, the system is not fully compatible with the client's website and Lavasoft must continue to work on it and introduce "fixes."

QUESTIONS

1. What went wrong with the project?
2. Where mistakes were made in the project initially?
3. How were problems allowed to persist and go uncorrected for so long?

Case 4.4 Proposed Gold Mine in Canada: Phased Project Planning

July 12, 2006: Peter's firm acquires the rights to an ore body in the Canadian Shield region. The firm is considering developing a new mine there, and Peter is responsible for proposing a project plan to the board in September. The mine will take a few years to reach full production, and there is much uncertainty as to the price of gold when that happens. Peter includes in his proposal a history of gold prices (Figure 4.11).

August 2, 2006: Peter meets with Bruce, a mining engineer with two decades of experience in Australian gold mines, and Sam, a geologist who, a few years back, did exploratory work on gold deposits in the Canadian Shield region. They discuss known facts about the ore body, the likelihood of unforeseen geological phenomena that could jeopardize mine development, production figures that might be achieved, and production costs and technical problems that might be experienced in extracting gold from the ore. A quick calculation shows that 300,000 ounces of gold per year at $700 per ounce would be very lucrative, but a figure of 150,000 ounces at $400 per ounce, 3 years from now, would lead to large losses that could ruin the company. Current information about the ore body is inadequate, however, and it will be necessary to drill explora-

tion holes to learn more about the general geology of the area.

Peter summarizes:

> To the best of our knowledge, we could produce anywhere between 150,000 and 300,000 ounces a year. The capital cost for developing the shaft will be US $150 million to $260 million, and annual operational costs could be $60 million to $100 million. Exploration to provide information on the ore body would require drilling 200 exploration holes at a cost of somewhere between $1.2 million and $1.6 million. Rock samples from these holes will be analyzed in a laboratory to determine the gold content.

Peter instructs Sam to review the data from his previous exploration work and to prepare a report of his recommendations concerning the future exploration. He is authorized to spend no more than $25,000 on this "paper exercise." They agree that, should the exploration holes yield good results, a "demonstration shaft" will be sunk to haul out a sample of 30,000 tons of ore to be processed to extract gold. Results from this demo would increase confidence about the amount of

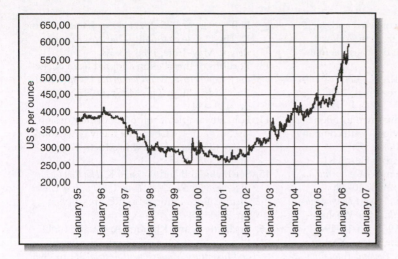

Figure 4.11
Gold prices.

gold present, reduce uncertainty about processing the ore, and provide a good indication of potential yields. They estimate that the demo shaft and analysis would cost $18 million to $25 million, some of which, however, could be deducted from the cost of the full-fledged mine—should it go ahead. Only if these results are positive—and the gold price is relatively high and stable as of that stage—would the development of a full-fledged shaft be authorized.

QUESTIONS

1. List the phases of the project and indicate the minimum and maximum cost of each phase as foreseen in August 2006.
2. "While estimates for the distant future are very 'broad brush,' it is always possible to make relatively accurate estimates for the imminent phase of a project." Explain.
3. Describe how each of the proposed project phases will help reduce the risk of the project.
4. Comment on the problem that, once money has been allocated to the process, people might become "hooked" into the project and be tempted to go ahead regardless of high risks.
5. How would you determine the value of accurate estimates for the number of ounces that could be mined and for costs?
6. Would you trust any internal rate of return or net present value estimates at this time?

NOTES

1. For advice in naming projects, see Gause D and Weinberg G. *Exploring Requirements: Quality Before Design.* New York, NY: Dorset House; 1989. pp. 128–134.
2. See Frame JD. *Managing Projects in Organization.* San Francisco, CA: Jossey-Bass; 1988. pp. 146–151.
3. Hajek V. *Management of Engineering Projects*, 3rd edn. New York, NY: McGraw-Hill; 1984. pp. 35–37; Whitten N. *Managing Software Development Projects*, 2nd edn. New York, NY: John Wiley & Sons; 1995. pp. 250–255.
4. Connell J and Shafer L. *Structured Rapid Prototyping.* Upper Saddle River, NJ: Yourdan Press/Prentice Hall; 1989.
5. Sliger M. *Relating PMBOK Practices to Agile Practices*, at StickyMinds.com, http://www.stickyminds.com/sitewide.asp?Function=e detail&ObjectType=/COL&ObjectId=10365 &tth=DYN&tt=siteemail&iDyn=2%20to%20 Agile%20Practices, accessed Feb. 17, 2010.
6. Portions adapted from Sabbagh K. *Twenty-First Century Jet: The Making and Marketing of the Boeing 777.* New York, NY: Scribner; 1996.

7. Based upon information collected and documented by Cary Morgen from interviews with managers of Jamal Industries (factual case, fictitious name).

8. Cusumano M and Selby R. *Microsoft Secrets*. New York, NY: Free Press; 1995. pp. 192–207.

9. Based upon an actual company relocation and data collected from interviews with company managers by Pam Paroubek.

10. This example is adapted from Harris KL. Organizing to overhaul a mess. *California Management Review* 17(3); 1975: 40–49.

11. Based upon Chapman RL. *Project Management in NASA: The System and the Men*. Washington, DC: NASA, SP-324; 1973. pp. 13–19.

12. Sources for this section: Bounds G, Yorks L, Adams M, and Ranney G. *Beyond Total Quality Management*. New York, NY: McGraw–Hill; 1994. pp. 275–282; Hauser J and Clausing D. The House of Quality. *Harvard Business Review* May–June; 1988: 63–73.

13. Portions of this section adopted from Nicholas J. *Competitive Manufacturing Management*. Burr Ridge, IL: Irwin/McGraw-Hill; 1998. pp. 428–434.

14. For an example of computer printer design, see Survant TG. Changing the way we think is key to successful new products. *Target* 11(2); 1995: 9–15.

15. See Bicknell B and Bicknell K. *The Road Map to Repeatable Success: Using QFD to Implement Change*. Boca Raton, FL: CRC Press; 1995. pp. 97–110.

16. Lockamy A and Khurana A. Quality function deployment: a case study. *Production and Inventory Management Journal* 36(2); 1995: 56–59.

Part III

Systems and Procedures for Planning and Control

*P*roject management extends far beyond defining project objectives and requirements; it involves forming a project organization, identifying the necessary tasks and the resources to do them, and providing leadership to get the tasks done. Overall project objectives and system requirements need to be articulated into detailed plans, schedules, and budgets to accomplish the objectives and requirements. Measures are then needed to make sure the plans and schedules are carried out as intended.

Over the years, an impressive collection of methods has been developed to help project managers define, plan, and direct project work. The next eight chapters describe these methods, which include techniques and procedures for specifying, scheduling, and budgeting project activities, assessing risks, organizing and keeping records, and monitoring and controlling work to achieve project quality, time, and cost requirements.

Procedures should be conducted within a framework to ensure that everything needed is accounted for, properly organized, and executed. These frameworks and the structures, activities, and systems that comprise them—work breakdown structures, cost accounting systems, information systems, and many others—are described in this section of the book.

Chapters in this section address all nine PMBOK knowledge areas: Chapters 5 and 11, *integration management*; Chapter 5, *scope management* and *human resource management*; Chapters 6 and 7, *time management*; Chapter 8, *cost management*; Chapter 9, *quality management*; Chapter 10, *risk management*; Chapter 11, *communication management*; and Chapters 5, 11, and 12, *procurement management*.

Planning Fundamentals

> *Big fleas hath smaller fleas*
> *upon their backs to bite 'em.*
> *And these fleas have smaller fleas*
> *And so ad infinitum.*

—*Jonathan Swift*

Every project is somewhat unique since it is aimed toward an end-item or result that is itself in some way unique. Because of its uniqueness, basic questions about the project must be addressed and satisfactorily answered before work can begin. Answering these questions such that the project will achieve its goals is the function of project planning.

There are two essential parts to project management: (1) During the conception and definition phases a *plan is prepared* that specifies the project requirements, work tasks, responsibilities, schedules, and budgets; (2) during the execution phase, the work in the *plan is performed* and project *progress is tracked* versus the plan. This chapter gives an overview of the first part, and covers the topics of scope and work definition, elemental scheduling, and procurement management.

5.1   PLANNING STEPS

After a business need, contract request, or RFP has been received, top management releases funds to prepare an initial plan, schedule, and cost estimate for the project proposal. Approval of the project and the signing of a contract authorize the project to begin, starting with the definition of system requirements and preparation of a project master plan. For internal projects, a *project charter* is sent to stakeholders to announce and briefly describe the project.

The project manager, if not already assigned or involved, is now identified to oversee the planning process and produce a plan that elaborates on any earlier plans as prepared for the proposal, business case study, or charter.

Because each project is unique, there is never an *a priori*, established way of how the project should be done. Each project poses new questions regarding *what*, *how*, by *whom*, in *what order*, *for how much*, and by *when*, and the purpose of planning is to answer them. The planning process answers the questions in the following steps:

1. **What?**
   The process defines the project *objectives*, *scope*, and *system requirements*. These specify the project deliverables, end-items, and other sought results, as well as the time, cost, and performance targets.
2. **How?**
   It defines the *work activities*, tasks, or jobs to be done to achieve the objectives and requirements. These activities include everything necessary to create and deliver the end-item or deliverables, including planning, control, and administration activities.
3. **Who?**
   It specifies the *project organization*—the individuals or departments, subcontractors, and managers that will perform and manage the work, and specifies their responsibilities.
4. **When, in what order?**
   It creates a *schedule* showing the timing of work activities, deadlines, and milestone dates.
5. **How much and when?**
   The process creates a *budget* and *resource plan* to fund and support the project.
6. **How well?**
   It specifies a method for tracking and controlling project work, which is necessary to keep the project conforming to the schedule, budget, and user and system requirements.

This chapter and the next seven chapters discuss these steps in detail.

5.2   THE PROJECT MASTER PLAN

Project planning begins early in the project life cycle—in most cases with preparation of the proposal. While preparing the proposal a rudimentary project team is organized, and the team prepares a brief summary plan for inclusion in the proposal. This plan is prepared using the same, albeit more abbreviated, procedures as are used to develop more elaborate and detailed project master plans. The difference between a proposal summary plan and a project master plan is that the former is aimed at the customer, while the latter is aimed at the project team.[1] The planning effort in preparing the proposal is directed at estimating the project duration, cost, and needed resources. The proposal summary plan includes just enough information about the project and price to enable the customer to make a decision.

In contrast, the project master plan lays out specifics of the project that will serve as a roadmap to *guide* the project team throughout the project execution. As mentioned in Chapter 4, usually the plan contains details only for the immediate upcoming phase of the project, about which the most is known. Details for later project phases are filled in later as more information becomes available.

Contents of Master Plans

Contents of master plans vary depending on the size, complexity, and nature of the project. Figure 5.1 shows a template for a typical master plan as outlined in Chapter 4.[2]

Elements of a Project Master Plan

I. Scope, Charter, or Statement of Work
Overview description of the project oriented towards management, customer, and stakeholders. Includes a brief description of the project, objectives, overall requirements, constraints, risks, problem areas and solutions, master schedule showing major events and milestones.

II. Management and Organization Section.
 A. Project management and organization: key personnel and authority relationships.
 B. Manpower: Workforce requirements estimates: skills, expertise, and strategies for locating and recruiting qualified people.
 C. Training and development: Executive development and personnel training necessary to support the project.

III. Technical Section. Major project activities, timing, and cost.
 A. High-level **user requirements** and **system requirements.**
 B. **Work breakdown structure**: Work packages and detailed description of each, including resources, costs, schedules, and risks.
 C. **Responsibility assignments**: List of key personnel and their responsibilities for work packages and other areas of the project.
 D. **Project schedules**: Generalized project and task schedules showing major events, milestones, and points of critical action or decision.
 E. **Budget**: Control accounts and sources of financial support: Budgets and timing of all capital and developmental expenses.
 F. **Quality plan**: Measures for monitoring quality and accepting results for individual work tasks, components, and end-item assemblies.
 G. Areas of uncertainity, and **risk plan**: Risk strategies, contingency and mitigation plans for areas posing greatest risk.
 H. **Work review plan**: Procedures for periodic review of work, what is to be reviewed, by whom, when, and according to what standards.
 I. **Testing plan** (may be included in work review plan): Listing of items to be tested, test procedures, timing, and persons responsible.
 J. **Change control plan**: Procedures for review and handling of requests for changes or defacto changes to any aspect of the project.
 K. **Documentation policy/plan**: List of documents to be produced, format, timing, and how they will be organized and maintained.
 L. **Procurement policy/plan**: policy, budget, schedule, plan, and controls for all for goods, work, and services to be procured externally.
 M. **Implementation plan**: Procedures to guide customer conversion to or adoption of project deliverables.

Figure 5.1
Template for project master plan.

Depending on the customer and type of project contract, the plan might require additional items not outlined here;[3] in small or low-cost projects it is possible to bypass some of the items, being careful not to overlook the crucial ones. It is good practice to carefully review every item in the template, even if only to verify that some are "N/A" (not applicable). An example project master plan for the LOGON Project is at the end of the book in Appendix C.

You might notice similarities between the sections of the plan and the contents of the proposal described in Figure 3.6. Although the format is different, indeed there are similarities. Sometimes the proposal, after revision to reflect updates, agreements, and contract specifications, becomes the project master plan. More often, however, the proposal serves as an outline for the master plan, and the master plan is more expansive than the proposal. Because the primary audience of the master plan is the project team and not the customer, the sections on work definition, schedule, and budget in the plan are much more detailed than in the proposal.

As illustrated in the following example, sometimes development of the project master plan is an evolutionary, multidisciplinary process.

Example 5.1: Developing a Project Plan for LOGON Project at Iron Butterfly Company

Iron Butterfly Company is a medium-sized engineering and manufacturing firm specializing in warehousing and materials handling systems. It purchases most of the subsystems and components for its product systems from vendors and then combines them to meet customer requirements. The company was awarded a large contract for a robotic system to place, store, retrieve, and route shipping containers by the MPD Company. The system, called the Logistical Online System, LOGON, is to be developed and installed at MPD's Chicago distribution center. Iron Butterfly is responsible for design, assembly, and installation of the system. Two of its contractors, CRC and CreativeRobotics, will provide the computer and robotics systems as well as assistance with their design, installation, and checkout. Frank Wesley is the project manager, and was also in charge of preparing the proposal.

Most of the project master plan for LOGON originated in Iron Butterfly's project proposal. In preparing the proposal, engineers from Iron Butterfly, CRC, and CreativeRobotics worked together to design a system that covered all of MPD's requirements. The design included schematics, operational specifications, and a bill of materials. From the design, managers at CRC and CreativeRobotics estimated the labor expertise needed and the costs for parts and labor. At Iron Butterfly, Frank Wesley and his engineers prepared a work breakdown structure (WBS) and estimates for their own time and costs. He then combined these with CRC's and CreativeRobotics' estimates to arrive at an overall plan, schedule, and price for the proposal.

After winning the contract, Frank met with his project engineer and managers from the fabrication, software, and purchasing departments to review the design, project plan, costs, and schedules, and to prepare a detailed master plan. This plan contained much the same information as the proposal, but was updated and expanded to include schedules for procured materials and parts, plans for labor distribution across work tasks, a task responsibility matrix, a detailed WBS and associated budget, and a master schedule.

In the LOGON project the master plan evolved in stages: it was initially created during proposal preparation, but was then expanded and modified after contract signing. In many projects, however, particularly for large, complex systems, the proposal serves only as a reference, and the bulk of project planning happens *after* the contract is signed (i.e., in the definition phase). In such cases, project planning is itself a significant effort that requires substantial time and labor.

Learning from Past Projects

Oftentimes organizations approach each project as being *too* unique and ignore the lessons of history—the mistakes, solutions, and lessons learned of the past.[4] No project is ever totally unique, so in developing the project plan it makes sense to refer to earlier, similar projects, their plans, procedures, successes, and failures. Ideally the project manager is provided with planning assistance in the form of lessons learned, best practices, suggested methodologies and templates, and even consultation based upon experience from past projects. Sometimes the project manager receives this assistance from the project management office (PMO), described in Chapter 16. Lessons learned and best practices are compiled from the *post-project summary* or *project post-mortem* reports of past projects; these are formal retrospective reports created at project termination that describe what went well, what went wrong, and any lessons derived from the project experience (described in Chapter 12). They provide useful guidance in planning future projects, and help managers avoid reinventing the wheel and repeating mistakes.

5.3 SCOPE AND STATEMENT OF WORK

Project planning starts with defining the objectives, deliverables, and major tasks of the project; in combination, these determine the overall size of the project and the range or extent of work it encompasses—the concept of *project scope*. Determining the project scope happens during project conception, first when the project is initiated and during preparation of the RFP and the proposal, and again during project definition. In each case, user needs and requirements are compared to time, cost, resource, and technology constraints to determine what the project should and can encompass. The process of setting the project scope is called scope definition.

Scope Definition

Scope definition involves specifying the breadth of the project and the full span of its outputs, end-results, or deliverables. The defined end-items to be produced or delivered by the project are termed "inclusions," meaning they are *included* in the project. To ensure clarity, the items, conditions, or results *not* to be included in the project, i.e., "exclusions," are also defined; for example, a project to construct a building might exclude the building's landscaping and interior decorating. Distinguishing between inclusions (contractor responsibilities) and exclusions (possible customer responsibilities) prevents misunderstanding and false expectations.

Scope definition focuses primarily on determining outputs and deliverables, not on time and cost. Of course, time and cost delimit or dictate the potential deliverables; as such, in the scope definition they must be accounted for as "constraints."

The outcome of scope definition is a *scope statement* that describes the main deliverables of the project, criteria for acceptance of the deliverables, assumptions and constraints (to provide rationale as to why the project has these deliverables and not others), functions to be fulfilled by the deliverables, brief background about the problem being addressed or the opportunity being exploited, project objectives, user requirements or high-level specifications, and high-level project tasks or major areas of work. The input information for scope definition includes a set of user needs and requirements, a business case or other expression of needs, and constraints and assumptions; ideally the principal subsystems and components of the end-item will have been identified and also serve as inputs. Everything to be included as part of the project or contract, including support and side-items, as well as work areas or deliverables *not to be included* in the project (exclusions), are mentioned. The scope statement sometimes also lists outcomes or consequences to be *avoided*, such as negative publicity, interference with other systems, pollution, or damage to the natural environment. Rather than repeat the detailed requirements and specifications, the scope statement normally refers to or incorporates other documents that contain them.

When the project is unique, the preliminary scope statement defined during project initiation might be somewhat vague; it should, however, be expanded and clarified during project definition as detailed plans for the first phase of the project are being developed. For programs and large projects, separate scope statements are developed for the overall program and the individual projects that comprise the program.

Once the scope statement has been approved, it becomes a controlled document that can be modified only through a formal change process (Chapters 9 and 11).

Example 5.2: Scope Statement for the LOGON Project

The RFP for the LOGON project (See Appendix A at the back of this book) sent by Midwest Parcel Distribution Company (MPD) specifies "The Contractor shall be responsible for furnishing expertise, labor, materials, tools, supervision, and services for the complete design, development, installation, check-out, and related services for full operational capability of the LOGON system." It also specifies the technical performance requirements for the system, as well as project exclusions, i.e., "Removal of existing storage, placement, and retrieval equipment will be performed under separate contract."

Upon receiving the RFP, Iron Butterfly Company, one of the proposing contractors, decided that the best way to meet MPD's needs would be with a system that employs robotic transporter units for placing and retrieving containers as instructed by a neural-network system. Iron Butterfly analyzed MPD's technical and budget requirements and, after a preliminary system design effort, created the following scope statement for its LOGON proposal.

1. Project background: (Short description of MPD's Chicago distribution facility, and of the purpose and objectives of the LOGON system).
2. Description of the work to be done: design, fabrication, installation, test, and checkout of a transport, storage, and database system for the automatic placement, storage, and retrieval of standardized shipping containers.
3. Deliverables and main areas of work:
   a. *Overall system*: Create basic design. Reference requirements A and B.
   b. *Racks and storage-bucket system* (termed "Hardware A"): Develop detailed design. Storage-bucket system is Model IBS05 adapted to requirements C.1 through E.14.
   c. *Robotic transporter units and track system* (termed "Hardware B"): Develop detailed design. RBU is Model IBR04 modified to meet requirements F.1 through G.13.
   d. *Neural-network*, database, and robotic-controller system: Develop software specifications. Reference requirements H.1 through H.9 and K.3.
   e. *Hardware A and Hardware B*: Procure software, subassemblies, and components. Reference requirements K.1 through L.9.
   f. *Hardware A and Hardware B*: Fabricate at IBC site. Reference requirement M.
   g. *Overall system*: Install and check-out at MPD site. Reference requirement Y.

Items (a) through (g) above represent deliverables for different stages of the project; associated with each are specific requirements (i.e., "reference requirements") listed in separate documents appended to the scope statement. For example, the detailed designs noted in points 3(b) and 3(c) include reference to requirements C.1 through E.14 and F.1 through G.13. The requirements must be sufficiently comprehensive to enable subcontractors to produce the specified systems and components. Elsewhere, the scope statement lists any project exclusions as noted in the RFP or identified by Iron Butterfly.

The scope statement is the reference document for all project stakeholders; it becomes the basis for making decisions about resources needed for the project, and, later, determining whether or not required or requested changes to work tasks and deliverables fall within the agreed-upon project scope. A common tendency in projects is *scope creep*, which means the project keeps growing due to changes in the number and/or size of deliverables. Scope creep, if not controlled, can lead to runaway project budgets and schedules.

The project scope statement appears in many places, such as project proposals, charters, and plans. Often the scope statement is incorporated into the statement of work.

Statement of Work

The statement of work is a description of the project; it includes a scope statement, but often goes far beyond that. It describes, for example, deliverable specifications and requirements; deliverable schedules; management procedures for communication, planning, and handling risks and changes; project budget; and key personnel responsible for administrative and work tasks. As such, the SOW is effectively a mini- or high-level version of the project master plan.

The term SOW and its usage are commonly associated with *contracted* projects, and the SOW appears in documents associated with the contracting or procurement process. The RFP, proposal, contract, and project master plan all contain SOWs, each an updated, expanded, or more refined version of the SOW in the previous document. The project charter described in Chapter 4 might also contain a SOW.

5.4 WORK DEFINITION

Once project objectives and deliverables have been set in the scope statement, the next step is to translate them into specific, well-defined work activities; that is, to specify the tasks and jobs that the project team must *do*. Particularly for large, unique projects, it is easy to overlook or duplicate activities. To insure that every necessary activity is identified and clearly defined, and that no activities are missed, a procedure called the "work breakdown structure" is used.

Work Breakdown Structure

Complex projects consist of numerous smaller subprojects, interrelated tasks, and work elements. As the rhyme at the beginning of the chapter alludes, the main end-result or deliverable of a project can be thought of as a system that consists of subsystems, which themselves consists of components, and so on. The method for subdividing the overall project into smaller elements is called the *work breakdown structure* or *WBS*, and its purpose is to divide the total project into "pieces of work" called *work packages*. Dividing the project into small work packages makes it easier to prepare schedules and budgets and to assign management and task responsibilities.

Creating a WBS begins with dividing the total project into major categories. These categories then are divided into subcategories that, in turn, are each subdivided. With this level-by-level breakdown, the scope and complexity of work elements at each level of the breakdown gets smaller. The objective is to reduce the project into many small work elements, each so clearly defined that it can easily be planned, budgeted, scheduled, and monitored.

A typical WBS consists of the following four levels:

LEVEL	ELEMENT DESCRIPTION
1	Project
2	Sub-project
3	Activity
4	Work Package

Level 1 is the total project. Level 2 is the project broken down into several (usually 4–10) major elements or subprojects. These subprojects must conform to the deliverables or work areas specified in the scope statement, and all of them when combined must comprise the *total project effort*. Each subproject is broken down into activities at Level 3. If a further breakdown is necessary, that occurs at Level 4. When the project is part of a *program*, a fifth level is added at the top and the levels are renumbered: Level 1 is the program, Level 2 the project, and so on.

When the process is completed, tasks at the *bottom* levels, whatever the levels might be, are called *work packages*. In the table above, the term "work package" appears at Level 4, but that is for illustration only. The actual number of levels in the WBS varies by project, as do the actual names of the element descriptions at each level. (The level and names are often prescribed by the project methodology in use.) Figure 5.2 shows a typical WBS. Note the different levels and descriptions for each work element.

The WBS process happens somewhat naturally, starting with the list of user and system requirements. These requirements suggest the main system, end-item,

Figure 5.2
Elements of a WBS.

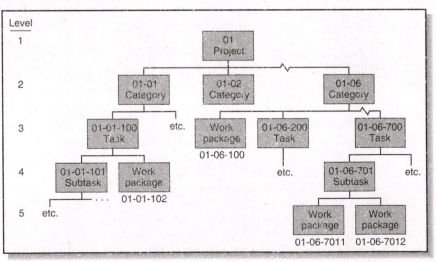

or deliverables of the project and the major subsystems and components; they also suggest which of these results will be met externally (by suppliers/subcontractors) and which internally. These major subsystems and components are boxes on the WBS. Those boxes are then each logically subdivided into smaller components of the system, and the work tasks to create or acquire them. For technical and engineering projects, the WBS should include all the configuration items (CIs) and major components of the system, as well as the work tasks to design, develop, build, and test them.[5]

The WBS becomes the basis for assigning project responsibility and contracting. For contracted work, responsibility for each subproject or activity is assigned to a subcontractor through a contract agreement between the subcontractor and the project manager. For internal projects, responsibility for each subproject or activity is assigned to an in-house department, through a formal agreement between the department manager and the project manager.

To avoid unnecessary complexity, the number of levels in the WBS should be limited. A five-level WBS might be appropriate for large projects, but for most small projects a three-level WBS is adequate. To help organize and track project activities, each work element is coded with a unique identifier or number. Usually the number at each level is based on the number at the next higher level. In Figure 5.2 Project "01" has six categories numbered 01–01 through 01–06; then, for example, category, 01–06 has seven tasks numbered 01–06–100 through 01–06–700. The project manager establishes the numbering scheme.

Figure 5.3 illustrates ways to create the WBS for constructing a house. The top part of the figure shows the main project end-item (Level 1) and the major categories of work (Level 2) necessary to build it. For the most part, the items at Level 2 are physical pieces or components of the house. In other words, they identify the deliverables or products to be produced. This is called a *product-oriented WBS*. By subdividing a project in this way—according to physical products or deliverables—it is easy to attach performance, cost, and time requirements to each and to assign responsibility for meeting them. That is, creating a WBS in this way assists in preparing other parts of the master plan, including the project budget and schedule. The bottom part of Figure 5.3 shows how the product-oriented WBS would be subdivided into four levels.

Sometimes the WBS or portions of it are *function-oriented* or *task-oriented* (rather than product-oriented). For example, the middle part of Figure 5.3 shows the project subdivided according to work functions (e.g., carpentry and plumbing), not deliverables. Functions or tasks such as management and overhead, design, engineering, training, and inspection that apply to multiple deliverables or to *integrating* multiple deliverables should be identified as separate work packages in the WBS. Whether the WBS uses product-, functional-, geographical- or task-based (or other) breakdown is a matter of preference, or is stipulated by the organization's project methodology or WBS templates.

During the WBS process, the questions "What else is needed?" and "What's next?" are constantly being asked. Supplementary or missed elements are identified and added to the WBS at appropriate levels. For example, the WBS in Figure 5.3 nowhere includes blueprints, budgets, and work schedules, even though the house cannot be built without them. These are deliverables associated with planning the project and designing the house, which could be included in the WBS by expanding Level 2 and inserting categories for "Design" and "Project Management," and then at Level 3 by inserting "blueprints" under Design and "budget and work schedules" under Project Management," respectively. Somewhere in the WBS, considerations such as site location, permits and licenses, environmental impacts, etc., must also be included.

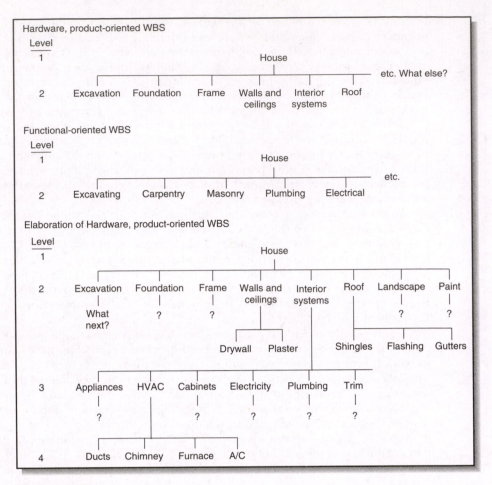

Figure 5.3
Example of WBS for building a house.

As described later, the WBS must also reflect any procured (contracted, outsourced) goods, materials or services.

Figure 5.4 exemplifies the WBS for a large engineering project where the main deliverable and many of its subsystems and components must be developed, built, integrated, and tested largely from scratch. Notice that some portions of it are product-oriented (vehicle, facilities), others are function-oriented (test/evaluation, project management/systems engineering).

The larger and less standardized the project, the easier it is to overlook something and the more valuable the WBS process is in avoiding that. In large projects the initial WBS is usually rather coarse and shows only the major products or work functions and the aspects of each to be allocated to specific contractors. Before work commences, however, details of each product or function must be more fully developed in the WBS.

Example 5.3: Process of Developing the WBS for the LOGON Project

The project manager and staff meet several times in brainstorming sessions to create the WBS for LOGON, first during proposal preparation to sort out key

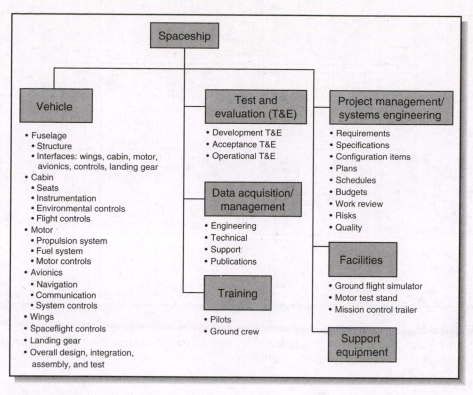

Figure 5.4
WBS for spaceship project.

deliverables and define the project scope, later during project definition to update the WBS and breakout the work packages into finer detail. In the first meeting they "rough out" the major categories of work and deliverables, identify the responsible functional areas, and create the scope statement (described in Example 2) that provides the Level 2 breakdown.

After contract signing, the project manager meets with managers from the functional areas that will be contributing to deliverables in the Level 2 breakdown. These managers then meet with their supervisors and technical staff to prepare a Level 3 breakdown. Where necessary, supervisors prepare a Level 4 breakdown.

Figure 5.5 shows a WBS that is part function-oriented (basic design, procurement, etc.) and part product-oriented (Hardware Part A, Hardware Part B, software, etc.). Where necessary, Level 2 items have been subdivided into Level 3 items, and Level 3 items into Level 4 items. The boxes at the bottom of the branches are "work packages," denoted by letters in parentheses. Notice the work packages are at different levels of the WBS; this is because each branch of the WBS is developed separately.

Work Packages

How far down does the breakdown go? Simply, for as far as needed to completely define all work necessary for the project. The work in each "box" or element of the WBS must be "well defined"; if it is not, then the box must be subdivided into smaller boxes. For a box to be "well defined" it should include the following:

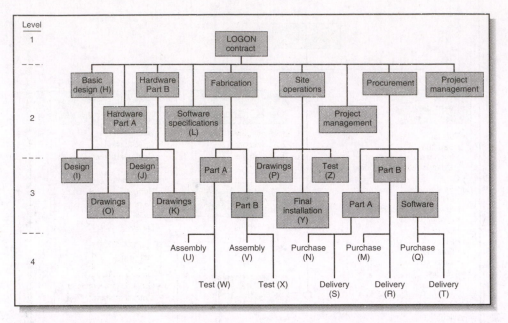

Figure 5.5
Work breakdown structure for the LOGON project. Work packages are lettered H through Z.

1. *Clear, comprehensive SOW*: Work task or activity to be done.
2. *Resource requirements*: Labor, equipment, facilities, and materials needed for the task.
3. *Time*: Estimated time to perform the task.
4. *Costs*: Estimated resource, management, and related expenses for the task.
5. *Responsibility*: Parties, individuals, or job titles responsible for doing and/or approving the task.
6. *Outcomes*: Requirements, specifications, and associated deliverables, end-items, or results for the task.
7. *Inputs*: Preconditions or predecessors necessary to begin the task.
8. *Quality Assurance*: Entry, process, and exit conditions to which the task must conform; as specified in the quality plan.
9. *Risk.* Uncertainty about time, cost, and resources associated with the task.
10. *Other*: Additional information as necessary.

These properties are summarized in Figure 5.6. If any of them cannot be defined for a given box, then the task or product in the box is too broad and must be

Inputs	Task	Outcomes
Predecessors	Statement of work	Deliverables
Preconditions	Time	Results
Resources	Cost	
Requirements/specifications	Responsibility	
	Quality assurance	
	Risk	

Figure 5.6
Properties of a work package.

broken down further. When all or most of the properties can be defined for a box or element, then the element is considered "well-defined" and, by definition, a *work package*.

The level of work breakdown must not, though, continue so far as to result in an unnecessarily large number of work packages. During the project each work package becomes the focal point for planning and control and, as such, involves paperwork, schedules, budgets, and so on. Thus, the larger the number of work packages, the greater the time and cost to manage them.

WBS Templates

A company that routinely performs similar kinds of projects might utilize a standardized WBS "template" at Level 2 or Level 3. The template is based upon experience from having done many of those kinds of projects. In some companies, the template is created and maintained by the project management office (PMO). Even with a template, however, it is good to remember that every project is somewhat unique, and that such uniqueness might not become apparent until Level 3 or 4. Hence, the WBS for a project should never be a mere template or complete copy of the WBS for a previous project, no matter how similar projects might seem. Nowhere is the saying "the devil is in the detail" more appropriate than in projects, and the WBS is *the* tool for identifying the details wherein the devil might be hiding. To reduce oversights, it is good practice to have two or more teams each create a WBS, and then to combine them into one.

Ideally, work packages represent jobs of about the same magnitude of effort and of relatively small cost and short duration compared to the total project. For example, DOD/NASA guidelines specify that work packages should be a maximum of 3 months' duration and not exceed $100,000 cost. But these are simply guidelines. Work package cost and duration depend on many factors, such as project size (smaller projects have smaller work packages).

Each work package represents a contract or agreement with a subcontractor, supplier, or internal functional unit. Although several functional or subcontracting units might share responsibility for a work package, ideally a work package has only one party responsible for it.

Example 5.4: Work Package Definition for LOGON Project

The LOGON project was divided into 19 work packages—the boxes lettered H through Z in Figure 5.5. Below is an example of the properties for a typical work package, Work Package X: Test of Hardware. Note how the defined properties correspond to those listed in Figure 5.6.

1. *Statement of work*: Perform checkout, operational test, and corrections as necessary for sign-off approval of four Batman robotic transporter units, Model IBR04.
2. *Resource requirements*: Labor (FT commitment, 3 weeks): test manager, two test engineers, three technicians.
   Procured materials: track for mock-up; all other materials on hand.
   Facility: Test room number 2 at Iron Butterfly for 3 weeks.
3. *Time*: Three weeks scheduled; (time critical) start December 2; finish December 23.
4. *Costs* (Control account RX0522):

Labor:	Manager, 75h+25% OH	$9,750
	Engineers, 1125h+25% OH	$135,000
	Technicians, 1125h+25% OH	$112,500
Material:		$70,000
Subtotal		$327,250
	10% G&A	$32,725
Total		$359,975

5. *Responsibility*:
   Oversee tests: B.J., manager of robotic assembly.
   Approve test results: O.B., manager of Fabrication Department.
   Notify of test status and results: J.M., project engineer; F.W.N., site operations.
6. *Deliverables*: Four tested and approved Batman robotic transporters, Model IBR04. Refer to specifications.
7. *Inputs*:
   Predecessor: Assembly of Batman robotic transporter (work package V).
   Preconditions: Test room setup for robotic transporter.
8. *Quality Assurance*: Refer to entry, process, and exit conditions for work package X in the LOGON quality plan.
9. *Risk*: RBU will fail test requirements because of assembly/integration problems/errors. Likelihood: low. Contingency reserve: Additional week included in the schedule.
10. *Specifications*: Refer to test document 2307 and LOGON contract spec sheets 28 and 41.
11. *Work orders*: None, pending.
12. *Subcontracts/purchase orders*: No subcontracts; P.O. 8967–987 for track tests.

A work package that produces a tangible deliverable or physical product as in the example should include specific start and finish dates for the work package.

WBS Process and the Integrated Project Plan

In an integrated project plan, important elements of the plan—requirements, work tasks, schedules, budgets, risk, quality, communications, procurement, and so on—are interconnected. Once created, such a plan provides managers a variety of ways to track and control the project, and to assess the impact of actions or problems regarding some elements of the plan on the other elements.

To better describe what an integrated plan is, we can compare it to what it is *not*, which would be: a list of work packages or tasks generated without much regard as to user requirements; a budget that does not account for the resources required of the project tasks; and a schedule where the tasks do match up with the tasks on the WBS or budget. To the outsider, it would appear that four people who never talked to each other about the project had each come up with, respectively, a list of work tasks, a list of needed resources, a schedule, and a budget. Amazingly, that is sometimes the way plans are created, with the result that requirements, tasks, resources, schedules, budgets, plans for risks, and so on are seemingly independent and unrelated.

One noticeable feature about an integrated project plan is that the same list of work packages or tasks reappears throughout the different elements of the plan. The list of work tasks developed in the WBS is used to create, and appears in, schedules, budgets, and most other elements of the plan.

The process of creating the WBS and the resulting list of work packages thus integrates various elements of the project plan and project control in several ways:[6]

1. Managers, subcontractors, and others responsible for the project are identified during the WBS process and involved in defining the work. Their involvement helps ensure completeness of work definition and gains their commitment to that work.
2. Work packages in each phase are logically related to those in earlier and later phases; this ensures that predecessor requirements are met and no steps overlooked.

3. Work packages identified in the WBS become the basis for budgets and schedules. The project budget is the sum of budgets for the work packages plus overhead and indirect expenses. The project schedule is a composite of the schedules for the work packages.
4. The project organization is formed around the work packages, with resources and management responsibility assigned to each work package.
5. The project is managed by managing people working on the individual work packages.
6. The project is controlled by controlling the work packages. During project execution, work completed and costs accrued are compared to schedules and budgets for the work packages, suggesting which work packages are in need of corrective action.

The integrated project plan is a systems approach to management—recognition that a project is a system of interrelated work elements, each of which must be defined, budgeted, scheduled, and controlled.

5.5 PROJECT ORGANIZATION AND RESPONSIBILITIES

Integrating WBS and Project Organization

During the WBS process, each work package is associated with the area of the project organization that will have functional or budget responsibility for it. An example is the LOGON project and its contractor, Iron Butterfly Company, represented in Figure 5.7: on the left is the company organization structure; across the top is the project WBS. For projects where the work is contracted (performed externally), the organization structure on the left would show contractors and suppliers instead of departments. Shown at the intersection of each department and work package is a box signifying a *control account* or *cost account*. Each account represents assignment of responsibility for a particular task or work package to a department. The account can represent a work package or portion of one; just like the work package, it includes a schedule and budget, resource needs, deliverables, requirements, and the manager or supervisor responsible for it. Each control account integrates the WBS with the project organization and represents an agreement or contract with departments or subcontractors to fulfill work package requirements. Control accounts are described further in Chapter 8.

Responsibility Matrix

The individuals responsible for work packages are shown in a chart called the *responsibility matrix* or assignment matrix. Figure 5.8 shows the responsibility matrix for the LOGON project. The rows represent the work packages or major project tasks and activities identified in the WBS. The columns represent the persons, groups, departments, or contractors responsible for them. Letters within the matrix symbolize the *kind* of responsibility: primary (ultimate accountability for the work package); secondary (assistance or help); notification (must be notified about the work package's status); and approval (has authority to approve or reject work package deliverables). Note that for each task one, and only one, person is assigned primary responsibility. The matrix can also be used to signify who will *do* the work, and any other conceivable kind of responsibility.

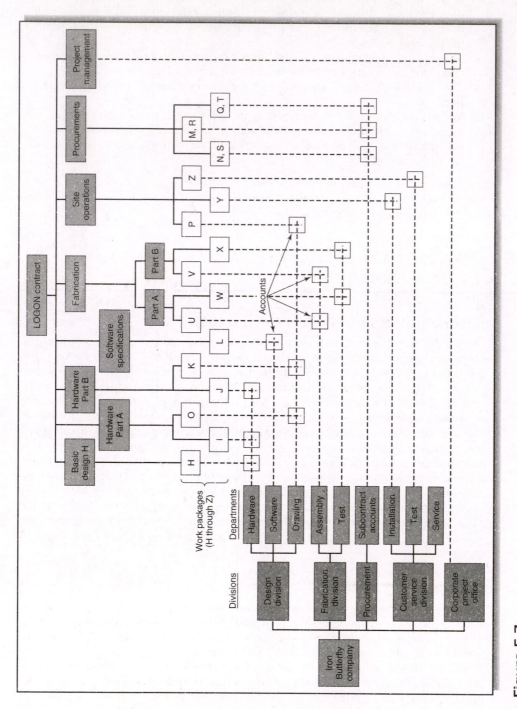

Figure 5.7
Integration of WBS and project organization.

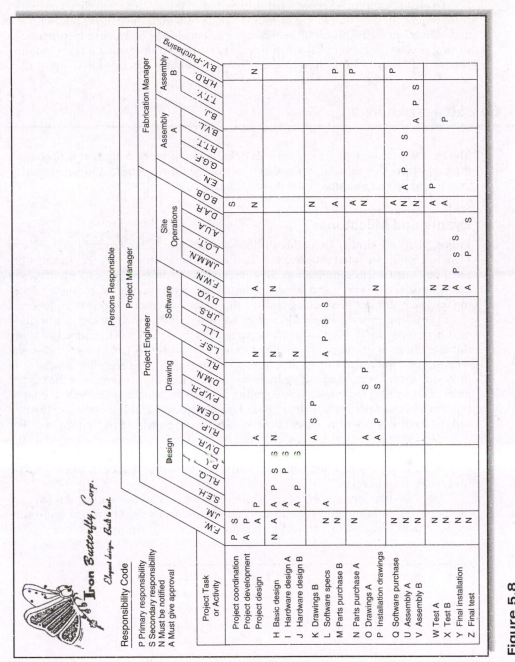

Figure 5.8
Sample responsibility matrix for LOGON project (with initials of persons responsible).

179

From the matrix, everyone associated with the project can easily see who is responsible for what. This helps avoid people shirking responsibility and "passing the buck."

To ensure everyone knows what is expected of them, and what they can expect from others, the people, groups, or companies identified in the matrix should review and consent to the responsibilities. The assignments in the matrix can be roughed in during project conception, and then detailed and firmed up during a team-building session held shortly after project kickoff. Team building is described in Chapter 15.

5.6 SCHEDULING

The next logical step after requirements definition and work definition is to *schedule* the project work tasks. A schedule shows the timing for work tasks and when specific events and project milestones should take place.

Events and Milestones

Project plans are similar to roadmaps: they show not only how to get to where you want to go, but also what progress you have made along the way. Work packages are what you must do; in combination, they are the road to project goals. Along that road are signposts called *events* and *milestones* that show how far you have progressed. Passing the last event signifies having reached the final destination: project completion.

Events and milestones should not be confused with work packages, activities, or other kinds of tasks. A task or work package is the actual work planned or being done, and represents the *process* of doing something (such as *driving* a car to get somewhere); it consumes resources and time. In contrast, an *event* signifies a *moment in time*—the instant when something happens. In a project, events represent the *start* or *finish* of something (equivalent to beginning a trip or arriving at an intermediate destination). In most project schedules, each task is depicted as a line segment; the two ends of the line segment represent the events of starting and completing the task. For example, in Figure 5.9 the line segment labeled "Task A" represents the time to do the task, and events 1 and 2 represent the moments when Task A is started and finished, respectively. In project schedules, each event is attached to a specific calendar date (day, month, and year).

There are two kinds of events in projects: interface and milestone.[7] An *interface event* denotes the completion of one task and simultaneous start of one or more subsequent tasks. Event 4 in Figure 5.9 is an interface event. An interface event often

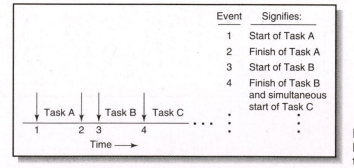

Figure 5.9
Relationship between tasks and events.

represents a change in responsibility: one individual or group completes a task and another individual or group starts the next task. It usually signifies approval of the task just completed, and readiness to begin subsequent tasks.

A *milestone event* represents a major project occurrence, such as completion of a phase or several critical or difficult tasks, approval of something important, or availability of crucial resources. Milestone events signify progress, and as such they are important measures. Often, approvals for system requirements, preliminary design, detailed design, or completion of major tests are considered milestones; they signify the project is ready to proceed to the next phase of the systems development cycle. Failure to pass a milestone is usually a bad omen, followed by changes to the budget and schedule.

Kinds of Schedules

The two most common kinds of schedules are the project schedule and the task schedule. Project managers and upper management use the *project schedule* (or project *master* schedule) to plan and review the entire project. This schedule shows all the major project activities, but not much detail about each. It is first developed during project initiation, and is continually refined thereafter. Managers develop the project schedule in a top-down fashion, first scheduling the tasks identified from the WBS or in the scope statement. Later, they refine the schedule in a bottom-up fashion, taking into account the more detailed task schedules developed by functional managers. When the project is performed in phases, the schedule for each phase must be sufficiently detailed to enable management to authorize work on the phase to commence.

A *task schedule* shows the specific activities necessary to complete a work package. It is created for people working on a specific task, and enables lower-level managers and supervisors to focus on the task and not be distracted by other tasks with which they have no interaction. Task schedules are prepared by functional managers or subcontractors, but incorporate interface and milestone events as specified on the project master schedule. Project and task schedules are prepared and displayed in many ways, including with Gantt charts.

5.7 PLANNING AND SCHEDULING CHARTS

Gantt Charts

The simplest and most commonly used scheduling technique is the *Gantt chart* (or bar chart), named after the management consultant Henry L. Gantt (1861–1919). During World War I Gantt worked with the US Army to find a way to portray visually the status of the munitions program. He realized that time was a common denominator to most elements of a program plan, and that it would be easy to assess progress by viewing each element's status with respect to time. His approach, which came to bear his name, became widely adopted in industry, and is used today in a variety of ways.

The chart consists of a horizontal scale divided into time units—days, weeks, or months—and a vertical scale showing project work elements—tasks, activities, or work packages. Figure 5.10 shows the Gantt chart for work packages in the LOGON project. Listed on the left-hand side are work packages, and along the bottom are work weeks. The starting and completion times of packages are indicated by the beginning and ending of each bar.

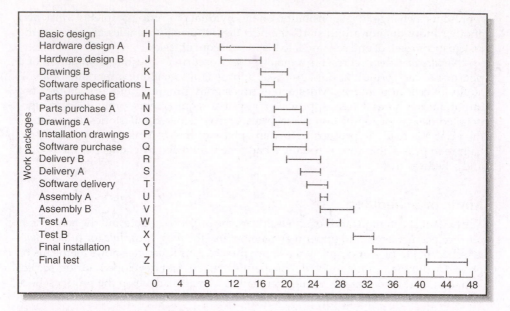

Figure 5.10
Gantt chart for LOGON project.

Preparation of the Gantt chart comes after a WBS analysis and identification of work packages or other tasks. During WBS analysis, the functional manager, contractor, or others responsible for a work package estimate its time and any prerequisites. The work elements are then listed in sequence of time, taking into account which elements must be completed before others can be started.

As an example, consider how the first nine work elements in Figure 5.10 (work packages H through P) are scheduled. In every project there is a precedence relationship between the tasks (some tasks must be completed before others can begin), and this relationship must be determined before the tasks can be scheduled. These are the "predecessor" inputs mentioned earlier in the discussion of work package definition. Suppose that during the WBS analysis for LOGON it was determined that before work elements I and J could be started, element H had to be completed; that before elements K, L, and M could be started, element J had to be completed; and that before elements N, O, and P could begin, element I had to be completed. That is:

BEFORE THESE CAN BE STARTED . . .	THIS MUST BE COMPLETED
I, J	H
N, O, P	I
K, L, M	J

This sequencing logic is used to create the Gantt chart. Thus, as shown in Figure 5.11 (and given the times shown for the work packages), only after element H has been completed—i.e., after week 10—can elements I and J be started; only after element J has been completed—after week 16—can elements K, L, and M be started; and only after element I has been completed—after week 18—can elements N, O, and P be started. As each new work element is added to the chart, care is taken to locate it following completion of all of its predecessor work elements. This example uses work

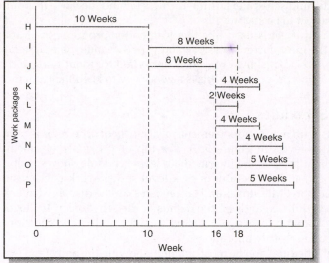

Figure 5.11
Setting up a Gantt chart.

packages as the elements being scheduled, but in fact any unit of work can be scheduled depending on the detail level desired.

Once the project is underway, the Gantt chart becomes a tool for assessing the status of individual work elements and the project as a whole. Figure 5.12 shows progress as of the "status date," week 20. The heavy portion of the bars indicates the amount of work that has been completed. The thinner part of the bars represents work unfinished or yet to be started. This method is somewhat effective for showing which of the work elements are behind or ahead of schedule. For example, as of week 20, work element N is on schedule, element O is ahead of schedule, and elements K, L,

Figure 5.12
Gantt chart for LOGON project showing work progress as of week 20.

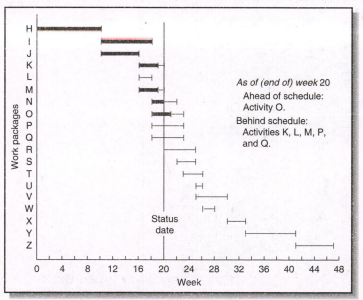

M, P, and Q are behind schedule; L is the furthest behind, because it should have be completed but has yet to be started.

When the Gantt chart is used like this to monitor progress, the information it reflects must be the most current possible, and the chart must be updated on a daily or at least weekly basis. Tracking progress is important for identifying and rectifying problems, and posting progress like this is a good way to keep the team motivated.

Hierarchy of Schedules

For large projects with many work elements a *hierarchy* of schedules is used, as illustrated by the three levels in Figure 5.13. The top or project-level schedule shows subprojects within a project, the intermediate-level schedule shows major activities within a subproject, and the bottom or task level shows work packages or smaller tasks within an activity. Milestones and target dates can be displayed at any level.

Each level schedule expands on the details of the schedule at the level above it. Intermediate- and bottom-level schedules are used for project and functional managers to plan labor and resource allocations.

Bottom-level schedules are the most detailed, showing the daily (and even hourly) schedules of the tasks within work packages. These are used by work-package leaders, and correspond to the task schedules mentioned earlier. Figure 5.14 is a multilevel schedule, showing both the higher-level project activities (denoted by "summary" bars) as well as the detailed tasks within each activity (denoted by "task" bars).

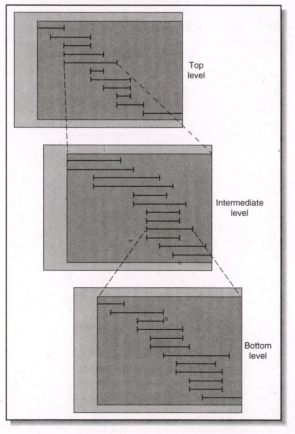

Figure 5.13
A hierarchy of schedules.

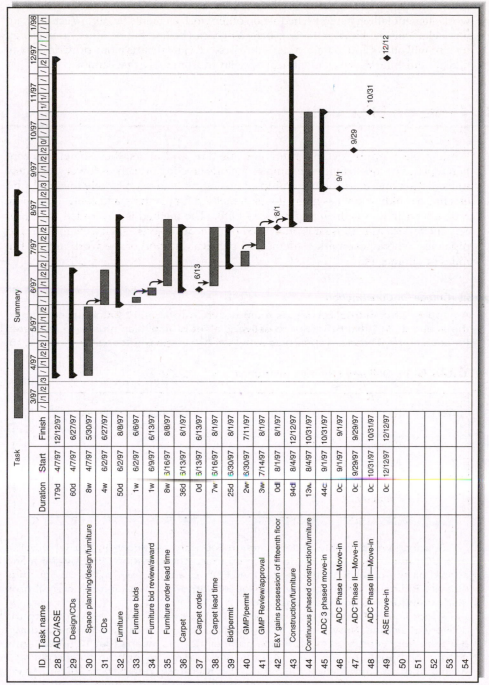

ID	Task name	Duration	Start	Finish
28	ADC/ASE	179d	4/7/97	12/12/97
29	Design/CDs	60d	4/7/97	6/27/97
30	Space planning/design/furniture	8w	4/7/97	5/30/97
31	CDs	4w	6/2/97	6/27/97
32	Furniture	50d	6/2/97	8/8/97
33	Furniture bids	1w	6/2/97	6/6/97
34	Furniture bid review/award	1w	6/9/97	6/13/97
35	Furniture order lead time	8w	5/16/97	8/8/97
36	Carpet	36d	5/13/97	8/1/97
37	Carpet order	0d	5/13/97	6/13/97
38	Carpet lead time	7w	6/16/97	8/1/97
39	Bid/permit	25d	6/30/97	8/1/97
40	GMP/permit	2w	6/30/97	7/11/97
41	GMP Review/approval	3w	7/14/97	8/1/97
42	E&Y gains possession of fifteenth floor	0d	8/1/97	8/1/97
43	Construction/furniture	94d	8/4/97	12/12/97
44	Continuous phased construction/furniture	13w	8/4/97	10/31/97
45	ADC 3 phased move-in	44c	9/1/97	10/31/97
46	ADC Phase I—Move-in	0c	9/1/97	9/1/97
47	ADC Phase II—Move-in	0c	9/29/97	9/29/97
48	ADC Phase III—Move-in	0c	10/31/97	10/31/97
49	ASE move-in	0c	12/12/97	12/12/97
50				
51				
52				
53				
54				

Figure 5.14
Multilevel schedule.

Disadvantages of Gantt Charts

A disadvantage of the Gantt chart is that it does not necessarily show the effects of one work element falling behind schedule on other work elements. In all projects, certain work elements depend upon others before they can begin; if these others are delayed then so will others and, possibly, the entire project. Gantt charts alone provide no way of distinguishing which elements can be delayed from those that cannot.

5.8 LINE OF BALANCE

While projects are by definition unique, one-time endeavors, they sometimes contain repetitive work activities. Examples include erecting numerous towers for a new transmission line, constructing multiple housing units that are largely identical, and erecting a building that has many floors. A method for planning and controlling these repetitive activities is the *line of balance*—LOB. (The method is also called the *Linear Scheduling Method* because it is often used on "linear projects" such as highways and pipelines, where post markers depict the physical location of the work in terms of miles or kilometers.)

Example 5.5: Cranes for Construction

A supplier of construction cranes must deliver a total of 12 cranes according to the schedule in Table 5.1. Prior to delivery, a set of activities must be completed for each crane. These are shown as activities A–F in the Gantt chart in Figure 5.15.

Table 5.1 Delivery schedule for cranes

WEEK	DATE	DELIVERY QUANTITY	CUMULATIVE DELIVERY QUANTITY
1	February 7	1	1
2	February 14	2	3
3	February 21	4	7
4	February 28	5	12

Suppose we look only at deliveries on February 14; according to Table 5.1, a total of three cranes must be delivered by then. The questions is: How far along should all the other activities be by then? For example, how many power units (activity B) should be bought by then (assuming one power unit per crane), how many components procured, and so on?

According to Figure 5.15, a power unit must be bought 2 weeks prior to the delivery of a crane. Now, look at the right-hand column of Table 5.1: moving down 2 weeks from February 14 shows the number 12; this means that 12 power units need to be bought by February 14. Activities A and C must both be completed 3 weeks prior to crane delivery (Figure 5.15); therefore, referring to Table 5.1, we see that 12 sets of "other components" must be procured (activity C) and 12 sets of structural components must be fabricated (activity A) by February 14. In the same manner, since operators must be trained (activity E) 1 week before delivery, moving down 1 week from February 14 in Table 5.1 shows that seven operators to be trained by February 14. Likewise, we see that seven cranes (activity D) must

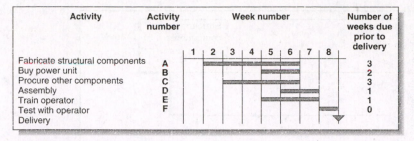

Figure 5.15
Gantt chart of tasks for delivery of one crane.

be assembled by February 14. Also, since tests with operators (activity F) involve zero lead time, three tests should be completed by then.

Figure 5.16 summarizes the LOB—the number of deliverables (completed units) per activity as of February 14. For the cost center, function, or supplier responsible for each activity, the LOB provides information necessary to estimate needed resources and plan work.

An alternate to Figure 5.16 is a diagram showing the number of units to be completed by a specific activity per time period. For example, dates and quantities for fabricated structural components (activity A) and assembled cranes (activity D) are illustrated in Figure 5.17. The same kind of figure can be used to monitor actual units completed, and to track progress versus planned units.

5.9   PROCUREMENT MANAGEMENT[8]

Most projects involve procurement of goods, materials, and subcontracted work. Indeed, in some projects everything is "procured" and virtually nothing is done or produced "internally." Whether project work should be done internally or procured from outsiders is the result of a make-or-buy analysis of the project end-item, subsystems, components, or other project deliverables, and of work packages and tasks identified in the WBS.

Certainly, the management of procured materials and outsourced work is every bit as important to project success as work done internally: procured items that run

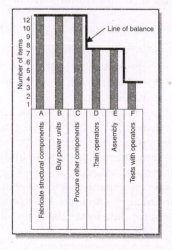

Figure 5.16
Number of deliverables required by 14 February per type of activity.

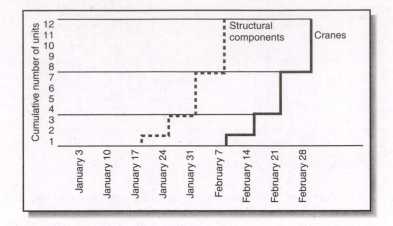

Figure 5.17
Alternative presentation of a Line of Balance schedule.

over budget or behind schedule, or fail to meet requirements, cause cost and schedule overruns for the entire project. This is the role of *procurement management*, which refers to planning and control of the following:[9]

1. Equipment, materials, or components designed and built by vendors *specifically* for the project. These procured items might involve portions of work packages or entire work packages (e.g., design work, environmental study, soil analysis). Major portions of the project might be wholly outsourced in a "turnkey" arrangement (i.e., subcontractors fully design, build, and install major equipment or components for the project end-item).
2. *Off-the-shelf* (OTS) equipment and components supplied by vendors. These represent products that are readily available and not produced specifically for the project.
3. Bulk materials (cement, metal tubing or framing, wire, stone, piping, etc.).
4. Consumables (nails, bolts, rivets, fuel) or tools for construction or fabrication.
5. Equipment for construction or fabrication not already owned by the contractor; this includes cranes, supports, scaffolding, and equipment for machine-shops, welding, and testing.
6. Administrative equipment not already owned by the contractor; this includes computers and project office facilities and equipment.

To simplify, we lump these items together here and refer to them as procured goods, work, or services (GWS). Goods refers to raw materials or produced items, work means contracted labor, and services means consulting.

The term "procurement" represents activities related to purchased, bought, or subcontracted items, although other terms are also used, but with the following distinctions: whereas "acquisition" refers to the purchase of an *entire complex system* that is not well defined (including its design, development, ramp-up, and production), and "buying" refers to the purchase of a standardized (off-the-shelf) *item or part*, "procurement" refers to the purchase of a component or subsystem (*less than entire system*)—including its design and/or production—according to specifications provided by the customer. Hence it would be appropriate to say the "acquisition of a nuclear power plant," the "procurement of an automatic shut-down safety device," and "buying a batch of standard 1-inch nails."

Procurement management includes almost everything associated with contracting and contract administration: soliciting bids and selecting contractors, establishing legally binding contracts between parties, managing the execution of the contracts, and closing out of contracts. The first few of these topics will be covered here, and the others in Chapters 11 and 12.

Soliciting and Evaluating Bids

Once the decision is made to procure GWS, potential vendors are solicited to offer bids or proposals. A customer who has a long-term relationship with a supplier or contractor will usually approach the contractor and negotiate a contract. This is called *sole sourcing*, because only one contractor is considered for the contract. When the scope of the project is somewhat simple and the requirements are well defined, the customer can advertise for bids in newspapers and other media using an RFP or RFQ (Request for Quotation, a simple price quote). For a large and somewhat undefined system that requires design work or other intellectual input, an RFP or IFB (invitation for bid) is sent to a short list of qualified suppliers. The RFP or IFB might be preceded by an RFI, a request for information to determine whether the contractor is qualified and should be sent an RFP. Sometimes the RFP is accompanied by a *bidder's* or *contractor's conference* to explain the background and scope of the project, documentation required from contractors, and contractual requirements. Acceptance of a bid will result in a formal contract, with content and conditions as described in Chapter 3. When the procured item is hardware, the contract should specify at what point the supplier is no longer responsible for damages and the buyer becomes responsible.

The basic types of contracts are described in Chapter 3, although certain industries require specific contract formats.[10] Procurement management is a specialized function that requires legal and contract administration skills; in some organizations, a specialized procurement division handles it.[11]

Procurement Planning and Scheduling

The first step in procurement planning is to estimate the procured GWS needs for the project—the items, labor, or services mentioned above. Associated with every work package are procured GWS requirements, some of which will be shared with other work packages. Items to be procured are identified during the WBS process, either from planning the work and resources needed for particular work packages, or from knowing that whole work packages must be outsourced. In the former case, managers responsible for each work package identify the GWS within the package that must be procured (e.g., the work package "build wing" will require procuring fiberglass, aluminum, and other materials from suppliers); in the latter case, managers will recognize that certain (sometimes significant) portions of the project (*entire* work packages) will have to be outsourced (e.g., the work package "develop rocket motor" will require development, fabrication, and testing—*all* to be provided by a contractor).

Associated with each procured item is a schedule specifying when the item is needed and when procurement activities must begin. Everything to be procured in the project must be scheduled in advance to allow enough time to conduct the RFP/proposal/supplier-selection process (described in Chapter 3), and for suppliers to deliver (or design, build, and then deliver) the items at the times needed. Figure 5.18 shows the considerations in scheduling a procured GWS item. The schedule is prepared by working backwards, starting with event 10, the date when the item *must* be available for the project. This schedule is then integrated with the project schedule to assure that

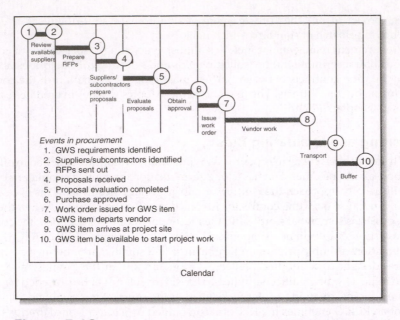

Figure 5.18
Procurement activities schedule.
Adapted from Joy PK. *Total Project Management*. Delhi: Macmillan India Limited; 1992. p. 383.

the procurement process happens far enough in advance so that the item will be available when needed. This scheduling procedure is repeated for all procured GWS items.

Of course, preparing such a schedule requires knowing the lead times for each of the procurement activities—the time needed, for example, for suppliers and subcontractors to prepare proposals, for the project manager to evaluate the proposals and issue contracts and work orders, and for suppliers/subcontractors to fulfill the work orders (which could involve their designing, building, and testing of equipment or components). It is not uncommon, especially in international projects, for these times to be grossly underestimated and, subsequently, the project to be delayed.

The schedule in Figure 5.18 starts at the point where GWS requirements have been identified. To get to that point, however, the system requirements and specifications must first have been defined—another reason for careful definition of the system early in the project life cycle.

Procured GWS require the same treatment in project planning as internal aspects of the project; hence matters such as the responsibility, budget, quality, and risk for procured items must also be addressed in the plan. These topics are discussed in later chapters.

Logistics Plan

Logistics relates to the transport and storage of materials. In projects that are materials-intensive, the loading, unloading, transportation, inspection, clearances and approvals, and storage of materials can be major issues. For example, consider a large construction project and the importance of timing the arrival of materials (steel, pipes, concrete slabs) to coincide with when those materials will be needed for the building. Obviously the materials cannot arrive late, because that will delay the project. But equally serious is when the materials arrive early. Where do you *put* them? In congested urban areas there simply is no space, and even when there is, materials delivered early are subject to damage, deterioration, and theft. Whenever GWS items cannot be scheduled to arrive *just in time* (exactly when needed), provision must made to store and protect them.

5.10 SUMMARY

The purpose of project planning is to determine the way in which project goals will be achieved—what must be done, by whom, when, and for how much.

The project scope statement and WBS are ways that managers and planners answer the question: "What must be done?" The scope statement outlines the main areas of work to be done and the deliverables or end-items. It appears commonly in two places, the SOW or the project charter. The SOW is a summary description of the project used for contracted work; it appears in the RFP, proposal, contract, and project master plan. The charter is a document used for internal projects to describe, announce, and formally authorize the project.

The WBS process subdivides the project into work packages or other work elements, each small enough to be well understood, planned, and controlled. Most elements and functions of project management—scheduling, budgeting, resource allocation, tracking, and control—are subsequently carried out with reference to the WBS and work packages.

The responsibility matrix integrates the project organization with the WBS; it prescribes which units and individuals, both internal and subcontractors, have project responsibility, and the kind of responsibility for each. It is valuable for achieving consensus, ensuring accountability, and reducing conflict among project participants.

Project schedules show the timing of work, and are the basis for resource allocation and performance tracking. Depending on the amount of detail required, different types of schedules are used: project-level schedules show only high-level tasks and work packages; task-level schedules show the jobs needed to complete individual work packages. The most common form of schedule is the Gantt chart. As a visual planning device it is effective for showing when work should be done and whether work elements are behind or ahead of schedule.

Project plans must account for all resources and work necessary for the project, including those procured (provided by suppliers and contractors). Procured items and the procurement process must be included in all elements of the project plan—the WBS, schedule, responsibility matrix, budget, and so on.

The concepts and techniques in this chapter are foundation tools for planning and scheduling. The next few chapters look at additional techniques for planning and scheduling. Later chapters address the role of the WBS, work packages, and schedules in cost estimating, budgeting, and project control.

REVIEW QUESTIONS AND PROBLEMS

1. What questions need to be answered every time when a new project is planned? What are the steps in the planning process that answer these questions?
2. What is the purpose of a project master plan? At what stage of the project should this plan be prepared?
3. Can a project be undertaken without a master plan? What are the possible consequences?
4. Which aspects of the master plan might be eliminated for projects with small

budgets? Which might be eliminated for short-duration projects (a few weeks or months) with relatively few tasks?

5. A section addressing "Risk and Uncertainty" is often left out of the project master plan. What are the potential pitfalls of doing this?

6. What is the purpose of the project scope statement? What information is used to create the scope statement? How is the scope reflected on the WBS?

7. What is the statement of work? In what documents does the SOW appear?

8. What are differences and similarities between the SOW and the project charter?

9. Think of a somewhat complicated endeavor you are familiar with and develop a WBS for it. (Examples: wedding, high school reunion, questionnaire survey, movie or stage play, etc.). Now repeat this for a complicated job you are not familiar with. At what point do you need assistance from "functional managers" or specialists to continue the breakdown?

10. How do you know in a WBS when you have reached a level where no further breakdown is necessary?

11. Could the WBS in Figure 5.5 have started with different Level-2 elements and still result in the same work packages? In general, can different WBS approaches give similar results?

12. In what ways is the WBS important to project managers?

13. What is the role of functional managers in developing a WBS?

14. What is the impact of altering the WBS after the project has started?

15. What should a "well-defined" work package include?

16. What is the relationship between the WBS and organization structure? In this relationship, what is the meaning of a "control account?"

17. Figure 5.8 shows some possible types of responsibilities that could be indicated on a responsibility matrix. What other kinds of responsibilities or duties could be indicated?

18. Construct a responsibility matrix using the WBS you developed in question 9. In doing this, consider the project organization and the managerial/technical staff to be assigned and their duties.

19. What function does the responsibility matrix serve in project control?

20. Can a responsibility matrix seem threatening to managers and others? Why?

21. Distinguish an event from an activity. What problems can arise if people on a project confuse these terms?

22. Distinguish an interface event from a milestone event. Give some examples of each. When is an interface event also a milestone event?

23. How are project-level and task-level schedules prepared? What is the relationship between them? Who prepares them?

24. Construct a Gantt chart similar to the one in Figure 5.10, using the following data:

Task	Start Time (weeks)	Duration (weeks)
A	0	5
B	6	3
C	7	4
D	7	9
E	8	2
F	9	8
G	12	7

When will task G be completed?

25. How would the Gantt chart you drew in question 24 have to be changed if you were told that C and D could not begin until B was completed, and that G could not begin until C was completed? What would happen to the project completion time?

26. Is the Gantt chart adequate for planning and controlling small projects?
27. In a hierarchy of schedules, how does changing a schedule at one level affect schedules at other levels?
28. How do you decide when more than one level of schedule is necessary?
29. If a hierarchy of schedules is used in project planning, explain whether there should be a corresponding hierarchy of plans as well.
30. What aspects of the project fall under "procurement management?" Why is managing procured items just as important to project success as managing internal items? What are the issues in scheduling procured items?
31. Consider this statement: The management of procured items can pose greater difficulties than managing internal items. Do you agree or disagree, and why?

QUESTIONS ABOUT THE STUDY PROJECT

1. Describe the project master plan for your project (the plan developed at the *start* of the project). What are the contents? Show a typical master plan.
2. Who prepared the plan?
3. At what point in the project was the plan prepared?
4. What is the relationship between the master plan and the project proposal? Was the plan derived from the proposal?
5. Is there a project scope statement? Who prepared it? Do major areas of work and deliverables of the project correspond to the scope statement?
6. Is there an SOW or project charter? Describe its purpose and contents.
7. How, when, and by whom was the work breakdown structure (WBS) prepared? Describe the process used in preparing the WBS.
8. Where in the WBS is project management included?
9. Was the work package concept used? If so, describe what a work package includes. How are work packages defined?
10. How were ongoing activities such as management, supervision, inspection, and maintenance handled in the WBS? Was there a work package for each?
11. How were responsibilities in the WBS assigned to the project organization (i.e., how did the functional areas become involved in the project)?
12. How were individuals assigned to the project? Describe the process.
13. Was a responsibility matrix used? Show an example.
14. How were activities in the WBS transferred to a schedule? How were times estimated? Who prepared the schedules?
15. Show examples of project-level and task-level schedules. Who prepared each? How were they checked and integrated?
16. What are the procured GWS in the project? Were these items managed differently than in-house aspects of the project? How were they first identified and then integrated into the project plan? Did procured items pose any difficulties to the project?

Case 5.1 Barrage Construction Company: Sean's WBS

Sean Shawn was recently appointed project planner at Barrage Construction, a company that specializes in custom-made garages. He had worked 2 years in the HR department while completing his MBA, and now occupies a place in the newly created project office. Barrage is considering branching out to building standard two-car and three-car garages as well as its usual customized garages, and asked Sean to determine the feasibility of moving into this market. Skimming a book on project management, he discovered the WBS concept and decided it would be helpful for developing cost estimates for the standard garages. He had never worked on a garage construction project, but felt he knew the process well enough from having talked to company employees. He sat down and drew the WBS in Figure 5.19. To estimate costs for each work category in the WBS, he reviewed company cost records from three recent two-car garage projects he thought similar to the standard garages, computed the average, and then apportioned the costs among the categories in the

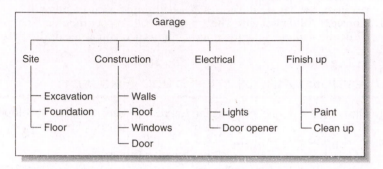

Figure 5.19
Sean's garage project WBS.

WBS. The company had no actual cost records for a three-car garage, so as an estimate he increased the estimate for the two-car garage by 50 percent. When he summed the costs for all the categories he arrived at a total of $43,000 for a two-car garage and $64,500 for a three-car garage. Compared to competitors, he discovered, these costs were 10 percent higher than their *prices*. However, because his estimates had been based on custom garages, he believed they might be at least 20 percent higher than for standard garages. He thus reduced his estimate by 20 percent and concluded that Barrage would be able to price its garages competitively and still make a 10 percent profit.

QUESTION

What is your opinion of Sean's approach to creating a WBS and estimating project costs? Please elaborate.

Case 5.2   *Startrek Enterprises, Inc.: Deva's Project Plan*

Deva Patel, project manager at Startrek Enterprises, Inc., is planning and coordinating the company's move to a new building currently under construction. Deva wants the move to commence as soon as the building is ready for the estimated June 1 occupancy—still 2 months away. The entire move, which will affect 4 departments and 600 people, is to be completed within 1 week. Because timing is critical, Deva starts her planning by preparing a Gantt chart. At the project level, she draws a bar 1 week (7 days) long and then subdivides it into three major categories: (1) pack office supplies, equipment, and furniture (3 days allotted); (2) move everything (2 days allotted); and (3) unpack and arrange it at new location (2 days). She then estimates the total number of boxes, equipment, and furniture that will have to be moved in 2 days, gives the estimate to a moving contractor, and receives a price quote. To assist in packing and unpacking boxes and equipment, Deva intends to hire temporary workers. She estimates the number of workers needed, gives it to a temp agency, and receives a price quote.

Deva shows the completed plan to her manager and asks him to review it. The plan consists of the Gantt chart and a budget that is largely based on the price quotes from the moving company and the temp agency.

QUESTIONS

1. What do you think about Deva's approach to scheduling work and estimating the costs?
2. If you were Deva's manager, would you consider her plan comprehensive?
3. How would *you* prepare a plan for the move, and what would your plan include?

Case 5.3   *Walter's Project Plan*

Walter has just been assigned to manage a project—his first experience as a project manager. The project involves developing an end-item that must meet a long list of requirements, but after reviewing the project SOW and requirements list the first thing Walter wonders is, who is going to be on his project team? He asks his manager, who gives him the names of three people in the department who are available to work on the project.

Next, Walter starts thinking about what each of the three people on the team will do. He feels that for a project to be successful, team members should each be assigned to tasks they are the most qualified or experienced to do. Since he has worked with the people before, he knows a little about their individual expertise. He sits down to prepare a list of tasks for each person; as he considers each person, he thinks about things that need to be done in the project and selects those things he thinks are best suited to the person. When he has finished creating the lists, he sees that person one has 11 tasks, while persons two and three have

4 tasks and 5 tasks, respectively. To balance out the workload, he takes 4 of the tasks from person one and splits them between the other two. He is pleased because he feels, with 7, 6, and 7 tasks, respectively, the team members will each have roughly the same amount of work.

On each list he then arranges the tasks in the approximate sequence they must be done.

The next day Walter meets with the team and gives them the lists of tasks. He asks that they estimate the time they will need to do each of the tasks and that they meet as a group to figure out how their tasks are interrelated and create a Gantt chart. He feels that by requiring team members to estimate task times and create their own schedule, the estimates and schedule will be realistic and accurately reflect the timing of the project.

Walter stops by his manager's office and eagerly reports that his "project plan" is soon forthcoming, to consist of a Gantt chart and lists of responsibilities for project team members.

QUESTIONS

1. Discuss Walter's approach to (a) defining work (creating task lists), (b) creating the schedule, and (c) assigning responsibility.
2. What do you think of Walter's approach to "balancing the workload" among the team members?
3. Do you think the Gantt chart will realistically reflect work that must be done in the project? Do you think the project will be able to satisfy the SOW and requirements?
4. How else might Walter have gone about defining work tasks, creating the schedule, and assigning responsibility?

NOTES

1. Some organizations use the term "project charter" to refer to a "master plan." Our preference is for the more common usage—i.e., the charter is a somewhat brief document to announce and authorize the decision to undertake a project, while the master plan is a comprehensive document that will guide the project team though project execution.
2. Contents of master plans are listed in Cleland DI and King WR. *Systems Analysis and Project Management*, 3rd edn. New York, NY: McGraw-Hill; 1983. pp. 461–469; Allen J and Lientz BP. *Systems in Action*. Santa Monica, CA: Goodyear; 1978. p. 95; Kerzner H. *Project Management*, 10th edn. New York, NY: Wiley; 2009. pp. 459–463.
3. See, for example, Cleland and King, *Systems Analysis and Project Management*, pp. 461–69.
4. Seymour Sarason, in *The Creation of Settings and The Future Societies* (San Francisco, CA: Jossey-Bass; 1972) argues the importance of knowing the beginnings, origins, and history of any new "setting" before initiating work; especially important is to anticipate and prepare for possible struggles, obstacles, and conflicts that may be encountered.
5. In technical projects, the subsystems and components—the "configuration items" (CIs)—are identified during preliminary design studies in systems engineering, described in Chapter 2.
6. Cleland and King, *Systems Analysis and Project Management*, p. 258.
7. Archibald R. *Managing High-Technology Programs and Projects*. New York, NY: John Wiley & Sons; 1976. pp. 65, 156.
8. Portions of this section are adapted from Joy, PK. *Total Project Management*. Delhi: Macmillan India Limited; 1998. pp. 378–400.
9. *Ibid*, pp. 378–380.
10. Examples: NEC or New Engineering Contract, The Institution of Civil Engineers, *The Engineering and Construction Contract*. London: Thomas Telford; 1995; and FIDIC, International Federation of Consulting Engineers, Lausanne, Switzerland, http://www1.fidic.org.
11. Whittaker R. *Project Management in the Process Industries*. New York, NY: John Wiley & Sons; 1995.

Chapter 6

Project Time Planning and Networks

> *I know why there are so many people who love chopping wood.*
> *In this activity one immediately sees the results.*
>
> —Albert Einstein

> *You can't always get what you want.*
>
> —Rolling Stones

Project scheduling involves much more than just displaying tasks on a Gantt chart. It is an integral part of project planning, an often trial-and-error process of adjusting work tasks to satisfy resource constraints while trying to meet project deadlines. Gantt charts are good for communicating project schedules, but they are limited as a planning tool because they do not explicitly show how activities are related or how delaying activities or shifting resources affects the overall project. The network methods described in this chapter do not have these limitations; they clearly show interdependencies and what happens to the project when resources are altered or activities delayed. This chapter and the next discuss the most widely used network-based approaches to project scheduling and planning.

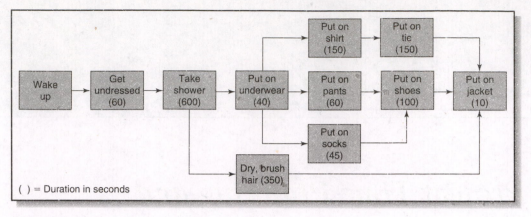

Figure 6.1
Network diagram for getting up and getting dressed.

6.1 NETWORK DIAGRAMS

A network diagram shows a group of activities or tasks and their logical relationships – i.e., the "precedence relationships" or "dependencies" among the tasks. Figure 6.1 is a network diagram for "getting up in the morning and getting dressed" (for a male). The boxes represent activities or tasks, and the arrows connecting them show the order in which they should occur – for example, put on shirt *before* tie, put on pants *and* socks *before* shoes, etc. (The diagram in Figure 6.1 is of course intended for illustration only; any real life attempt to plan work in such detail would be "micromanagement" and a real time-waster!) Ordinarily for a project, the boxes shown in the network would be the activities or work packages as defined in the work breakdown structure (WBS). Depending on the desired detail, however, the activities in the network can represent work at any level, including projects in a program, subprojects belonging to a project, or the work packages belonging to a project, project phase, subproject or specific facility.

Networks also show *events*. As described in Chapter 5, an event represents an *instant* in time, an "announcement" that something has happened or will happen. Typically it signifies the start of an activity or the end of an activity. An activity with a very short duration may also be regarded as an event. An important event such as completion of a project phase is a *milestone*.

Two methods for constructing network diagrams are *activity-on-node* (*AON*), also called the *precedence diagramming method* (*PDM*), and *activity-on-arrow* (*AOA*). Both were developed independently during the late 1950s. Our discussion will center on the more commonly used AON method. The AOA method is addressed in Appendix I to this chapter.

Activity on Node (AON) (or PDM) Diagrams

Figure 6.2 shows an activity as represented in the AON method. The *node* (the box in the figure) is the activity; inside the node is information about the activity, such as its duration, start time, and finish time.

To construct an AON network, start by drawing the first activity in the project (e.g., "wake up"). From this activity, draw lines to the activities that happen next. As

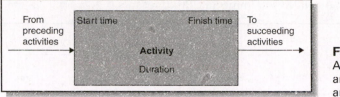

Figure 6.2
AON Presentation for an activity and its start and finish events.

shown in Figure 6.1, activities are added one after another, in sequence or parallel, until the last activity is included.

But before you can actually create a network, you must first know each activity's relationship to the other activities – for example:

- What activities are its predecessors?
- What activities are its successors?
- What activities can be done at the same time as it?

In a network, every activity except the first one has *predecessors*, which are activities that must be completed ahead of it; in Figure 6.1, for example, "put on shirt" is a predecessor for "put on tie." Similarly, every activity except the last one has *successors*, which are activities that cannot begin until the current activity is completed; "put on tie" is a successor of "put on shirt," which is a successor of "put on underwear," and so on.

It is important to distinguish between mandatory and discretionary predecessor/successor dependency relationships:

Mandatory: the sequence of two activities (which activity should precede the other) cannot be reversed. The relationship between "put on socks" and "put on shoes" in Figure 6.1 is an example.

Discretionary: the sequence is a matter of choice. For example, the order of "dry, brush hair" and "put on jacket" *can* be reversed. If need be, a discretionary dependency can be eliminated and activities overlapped to speed up the project. This is called *fast tracking*.

In another kind of dependency, called external dependency, an activity must follow some event or activity that is not in the network. For instance, in Figure 6.1 the activity "take umbrella" might be added at the end of the network, but only if rain is forecast. External dependencies can be either mandatory or discretionary.

Sometimes only the *immediate predecessors* are used to construct the network. An immediate predecessor is an activity that *immediately* precedes another activity. For example, "wake up" and "get undressed" are predecessors for "take shower," but only "get undressed" is an immediate predecessor. (The logic is, to "get undressed" you have to first "wake up".) Given the immediate predecessor information, it is easy to construct the network. In Table 6.1 this is done by starting with the first activity in the project (the one with no immediate predecessors) –"get undressed" – then connecting it to the activity that has "get undressed" as its immediate predecessor, which is "take shower". Next come "put on underwear" and "dry, brush hair," since "take shower" is *their* immediate predecessor. Continuing in this fashion, the result is the diagram in Figure 6.1. To make sure that no dependency is overlooked, check over the list of immediate predecessors to ensure that *all* of them are accounted for.

Table 6.1 Activities and Immediate Predecessors

ACTIVITY	IMMEDIATE PREDECESSORS	DURATION (SECONDS)
Get undressed	—	60
Take shower	Get undressed	600
Put on underwear	Take shower	40
Dry, brush hair	Take shower	350
Put on shirt	Put on underwear	150
Put on pants	Put on underwear	60
Put on socks	Put on underwear	45
Put on tie	Put on shirt	150
Put on shoes	{ Put on pants Put on socks	100
Put on jacket	{ Put on tie Put on shoes Dry, brush hair	10

Once the network is constructed, it is easy to see which activities are sequential and which are parallel. Activities that have a predecessor–successor relationship are *sequential* activities – one follows the other. For example, "take shower," "put on underwear," and "put on shirt" are sequential activities because they come one after the other. Two or more independent activities that can be performed at the same time are *parallel* activities. For instance, "put on shirt," "put on pants," "dry, brush hair," and "put on socks" are parallel because they can be done *all at the same time* (which, in this example, would be difficult to do) or in *any* order. Once the network has been completed, check the relationships among activities for completeness and logical consistency.

A second example is given in Table 6.2. The network diagram for this project, shown in Figure 6.3, begins at Activity A. Since Activities B and C both have A as their

Table 6.2 Activities and Immediate Predecessors

ACTIVITY	IMMEDIATE PREDECESSOR
A	—
B	A
C	A
D	B, C
E	B, C

Figure 6.3
AON Presentation for an activity and its start and finish events.

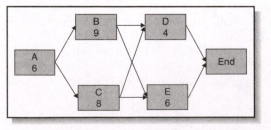

common immediate predecessor, both are connected directly to A. Then, because D has two immediate predecessors, B and C, it is connected to both of them; similarly, so is Activity E. Each node is labeled to identify the activity code and its duration.

In general, good practice dictates that a network should always have only one "start" and one "end" node, each a single place on the network to represent the start and end of the project. Whenever a project has multiple nodes at the start or end of the network, then a single node should be inserted before or after them, respectively. In Figure 6.3, for example, a single end node (with implied zero duration) has been inserted after Activities D and E. Without this node, the mistaken understanding might be that the project ends upon completion of either Activity D or Activity E. The "end" node means that the project ends when *both* D and E are completed.

As a final example, Table 6.3 shows the immediate predecessors for the LOGON project using work packages from the WBS in Chapter 5. Figure 6.4 shows the corresponding network.

Table 6.3 Activities and Immediate Predecessors for LOGON Project

ACTIVITY	DESCRIPTION	IMMEDIATE PREDECESSORS	DURATION (WEEKS)
H	Basic design	—	10
I	Hardware design for A	H	8
J	Hardware design for B	H	6
K	Drawings for B	J	4
L	Software specifications	J	2
M	Parts purchase for B	J	4
N	Parts purchase for A	I	4
O	Drawings for A	I	5
P	Installation drawings	I, J	5
Q	Software purchases	L	5
R	Delivery of parts for B	M	5
S	Delivery of parts for A	N	3
T	Software delivery	Q	3
U	Assembly of A	O, S	1
V	Assembly of B	K, R	5
W	Test A	U	2
X	Test B	V	3
Y	Final installation	P, W, X	8
Z	Final system test	Y, T	6

*Work packages from WBS, Figure 5.5.

Note that Tables 6.1, 6.2, and 6.3 used in the network examples include only the immediate predecessors for each activity. While it would have been okay to show *all* the predecessors for each activity in these tables, much of that information would have been unnecessary. For example, had Table 6.2 shown the predecessors for Activity D as A, B, and C, that would have been correct but also unnecessary because A is the predecessor for B and C, hence listing A would have been redundant. The point is, once dependencies have been thoroughly checked, only the immediate predecessors for each activity need be known to construct a network.

Creating a Network

A network is created using a list of activities from the WBS and their predecessors. If done by hand, the process is trial and error and the network might have to be redrawn several times before it is correct. Even if done by computer, good practice is to first

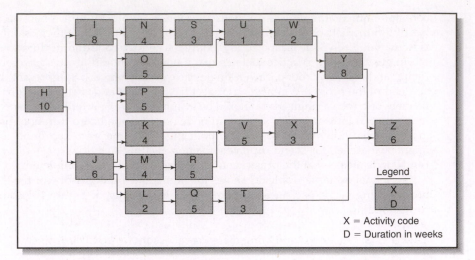

Figure 6.4
Network diagram for LOGON project.

sketch out the network by hand to create an initial ("coarse grain") network and then enter the data into a computer. This affords the project manager an intuitive "feel" for the project. The activities can be clustered into the higher-level subnetworks that represent, for example, subprojects, work packages or project phases. Project phases are normally conducted in series, although, as mentioned, discretionary dependencies can be eliminated so phases overlap and are *fast tracked*. (Even when phases overlap, however, it is still necessary to define their start and end points so that management can authorize the phases and approve milestone payments.)

In big projects the network might show detailed activities for early phases, but only rough clusters of activities for later phases. As a phase moves toward completion, details for activities in the next phase are added. This phased approach (called *phased project planning, progressive elaboration*, or *rolling wave planning*) reduces the complexity of the network for a large project.

Computer software for creating networks is a convenience in small projects but a necessity in large projects. The resulting network should be reviewed for accuracy, omissions, and mistakes. As a rule, the network should be created only after a suitable scope statement and WBS have been developed (i.e., the list of work tasks should be created before—not while—the network is created). Afterward a Gantt chart can be developed, as explained later.

6.2   THE CRITICAL PATH

Project networks are important tools for project planning and control. They are useful for determining *how long* the project will take (the *expected project duration*), *when* each activity should be scheduled to start and finish, and the *likelihood* of completing a project on time.

In general, the expected project duration, T_e, is determined by finding the *longest path* through the network. A "path" is any route comprised of one or more activities connected in sequence. The longest path from the project start node to the end node is called the *critical path*; its length is the expected project duration. Should any activity that forms part of the critical path (critical activity) take longer than planned (because of delays, interruptions, lack of resources, etc.), the entire project will take longer than planned.

This concept is illustrated in the following example. The firm of Kelly, Applebaum, Nuzzo, and Earl, Assoc. (KANE) is working on the Robotics Self-Budgeting (ROSEBUD) project. Figure 6.5 shows the network. (Parts (a) and (b) of Figure 6.5 are very similar; for now, look only at (a).) The first phase in the project is systems design (Activity J), followed by the simultaneous phases of (1) purchase, assembly, and installation (Activities M–V–Y), and (2) software specification and purchase (L–Q). The last phase of the project is system test and user test of the hardware and software (W–X).

How long will this project take? The first activity, J, takes 6 weeks; after J has been completed, activities on the paths M–V–Y and L–Q can begin. It will take $4+6+8=18$ weeks to do the activities on path M–V–Y, and $2+8=10$ weeks to do the activities on path L–Q. Because Activity J takes 6 weeks, path M–V–Y will be completed in $6+18=24$ weeks, and path L–Q will be completed in $6+10=16$ weeks. The diagram implies that for Activity W to begin, *both* Activity Y and Activity Q must be finished. Thus, the earliest Activity W can begin is after 24 weeks. Activity W will be completed 1 week later, and Activity X (user test) will be completed 1 week after that. Thus, the duration (denoted as T_e) of the ROSEBUD project is $T_e = 24+1+1 = 26$ weeks.

Notice from Figure 6.5(a) that there are two paths from the start node (J) to the end node (X). The shorter path, J–L–Q–W–X, is 18 weeks; the longer path, J–M–V–Y–W–X, is 26 weeks. In general, *the longest path—called the critical path—gives the project duration*. The critical path is highlighted in the example, where the critical activities are the ones with darker "framed" boxes.

Figure 6.5
Network for ROSEBUD project.

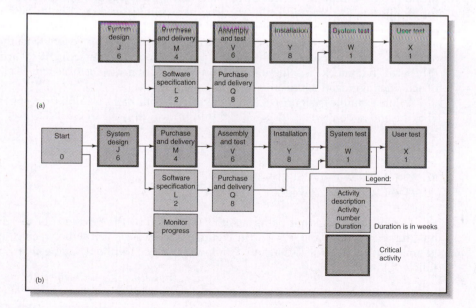

Should it be necessary to reduce the project duration, any reduction in effort (e.g., reducing the time for an activity) must happen on the critical path. Shortening any critical activity by, say, 1 week would have the effect of shortening the project duration by 1 week. In contrast, shortening activities *not* on the critical path would have no effect on project duration. For example, if L or Q is reduced by 1 week, then Activity Q will be completed in Week 15 instead of Week 16; but since Activity W must still wait on completion of Activity Y—which won't happen until after Week 24—there will be no change in project duration.

As mentioned, the critical path is important for another reason: *any* delay among the activities in the critical path will result in a delay in the project completion. Should any critical activity be delayed by, say, 1 week, the project completion will be delayed by 1 week. Note, however, that non-critical activities *can* be delayed somewhat without delaying the project. In fact, in the example, non-critical activities L and Q together can be delayed by up to 8 weeks. This is because normally they will be completed in 16 weeks, which is 8 weeks earlier than the activities on path M–V–Y will be completed, which is 24 weeks. In other words, although activities on path L–Q can be completed in as early as 16 weeks, it is okay if they are completed in as late as 24 weeks. Thus, the critical path shows the project manager which activities are most critical to completing the project on time. In order to prevent delays, the project manager should focus on the critical activities.

Although the critical path is important, that doesn't mean it should receive *exclusive* focus. Whenever a non-critical activity is delayed, the length of the path for that activity gets longer. When the length of a non-critical path grows to exceed the critical path, the former non-critical path becomes critical and the (former) critical path becomes non-critical! In other words, the critical path changes.[1] These changes can happen without warning, and leave the project manager focused on the wrong activities. One solution is to provide warning signals when non-critical activities are at risk of becoming critical; this is done in the *critical chain* method, discussed in Chapter 7.

Figure 6.5(b) illustrates an activity that "spans" multiple other activities, called a *hammock*. The activity "Monitor progress" is a hammock because it covers all activities in the project except "User test," implying that the project manager is responsible for monitoring the progress on every activity except "User test." The duration of a hammock is determined by the duration of the longest path of activities over which it spans, which in Figure 6.5(b) is $6 + 4 + 6 + 8 + 1 = 25$ weeks. Note, however, that although a hammock spans a portion of the longest path, it is not considered a critical activity. (The term "hammock" is sometimes also used to describe a *summary activity*; e.g., a set of activities aggregated into one work package.)

A final example is Figure 6.6. This network has four paths leading from start node H to the end node Z:

a. H–J–P–Y–Z = 35 weeks
b. H–J–K–V–X–Y–Z = 42 weeks
c. H–J–M–R–V–X–Y–Z = 47 weeks
d. H–J–L–Q–T–Z = 32 weeks.

The longest of the four paths is Path c (indicated by the "shaded" boxes); hence c is the critical path and $T_e = 47$. (In Figure 6.6, notice the arrow between X and Z is unnecessary: if Z follows Y and Y follows X, it goes without saying that Z must follow X.)

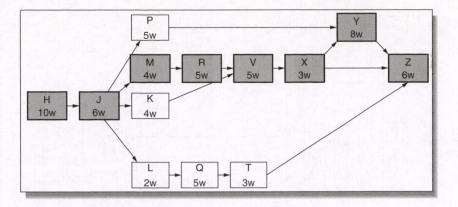

Figure 6.6
Example network showing the critical path as (developed with Project Scheduler 8.5 software).

Multiple Critical Paths

Can a project have more than one critical path? There is no reason why not. Suppose the duration of Activity L in Figure 6.6 were 17 weeks instead of 2 weeks. In that case, the durations of path M–R–V–X–Y and path L–Q–T would both be 25 weeks, and the project would have *two* critical paths, both with duration 47 weeks. The entire project would be delayed if a delay were to occur on *either* critical path. If, however, the project duration had to be *shortened* to less than 47 weeks, it would be necessary to shorten *both* critical paths. A problem with multiple critical paths is that they dilute management focus: more things are of critical importance.

Early Times: Early Start (ES) and Early Finish (EF)

Scheduling each activity in a project involves, at minimum, specifying when the activity must be started and finished. The scheduling procedure depends on whether the project is assumed to start "at Time 0" or "on Day 1." The procedure below is based on the more common "Time 0" assumption; Appendix II to this chapter describes scheduling under the "Day 1" assumption.

The formula for computing finish time given start time and duration is:

$$\text{Finish time} = \text{Start time} + \text{Duration}$$

These start and finish times for an activity are represented on the network by two "early times": (1) the *early start time* (ES), and (2) the *early finish time* (EF); these represent the earliest possible times that the activity can be started and completed.

But the ES of an activity depends on the finish times of its immediate predecessors. These times are found by summing the durations of the predecessor activities along the paths leading to the activity in question; when more than one path leads to an activity, the ES of the activity will be determined by the *longest path* leading to the activity. This is shown in Figure 6.7. Suppose the ES for the first activity, H, is 0 (meaning the project starts at time 0). Since the duration is 10 weeks, the early finish, EF, of H must be Week 10. This was determined from the formula:

$$EF = ES + \text{Duration}$$

Figure 6.7
Example network showing ESs and EFs.

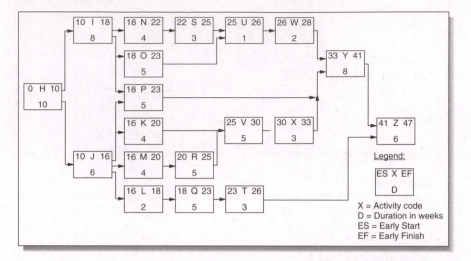

In Figure 6.7, ES is shown in the upper left of each node and EF on the upper right.

Given that for Activity H the EF is Week 10, for Activity J the ES will be at Week 10 and the EF at Week 16. Similarly, ES for activities K, M, and L will be Week 16. For Activity V, the ES will occur after all of its immediate predecessors have been completed: the length of the path going through Activity K is $10+6+4=20$, which is the EF for Activity K; the length of the path going through activities M and R is $10+6+4+5=25$, which is the EF for Activity R. Thus, the ES of Activity V will depend on the longer of the paths leading to it, which is through Activity R. Since EF for Activity R is Week 25, ES for Activity V is Week 25. The same happens at Activity P: ES = Week 18, which is computed by using the longest path leading to it—the path through Activity I.

For Activity Y to start, all three of Y's immediate predecessor activities, W, P, and X, must have been completed. Hence, the earliest that Activity Y can be started is in Week 33. For Activity Z the ES is at the start of Week 41 and EF is at the end of Week 47. Notice, 47 weeks is also the project duration, T_e.

In summary, ESs and EFs are computed by taking a "forward pass" through the network. When an activity has only one immediate predecessor, its ES is simply the period following the EF of the predecessor. When an activity has several immediate predecessors, its ES is based on the *latest* EF of all its immediate predecessors.

Late Times: Late Start (LS) and Late Finish (LF)

As discussed, a non-critical activity can be delayed without delaying the project; the question is: How much can it be delayed? To answer that we must determine the "late times"—that is, the latest allowable times that the activity can be started and finished without delaying the project completion. Just like the ES and the EF, every activity has a *late start* time, LS, and a *late finish* time, LF.

Refer to Figure 6.8. To determine the late times, begin by assigning a *target completion date*, T_s, to the *last node* in the network. For projects that have to be completed *as soon as possible*, the date for T_s is the same as the T_e calculated in the forward pass; this is the EF of the last activity. For projects with a due date set by the customer or the sponsor, T_s is the due date, not the calculated T_e value.

To determine the late times, start at the *last activity* in the network and make a "backward pass" through the network using the formula:

$$LS = LF - Duration$$

In Figure 6.8, start with Activity Z. If T_s is 47 weeks, then LF for Activity Z is 47 and LS is $47 - 6 = 41$; i.e., Activity Z must start in Week 41 for the project to end in Week 47. Continuing backward, for Activity Y (and Activity T) the LF is 41 weeks, and LS for Y is $41 - 8 = 33$. Continue moving backward like this through each path, computing LF and LS for each activity.

Whenever we encounter an activity that has *multiple* paths leading back to it (i.e., it has multiple immediate successors), it is the *longest backward path* that determines the activity's LF; in other words, it is the immediate successor with the longest path leading back to it that determines the activity's LF. The successor with the longest path leading back to it also has the *smallest LS*. Thus, the smallest LS of all immediate successors determines an activity's LF. For example, Activity J has four paths leading back to it and four immediate successors:

- For Activity P the LF is 33 weeks (because LS for Activity Y is Week 33); thus LS for P is $33 - 5 = 28$

- For Activity K the LF is 25 weeks (because LS for Activity V is Week 25); thus LS for K is $25 - 4 = 21$ weeks

- Similarly, for Activity M, LF is 20, so LS $= 20 - 4 = 16$ weeks

- For Activity L, LF $= 33$ and LS $= 33 - 2 = 31$ weeks.

Figure 6.8
Example network showing LFs and LSs.

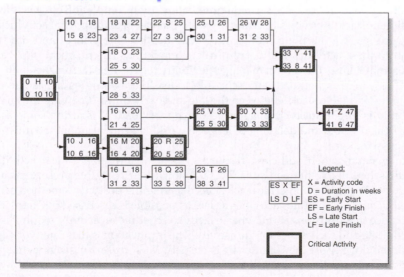

Since the successor of Activity J with the smallest LS is Activity M (LS = 16), the LF for Activity J is 16; this is the latest Activity J can be finished to allow enough time to complete the longest sequence of remaining activities M–R–V–X–Y–Z by the target date of 47 weeks.

In summary, calculations for LFs and LSs start at the last node of the project network and work backward. When an activity has more than one path leading back to it, the smallest value of LS among all its immediate successors is the basis for determining the activity's LF. Having completed both forward and backward passes through the network, we now have the earliest possible and latest allowable scheduled times for every activity in the network. Once the forward and backward pass calculations have been completed, the durations of hammock activities become evident.

Total Slack

Referring to Figure 6.8, notice that for most activities ES and LS are not the same. The difference between LS and ES (or LF and EF) is referred to as *total slack*, "total float," or simply "slack" or "float" of an activity. Slack is the amount of allowable deviation between when an activity *must* take place at the latest and when it *can* take place at the earliest; it is the amount of time an activity can be delayed without delaying the project:

$$\text{Total slack} = EF - ES$$
$$= LF - LS$$

In Figure 6.8 the total slack for Activity H is $0 - 0 = 0$ weeks; for Activity I it is $15 - 10 = 5$ weeks, and so on. Notice that activities on the critical path in Figure 6.8 have zero slack; hence, these activities cannot be delayed by any amount without delaying the project. (The case where critical activities *do* have some slack is discussed later.) The activities that *do have* slack (which, as it turns out, are the *non-critical activities*) can be delayed by their slack time without delaying project completion.

When activities lie in sequence on a path, a delay in earlier activities will result in a delay to later ones; this is the equivalent of reducing slack for the remaining activities. In Figure 6.8, for example, activities L, Q, and T all lie on the same path and all have the same slack of 15 weeks. But if Activity L is delayed 5 weeks, then activities Q and T will also be delayed 5 weeks and thus will have only 10 weeks of slack remaining, not 15. If, in addition, Activity Q is delayed 10 weeks, then Activity T will have no remaining slack and must be started immediately upon completion of Q. Having used up all their slack, Activities L, Q and T would then all become critical activities.

Once slack is used up, non-critical activities become critical and any further delays to these activities will delay project completion. The practical implication of slack is that it gives the project manager flexibility regarding exactly when non-critical activities can be scheduled: any schedule is feasible as long as it lies somewhere within the available slack—between the late and early times. Knowing the amount of flexibility is important for managing resource workload. By starting some activities as early as possible and delaying others, the workload can be smoothed; this concept is discussed later.

In general, when sufficient resources are available, non-critical activities are usually scheduled to happen as early as possible (their ESs); this preserves slack and minimizes the risk of non-critical activities delaying the project. (A method called the *critical chain* that schedules activities as late as possible is discussed in Chapter 7.)

Notice that decisions about when exactly to schedule an activity require knowing both the late and early times for the activity. The implication is that a network analysis should be done *before* the Gantt chart is created. Most project management software develops networks and Gantt charts simultaneously and schedules activities using the early start times. As discussed later, however, activities should not always be scheduled according to the early times.

Free Slack

While *total slack* refers to the amount of time an activity can be delayed without delaying *the project*, the term *free slack* refers to the time an activity can be delayed without delaying *the start of any successor activity*. Free slack of an activity is determined by the formula:

Free slack for activity = ES (earliest successor) − EF (activity)

For example, in Figure 6.8 Activity I has a total slack of 5 weeks but free slack of 0 weeks because *any* delay in it will delay the start of activities N, O, and P. Activity O, on the other hand, has free slack of 2 weeks, because its EF of 23 can be delayed to 25 without delaying the ES of its successor, Activity U, which is 25.

Knowing the free slack, managers can readily identify activities where slippages immediately impact other activities. When an activity has zero free slack, *any* slippage will cause at least one other activity to also slip. If, for example, Activity L slips, then so will Q and T, and teams working in Q and T (specified in the responsibility matrix) must be notified of the delay.

As with total slack, the amount of free slack available to an activity assumes the activity starts at its ES time. Thus, the free slack for Activity O is 2 weeks as long as Activity I, its immediate predecessor, is completed at EF = 18. If Activity I is delayed by any amount, then Activity O's free slack will be reduced by the same amount.

Free slack is important because many activities are scheduled to start as soon as possible and resources are booked to be available on these dates. If an activity is delayed, it can delay other activities and disrupt the schedules of everyone who planned to work on those activities. Moreover, such delays extend the period over which resources (e.g., equipment contracted at a daily or hourly rate) are needed and can lead to cost overruns.

Table 6.4 summarizes these concepts, showing ES, LS, EF, and LF, and total and free slack for the LOGON project in Figure 6.8. Notice that for activities on the critical path the total slack and free slack times are zero.

The Effect of Project Due Date

In discussing total slack we assumed that the target completion date, T_s, was the same as the earliest expected completion date, T_e. But in fact the target completion date can be set to make it either later or earlier than T_e to reflect the wishes of the customer.

Setting the target date to *later* than T_e has the effect of *increasing* total slack for every activity in the project by the amount $T_s - T_e$. Although no longer zero, the slack on the critical path will still be the *smallest* slack anywhere in the network. For example, if the target completion date T_s for the project in Figure 6.8 were increased to 50 weeks, then the total slack in Table 6.4 would be $50 - 47 = 3$ weeks for all critical activities and 3 *additional* weeks for all non-critical activities.

If T_s is set *earlier* than T_e, then the total slack times everywhere in the project will be reduced by the amount $T_s - T_e$ and activities along the critical path will have *negative* slack times. The size of this negative slack is the amount of time by which the project duration must be reduced to meet the customer target date. (Note that altering T_s has no influence on free slack times: these depend on early start and early finish times, both of which are affected by the same amount when changing T_s.)

In general, projects have to be completed either as soon as possible or by a predetermined due date. For projects that have to be completed as soon as possible,

Table 6.4 LOGON Project Time Analysis (from Figure 6.8)

Activity	Duration (weeks)	Start Node		Finish Node		Slack		Note
		ES (Start of week)	IS (Start of week)	EF (Start of week)	IF (Start of week)	Total*	Free**	
H	10	0	0	10	10	0	0	CP
I	8	10	15	18	23	5	0	
J	6	10	10	16	16	0	0	CP
K	4	16	21	20	25	5	5	
L	2	16	31	18	33	15	0	
M	4	16	16	20	20	0	0	CP
N	4	18	23	22	27	5	0	
O	5	18	25	23	30	7	2	
P	5	18	28	23	33	10	10	
Q	5	18	33	23	38	15	0	
R	5	20	20	25	25	0	0	CP
S	3	22	27	25	30	5	0	
T	3	23	38	26	41	15	15	
U	1	25	30	26	31	5	0	
V	5	25	25	30	30	0	0	CP
W	2	26	31	28	33	5	5	
X	3	30	30	33	33	0	0	CP
Y	8	33	33	41	41	0	0	CP
Z	6	41	41	47	47	0	0	CP
(1)	(2)	(3)	(4)	(5)	(6)	(7)	(8)	

Total slack, $(7) = (4) - (3) = (6) - (5)$
Free slack, $(8) = [(3)$ of earliest successor$] - (5)$

*Total slack is the spare time on an activity that, if used up and the activity is delayed any further, delays successors and affects the end date of the project as a whole.

**Free slack is the spare time on an activity that, if used up, does not affect the early start time of any succeeding activities (i.e., will not affect the total slack or delay any successor).

the project manager does a forward-pass calculation through the network, then commits to the resultant T_e. For projects that must meet a predetermined due date, the project manager substitutes T_s at the last event, then works backwards through the network, noting the feasibility of speeding up activities in the project to eliminate negative slack times on the critical path.

6.3 Gantt Charts and Calendar Schedules

Converting the information from tables such as Tables 6.2 or 6.3 into a network with start and finish times is a simple procedure that requires no management decisions and is readily performed by computer software. To be usable, however, the times in the network must be converted into dates (day, month, and year) on either a Gantt chart or an actual calendar. But converting network times to a Gantt or calendar schedule is *not* a simple procedure and *does* require management decisions.

For starters, the Gantt or calendar schedule must account for *non-working time* such as weekends, holidays, and vacations. Figure 6.9 shows the LOGON project schedule as produced by Microsoft Project software and incorporating time off for weekends and holidays.

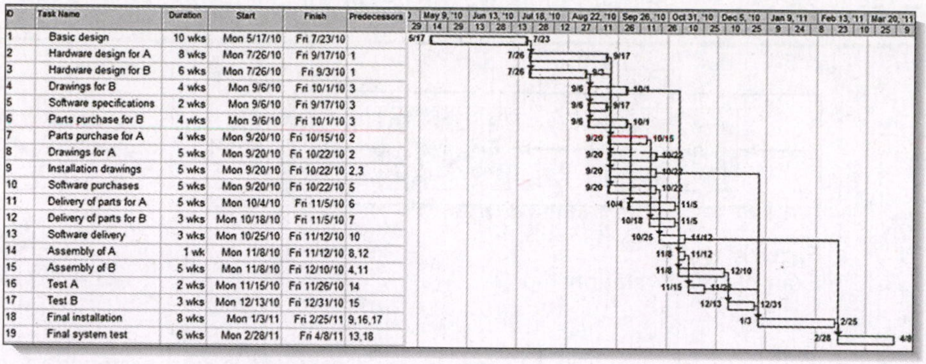

ID	Task Name	Duration	Start	Finish	Predecessors
1	Basic design	10 wks	Mon 5/17/10	Fri 7/23/10	
2	Hardware design for A	8 wks	Mon 7/26/10	Fri 9/17/10	1
3	Hardware design for B	6 wks	Mon 7/26/10	Fri 9/3/10	1
4	Drawings for B	4 wks	Mon 9/6/10	Fri 10/1/10	3
5	Software specifications	2 wks	Mon 9/6/10	Fri 9/17/10	3
6	Parts purchase for B	4 wks	Mon 9/6/10	Fri 10/1/10	3
7	Parts purchase for A	4 wks	Mon 9/20/10	Fri 10/15/10	2
8	Drawings for A	5 wks	Mon 9/20/10	Fri 10/22/10	2
9	Installation drawings	5 wks	Mon 9/20/10	Fri 10/22/10	2,3
10	Software purchases	5 wks	Mon 9/20/10	Fri 10/22/10	5
11	Delivery of parts for A	5 wks	Mon 10/4/10	Fri 11/5/10	6
12	Delivery of parts for B	3 wks	Mon 10/18/10	Fri 11/5/10	7
13	Software delivery	3 wks	Mon 10/25/10	Fri 11/12/10	10
14	Assembly of A	1 wk	Mon 11/8/10	Fri 11/12/10	8,12
15	Assembly of B	5 wks	Mon 11/8/10	Fri 12/10/10	4,11
16	Test A	2 wks	Mon 11/15/10	Fri 11/26/10	14
17	Test B	3 wks	Mon 12/13/10	Fri 12/31/10	15
18	Final installation	8 wks	Mon 1/3/11	Fri 2/25/11	9,16,17
19	Final system test	6 wks	Mon 2/28/11	Fri 4/8/11	13,18

Figure 6.9
LOGON project schedule adjusted for holidays and weekends.

In addition, a calendar schedule must account for issues that require analysis and management decisions; examples include:

- *Resource constraints*: a work package is delayed because the resources it needs are unavailable or must be shared with or, parallel activities
- *Cash flow*: the procurement of an expensive equipment item is delayed in order to defer cash outlay, improve cash flow, or await an exchange rate improvement
- *Risk of changes*: a design activity is postponed due to changes in project scope, developing technologies, or design activities
- *Logistics*: the acquisition of a bulky item for construction is delayed until space becomes available at the construction site.

Computer software can readily generate the project network, Gantt chart, and calendar schedule, but unless issues like those listed above are accounted for, the project schedule will be infeasible, unworkable, or too risky. The point is, project scheduling involves more than merely creating a computer-generated version of the project network; it requires analysis and management judgment. Thus, the Gantt chart should be created only *after* a network analysis has been done, early and late dates determined, and issues and constraints surrounding the project accounted for.

6.4 Management Schedule Reserve

Usually, the contractual or committed target completion time T_s is *not* simply the estimated completion time T_e plus allowance for non-working time; instead, it is some time *after* that and includes a *management schedule reserve* or *time buffer*. This chapter has treated activity and project durations as if they are fixed. Of course, each project is unique, and until it has actually been completed its duration is no more than an estimate. All durations (of projects and of the activities that compose them) are subject to uncertainty; the more unusual the project, the larger the uncertainty. To account for that uncertainty, a management schedule reserve is created. This reserve constitutes a "safety buffer" or "time buffer" the project manager can use to offset project delays. Time buffers are discussed in Chapter 7.

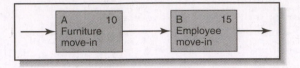

Figure 6.10
Example of FS relationship.

The network scheduling procedures discussed so far assumed a sequential relationship wherein the start of an activity is predicated upon the completion of its immediate predecessors. Such is the case illustrated in the diagram in Figure 6.10, where Activity B starts upon completion of Activity A. This strict start-only-when-predecessors-are-finished relationship is called *finish-to-start*, *FS*. The limitation of this assumption is that it precludes those kinds of tasks that can be started when their predecessors are only *partially* (but not fully) completed. For example, when a company relocates to a new facility, the activity "employee move-in" should be able to start after *some* of the activity "furniture move-in" has been done; i.e., "employee move-in" can begin *before* its immediate predecessor "furniture move-in" has been completed. The precedence diagramming method (PDM) allows for this and similar such situations. Besides the usual FS relationship, PDM permits the logical relationships of start-to-start (SS), finish-to-finish (FF), and start-to-finish (SF). It also allows for lags between times when activities must be started or finished. These relationships are described next.

Start-to-Start (SS)

In an SS relationship between two activities A and B, the start of B can occur at the earliest *n* days after the start of its immediate predecessor, A. This is diagrammed in Figure 6.11. The *n* days delay is called *lag*. In the case of acceleration instead of a delay, *lead* is used instead of lag (lead is the mathematical negative of lag).

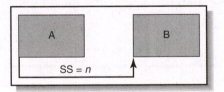

Figure 6.11
PDM representation of SS relationship with *n* day lag.

Using the example from Figure 6.10, suppose that "employee move-in" can begin 5 days after the start of "furniture move-in;" the network diagram and associated Gantt chart for the two activities would appear as in Figure 6.12.

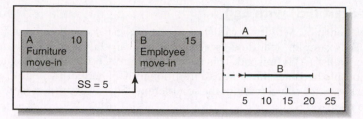

Figure 6.12
Example of SS relationship.

Finish-to-Finish (FF)

In an FF relationship between two activities A and B, B will finish *n* days at the latest, after A finishes. An illustration is provided in Figure 6.13, where "paint parking lines" (B) must be finished within 5 days after "lay asphalt" (A) has been finished. When two or more activities must finish at the same time, an FF relationship with zero lag is used.

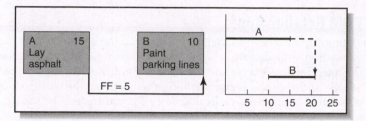

Figure 6.13
Example of FF relationship.

Start-to-Finish (SF)

In an SF relationship, the finish of Activity B must occur at the latest *n* days after the start of Activity A. For example, "phase out old system" (B) cannot be finished until 25 days after "test new system" (A) begins. This is shown in Figure 6.14.

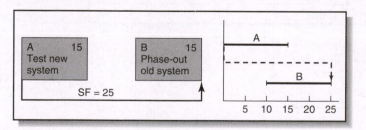

Figure 6.14
Example of SF relationship.

Finish-to-Start (FS) with Lag

In an FS relationship, Activity B can start at the earliest n days after the finish of Activity A. For example, "tear down scaffolding" (B) can start no sooner than 5 days after "plaster walls" (A) is finished. This is shown in Figure 6.15. Note that when $n=0$, the FS relationship becomes the same as a traditional AON network schedule wherein the start of a successor coincides with the completion of its latest predecessor, with no lag between them.

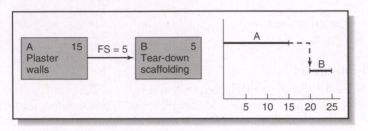

Figure 6.15
Example of FS relationship.

Multiple PDM Relationships

Two PDM relationships can be used in combination. Having both SS and FF is a rather common combination; an example is illustrated in Figure 6.16. Notice in the figure that because B must be finished no later than 10 days after A finishes, the start of B must occur at Day 10. Suppose B is an *interruptible* activity (i.e., the work in B does not have to be performed contiguously). In that case, B could instead be started 5 days after the start of A *and* be finished 10 days after the finish of A. This is represented in Figure 6.17. The assumption is that the 15 days of work for B will be performed sometime within the 20 days allowed for it between Day 5 and Day 25.

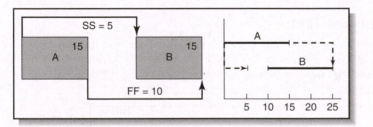

Figure 6.16
Schedule for non-interruptible activity B.

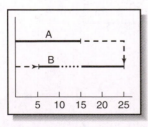

Figure 6.17
Schedule for interruptible activity B.

Notice that the 20 days scheduled for Activity B gives two possible slack values for that activity, LS – ES = 5 or LF – EF = 0. PDM usually observes the smallest slack value, in this case 0.

Example 6.1: PDM in ROSEBUD Project

Figure 6.18 shows the usual (FS=0) network diagram for the ROSEBUD project and Figure 6.19 shows the corresponding time-scaled network, which is a form of Gantt chart wherein dependencies among the activities are shown explicitly.

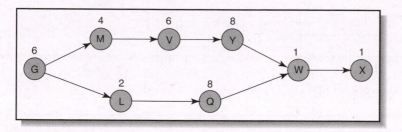

Figure 6.18
AON diagram for ROSEBUD project.

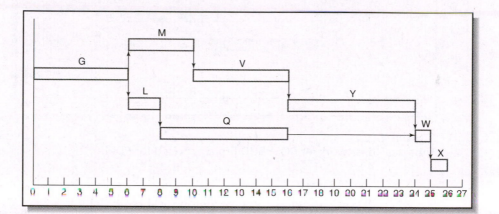

Figure 6.19
Time-scaled network for ROSEBUD project.

The network will now be altered to permit the following special (non-FS) relationships:

1. Activity L can begin 3 days after Activity G begins, but it cannot be finished until G is also finished.
2. Activity Y can begin 2 days after Activity V begins, but it cannot be completed until at least 6 days after V is completed.
3. Activity W can begin 5 days after Activity Y begins, but it cannot be completed until Y is also completed.
4. Activity X cannot be started until at least 1 day after Activity W is completed.

The PDM network in Figure 6.20 shows these relationships. Figure 6.21 shows the time-scaled network assuming earliest start dates and allowing for interruptions in activities.

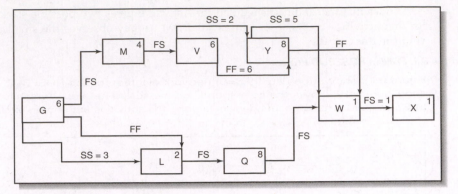

Figure 6.20
PDM network for ROSEBUD project.

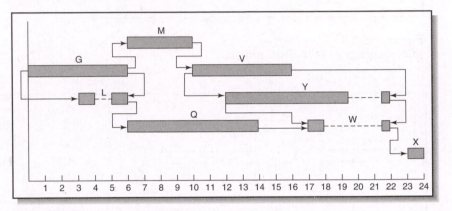

Figure 6.21
Time-scaled network for ROSEBUD project revised for PDM.

A traditional FS network can handle relationships where FS > 0 by creating artificial activities, but it has no way of incorporating SS, FF, or SF; thus, the obvious advantage of non-FS PDM networks is that they permit a greater degree of flexibility. The trade-off is that the networks are more complex and require greater care both in their creation and interpretation. Because activities do not follow a neat FS sequence, finding the critical path and slack times is not so simple either. Complex precedence relationships also cause counterintuitive results. For example, in a simple FS network the way to reduce the project completion time is to reduce the duration of activities along the critical path; however, doing the same thing in a non-FS network does not necessarily produce the desired result. In the previous example, the critical path is path G–M–V–Y–W–X. Suppose we decide to reduce the time on Activity Y. Because of the precedence requirement that Y cannot be finished sooner than 6 days before V is finished, the completion date of Y cannot be changed. Thus, any shortening of the duration of Y serves to *move back* the start date of Y. Because of the precedence requirement, moving back the start date of Y results in moving back the start date of W and, as a result, the start date of X. In other words, shortening critical Activity Y actually causes an *increase in the project duration*.

In general, interpreting a non-FS network with lag or lead relationships requires more care than ordinary AON networks. However, these and other difficulties are relatively inconsequential when the PDM network is generated with project management software.

6.6 SCHEDULING WITH RESOURCE CONSTRAINTS

Every activity requires working capital, people, equipment, material, and even space. Until now, our coverage of scheduling has assumed implicitly that such resources would always be available when needed. But of course resources are not always available. We now consider scheduling with resource constraints, and the effect of constraints on workload and project duration.

Resource Availability and Project Duration

In many cases, the availability of skilled workers, equipment, and working capital dictate whether activities can be scheduled at their early times or must be delayed. This is especially true when multiple activities that require the same resource are scheduled for the same time. When resources are not sufficient to satisfy the needs of all of them, some activities must be delayed. Figure 6.22 illustrates; (a) shows the network and (b) shows the project schedule, not accounting for the resources. Suppose Activities B and C both require the same resource, but the resource can be applied to only one of them at a time. The project is *resource constrained*. In that case, the schedule must be revised; Figure 6.22(c) shows two alternatives.

In general, projects tend to be either *resource constrained* or *time constrained*. A resource-constrained project is one where the resources are limited in some way and the project completion date is determined by the availability of those resources. A time-constrained project is one that *must* be completed by a certain due date, and sufficient resources must be found to enable the project to meet that date. A project that is both resource constrained and time constrained might not be able to meet the required completion date.

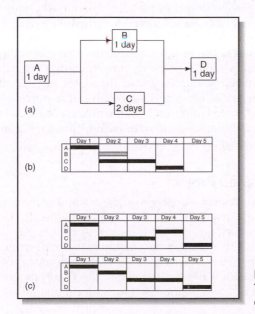

Figure 6.22
The effect of a constrained resource on schedule.

Resource Allocation, Workload, and Loading

The terms resource allocation, workload, and resource loading convey related but different concepts. *Resource allocation* refers to assigning one or more resources to an activity or project. *Workload* refers to the amount of work imposed on a resource. *Resource loading* refers to the amount of a particular resource needed to conduct all the activities in a project to which the resource is allocated. For an *individual resource* (such as a person), the workload can be specified either as a percentage of the resource's full workload potential or, more commonly, as units such as labor-hours. For a *facility* or *labor category* (such as a department or pool of workers with a specific skill), the workload is specified in terms of number of workers. Since people in a labor category (such as "computer programmer") rarely have exactly the same skills, ordinarily it is better to allocate a specific person (a specific programmer) rather than a labor category to an activity. (The usual assumption when allocating from a labor category is that everyone in the category is equally capable, though often after the work begins it becomes evident that not all workers are equally capable.) The workload that an individual can handle in a year is computed as the number of working days (excluding holidays and all types of leave) times the number of productive (working) hours per day. Many companies have guidelines stating the number of hours an individual should work on projects per week, month, or per year. In a matrix organization, functional managers are responsible for ensuring that each worker's time is well utilized and her workload does not exceed a recommended maximum.

Workload is always from the perspective of the particular resource; in contrast, loading is from the perspective of the *project*. It is the number of hours, people, or other units of a particular resource needed at a given time in a project (or in multiple concurrent projects). Resource loading is important because virtually all resources are finite and many are scarce. Thus, the resource loading (total amount of the resource needed for a project or projects at a given time) cannot exceed the amount available. When resources are scarce, their allocation is constrained, and sometimes activities in a project must be rescheduled to accommodate the scarcity. The example in Figure 6.22 was such a case: Activities B and C require the same resource, but the resource cannot be used in both at the same time. Resources available in sufficient quantity do not pose an issue (air is an example—unless the project is being conducted under water or in outer space where air is limited) and can be ignored for scheduling purposes.

The following sections consider two cases where the project schedule must be altered to accommodate resources. The first is called *resource leveling* in a *time-constrained project*. In this case, there is enough of the resource to complete the project on time; however, the amount of the resource needed fluctuates throughout the project, making it difficult to manage the resource. The objective of resource leveling is to level the amount of the resource needed throughout the project. The second case is the situation mentioned before: *the resource-constrained project*—not having enough of a resource to do multiple activities at the same time.

Leveling of a Time Constrained Project

Because the loading for a particular resource depends on the amount of the resource needed by project activities and the start and finish dates of those activities, the loading for a particular resource tends to vary throughout a project. A common resource-loading pattern in a project is a steady build-up in the amount of the resource needed, a peak, and then a gradual decline. Thus, relatively little of the resource is needed early and late in the project, but much is needed in the middle. This is problematic for functional managers who are responsible for a stable, uniform pool of workers

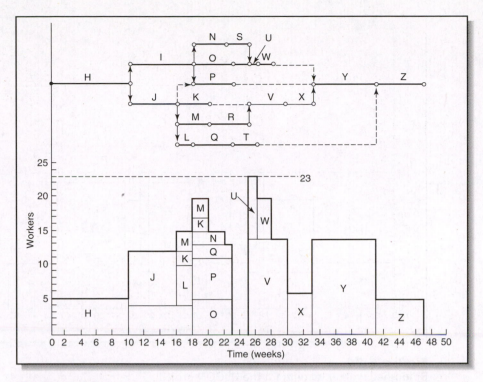

Figure 6.23
Schedule and corresponding worker loading for the LOGON project.

and equipment, because it results in periods where the pool is underworked or overworked. Certainly better would be a relatively uniform workload on the resource pool. This is the purpose of resource leveling: to alter the schedule of individual project activities such that the resultant amount of a required resource is somewhat uniform throughout the project.

Figure 6.23 shows the loading of a resource for the LOGON project—the resource being a particular skill or trade (programmer, steel worker, etc.). The diagram is created from the schedule in Figure 6.23 and the weekly labor requirements in Table 6.5 by adding the requirements for all activities scheduled each week, on a week-by-week basis. For example, for the first 10 weeks only Activity H is scheduled, so the loading for those weeks stays at five workers (the weekly requirement for H). Over

Table 6.5 LOGON Project Weekly Labor Requirements

ACTIVITY	H	I	J	K	L	M	N	O	P	Q	R	S	T	U	V	W	X	Y	Z
Duration (weeks)	10	8	6	4	2	4	4	5	5	5	5	3	3	1	5	2	3	8	6
Weekly Labor Requirements (workers)	5	4	8	2	6	3	2	5	6	2	0	0	0	9	14	6	6	14	5
Weekly Equipment Requirements (hours)	8	2	6	1	2	2	0	0	6	0	4	4	0	8	8	8	8	8	8

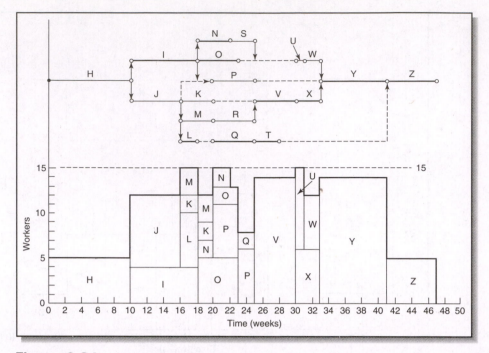

Figure 6.24
Smoothed worker loading for the LOGON project.

the next 6 weeks, activities I and J are scheduled, so the loading becomes $4+8=12$, and so on.

Looking at Figure 6.23, you can see that the loading for the LOGON project might pose a problem because it fluctuates so much, varying from a maximum of 23 workers in Week 26 to a minimum of zero workers in Weeks 24 and 25 (since activities R, S and T do not require any workers). The problem facing the manager allocating these workers to LOGON is what to do with excess workers during slow periods and where to get additional workers during busy periods.

One way to handle the problem is to adjust the worker loading so it is more "level." This is done by "juggling" activities, by taking advantage of slack times and delaying non-critical activities after their early times so as to reduce workload peaks and fill in workload valleys. For example, the somewhat smoothed workload in Figure 6.24 is achieved by delaying activities P and Q each by 2 weeks, and U and W each by 5 weeks.

Although resource leveling is often necessary to ease difficult-to-manage workload situations, it potentially increases the risk of project delays since delaying activities reduces slack time. In Figure 6.24, delaying activities U and W makes them critical, and thereafter a delay in either will delay the project.

Splitting Activities, Multi-tasking, and Hand-Over Points

In the previous example, an even more uniform loading could have been achieved if each activity were split and the pieces scheduled at different times. Whether this is feasible depends on whether a job, once started, can be interrupted and then restarted later. As discussed earlier, definition of project activities and work packages takes place during the WBS process, and the resultant activities become the basis for

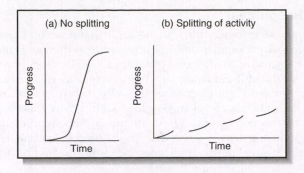

Figure 6.25
The effect of splitting of an activity on duration.

establishing schedules, budgets, and so on. Once an "activity" has been defined in the WBS, it cannot be arbitrarily "split" later on.

Although activity splitting can lead to a more uniform loading, the downside is that it can lead to wasted time and longer activity durations. Figure 6.25 illustrates what happens when an activity is split. Uninterrupted, the activity starts slowly but then builds momentum as it moves ahead. Split, each piece starts slowly and never gathers momentum. The sum of the durations of the pieces in (b) exceeds the duration in (a). The effect, known as *multi-tasking*, leads to slower-paced work on average, and extends the activity duration. The moral is, once an activity has been started, it is usually better to finish it uninterrupted.

Multitasking wherein the work is stopped and then resumed should not be confused with work that continues uninterrupted but has multiple *hand-over points*. The hand-over concept is illustrated in Figure 6.26, where the design and build activities each proceed uninterrupted, though multiple hand-over points (called "laddering") enable the build activity to start and continue well before the entire design activity (encompassing Design A + Design B + Design C) is completed. Although the activities appear to be split (Design A, Design B, Build A, Build B, etc.), in fact they are not since there is no time lag in between. The method greatly shortens the project duration and facilitates interaction between designers and builders; this is the concurrent engineering approach described in Chapters 4 and 13.

Figure 6.26
Multiple hand-over points of an uninterrupted activity.

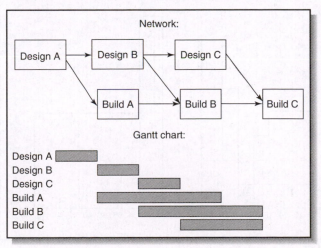

Leveling Multiple Resources

Leveling is easy for a single resource, but can be difficult for several resources simultaneously. Because work packages usually require resources from more than one functional unit or subcontractor, a schedule that provides a level loading for one unit may cause overloading or difficult-to-manage fluctuations for others. For example, based on the weekly equipment requirements for LOGON shown in Table 6.5, the schedule that provides the somewhat level worker loading in Figure 6.24 yields the erratic equipment loading shown in Figure 6.27. An attempt to smooth the equipment loading by adjusting or delaying activities will disrupt the worker loading. (As you can verify, the schedule in Figure 6.23 that produces the erratic loading for workers yields a relatively balanced loading for equipment.)

It is impossible to completely level the load for all resources at once. The best results arise from applying the scheduling equivalent of the "Pareto optimum"—that is, schedule the activities in the best interests of the project while trying to minimize the number of conflicts and problems in the departments and organizations that supply the resources. When considering multiple resources simultaneously, the schedule focuses on leveling "priority" resources—resources where irregular loadings are the most costly to the organization or demoralizing to workers. The financial and social costs associated with hiring, overtime, and layoffs often dictate that "human resources"—the workers—be given the highest priority. Many project software packages perform scheduling analysis that permits simultaneous leveling of multiple resources.

Delaying activities is one method to level resources; others are:

- Eliminating some work segments or activities (reduce project scope)

- Substituting resources

- Substituting less resource-consuming work activities.

These methods eliminate or alter work activities to consume fewer or different resources. For example, when the most qualified workers are not available, either eliminate the work that requires their expertise or use less qualified workers. These

Figure 6.27
Equipment loading for the LOGON project.

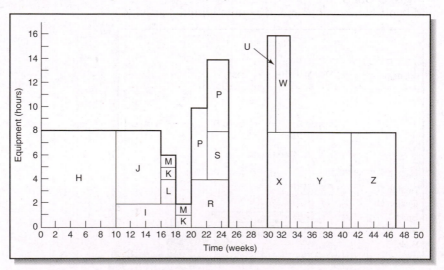

options, however, might compromise the scope or quality of the work and increase the risk of the project not meeting requirements.

Leveling of a Resource-Constrained Project

What happens when the number of personnel, pieces of equipment, or amount of working capital available restricts a schedule? This is a resource-constrained project. Activities in the project must be scheduled so that the loading of a particular resource to the activities does not exceed the available maximum. The focus differs from time-constrained resource leveling, because the issue is not the resource's loading *variability* but its maximum requirement. As each activity is to be scheduled, the sum of its required resources plus the required resource for activities already scheduled at the same time must be checked against the amount available. The problem is more than just leveling of resources; it involves rescheduling jobs, delaying them until such time when resources become available.

In the LOGON project, for example, suppose only 14 workers are available in any given week. The "leveled" schedule in Figure 6.24 results in a maximum loading of 15 workers. In this case, it is not possible to reduce the maximum loading to any number less than 15 and still complete the project in 47 weeks. To reduce the loading to the 14-worker maximum, some activities will have to be delayed beyond their late start dates, which will delay the project. With a problem like this something has to give, since it is not feasible to both satisfy the resource restriction *and* complete the project in 47 weeks. Figure 6.28 shows a schedule that satisfies the 14-worker constraint. This schedule was determined by trial and error, making certain not to violate either the precedence requirements or the 14-worker limit. Notice that the project now requires

Figure 6.28
Schedule and corresponding worker loading for the LOGON project with 14-worker constraint.

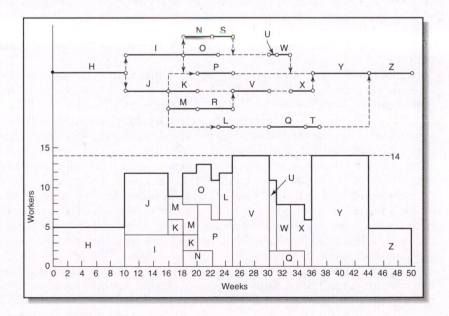

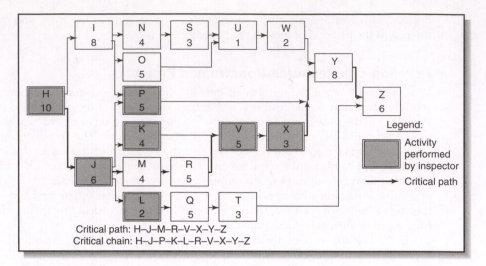

Critical path: H–J–M–R–V–X–Y–Z
Critical chain: H–J–P–K–L–R–V–X–Y–Z

Figure 6.29
Activities in the LOGON project involving the resource of technical inspector.

50 weeks to complete, because Activity X had to be delayed 3 weeks beyond its late start date.

As the example shows, a resource needed by multiple activities can dictate the project duration and override the critical path time. Consider another example, again from the LOGON project. Suppose one important project resource is a technical inspector. The employee has skills to inspect and approve a variety of activities; however, his work is exacting, which prevents him from working on more than one activity at a time. Suppose the activities in which he will be working are H, J, P, K, L, V, and X. These activities are highlighted in Figure 6.29. Because he can work on them only one at a time, he must do the activities sequentially. Summing the durations of these activities gives the time required for him to inspect all of them: 35 weeks. Add to this the times for the last two activities, Y and Z, and the total is 49 weeks. Thus the project duration will be 49 weeks, not the 47 weeks determined by the critical path.

Goldratt calls the path connecting activities that require the same constrained resource the *critical chain* (here, H–J–P–K–L–V–X) and distinguishes them from the critical path (H–J–M–R–V–X plus Y and Z).[3] Referring back to the example in Figure 6.22, the critical path is A–C–D but the critical chain is either A–C–B–D or A–B–C–D. The significance of this is that when activities must be delayed and performed sequentially due to a constrained resource, the sum of the durations of those activities, the critical chain, normally exceeds the length of the critical path, and it is the critical chain—*not* the critical path—that sets the project duration. This is discussed in Chapter 7.

Scheduling with constrained resources involves decisions about which activities can be scheduled immediately and receive resources, and which should be delayed until resources are available. Project management software uses procedures based on simple rules (called *heuristics*) for scheduling with constrained resources; some of these are discussed in the next chapter.

The constrained-resource problem also occurs in multi-project organizations that draw resources from a common pool. To schedule activities for any one project, managers must account for the resource requirements of other, concurrent projects.

The result is that schedules for some projects are determined in part by when resources will be freed up from other, higher priority projects.

6.7 CRITICISMS OF NETWORK METHODS

Network methods have been criticized because they incorporate assumptions and yield results that are sometimes unrealistic. For example, they assume that a project can be completely defined upfront in terms of identifiable activities with known precedence relationships. In many projects, however, not all work can be anticipated or clearly defined at the start. Rather, the project "evolves" as it progresses. But this is a problem with scope planning and activity definition, not scheduling.

A related problem is that activities and durations in a schedule sometimes require regular modification; this happens when there are too many activities in the network or the activities are not well defined. These problems can be addressed by initially creating a "rough" schedule and then developing more detailed schedules in a phased approach, as discussed in Chapter 4, and by avoiding "proliferation" of activities, i.e., keeping the number of activities in the schedule to the essential minimum as prescribed in the work definition guidelines in Chapter 5.

Another criticism relates to the fact that it is sometimes difficult to demarcate one activity from the next, and the point of separation is more or less arbitrary. This means that successors can sometimes be started before predecessors are finished, and the two "overlap" in the sequence. But again, this is not really a problem. PDM allows for overlap of activities, and hand-over points treat activities as if they did overlap.

In summary, the shortcomings of networks are actually shortcomings in project planning. It can be argued (and innumerable project managers will attest) that network methods, though not perfect, offer a good approach for analyzing and creating project schedules.

6.8 SUMMARY

The advantage of networks is that they clearly display the interdependencies of project activities and show the scheduling impact that activities have on each other. This feature enables planners to determine critical activities and slack times, which is important in project planning and control. Knowledge of critical activities tells managers where to focus; knowledge of slack enables them to address the problems of non-uniform resource requirements and limited resources. The PDM method allows for a variety of relationships between project activities to better reflect the realities of project work.

Chapter 7 describes other well-known and more advanced network scheduling methods: PERT, simulation, time–cost trade-off analysis (CPM), and the critical chain method.

Summary List of Symbols

T_e	Expected Project Duration: The expected length of the project
T_s	Target Project Completion Date: The contracted or committed date for project completion
ES	Early Start for an Activity: The earliest feasible time an activity can be started
EF	Early Finish for an Activity: The earliest feasible time an activity can be completed

LS	Late Start: The latest allowable time an activity can be started to complete the project on target
LF	Late Finish: The latest allowable time an activity can be completed to complete the project on target
t	Activity Duration: The most likely or best guess of the time to complete an activity
FS = n	Finish-to-Start: An activity can start no sooner than n days after its immediate predecessor has finished
SS = n	Start-to-Start: An activity can start no sooner than n days after its immediate predecessor has started
SF = n	Start-to-Finish: An activity can finish no later than n days after its immediate predecessor has started
FF = n	Finish-to-Finish: An activity can finish no later than n days after its immediate predecessor has finished

Summary Illustration Problem

AON representation:

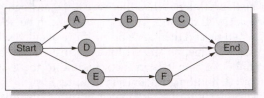

						SLACK	
ACTIVITY	TIME	ES	EF	LS	LF	TOTAL	FREE
A	2.0	0	2.0	0	3.0	1.0	0
B	5.0	2.0	7.0	3.0	8.0	1.0	0
C	2.0	7.0	9.0	8.0	10.0	1.0	1.0
D	5.0	0	5.0	5.0	10.0	5.0	5.0
E*	5.0	0	5.0	0	5.0	0	0
F*	5.0	5.0	10.0	5.0	10.0	0	0

*Activities on critical path

APPENDIX I: AOA DIAGRAMS

The chapter described the AON method of network diagramming. Besides this method, another diagramming method is the *activity-on-arrow (AOA)* or *arrow diagramming* technique. The major feature that distinguishes AOA from AON is the way activities and events are denoted on the network. Figure 6.30 shows the AOA representation for one activity and its events.

Figure 6.30
AOA representation for an activity and its start and finish events.

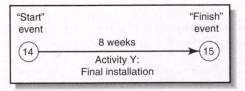

In the AOA method, an activity is represented as a directed line segment (called an *arrow*) between two nodes (or circles). As shown in Figure 6.30, the nodes represent the start and finish events for an activity, and the arrow between them represents the activity. The number inside each node merely identifies the event. Each event must have its own unique number. In the example, the numbers 14 and 15 were chosen arbitrarily. Node 14 means "start Activity Y" and node 15 means "finish Activity Y."

The arrowed line and the number above it represent the activity, though the length of the line has no significance. As in AON networks, an AOA network should have only *one origin* event and *one terminal* event. All arrows must point generally toward the right end of the network; the arrows cannot double back.[4]

As in the AON method, the activities follow a sequential order as defined by their immediate predecessors. When an activity has more than one immediate predecessor, the network must show that it cannot be started until *all* of its immediate predecessors have been completed. This is the purpose of a special kind of activity called a "dummy."

Dummy Activities

A *dummy activity* is used to illustrate precedence relationships in AOA networks. It serves only as a "connector"—it is not a "real" activity, and represents neither work nor time. The following example demonstrates the need for dummy activities in an AOA network.[5]

An engineer decides to write a new computer program and to buy a new computer to run it on. The activities and their dependencies are illustrated in the AON network in Figure 6.31. The dependencies (excluding ones from start and to end nodes) are:

1. Pay for the computer after buying the computer
2. Install the computer program after writing the program *and* after buying the computer.

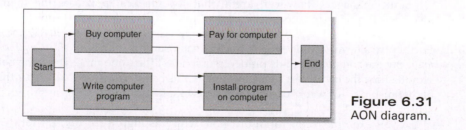

Figure 6.31
AON diagram.

The AOA network for this project is shown in Figure 6.32. Note that to show the dependencies "install program" after "buy computer" and "write program" requires a dummy activity (the dashed arrow) between node V and node Y. This dummy links "install program" to its two immediate predecessors, "buy computer" and "write computer program." Notice that the overall network has only one "Start" node and one "End" node.

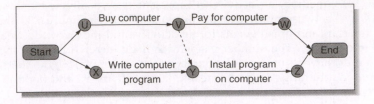

Figure 6.32
Figure 6.31 converted to AOA diagram.

AON versus AOA

AON networks are constructed without use of dummies, so they are simpler and easier to construct and interpret than AOA networks; as a consequence, they are more popular. But because AOA diagrams use line segments (the arrows) to represent the flow of work and time, they can easily be converted into time-scaled networks that look like Gantt charts. Some project software packages create time-scaled networks, and some create both AOA and AON network diagrams. For a particular project, only one method should be used.

APPENDIX II: ALTERNATE SCHEDULING METHOD: STARTING THE PROJECT AT DAY 1

The scheduling technique illustrated in this chapter is the usual approach to introduce network scheduling. The method assumes that the project *begins at time zero*, and that a *successor activity begins immediately upon finishing its predecessors*. The method is simple and is mathematically correct.

Some managers, however, argue that for practical purposes the method is incorrect. Project managers speak of the "first day" of the project, not the "zeroth day." Thus, they say, the project start time should be indicated as Day 1, not Day 0. Further, whenever activities are in series, each successor activity *starts on the period following* the completion of its predecessors, not at the same time. Thus, the network would show the early start time of an activity as being a day (or week) later than the early finish day (or week) of its latest predecessor. Realistically, this approach makes sense.

As an example, refer to Figure 6.33, which is Figure 6.8 revised for "Day 1" assumptions. Activity H is the first activity in the project and lasts 10 days. Using the Day 1 scheme, for Activity H ES = 1. In making the forward pass through the network, computationally EF = ES + Duration − 1. Thus, EF = 1 + 10 − 1 = 10. The ES for Activity H's successors, Activity I and Activity J, is on the *next* day, i.e., ES = 11.

Using the assumptions of course affects the late times too. Making the backward pass through the network, LS = LF − Duration + 1. Thus, for Activity I with Duration 8, if LF = 18 then LS = 18 − 8 + 1 = 11. The immediate predecessor of Activity I, Activity H, must finish the day before this, so LF = 10 for Activity H.

The Day 1 scheme does not impact the computation of total slack, which remains

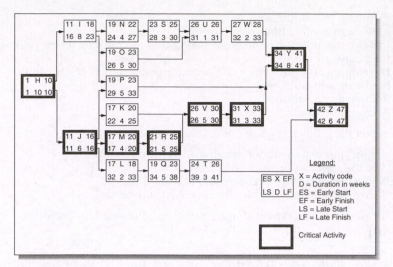

Figure 6.33
Figure 6.8 adjusted for "Day 1" assumptions.

the simple difference between early and late start times or early and late finish times. It does, however, change the computation of free slack:

$$\text{Free slack for an activity} = \text{ES (earliest successor)} - \text{EF (activity)} - 1$$

Project management scheduling software uses actual dates, not elapsed times, and the project start will be indicated by the date of the first day (or week) of the project. Throughout the network, the start dates of successor activities will be shown as the next period (day or week) after the finish dates of their successors.

REVIEW QUESTIONS AND PROBLEMS

1. What are the advantages of networks over Gantt charts?
2. Draw a network diagram of your college studies, starting with enrolment and finishing with graduation. Indicate the courses, projects, and exams, as well as precedence relationships where applicable.
3. How is a WBS used to create a network and what role does a scope statement play?
4. Can a Gantt chart be created from a network? Can a network be created from a Gantt chart? Which is the preferred way? Explain.
5. Why is it vital to know the critical path? Explain the different ways the critical path is used in network analysis and project planning.
6. Explain the difference between total and free slack.
7. Explain the difference between ES, EF, LS, and LF.
8. Consider each of the following projects:
   a. Composing and mailing a letter to an old friend
   b. Preparing a five-course meal (you specify the course and dishes served)
   c. Planning a wedding for 500 people
   d. Building a sundeck for your home

e. Planning, promoting, and conducting a rock concert
f. Moving to another house or apartment
g. Developing, promoting, manufacturing, and distributing a new packaged food item
h. Developing and installing a computerized information system, both hardware and software
i. Remodeling a bathroom
j. Adding a bedroom to a house.

Now, answer the following questions for each project:

1. Using your experience or imagination, create a WBS.
2. List the activities or work packages.
3. Show the immediate predecessors for each activity.
4. Draw the network diagram (using the AON scheme).

9. Draw the AON network diagrams for the following four projects:

Project 1		Project 2	
Activity	Immediate Predecessor	Activity	Immediate Predecessor
A	—	A	—
B	A	B	A
C	A	C	A
D	B	D	B
E	D	E	B
F	D	F	C
G	D	G	D
H	E, F, G	H	D
		I	G
		J	E, F, H, I

Project 3		Project 4	
Activity	Immediate Predecessor	Activity	Immediate Predecessor
A	—	A	—
B	A	B	—
C	—	C	—
D	—	D	C
E	D	E	A
F	B, C, E	F	B
		G	E
		H	F, G, J
		I	A
		J	D, I

10. Refer to Figure 6.1 in the text.
   a. If the person wants to get more sleep by waking up later, which of the following steps would be useful?
      i. Put socks on faster
     ii. Put tie in pocket to put on later
    iii. Put shoes on faster
     iv. Buy a hair dryer that works faster.
   b. Calculate the total float and free float of the activity "Put on socks."

11. Eliminate redundant predecessors from the following lists so only immediate predecessors remain.

a.

Activity	Predecessor
A	—
B	—
C	—
D	B
E	C
F	A
G	B, D, C, E
H	A, B, C, D, E, F, G

b.

Activity	Predecessor
A	—
B	A
C	A
D	A, B
E	A, B
F	A, C
G	A, B, C, D, E, F
H	A, B, C, D, E, G

c.

Activity	Predecessor
A	—
B	—
C	A
D	A
E	B
F	B
G	A, C
H	A, B, D, F
I	B, F
J	C, D, E, F, G, H, I

12. Use Figures 6.5 (a & b) to draw Gantt charts for the ROSEBUD project.
13. Some projects have a fixed due date while others have to be finished as early as possible, and the project manager only makes commitments on the completion date once she and her project management team have scheduled the project. Explain how the backward pass differs for these two project types.
14. Explain how it is possible that there can be slack on the critical path. What is the implication of negative slack on the critical path?
15. In the development of a new (first of its kind) complex system, the design of a certain subsystem has large slack. Sufficient resources are available for either an early start or a late start. Discuss the pros and cons of early and late starts. Consider the risk of delaying the project, the risk of changes in the design, management focus, cash flow, and any other factor that you can think of.[6]

16. What limitations of simple AON networks does non-FS PDM overcome? What limitations does it not overcome?
17. Give examples of applications of non-FS PDM. Take a project you are familiar with (or invent one) and create a PDM network.
18. For the PDM network in Figure 6.20, calculate ES, EF, LS, and LF for all activities.
19. To produce a manual, John has to write the text, after which Ann has to draw sketches and typeset the document. John can start with any section of the book (i.e., he does not have to start with Section 1). The work has to be done within 95 days. The network diagram below shows the precedence relationships and duration of each activity. Draw a Gantt chart to show how the work can be done within 95 days. Take into account that both John and Ann are able to attend to only one task at a time.[7]

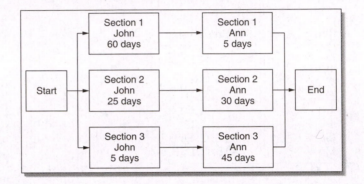

20. Why is leveling of resources preferred to large fluctuation of workload? What negative result could resource leveling cause?
21. Describe how resource leveling of a resource-constrained project differs from resource leveling in a time-constrained project.
22. The requirements for systems analysts and programmers for the GUMBY project are as follows:

Activity	J	M	V	Y	L	Q	Z
Predecessors	—	J	M	V	J	L	Y,Q
Duration (weeks)	6	4	6	8	2	8	2
Systems Analysts (weekly)	8	5	3	2	5	3	5
Programmers (weekly)	3	4	2	3	3	2	3

   a. Compute ESs, LSs, and total slack times.
   b. Then show the separate resource loadings for systems analysts and programmers, assuming early start times.
   c. Suppose the maximum weekly availability is eight systems analysts and five programmers. Can activities be scheduled to satisfy these constraints without delaying the project?
23. Level the resources for a project with the workload diagram below. In the time-phased diagram at the top of the diagram, dotted lines indicate slack.[8] Discuss pros and cons of the alternatives available.

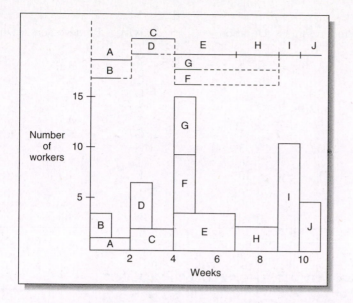

24. Discuss the implications of resource allocation for organizations involved in multiple projects.
25. Show that the schedule in Figure 6.23 (which produced an erratic loading for workers) yields a more balanced loading for equipment than the one shown in Figure 6.27.
26. Suppose in Figure 6.20 everything is the same except Activity Y can start 4 days after Activity V starts, but cannot be finished until 6 days after Activity V is finished. Show how this changes the values for ES, EF, LS, and LF.
27. Redraw Figure 6.6 using the AOA method.
28. For each of the following predecessor tables:
    • Draw a corresponding AON network.
    • Compute ES and EF for each activity.
    • Compute LS and LF for each activity. Find the critical path.
    • Determine the total slack and free slack.

a.

Activity	Predecessors	Duration
A		6
B		3
C	A	9
D	B	5
E	B	4
F	D	2
G	E	8

b.

Activity	Predecessors	Duration
A		3
B	A	8
C	B	9
D	C	3
E	B	2
F	E,H	4
G	A	6
H	G	5
J	D,F	1

c.

Activity	Predecessors	Duration
A		9
B	A	2
C		8
D	C	8
E	B,D	7
F	E	4
G	C	4
H	B,D.G	3
J		6
K	J	10
M	G,K	3
N	H, M	6

d.

Activity	Predecessors	Duration
A		10
B	A,E	9
C	B,N	15
D	C	7
E		5
F	A,E	6
G	K,F	7
H	G	12
J		12
K	E,J	4
L	K, F	11
M	L	8
N	E,J	7

QUESTIONS ABOUT THE STUDY PROJECT

1. Were networks used for scheduling? If so, describe the networks. Show examples. What kind of computer software system was used to create and maintain them? Who was responsible for system inputs and system operations? Describe the capabilities of the software system.
2. At what point in the project were networks created? When were they updated?
3. Was all detail planning done upfront or was a phased approach followed?
4. How was the schedule reserve determined and included into the schedule?
6. Was the workload on resources made visible?
7. If the project was done within a matrix structure, how did communication between the functional and project managers take place?
8. Did the functional manger(s) take responsibility for workload on resources?
9. Was resource leveling done?
10. Were there any complaints about unrealistic workloads?

Case 6.1[9] Network Diagram for a Large Construction Project

The table below lists activities for constructing a bridge over an operational railway line, similar to the bridge described in Case 10.3.

Activity No	Activity Description	Duration (months)	Predecessors
A	Detailed site investigation and survey	2	—
B	Detailed planning	6	A
C	Detailed design	6	B
D	Preparation of site	4	C
E	Relocate services	3	C
F	Re-align overhead track electrification	4	C, E

G	Access road and ramp construction	1	D
H	Piling	2	G
J	Construct foundations and abutments	3	H
K	Construct temporary supports to support bridge deck during construction	2	F, G
L	Fabrication planning of structural steel components	2	C
M	Manufacture structural steel components (off-site)	2	L
N	Transport structural steel components and erect on-site	1	M
P	Erect pylons and fill with concrete	2	J
Q	Construct main span deck on pre-cast concrete beams	3	H, K, N, P
R	Install stay-cables and lift the bridge deck off temporary supports	3	Q
S	Remove temporary supports	1	R
T	Electrical system installation	1	S
U	Roadway surfacing (paving)	2	S
V	Finishing and ancillaries	2	T, U
W	Commissioning – cut-over	1	V
X	Formal hand-over & ceremony	1	W
Y	Project sign-off	1	X
Z	Administrative closure	1	W
AA	Project End	0 (milestone)	Y, Z

1. Construct a network diagram for the project.
2. Do forward and backward pass calculations to indicate early and late start and finish times.
3. Indicate the critical path.
4. Indicate the total and free slack of each activity.

5. The following resources are required to perform the activities. Allocate the resources to the activities and indicate the workload on the resources. If needed, adjust the schedule.

Activity No	Activity Description	Resources
A	Detailed site investigation and survey	Surveyors, Engineering, Project Manager
B	Detailed planning	Project Manager, Engineering, Construction, Contractors
C	Detailed design	Engineering
D	Preparation of site	Construction
E	Relocate services	Engineering
F	Re-align overhead track electrification	Engineering, Contractors
G	Access road and ramp construction	Construction
H	Piling	Construction, Contractors
J	Construct foundations and abutments	Engineering, Construction
K	Construct temporary supports to support bridge deck during construction	Engineering, Construction
L	Fabrication planning of structural steel components	Engineering, Manufacturer
M	Manufacture structural steel components (off-site)	Engineering, Manufacturer
N	Transport structural steel components and erect on-site	Transporter, Engineering
P	Erect pylons and fill with concrete	Construction, Engineering
Q	Construct main span deck on pre-cast concrete beams	Construction, Engineering
R	Install stay-cables and lift the bridge deck off temporary supports	Construction, Engineering
S	Remove temporary supports	Construction, Engineering
T	Electrical system installation	Construction, Engineering

U	Roadway surfacing (paving)	Contractor, Engineering
V	Finishing and ancillaries	Contractors, Engineering
W	Commissioning – cut-over	Project Manager, Engineering, Construction, Contractors
X	Formal hand-over & ceremony	Project Manager, Engineering, Construction, Contractors
Y	Project sign-off	Project Manager, Engineering
Z	Administrative closure	Engineering
AA	Project End	Project Manager

NOTES

1. Duncan WR (ed). *A Guide to the Project Management Body of Knowledge.* Newton Square, PA: Project Management Institute Standards Committee; 1996. The definition of the critical path in later editions of this document does not say that the critical path can change; this does not alter the fact that it does.
2. For more about PDM scheduling, see Dreger JB. *Project Management: Effective Scheduling.* New York, NY: Van Nostrand Reinhold; 1992.
3. Goldratt EM. *Critical Chain.* Great Barrington, MA: North River Press; 1997.
4. Loops back are permitted in a special form of network analysis called GERT.
5. Adapted from Gordon JD and Villoria RL. *Network-Based Management Systems (PERT/CPM).* New York, NY: John Wiley & Sons; 1967.
6. Steyn H (ed.). *Project Management: A Multi-disciplinary Approach.* Pretoria: FPM Publishing; 2003. Reproduced with permission.
7. *Ibid.*
8. *Ibid.*
9. *Ibid.*

Chapter

Advanced Project Network Analyses and Scheduling

> *Look beneath the surface: never let a thing's intrinsic qualities or worth escape you.*

—MARCUS AURELIUS,
Meditations

*T*he scheduling methods discussed in Chapter 6 assume that activity times are known and fixed, ignoring the fact that in reality they are estimated and are variable. This chapter discusses the implications of variable activity times on project schedules and the PERT and critical-chain methods for handling uncertainty in project completion dates. It also covers methods for reducing the project duration, starting with CPM.

7.1 CPM AND TIME–COST TRADE-OFF

The *critical path method* (CPM) is a systematic approach for allocating resources among activities to reduce project duration for the least cost. Developed in 1957 by the DuPont Company, Remington Rand, and Mauchy Associates for DuPont plant construction, it is a mathematical procedure for estimating the trade-off between project duration and project cost.[1]

Example 7.1: The House Built in Less Than Four Hours[2]

With virtually unlimited resources and meticulous planning and control, a project can be done *very* fast. On March 13, 1999, the Manukau (New Zealand) Chapter of Habitat for Humanity (the non-profit organization dedicated to eliminating poverty housing) set the new record for building a house: 3 hours and 45 minutes.

The project specifications included construction of a four-bedroom house on an established foundation (Figure 7.1). It incorporated prefabricated wall panels, wooden floor, roofing iron, ceilings, decks, and steps. Doors, windows, a bath, a toilet, and plumbing, as well as the electrical system, had to be installed and ready for use; walls, ceilings and window frames had to be painted; carpets had to be laid and curtains hung. The specifications also included a path to the front door, letter box, installed clothes line, wooden fence around the yard, three trees planted, and a leveled lawn with grass. The new owners, Mr and Mrs Suafoa, watched the construction with their four children while CNN filmed the event. The house was inspected, passed all local building codes, and the keys were handed over to the family.

Figure 7.1
The house built in less than 4 hours.
Photograph courtesy of Habitat for Humanity.

What made the speedy completion possible? First were abundant resources: 150 people (mostly volunteers). Second was the comprehensive and meticulous preparation: 14 months of planning, including many iterations of network analysis. The detailed plan was recorded on special task sheets so that team leaders could hand over tasks from one to another without deliberation. With so many people and construction material items at the site, workspace was at a premium. A crane was provided to lift the wooden roof frame onto the wall structure. Third was a systematic computerized method for planning, monitoring, and controlling the project that included the critical-chain method and time buffers. (The bathroom-fitting task was estimated to take 30 minutes, but took 1 hour; the 30-minute overrun was absorbed in the project buffer.) The final factor was the use of suitable technology, including prefabricated walls and components.

Time–Cost Relationship

CPM assumes that the time to perform a project activity varies depending on the amount of effort or resources applied; project duration can be shortened by applying more resources (labor, equipment, etc.) to particular activities. Projects can be sped up by adding resources, but doing so increases the cost.

Ordinarily, work on any given activity in a project is performed at a *normal* (usual and customary) work pace. This is the "normal" point shown in Figure 7.2. Associated with this pace is the *normal time*, T_n—i.e., how long the activity will take under normal work conditions, and the *normal cost*, C_n, which is the cost of doing the activity in the normal time. (The normal pace is assumed to be the most efficient and thus *least costly* pace. Extending the time beyond the normal pace will not produce additional savings and might increase the cost.)

To reduce the time to complete the activity, more resources are applied in the form of additional personnel or overtime. As more resources are applied, the duration shortens but the cost increases. When the maximum effort is applied so that the activity can be completed in the shortest possible time, the activity is said to be *crashed*. The crash condition (see Figure 7.2) represents not only the shortest duration, but the *most costly* as well. For some activities, however, there is no time–cost trade-off; an activity that is *process limited* requires a specific time that cannot be changed regardless of resources. An example is the time needed to ferment wine or cure concrete.

As illustrated in Figure 7.2, the points for completing an activity under normal conditions and crash conditions define two theoretical extremes. The line connecting the points, called the *cost slope*, represents the time–cost relationship or marginal trade-off of cost-to-time for the activity. The time–cost relationship for every activity is unique, and can be linear, curvilinear (concave or convex), or a step function. Because the shape of the actual time–cost relationship is usually unknown, it is often assumed to be linear.[3] Given this assumption, the formula for the cost slope is:

$$\text{cost slope} = \frac{C_c - C_n}{T_c - T_n}$$

where C_c and C_n are the crash and normal costs, respectively, and T_c and T_n are the crash and normal times for the activity. The cost slope is how much it would cost to speed up or slow down the activity.

Using the formula, the cost slope for the activity in Figure 7.2 is $3K per week. Thus, for *each week* the activity duration is reduced from the normal time of 8 weeks,

Figure 7.2
Time–cost relationship for an activity.

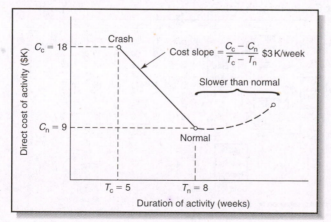

the cost will increase by $3K. Completing the activity 1 week earlier (from 8 weeks to 7 weeks) would alter the cost from the normal cost of $9K to the "sped up" cost of $9K + $3K = $12K; completing it another week sooner (in 6 weeks) would increase the cost to $12K + $3K = $15K; completing it yet another week sooner (in 5 weeks) would increase the cost to $18K. According to Figure 7.2, this last step puts the activity at the crash point, the shortest duration for the activity.

Reducing Project Duration: Shorten the Critical Path

The cost–slope concept can be used to determine the least costly way to shorten a project. Figure 7.3 illustrates this with an example. Start with the preliminary project schedule by assuming a normal pace for all activities; therefore, the project in the figure can be completed in 22 weeks at an expense of $55K. Suppose we want to shorten the project duration. Recall from Chapter 6 that the *project duration is the length of the critical path*. Because the critical path A–D–G is the longest path (22 weeks), to shorten the project it is necessary to shorten a critical activity—A, D, or G. Reducing an activity increases its cost, but because the reduction can be made *anywhere* on the critical path, the increase is minimized by selecting the activity with the smallest cost slope, which is Activity A. Reducing A by 1 week shortens the project duration to 21 weeks and adds $2K (the cost slope of A) to the project cost, bringing it to $55K + $2K = $57K. This step does not change the critical path, so, if need be, an additional week can be cut from A to reduce the project duration to 20 weeks for a cost of $57K + $2K = $59K.

With this second step, the nature of the problem changes. As the top network in Figure 7.4 shows, shortening A uses up all of the slack on Path B–E, so the network now has two critical paths: A–D–G and B–E–G. Any further reduction in project duration must be made by shortening *both* paths, because shortening just one would leave the other at 20 weeks. The least costly way to reduce the project to 19 weeks is to reduce both A and E by 1 week, as shown in Figure 7.4(b). The additional cost is $2K for A and $2K for E, so the resulting project cost would increase to $59K + $2K + $2K = $63K. This last step reduces A to 6 weeks, its crash time, so no further reductions can be made to A.

If a further reduction in project duration is desired, the least costly way to shorten both paths is to reduce G. In fact, because the slack on the non-critical path C–F is 3 weeks, and because the crash duration for G is 2 weeks (which means, if desired, 3

Figure 7.3
Time–cost trade-off for example network.

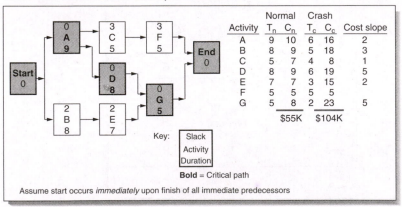

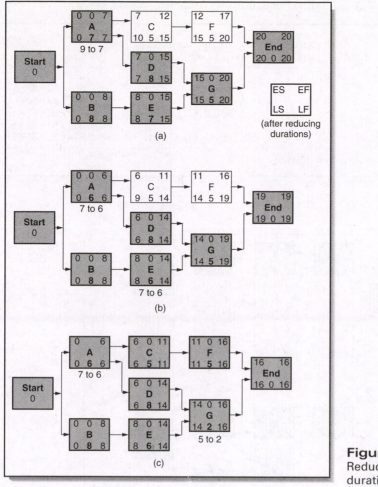

Figure 7.4
Reducing project duration.

weeks *can* be taken out of G), the project can be reduced to 16 weeks by shortening G by 3 weeks, as indicated in Figure 7.4(c). This adds $5K per week, or 3 × $5K = $15K, to the project cost. With this last step, all slack is used up on Path C–F, and all the paths in the network (A–C–F, A–D–G, and B–E–G) become critical.

Any further reductions desired in the project must shorten *all three critical paths* (A–C–F, A–D–G, and B–E–G). As you may wish to verify, the most economical way to reduce the project to 15 weeks is to cut 1 week each from E, D, and C, bringing the project cost up to $86K. This step reduces the time of C to its crash time, the shortest possible project duration. The sequence of steps is summarized in Table 7.1.

Shortest Project Duration

The time–cost procedure described determines which activities to speed up, step-by-step, so as to reduce the project duration. This stepwise reduction of the project duration eventually leads to the shortest possible project duration and its associated cost. However, if we want to directly find the *shortest possible project duration* and avoid the intermediate steps, a simpler procedure is to simultaneously crash *all* activities at once. This, as Figure 7.5 shows, also yields the project duration of 15 weeks. However,

Table 7.1 Duration Reduction and Associated Cost Increase

Step	Duration (T_e, weeks)	Activities on CP with Least Cost Slope	Cost of Project (K$)
1*	22		$55
2	21	A ($2)	$55 + $2 = $57
3	20	A ($2)	$57 + $2 = $59
4	19	A ($2), E ($2)	$59 + $2 + $2 = $63
5, 6, 7	18, 17, 16	G ($5	$63 + $5 + $5 + $5 = $78
8	15	E ($2), D ($5), C ($1)	$78 + $2 + $5 + $1 = $86

*Duration and cost using normal conditions.

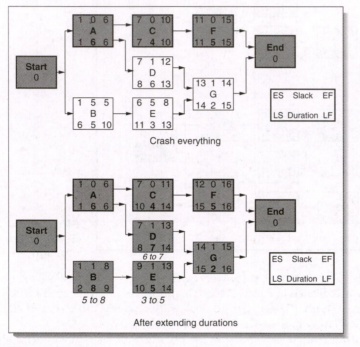

Figure 7.5
Example network using crash times.

the expense of crashing all activities, $104K (see table in Figure 7.3) is artificially high because, as will be shown, *not* all activities need to be crashed to finish the project in the shortest time.

The project duration of 15 weeks is the time along the critical path. Because the critical path is the longest path, other (non-critical) paths are of shorter duration and, consequently, have no influence on project duration. Thus, it is possible to "stretch" or increase any non-critical activity by a certain amount without lengthening the project. In fact, the non-critical activities can be stretched until all the slack in the network is used up.

Just as reducing an activity's time from the normal time increases its cost, so *extending* its time from the crash time *reduces* its cost. As a result, by extending non-critical jobs the project crash cost of $104K can be reduced. To do so, start with those non-critical activities that will yield the greatest savings—those with the greatest cost slope. Notice in Figure 7.5(a) that because Path B–E–G has a slack of 5 weeks, activities along this path can be stretched by up to 5 weeks without extending the project. Three weeks can be added to Activity B (bringing it to the normal duration of 8 weeks) without lengthening the project. Also, 2 weeks can be added to E and 1 week to D, both without changing the project duration. The final project cost is computed by subtracting the savings obtained in extending B by 3 weeks, E by 2 weeks, and D by 1 week from the initial crash cost.

$$\$104K - 3(\$3K) - 2(\$2K) - 1(\$5K) = \$86K$$

In general, to obtain the shortest project duration, start by crashing all activities, and then extend the non-critical activities with the greatest cost slopes to use up available slack and obtain the greatest cost savings. An activity can be extended up to its normal duration, which is assumed to be its least-costly time (Figure 7.2).

Total Project Cost

The previous analysis dealt only with direct costs—costs immediately associated with individual activities that increase directly as resources are added to them. But the cost of conducting a project includes more than direct activity costs; it also includes *indirect* costs such as administrative and overhead charges. (The distinction between direct and indirect cost is elaborated upon in the next chapter.) Usually, indirect costs are a function of, and increase proportionately to, the duration of the project. In other words, *indirect costs*, in contrast to direct costs, *decrease as the project duration decreases*.

The mathematical function for indirect cost can be derived by estimation. As an illustration, suppose indirect costs in the previous example are approximated by the formula

$$\text{Indirect cost} = \$10K + \$3K(T_e)$$

where T_e is the expected project duration in weeks. This is represented by the indirect cost line in Figure 7.6. Also shown is the *total project cost*, which is computed by summing indirect and direct costs. Notice from the figure that by combining indirect costs and direct costs it is possible to determine the project duration that gives the lowest total project cost. Figure 7.6 shows that, from a cost standpoint, 20 weeks is the "optimum" project duration.

In addition to direct and indirect costs, another cost that influences total project cost (and hence the optimum T_e) is any *contractual incentive*, such as a *penalty charge* or a *bonus payment*. A penalty charge is a late fee imposed on the contractor for not completing a deliverable on time. A bonus payment is a reward—a cash inducement—for completing work early. The specific terms of penalties and bonuses are specified in incentive-type contracts such as described in the Appendix to Chapter 3.

In the previous example, suppose the contract agreement is to complete the project by Week 18. The contract provides for a bonus of $2K per week for finishing before 18 weeks, and a $1K per week penalty for finishing after 18 weeks. Figure 7.7 shows these incentives and their influence on total project cost. Notice that even with incentives, the optimum duration (for the contractor) is at 19 or 20 weeks, not the contractual 18 weeks. This example reveals that a formal incentive agreement alone is not necessarily enough to influence performance. For the incentive to motivate the

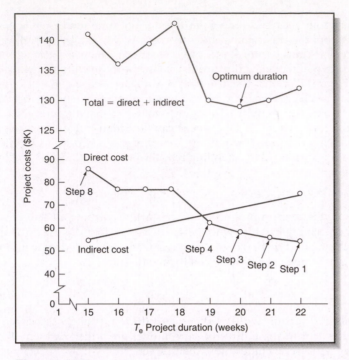

Figure 7.6
Total time–cost trade-off for the project.

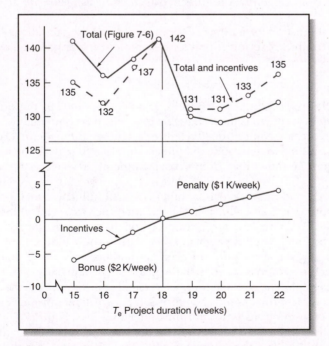

Figure 7.7
Time–cost trade-off for the project with incentives.

contractor it must have "teeth"—in other words, it should be of sufficient magnitude with respect to other project costs to affect contractor performance. Had the penalty been raised to $3K (instead of $1K) per week for finishing after 18 weeks, the contractor's optimum duration would have shifted to 16 weeks.

7.2 VARIABILITY OF ACTIVITY DURATION

Suppose you are driving to somewhere; Figure 7.8 shows the estimated time it will take you to get there and the variability in that time. If everything goes well (little traffic and no mechanical problems), you will get there very quickly; this is the "Optimistic Duration." Most likely, however, it will take you longer than that. This is shown by the "Most Likely Duration" time of 30 minutes. Of course, it could take longer than this—say, when traffic is congested or, worse, you are involved in an accident. Note in the figure that the area below the curve to the left of the Most Likely Duration is much less than to the right of it. This indicates that the chances of you arriving later than the Most Likely time are greater than the chances of you arriving earlier.

Like your travel time, the activity durations in a project are variable. The question is: Given that you cannot say for sure when each activity will be completed, how can you possibly say when the project will be completed?

The scheduling approach discussed in Chapter 6 ignores variability and assumes that activity durations are constant; this is called the *deterministic* approach. In the following sections, we consider what happens when the activity durations are variable; this is called the *stochastic* approach.

Variability Effects on a Project Network

Figure 7.8 relates to a single activity. In a project, some activities will be completed earlier than expected, others later. When activities are combined in a network, however, the early activities and late activities do not average out: in general, *it is only the late activities that impact the project completion.* This is one reason why projects tend to take longer than estimated.

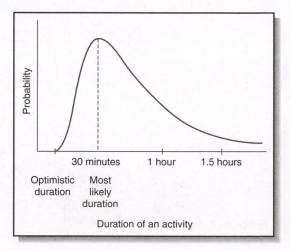

Figure 7.8
Variability of activity duration.

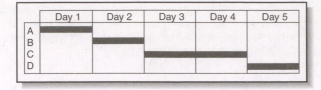

Figure 7.9
Activities delayed if Activity
A is delayed.

Consider, for example, Activity A in Figure 7.9. If Activity A takes longer than planned, it will delay Activity B, which in turn will delay Activities C and D and, thus, the completion of the project. Suppose, however, that Activity A were finished *earlier* than planned. In that case would Activity B start earlier? Not necessarily. Resources needed for Activity B, such as people and equipment, would likely have other commitments, which would likely preclude Activity B starting before the scheduled start date.

Consider a second example. Most project networks consist of several paths that merge together into a critical path. Figure 7.10(a) illustrates a project with two critical paths, each with a 50 percent chance of finishing on time. The probability that the project will finish on time is the probability that both paths will finish on time, or $0.5 \times 0.5 = 0.25$ or 25 percent. Figure 7.10(b) shows five paths merging (which is typical of what happens near the end of project networks), each with a 50 percent probability of finishing on time. The probability of finishing the project on time is now $(0.5)^5$, or about 3 percent. This effect is called *merge bias* or *merge-point bias*.

Chapter 6 addressed the fact that the critical path is not necessarily stable but can change if non-critical activities take longer than planned or critical activities take less time than planned. Either case can result in the project being delayed.

Several methods have been developed to help grapple with the uncertainty about when a project will be completed. These are addressed in the following sections, starting with PERT.

7.3 PERT

The PERT method was developed explicitly for application in projects where the activity durations are uncertain. It originated during the US Navy's Polaris Missile System program—the perfect example of a complex research and development program with much uncertainty as to the kind of research to be done, the stages

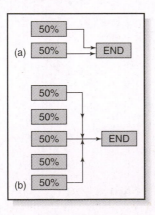

Figure 7.10
Activities delayed where paths merge.

of development needed, and how fast they can be completed. Projects like this are contracted while developments are still unfolding and before many of the problems in technology, materials, and processes have been identified. The duration of the project is uncertain, and there is great risk the project will overrun the target completion time.

To provide a degree of certainty in the duration of the Polaris program, a special operations research team was formed in 1958 with representatives from the Navy's Special Projects Office, the consulting firm of Booz, Allen, and Hamilton, and the prime contractor Lockheed Missile Systems. The method they devised was called PERT (Program Evaluation and Review Technique).[4]

PERT is a technique to estimate the likelihood (or probability) of a project finishing on time. The purpose of PERT is to analyze the project network (and the Gantt charts resulting from the network), not to create a schedule. The method provides insight into the likelihood of finishing a project by a certain time, though it says nothing about how to increase that likelihood or reduce the duration of a project.

Three Time Estimates

The network methods discussed in Chapter 6 determine the critical path and slack times using *best estimates* for activity duration. PERT, however, addresses uncertainty in the durations by using three time estimates—*optimistic*, *most likely*, and *pessimistic*. Presumably the three estimates are obtained from people who are most knowledgeable about difficulties likely to be encountered and the potential variability in time; usually they are expert estimators or the people who will perform or manage the activity.

The three estimates are used to calculate the *"expected time"* for an activity. The range between the optimistic and pessimistic estimates is a measure of variability that permits making statistical inferences about the likelihood that project events will happen by a particular time.

As seen in Figure 7.11, the *optimistic time, a,* is the minimum time for an activity—the situation where everything goes well and there is little hope of finishing earlier.

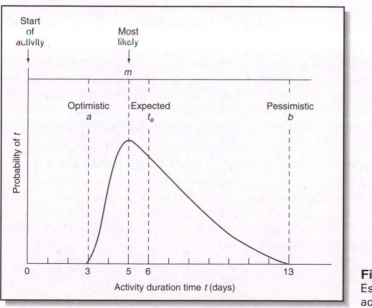

Figure 7.11
Estimating
activity duration.

A normal level of effort is assumed, with no extra personnel. The *most likely* time, *m*, is the time that would occur most often if the activity were repeated. Finally, the *pessimistic* time, *b*, is the maximum time for an activity—the situation where bad luck is encountered at every step. The pessimistic time includes likely problems in work, but not highly unlikely events such as natural disasters.

The three estimates in Figure 7.11 are related in the form of a *Beta* probability distribution with parameters *a* and *b* as the end-points and *m*, the most frequent value. The Beta distribution is used because it is unimodal (has a single peak value) and not necessarily symmetrical—properties that seem desirable for a distribution of activity durations.[5] Note that whereas the distribution in Figure 7.8 had no end-point on the right-hand side, the curve in Figure 7.11 disallows very unlikely events and has end-point *b*.

Based on this distribution and the three time estimates, the *mean* or *expected* time, t_e, and the *variance, V*, of each activity are computed with the following formulas:

$$t_e = \frac{a + 4m + b}{6}$$

$$V = \left(\frac{b - a}{6}\right)^2$$

Since $V = \sigma^2$,

$$\sigma = (b - a)/6$$

The expected time, t_e, represents the point on the distribution in Figure 7.11 with a 50–50 chance that the activity will be completed earlier or later than it. In the figure,

$$t_e = \frac{3 + 4(5) + 13}{6} = 6 \text{ days}$$

The variance, *V*, is a measure of variability in the activity duration:

$$V = \left(\frac{13 - 3}{6}\right)^2 = (1.67)^2 = 2.78$$

The larger *V*, the less reliable t_e, and the higher the likelihood the activity will be completed much earlier or much later than t_e. This simply reflects that the farther apart *a* and *b*, the more dispersed the distribution and the greater the chance that the actual time will significantly differ from the expected time. In a routine (repetitive) job, estimates of *a* and *b* are close to each other, *V* is small, and t_e is more likely.

Probability of Finishing by a Target Completion Date

The expected time t_e, is used in the same way as the estimated activity duration was used in the deterministic networks in Chapter 6. Because statistically the expected time of a sequence of independent activities is the sum of their individual expected times, the expected duration of the *project, T_e*, is the sum of the expected activity durations along the critical path:

$$T_e = \sum_{CP} t_e$$

where each t_e is the expected time of an activity on the critical path.

PERT uses a stochastic approach; hence the project duration is not considered a point but rather an estimate subject to uncertainty owing to the uncertainties of the activity durations along the critical path. Because the project duration T_e is computed as the sum of expected activity durations, it follows that T_e is also an expected time. The project duration can be thought of as a probability distribution with an *average* of T_e. Thus, the probability of completing the project sooner than T_e is 50 percent, and so is the probability of completing it later than T_e.

The variation in the project duration distribution is computed as the sum of the variances of the activity durations along the critical path:

$$V_P = \sum_{CP} V$$

where V is the variance of an activity on the critical path. (For justification, refer to the Appendix to this chapter.)

These concepts are illustrated in the AOA network in Figure 7.12.

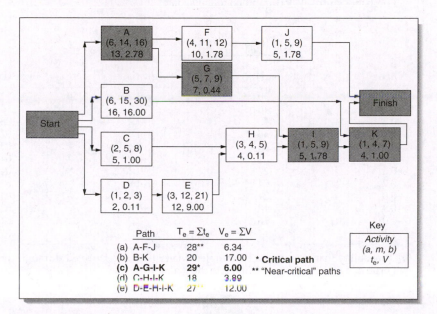

Figure 7.12
PERT network with expected activity durations and activity variances.

The distribution of project durations is assumed to be the normal, the familiar bell-shaped curve (refer to Appendix for justification). Given this assumption, it is easy to determine the probability of meeting any specified project target completion date, T_s.

As examples, consider two questions about the project shown in Figure 7.12: (1) What is the probability of completing the project in 27 days? (2) If we want to make a commitment on project duration and to be 95 percent sure, what duration should we quote? Both questions can be answered by determining the number of standard deviations that separate T_s from T_e. The formula for the calculation is:

$$z = \frac{T_s - T_e}{\sqrt{V_P}}$$

To answer the first question, use $T_s = 27$ days. From the network, the expected project duration, T_e, is computed as 29 days. Therefore,

$$z = \frac{27 - 29}{\sqrt{6}} = -0.82$$

The probability of completing the project within 27 days is equal to the area under the normal curve to the left of $z = -0.82$. Referring to Table 7.2(a), the probability is about 21 percent.

To answer the second question (duration with a 95 percent certainty): using Table 7.2(b), for a probability of 0.95 the z value is 1.6. As before, we calculate

Table 7.2   Normal Distribution Function for Completing a Project by Time T_s

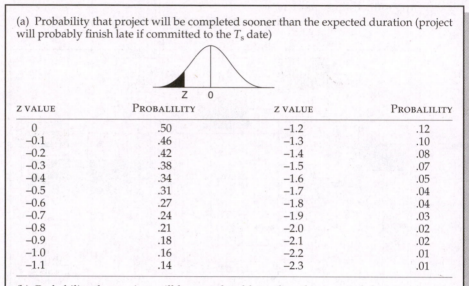

(a) Probability that project will be completed sooner than the expected duration (project will probably finish late if committed to the T_s date)

Z VALUE	PROBALILITY	Z VALUE	PROBALILITY
0	.50	−1.2	.12
−0.1	.46	−1.3	.10
−0.2	.42	−1.4	.08
−0.3	.38	−1.5	.07
−0.4	.34	−1.6	.05
−0.5	.31	−1.7	.04
−0.6	.27	−1.8	.04
−0.7	.24	−1.9	.03
−0.8	.21	−2.0	.02
−0.9	.18	−2.1	.02
−1.0	.16	−2.2	.01
−1.1	.14	−2.3	.01

(b) Probability that project will be completed later than the expected duration (project will probably finish early if committed to the T_s date)

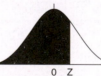

Z VALUE	PROBALILITY	Z VALUE	PROBALILITY
0.0	.50	1.2	.88
0.1	.54	1.3	.90
0.2	.58	1.4	.92
0.3	.61	1.5	.93
0.4	.66	1.6	.95
0.5	.69	1.7	.96
0.6	.72	1.8	.96
0.7	.76	1.9	.97
0.8	.79	2.0	.98
0.9	.82	2.1	.98
1.0	.83	2.2	.99
1.1	.86	2.3	.99

$$1.6 = \frac{T_s - 29}{\sqrt{6}}, \text{ so } T_s = 33 \text{ days}$$

In other words, it is "highly likely" (95 percent probable) that the project will be completed within 33 days. Note that since we are working with values that are merely estimates, it does not make sense to compute figures of great precision.

Near-Critical Paths

The PERT procedure has been criticized for providing overly optimistic results—a criticism that is well-justified, since it does not account for the effect of merge-point bias.[6] Notice in the example in Figure 7.12 that two paths are "near critical" in length. The variance of these paths is large enough that either could easily become critical by exceeding the 29 days of the original critical path. In fact, as you may wish to verify using the statistical procedure described previously, the probabilities of *not* completing Path (a) (A–F–J) and Path (e) (D–E–H–I–K) within 29 days are 34 percent and 29 percent, respectively. So there is more than a slight chance that these paths could become critical. The warning is: putting too much emphasis on the critical path can lead to ignoring paths that are near-critical in length, paths that could themselves become critical and jeopardize the project completion date.

Furthermore, the 50 percent probability of completing the project within 29 days, as presumed with the normal distribution, is overly optimistic. Because *all* activities in the network must be completed before the project is finished, the probability of completing the project within 29 days is the same as the probability of completing *all* five paths within 29 days. Although the probability of completing Paths (b) and (d) within 29 days is close to 100 percent, the probabilities of completing Paths (a) and (e) within that time are 66 percent and 71 percent, respectively, and the probability of completing (c), the critical path, is only 50 percent. So the chance of completing all paths within 29 days is the product of the probabilities $1.0 \times 1.0 \times 0.66 \times 0.71 \times 0.5$, or less than 25 percent.

Meeting the Target Date

PERT analysis provides the project manager with a level of confidence in estimating the project end date, which is useful when negotiating with customers and other stakeholders. Clearly, one way to increase confidence in the end date is to delay it, but when the end date is fixed and cannot be delayed, the only alternative is to revise the project network so as to shorten the critical and near-critical paths. Possible ways to do this include:[7]

1. Look for opportunities to fast track activities on the critical path (i.e., overlap activities on the critical path). This implies scheduling an activity to start before its predecessors are completed. An alternative is to split the predecessors into sub-activities, and start the successor when only some of the sub-activities have been completed.
2. Add more resources to critical activities (e.g., transfer resources from activities that have large slack times to critical and near-critical activities).
3. Substitute time-consuming activities with ones that are less so, or delete activities that are not absolutely necessary.

Each of these has drawbacks. Fast-tracking increases the risks of making mistakes and having to repeat activities. Adding resources to speed up activities increases the cost. Transferring resources between activities requires changes to plans and schedules, increases administrative costs, disrupts resources, and aggravates the functional managers who supply the resources. The final alternative, substitution or elimination of activities, jeopardizes project performance, especially when it equates to making "cuts" or using poorer-quality materials or less-skilled labor.

Criticisms of PERT[8]

The PERT method has been criticized because it is based upon assumptions that sometimes yield problematical results. For example, it ignores human behavior and assumes that whenever an activity is completed earlier than scheduled that succeeding activities will start straight away—ignoring the fact that resources might not be available or that people procrastinate.

PERT assumes that activity durations are independent. But whenever resources are transferred from one activity to another, then the durations of both activities are changed. Activity durations are usually not independent: one's gain is another's loss.

PERT also assumes that three activity estimates are better than one. Unless based upon good historical data, the three estimates are still *guesses*, which might not improve over a single "best" guess. An advantage of the pessimistic estimate, however, is that it allows for the possibility of possible setbacks, which a single estimate cannot.

Accuracy of estimates often depends on experience. Whenever a database can be formed based upon experience from similar activities from previous projects, a "history" can be developed for each kind of activity that can be used to estimate the durations for future similar activities. In fact, reliance on good *historical data* for estimating times makes the PERT method appropriate for projects that are somewhat "repeatable" (and less so for the research and first-of a-kind projects for which it was originated). Because of this, the PERT method tends to be used in construction and standardized engineering projects, but seldom elsewhere.

Some of PERT's shortcomings are addressed by simulation.

Monte Carlo Simulation of a PERT Network

Monte Carlo computer simulation is a procedure that takes into account the effects of near-critical paths and merge-point bias. Durations for project activities are randomly selected from probability distributions, and the critical path is computed from these times. The procedure is repeated thousands of times to generate a distribution of project durations. It gives an "expected" project duration and standard deviation that is more reliable and accurate than simple PERT computations, and it also gives the probabilities of other paths becoming critical.[9]

Simulation allows the use of a variety of probability distributions besides Beta, including distributions based upon empirical data. As a result, the generated project durations more accurately represent the range of expected durations than does the single-network PERT method.

Simulation can also be used to avoid some limitations of PERT assumptions, such as independence of activity durations and normality of the project duration distribution. The following example from Evans and Olson illustrates usage of the three time estimates in a simulation to assess the likelihood of project completion time.[10]

Example 7.2: Simulation to Determine Project Duration

Consider the project activities and time estimates in Table 7.3 and the project network in Figure 7.13.

Table 7.3 Activities and Time Estimates

	Activity	Predecessors	Minimum	Most Likely	Maximum	t_e	V
A	Select steering committee	—	15	15	15	15	0
B	Develop requirements list	—	40	45	60	46.67	11.11
C	Develop system size estimates	—	10	14	30	16	11.11
D	Determine prospective vendors	—	2	2	5	2.5	0.25
E	Form evaluation team	A	5	7	9	7	0.44
F	Issue request for proposal	B, C, D, E	4	5	8	5.33	0.44
G	Bidders' conference	F	1	1	1	1	0
H	Review submissions	G	25	30	50	32.5	17.36
I	Select vendor short list	H	3	5	10	5.5	1.36
J	Check vendor references	I	3	3	10	4.17	1.36
K	Vendor demonstrations	I	20	30	45	30.83	17.36
L	User site visit	I	3	3	5	3.33	0.11
M	Select vendor	J, K, L	3	3	3	3	0
N	Volume sensitive test	M	10	13	20	13.67	2.78
O	Negotiate contracts	M	10	14	28	15.67	9
P	Cost–benefit analysis	N, O	2	2	2	2	0
Q	Obtain board of directors' approval	P	5	5	5	5	0

Source: Evans J and Olson, D. *Introduction to Simulation and Risk Management*. Upper Saddle River, NJ: Prentice Hall; 1998. p. 116. Reproduced with permission.

The critical path is B–F–G–H–I–K–M–O–P–Q; summing t_e and V on this path gives a project duration of 147.5 days with a variance of 56.63.

Suppose the customer would prefer that the project is completed within 140 days. Using the PERT method, the probability of completing the project within 140 days is found from

$$Z = \frac{140 - 147.5}{\sqrt{56.65}} = -0.996$$

Referring to Table 7.2, the probability is about 16 percent.

Figure 7.13
Project network.

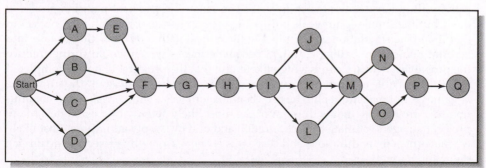

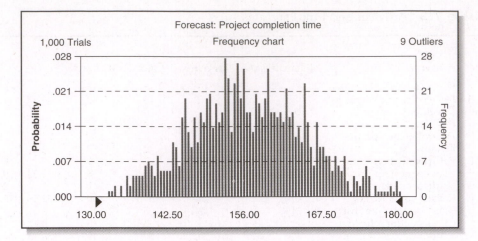

Figure 7.14
Crystal Ball simulation results for project completion times.

Using the simulation program Crystal Ball to generate the completion times for 1,000 replications of the project yields the distribution in Figure 7.14 (various other programs, such as Risksim, @Risk, Arena, and Simul-8, can also be used).[11]

The simulation distribution has a mean of 155 days, and gives a probability of completing the project in 140 days of about 6.9 percent (the sum of the probabilities to the left of 140 on Figure 7.14). It is thus unlikely that the project will be finished in less than 140 days, and only 50 percent likely that it will be completed within 155 days, which is 7.5 days longer than the PERT estimate of 147.5 days.

Simulation provides more accurate, realistic results than PERT because it compensates for non-critical paths that can become critical. However, like PERT, it is merely a method for analyzing schedules, not for creating them (such as network diagrams and Gantt charts); it is also based upon guesses or best estimates. It is a "better" analysis tool than PERT, but, like PERT, does not eliminate the uncertainty associated with scheduling, or say what to do to reduce project risk; other tools are needed for that, as discussed in Chapter 10.

Why Projects Are Often Late

The project manager might face considerable risk when committing to a due date based solely on the duration of the critical path. For example, a Monte Carlo simulation was used to calculate the probability of finishing a project given the critical path activity durations shown in Figure 7.15. The most likely critical path length is 130 days, but the simulation reveals only a 15 percent chance of finishing the project in that time. The simulation was applied to the critical path only, and did not take into account non-critical paths that might become critical—which would further reduce the probability. Thus, there is a high likelihood that the project will not be completed in 130 days. While individual m values might be considered "realistic," the sum of the m values is not realistic at all! The project manager faces a similar risk when committing to a project cost that is the sum of the most likely activity cost estimates. Many project managers estimate project duration and cost by simply adding up most likely estimates of activity durations and costs; this is one reason why projects overrun due dates and budgets.

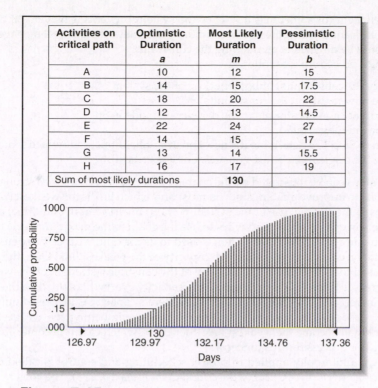

Activities on critical path	Optimistic Duration	Most Likely Duration	Pessimistic Duration
	a	m	b
A	10	12	15
B	14	15	17.5
C	18	20	22
D	12	13	14.5
E	22	24	27
F	14	15	17
G	13	14	15.5
H	16	17	19
Sum of most likely durations		**130**	

Figure 7.15
Simulation results show low probability of finishing within critical path time.
Generated by means of Crystal Ball software, assuming triangular distributions.

Another reason for overruns is human behavior. During the feasibility or proposal (tendering) stage of the project, champions and supporters do their best to "sell" the project. Everyone is optimistic. Of course, without such optimism many an important project would never have gotten off the ground. While optimism gains the necessary buy-in from stakeholders, it also leads to underestimating project duration and cost. The Channel Tunnel is an example. Originally, it was estimated that 30 million people and 100 million tons of freight would be transported through the Chunnel *per year*.[12] This claim proved slightly exaggerated: in the first *5 years* the actual numbers were 28 million people and 12 million tons of freight. The cost, initially estimated at £7.5 billion, ultimately reached £15 billion, and the project took nearly 18 months longer to complete than originally estimated.

There are some other important reasons why projects finish late, and ways to avoid them; these are discussed in the next sections.

7.4 THEORY OF CONSTRAINTS AND CRITICAL CHAIN METHOD

The theory of constraints (TOC) is a systems approach to improving the performance of business systems.[13] A premise of TOC is that every system has a goal, and that often only one element (or sometimes a few) of the system prevents achievement of that goal. This element is called the *system constraint*; to achieve the goal, all management efforts should be directed at eliminating the constraint.

The TOC procedure is as follows:

1. Identify the constraint(s) or bottleneck(s) of the system
2. Decide how to exploit the constraint(s)
3. Subordinate non-constraints to the decision(s) made in Step 2
4. Elevate the constraint(s)
5. Return to Step 1 to determine if a new constraint has appeared (which would render the original one a non-constraint or less critical).

These steps can be illustrated by the analogy of a chain. A chain is as strong as its weakest link; to improve a chain, first you must find which link is the weakest (Step 1). Step 2 aims at the optimal use of the system without investment in additional capacity; in the chain example, you find ways to use the chain to the maximum load for the weakest link. In Step 3, the entire system is used to its maximum capacity by ensuring that the load on every link is equal to the capacity of the weakest link. Once the entire system is used to its maximum, the capacity of the constraint (strength of the weakest link) is increased (Step 4). This will enable the capacity everywhere (load on the links) to also be increased. Note, however, that the system's capacity is increased only *after* its existing capacity has been fully utilized. Upon strengthening the weakest link, another link will become the weakest link (Step 5), in which case it becomes the new constraint. The process returns to Step 1.

The TOC philosophy applied to project scheduling and control is called *critical chain project management (CCPM)* or the *critical chain method (CCM)*. The constraint for an individual project is its *duration* or due date, and the aim of the method is to reduce the duration, or guarantee hitting the due date.[14] CCPM acknowledges the stochastic nature of activity durations, and also takes into account the impact of human behavior on project scheduling and execution. It can be applied to single projects and to multiple, concurrent projects.[15]

Consider the activities for the project shown in Table 7.4 and Figure 7.16. The critical path, P–Q–R–Z, is 32 days long. Step 1 identifies this duration, 32 days, as the constraint. Step 2 involves deciding how to exploit the constraint—how to reduce the duration of the critical path so the project can be completed as fast and prudently as possible.

Commitment to Due Dates

With traditional network-based methods, people working in each activity in the project must *commit* to completing the activity by a target date, even though the

Table 7.4 Activities for Small System Development Project

ACTIVITY DESCRIPTION (FROM WBS)	ACTIVITY CODE	DURATION (DAYS)	RESOURCES
Design Subsystem A	P	8	Design Team A
Manufacture Subsystem A	Q	12	Technician
Test Subsystem A	R	8	Test team
Design Subsystem B	S	4	Design Team B
Build Subsystem B	T	20	Technician
Assemble Subsystems A and B	Z	4	Technician

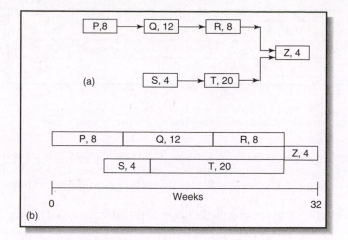

Figure 7.16
(a) AON network for activities in Table 7.4.
(b) Time-scaled network for activities in Table 7.4.

activity duration is uncertain. There might be penalties for finishing late (and rewards for finishing early). Out of fear of finishing late, people responsible for an activity often provide a relatively pessimistic or "padded" time estimate. This behavior is quite normal, although it results everywhere in inflated estimated activity durations (t_e) and, hence, longer duration projects. The TOC approach to avoiding padding is simply this: do not require people responsible for activities to commit to due dates. Encourage them to work in earnest, but do not hold them to a target date. In requesting time estimates, ask people to provide the most "realistic" time, meaning the time with a 50 percent chance of being longer and 50 percent chance of being shorter.

Project Buffer and Feeding Buffers

But, you ask, what happens if activities get delayed? Won't that delay the project? To protect against delays, a *project buffer* (time contingency) is placed at the end of the project. The date at the end of the buffer is the date to which the project manager commits to completing the project. (Note: the project manager commits to a date for completing the project, but, as mentioned, people responsible for the activities in the project do not commit to dates; they just try to complete their activities speedily.) Now you ask, won't adding a time buffer lengthen the project? The answer is no, because when the project manager receives the "customary" time estimates for activities she *cuts them in half!* The rationale is that most people submitting time estimates build into them contingency (i.e., they pad the estimate) to allow for uncertainty. Reducing the estimate by 50 percent removes that contingency. (It should be noted, however, that when the project manager thinks she has received a "realistic" estimate—i.e., an estimate that is not padded—she does not cut it in half). Reducing the estimate by 50 percent removes that contingency, but that is okay, because the project buffer provides for any needed contingency.

To illustrate, look at Figure 7.17, where the durations in Figure 7.16 everywhere have been cut in half. The total number of days cut from the critical path P–Q–R–Z, 16 days (4+6+4+2), becomes the project buffer. Note also in the figure the presence of a *feeding buffer*, which is the sum of the number of days removed from the non-critical

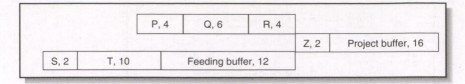

Figure 7.17
Schedule with contingencies reserves allocated to the project manager.

path S–T, 12 days (2 + 10). In general, CCPM calls for a single project buffer at the end of the critical path as well as a feeding buffer located wherever a non-critical path feeds into the critical path. The feeding buffer protects against delays in non-critical activities.

While project buffers and feeding buffers bear a resemblance to slack, they are *not* slack. Whereas with traditional methods activities are scheduled as early as possible and slack may be used to delay activities when necessary, in CCPM non-critical activities are planned to start *as late as possible*, but with buffers. (During *execution*, however, work starts on the scheduled date or *as soon as possible*). The buffers belong to the project manager, and only she can allocate time from them, which happens whenever an activity exceeds its estimated "expected" duration. Since every activity has only a 50 percent chance of exceeding its expected duration, the buffers provide more than enough time to compensate for delayed activities.

In fact, the size of the buffer can be reduced substantially for two reasons. The first is the mathematical effect called *aggregation*, which in a project means that it is extremely unlikely that *all* activities will experience bad luck and that many will finish ahead of the planned expected time, t_e. When the time usually allowed to "pad" each activity is cut from the activity and is instead included in a single buffer at the end of the project, the size of the required buffer ends up being substantially less than the total padding removed from all the activities. The aggregation effect—well known in risk management—is explained in the Appendix to this chapter. The second reason why the buffer size can be reduced stems from the obverse of Parkinson's Law, which states that "work expands to fill the time available." By removing padding from each activity, people have less time to do the work, and hence tend to work faster than when they have more time. For these reasons, the buffer sizes can be reduced. In Figure 7.18, they have been reduced by 50 percent.

The project manager commits to completing the project on or before the date at the end of the project buffer (Week 28 in the example), although the project team works to complete the project on or before the date at the *start of* the project buffer (Week 20). In theory, there is a high likelihood that this project will be completed *in less than 28 weeks*. With the critical path method, there is a high likelihood the project will be completed *after* the critical path duration, which is *32 weeks*.

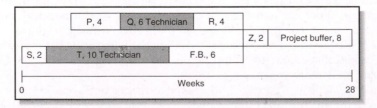

Figure 7.18
Schedule with buffer sizes reduced.

Worth repeating is that in CCPM the project manager commits to the completion due date (at the end of the project buffer), while people responsible for individual activities *do not* commit to any due dates; they just try to complete their activities within the time estimates they provided.

Critical Chain

Figure 7.18 reveals a potential problem, though: activities Q and T both use the same resource (the "technician"). Assume each requires her full-time attention; to allow for that, the schedule is adjusted as shown in Figure 7.19 (putting Activity Q before T would be another possible schedule). In the adjusted schedule, path S–T–Q–R–Z is the *critical chain*, defined as the path connecting activities that require the same constrained resource. The critical chain is not necessarily the longest path in the network, although whenever the length of the critical chain plus buffers exceeds the length of the critical path the critical chain, *not* the critical path, determines the project duration. Traditional network methods address the resource-conflict problem by means of resource leveling, although the result will not necessarily be the same as with CCPM. Note that the feeding buffer (F.B.) is 4 days, not 2. The reason is because it follows only one activity, P, and hence the principle of aggregation does not apply. Ultimately, the size of the buffer is at the manager's discretion, and whatever she decides.

If the schedule does not meet a predetermined due date, or upper management wants the project completed sooner, additional resources must be added. But additional resources are costly; hence CCPM attempts first to make full use of whatever resources are currently available.

Figure 7.19
Schedule adjusted so that every resource performs only one task at a time.

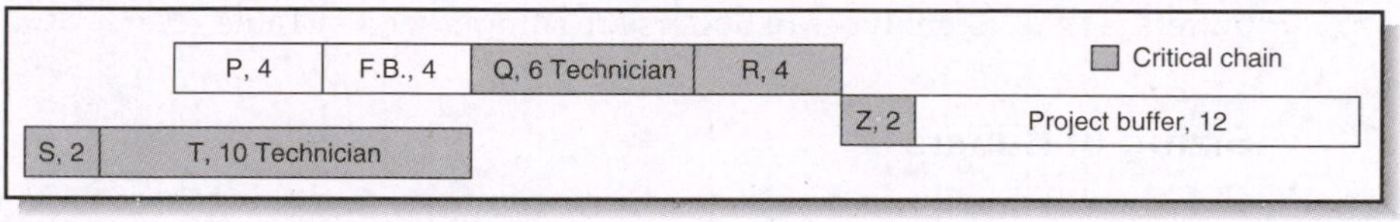

Resource Buffers: Capitalizing on Good Luck

Mentioned earlier was the fact that whenever activities finish late their successors start late, but whenever they finish early their successors *don't necessarily* start early. Resources such as people and equipment that have been scheduled to work at a date often are not available earlier than that because they are working on something else. As a consequence, whenever bad luck occurs the project is delayed; whenever good luck occurs it makes no difference!

In CCPM, the project team is able to capitalize on good luck (predecessors finishing early) through use of *resource buffers*. Unlike project and feeding buffers, resource buffers do not add time to the schedule. A resource buffer is a *countdown* signal or warning to alert resources that an activity on the critical chain will possibly finish earlier than planned and to *be prepared to start early*. This is in accordance with TOC Step 2 (exploit the constraint). In a marathon relay race, each runner is prepared to accept the baton from the previous runner, regardless when the latter is expected to arrive; likewise, resources on the critical chain are prepared to take advantage of good luck—i.e., to start earlier than scheduled. In practice, a resource buffer can take the form of a series of e-mail or other messages to resources, counting down the time remaining

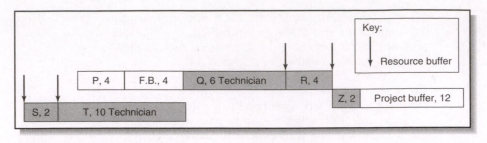

Figure 7.20
Resource buffers providing countdown on when to start critical activities.

before they must be ready to start a critical activity. The locations of resource buffers are illustrated in Figure 7.20.

Note that resource buffers are inserted only on the critical chain, since feeding buffers are able to deal adequately with the uncertainty on non-critical paths. Note also there is no resource buffer between Activity T and Activity Q, since the same resource (technician) does both and, obviously, needs no advance notification about when she will finish Activity Q and must start Activity T.

Milestone Buffers

Sometimes milestone deadlines are set at intermediate times in the project, such as at the scheduled completion dates for project phases. In that case, a *milestone buffer* is inserted before each milestone. When milestone buffers are used, the size of the project buffer is reduced; in effect, the project buffer is divided up among the milestone buffers. The different types of buffers are summarized in Table 7.5.

Sizing of Buffers

CCPM relies heavily on project and feeding buffers, so making them the right size is important. Goldratt suggests that activity durations be cut by 50 percent and that the project buffer be half the duration of the resulting longest path.[16] The method, which reduces the project duration by 25 percent, was illustrated in the example above, and is referred to as the "50 percent of chain" and "cut and paste" method.

Table 7.5 Summary of Buffer Types for a Single Project

Buffer Type	Function of the Buffer
Project buffer	Comprised of aggregated contingency reserves taken from activities on the critical chain; provides a contingency reserve between the earliest completion date possible and the committed date
Milestone buffer	Similar to a project buffer but used when a project phase or milestone has a fixed due date
Feeding buffer	Comprised of aggregated contingencies taken from non-critical paths; stabilizes the critical chain by preventing non-critical activities from delaying critical activities
Resource buffer	An early warning or "count down" to the start of a critical activity that ensures that resources are ready to do work on the critical chain as soon as all preceding activities have been completed

As explained in the Appendix to this chapter, the amount by which the duration can be reduced is proportional to the square root of the number of activities in the chain. When a path consists of many activities, a buffer of 50 percent of the path length is too large.[17] Newbold proposes the *square root of sum of squares (SSQ)* method, where the buffer size is set to the square root of the sum of squares of the difference between the low-risk duration and the mean duration for each task along the longest path leading to the buffer.[18] Others have suggested additional methods.[19]

Effects of Human Behavior

Projects take longer than necessary for many reasons, including the following.

First, people build *padding* into time estimates. The effect of padding gets worse as each manager in the WBS adds to the padding. If the person responsible for an activity pads the time by 10 percent and each person higher in the WBS also pads it by 10 percent, the padding at the project level would be $(1.1)^n$ where n is the number of WBS levels. For a WBS of five levels, this yields a total contingency of 60 percent. If each adds in 15 percent, the total contingency for the activity would be 101 percent.

Second, people *multitask*. For example, a contractor has three independent projects, X, Y, and Z, each of expected duration 10 weeks. The contractor is anxious to finish *all* of them as soon as possible, so he divides each into small pieces so that, in a sense, he can work on all of them at the same time. But in doing so, he actually delays the completion of two of the projects. If he had scheduled the projects sequentially, X first, Y second, and Z last, without interruption, then, as shown in Figure 7.21(a), he would finish X at Week 10, Y at Week 20, and Z at Week 30. But when he breaks up the projects into segments of, say, 5-week periods, and alternates working among them, he increases the *elapsed time* for each project from 10 weeks to 20 weeks. As illustrated in Figure 7.21(b), the result is that two of the projects are delayed: X finishes in Week 20 and Y finishes in Week 25. In general, the more the activities or projects are broken up and intermixed with other projects, the greater the elapsed time to finish any of them.

Compounding the effect is that this practice precludes people from building the momentum they would have gained by focusing uninterrupted on only one task. This effect was illustrated in Figure 6.25.

Multitasking conflicts with TOC Step 2 (exploiting the constraint) and Step 3 (subordinating everything else to the constraint). By focusing on just one activity at a time, the activity can be completed faster, successor activities started earlier, and the project finished sooner.

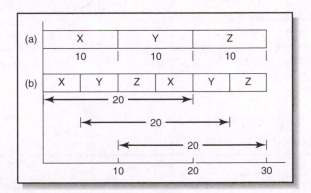

Figure 7.21
Effect of multitasking on elapsed and completion times.

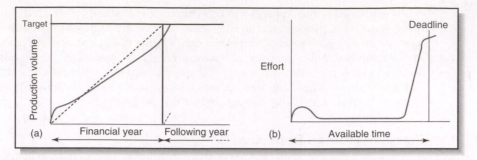

Figure 7.22
Students' syndrome (a) in a production and (b) in a project.

A third reason projects take longer than necessary is that people procrastinate and waste available slack.[20] Given a choice between two scheduled times, one early and one late, people often choose to *wait* until the late one; this automatically eliminates slack, puts activities on the critical path, and increases the likelihood of project delay. Whenever people perceive slack, they are less motivated to complete an activity early. The effect is called the "students' syndrome," reflecting the initial enthusiasm with which students tackle a course, which soon wanes, only to resume just before the final examination. A similar effect happens in production and project environments, shown in Figure 7.22.

Shortening activity durations and scheduling activities as late as possible (with buffers) reduces the tendency to procrastinate.

The Challenge of CCPM: Changing Behavior

A belief in most project organizations is that because the project manager has to commit to a due date, everybody in the project must also commit to due dates. In CCPM, the premise is that only the project manager needs to commit to a date; everyone else works toward realistic estimates. While CCPM can often be used on small projects without everyone accepting this, such is not the case for major projects. Since most people are accustomed to working toward deadlines, this requires no less than a cultural and behavioral change at all levels of the organization, including top management. Senior managers and customers who do not understand the principles of CCPM will try to trim or eliminate the project buffer.

Software Support for CCPM[21]

Many project management software systems include provision for CCPM, and many others accept add-ons that make them compatible with CCPM. MSProject supports the critical-chain method only if the Prochain™ add-in is used. The Sciforma™ and Concerto™ software fully support CCPM.

7.5 ALLOCATING RESOURCES AND MULTIPLE PROJECT SCHEDULING

Organizations in construction, consulting, systems development, and maintenance commonly use a pool of shared equipment and skilled workers from which all projects draw. In matrix organizations (Chapter 13), projects share resources from the same functional departments. This section addresses the matter of scheduling multiple projects that share constrained resources.

Multiple projects that share resources must be planned and scheduled such that in combination they do not exceed the resources available in the shared pools. Although these projects might in all other ways be considered independent, the fact that they share resources means they are at least somewhat dependent.

As might be expected, the problem of scheduling multiple concurrent projects is analogous to scheduling multiple concurrent activities within a single project, but with modification to account for the economic, technical, and organizational issues that arise when dealing with multiple projects (see Chapter 17).

First, each project has its own target completion date, and all the projects must be scheduled to finish as close to those dates as possible to avoid deferred payments, penalty costs, or lost sales and revenues. Further, when projects are interdependent, then delays in one project can have a ripple effect on others; e.g., the delay of a satellite development and launch project will subsequently cause the delay of a telecommunications project. In any case, scheduling of multiple projects requires first determining the relative priority among the projects to determine which project should get "first dibs" on scarce resources.

Because most organizations prefer to maintain a uniform level of personnel and other resources, the combined schedules for multiple projects ideally result in a uniform loading of these resources. In other words, the resource loading for the combined projects is ideally flat. In theory, projects are scheduled such that as resources are released from one project they are assigned to others. This minimizes costs associated with hiring, layoffs, and idle workers and facilities, and helps maintain efficient use of resources and worker morale.

When many activities are ready to start, and all require the same resource, to which activities should the resource be allocated? When 10 tasks are ready to start, the number of possible sequences in performing them is 10!, or more than 3.6 million. If n activities are ready to start and all of them require m resources, the number of possible schedules would be $(n!)^m$. Optimization using normal polynomials requires intolerably large amounts of computing time and is usually not feasible (the problem is "NP hard"). Heuristic methods, on the other hand, provide simple, acceptable solutions.[22]

Heuristic Methods for Allocating Resources to a Project

A heuristic is a procedure based upon a simple rule. Heuristic methods for allocating resources to projects often employ decision rules called *priority rules* or *dispatching rules*. While these methods do not produce optimal schedules, they do produce schedules that are good enough for most situations.

Heuristics methods start with early and late times as determined by traditional network methods, and then analyze the schedule for the required resources (i.e., the resource loading). Whenever a resource requirement exceeds the constraint, the heuristic determines which activity gets high priority and receives the resource. The most common heuristic rules for determining scheduling priority are:

a. *As soon as possible*: activities that *can* be started sooner are given priority over (or scheduled ahead of) those that can be started later
b. *As late as possible*: activities that can be finished later are given lower priority than those that must be finished earlier
c. *Most resources*: activities requiring more resources are given priority over those requiring fewer resources
d. *Shortest task time*: activities of shorter duration are given priority over those of

longer duration (sometimes referred to as *shortest activity duration, shortest processing time* or *shortest operating time*)

e. *Least slack*: activities with less slack are given priority over those with more slack; critical path activities thus have highest priority (this rule is also referred to as *slack time remaining*)

f. *First come first served*: activities that arrive earlier or require the resource earlier are given priority

g. *Earliest due date*: this rule is used where a resource is to be allocated to more than one project. The project with the earliest target completion date is given priority. Alternatively, the activity with the *earliest next operation* is given priority.

Numerous other priority rules have been defined.[23] All of them are subordinate to precedence requirements; i.e., regardless of the rule, the resulting schedule will not violate predecessor–successor relationships. Most project management software employs some combination of these rules (e.g., using "shortest task time," then using "as soon as possible" as a tie breaker). Figure 7.23 shows examples of the above rules

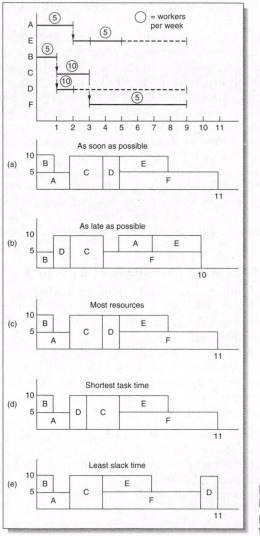

Figure 7.23
Results of several priority rules on project schedule and completion times.

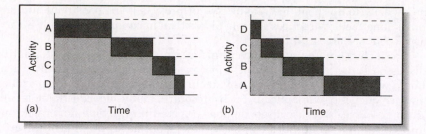

Figure 7.24
The shortest task time rule reduces waiting time. (a) Longest task first.
(b) Shortest task first.

(a) through (e) and their impacts on the project schedule, assuming a constraint of 10 workers per week maximum.

As Figure 7.23 shows, the rules yield different results, some better than others. In general, with the *as late as possible* rule, everything occurs at its latest date; the drawback of this is that a delay in any activity will delay the project. In contrast, the *least slack rule* is good since it reduces the risk of non-critical activities delaying critical ones.

The *shortest task time* rule is good when multiple projects must be executed at once, since it allows people responsible for succeeding activities to perform them sooner. Figure 7.24 shows what happens when tasks are scheduled *longest task first* versus *shortest task first*. As represented by the area under the bars, the total waiting time in Figure 7.24(b) is much less than in Figure 7.24(a). The rule says: when you have several things to do, do the shortest ones first.

The typical scheduling goal is to complete the project by the target completion date, although that is sometimes not possible, regardless of the priority rule. For example, suppose the target completion date for the project in Figure 7.23 is 9 weeks—the critical path length. Given the constrained-resource level of 10 workers, none of the heuristics in the example meets this target, although one of them ("as late as possible") results in 10-week completion.

7.6 TOC METHOD FOR ALLOCATING RESOURCES TO MULTIPLE PROJECTS[24]

As much as 90 percent (by value) of all projects is carried out in multi-project environments.[25] In the TOC method, the constraint for an individual project is its duration. When multiple projects are involved, the goal is to do them as fast as possible, and the constraint is the rate of flow of the projects through the system. TOC provides a heuristic for scheduling the start of new projects so as to maximize the flow of all projects. The heuristic is based upon the five steps mentioned earlier.

Step 1: Identify the Constraint

What prevents a company from making more money through projects? If the contractor has few projects on the order books, the constraint might be limited market share or the size of the market. But if the contractor has more demand for projects than the capacity to do them, the rate of flow of projects is the constraint and anything constricting the flow reduces the rate to less than maximum. Often this is caused by insufficient resources.

Production environments such as manufacturing "job shops" use priority rules (discussed earlier) to select the next job on which a resource (usually a machine) should work. In job shops, it is easy to identify the constraint—it is the machine ahead of which queues of work pile up. Such a resource, the system constraint, is called the "drum resource," because it sets the tone or pace of everything flowing through the process. The TOC philosophy emphasizes the importance of keeping the constrained (drum) resource busy, preventing starvation and blockage from reducing the flow.[26] To ensure this, *drum buffers* are used. Application of the drum resource method to project management is described elsewhere.[27]

Experience with the implementation of TOC in project environments in recent years, however, suggests that while a specific resource might be identified as the constraint in a multi-project environment, often the real constraint is something *other* than such a resource. In practice, the identified constraints might be different for the *planning* of a set of projects than for their *execution*. Typical such constraints are discussed next.

In a sequence of activities, regardless of the actual constraint, an activity near the end of a project may be chosen to substitute for the constraint.[28] For *planning* a set of projects, a *rule* regarding the scheduling of this chosen activity may be used as proxy for the constraint of the set of projects. For example, in one electronics company that conducts multiple, concurrent projects, all projects must pass through "final integration" just before closeout. A specialist engineer was identified as the resource with the highest workload in final integration, but rather than using that workload as the drum constraint to stagger the projects, it was decided instead to use the rule of *only three projects in final integration at a time*. In Figure 7.25(a), the shaded activities represent final integration in nine projects. To ensure there are always three projects in final integration, 2.1 starts as soon as 1.1 is completed, 2.2 starts as soon as 1.2 is completed, and so on. This was the constraint for *planning* sets of projects. For *executing* the sets of projects, the typical constraint is the time that managers have available to spend on managing projects.

Step 2: Decide How to Exploit (Utilize) the Constraint

Assume the constraint is the rule "only three projects in final integration." This rule then serves as the guideline for exploiting the constraint for planning purposes, which would be to stagger the release of project work in such a way that there is always at least one project ready and waiting to enter the stage of final integration. *Capacity buffers*, inserted as shown in Figure 7.25(b), are used to determine the moment when project work should be released such that when final integration for one project is completed, another project is waiting to begin final integration. This ensures that the constraint does not become idle (is "exploited") and that there will always be three projects in final integration, as shown in Figure 7.25(a). The schedule of when a project should be ready for final integration to start, combined with the duration of each project, determines when each project should be released into the system.

Note that a capacity buffer does not increase the duration (time from start to finish) of an individual project; it merely ensures that a project will start on time. The capacity buffer is therefore not monitored and reported like project or feeding buffers; its sole purpose is to support the staggering rule.

In the event that the final integration stage is completed early, resource buffers (discussed earlier) will ensure that subsequent projects can be accelerated accordingly to start early.

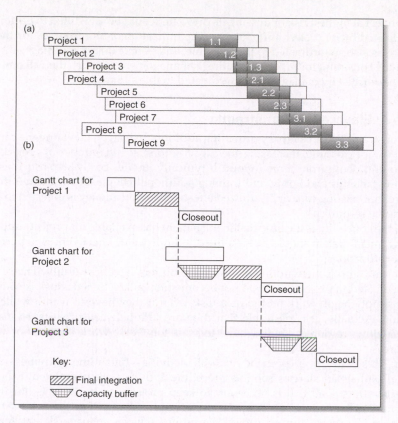

Figure 7.25
Capacity buffer used to stagger projects.

Because fewer projects are being worked on, staggering them in this way reduces the workload on most resources, reduces multitasking across projects, improves the flow of projects, and ensures meeting commitments to customers.

If the time that managers need to effectively manage projects is the constraint for *executing* the set of projects, then measures must be taken to increase the time they have available for this purpose (managers should, for example, not be spending time trying to keep all resources busy all the time). If lack of management support during execution is the constraint on the flow of projects, then this constraint has to be removed. This is effectively achieved through the steps discussed below.

Step 3: Subordinate Everything Else to Decisions Regarding the Constraint

During scheduling, the release of projects (authorization to start) is based on the load on the constraint. If the company decides that it should have only three projects in the integration phase, the proxy constraint would be the rule "three projects in integration." Each new project would be slotted to start integration at whatever time is necessary to maintain the three-project-maximum load in integration. The schedules of individual projects are therefore subordinated to the schedule of the multi-project constraint—i.e., the rule regarding the number of projects in the integration phase.

The project at highest risk of missing its due date would be scheduled to be done first, as indicated by its project buffer status. The utilization of all resources for the set of projects is also subordinated to the schedule, and people do not multitask.

If the constraint for project execution is management support, then all other work to be performed by managers is subordinated to this support role.

Step 4: Elevate the Constraint

The constraint is "elevated" by providing additional capacity. Elevating the constraint involves, for example, increasing the capacity to raise the number of projects in the integration phase from three to four. It typically implies costly steps such as building new facilities and hiring and training additional people. Steps 2 and 3 therefore ensure that existing capacity is utilized effectively before money is invested to acquire additional resources.

If the constraint is the time that management has available for project support, the management system should be simplified to improve its effectiveness in performing support functions.

In multi-project environments, resource buffers have less utility. The resources are dedicated to projects; they do not become unavailable when a task is completed. They simply begin work on the next task, even if they have to wait a while before starting. Actually, it is desirable that they are idle between projects: to maximize project flow, resources should have to wait for work; work should not wait for resources.

In this way, it is possible that all activities (including activities on non-critical paths) can start as soon as preceding activities are completed. Monitoring project buffers is all that is necessary to keep projects on track (as is illustrated in Chapter 11, Example 11.4). Tracking project buffers simplifies the project tracking and control process during project execution, relieves managers' workload, and increases the time available to support other projects. In turn, this elevates the constraint for project execution—the time managers have available to make better flow decisions.

Step 5: Return to Step 1

Adding resources might remove the constraint, in which case a new constraint would be identified and the process repeated. Sometimes, however, the new constraint would be too disruptive, in which case the extant constraint is allowed to remain and *not* be elevated.

Discussion

One company has simplified the TOC method for managing multiple projects by using only three rules:

Rule 1: During planning, stagger the release of projects
Rule 2: Plan aggressive project durations using project buffers only one-third the length of the critical chain
Rule 3: During execution, (a) ensure that activities are executed according to priorities indicated by buffer status (Chapter 11, Example 11.4), and (b) minimize buffer consumption by doing all tasks as soon as possible.[29]

How good are TOC heuristics for planning compared to traditional priority rules? The answer is somewhat equivocal, and for some simple projects the results are the same. An exploratory experiment where the heuristic was compared with the often-used least slack rule showed the TOC heuristic gave better results,[30] but another experiment revealed poorer results.[31] Although the TOC method is based on logic and seems to make sense, verification in practice would require empirical research from a variety of industrial different settings, which has yet to be done.

7.7 DISCUSSION AND SUMMARY

This chapter has covered project scheduling methods that address time constraints, resource constraints, uncertainty about activity and project durations, and multiple projects sharing resources. The methods offer ways to accelerate projects and reduce uncertainty about completion dates. Unlike the simpler techniques, such as Gantt charts and critical path networks generated by inexpensive software, the methods described in this chapter have gained fewer acceptances and are applied mainly in relatively sophisticated industries. All the methods have limitations, yet all have merits and contribute to an understanding of project time management and improved competitiveness.

- CPM is a network-based method for analyzing the effect of project duration on cost. It enables managers to determine the least costly way of reducing project duration to complete the project by a due date or in the shortest time.

- The PERT method enables managers to gauge project risk by estimating the probability of finishing a project by a predetermined due date. The method, however, considers only the current critical path, and ignores non-critical paths that could become critical. Monte Carlo simulation accounts for the possibility of any path becoming critical and overcomes this limitation.

- The critical-chain method, CCPM, based on the Theory of Constraints (TOC), aims at reducing project duration. Using time buffers, it transforms a stochastic problem into a relatively simple deterministic one. Unlike critical path scheduling, which normally schedules non-critical activities as early as possible, CCPM schedules them as late as possible but with buffers. With other methods, variability in activity durations leads to changes in the critical path without warning, but in CCPM, buffers provide relative stability to the critical chain—the path connecting activities that require the same constrained resource—and certainty about the completion time. CCPM is conceptually sound and offers a practical and relatively simple way to schedule projects, but the method requires a shift in human behavior since nobody but the project manager is required to commit to due dates. Many managers find that concept hard to swallow.

- Multi-project scheduling presents special challenges, one being the allocation of scarce resources to concurrent projects. The traditional way to allocate resources among projects (and among activities *within* projects) is to use priority rules. The TOC way aims to allow as many concurrent projects as possible by improving the flow of projects through the system.

- All the methods in this chapter are supported by commercial software systems, which simplify their application and eliminate computational difficulties. However, as with all management methods, appropriate application of the techniques assumes a sound understanding of the principles that underlie them, and management support.

Summary List of Symbols

N	Number of activities on the critical path
C_n	Normal Activity Cost: the direct cost of completing an activity under normal work effort; usually, the lowest cost for completing an activity
C_c	Crash Activity Cost: the direct cost of completing an activity under a crash work effort; usually, the highest cost for completing an activity
T_n	Normal Activity Duration: the expected time to complete an activity under normal work effort; usually, assumed to be the longest time the work will take
T_c	Crash Activity Duration: the expected time to complete an activity under a crash work effort; the shortest possible time in which the work can be completed
t_e	Expected Activity Duration: in PERT, the mean time to complete an activity, based on optimistic (a), most likely (m), and pessimistic (b) estimates of the activity duration
T_e	Expected Project Duration: the probability of finishing earlier than this time is 50 percent and the probability of finishing later than this value is 50 percent
T_s	Target Completion Time for Project: a time specified for project completion
V	Variance of an Activity: the variability in expected activity duration
V_p	Variance of the Project Duration: the variability in the expected project duration

APPENDIX: THE CENTRAL LIMIT THEOREM AND ITS IMPLICATIONS

The PERT and CCPM both utilize the Central Limit Theorem.

Theorem[32]

Suppose n independent tasks are to be performed in sequence (e.g., on a critical path). The term *independent* means that the duration of one activity does not influence the durations of any of the other activities (it does *not* refer to predecessor/successor dependencies in a network).

Let $t_1, t_2, t_3 \ldots t_n$ be the actual times to complete these activities; these are random variables, each with a distribution.

Let the *means* of these variables be $t_{e1}, t_{e2}, t_{e3}, \ldots t_{en}$, and let the *variances* be $V_{t1}, V_{t2}, V_{t3}, \ldots V_{tn}$. Now define T (also a random variable) to be the sum:

$$T = t_1 + t_2 + t_3 + \ldots + t_n$$

If n is a *large number*, the distribution of T is *approximately normal* with mean T_e

$$T_e = t_{e1} + t_{e2} + t_{e3} \ldots + t_{en}$$

and variance V_p

$$V_p = V_{t1} + V_{t2} + V_{t3} + \ldots + V_{tn}$$

or

$$V_p = \sum_{CP} V$$

Therefore, the mean of the sum equals the sum of the individual means, and the variance of the sum equals the sum of the individual variances. In addition, the distribution of the sum of activity durations is a normal distribution, regardless of the shapes of the distributions of the individual activity durations, as illustrated in Figure 7.26.

Application to PERT

Given that the most likely (or modal) duration of an activity is m, the optimistic value is a and the pessimistic value is b, the mean expected duration of each activity

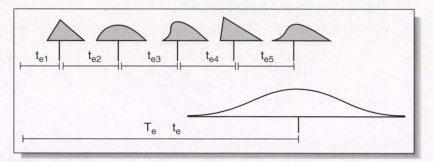

Figure 7.26
The distribution of the sum of skewed distributions is a normal distribution (not to scale).

$$t_e = (a + 4m + b)/6$$

and the variance of each activity

$$V = \left(\frac{b - a}{6}\right)^2$$

Given the mean and variance for every activity on the critical path, the distribution for the sum of the activities on the critical path can be obtained, *provided* the two assumptions of the Central Limit Theorem apply: the activity durations are independent, and there is a "large number" of activities. In project scheduling, the values employed in the calculations are estimates (hence assumed to be independent) and five or more activities is considered a "large" number.

The value of 6 in the variance formula is based on the assumption that the optimistic duration a is the *shortest possible* duration (0 percent chance of the duration being shorter) and the pessimistic duration b is the *longest possible* duration (0 percent chance of it being longer). In other words, the distribution curve intersects the time-axis at these points as indicated in Figure 7.11. If, however, a is defined as a value with 5 percent chance of the duration being less than this, and b as a value with 5 percent chance of the duration being longer than this, as indicated in Figure 7.27, then the value in the above formula for V changes from 6 to 3.2.

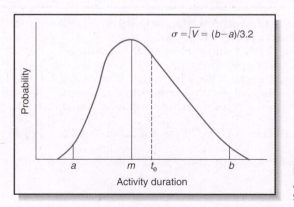

$$\sigma = \sqrt{V} = (b - a)/3.2$$

Activity duration

Figure 7.27
Activity durations with 5th and 95th percentile values.

The Principle of Aggregation[33]

One justification in CCPM for making project and feeding buffers smaller than the sum of the contingency reserves removed from individual activities derives from the Central Limit Theorem. If a number of independent probability distributions are summed, the variance of the sum equals the sum of the variances of the individual distributions. Therefore, if n independent distributions with *equal* variance V are summed, it follows that:

$$V_p = n \cdot V$$

where V_p is the variance of project duration.

The standard deviation σ can be used as an indication of risk and, correspondingly, the amount of contingency reserve required. Since $\sigma^2 = V$, then for the aggregated activities,

$$\sigma_p = (n)^{1/2} \cdot \sigma$$

where σ_p is the standard deviation of project duration.

In the absence of aggregation:

$$\sigma_p = n \cdot \sigma$$

Because $(n)^{1/2}$ is significantly smaller than n, the effect of aggregating independent risks is significant. The higher the number of risks that are aggregated, the more marked the effect. CCPM applies the principle of aggregation to project schedule risks: contingency reserves for individual activities are reduced so that activity durations are challenging but realistic. The contingencies removed from individual activity durations are replaced by a single contingency reserve or "buffer" for the overall project. Because of the aggregation effect, this buffer can be smaller than the sum of the individual contingencies removed from the individual activities. The larger the number of activities on the critical path, the more the project buffer can be reduced.

If the Central Limit Theorem is used to size a project buffer, the probability of the project finishing on time should correspond to the probability indicated by a PERT analysis. The reduction in project duration is dependent on human behavior.

Some authors[34] apply the principle of aggregation to project cost, but before the advent of critical chain there was little evidence of its formal application to project schedules.

REVIEW QUESTIONS AND PROBLEMS

1. Define crash effort and normal effort in terms of the cost and time they represent. When would a project be crashed?
2. How do CPM and PERT differ? How are they the same?
3. What does the cost slope represent?
4. The cost slope always has a negative value. What does this indicate?
5. Time–cost trade-off analysis deals only with direct costs. What distinguishes these costs from indirect costs? Give examples of both direct and indirect costs.
6. What are the criticisms of CPM? How and where is CPM limited in its application?
7. The project network and associated costs (T in days, C in $1,000s) are shown below.

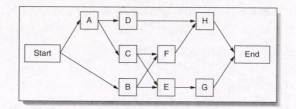

	Normal		Crash		
Activity	T_n	C_n	T_c	C_c	Cost slope
A	4	210	3	280	70
B	9	400	6	640	80
C	6	500	4	600	50
D	9	540	7	600	30
E	4	500	1	1100	200
F	5	150	4	240	90
G	3	150	3	150	—
H	7	600	6	750	150

a. Verify that the normal duration is 22 days and that the direct cost is $3,050.
b. What is the least costly way to reduce the project duration to 21 days? What is the project cost?
c. What is the least costly way to reduce the duration to 20 days? What is the project cost?
d. Now, what is the *earliest* the project can be completed and what is the least costly way of doing this? What is the project cost?

8. The project network and associated costs (T in days, C in $1,000s) are shown below.

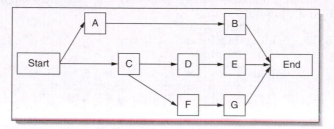

	Normal		Crash		
Activity	T_n	C_n	T_c	C_c	Cost slope
A	6	6	3	9	
B	9	9	5	12	
C	3	4.5	2	7	
D	5	10	2	16	
E	2	2	2	2	
F	4	6	1	10	
G	8	8	5	10	

a. What is the earliest the project can be completed under normal conditions? What is the direct cost?
b. What is the least costly way to reduce the project duration by 2 days? What is the project cost?
c. What is the *earliest* the project can be completed and what is the least costly way of doing this? What is the project cost?

9. The following table gives information on a project (T in days, C in $1000s).

Activity	Immediate predecessors	Normal		Crash	
		T_n	C_n	T_c	C_c
A	—	6	10	2	38
B	—	4	12	4	12
C	—	4	18	2	36
D	A	6	20	2	40
E	B, D	3	30	2	33
F	C	10	10	6	50
G	F, E	6	20	2	100

a. Draw the network diagram. Under normal conditions, what is the earliest the project can be completed? What is the direct cost? What is the critical path?
b. What is the cost of the project if it is completed 1 day earlier, and 2 days earlier?
c. What is the earliest the project can be completed? What is the lowest cost for completing it in this time?
d. If overhead (indirect) costs are $20,000 per day, for what project duration are total project costs (direct + indirect) lowest?

10. Has variability in a time estimate ever caused you to be late for an appointment? Describe.

11. A procurement officer finds that the delivery time for a specific item is never less than 5 days. The worst case scenario is that it takes 30 days for the item to arrive. A delivery lead time of 10 days is more frequent than any other.
a. Calculate the expected delivery time.
b. What estimate would you give for its variance?
c. What factors would you take into account when deciding the amount of time to be allowed for in the project plan for delivery of the item?

12. Given the immediate predecessors and a, m, b for each activity in the tables below, compute:
a. t_e and V for each activity
b. ES, EF, LS, and LF for each activity.
c. T_e and V_p for the project.

Activity	Predecessors	a	m	b
A	—	7	9	11
B	A	1	2	3
C	A	7	8	9
D	B	2	5	11
E	C	2	3	4
F	C	1	4	8
G	D, E	6	7	8
H	F, E	2	6	9

Activity	Predecessors	a	m	b
A	—	2	4	6
B	—	2	2	3
C	—	4	8	10
D	A	4	6	7
E	A, B	7	9	12
F	D, E	1	2	3
G	C	2	3	4

13. Refer to the first network in the above problem.
a. What is $P(T_e < 23)$?
b. What is $P(T_e < 32)$?
c. For what T_s is the probability 95 percent that the project will be completed?

14. For the network in Figure 7.12, what is the probability of completing each of the five paths within 30 days? What is the probability of completing them *all* within 30 days?

15. How would you use buffers to ensure that you are on time for appointments? What factors would you take into account when you make a decision on the size of the buffer?

16. Explain in your own words how the principle of aggregation plays a role in reducing project duration.

17. The diagram below was drawn before it became clear that Mary would have to perform both Activity B and Activity F.[35]

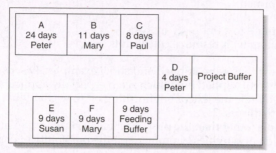

   a. With the realization that Mary has to do the two tasks, indicate two possible critical chains.
   b. Reschedule the work and indicate the position and the size of the feeding buffer.

18. Refer to the network in Number 19 in "Review Questions and Problems" for Chapter 6.
   a. Indicate the critical chain on the diagram.
   b. Which one of the two resources is the constraint?
   c. Construct Gantt charts for this example based on the following heuristics: the shortest task time rule, the least slack rule, and the TOC heuristic.
   d. Assume that the schedule indicates durations from which contingency reserve has been removed. Insert a project buffer and feeding buffers as required.

19. Refer to Figure 7.20. Scheduling Activity Q before Activity T would also have been a way to resolve the resource contingency. Explain why this alternative was not selected.

20. Consider the data about project activities given in the table below.[36]
   a. Schedule the work in such a way that each person always has only one task to perform (do not reduce the durations of activities or insert buffers as yet).
   b. Indicate the critical chain.
   c. Indicate where the feeding buffers should be inserted.
   d. What is the difference in the lengths of the critical path and the critical chain?

Activity	Predecessor(s)	Duration (days)	Resources
A	—	2	John
B	A	3	Sue
C	—	3	Sue & John
D	C	2	Al
E	D, J	3	Sue & Al
F	E, B	2	John
G	F	2	Ann
H	—	4	Sue
J	H	2	Al

21. Discuss the implications of resource allocation for organizations involved in multiple projects.
22. Discuss the differences between fast-tracking, concurrent engineering, and crashing.
23. Write an essay on the reasons why projects are often late.

QUESTIONS ABOUT THE STUDY PROJECT

1. In the project you are studying, discuss which of the following kinds of analysis were performed:
   a. PERT
   b. CPM/time–cost trade-off analysis
   c. Scheduling with resource constraints
   d. CCPM.
2. Discuss how they were applied and show examples. Discuss those applications which were not applied but which seem especially applicable to the project.
3. How do you rate the risk of not finishing on time, and what are the factors contributing to this risk?
4. Were people (other than the project manager) required to make commitments on the duration of activities? Comment on the possibility of changing this behavior.

Case 7.1   Bridgecon Contractors

Bridgecon Construction Company specializes in the detailed design and construction of steel and concrete bridges. The first phase of the company's project management methodology, Initiation, includes identification of project opportunities and assessment of each project's risks and alignment with strategic goals. Bridgecon's marketing department identified an opportunity: a well-known bridge architect recently completed the concept design for a cable-stayed bridge intended to cross over electrified railway lines. Senior managers felt the company could handle the project and decided to pursue it; this marked the end of the first phase.

The project next enters the second phase, Estimating, which includes site visits by the estimating team, review of available resources and skills, detailed risk assessment, and preparing a preliminary plan for detailed design, procurement, logistics, and construction. The phase includes activities A and B in Table 7.6, which are necessary to prepare the bid for building the bridge. The phase concludes with a presentation to the customer, the rail authority.

The project manager and the estimating team meet with the architect and structural engineers who produced the concept design to acquaint themselves with the design. They then meet with subcontractors who they might choose to construct the pilings and fabricate steel components.

Following these meetings the "Initial Duration Estimate" and "Initial Cost Estimate" are completed, shown in Table 7.6.

The RFP (request for proposal) for building the bridge says acceptance of the plan by the rail authority is one criterion for selecting a contractor. Early on it becomes evident that starting with activity D and until the completion of activity S, operation of one of the railway lines under the bridge will be impaired, although an informal discussion with the rail authority indicates that this might be acceptable. During a subsequent meeting, however, the rail authority expresses concern that the impairment will last 17 weeks, and requests Bridgecon to find ways to reduce that time. The estimating team suggests the following possibilities:

- The duration of activity N could be reduced from 1 week to half a week by using additional trucks. The additional cost would be $33,000.

- An alternative subcontractor for piling is approached. This subcontractor says it will be able to halve the time of Activity H for a total cost of $960,000.

- Two ways are identified to shorten the duration of activity D. First, additional temporary workers could be employed. This would reduce the duration to 3 weeks, and increase

Table 7.6 Activities for Constructing the Cable-Stayed Bridge

ACTIVITY	ACTIVITY DESCRIPTION	INITIAL DURATION ESTIMATE	PREDECESSORS	INITIAL COST ESTIMATE ($1000)
A	Detailed site investigation and survey	2	—	17
B	Detailed planning	6	A	16
C	Detailed design	6	B	557
D	Preparation of site	4	C	47
E	Relocate services	3	C	28
F	Re-align overhead track electrification	4	C, E	650
G	Access road and ramp construction	1	D	63
H	Piling	2	G	820
J	Construct foundations and abutments	3	H	975
K	Construct temporary supports to support bridge deck during construction	2	F, G	720
L	Fabrication planning of structural steel components	2	C	13
M	Manufacture structural steel components (off-site)	2	L	1320
N	Transport structural steel components and erect on-site	1	M	433
P	Erect pylons and fill with concrete	2	J	840
Q	Construct main span deck on pre-cast concrete beams	3	H, K, N, P	2800
R	Cable-stay installation and lift the bridge deck off temporary supports	3	Q	875
S	Removal of temporary supports	1	R	54
T	Electrical system installation	1	S	147
U	Roadway surfacing (paving)	2	S	142
V	Finishing and ancillaries	2	T, U	76
W	Commissioning – cut-over	1	V	11
X	Formal hand-over & ceremony	1	W	9
Y	Project Sign-off	1	X	1
Z	Administrative closure	1	W	4
AA	Project End (Milestone)	0	Y, Z	
				10621

the cost to $147,000. Second, a team of workers highly skilled in this procedure (and their equipment) could be temporarily reallocated from another project. Adding this team and temporary workers to the original team could lead to completing the work in 1 week. The manager of the other project estimates that the reallocation would cause him to forfeit an incentive fee of $150,000 for finishing his project early. The managers of the two projects

agree that, should the reallocation be made, the value of incentive fee would be booked as a cost against the cable-stayed bridge project and transferred as a bonus to the other project.

- The duration of activity F can be reduced to 3 weeks, but would increase the activity's cost to $730,000. It could be reduced to 2 weeks, but would cost $820,000.

- The duration of activity Q can be reduced to 2 weeks, but the activity would cost $2,929,000.

1. Compile a list showing the reduced periods for impairment of the rail operation and the associated additional costs.

2. Comment on the implications that crashing might have on the risk of not meeting the committed due date.

Case 7.2 The LOGON Project

After signing the contract, the management at Midwest Parcel Distribution (MPD) discovers that for many reasons it would be advantageous to complete the project in 40 weeks. It is too late for MPD to "require" the contractor Iron Butterfly to complete it in that time, but nonetheless it discusses the possibility with Iron Butterfly Company's project manager, Frank Wesley. Reviewing the network diagram (Figure 7.28), Frank checks the feasibility of this and then asks his managers and technical staff to give him three time estimates for every activity in the project. The estimates are given in Table 7.7.

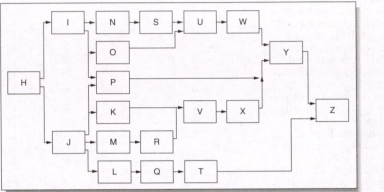

Figure 7.28
LOGON Project.

Table 7.7 Time Estimates for LOGON Project

ACTIVITY	OPTIMISTIC DURATION (WEEKS)	MOST LIKELY DURATION (WEEKS)	PESSIMISTIC DURATION (WEEKS)
H	10	10	10
I	8	8	16
J	1	6	6
K	4	4	4
L	2	2	2
M	2	4	5
N	4	4	10
O	5	5	5
P	5	5	5
Q	5	5	5
R	2	5	5
S	3	3	6
T	3	3	3
U	1	1	2
V	3	5	5
W	2	2	8
X	3	3	3
Y	8	8	8
Z	6	6	6

QUESTIONS

1. Determine the most likely project duration.
2. What is the probability of finishing within 40 weeks?
3. Do you foresee any significant risk of a delay that the calculations for (1) and (2) above do not take into account?
4. What is the applicability of the Central Limit Theorem (CLT) to this problem? Select one answer from below and explain:
   a. The CLT does *not* apply because Activity Z is dependent on Activity Y, Activity Y is dependent on Activity W, and so on.
   b. The CLT does *not* apply because human behavior is not taken into account.
   c. The CLT *does* apply, provided that the duration of any activity does not influence the duration of any other activity.
   d. The CLT does *not* apply because the number of activities on the critical path is too small.

NOTES

1. CPM first appeared in the article by its originators: Kelley J and Walker M. *Critical Path Planning and Scheduling*. Boston, MA: Eastern Joint Computer Conference; 1959. pp. 160–173.

2. A. Y. Goldratt Institute, group e-mail messages sent 17 and 18 March 1999; Larry English, Habitat for Humanity, January 2007, Pretoria, South Africa; Habitat for Humanity, *The Fastest House in the World,* accessed January 2007 from http://www.habitat.org/newsroom/1999archive/insitedoc004016.aspx?print=true.

3. For a piece-wise approximation for non-linear relationships, see Wiest J and Levy F. *A Management Guide to PERT/CPM: with GERT/PDM/DCPM and Other Networks*. Englewood Cliffs, NJ: Prentice Hall; 1977. pp. 81–85. The relationship between number of workers and activity duration is non-linear; i.e., cutting the number of workers in half will not double the time but might increase it by, say, 50–150 percent, depending on the task. See Brooks F. *The Mythical Man Month: Essay on Software Engineering*. Reading, MA: Addison-Wesley; 1995. pp. 13–36

4. The method first appeared in the article by the originators of PERT: Malcolm D, Roseboom J, Clark C, and Fazar W. Application of a technique for research and development program evaluation. *Operations Research* 7(5); 1959: 646–670.

5. Wiest and Levy, *A Management Guide to PERT/CPM: with GERT/PDM/DCPM and Other Networks*.

6. See Klingel A. Bias in PERT project completion time calculation for real networks. *Management Science* 13; 1966: 194–201.

7. See Miller R. *Schedule, Cost, and Profit Control with PERT*. New York: McGraw-Hill; 1963. p. 58; Kerzner H. *Project Management: A Systems Approach to Planning, Scheduling, and Controlling*, 10th edn. Hoboken, NJ: John Wiley & Sons; 2009. p. 529.

8. See Krakowski M. PERT and Parkinson's Law. *Interfaces* 5(1); 1974; and Vazsonyi A. L'Historie de la grandeur et de la decadence de la methode PERT. *Management Science* 16(8); 1970 [written in English]. Other problems of PERT/CPM are described by Kerzner, *Project Management*, pp. 519–522; Miller, *Schedule, Cost, and Profit Control with PERT*, pp. 39–45; and Wiest and Levy, *A Management Guide to PERT/CPM*, pp. 57–58, 73, 166–173. References to human behavior are in the critical-chain literature referenced in this chapter.

9. See Van Slyke R. Monte Carlo methods and the PERT problem. *Operations Research* 11(5); 1963: 839–860.

10. Adapted with permission from Evans J and Olson D. *Introduction to Simulation and Risk Analysis*. Upper Saddle River, NJ: Prentice Hall; 1998. pp. 111–120.

11. Crystal Ball is a registered trademark of Decisioneering, Inc.; for information, see decisioneering.com. RiskSim is a trademark of Treeplan.com.; see www.treeplan.com. For @Risk, see www.palisade.com. For Arena, see www.rockwellautomation.com. For Simul8, see www.simul8.com

12. Cleland D. *Project Management—Strategic Design and Implementation*, 2nd edn. New York, NY: McGraw-Hill, Inc.; 1994. p. 7.

13. Goldratt E. *What Is This Thing Called Theory of Constraints and How Should It Be Implemented?* New York, NY: North River Press, Inc.; 1990.

14. Pittman P. *Project Management: A More Effective Methodology for the Planning and Control of*

Projects. Georgia: PhD dissertation, University of Georgia; 1994; Goldratt EM, *Critical Chain*. Great Barrington, MA: North River Press; 1997.

15. Walker E. *Planning and Controlling Multiple, Simultaneous, Independent Projects in a Resource Constrained Environment*, Georgia: PhD dissertation, University of Georgia; 1998. A TOC method for allocating resources to multiple projects was developed in this study, and subsequently has been developed further.

16. Goldratt E, *Critical Chain*, p. 156.

17. Herroelen W and Leus R. On the merits and pitfalls of critical chain scheduling. *Journal of Operations Management* 7; 2001: 559–577; Leach L. *Critical Chain Project Management*, 2nd edn. Norwood, MA: Artech House, Inc., 2003; Geekie A and Steyn H. Buffer sizing for the critical chain project management method. *South African Journal of Industrial Engineering* 19(1); 2008: 73–88.

18. Newbold R. *Project Management in the Fast Lane—Applying the Theory of Constraints*. New York, NY: St Lucie Press; 1988.

19. Tukel I, Rom W, and Eksioglu SD. An investigation of buffer sizing techniques in critical chain scheduling. *European Journal of Operational Research* 172; 2006: 401–416; see also Trietsch D. The effect of systemic errors on optimal project buffers. *International Journal of Project Management* 23; 2005: 267–274; Shou Y and Yeo K. Estimation of project buffers in critical chain project management. *Proceedings of the IEEE International Conference on Management of Innovation and Technology (ICMIT)*; 2000: 162–167.

20. Goldratt, *Critical Chain*.

21. For Prochain software, see www.prochain.com; for Sciforma software, see www.sciforma.com; for Concerto see www.realization.com.

22. Tsai D and Chiu H. Two heuristics for scheduling multiple projects with resource constraints. *Construction Management and Economics* 14(4); 1996: 325–340; Al-Jibouri S. Effects of resource management regimes on project schedule. *International Journal of Project Management* 20(4); 2002: 271–277; as well as Chelaka M, Abeyasinghe L, Greenwood D, and Johansen D. An efficient method for scheduling construction projects with resource constraints. *International Journal of Project Management* 19(1); 2001: 29–45.

23. Panwalkar S and Iskander W. A survey of scheduling rules. *Operations Research* 25(1); 1977: 45–61.

24. Viljoen P. Goldratt Schools, Personal communication, Pretoria, SA, May 2007 and May 2010.

25. Turner J. *The Handbook of Project-Based Management*. London: McGraw-Hill; 1993.

26. Goldratt E and Cox J. *The Goal*, 2nd revised edn. Croton-on-Hudson, NY: North River Press: 1986.

27. Newbold R. *Project Management in the Fast Lane—Applying the Theory of Constraints*. Boca Raton: St Lucie Press; 1998; and Leach, LP. *Critical Chain Project Management*, 2nd edn. Norwood, MA: Artech House, Inc.; 2003. See also Steyn H. Project management applications of the theory of constraints beyond critical chain scheduling. *International Journal of Project Management* 20(1); 2002: 75–80.

28. In Goldratt E and Cox J, *The Goal*; also in Goldratt E and Fox R. *The Race*. Croton-on-Hudson, NY: North River Press; 1986. The notion of using the constraint (drum) to set the pace is described.

29. Adapted from training material of Realization. See www.realization.com.

30. Dass S and Steyn H. An exploratory assessment of project duration in multiple-project schedules where resources are allocated by the theory of constraints method. *South African Journal of Industrial Engineering* 17(1); 2006: 39–54.

31. Cohen I, Mandelbaum A, and Shtub A. Multi-project scheduling and control: a process-based comparative study of the critical chain methodology and some alternatives. *Project Management Journal* 35(2); 2004: 39–50.

32. Moder J and Philips C. *Project Management with CPM and PERT*. London: Van Nostrand Reinhold Co.; 1985.

33. See Steyn H. An investigation into the fundamentals of critical chain project scheduling. *International Journal of Project Management* 19; 2000: 363–369.

34. See, for example, Turner J. Controlling progress with planned cost or budgeted cost. *International Journal of Project Management* 18(3); 2000: 153–154.

35. Adapted from Steyn H. (ed.). *Project Management—A Multi-disciplinary Approach*. Pretoria: FPM Publishing; 2003.

36. *Ibid.*

Chapter

Cost Estimating and Budgeting

A billion here and a billion there. Pretty soon it starts to add up to real money.

—SENATOR EVERETT DIRKSEN

Cost estimates, budgets, WBSs, and schedules are interrelated. Ideally, cost estimates are based upon elements of the WBS and are prepared at the work package level. When the cost cannot be estimated because it is too complex, the task is broken down further until it can. When the cost cannot be estimated because the work is ill-defined or uncertain, the estimate is initially based upon judgment and later is revised as information becomes available. Project schedules dictate the need for resources and the rate of expenditures, but the converse is also true: constraints on resources and working capital dictate the schedules. Imposing practical constraints on costs is necessary to create realistic project budgets. Failing to do so results in projects being completed at exorbitant expense, or prematurely terminated for lack of funds. Both occurrences are relatively commonplace.

Cost estimating, budgeting, and control are sometimes thought to be the exclusive concerns of cost specialists, planners and accountants, but in projects they should be the concern of everyone. Project participants who are closest to the sources of costs—engineers, scientists, systems specialists, architects, or others—should be involved in the estimating and budgeting process. Commonly, however, these same people are disdainful of budgets, and ignorant about how they work or why they are necessary.

The project manager, of course, must also be involved. Although she does not need to be a financial wizard, she does need to be skillful in organizing and using cost figures. The project manager oversees the cost estimating and budgeting process, though often with the assistance of a staff cost accountant. On most technical projects, the *cost engineer* reviews the deliverables and requirements, assesses the project from both cost and technical points of view, and advises the project manager. Cost engineering is discussed later.

8.1 COST ESTIMATES

The initial cost estimate can seal the project's financial fate. When project costs are overestimated, the contractor risks losing the job to a lower-bidding competitor. Worse is when they are underestimated. A $50,000 fixed price bid might win the contract, but obviously the contractor will lose money if the project ends up costing $80,000. Underestimating is often accidental—the result of being overly optimistic, although sometimes it is intentional—the result of trying too hard to beat the competition. In a practice called *buy in*, the contractor reduces an initially realistic estimate just enough to win the contract, hoping to cut costs or renegotiate a higher price after the work is underway. The practice is risky, unethical, and, sadly, relatively commonplace. In large capital projects, the tendency is to underestimate costs so as to get the funding needed to launch the project (and afterward soon to forget the estimate).

But a very low bid can also signify that in the estimate the contractor cut corners, left things out, or was just sloppy. The consequences for both client and contractor can be disastrous, ranging from suffering a loss to bankruptcy. Cost estimates are used to develop budgets. After the project begins, actual costs are compared to estimated costs (indicated by the budget) as one measure of the project's work performance. Without good estimates, it is impossible to evaluate work efficiency or to determine in advance how much the project will cost at completion.

8.2 COST ESCALATION

Accurate cost estimating can be difficult because it begins during project conception and before much is known about the project. The less well defined the project, the greater the chances that estimated costs will substantially differ from actual costs. As a rule, the estimate will be too low and the project will suffer a cost overrun. The amount by which actual costs grow to exceed initial estimates is referred to as *cost escalation*.[1]

Some escalation can be expected, and up to 20 percent is relatively common. Usually, the larger and more complex the project, the greater is the potential for escalation. The costs of cutting-edge technology and research projects frequently escalate by upwards of several hundred percent. The Concorde supersonic airliner exceeded the original estimate by a factor of five, nuclear power plants often exceed estimates by a factor of two or three, and NASA spacecraft often exceed estimates by a factor of four to five.

Figure 8.1 shows a plot of percent cost overrun versus year of decision to build for 111 transportation-related projects spanning approximately 80 years.[2] The study from

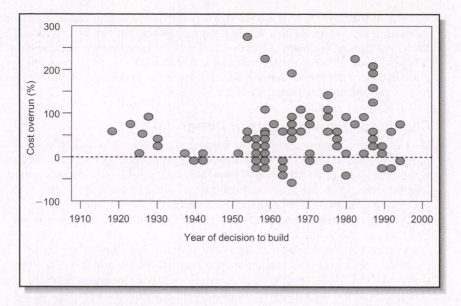

Figure 8.1
Projects versus percent cost overrun.
From Flyvbjerg B, Bruzelius N, and Rothengatter W. *Megaprojects and Risk: An Anatomy of Ambition*. Cambridge: Cambridge University Press; 2003, reprinted with permission.

which this plot was taken also looked at 246 other projects and got a similar picture. Clearly, overruns have been, and remain, common. How does that happen? There are many reasons.

Uncertainty and Lack of Accurate Information

Much of the information needed for accurate estimates is simply not available when costs are first estimated. In NASA, for example, lack of well-defined spacecraft design and unclear definition of experiments are the principal reasons for cost overruns. Not until later, when the design is finalized and work activities are well defined (during the definition phase or later), can material and labor costs be accurately determined. In most research and development projects the activities are unpredictable, of uncertain duration, or must be repeated.

Sometimes, though, the uncertainty stems from lack of effort. In general, management should strive for the clearest, most definitive scope of work and project objectives. The clearer the scope, objectives, requirements, and work definition, the more accurate are the cost estimates.

During the project, whenever necessary changes in product design or project schedules occur due to product concept changes, developmental barriers, strikes, legal entanglements, or skyrocketing wage and material costs, the original cost estimate should be updated and become the new baseline for tracking and controlling project costs.

To allow for uncertainty, an amount called a *contingency fund* or *budget reserve* is added to the original estimate.[3] This is the budget equivalent of the *schedule reserve* or *buffer* mentioned in Chapter 7. The contingency amount is proportional to the uncertainty of the work; the greater the uncertainty, the larger the contingency. The project manager controls the fund and its allocation to cover cost overruns.

The contingency fund is intended primarily to offset small variations arising from estimating errors, omissions, minor design changes, and small schedule slippages. Each time the cost estimate is updated, so too is the contingency fund. The fund is not a "slush" fund. When no longer needed as intended, it should be cut from the project budget; otherwise, the tendency is for costs to rise to expend whatever remains in the fund. Contingencies are discussed later.

Changes in Requirements or Design

Cost escalation also occurs due to discretionary, non-essential changes to system requirements and plans. These changes come from a change in mind, not from oversights, mistakes, or environmental mandates that would make them imperative. The routine tendency is for users and contractors alike to want to modify systems and procedures—to make "improvements" to original plans throughout the project life cycle. Such changes are especially common in the absence of thorough planning or strict control procedures.

Contracts occasionally include a *change clause* that allows the customer to make certain changes to contract requirements—sometimes for additional payment, sometimes not. The clause allows the customer flexibility to incorporate requirements not envisioned at the time of the original contract agreement. It can be exercised at any time, and the contractor is obligated to comply. Any change, however, no matter how small, causes escalation; it usually involves a combination of redesign or reorganizing work, acquiring new or different resources, altering plans, and undoing or scrapping earlier work. The further along the project is, the more costly the change. When accumulated, even small changes have a substantial effect on schedules and costs. Formal *change control* procedures, as described in Chapter 11, help reduce the number of changes and contain escalation.

Economic and Social Factors

Even with good initial estimates and few changes, cost escalation occurs because of social and economic forces beyond the contractor's or user's influence. Labor strikes, legal action by interest groups, trade embargoes, and materials shortages all serve to stifle progress and increase costs, but cannot be precisely anticipated or factored into plans and budgets. Whenever work is suspended or interrupted, administrative and overhead costs continue to mount, interest and leasing costs on borrowed capital and equipment continue to accrue, and the date when payback begins and profit is earned is delayed. Rarely can such problems be anticipated and their impacts incorporated into the contingency fund.

One economic factor that influences cost escalation and project profitability is *inflation*.[4] The contractor might try to offset escalation from inflation by inflating the price of the project, although the actions of competitors or federal restrictions on price increases often preclude doing that. Some protection from inflation may be gained by including clauses in the contract that allow wage and material cost increases to be appended to the contract price,[5] but the protection may be limited. Inflation is not one-dimensional; it varies with the labor, materials, and equipment employed, and by geographical region and country. Subcontractors, suppliers, and clients use different contracts that have different inflation protection clauses and that might be advantageous or disadvantageous to other parties in the project.

Inflation also causes cash flow difficulties. Even when a contract includes an inflation clause, payment for inflation-related costs must be tied to the publication of inflation indices, which always lags behind inflation. Contractors pay immediately for the effects of inflation, but are not are reimbursed for these effects until later.

Trend analysis of inflation in the industry and economy can improve the accuracy of cost estimates. In long-term projects, wage rates should be forecast; this is done by starting with best estimates of wage costs in current dollars, and then applying inflation rates over the project's length.

In international projects, costs escalate due to changes in *exchange rates*. When the costs are incurred in one currency but paid for in another, a change in the exchange rate will cause the relative values of costs and payments to change, resulting in a the cost or price escalation. This topic is discussed in Chapter 18.

Cost estimates are based upon prices at the time of estimating. Thus, whenever inflation rates become known, the estimates should be adjusted so as to provide a valid baseline from which to identify cost variances and take corrective action.

Inefficiency, Poor Communication, and Lack of Control

Cost escalation also results from work inefficiency, poor management and planning, poor communication, lack of supervision, and weak control. In large projects especially, these lead to conflicts, misunderstandings, duplication of effort, and mistakes. This is *one* source of escalation where management has substantial influence. Careful work planning, tracking and monitoring of activities, and tight control improve efficiency and contain cost escalation.

Ego Involvement of the Estimator

Cost escalation also comes from the *way* people estimate. Many people are overly optimistic and habitually underestimate the time and cost it will take to do a job, especially in areas where they have little experience. Have you ever estimated the time it would take for *you* to paint a room or tile a floor? How long did it *really* take? People often confuse the estimate with a *goal*; they think an estimate is what a job *should* take, not an honest prediction of what it *will* take. The more the estimator's ego is involved in the job, the less reliable the estimate. Sometimes, of course, the opposite happens: worried about overrunning the estimate, they "pad" it.

Companies avoid the problem by employing professional cost estimators; these are not the same people who will do the work. Remember the earlier contention about involving project participants in planning the project? Experienced workers are usually much better at estimating time and materials than they are costs. So the doers (those who do the work) should define the work and estimate the needed resources and time, but the professionals should estimate the cost. A cost estimate should never be based upon a goal; thus, estimators must be positioned organizationally so that others will not coerce them into providing the numbers they want.[6]

Project Contract

Chapter 3 describes the relative merits of different forms of contracts, some of which are relevant to project cost escalation.[7] Consider, for example, the two basic kinds of contracts: fixed price and cost-plus. A fixed price agreement gives the contractor an incentive to control costs because, no matter what happens, the amount paid for the project remains the same. In contrast, a strictly cost-plus contract offers little incentive to control costs. In fact, when profit is computed as a percentage of costs (rare these days), the contractor is motivated to "allow" costs to escalate. Other forms of agreements, such as incentive contracts, permit cost increases, but encourage cost control and provide motivation to minimize escalation.

Bias and Ambition[8]

Finally, it is human nature for the champions of projects to be optimistic about their projects. In fact, without champions most projects would never start and everyone might be worse off. That optimism, however, can lead to overestimating benefits and underestimating costs. Promoters of big projects know that if a project is important enough, sufficient funding to complete it will materialize, no matter the size of the overrun.

Example 8.1: Escalation of the Bandra-Worli Sea Link Project

January 1999—Government Clears Worli-Bandra Cable Bridge
February 2001—Worli-Bandra Sea-link Enters Crucial Stage
October 2002—Bandra-Worli Sea Link Toll To Be Costlier
October 2003—Bandra-Worli Sea Link May Hit A Dead End
January 2004—Bandra-Worli Sea Link Project Under Threat
July 2005—Sea Link In Trouble Over Extension
May 2006—Bandra-Worli Sea Link To Be Ready By 2008

The headlines from local news media refer to the Bandra-Worli Sea Link (BWSL) roadway and cable-stayed bridge in Mumbai—India's equivalent to San Francisco's Golden Gate Bridge, and a good example of megaproject woes. The 8-km bridge and its approaches bend 200 meters into the Arabian Sea to connect downtown Mumbai with its western suburbs. Travel time now takes about 30 minutes—half the time needed before the bridge was built.

The project was approved in early 1999 following 7 years of study; it was supposed to start in May, cost 650 crore (US $120M), and finish by mid-2001. But work did not begin until December, and by then the estimated completion date had slipped to mid-2002. Then came the monsoons, which brought the project to a near halt in 2000 and 2001. In late 2001, the project's prime consultant, Sverdrup, was dropped for failure to provide a "competent project engineer." The replacement, Dar Consultants, modified the bridge design by adding 2.8 km to its length and splitting the eight-lane main bridge into two four-lane roadways. By January 2002, the scheduled completion date had slipped to March 2004. In October, it was announced that project costs had increased by 50 crores; due to a "paucity of funds," work had to be slowed and the completion date was pushed back to September 2004. A year later, monsoons and rough seas again halted work, delaying the completion date to 2005. Meantime, complaints grew from fishermen concerned about the link's interference with their boats, and from environmentalists regarding its harm to marine ecology. In 2003, rains again stalled the project for many months. The project's primary contractor, Hindustan Construction Company, requested an additional 300 crores to cover delays and design changes, but the government balked and offered to pay only 120 crores. The controversy stalled the project for almost a year, though eventually funds materialized and the project resumed. By June 2005, the completion date had slipped to September 2006 and the project cost had risen to 1,306 crore. In May 2006 the completion date was pushed back again to April 2008, but it was not until June 2009 that the bridge was dedicated; in March 2010, all lanes opened to traffic. Estimated cost: 1,600 crore (US $336M).

As illustrated, schedule delays and cost escalation are inextricably connected. The 11-year history of the BWSL project saw a 9-year schedule slip and 150 percent cost increase. Contributing factors included unknowns (weather), changes in scope and requirements (bridge and roadway design), social factors (livelihood and environmental impact concerns), economics (growing land values and interest), and management issues (dismissal of a major contractor).

8.3 Cost Estimating and the Systems Development Cycle[9]

Project cost estimating happens throughout the project phases of conception, definition, and execution.

The first estimate is made during project conception. Since very little hard cost information is available at that time, the estimate is the least reliable that it will ever be. Uncertainty about the project cost and duration may be large, as illustrated by the largest "region of time–cost uncertainty" in Figure 8.2. How much the project will *really* cost and how long it will *really* take are very much open to question. The project is compared to other, similar projects, and an estimate is made based upon standards of what it should take—labor time, materials, and equipment—to do the job. When there are no similar projects or standards, initial estimates are largely "guesstimates" and might end up being nowhere close to actual costs.

If the project is unique and ill defined, uncertainty in cost estimates often dictates that contracts will be of the cost-plus kind. As more aspects of the system and project are defined, the material costs, labor times, and labor rates can be nailed down, and cost estimates become more reliable. When the system and project are fairly routine, the estimates are somewhat reliable and contractors are willing to accept incentive-type or fixed-price contracts. In fact, the awarding of contracts is sometimes put off until designs are somewhat complete and more accurate cost estimates are possible. This, of course, requires contractors to do a lot of front-end work without assurances that they will be awarded the job. Contractors required to bid before they can attain reliable estimates must include a contingency amount in the estimate, to cover the uncertainty.

Figure 8.2
Time–cost graph showing cumulative project cost and regions of time–cost uncertainty.

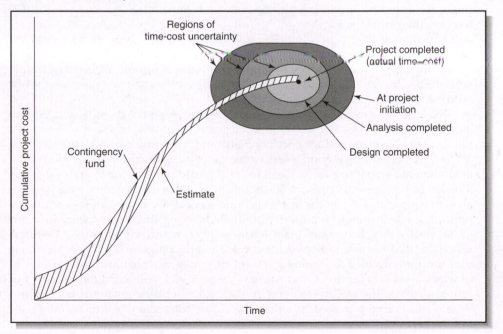

As the project moves into the middle and later phases, when work is being completed and funds expended, cost estimates become more certain. The shrinking time-cost uncertainty regions in Figure 8.2 illustrate this. As the uncertainty decreases, the amount in the contingency fund is reduced. A contingency starting out at 15 percent of the base project estimate might be decreased halfway through the project to 8 percent, then to 3 percent at the three-fourths mark, and then to 1 percent at final installation to cover minor corrections at sign-off.

As discussed in Chapter 4, usually a detailed plan is developed only for the most immediate, upcoming phase of the project (phased or rolling wave planning), and that plan will include a cost estimate and cost commitments for the phase. At the same time, every attempt is made to look beyond that phase and to develop a realistic cost estimate for the entire project.

Once developed and approved, the estimate for the project becomes the budget, and the baseline against which project progress and performance will be measured. It is thus bad practice to keep changing the estimate later in the project, because that destroys the purpose of a baseline—to measure progress and control costs. Sometimes, however, escalation factors render the estimate obsolete and mandate periodic revisions.

8.4 LIFE CYCLE COSTS

Life cycle costs (LCC) represent all the costs of a system, facility, or product throughout its life cycle, cradle to grave. The concept originated in military procurement, when it was realized that development of a system or product represents but the tip of the cost iceberg and that the costs to operate (e.g., fuel consumption) and maintain (e.g., parts replacement) it are usually far greater. Whereas the emphasis in this chapter is on *project costs*—i.e., costs incurred during the *project* phases of definition and execution—LCC include costs for the other phases of the system life cycle—the operation phase and eventual disposal of the end-item, and, sometimes, the conception phase too (initiation and feasibility).

Anticipating LCC is necessary because costs influence so many decisions. For example, suppose three contractors submit proposals to build a plant, and each proposal contains not only the plant's construction cost but also its expected operating costs. If the bids are similar in terms of construction costs and plant features, the one with the lowest operating costs will likely win.

The LCC similarly affect decisions regarding development projects, and feasibility studies should consider *all costs* for acquisition, operation, maintenance, and disposal of the system or product. For example, most US aerospace manufacturers in the 1970s were hesitant to develop a supersonic commercial aircraft because of cost and environmental impact concerns. Costs to develop and produce the aircraft were projected to be high, as were costs for operation and maintenance. At issue were whether enough people would pay the high ticket prices necessary for the airlines to make a profit, and whether enough airlines would purchase the aircraft for the manufacturers to make money. Ultimately, many felt the answer was no on both counts. Congress cancelled subsidies for developing the aircraft, and the program dissolved. Meantime the Europeans decided differently and went on to manufacture the Concorde, only 14 of which went into service. Concorde flew for nearly 27 years, and the last one was retired in 2003. The LCC were never recouped; had not the governments of Great Britain and France provided subsidies, the airlines and manufacturers would have lost money.

Key design decisions affecting the operation, maintenance, and disposal of a system are made early in the project life cycle—in the conception and definition phases. A product with a high development cost and purchase price becomes more appealing if it can be conceived and designed to have a relatively low operating cost. For example, a more fuel-efficient vehicle might be higher priced than less efficient vehicles, but customers readily pay the premium knowing that over the life of the vehicle they will recoup it through fuel savings and lower pollution. Of course, estimating LCC involves making assumptions about technology, market, and product demand, and relies on historical costs of similar systems and projects; still, it is a sensible way to approach projects, especially when there is a choice between alternative designs or proposals.

The LCC should also account for the time necessary to develop, build, and install the end-item—i.e., the time before the facility or system becomes operational or the product is "launched" to market. Time is important: it determines how soon the end-item will start to generate revenues, gain market share, and accrue profits or other benefits. The higher costs of speeding up the project are compared to the additional benefits gained from an early completion or product launch. Similarly, the *cost of disposal* at the end of the life cycle is also estimated; for facilities such as mines and nuclear power plants that require shut-down and rehabilitation after their useful lives, this cost can be substantial.

Analysis of LCC is also necessary for setting targets on development and operating costs, and making design trade-off decisions to achieve those targets. Example 8.2 provides an illustration.

Example 8.2: Life Cycle Costs for an Operational Fleet of Spaceships

(This illustration extends on previous SpaceShipOne examples, but the numbers are purely hypothetical.)

Having gained experience from SpaceShipOne, a larger spaceship and mothership are to be designed. The new spaceship will carry a pilot plus four paying passengers, go as high as 120 km, and be capable of 20 flights per year over an operational life of 5 years. The cost of developing and producing four of these spaceships and two motherships is estimated at $80 million. Meantime, a survey indicates that the number of people worldwide willing to pay the $190,000 ticket price to fly on these spaceships is at least 1,000 per year.

A "spaceline" that will use and maintain the spaceships is being created for a start-up cost of $10 million. Operational costs for the spaceline comprise two parts: annual costs for ground operations (reservations, personnel, ground facilities, etc.), and per-flight costs for flight operations (fuel, parts, repairs, etc., for the spaceship and the mothership). Ground operations costs are placed at $2 million/year, and per-flight costs at $0.4 million/flight. (These costs are assumed to be constant for every year and flight, respectively, although realistically they would vary up or down on depending on inflation, the learning curve, efficiencies, and economies of scale as more spaceships are added to the fleet. Annual revenues are assumed constant too, though realistically they would start out small and then grow until the full fleet of spaceships is operational). Given these costs and ignoring other factors (e.g., time value of money), what is the LCC for the venture?

Assumptions

Four spaceships @ 20 flights/year each = 80 flights/year (320 passengers/year, which lies well within the estimated annual demand). Five years of operation.

Costs

Development and manufacturing: $80 million.
Spaceline start-up: $10 million.
Ground operations: $2 million/year.
Flight operations: $0.4 million/flight.
Ticket price: $190,000 (marketing slogan: "Now YOU can go to space for under $200,000!").

LCC Model

LCC ($ million) = Development & production cost
+ Start-up cost + Operating cost (5 years)
= $80 + $10 + ([5 y × $2] + [5 y × 80 flights × $0.4])
= $260 million
Total revenues ($ million) = (5 y × 80 flights × 4 passengers × $0.190)
= $304 million

Bottom line: Assuming the assumptions are correct, revenues will exceed costs by $44 million.

All the numbers are estimates, but some are more certain than others. For example, based upon experience with SpaceShipOne, the development cost might be fairly certain, but due to lack of long-term operational experience the per-flight cost is fairly uncertain. Start-up and ground operations costs, if analogous to airline operations, might be somewhat certain, although passenger demand might be fairly uncertain.

The LCC model plays an important role in system design and development. Based on the model, sensitivity analysis can be performed to see what happens when costs increase or decrease to show best case, most likely, and worst case scenarios. The model can also be used to determine by how much and in what combination the costs must vary such that the enterprise becomes lucrative (or disastrous).

The LCC model is also used to set cost targets. If the decision is made to proceed with the $80 million development and production cost, then the project must be planned, budgeted, and controlled so as stay close to that amount. If the per-flight cost is set at $0.4 million, the project must strive to develop vehicles that will cost no more than that to operate. This will affect innumerable design decisions pertaining to many details. Early on, the design analysis must consider major alternatives (e.g., to carry five or six passengers, not four), and the expected costs, revenues, and benefits for each.

The best and only truly comprehensive approach to estimating and analyzing LCC is with a team of people that represents all phases of the system development cycle—a cross-functional team of designers, builders, suppliers, and users, i.e., a *concurrent engineering team*. Concurrent engineering for LCC is further discussed in Chapter 13.

8.5 COST ESTIMATING PROCESS

Estimate versus Target or Goal

Sometimes the word "estimate" is confused with "target" and "goal." It shouldn't. Whereas an estimate is a *realistic assessment* based upon known facts about the work, required resources, constraints, and the environment, and is derived from estimating methods, a target or goal is a desired outcome or commitment. Other than by chance, the estimate will *not* be the same as the target or goal. That said, once computed the estimate can be compared to a target value or goal, and the work tasks, resources, and schedules, etc., revised to bring the estimate closer to the target. The estimate should never be a simple plug-in of the target value.

Accuracy versus Precision

"Accuracy" represents the closeness of an estimated value to the actual value: the accuracy of a $99,000 estimate for a project that actually cost $100,000 is very good. In contrast, "precision" is the number of decimal places in the estimate. An estimate of $75,321 is more precise than one of $75,000 (though *neither* is *accurate* if the actual cost is $100,000). Accuracy matters more than precision: the aim is to derive the most accurate estimate possible.

Sometimes accuracy can be improved by employing a so-called *three-point estimate*, which combines optimistic (a), pessimistic (b), and most likely cost estimates (m) to arrive at an expected cost estimate—analogous to the PERT approach for computing expected time:

$$C_E = \frac{a + 4m + b}{6}.$$

Classifying Work Tasks and Costs

The cost estimating process begins by breaking the project down into work phases, such as design, development, and fabrication, or into work packages from the WBS. The project team, including members from involved functional areas and contractors, meets to discuss the work phases or packages and receive specific assignments.

The team looks for tasks in the project that are similar to existing designs and standard practices and can readily be adopted. Work is classified as *developmental*, or as an adaptation of existing, *off-the-shelf* (OTS) designs, techniques, or procedures. Developmental work involves uncertainty in design, testing, and fabrication, so cost estimating is more difficult compared with estimating for OTS items or duplicated work, which is straightforward and uses known prices or records of material and labor costs for similar systems or tasks. Overruns for developmental work are common, especially due to inaccurate labor estimates. It is thus often beneficial to make use of existing designs and technology as much as possible.

Estimated costs are classified as *recurring* and *non-recurring*.[10] Recurring costs happen more than once and are associated with tasks periodically repeated, such as quality assurance and testing. Non-recurring costs happen once, and are associated with development, fabrication, and testing of one-of-a-kind items or procurement of special items.

In a pure project form of organization, the project manager delegates the responsibility for the estimating effort, combines the estimated results, and presents the final figures to management. In a matrix organization, estimating is the joint responsibility of the project and functional managers; the project manager coordinates the effort and accumulates results.

Although this typifies the estimating process, the actual methods used will depend on the information available and the required accuracy of the estimate. Most estimates are made using variants of four methods: expert judgment, analogy, parametrics, and cost engineering.

Expert Judgment

An *expert judgment* is an estimate provided by an expert—someone who, from breadth of experience or expertise, is able to provide a reasonable ballpark estimate. It is a "seat of the pants" estimate used whenever lack of information precludes more rigorous cost analysis. Expert opinion is usually restricted to estimates made during the conception phase, and for projects that are poorly-defined or unique and for which there are no previous similar projects for comparison.

Analogous Estimate

An *analogous estimate* is developed by reviewing costs from previous, similar projects. The method can be used at any level: overall project cost can be estimated from the cost of an analogous project; work package cost can be estimated from analogous work packages; and task cost can be estimated from analogous tasks. The cost for a similar project or work package is analyzed and adjusted for differences between it and the proposed project or work package, taking into account differences in project scale, locations, dates, complexity, exchange rates, and so on. If, for example, the analogy project was performed 2 years ago and the proposed project is to commence a year from now, the analogy project cost must be adjusted to account for inflation and price changes during the 3-year interim. If the analogy project was in California and the proposed project will be in New York, the cost estimate must account for site and regional differences. If the "size" (scope, capacity, or performance) of the proposed task is twice that of the analogy task, then costs of the analogy task must be "scaled" up. But twice the size does not mean twice the cost, and the size–cost relationship must be uniquely determined.

Example 8.3: Estimating Project Costs by Scaling an Analogy Project

So-called process industries such as petrochemicals, breweries, and pharmaceuticals use the following formula to estimate the costs of proposed projects:

Cost (proposed) = Cost (analogy)[Capacity (proposed)/Capacity (analogy)]$^{0.75}$

where "proposed" refers to a new facility and "analogy" to an analogous facility. In practice, the exponent varies from 0.35 to 0.9, depending on the kind of process and equipment used.[11]

Suppose a proposed plant is to have a 3.5 million cum (cubic meter) capacity. Using an analogy project for a plant with 2.5 million cum capacity and a cost of $15 million, the estimated cost for the proposed plant is

$$\$15 \text{ million } [3.5/2.5]^{0.75} = \$15 \text{ million } [1.2515] = \$18.7725 \text{ million}$$

Because the analogy method involves comparisons to earlier, similar projects, it requires extant information about prior projects. Companies that are serious about using the method gather cost documentation and retain it on a database that classifies costs according to type of project, work package, task, and so on. When a new project is proposed, the database is accessed for cost details about similar projects and work packages. Of course, the basic assumption in the analogy method is that the analogy chosen is *valid*; sometimes that is where things go awry.

Example 8.4: A Case of Costly Mistaken Analogy[12]

In the 1950s and 1960s, when nuclear power plants first appeared in the US, General Electric and Westinghouse, the two main contractors, together lost a *billion* dollars in less than 10 years on fixed price contracts because they had underestimated costs. Although neither had expected to make money on these early projects, certainly they had not planned to lose so much either. The error in their method was assuming that nuclear power plants are analogous to refineries and coal power plants—for which the marginal costs actually get smaller as the plants get larger. But nuclear power plants are not like other plants. For one thing, they require more safeguards. When a pipe springs a leak in a coal power plant, the water is turned off and the plant shut down until the leak is fixed. In a nuclear plant the water cannot be turned off, nor the plant shut down; the reactor continuously generates heat and if not cooled will melt, cause pipes to rupture, and disperse radiation. The water-cooling system needs a back-up system, and the back-up system needs a back-up. Typical of many complex systems, costs for nuclear power plants increase somewhat exponentially with plant size—although in the early years of nuclear power nobody knew that.

Parametric Estimate

A *parametric estimate* is derived from an empirical or mathematical relationship. The method can be used with an analogy project (as in Example 8.3) to scale costs up or down, or it can be applied directly without an analogy project when costs are a function of system or project "parameters." The parameters can be physical features, such as area, volume, weight, or capacity, or performance features, such as speed, rate of output, power, or strength. The method is especially useful when early design features are first being set and an estimate is needed quickly.

Example 8.5: Parametric Estimate of Material Costs

Warren Eisenberg, President of Warren Warehousing, Inc., a facilities contractor, needs a quick estimate of the material cost of a new facility. His engineers investigate the relationship between several building parameters and the material costs for eight recent projects comparable in terms of architecture, layout, and construction material. Using the method of least squares (a topic covered in textbooks on mathematical statistics), they develop the following formula, which is a multiple regression model that relates material cost (y) to floor space (x_1, in terms of 10,000 sq. ft.) and number of shipping/receiving docks (x_2) in a building:

$$y = 201,978 + (41,490)x_1 + (17,230)x_2$$

The least squares method for this model indicates that the standard error of the estimate is small, which suggests that the model provides somewhat accurate cost estimates when compared to the actual cost of each of the eight projects.

A proposal is being prepared to construct a 300,000 sq. ft facility with two docks. The estimated material cost using the model is thus:

$$y = 201,978 + (41,490)(30) + (17,230)(2) = \$1,481,138$$

Cost Engineering

Cost engineering refers to a detailed cost analysis of individual cost categories at the work package or activity level. A bottom-up approach, it provides the most accurate estimates of all the methods, but it is also the most time-consuming. The method requires detailed work-definition information that, often, is not available early in the project. It first divides the project into activities or work packages (e.g., from the WBS), then divides each of these into cost categories. For small projects like Example 8.6, the approach is simple and straightforward.

Example 8.6: Cost Engineering Estimate for a Small Project

The project manager for the DMB project at Iron Butterfly Company is preparing a project cost estimate. He begins by breaking the project into eight work packages and creating a simple schedule. Three labor grades will be working on the project;

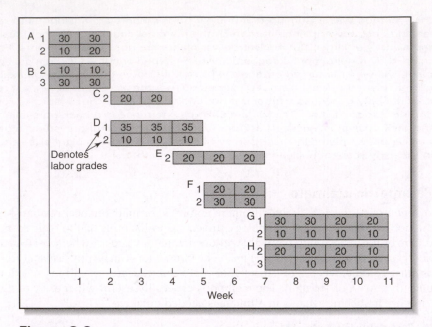

Figure 8.3
Schedule showing hours allocated to work packages by labor grade.

for each work package he estimates the needed number of labor hours per week for each grade. Hours per week per labor grade are represented inside the shaded boxes in Figure 8.3.

For each work package he also estimates the cost of material, equipment, supplies, subcontracting, freight charges, travel, and other non-labor costs. Table 8.1 is a summary of the labor hours and non-labor costs. The sum of the non-labor costs is $26,500.

Table 8.1 Labor Hours and Non-Labor Costs

| WORK PACKAGE | HOURS BY LABOR GRADE | | | NON-LABOR COSTS | | | |
	1	2	3	MATERIAL	EQUIPMENT	SUBCONTRACTS	OTHER
A	60	30		$500			
B		20	60		$1,000		
C		40			$500		$500
D	105	30			$500		
E		60				$4,500	
F	40	60		$8,000	$1,000	$5,000	$500
G	100	40		$1,500			$500
H		70	40		$1,000		$1,500
Total	305	350	100	$10,000	$4,000	$9,500	$3,000

For labor grades 1, 2, and 3, suppose the hourly rates are $10, $12, and $15, and the overhead rates are 90 percent, 100 percent, and 120 percent, respectively (overhead is an amount *added* to the labor cost; determining overhead rates is discussed later). Therefore, labor-related costs are:

Grade 1	305($10)(100%+90%)	= $5,795
Grade 2	350($12)(100%+100%)	= 8,400
Grade 3	100($15)(100%+120%)	= 3,300
		$17,495

The preliminary estimate for labor and non-labor costs is $17,495+$26,500= $43,995. Suppose the company routinely adds 10 percent to all projects to cover general and administrative expenses; this puts the cost at $43,995(1.1) =$48,395. If the contingency amount is also 10 percent, the total cost estimate for the DMB project is $48,395(1.1) =$53,235.

At the work package or lower level, detailed estimates are sometimes derived with the aid of *standards manuals* and *tables*. Standards manuals contain time and cost information about labor and materials to perform particular tasks. In construction, for example, the numbers of labor-hours to install an electrical junction box or a square foot of wall sections are both standards. To determine the labor cost of installing junction boxes in a building, the estimator starts with an estimate of the required number of boxes, multiplies this by the labor standard per box, and then multiplies that by the hourly labor rate. For software development, the industry standard is one person-year to create 2,000 lines of bug-free code.

For larger projects, the estimating procedure is roughly the same as that illustrated in Example 8.6 although more involved. First, the manager of each work package breaks the work package down into more fundamental or "basic" areas of work, such as "engineering" and "fabrication." Supervisors in each basic area then estimate the hours and materials needed to do the work. The engineering supervisor might further divide work into the tasks of structural analysis, computer analysis, layout drawings, installation drawings, and manuals, then for each task develop an estimate of the duration and the labor grade or skill level involved. In similar fashion, the fabrication supervisor might break the work down into materials (steel, piping, wiring), hardware, machinery, equipment, insurance, and so on, then estimate how much (quantity, size, length, weight, etc.) of each will be needed. Estimates of time and materials are determined by reference to previous, similar work, standards manuals, reference documents, and rules of thumb ("1 hour for each line of code"). The supervisors submit their estimates to the work package manager, who checks, revises, and then forwards them to the project manager.

The project manager and professional estimators on the project staff review the submitted time and material estimates to be sure that no costs were overlooked or duplicated, everyone understood what they were estimating, correct estimating methods were used, and allowances were made for risk and uncertainty.[13] The estimates are then aggregated as shown in Figure 8.4 and converted into dollars using standard wage rates and material costs (current or projected). Finally, the project manager adds in project-wide overhead (to cover project management and administrative costs) and company-wide overhead (to cover general company expenses) to arrive at a cost estimate for the total project. The accumulation of work package estimates (upward arrows in Figure 8.4) to derive the project estimate is called the "bottom-up" approach.

Contingency Amount

Contingency amounts are added to estimates to offset uncertainty. As mentioned, the less well defined or more complex the situation, the greater the required amount. Contingency amounts can be developed for individual activities or work packages,

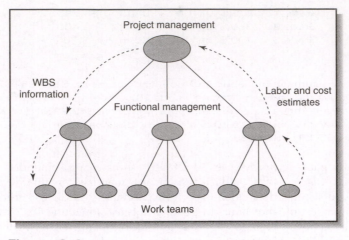

Figure 8.4
The estimating process.

or the project as a whole. *Activity contingency* is an amount estimated to account for "known unknowns" in an activity or work package, i.e., sources of cost increases that could or likely will occur; they include scrap and waste, design changes, increases in the scope, size, or function of the end-item, and delays due to weather. When the project budget is later established, this amount should be placed in a special budget, subdivided into work package accounts and strictly controlled by the project manager. The project manager sums the activity contingencies and adds them to the total project cost; this gives the *base estimate* for the project cost.

The project manager might add yet another amount to the base estimate, a *project contingency*, which is to account for "unknown unknowns"—external factors that affect project costs but cannot be pinpointed. Examples include unforeseen fluctuations in exchange rates, shortages in resources, and changes in the market or competition. Like activity contingencies, the project manager controls usage of the project contingency. Adding the project contingency to the base estimate gives the *final cost estimate*. This is the *most likely cost* for the project.

Besides the activity and project contingencies, the *corporation* might set aside an allowance to cover overruns. This amount, the *overrun allowance*, is added to the most likely cost to yield a cost where, as a rule, the probability of it being exceeded is less than 10 percent. The overrun allowance is controlled by program or corporate managers, and ordinarily is not available to the project manager without approval.

Top-down versus Bottom-up

In general, estimating can occur in two ways: top-down and bottom-up. Top-down refers to estimating the cost by looking at the project as a whole. A top-down estimate is typically based upon an expert opinion or analogy to other similar projects. Bottom-up refers to estimating the costs by looking at elements of the project—individual work packages and end-item components. Costs for each work package or end-item element are estimated separately and then aggregated to derive the total project cost. Example 8.6 is a bottom-up approach; Example 8.3 is a top-down approach. The two approaches can be used in combination: portions of a project that are well defined can be estimated bottom-up; other less-defined portions can be estimated top-down. The cost of each work package can also be estimated either way—by breaking the package into small elements and estimating the cost of each (bottom-up), or by making a gross estimate from analogy or expert opinion (top-down). The bottom-up method provides better estimates than the top-down method, but is more time consuming and requires more data.

Reconciling Estimates

The project manager submits the final cost estimate to company management along with forecasts showing the effects of potential escalation factors, such as inflation and risks. The estimate is compared against top management's *gross estimate*, the goal or target set by the company or customer. Management compares the final cost estimate to the gross estimate and either accepts it or mandates a revision. If the gross estimate is larger, the project manager reviews the work package estimates for possible oversights or over-optimism. If the final estimate is larger, the project manager reviews the work package estimates for incorrect assumptions, padding, and other sources of excess cost.

Reducing Costs

What happens if competition or insufficient funding forces management to reduce the project cost? All managers will want to retain their share of the budget, and none will want to see their funding or staff reduced. Non-managers, such as engineers, scientists, or systems analysts, are often unaware of cost constraints and will resist cuts. The project manager uses diplomacy and negotiation to convince everyone to look for ways to reduce costs. Failing that, *she* must find the ways and convince everyone to accept them.

To reconcile differences between gross and final estimates, managers sometimes exercise an across-the-board cut on *all* estimates. This is poor practice, because it fails to account for judgmental errors or excessive costs on the part of just a few units. It also unfairly penalizes managers who tried to produce fair estimates and were honest enough not to pad them. Such indiscriminate, across-the-board cuts induce everyone to pad estimates for their own protection.

Suppose you are the project manager and it is clear that the budget which management insists on is too small to do the work. There are two courses of action: either undertake the project and attempt wholeheartedly to meet the budget, or hand it over to another manager.[14] If you decide on the former, you should document and report your disagreement to top management; later, ways might be found to reduce costs and complete the project within budget. If the contract is cost-plus, then the risk for the contractor is low, since additional costs will be reimbursed. If the contract is fixed price and the budget is so underfunded as to likely require cutting corners or stalling the project, then you should suggest the project be cancelled or that another person be appointed project manager. Not only is this good business practice; it is also the ethical thing to do.

8.6 ELEMENTS OF BUDGETS AND ESTIMATES

Budgets and cost estimates are the same in that both state the cost of doing something. The difference is that the estimate comes first and is the basis for the budget. An estimate may have to be refined many times, but once approved it becomes the budget.

Organizations and work units are then committed to performing work according to the budget. It is the agreed upon amount for what the work should cost, and the baseline against which actual expenditures will be compared. Project budgets and fiscal operating budgets are similar; the difference is that the former covers the life of a project, the latter only a year at a time.

Estimates and budgets share the following elements:

- Direct labor expense
- Direct non-labor expense
- Overhead expense
- General and administrative expense
- Profit and total billing.

Direct Labor Expense[15]

Direct labor expense is the labor charge for the project. For each task or work package, an estimate is made of the number of people needed in each labor grade, and the number of hours or days for each. This gives the distribution of labor hours or days required per labor grade. The labor hours for the various grades are then multiplied by their respective wage rates. The work package budget in Figure 8.5 shows the wage rates for three labor grades and the associated labor hours time-phased over a 6-month period.

When the wage rate is expected to change over the course of the work, a weighted average wage rate is used. In Figure 8.5, suppose the initial rate for assistant is expected to increase from $20 to $25 in months 3, 4, and 5. Instead of $8,000, the labor cost for an assistant would be 100($20) + 100($25) + 100($25) + 100($25) = $9,500. The average wage rate would thus be $9,500/400 hours = $23.75/hour.

Figure 8.5
Typical 6-month budget for a work package.

Charge	Rate	Months[+]						Totals	
		1	2	3	4	5	6	Hours	Cost
Project CASTLE **Date** April 1, 1592 **Department** Excavating **Work package** Moat									
Direct labor									
Professional	$35/hour	50				50		100	3,500
Associate	$30/hour								
Assistant	$20/hour		100	100	100	100		400	8,000
Direct labor cost		1,750	2,000	2,000	2,000	3,750			11,500
Labor overhead	75%	1,312	1,500	1,500	1,500	2,813			8,625
Other direct cost*			100						100
Total direct cost		3,062	3,600	3,500	3,500	6,563			20,225
General/administrative	10%	306	360	350	350	657			2,023
Total costs		3,368	3,960	3,850	3,850	7,220			22,248
Profit	15%								
Billing total									

[+]Should extend for as many months as required by the project.
*Should be itemized to include costs for materials, freight, subcontracts, travel, and all other nonlabor direct costs.

Direct Non-Labor Expense

Direct non-labor expense is the total expense of non-labor charges applied directly to the task. It includes subcontractors, consultants, travel, telephone calls, computer time, material costs, purchased parts, and freight. This expense is represented in Figure 8.5 by the line "other direct cost." Material costs include allotments for waste and spoilage, and should reflect anticipated price increases. Material costs and freight charges sometimes appear as separate line items called *direct materials* and *overhead on materials*, respectively; computer time and consultants may appear as *support*.

Direct non-labor expenses also include necessities for installation and operation, such as instruction and maintenance manuals, engineering and programming documentation, drawings, and spare parts. Note that these are costs incurred only for a specific project or work package. Not included are the general or overhead costs of doing business, unless those costs are tied solely to the specific project.

On smaller projects, the direct non-labor expenses are individually estimated for each work package. In larger projects, a simple percentage rate is applied to cover travel and freight costs. For example, 5 percent of direct labor cost might be included as travel expense, and 5 percent of material costs as freight. These percentages are estimated in the same fashion as overhead rates, discussed next.

Overhead, General, and Administrative Expenses

Although direct expenses for labor and materials are easily charged to a specific work package, many other expenses cannot so easily be charged to specific work packages or even to specific projects. These expenses, termed *overhead* or *non-direct expenses*, are the costs of doing business. They include whatever is necessary to house and support the labor, including building rents, utilities, clerical assistance, insurance, and equipment. Usually, overhead is computed as a percentage of the direct labor cost. Frequently the rate is around 100 percent, but it ranges from as low as 25 percent for companies that do most of their work in the field to over 250 percent for those with laboratories and expensive facilities and equipment.

The overhead rate is computed by estimating the annual business overhead expense, then dividing by the projected total direct labor cost for the year. Suppose projections show that total overhead for next year will be $180,000. If total anticipated direct labor charges will total $150,000, then the overhead rate to apply is $180,000/150,000 = 1.20$. Thus, for every $1.00 charged to direct labor, $1.20 is charged to overhead.

This is the traditional accounting method for deriving the overhead rate, but for projects it results in an arbitrary allocation of costs; this is counterproductive for controlling project costs because most of overhead cost sources are not tied to any particular project. More appropriate for projects is to divide overhead costs into two categories: *direct overhead* for costs that can be allocated in a logical manner, and *indirect overhead* for costs that cannot. Direct overhead costs can be traced to the support of a particular project or work package; such costs are allocated *only* among the specific projects or activities for which they apply. For example, the overhead cost for a department working on four projects is apportioned among the four projects based on the percentage of labor time it devotes to each. The department's overhead cost is not allocated to projects it is not working on.

The other kind of overhead, indirect, includes general expenses for the corporation. Usually referred to as *general and administrative* expense, or *G&A*, it includes taxes, financing, penalty and warranty costs, accounting and legal support, proposal expenses, marketing and promotion, salaries and expenses of top management, and employee benefits. These costs might not be tied to any specific project, so they are allocated across all projects, to certain projects, or to parts of certain projects. For example, corporate-level overhead would be allocated across all projects, project management overhead on a per-project basis, and departmental overhead to specific project segments to which a department has contributed. Often, G&A overhead is charged on a time basis, so the longer the project duration, the greater the G&A expense for the project.

The actual manner in which indirect costs are apportioned varies in practice. The example for the SETI Company in Table 8.2 shows three methods for distributing indirect costs between two projects, MARS and PLUTO.[16] Notice that although company-wide expenses remain the same, the cost of each project differs depending on the method of allocating indirect costs.

Clients want to know the allocation method used by their contractors, and contractors should know the allocation method used by subcontractors. For example,

Table 8.2 Examples of Indirect Cost Apportionment

SETI COMPANY COMPANY-WIDE (INDIRECT COSTS)

Overhead (rent, utilities, clerical, machinery)	OH		120
General (upper management, staff, benefits, etc.)	G&A		40
	Indirect Total		*160*

Project costs	MARS Project	PLUTO Project	Total
Direct labor (DL)	50	100	150
Direct non-labor (DNL)	40	10	50
	90	110	200
		Direct Total	*200*
		Direct and Indirect Total	360

Some methods for apportioning indirect costs

I. Total indirect proportionate to total direct costs

	MARS Project	PLUTO Project	Total
DL and DNL	90	110	200
OH and G&A	72	88	160
	162	198	360

II. OH proportionate to direct labor only; G&A proportionate to all direct costs

	MARS Project	PLUTO Project	Total
DL	50	100	150
OH on DL	40	80	120
DNL	40	10	50
G&A on (DL and DNL)	18	22	40
	148	212	360

III. OH proportionate to direct labor only; G&A proportionate to DL and OH and DNL

	MARS Project	PLUTO Project	Total
DL and OH and DNL	130	190	320
G&A	16.25	23.75	40
	146.25	213.75	360

Method I in Table 8.2 is good for the client when the project is labor (DL) intensive, but bad when it is direct non-labor (DNL) intensive. Method III is the opposite, and gives a lower cost when the project is relatively non-labor intensive (i.e., when labor costs are low but material and parts expenditures are high). This can be seen by comparing MARS (somewhat non-labor intensive) to PLUTO (somewhat labor intensive).

Overhead costs appear in projects in different ways. Any overhead expense that *can* be traced to specific work packages should be allocated to them directly. These appear in the budget, as shown in Figure 8.5. Remaining overhead expenses that cannot be traced to specific work packages are assigned to a special "overhead" work package. This can be a single package for the entire project, or, if overhead costs can be tied to individual project stages or phases, a series of overhead work packages for each.

Profit and Total Billing

Profit is the amount left over after expenses have been subtracted from the contractual price. It can also be an agreed-to fixed fee or a percentage of total expenses, determined in part by the kind of contract, as discussed in the Appendix to Chapter 3. Total billing is the sum of total expenses and profit. Total billing and profit are included in estimates for the overall project, groups of work packages, and subcontracted work. They usually do not appear on budgets for lower-level work elements.

8.7 PROJECT COST ACCOUNTING SYSTEMS

A project is a system of sometimes hundreds or thousands of elements—workers, materials, and facilities—all which must be estimated, budgeted, and controlled. To expedite the process, reduce confusion, and improve accuracy, you need another system; in particular, one to help compute estimates, create, store and process budgets, and track costs. Such a system, called a *project cost accounting system (PCAS)*, is initially set up by the project manager, project accountant or PMO. While the main focus of the PCAS is on project costs, the system also assists tracking and controlling schedules and work progress. When a PCAS is combined with other project planning, control, and reporting functions, the whole system is referred to as the *project management information system (PMIS)*.

During project conception and definition, cost estimates of work packages are accumulated through the PCAS to produce a cost estimate for the project. This estimate later becomes the basis upon which the project and work package budgets are created.

After work on the project begins, the PCAS is used to accumulate, credit, and report project and work package expenditures. Time-phased budgets (see, for example, Figure 8.5) are created to help managers monitor costs and verify that the work has been completed and charged. The system also provides for revision of budgets.

The functions of the PCAS are summarized in Figure 8.6.

Example 8.7: A PMIS for Estimating Labor Requirements and Costs[17]

Sigma Associates is an architectural/engineering firm with a staff of 100 architects, engineers, and draftsmen. In 1978, the firm developed a PMIS to assist in estimating, planning, and scheduling.

Each potential project begins with the project manager creating a WBS to identify the main work packages. Using a menu in the PMIS, she reviews the

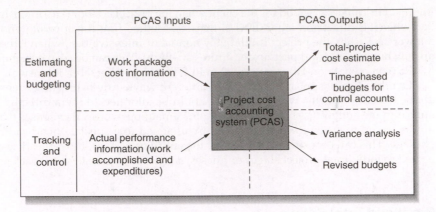

Figure 8.6
Elements of project cost accounting system.

history of similar work packages from previous projects, and the kind and amount of labor they required. By entering factors related to project size, construction costs, and type of client, she can estimate the labor requirements for every activity in the project. Using the PMIS, the project manager combines these labor estimates with requirements for existing projects to produce a 1-year manpower-loading forecast; this enables the project manager to determine whether or not sufficient labor is available. If it is not, the project manager uses the system to review options such as modifying the schedule, scheduling overtime, or leveling resources (as discussed in Chapter 6).

The labor requirements estimate is given to the comptroller, who, through the PMIS, applies existing or projected hourly rates to every activity. The comptroller then adds in employee benefits and labor overhead to produce an estimate for direct labor cost.

With information from the company general ledger, the comptroller computes the overhead rate, which he uses to charge the project for its share of company-wide expenses. Through the PMIS, he rolls up all of the estimated expenses to create an estimated total budget. Last, the comptroller analyzes the estimated budget along with the project plan for profitability. If the budget and plan show a reasonable profit and the comptroller and project manager both agree to the budget, the project is accepted. If not, a different plan is sought that maintains the same high-quality standards but is more profitable.

Time-Phased Budgets

Simultaneous control of schedules and costs can be difficult, and the project manager needs a way to keep track of where expenses are accruing, how well the project is progressing, and where problems are developing. One way is with a *time-phased budget*, which consolidates the project budget and the project schedule; this budget shows how budgeted costs are distributed over time according to the project schedule. Figure 8.5 is an example; it shows the distribution of costs over one 6-month period. Throughout the duration of the project the PCAS generates reports like this for each work package, allowing managers to compare budgeted costs and actual expenditures month by month.

For projects where a substantial amount of the costs originate from purchased items or services, a special time-phased budget is prepared for *procured* goods, work, and services. In large projects, this budget is controlled by a materials or procurement manager.

8.8 BUDGETING USING CONTROL (COST) ACCOUNTS[18]

In small projects, budgeting and cost monitoring is done using a single budget for the project as a whole. This budget, perhaps similar to the one in Figure 8.5, is used to compare actual costs with budgeted costs throughout the project.

On larger projects, however, a single, project-wide budget is too insensitive; once the project is underway and expenses begin to accrue, it would be difficult to quickly locate the sources of cost overruns. The better way is to subdivide the project budget into smaller budgets called *control accounts* or cost accounts. Large projects have tens of control accounts; very large projects have hundreds.

The control account is the basic project tracking in the PCAS. The accounts are set up in a hierarchy, similar or identical to the WBS. The lowest level control account usually corresponds to a work package, although when the number of work packages is very large, one account might represent several work packages combined. Like work packages, each control account includes:

- A work description
- A time schedule
- Who is responsible
- Material, labor, and equipment required
- A time-phased budget.

Control accounts are also established for project costs not readily attributable to any specific work packages. For example, for monies allocated for general purpose items, materials, or equipment that can be used by anyone or any work package, or for jobs such as administration, supervision, or inspection that apply across the whole project, separate control accounts are established. These accounts are usually set up for the duration of the project, or are extended period by period as needed or as funds are appropriated.

With a PCAS and control-account structure, it is easy to monitor cost performance for each work package, group of work packages, and the project as a whole. As an example, consider again the Robotics Self-Budgeting (ROSEBUD) project described Chapter 6. Figure 8.7 shows the WBS for the project, and the organization chart for the contractor, KANE & Associates. The shaded boxes represent locations of control accounts; notice that each represents all or part of a work package for which a functional area is responsible. For the same project, Figures 8.8 and 8.9 show, respectively, the time-phased budget portions of the control accounts for the programming department's contributions to work packages L and W.

The WBS for ROSEBUD consists of nine work packages performed by four functional departments, plus an additional work package for project management. During the estimating phase, each department submits a cost estimate for the work packages in its part of the project. Upon approval, with additions for overhead and G&A, each departmental estimate becomes a budget. Thus, the 10 shaded boxes in Figure 8.7 represent departments/work packages for which initial cost estimates were made and, subsequently, budgets and control accounts were established.

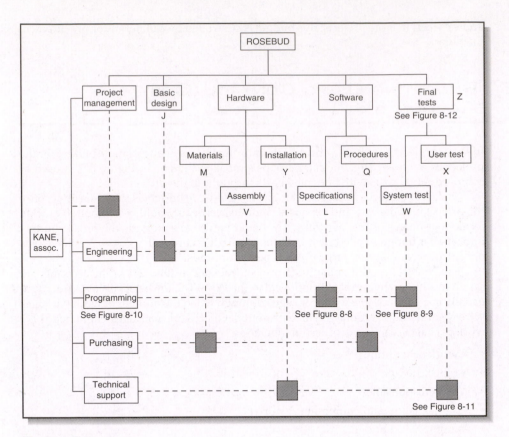

Figure 8.7
Integration of WBS and organization structure showing cost accounts. (See Figures 8.8 to 8.12 for details.)

8.9 COST SUMMARIES[19]

With the control account structure shown in Figure 8.7, high-level summary accounts can be developed by consolidating control accounts for the WBS and organizational hierarchies. Such consolidation is useful for monitoring the performance of individual departments and segments of the project. For example, consolidating accounts in Figure 8.7 horizontally results in a control account for each functional department. Figure 8.10 shows this with the time-phased budget for the programming department, which sums the budgets for work packages L and W (Figures 8.8 and 8.9).

Control accounts also can be consolidated vertically through the WBS. This would be useful for tracking and controlling individual work packages, clusters of work packages, or the project as a whole. Figure 8.12 illustrates the time-phased budget for final tests, which is the sum of the budgets for work packages W (Figure 8.9) and X (Figure 8.11).

The highest-level accounts are for the project and the company's contribution to the project. Figure 8.13 shows budgeted amounts aggregated vertically and horizontally. Through the PCAS and control account structure, deviations from budget

Project ROSEBUD   Date _____

Department Programming   Work package L– Software specifications

Charge	Rate	Months+						Totals	
		1	2	3	4	5	6	Hours	Cost
Direct labor									
Professional	$35/hour		130					130	4,550
Associate	$30/hour		50	100				150	4,500
Assistant	$20/hour			100				100	2,000
Direct labor cost			6,050	5,000					11,050
Labor overhead	75%		4,538	3,750					8,288
Other direct cost*									0
Total direct cost			10,588	8,750					19,338
General/administrative	10%		1,059	875					1,934
Total costs			11,647	9,625					21,272

+Should extend for as many months as required by the project.
*Should be itemized to include costs for materials, freight, subcontracts, travel, and all other nonlabor direct costs.

Figure 8.8
Budget for programming department for Work Package L.

identified at the project level or company level can readily be traced to the work packages and departments responsible. Chapter 11 will describe this. The PCAS and control account structure permit costs to be summarized in a variety of ways. Table 8.3, for example, shows the allocation costs by type among the five departments and nine work packages that comprise the ROSEBUD project.

Figure 8.9
Budget for programming department for Work Package W.

Project ROSEBUD   Date _____

Department Programming   Work package W– System test

Charge	Rate	Months+						Totals	
		1	2	3	4	5	6	Hours	Cost
Direct labor									
Professional	$35/hour						20	20	700
Associate	$30/hour						50	50	1,500
Assistant	$20/hour								0
Direct labor cost							2,200		2,200
Labor overhead	75%						1,650		1,650
Other direct cost*							0		0
Total direct cost							3,850		3,850
General/administrative	10%						385		385
Total costs							4,235		4,235

+Should extend for as many months as required by the project.
*Should be itemized to include costs for materials, freight, subcontracts, travel, and all other nonlabor direct costs.

Charge	Rate	Months+						Totals	
		1	2	3	4	5	6	Hours	Cost
Direct labor									
Professional	$35/hour		130				20	150	5,250
Associate	$30/hour		50	100			50	200	6,000
Assistant	$20/hour			100				100	2,000
Direct labor cost			6,050	5,000			2,200		13,250
Labor overhead	75%		4,538	3,750			1,650		9,938
Other direct cost*									0
Total direct cost			10,588	8,750			3,850		23,188
General/administrative	10%		1,059	875			385		2,319
Total costs			11,647	9,625			4,235		25,507

Project ROSEBUD Date _____
Department Programming Work package ALL

+Should extend for as many months as required by the project.
*Should be itemized to include costs for materials, freight, subcontracts, travel, and all other nonlabor direct costs.

Figure 8.10
Budget summary for programming department.

Charge	Rate	Months+						Totals	
		1	2	3	4	5	6	Hours	Cost
Direct labor									
Professional	$35/hour						10	10	350
Associate	$30/hour						40	40	1,200
Assistant	$20/hour								
Direct labor cost							1,550		1,550
Labor overhead	75%						1,163		1,163
Other direct cost*						1,200	2,107		3,307
Total direct cost						1,200	4,820		6,020
General/administrative	10%						120	482		602
Total costs						1,320	5,302		6,622

Project ROSEBUD Date _____
Department Technical support Work package X - User test

+Should extend for as many months as required by the project.
*Should be itemized to include costs for materials, freight, subcontracts, travel, and all other nonlabor direct costs.

Figure 8.11
Budget for Work Package X.

Charge	Rate	Months[+] 1	2	3	4	5	6	Totals Hours	Cost
Project ROSEBUD									
Department Technical support; Programming					Work package	(W + X) Final Tests		Date	
Direct labor									
Professional	$35/hour						30	30	1,050
Associate	$30/hour						90	90	2,700
Assistant	$20/hour								0
Direct labor cost							3,750		3,750
Labor overhead	75%						2,813		2,813
Other direct cost*						1,200	2,107		3,307
Total direct cost						1,200	8,670		9,870
General/administrative	10%					120	867		987
Total costs						1,320	9,537		10,857

[+]Should extend for as many months as required by the project.
*Should be itemized to include costs for materials, freight, subcontracts, travel, and all other nonlabor direct costs.

Figure 8.12
Budget summary for final tests.

Figure 8.13
Aggregation of cost account information by project and organization.

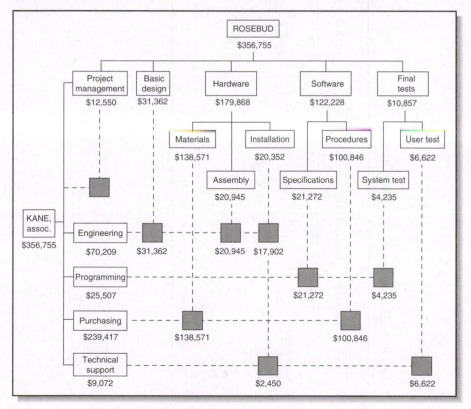

Table 8.3 Cost Summary for ROSEBUD Project

	Labor ($)				Overhead ($)				Materials	General and Administrative	Total Cost
	Engineering	Programming	Purchasing	Technical Support	Engineering	Programming	Purchasing	Technical Support			
Total project	22,800	13,250	2,230	2,850	22,800	9,938	1,673	2,138	235,236	31,290	356,755
Project management											12,550
Activity J	7,200				7,200				14,111	2,851	31,362
Activity L*		11,050				8,288				1,934	21,272
Activity M			1,100				825		124,050	12,596	138,571
Activity Q			1,300				818		89,700	9,168	100,846
Activity V	8,200				8,200				2,641	1,904	20,945
Activity Y	7,400			1,300	7,400			975	1,427	1,850	20,352
Activity W		2,200				1,650				385	4,235
Activity X				1,550				1,163		602	6,622

* Refer to Figure 8.8 to see, for example, how costs in this row were developed.

Questions arise during project planning about how expenditures vary throughout the project, which periods have the heaviest cash requirements, and how expenditures compare to income. To answer these and other such questions, it helps to analyze the estimated "pattern of expenditures" as derived for work package cost estimates and the project schedule. The following are examples.

Cost Analysis with Early and Late Start Times

A simplifying assumption used in cost estimating is that costs in each work package are incurred uniformly. For example, a 2-week, $22,000 work package is assumed to have expenditures of $11,000 per week. With this assumption, it is easy to create a *cost schedule* that shows the cost *each week* of the entire project.

As an example, look at Figure 8.14—the time-based network for the LOGON project using early start times. Then look at Table 8.4, which lists the LOGON work packages and the time, total cost, and weekly direct cost for each (where weekly direct cost is the total cost divided by the time; e.g., for Activity H it is $100K/10 weeks=$10K/week). Using the schedule, the cost for the project *each week* can be computed by summing the costs for all activities scheduled in that week. The procedure is the same as described in the Chapter 6 for determining the resource loading. According to the schedule, in the first 10 weeks only Activity H is scheduled, so the weekly cost stays at $10K. Over the next 6 weeks activities I and J are scheduled, so the weekly cost is their sum, $16K+$8K=$24K. Further along, in weeks 17 and 18, four work packages—I, K, L, and J—are scheduled, so the weekly cost is their sum total, $8K+$4K+$18K+$21K=$51K. These weekly costs, summarized in the third column in Table 8.5, represent the *cost schedule* for the project. The cumulative expense column in Table 8.5 represents the forecast total project cost for a given week. These costs are presented graphically in Figure 8.15.

Using the same procedure, project cost schedules and forecasts can be prepared based on *late* start times. Figure 8.16 is the time-based network for LOGON using late

Figure 8.14
Time-based network for the LOGON project using early start times.

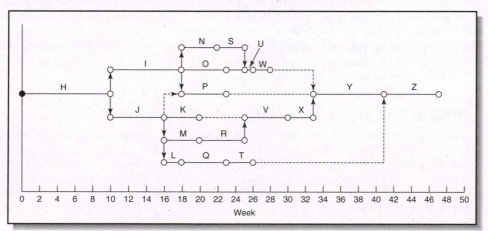

Table 8.4 Activities, Time, Cost, and Labor Requirements (Result of Work Breakdown Analysis)

Activity	Time (Weeks)	Total Cost ($K)	Weekly Direct Cost ($K)	Weekly Labor Requirements (Workers)
H	10	100	10	5
I	8	64	8	4
J	6	96	16	8
K	4	16	4	2
L	2	36	18	6
M	4	84	21	3
N	4	80	20	2
O	5	50	10	5
P	5	60	12	6
Q	5	80	16	2
R	5	0	0	0
S	3	0	0	0
T	3	0	0	0
U	1	14	14	9
V	5	80	16	14
W	2	24	12	6
X	3	36	12	6
Y	8	104	13	14
Z	6	66	11	5

Total Direct Cost—$990K

start times. The latter two columns of Table 8.5 are the late-start weekly and cumulative costs.

Given the early and late cost figures in Table 8.5 it is possible to analyze what effect delaying activities will have on project costs. By comparing weekly costs from early start times with those of late start times in Figure 8.17, the influence of schedule changes on project costs is readily apparent. The shaded region in the top figure represents the *feasible budget region,* the range of budgets permissible by changes in the project schedule. The lower part of the figure shows the impact on weekly costs from delaying activities.

When funding restrictions constrain project expenditures, cost schedules reveal the places where the schedule must be changed. For example, Figure 8.17 shows a peak weekly expense of $82,000 in Weeks 18 and 19. If a weekly budget ceiling of $60,000 per week were imposed on the project, then late start times would be preferred because they would result in a more "level" cost profile and peak expense of only $54,000. The method for leveling resources discussed in Chapter 6 is applicable to leveling project costs; costs are treated just as another resource.

Effect of Late Start Time on Project Net Worth

Owing to the time value of money, the cost of work done farther in the future has a lower net present worth than the same work if done earlier. Delaying activities in a lengthy project can thus provide substantial savings in the present worth of project costs. For example, suppose the duration of the LOGON is 47 *months* instead of the 47 weeks used so far. If the annual interest rate is 24 percent, compounded at 2 percent per month, the present worth for the project would be $649,276. This is computed by using the monthly expenses in Table 8.5 (again, assuming the weeks shown to be

Table 8.5 LOGON Project Weekly Expense Using Early Start Times ($1,000)

Week	Early Start Activities During Week	Early start Weekly Expense	Early Start Cumulative Expense	Late Start Activities during Week	Late Start Weekly Expense	Late Start Cumulative Expense
1	H	10	10	H	10	10
2	H	10	20	H	10	20
3	H	10	30	H	10	30
4	H	10	40	H	10	40
5	H	10	50	H	10	50
6	H	10	60	H	10	60
7	H	10	70	H	10	70
8	H	10	80	H	10	80
9	H	10	90	H	10	90
10	H	10	100	H	10	100
11	I, J	24	124	J	16	116
12	I, J	24	148	J	16	132
13	I, J	24	172	J	16	148
14	I, J	24	196	J	16	164
15	I, J	24	220	I, J	24	188
16	I, J	24	244	I, J	24	212
17	I, K, L, M	51	295	I, M	29	241
18	I, K, L, M	51	346	I, M	29	270
19	K, M, N, O, P, Q	83	429	I, M	29	299
20	K, M, N, O, P, Q	83	512	I, M	29	328
21	N, O, P, Q	58	570	I, R	8	336
22	N, O, P, Q	58	628	K, I, R	12	348
23	O, P, Q	38	666	K, R	4	352
24	—	0	666	K, R, N	24	376
25	—	0	666	K, R, N	24	400
26	U, V	30	696	N, O, V	46	446
27	V, W	28	724	N, O, V	46	492
28	V, W	28	752	S, O, V	26	518
29	V	16	768	S, O, P, V	38	556
30	V	16	784	S, O, P, V	38	594
31	X	12	796	U, P, X	38	632
32	X	12	808	W, P, X, L	54	686
33	X	12	820	W, P, X, L	54	740
34	Y	13	833	Y, Q	29	769
35	Y	13	846	Y, Q	29	798
36	Y	13	859	Y, Q	29	827
37	Y	13	872	Y, Q	29	856
38	Y	13	885	Y, Q	29	885
39	Y	13	898	Y, T	13	898
40	Y	13	911	Y, T	13	911
41	Y	13	924	Y, T	13	924
42	Z	11	935	Z	11	935
43	Z	11	946	Z	11	946
44	Z	11	957	Z	11	957
45	Z	11	968	Z	11	968
46	Z	11	979	Z	11	979
47	Z	11	990	Z	11	990

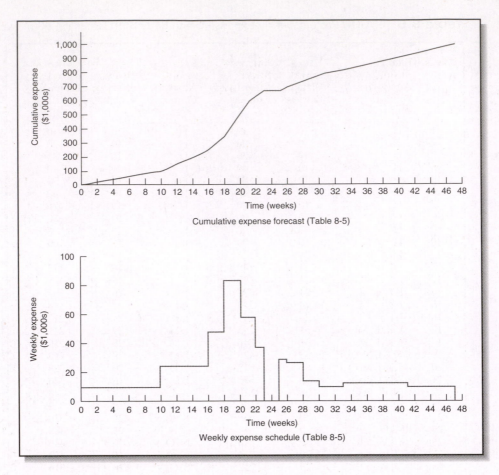

Figure 8.15
Planned weekly and cumulative expenses for the LOGON project.

Figure 8.16
Time-based network for the LOGON project using late start times.

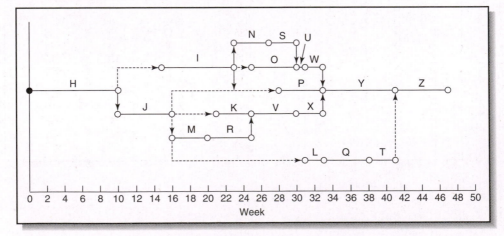

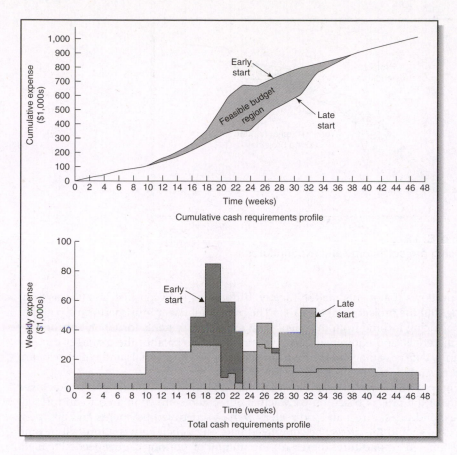

Figure 8.17
Comparison of cash requirements, early versus late start times.

months instead) and discounting the amounts back to time zero. Now, when the late start times are used instead, the present worth is only $605,915—a saving of $43,361.

Does this mean that activities should be delayed until their late start date? Not necessarily. Remember, delaying activities uses up slack time and leaves less extra time to deal with problems that could put the project behind schedule. Thus, whether or not an activity should be delayed depends on the *certainty of the work*. Activities that are unlikely to encounter problems can be started later to take advantage of the time value of money. Activities that are less familiar, such as research and development work, should be started earlier to retain slack that might be needed to absorb unanticipated delays. (This assumes the critical path method; CCPM relies on resource buffers that preclude the need for slack). Also, whether or not to delay activities will depend on the schedule of customer payments. If payments are tied to project milestones, then activities tied to those milestones cannot be delayed. Other factors to consider when deciding which activities to delay are discussed in Chapter 6.

Cash Flow

A problem the project manager often faces is maintaining positive cash flow—i.e., assuring that the cumulative cash inflows (payments received) exceed the cumulative

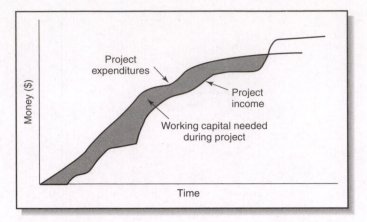

Figure 8.18
Balancing project income and expenditures.

cash outflows (payments made). Ideally, differences between cash in and cash out throughout the project will be small.[21] The project manager must perform a juggling act, balancing income from the client with expense payments for labor, subcontractors, materials, and equipment. To help maintain this balance the manager can, for example, take advantage of the time lag between when materials and equipment are acquired and the payments for them are required.

Figure 8.18 shows an example of forecast cash flow. All sources of income over the life of the project based on contractual agreements are compared to all foreseeable expenditures, direct and indirect, as well as scheduled payments and any penalty costs, should the project be completed late. The deficit between forecast income and estimated expenditures represents the amount of working capital needed to meet payment commitments. Based upon this cash flow forecast, a *funding plan* should be created to ensure sufficient working capital is available throughout the project.[22]

As mentioned, customer payments are sometimes made at milestones tied to completion of deliverables or project phases. Such payments help the contractor to cover his costs. The drawback, however, is that should the project encounter serious problems, an unscrupulous contractor, having already received several payments, can simply walk away from the job and leave the customer in a fix! One way for the customer to keep "hold" on the contractor is to withhold back a significant portion of the agreed upon payment, called *retention money*, until all work is satisfactorily completed. A second way is to withhold some portion of the final payment, called a *performance guarantee*, for a period following handover of the end-item until all defects discovered by the customer have been rectified.

8.11 SUMMARY

Cost estimation and budgeting are part of the project planning process. Cost estimation logically follows work breakdown and precedes project budgeting. Accurate cost estimates are necessary to establish realistic budgets and to provide standards against which to measure actual costs; they are thus crucial to the financial success of the project.

Costs in projects have a tendency to escalate beyond original estimates. Defining clear requirements and work tasks, employing skilled estimators, being realistic in estimating, and anticipating escalation causes such as inflation all help to minimize escalation. Estimate accuracy is partly a function of the stage in the project life cycle during which the estimates are prepared; the further along the cycle, the easier it is to produce accurate estimates. However, accurate estimates are needed early in the project, and this accuracy can be improved by clearly defining project scope and objectives, and subdividing the project into small tasks and work packages. In general, the smaller the work element being estimated and more standardized the work, the greater the accuracy of the estimate. The aggregate of cost estimates for all the work elements plus overhead costs becomes the cost estimate for the overall project. The approved estimates become budgets after contingency reserves have been added.

The project budget is subdivided into smaller budgets called control accounts. Control accounts are derived from the WBS and project organization hierarchies, and are the budget equivalent to work packages. In large projects, a systematic methodology or project cost accounting system (PCAS) is useful for aggregating estimates and maintaining a system of control accounts for budgeting and control.

Cost schedules are derived from time-phased budgets, and show the pattern of costs and expenditures throughout the project. They are used to identify cash and working capital requirements for labor, materials, and equipment.

Forecast project expenditures and other cash outflows are compared to schedule payment receipts and income sources to predict cash flow throughout the project. Ideally, expenditures and income are balanced so that the contractor can maintain a positive cash flow. The forecasts are used to prepare a plan that guarantees adequate funding support for the project.

REVIEW QUESTIONS AND PROBLEMS

1. Why are accurate cost estimates so important, yet so difficult, in project planning? What are the implications and consequences of overestimating costs, and of underestimating costs?
2. Define cost escalation. What are major sources of cost escalation?
3. What is the purpose of a contingency fund (management reserve)? How is the contingency fund used and controlled?
4. Describe what the term "phased (rolling wave) project planning" means.
5. How do changes in requirements cause cost escalation?
6. How does the type of contractual agreement influence the potential for cost escalation?
7. What is the relationship between phases of the project life cycle and cost escalation?
8. Explain what life cycle costs are, and how they are different from project costs.
9. Explain the difference between a cost estimate and a cost target. What are the problems in confusing the two—in using cost targets as cost estimates?
10. Explain the difference between accuracy and precision. Give two examples that illustrate the difference.
11. For each of the following estimating methods, briefly describe the method, when it is used, and the estimate accuracy it provides:
    a. Expert opinion
    b. Analogy
    c. Parametric
    d. Cost engineering.

12. Describe the process of using the WBS to develop cost estimates. How are these estimates aggregated into total project cost estimates?
13. What is the role of the functional units and subcontractors in cost estimating?
14. Describe the different kinds of contingency amounts, and the purposes each serves.
15. Describe the PCAS. What is its purpose, and how is it used in project planning?
16. What is a time-phased budget? What is the difference between a budget and a cost estimate?
17. Distinguish recurring costs from non-recurring costs.
18. What are six cost elements shared by most estimates and budgets?
19. How are direct labor expenses determined?
20. What expenses are included under direct non-labor?
21. How is the overhead rate determined?
22. What is a control account, and what kinds of information does it contain? How does a control account fit into the structure of the PCAS?
23. How are control accounts aggregated horizontally and vertically? Why are they aggregated like this?
24. How are time-based forecasts prepared, and how are they used?
25. What are the reasons for investigating the influence of schedules on project costs? What is the feasible budget region?
26. What might happen if top management submitted a bid for a project without consulting the business unit or department to be involved in the project?
27. Refer to Case 5.1, the Barrage Construction Company, in Chapter 5. The project manager Sean Shawn employed the analogy with adjustment method to estimate the cost of constructing a three-car garage. Specifically, he started with the cost of an average two-car garage, $43,000, and increased it by 50 percent to $64,500. Comment on the likely accuracy of the three-car garage estimate. Suggest a different approach that might yield a more accurate cost estimate, and then use this approach and made-up time and cost figures to compute the estimate. Argue why your estimate is better than Sean's. See Chapter 5, Figure 5.19, for Sean's WBS.
28. The example in Table 8.2 shows three possible ways of apportioning total direct costs. Using the same example, suppose the direct non-labor (DNL) cost and G&A are broken down as follows:

Direct Non-Labor

	MARS	PLUTO		G&A
Materials	30	5	Freight	8
Other	10	5	Other	32
	40	10		40

Assuming all remaining costs shown in Table 8.2 are unchanged, compute the project costs for MARS and PLUTO using the following apportioning rules:
a. Overhead (OH) is proportionate to direct labor (DL).
b. Freight G&A is proportionate to materials.
c. Other G&A is proportionate to DL, OH, DNL, and freight.
29. Chapter 7 discussed the impact of crashing activities and the relationship of schedules to cost. The method assumes that as activity duration is decreased, the direct cost increases owing to the increases in direct labor rates from overtime. Overhead rates also may vary, although the overhead rate is often *lower* for overtime work. For example, the overhead rate may be 100 percent for regular time but only 20 percent for overtime. In both cases, the overhead rate is associated with the wage rate being used.

Suppose that in the MARS project in Table 8.2, 1,000 direct hours of labor are required at $50 per hour, and the associated overhead rate is 100 percent for regular time. Now suppose an overhead rate of 10 percent and overtime wage rate of time-and-a-half.

Compare the project cost if it were done entirely on regular time with the cost if it were done entirely on overtime. Which is less expensive?

30. Use the table below and the network in Figure 8.19 to answer questions about the ARGOT project:

Activity	Time (wks)	Weekly Cost ($K)	Total ($K)
A	4	3	12
B	6	4	24
C	3	5	15
D	4	5	20
E	8	3	24
F	3	4	12
G	2	2	4
			111

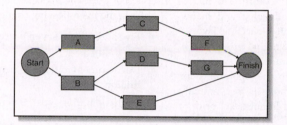

Figure 8.19

a. Compute the ESs and LSs for the project. Assume T_s is the same as the earliest project completion date.
b. Construct a time-based network for the project such as Figure 8.14 (use early start times).
c. Construct two diagrams similar to those in Figure 8.15 showing the weekly and cumulative project expenses.

31. Using the data in problem 30, repeat Steps b and c using late start times. Then identify the feasible budget region using the cumulative curves.

32. Explain retention money and performance guarantee.

QUESTIONS ABOUT THE STUDY PROJECT

1. How were project costs estimated? Who was involved? Describe the process.
2. When did estimating take place? How were estimates checked and accumulated? How were they related to the WBS?
3. What, if any, were the principle causes of cost escalation in the project?
4. Was a life cycle cost analysis performed? If so, who did it, when, and using what methods? How did the analysis affect the design, development, and production of the project deliverables or main end-item?
5. How often and when were cost estimates revised during the project?
6. How were overhead costs determined? What basis was used for establishing overhead cost rates?
7. How were estimates tallied to arrive at a total project cost estimate? Who did this?
8. What kind of project cost accounting system (PCAS) was used? Was it manual or computerized? Describe the system and its inputs and outputs. Who maintained the system? How was it used during the project?

9. Describe the process of creating the project budget. Show a sample budget (or portion thereof).
10. How were management and supervisory costs handled in the budget?
11. Was the project budget broken down into control accounts? If so:
   a. How were they related to the work packages and WBS, and
   b. How were they tied into the PCAS?
12. What kinds of costs summaries were prepared? Who were they sent to? How were they used? Show some examples.
13. Did the PCAS produce time-phased cost schedules and forecasts? Show some examples. How were they used by the project manager?

Case 8.1 Life Cycle Costs for Fleet of Tourist Spaceships

At the time of writing, Burt Rutan and Sir Richard Branson had teamed up to form The Spaceship Company, which will develop and manufacture commercial spacecraft (SpaceShipTwo, or SS2), launch aircraft (WhiteKnightTwo, or WK2), and support equipment. Branson's "spaceline," Virgin Galactic, will handle the operations for space tourist flights. Their hope is to eventually reduce by half the proposed initial ticket price of $190,000.

No information has been released about development and operating costs for the spaceline and equipment, so the figures used in this case are

guesses. Refer to Example 8.2 for *hypothetical* life cycle costs for the spaceline and spaceship fleet, but assume the following changes to the numbers:

- Five spaceships, seven passengers per spaceship
- Development and manufacturing costs, $120 million
- Flight operations cost: $0.5 million/flight
- Ticket price: $190,000 for passengers on the first 100 flights, then $150,000 for passengers on the next 100, and $100,000 for passengers on flights thereafter.

QUESTIONS

1. Assuming all other numbers from Example 8.2 are the same, what is the "bottom line" profit of the venture for 5 years of operation?
2. If the profit goal is $70 million:
   a. What is the maximum development and production cost for the fleet?
   b. What is the maximum per-flight operational cost (note: assume $120 million development/production cost)?

3. Brainstorm. What are some ways that the development cost might be reduced? What are some possible design decisions for the spacecraft and mothership that would reduce the per-flight operational cost? Next, research articles and news releases about SS2 and WK2 to see what the developers, Scaled Composites and The Spaceship Company, have been doing to contain costs.

Case 8.2 Estimated Tunnel Costs for the Chunnel Project[23]

Before construction began on the English Channel Tunnel (Chunnel) Project, the banks underwriting the project hired consulting engineers to review cost estimates prepared by the contractors. The consultants concluded that the tunneling estimates were 20 percent too high.

Their analysis was based on comparisons of costs from recent European tunnel projects, including 50 German railroad tunnels ranging in length from 400 m to 11 km, to the Chunnel, which would be 49 km in length. The costs of the tunnels ranged from £55 to £140 per cubic meter (cum) of open tunnel; the cost of the Chunnel was estimated at £181 per cum on the British side of the channel and £203 on the French side (the difference owing to more difficult conditions on the French side). The Chunnel is actually three interconnected tunnels—one for trains going in each direction, and a smaller service tunnel in between them. Note, however, that the cost estimates are per cubic meter of tunnel, so, *presumably*, differences in tunnel lengths and diameters are not major factors. Why might the estimates for the Chunnel be so much higher per cum than the costs for the analogy projects? Discuss possible, logical adjustments to the analogy tunnel project costs to arrive at a cost estimate for the Chunnel tunnel.

Notes

1. See Harrison F. *Advanced Project Management*. Aldershot: Gower; 1981. pp. 147–148.
2. Flyvbjerg B, Bruzelius N, and Rothengatter W. *Megaprojects and Risk: An Anatomy of Ambition*. Cambridge: Cambridge University Press; 2003. p. 16.
3. See Archibald R. *Managing High-Technology Programs and Projects*. New York, NY: Wiley; 1976. pp. 167–168.
4. Harrison, *Advanced Project Management*, pp. 148–152.
5. *Ibid.*, pp. 172–173, gives an example of an escalation clause.
6. Politically, how independent should the estimators be? So independent, says DeMarco, that the project manager has "no communication with the estimator about how happy or unhappy anyone is about the estimate." DeMarco T. *Controlling Software Projects*. New York, NY: Yourdon Press, 1982. p. 19.
7. A more complete discussion is found in Harrison, *Advanced Project Management*, pp. 162–171.
8. Flyvbjerg B, Bruzelius N, and Rothengatter W. *Megaprojects and Risk: An Anatomy of Ambition*.
9. Harrison, *Advanced Project Management*, pp. 154–161.
10. Archibald, *Managing High-Technology Programs and Projects*, p. 171.
11. Dingle J. *Project Management: Orientation for Decision Makers*. London: Arnold/John Wiley & Sons; 1997. p. 105.
12. Pool R. *Beyond Engineering: How Society Shapes Technology*. New York, NY: Oxford University Press; 1997; Heppenheimer TA. Nuclear power. *Invention and Technology* 18(2); 2002: 46–56.
13. A complete discussion of the cost review procedure is given by Kerzner H. *Project Management: A Systems Approach to Planning, Scheduling, and Controlling*, 10th edn. New York, NY: Wiley; 2009. pp. 592–595.
14. Rosenau M. *Successful Project Management*. Belmont, CA: Lifetime Learning; 1981. p. 91.
15. Kerzner, *A Systems Approach to Planning, Scheduling, and Controlling*, pp. 580–584, thoroughly discusses labor costing in projects. This example is derived from Kerzner.
16. This example is derived from a similar one in Rosenau, *Successful Project Management*, pp. 89–91.
17. This example is derived from Wilson T and Stone D. Project management for an architectural firm. *Management Accounting* October; 1980: 25–46.
18. See Harrison, *Advanced Project Management*, pp. 199–202, for further discussion of cost accounts.
19. The kinds of cost summaries used often depend on the kind available in the software, though many software packages permit customizing of reports.
20. Wiest J and Levy F. *A Management Guide to PERT/CPM*, 2nd edn. Upper Saddle River, NJ: Prentice Hall; 1977. pp. 90–94.
21. Harrison notes that balancing cash in foreign contracts is especially difficult because "In many cases, the profits from [currency dealings] can exceed the profits from the project; [if funds are] not managed effectively, the losses from foreign currency commitments can bring about large losses on a project and lead to bankruptcy." See Harrison, *Advanced Project Management*, p. 185.
22. See Archibald, *Managing High-Technology Programs and Projects*, p. 168.
23. Fetherston D. *The Chunnel*. New York, NY: Times Books; 1997. pp. 141–142.

Chapter

Project Quality Management

> *I have offended God and mankind because my work didn't reach the quality it should have.*
>
> —Leonardo da Vinci

*P*roject success is measured in terms of how well a project meets budgetary, schedule, and performance requirements. Performance requirements generally relate to project stakeholders' needs and expectations about the functioning and performance of the end item or deliverables. A high-quality project is one that meets performance requirements, satisfies its stakeholders and society at large, and causes no harm to the environment.

9.1 THE CONCEPT OF QUALITY

In the 1950s, *quality* was viewed as the process of inspecting products that had already been produced in order to separate the good ones from the bad (defective or sub-par). But in the current business environment, so the thinking goes, you have to *prevent* defects and failures rather than inspect for them; i.e., you cannot make it right by inspection. You have to focus on *processes* to ensure things are done right the first time, every time, and on a *culture* where everybody is quality-focused.

But in the pursuit of being competitive, project teams often seek ways to accelerate schedules and cut costs, even though this commonly results in more rework, more mistakes, greater workload for the project team, and a "quality meltdown." They become preoccupied with lowering costs and shortening schedules, even though ". . . the bitterness of poor quality lives long after the sweetness of cheap price and timely delivery has been forgotten."[1]

An example is the space shuttle Challenger. On January 28, 1986, defective seals allowed flames to breach the joint in a rocket motor and ignite the main fuel tank shortly after launch, causing a massive explosion and killing the seven astronauts onboard. While engineers had previously warned managers about the risk of this happening, the launch proceeded on time because of a promise to politicians; for the sake of meeting a schedule, quality was compromised.

In contrast, consider Tower Bridge in London (Figure 9.1).[2] Four years late and costing nearly twice the estimated £585,000 when it opened in 1894, it has withstood the test of time. Originally designed and built to enable pedestrians and horse-drawn vehicles to cross the River Thames, it now carries 10,000 vehicles per day and is a major tourist attraction. The bridge has survived floods, pollution, and the bombs of World War II—problems its original designers never considered. In terms of time and cost, the project was a failure; in terms of quality, it has been a raving success. Another example of quality is a 120-foot arched bridge located not far from Beijing. Built in AD 605, it has withstood floods, earthquakes, and combat.

What is Quality?

Quality implies meeting specifications or requirements, but it also means more than that. While meeting project specifications will usually prevent a customer from taking a contractor to court, specifications alone cannot ensure that the customer will be satisfied with the end result or the contractor will receive gratitude or win repeat business.

Ideally, a project aims *beyond* specifications and tries to fulfill customer expectations—including those not articulated; it aims at delighting the client. A common weakness of project managers is they assume that customer needs, expectations, and requirements are readily evident or will require little effort to research and specify.

Figure 9.1
London Tower Bridge.
Photograph courtesy of Herman Steyn.

Fitness for Purpose

The term "quality" implies that a product or deliverable is *fit for the intended purpose*. Fitness normally involves a wide range of criteria, such as performance, safety, reliability, ease of handling, maintainability, logistical support, and no harmful environmental impacts. While an item such as an expensive piece of clothing might have superior style, material, or workmanship, the customer will also consider its *value for money* and whether it is priced correctly for the intended purpose. Optimizing only one aspect of a product—fitness for purpose, client satisfaction, value for the money, or strategic benefit to the organization—will not result in overall optimal product; the project manager must seek to balance the multiple aspects of an end-item and define specifications so as to reflect that compromise.

Absence of Defects

Quality also implies an absence of defects, which is why people often associate the terms *quality* and *defect*. A defect is a *nonconformity*—something other than what the customer had expected, a problem or mistake. One way to achieve quality is to identify and correct as many nonconformities as possible, and to identify them as soon as possible. In general, the longer a nonconformity persists before it is discovered, the more costly it is to remedy or remove it. It might be relatively easy and inexpensive to fix a defect in a component part, but it is usually more expensive to fix it after the component has been put into an assembly, and even more expensive after the assembly has been imbedded inside a system. The defect is most expensive when it causes a product or system to malfunction or fail while in use by the customer.

But "absence of defects" requires qualification, and the presumption that zero defects equates to high quality is not always true. A quality project is one that satisfies multiple requirements, and devoting too much attention to any particular one, such as eliminating *all* defects, may detract from fulfilling other requirements that are more important.[3] For example, in most projects the requirements relate to time, cost, and performance. When the schedule must be maintained, trying to remove *all* defects can prove exceptionally costly. The customer might prefer to keep costs down and hold to the schedule rather than eliminate all defects. Of course, in some cases it is necessary to eliminate virtually every defect.[4] Even the most minor defect in an air traffic control system or artificial human heart can result in injury or loss of life. The point is, it depends on the customer. In many cases the customer would prefer a deliverable completed on time, at lower cost, and with a *few* minor defects to one completed late, at higher cost, but with no defects.

Good Enough Quality

In removing defects, emphasis is on those defects that would prevent the system from meeting its most important requirements. This is the concept of "good enough quality"—the default criteria when priorities on performance requirements, time, and cost preclude meeting all the requirements and force the project team into meeting only those that are most important. Says Bach, creating systems "of the best possible quality is a very, very expensive proposition, [though] clients may not even notice the difference between the best possible quality and pretty good quality."[5] The customer, of course, must be able to judge what is "good enough," and to do that must be constantly updated about project progress, problems, costs, and schedules.

In the ideal case, everyone on the project team contributes to quality; each:

1. Knows what is expected of him or her
2. Is able and willing to meet those expectations
3. Knows the extent to which he or she meets the expectations
4. Has the ability and authority to take necessary corrective actions.

Such conditions require quality-focused leadership, training, and motivation efforts. Once everyone starts contributing, however, attention to quality becomes automatic and requires little influence from the project manager.

What Quality Is *Not*

Quality implies that the product is fit for the purpose. But fit for purpose does not necessarily relate to the expense, reliability, or number or sophistication of features, all which refer to the *grade* of the product. In other words, *quality* and *grade* are not the same. For example, coal mines produce different grades of coal. The highest grade is used in steel-making, while lower grades are used in chemical products and coal-fired power stations. Even though the coal for a power plant is lower grade than that for steel-making, it is the appropriate—and hence best-quality—coal for the purpose. In fact, it would be inappropriate and uneconomical for power plants to use higher-grade coal. Of course, the *coal mines* should strive for *high-quality processes* to deliver all grades of coal to meet the specifications and requirements of all of their clients, including specifications for price and reliable delivery.

Quality Movements and Progress

What might be called the "quality revolution" started in the 1950s in Japan under the influence of an American consultant, Dr W. Edwards Deming. He proposed a philosophy of quality that included continuous improvement, skills training, leadership at all levels, elimination of dependency on inspections, reliance on single-source (rather than many-source) suppliers, and use of sampling and statistical techniques. Since then a number of other quality movements have come and gone—some that could be described as fads. The most lasting and popular movement since the 1980s is *total quality management* (TQM). TQM is a set of techniques and more—it is a mindset, an ambitious approach to improving the total effectiveness and competitiveness of an organization. The key elements of TQM are identifying the mission, goals, and objectives of the organization; acting in ways consistent with those goals and objectives; and focusing on customer satisfaction. TQM involves the total organization, including teams of frontline workers and visible support from top management. Quality problems are systematically identified and resolved to continuously improve processes. In projects, this purpose is served by project reviews and closeout sessions, discussed later.

Another management philosophy called *just in time* or *lean production* complements TQM. In a business environment, lean recognizes that quality problems originate from "broken processes." It provides methods and tools to analyze processes and expose and eliminate sources of non-value added waste in processes. The lean approach includes relatively easy to implement methods to improve quality and reduce costs and lead times.[6] The difficult aspect of implementing lean is that it requires developing a culture where employees everywhere have the authority and skills to continuously improve their processes—an unusual concept for many organizations. The principles of lean production originated at Toyota in the Toyota Production System (TPS), and have been successfully adopted around the world. In some industries (e.g., autos and electronics), virtually all the big players have adopted lean production. In project environments, lean production methods are being applied to product development and construction.[7]

Another influential quality movement is *Six Sigma*, started in the 1980s at Motorola and later popularized by General Electric. Advocates claim that Six Sigma provides a more structured approach to quality than TQM. The term "Six Sigma" refers to the fact that in a normal distribution, 99.99966 percent of the population falls within -6σ to $+6\sigma$ of the mean, where "σ" is the standard deviation. If the quality of a process is controlled to the Six Sigma standard, there will be less than 3.4 *parts per million* defects in the process—near perfection!

But the Six Sigma approach goes beyond statistics, and is a philosophy for reducing process variability. It includes a five-step process for improving existing processes, and another five-step process for designing new processes and products, both aimed at Six Sigma quality levels. The first process is called DMAIC (Define, Measure, Analyze, Improve, Control), and involves the steps of defining the best measures to improve a process, implementing those measures, tracking the measures, and reducing defects so that fewer outcomes fail to meet specifications. The second process, which focuses on design, employs a similar process called DMADV—Define, Measure, Analyze, Design, and Verify. In projects, the Six Sigma approach translates into defining clear deliverables that relate to the mission of the organization and are approved by management. The DMAIC process is sometimes used as the project methodology, wherein the five steps of the process define the stages of the project.

Project Quality Management

Project quality means quality of the project end-item, deliverable, or product. Quality of the end-item or product starts with clearly defined product or system requirements that both the contractor and customer agree upon. If the customer provides requirements or specifications that seem unrealistic, the contractor should review them with the customer and alter them so the desired end-result can realistically be achieved. The final agreed upon specifications should reflect the customer's expectations, the product's fitness for the intended purpose, and any negotiated compromises. Comprehensive specifications for the deliverable should be included in the project scope definition.

Management to achieve project quality, i.e., *project quality management*, includes quality management processes as well as techniques to reduce the risk of products or deliverables not meeting requirements. The following sections discuss these processes and the techniques.

9.2 PROCESSES OF PROJECT QUALITY MANAGEMENT

Project quality management consists of three processes: quality planning, quality assurance, and quality control (Figure 9.2). *Quality planning* guides future quality activities; it sets the requirements and standards to be met and the actions necessary to meet them. *Quality assurance* performs the planned quality activities and ensures the project utilizes processes necessary to meet quality standards and end-item requirements. *Quality control* ensures that quality assurance activities are performed according to quality plans, and that requirements and standards are being met. You can think of quality control as the "medicine" to eliminate existing nonconformities and

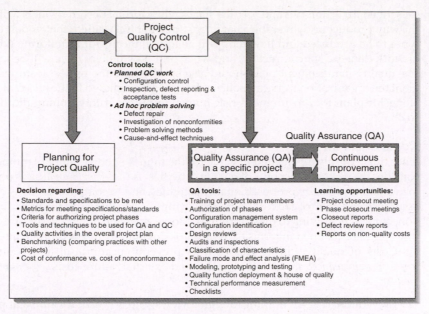

Figure 9.2
The project quality management process.

quality planning and assurance as the "healthy lifestyle" to prevent nonconformities in the first place.

As shown in Figure 9.2, project quality control overarches quality planning and quality assurance. The role of quality control is to ensure that quality assurance happens according to the quality plan. Quality assurance aims to ensure there are appropriate quality standards for a project, and to take advantage of learning opportunities from completed projects for continuous improvement of future projects.

Quality Planning

Quality planning should provide confidence that everything necessary to ensure quality has been thought through. It has two aspects: (1) establishing project quality management procedures and policies for the entire organization; and (2) establishing a quality plan as part of the project master plan for each project.

Responsibility for establishing organization-wide policies and procedures to improve project quality management typically falls on functional managers, especially the quality manager. Projects often employ quality standards that already exist in the organization, such as the ISO 9001 standard, in a quality management system.[8] For design and development projects, this standard prescribes that an organization shall set procedures for (a) the design and development stages; (b) the necessary reviews, verifications, and validations appropriate to each of the stages; and (c) the responsibilities and authorities for the stages.

Planning for quality in each project should be a part of the project planning process. Identifying, scheduling, budgeting, and assigning responsibility for quality assurance and control activities is done utilizing the same principles and methods as for other project activities, discussed in Chapters 4–8. The quality management plan for the project should specify for each phase of the project the requirements to be met to authorize the next phase. It should specify the quality techniques that will be used (described in sections 9.3 and 9.4), the stages when formal design reviews will be held, the way product or deliverable characteristics will be classified, the models or prototypes to be produced and how they will be tested, means for monitoring the quality of work done by subcontractors, and when and how deliverables will be inspected. The quality management plan should also specify how the project team will implement the organization's quality policies. It should be included in the *project master plan* alongside plans for procurement, risk, human resources, safety, communications, and so on.

Costs of Quality

Since quality is always related to value for the money spent, quality planning should consider the costs and benefits of quality activities. A *cost–benefit analysis* is performed to evaluate and justify proposed quality activities, and to compare the costs of quality assurance and control activities with the savings or benefits from fewer or eliminated nonconformities owing to those activities. Money spent on quality assurance and control should be justified in terms of reduced risk of not meeting requirements.

Costs of quality can be classified as prevention, appraisal and control costs (*costs of conformance*), and internal failure and external failure costs (*cost of nonconformance*):

1. Prevention: costs of training, design reviews, and any activity aimed at preventing errors; includes cost of quality planning.
2. Appraisal and control: costs of evaluating products and processes, including product reviews, audits, tests, and inspections.
3. Internal failure: costs associated with nonconformities discovered by the producer; includes costs for scrap, rework, and retest.
4. External failure: costs incurred as a result of product failures after delivery to the customer; includes costs for replacements, warranty repairs, liability, lost sales, and damaged reputation.

While the costs of quality for a company with a sound quality management system can be as little as 2 percent of the company proceeds, for a company with a poor quality management system they can exceed 20 percent.[9] It therefore makes sense to invest in a good quality management system—i.e., to spend more on design reviews, audits, training, and modeling and testing so as to spend less on internal and external failures.

For projects, the costs of external failures occur after the project is completed, whereas the costs of prevention, appraisal, and control are incurred during the project. Therefore, costs for prevention, appraisal, and control should be estimated, included in the project plan, and covered in the project budget. They are among the many costs the project manager must justify to management and the customer.

Quality Assurance

Project quality assurance relates to the execution of the project quality management plan. It reduces the risks related to not meeting desired features or performance requirements of deliverables.

As shown in Figure 9.2, quality assurance covers the following:

1. Activities performed *in a specific project* to ensure that requirements are being met and that the project is being executed according to the quality plan.
2. Activities that contribute to the continuous improvement of current and *future projects*, and to the project management maturity of the organization.

Quality assurance should provide confidence that everything necessary is being done to ensure the appropriate quality of project deliverables.

Continuous Improvement and Project Post-Completion Reviews

You might say that continuous improvement is the foundation to progress: without it, humankind would not have moved beyond the Stone Age. Project organizations that strive to continually improve their technical operations and managerial processes conduct a formal closeout or *post-completion review* for every project. The review happens upon completion of the project or, ideally, upon completion of each phase of the project. Its purpose is to understand what happened, and to learn lessons that can be applied to other projects to avoid repeating mistakes. The reviews enable the organization to improve its technical processes and project management.

The project manager's responsibility during reviews is to facilitate candid and constructive discussion about what happened—what worked and what did not—and to make sure that everyone participating is heard. The discussion is formally documented, and a list of lessons learned created. This process is essential for continuous improvement, though often it is neglected because people lose interest as the project winds down or they become busy on new, upcoming projects. As a result, organizations repeat mistakes, reinvent the wheel, and do not learn from their experiences.[10] Post-completion reviews are covered further in Chapter 12.

Quality Control

Quality control is the ongoing process of monitoring and appraising work, and taking corrective action so as to achieve the planned quality outcomes. The process also verifies that quality assurance activities are being performed according to the quality plan, and that project requirements and specifications are being met. Whenever nonconformities are uncovered, the causes are determined and eliminated. In the same way that the quality plan should be integrated with other aspects of project plan, quality control should be integrated with the other aspects of project control. Quality control cannot happen in isolation; it must be integrated with scope control, cost control, progress control, and risk control. It is a responsibility of the project manager.

Quality control can be contrasted to *scope verification*: whereas scope verification refers to the acceptability of project deliverables *by the customer*, quality control refers to conformance to specifications as set *by the contractor*. Whereas quality control refers to verifying adherence to specifications and standards previously set, scope verification also includes verifying *acceptability* of those specifications and standards.

The quality control process includes inspections to verify that deliverables are meeting specifications as well as acceptance tests before handover of deliverables to the customer. In the event that a minor feature does not meet specification, the contractor might request a waiver or deviation that would release the nonconforming item from the specification. A *waiver* applies to an unplanned condition that is discovered only after the item has been produced. It authorizes a temporary nonconformity, such as a scratch discovered on the paint of a hardware item. A *deviation* is also a temporary departure from specification, but it is obtained beforehand. For example, if a specified material is temporarily unavailable, the contractor can apply for a deviation to allow usage of an alternative material. A nonconformity can also be classified a *modification*, which is a change to the specification that is considered permanent.

Control activities, as illustrated in Figure 9.2, include both planned quality control activities and *ad hoc* problem-solving. Planned activities include, for example, site inspections on a construction project, tests on a product component, or an audit of a supplier to ensure that it is using correct materials. *Ad hoc* problem-solving refers to handling problems and risks as they emerge. Techniques for analysis and problem solving are discussed later.

Quality of Procured Items

Quality requirements for most items procured from suppliers are set by industry standards, in which case the main criterion for choosing a supplier is price. To buy a batch of standard items such as bolts, the procurement officer obtains quotes from a number of suppliers and picks the least expensive. When the batch arrives, an inspector checks the bolts to determine if they are acceptable. However, when procuring a system or item that must be newly developed, there likely is no industry standard. In that case, the purchaser has to work with the item's supplier and assist in planning for the quality assurance and control to assure the item meets specifications.

Of course, even for procurement of standard items, far better than selecting the least expensive supplier is selecting a supplier that has proven capability and willingness to meet the contractor's requirements, and then seeking to develop a mutually beneficial long-term relationship with the supplier. The two parties work together as partners, and share responsibility for each other's success. Establishing this kind of relationship is not always easy, especially when the supplier is much larger than the contactor, or does not value the relationship or consider the contracted work a priority.

Contractors often invest heavily to make sure they get the appropriate-quality procured subsystems and components. A contractor often has a special vendor quality section within its procurement division to manage quality assurance of all its procured items—including their development and manufacture or construction. The purpose of this section is to assist in selecting suppliers, monitoring suppliers' processes to ensure quality, and performing inspections and acceptance tests of purchased items. Other responsibilities are described next.

Example 9.1: Companies Working Together for Quality Assurance and Control

Company A develops and manufactures mining vehicles. It is working on a new vehicle, and must choose a supplier to develop, manufacture, and support a transmission for the vehicle. The company's vendor quality section and procurement staff review proposals from supplier candidates, and select Company B to provide the transmissions. Company A's engineering division develops a functional specification for the transmission that includes performance characteristics, maintenance requirements, interfaces with other parts of the vehicle, and test requirements. The vendor quality section then works with Company B to ensure that Company B's engineers will be using appropriate processes for cost-effective compliance with the specification, and that before any transmissions are shipped they will be tested according to Company A's functional specification for compliance to performance criteria.

9.3 TECHNIQUES FOR QUALITY ASSURANCE DURING SYSTEM DEVELOPMENT

In phased project planning, authorization of a phase implies that plans for the phase have satisfied pre-specified criteria, one criterion being that the plans include sufficient measures for quality assurance. System developers employ a variety of such measures, as discussed in this section.

Configuration Management[11]

During design and development of a system vast amounts of information are generated for use in the design process, and later for manufacturing (or construction), maintenance, and support. The information can include many hundreds or thousands of documents (specifications, schematics, drawings, etc.), each likely to be modified in some way during the project. Keeping track of all the changes and knowing which version is the most current for every item can be difficult. Thus, any project aimed at delivering a technical product needs a system or process to keep up with and manage all the information; such is the purpose of *configuration management*.

Configuration management includes policies and procedures for monitoring and tracking design information and changes, and ensuring that everyone involved with the project (and, later, the operation of the deliverable) has the most current information. Policies and procedures that form the configuration management system for a project should be included in the quality plan. As with all procedures, the best configuration management system is whatever permits the desired level of control and is the simplest to implement. The two main aspects of configuration management are configuration identification and configuration control.

Configuration Identification

Configuration identification is an inherent part of systems design, and involves defining a system's overall structure and its subsystems and components. Mentioned in Chapter 2, any subsystem, component, or part that is to be tracked and controlled as an individual entity throughout the life cycle of the system is identified as a *configuration item* (*CI*). A CI can be a piece of hardware, a manual, a parts list, a software package, or even a service. Any subsystem that is procured is also treated as a CI. Every physical and functional characteristic that defines and is important for controlling the CI is identified and documented. Ultimately, every functional and physical element of the end-item system should be associated in some way with a CI, either as a CI in its own right or as a component within a subsystem that has been identified as a CI. Ideally, each CI is small enough to be designed, built, and tested individually by a small team.

Master copies (electronic or paper) of the configuration documents for every CI are retained in a secure location (the "configuration center") and managed by someone not involved in the functions of design, construction, manufacture, or maintenance. (Documentation about design premises, assumptions, and calculations are not considered configuration documents, and are retained elsewhere by the design authority.)

Any modifications, waivers, or deviations to a CI are recorded so that all CI documentation reflects the "as-built" status of the system. In the case of a deliverable such as a building, ship, or other one-of-a-kind system that becomes operational, the "as-built" specification will later be used in its operation and maintenance. Where multiple units are produced (e.g., cars, airplanes, appliances) and modifications and improvements are introduced over time, the specific configuration for each individually produced unit must be known, which requires that each specific CI in the product must be traceable to its specific "as-built" specifications. This is necessary so that, for example, the correct spare parts, training, and operating manuals can be supplied, and problems can be traced and analyzed in the event of accidents, customer complaints, or claims regarding product liability. This concept of "traceability" was introduced in Chapter 4, and is illustrated in the following example.

Example 9.2: Traceability and the Apollo Spacecraft[12]

To establish the reliability of an item, either many of the items are tested until one fails, or the required reliability is designed-in through methods of engineering analysis. Either way, to assure reliability everything about the item must be known—its manufacturing process, the composition of it parts and materials, and even the sources of those materials. For the Apollo space mission, the goal of achieving mission success was set at 99 percent and crew survivability at 99.9 percent. To meet such high-level goals, every CI (subsystem, component, part, etc.), as it moved through the design and manufacturing process, was accompanied by a package of documents that established its genealogy and pedigree. The saying went, "If you ordered a piece of plywood, you wanted to know from which tree it came." Half-inch bolts for the Apollo spacecraft involved an 11-step manufacturing process with certification tests at each step. Every bolt was subjected to rigorous testing, as were the steel rods from which they were made, the billets from which the rods were extruded, and the ingots from which the billets were forged. Everything about the processes and tests for the bolts was documented, including the source of the iron for the bolts—Minnesota—and even the mine and the mine shaft. Such extreme tracking and control is necessary to insure high reliability and enable problem diagnosis in case things go wrong. But it comes with a price—which is why bolts available for 59 cents at the hardware store cost $8 or $9 apiece on rockets and spacecraft.

Configuration Control

Configuration control, the second aspect of configuration management, concerns more quality control than quality assurance, but is covered here for the sake of continuity. The design of a system is normally specified by means of a large number of documents, such as performance specifications, drawings, manuals, and testing procedures, that are generated during the design process. As the design evolves these documents are subject to change, and an orderly scheme is needed to manage and keep track of all the changes. Such is the purpose of configuration control.

Configuration control is based on the following principles:

1. Any organization or individual may request a change—a modification, waiver, or deviation.
2. The proposed change and its motivation should be documented. Standard documents exist for this purpose: for modifications, the document is called a *change proposal, change request, change order,* or *variation order.*
3. The impact of the proposed change on system performance, safety, and the environment is evaluated; so is its impact on other hardware items, software, manuals, and methods of manufacturing or construction and maintenance.
4. The change is assessed for feasibility; this includes estimating the resources needed to implement the change, and the impact of the change on schedules.
5. The group responsible for approving or rejecting the proposed change is the *configuration board* (CB) or *configuration control board* (CCB). The board usually includes the chief designer and representatives from manufacturing or construction, maintenance, and other important stakeholders, and is often chaired by the project manager or program manager.
6. Upon approval of the proposed change, the work required to implement the change is planned. This planning includes taking action with regard to the disposition of anything that might be affected by the change, including spare parts, equipment and processes for manufacturing or construction, and manuals and other documentation.
7. The implemented change is verified to ensure it complies with the approved change proposal.

Change requests are sometimes classified as Class I or Class II. Class I requests can be approved by the contractor or the developer; Class II changes must be approved by the client. Configuration control is an aspect of project control and, in particular, change control, both discussed in Chapter 11.

Design Reviews

The fate of a deliverable is set in its design, so the project manager must ensure that the proposed design is acceptable in all respects. Such is the purpose of *design reviews*—to ensure that the users' requirements and assumptions have been correctly identified, and that the proposed design is able to meet the requirements in an appropriate way. Design reviews (not to be confused with *general project reviews*, described in Chapter 12) provide confirmation of design assumptions (e.g., load conditions), data used in the design process, and design calculations. Reviews should ensure that all important life-cycle aspects of the project end item have been addressed and pose no unacceptable risks. In particular, reviews serve as checks for:

1. Omissions or errors in the design
2. Compliance to regulations, codes, specifications, and standards
3. Cost of ownership
4. Safety and product liability
5. Reliability
6. Availability
7. Ability to be constructed or manufactured (manufacturability)
8. Shelf life
9. Operability
10. Maintainability
11. Intellectual property rights
12. Ergonomics.

The reviews involve representatives from all disciplines, functions, and users who are or will be connected to the deliverable throughout its life cycle and often include outside designers and subject matter experts. (This relates to the concurrent engineering process, discussed in Chapters 4 and 13.) For example, a design review of a production facility (e.g., chemical plant, mine, or factory) would include:

- Representatives from the technical support area that will eventually be responsible for maintaining the facility

- Representatives from the company that will build the facility

- Representatives from the marketing, procurement, legal services, and quality areas that in some way will occupy, make use of, or have to deal with the consequences of the facility.

When conducted early in the conceptual phase, the reviews involve representatives from only a few functions; as the project progresses to later phases, they involve representatives from more functions. For the design of a simple part or component, a single review upon completion of the design— but preceding manufacture—might be sufficient. In the case of a complex system, however, it will be necessary to convene several reviews at successive stages of the project. The *quality plan* should indicate when these reviews will be held, the participants in each, who will chair them, and to what extent the designer is bound to comply with the reviewers' directions or recommendations. The review dates, topics, and attendees should be noted in the project *communication plan*, discussed in Chapter 12.

Formal Reviews

Formal design reviews are planned events, ideally chaired by the project manager or someone else *not* directly involved in the design of the end-item. For projects aimed at developing and delivering a product, there are commonly four reviews:

1. *Preliminary design review*: review of the functional design to determine if the concept and planned implementation meet the basic operational requirements.
2. *Critical design review*: review of the details of the hardware and software design to ensure they conform to the preliminary design specifications.
3. *Functional readiness review*: (for high-volume or mass-produced products only), evaluation of tests performed on early-produced items to check the efficacy of the manufacturing process.
4. *Product readiness review*: comparison of manufactured products to specifications to ensure that design control documents will result in products that meet requirements.

Formal reviews serve other purposes too: to minimize risk, identify uncertainties, assure technical integrity, and assess alternative design and engineering approaches. Unlike peer reviews, formal reviews are overseen and conducted by a group of outsiders who use information accumulated by the project team. These outsiders are technical experts or experienced managers who are familiar with the end-item and workings of the project and project organization, but are *not* formally associated with the project organization or its contractors. Since a formal review may last for several days and require considerable preparation and scrutiny of results, the tasks and time necessary to prepare and conduct the review and obtain approvals should be incorporated in the project schedule.

Since a prerequisite for each design review is thorough design documentation, common practice is to convene a "pre-review meeting" during which the design team gives the review team an overview of the proposed design; documentation about the design premises, philosophy, assumptions, and calculations; and specifications and drawings. The review team is then allowed time (typically 14 days) to evaluate the design and prepare for the formal review meeting. Sometimes the review team uses a checklist to ensure that everything important is covered. In recent years, the Internet has become an effective medium for conducting design reviews.[13]

Informal Design Reviews

Although formal reviews are sometimes necessary, as much as possible the project manager should encourage informal design reviews too, including informal discussions among designers, and between designers and other stakeholders. Good suggestions can originate anywhere, but it is up to the designer to decide whether or not to use them. Draft designs, reports, and other deliverables should be presented regularly and (ideally) voluntarily to peer designers and others for informal review. In a healthy quality culture, *brainstorming* is commonly used to evaluate and edit not only designs, but also reports and other deliverables of all kinds. The principle behind brainstorming is to freely generate as many ideas as possible, and to withhold any form of evaluation or criticism until after numerous ideas have been generated. Only later are the ideas assessed and the good ones separated from poor ones.

Example 9.3: Formal and Internal Reviews in the Mars Pathfinder Project[14]

Outside review boards conduct formal reviews for all major NASA projects. These reviews are important, since a project's termination or continuation can depend on the board's findings. Preparation for a formal NASA review can take an enormous amount of time. Senior project management for the Mars Pathfinder project (see also Example 11.5, Chapter 11) estimated that preparation for one such review, the *critical design review*, would require about *6 weeks* of devoted attention. This would divert time from the actual management of the project, which, paradoxically, could increase the likelihood of the project falling behind schedule and failing the review. To prepare for the formal review, project manager Brian Muirhead ordered an internal review.

In contrast to formal reviews, internal (or peer) reviews address a narrow range of topics and require only a few days preparation. The value of these reviews lies in making sure that everyone understands the decisions being made, nothing is overlooked, and the project is kept on track. Over 100 internal reviews were conducted during the 3-year Pathfinder development.

The internal review revealed a slew of problems, including lack of progress in defining system interfaces, rapid growth in the mass of the Mars lander (the prototype weighed too much), and a shortage of good engineers. These findings did little to inspire confidence about the project's ability to pass scrutiny in the formal design review.

The verdict from a critical design review is an all-or-nothing decision. The project earns either a passing or failing grade. A failing grade initiates a cancellation review that can result in project termination. A project such as Pathfinder could be canceled if the budget were to overrun by as little as 15 percent. The Pathfinder design review board comprised 25 consultants and seasoned managers from NASA and the Jet Propulsion Laboratory (JPL, the site responsible for most of the Pathfinder design work), none of whom was associated with the project.

Besides determining the future of a project, formal design reviews serve another purpose: to give the project a kick in the pants. Preparation for each review is a laborious endeavor, and forces the project team to make decisions about unresolved issues. Formal reviews may be held three or four times during the project.

The review board for the Pathfinder was not happy with many aspects of the project, but did not initiate a cancellation review. Instead, the board approved the project, but instructed Pathfinder managers to be more critical of designs, focus less on performance and more on cost, and stop obsessing over business innovations. These recommendations later proved useful, and helped to make the Pathfinder project one of the most successful in the history of space exploration.

Regardless of the competency of the design staff, design reviews are significant to quality. There is always more than one means to an end, and no designer can be expected to think of all of them. Even the most capable people overlook things. Mature designers appreciate the design review process in terms of the networking experience, innovative ideas provided by others, knowledge gained, and reduction of risks, but less mature designers tend to feel insulted or intimidated by it. It is human nature for people to be less than enthusiastic about others' ideas, and to resist suggested changes to their own. The design review process seeks to achieve "appropriate quality," a balanced compromise between insiders and outsiders, and to refrain from faultfinding or perfecting minor features.

Audits

Unlike design reviews, which relate specifically to the design of a product, audits are broad in scope and include a variety of investigations and inquiries. The main purpose of audits is to verify that *management processes* comply with prescribed processes, procedures, and specifications regarding, for example, system engineering procedures, configuration management systems, contractor warehousing and inventory control systems, and safety procedures. They are also used to verify that *technical processes* such as welding adhere to prescribed procedures, and to determine *project status* based upon careful examination of certain critical aspects of the work. Any senior stakeholder, such as the customer, program manager, or executive, can request an audit. Like formal design reviews, they are relatively formal, and normally involve multifunctional teams. Unlike design reviews, where innovative can ideas originate, audits focus strictly on verifying that processes are is being done as required. The auditor can be an internal staff member or an external party who is deemed to be credible, fair, honest, and unbiased.

Audit preparation begins with an agreement between the auditor and stakeholder requesting the audit, as to the audit's scope and schedule, and the responsibilities of the audit team. The audit team prepares for the audit by compiling checklists, and sometimes attending a briefing session to learn about the project. The auditor is required to prepare a report within a few days following the investigation that details any nonconformities found, rates the importance of the nonconformities, describes the circumstances under which they were found and the causes (if known or determinable), and provides suggestions for corrective action. While the focus is on uncovering nonconformities, commendable activities are sometimes also noted in the audit report. A typical thorough audit will take 1–2 weeks.

Classification of Characteristics

A project end-item or deliverable is "specified" or defined in terms of a number of attributes or characteristics, including functional, geometrical, chemical, or physical properties. Characteristics—often specified quantitatively—usually include tolerances of acceptability. In a complex system, numerous characteristics are defined on drawings and other documents. The Pareto principle (discussed later) states that the large majority of problems are caused by a relative few sources. Therefore, the cost-effective way to address quality assurance is to attend to characteristics that most seriously impact quality problems or failures. This is not to say that other characteristics are ignored, but that limited resources for inspection and acceptance testing should first be directed at those items classified as most crucial or problematic.

Characteristics are typically classified into four categories: *critical, major, minor,* and *incidental* (or, alternatively, *critical, major A, major B,* and *minor*). The *critical* classification is reserved for characteristics where nonconformance would pose safety risks or lead to system failure. Quality plans often specify that items with critical characteristics be subject to 100 percent inspection. The *major* classification is for characteristics where nonconformance would cause the loss of a major function of the deliverable. The *minor* classification is for characteristics where nonconformance would lead to small impairment of function or to inconvenience with manufacturability or serviceability. Characteristics classified as *incidental* would have minimal effect or relate to relatively unimportant requirements.

The classification of characteristics is assigned by the designers of each system who collaborate with the designers of the next higher-level system, designers of interfacing systems, and staff from manufacturing or construction. Together they analyze design characteristics regarding safety and other requirements and classify them using a set of ground rules.

Classification of characteristics should not be confused with the classification of *defects*. In a welded structure, for example, the specified characteristics might include the "absence of cracks or impurities" in the weld metal. A crack (that could lead to catastrophic failure) would be classified as "very serious," whereas a small amount of impurity in the weld (that would not affect the integrity of the structure) would be classified as "minor."

Characteristics classifications are sometimes listed in a separate document, although it is more practical to show the classifications directly on drawings and other specifications using symbols such as "C" for critical, "Ma" for major, "Mi" for minor, and so on. Absence of a symbol normally indicates the lowest priority, although sometimes even the lowest classification is denoted with a symbol as well. Only a small percentage of characteristics should be classified as critical. A large number of characteristics classified as critical could be a sign of poor design: when everything is critical, nothing in particular is critical!

Characteristics classification serves as a basis for decisions regarding modifications, waivers, and deviations at all levels of a system. For example, the characteristics classification for a higher-level system provides guidance to designers of the lower-level subsystems and components that comprise the system. Classifying the braking performance of an automobile as critical (e.g., an automobile traveling at 25 miles per hour should be able to stop within 40 feet on dry pavement) tells designers of the braking system to classify the brake's components as critical as well. Failure mode and effect analysis (FMEA) sometimes plays a role in the classification process.

Failure Mode and Effect Analysis

A system can potentially fail as the result of a variety of conditions, such as the short-circuiting, cracking, collapsing, or melting of its components, or inadequate, missing, or incorrect steps and procedures in its design, production, or operation. FMEA is a technique to determine the ways (modes) a technical system might fail, and what effects the identified failures would have on the system's performance, safety, and environment.

The FMEA procedure is normally used during the early stages of system development; it involves the following steps:

1. List the *relevant components* of the system.
2. Identify all the *possible ways* that the component or system might fail (the *failure modes*). This is best done by a team brainstorming the failure modes. For each failure mode, the causes and conditions under which it is likely to occur are also listed.
3. Assign a *probability* of occurrence to each failure mode.
4. Describe and assess the probable *effects* (or impacts) of each failure mode on the performance and safety of the system, and on the environment.
5. Assess the *severity* or seriousness of the effects.
6. Compute the *criticality* of each failure mode. Criticality is a function of both the probability of the failure and the seriousness of the effects.
7. Prepare a plan to circumvent the failure mode, mitigate the effects of failure, or respond in case the failure occurs. When conformance to a specific characteristic is necessary to prevent failure, the characteristic is classified as critical.

Table 9.1 illustrates. In the columns "Sev" (severity), "Prob" (probability), and "Det" (detectability—whether the potential failure will be easy or difficult to detect), each potential failure mode is rated 1 to 10. RPN (risk priority number), which is the criticality of the failure mode, is computed as:

$$RPN = Sev \times Prob \times Det$$

Items are then categorized by RPN; the highest RPN's have the highest priority.

Although a failure by itself might not be critical, combined with other failures it could be very serious. The Chernobyl disaster is an example where a chain of errors (each alone not very serious) led to catastrophic failure—the meltdown of a nuclear

Table 9.1 FMEA Table

Potential
Failure Mode and Effects Analysis
(Design FMEA)

System _____
Subsystem _____
Component _____
Design Lead _____
Core Team _____

Key Date _____

FMEA Number _____
Prepared By _____
FMEA Date _____
Revision Date _____
Page _____ of _____

Item/ Function	Potential Failure Mode(s)	Potential Effect(s) of Failure	S E V	Potential Cause(s)/ Mechanism(s) of Failure	P R O B	Current Design Controls	D E T	R P N	Recommended Action(s)	Responsibility & Target Completion Date	Action Results				
											Actions Taken	New Sev	New Occ	New Det	New RPN

336

reactor. Thus, FMEA must consider *combinations* of failures modes as well individual failure modes. Besides use in design and engineering analysis, FMEA can also be used to identify issues affecting project costs and schedules; it is also a tool in project risk management, described in Chapter 10.

Modeling and Prototyping

Designers use various kinds of models—computer simulation models, mathematical models, three-dimensional scale models, full-scale prototypes—to gain a better impression of how the final product, system, or subsystem will look and perform. Models and prototypes are also used in marketing to enable customers to "envision" the product or system. A full-scale wooden or plastic mock-up of the driver's cab for a truck or the cockpit of an airplane, for example, helps the producer sell the product and obtain suggestions or criticisms about it.

In product development projects, models help reduce the risk of failure to meet technical requirements. As shown in Table 9.2, the kinds of models built and tested and the risks they eliminate coincide with the project phases. Projects for the development of large processing plants often use models in a similar fashion (Table 9.3). Models for those projects usually start out as laboratory equipment, but ultimately grow in sophistication and capacity to enable a pilot operation and then a demonstration plant that closely replicates the proposed facility.

Table 9.2   Phases of Equipment Development

PROJECT PHASE	MODEL BUILT AND TESTED	OBJECTIVES RELATING TO THE ELIMINATION OF RISKS	RISKS ELIMINATED
Concept	Exploratory development model (XDM) (Breadboard models); such models could be built for the entire system or for specific high-risk subsystems	Proof that the new concept would be feasible	The risk that the concept would not be feasible
Validation	Advanced Development Model (ADM)	Proof that the product would perform according to specifications and interfaces well with other systems (form, fit and function)	The risk that the performance of the system and its interfaces with other systems would not be acceptable
Development	Engineering Development Model (EDM) manufactured from the intended final materials	Proof of reliability, availability, and maintainability	The risk of poor operational availability or reliability
Ramp-up	Pre-production models (PPM)	Proof that the product could be manufactured reliably in the production facility and could be deployed effectively	The risk of unforeseen problems in manufacturing

Table 9.3 Phases for Development of Process Plants

PROJECT PHASE	OBJECTIVE
Laboratory experiments	To prove the basic concept
Pilot plant	To learn how the process works when scaled up To provide inputs for the design of the final plant
Demonstration plant	To provide a full-scale plant that demonstrates to potential customers the economic feasibility as well as operational aspects

The kind of models used, whether full-scale physical mock-ups, scale models, mathematical models, computer simulation models, breadboards, or prototypes, depends on the information needed versus the expense of creating and using models. For a small product comprising only a few components, building and testing a full-scale model that closely resembles the final product is usually cost-effective; for a large, complex system, it usually is not and a computer simulation model is more effective.

Example 9.4: Modeling the Form and Fit of Boeing 777 Components[15]

One of the most pervasive problems in the development of large aircraft is aligning vast numbers of parts and components so that no interference or gaps between them will occur during assembly. In the mid-1980s, Boeing invested in three-dimensional CAD/CAM (computer-aided design/computer-aided manufacture) technology that would enable designers to see components as solid images and simulate their assembly into subsystems and systems on computer screens. By 1989, Boeing had concluded that "digital preassembling" of an airplane could significantly reduce the time and cost of rework that usually accompanies introducing a new airplane into the market. In 1990 it launched the Boeing 777 twinjet program, and began involving customers, design engineers, toolmakers, manufacturing representatives, and suppliers in the concurrent engineering design process (see Example 4.5, Chapter 4). The physical geometry of the plane's components was determined with CAD/CAM technology instead of with physical mock-ups, which are time-consuming and expensive to build. One result was that changes and rework in the 777 program were reduced by 50 percent.

Testing of Prototypes and Models

As shown in Table 9.2, a goal of building and testing models is to systematically reduce the risk that the final product will not be satisfactory. Data gathered from models reveal design shortcomings and assist in later stages of development. Data from experiments with models about stresses and strains in components, for example, suggest potential failure modes in the final product.

For products that will be manufactured in quantities, the design should be verified by means of *qualification tests* before manufacturing begins. Qualification tests happen the opposite way to design: while the typical design process starts with the overall system design and cascades down to the design of individual subsystems and components, qualification testing starts with testing and qualification of individual components, then builds up to the testing of subsystems and, finally, of the full system.

Quality control involves performing the tasks defined in the quality management plan, plus undertaking any other necessary corrective actions to assure quality. It involves use of a variety of techniques, as discussed next.

Inspection and Acceptance Testing of the Final Product

Whereas testing of models and prototypes provides information for design and development, acceptance testing of deliverables and the final product verifies that the product meets specifications. Characteristics classified as critical are always inspected, but those classified as minor or incidental are not. In automobile production, for example, the braking and steering performance of every vehicle is tested. For items produced in large quantities, a few might be subjected to destructive tests (i.e., tested until they break); items produced one-of-a-kind or in a small batch are subjected to nondestructive inspection and testing.

Although testing the end-results from a production process does not fall under the realm of *project* quality management *per se*, the deliverable of any development project where the end-result is to be mass-produced would include the testing procedures and other quality assurance processes to be used in producing the item. Product designers who are intimately familiar with key characteristics of the product and its components are best suited to specify the ways those components should be quality checked after production begins. For components or materials produced in high volume, sampling is commonly used to reduce the cost of inspection. Based on the results of tests from a few samples, a statistical inference is made about the quality of the entire batch or process. Obviously, sampling is mandatory when the testing destroys the product.

Tools of Quality Control

In the 1980s, Kaoru Ishikawa of Tokyo University defined the basic tools of quality control.[16] The tools Ishikawa defined aim at identifying the sources of defects and nonconformities in products and processes; they are applicable for identifying sources of and resolving problems of all kinds, including problems associated with risks. Although developed in a production environment (Kawasaki Steel Works), several of the tools he defined are nonetheless applicable to projects.[17] We discuss some of these tools below.

Run Chart

A run chart is a graph of observed results plotted versus time to reveal possible trends or anomalies. The plot of schedule performance index versus cost performance index illustrated in Figure 11.11 is a form of run chart that tracks project performance and shows if it is improving or worsening in terms of schedule and cost.

Control Chart

Control charts are widely used for tracking and controlling repetitive processes and detecting process changes. For projects that include the development of production processes, one deliverable would be specifying the relevant charts for controlling the quality of the process. Readers involved in projects aimed at the delivery of repetitive operating systems should refer to books on statistical control techniques, such as *Juran's Quality Control Handbook*.[18]

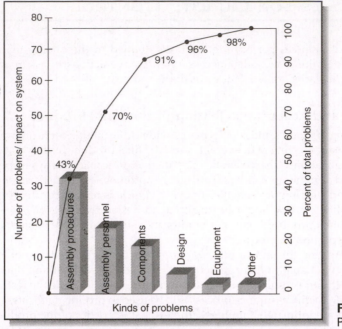

Figure 9.3
Pareto diagram.

Pareto Diagram

Vilfredo Pareto, a nineteenth-century Italian economist, formulated "Pareto's Law" of income distribution, which states that the distribution of income and wealth in a country follows a regular pattern: 80 percent of the wealth is owned by 20 percent of the people. This principle, also dubbed the "80/20 rule," has since been found to apply in principle to a wide variety of situations, including those relating to quality. Quality consultant Dr Joseph Juran posited, in the late 1940s, that the large majority of defects result from a relative few causes, and thus, for economic reasons, it makes sense to identify the vital few causes of the bulk of defects and to direct efforts at removing them.

Figure 9.3 is a Pareto diagram. Across the bottom part of the diagram is a histogram showing the number of problems versus the sources of the problems; the diagonal line crossing the figure is the cumulative effect of the problems (corresponding to the scale on the right). As shown, the first kind of problem accounts for 43 percent of the problems; the first and second combined account for 70 percent. Thus, resolving just the first two kinds of problems would eliminate 70 percent of the problems.

In project environments, Pareto analysis is used to identify sources of the most problems—the sources most in need of attention.

Cause-and-Effect Techniques

Cause-and-Effect Diagram

Quality problems and risks are often best addressed through the collective experience of project team members. Team members meet to brainstorm ideas about problems, and these ideas are recorded on a *cause-and-effect* (CE) *diagram* (also called a fishbone or Ishikawa diagram), which is a scheme for arranging the causes for a specified effect in a logical way. Figure 9.4 shows a CE diagram to determine why a control system

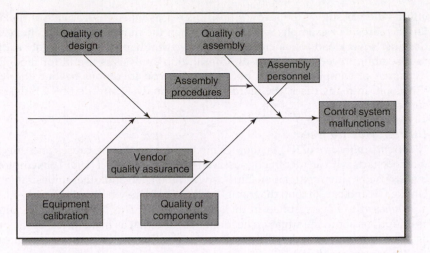

Figure 9.4
Cause-and effect (fishbone or Ishikawa) diagram.

malfunctions. As the team generates ideas about causes, each cause is assigned to a specific branch (e.g., "assembly procedures" on the Quality of Assembly branch). CE diagrams and brainstorming can be used in two ways: (1) given a specified or potential outcome (*effect*), to identify the potential *causes*; and (2) given a cause (or a risk), to identify the outcomes that might ensue (*effects*). Identifying problem causes is an obvious first step to resolving problems.

Causal Loop Diagram

A *causal loop diagram* can be used to portray the causes of a certain problem or the influence several variables in a complex system have on one another.[19] In Figure 9.5, variables in the diagram are connected by arrows to indicate cause–effect relationships. The positive and negative signs represent the direction in which the variable at the arrow's head changes when the variable at the arrow's tail changes. A positive sign indicates a reinforcing effect—the variable at the arrow's head increases when the variable at the arrow's tail increases. A negative sign indicates a negative

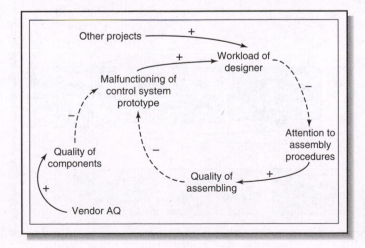

Figure 9.5
Casual loop diagram for control system problem.

effect—the variable at the arrow's head decreases when the variable at the arrow's tail increases. For example, in Figure 9.5, when the number of projects increases the designer's workload also increases, and when that happens the designer's attention to assembly procedures decreases. Causal loop analysis is useful for modeling the dynamics of complex systems, but it involves considerations beyond the scope of this book. In many cases, the more superficial analysis afforded by CE diagrams is sufficient.

Current Reality Tree

A *current reality tree* (CRT) is another method for analyzing causes and effects. The method starts with an identified (observed) undesirable *effect* (UDE) or symptom, and then is used to identify relationships between the UDE and other undesirable effects. Unlike CE and causal loop diagrams, a CRT considers whether the causes identified are *sufficient* to have resulted in the specified UDE. This "hard logic" requires that assumptions about the situation be identified, and that as many facets of the problem as possible be uncovered, which leads to the identification of underlying causes (root causes or core problems).[20]

For example, suppose one possible source of a malfunctioning control system is the procedure to assemble the system. Figure 9.6 shows the CRT for the situation; it is read from the bottom to the top as follows: entities 100, 200, 300, and 400 are causes for the UDE numbered 500. The oval around the arrows indicates that these four entities are sufficient to have caused UDE 500. In the same way, entities 100, 500, 600, 700, and 800 are sufficient to have caused UDE 900.

The CRT method requires more effort than simple CE analysis, and hence is usually applicable to problems considered more severe (the 20 percent of the causes that lead to 80 percent of the problems). It is one of several "tree techniques" described in the literature on theory of constraints, including the *future reality tree* (the desired

Figure 9.6
Example of a CRT.

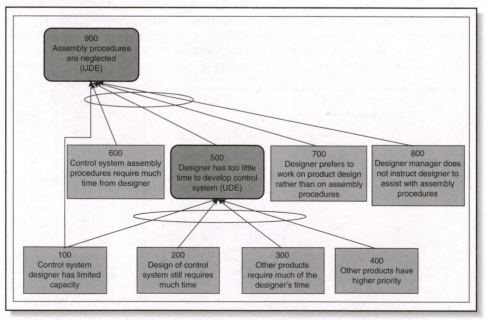

future situation after a problem has been resolved), the *prerequisite tree* (the means for overcoming barriers), and the *transition tree* (a problem-solving process).[21]

Other Tools for Quality Assurance and Control

Described elsewhere in this book are planning and control methods that also apply to quality assurance and control. For example, much quality assurance effort in a product design project is directed at focusing the project team on customer requirements, and making sure those requirements do not become distorted or misinterpreted as the project moves from stage to stage and the work changes hands. Quality function deployment (QFD), discussed in Chapter 4, addresses quality as a method for defining customer requirements and ensuring that the design and production process remains focused on those requirements. Technical Performance Measurement (TPM), discussed in Chapter 11, can also be considered a quality assurance technique.

Likewise, the checklists described earlier for preparing plans, assessing risks, and monitoring progress assist in quality by assuring that important issues are not overlooked. Such checklists are used for inspections, testing, design reviews, and FMEA. One disadvantage of checklists is that people come to rely on them and, thus, ignore issues *not* on the list. The last item on every checklist should be "Now, list all the perceived important items not on this checklist, and check them too!"

9.5   SUMMARY

Project schedules, budgets, and quality management address the three dimensions of project goals: to finish on time and on budget, and to satisfy requirements. Project quality takes into account compliance of deliverables to specifications, fitness for the purpose, and customer expectations. It does not necessarily imply the highest grade, most product features, or even zero defects. What it does imply is whatever is "best" based upon customer expectations and the intended use of the deliverable.

Quality management includes three processes: *quality planning*, *quality assurance*, and *quality control*. Quality planning is a part of project planning, and involves setting standards and specifications to be met, identifying quality-related activities in the project, and scheduling and budgeting of these activities. Quality assurance is performing the planned quality activities and ensuring that the project utilizes whatever resources are necessary to meet the requirements. Quality control is the ongoing process of monitoring and appraising work for quality assurance, and taking corrective action. It is a part of project control, and includes inspection, testing, and *ad hoc* problem-solving.

Project management has benefited primarily from the quality philosophies of TQM and Six Sigma, both of which emphasize continuous improvement. In a project environment, the quality assurance process and systematic project closeouts with documented lessons learned support continuous improvement.

Project management has also benefited from many of the techniques popularized by the so-called quality movements, including statistical methods and basic problem-solving tools used for manufacturing and production. Beyond these, however, project quality management utilizes techniques applicable to all engineering and technical endeavors, including design reviews, configuration identification, classification of characteristics, and FMEA, as well as experimenting, modeling, and prototyping. Many of the techniques are also applicable to project risk management, the subject of Chapter 10.

REVIEW QUESTIONS AND PROBLEMS

1. Describe your understanding of "quality."
2. A Rolls Royce is a high-quality vehicle. Is this always true? Consider different users and uses.
3. How does compliance to specification differ from satisfying requirements?
4. What is the difference between *satisfying requirements* and *fitness for purpose*? Explain.
5. Explain the difference between *quality* and *grade*.
6. How does the role of the quality manager (a functional manager) regarding quality planning differ from that of the project manager?
7. Indicate for each of the following whether to apply for a modification, a deviation, or a waiver:
   a. The supplier of oil filters to an automobile manufacturer says it plans to terminate production of a filter to be used on a car that is being developed.
   b. An inspector has discovered a kink in reinforcing steel. A structural engineer says that, while the steel will not comply with her drawings, the kink will have no negative effect on the strength of the steel.
   c. A damaged ship has to be repaired. The corrosion protective coating specified is not available; however a more expensive (but acceptable) coating is available.
8. Describe the differences between design reviews and audits.
9. Discuss how design reviews contribute to the approach of concurrent engineering.
10. Explain how a narrow tolerance on a manufacturing drawing differs from the characteristic being classified as critical or major.
11. Explain how classification of *defects* differs from classification of *characteristics*.
12. Discuss the relationship between project risk management and project quality management.
13. Describe how FMEA resembles the risk management approach described in Chapter 10.
14. Perform an FMEA analysis on an electric kettle with cord and plug.
15. How do client tests for acceptance differ from tests to obtain design information?
16. How would you expect the bars of a Pareto diagram to change as the result of an improvement program?
17. How does the information on the x-axis of a Pareto diagram in project control differ from the information on the x-axis of a Pareto diagram constructed to analyze defects in a mass production environment?
18. Describe the pros and cons of CE diagrams, causal loop diagrams, and CRT.
19. Why does it make sense to construct a Pareto diagram before constructing a CRT?

QUESTIONS ABOUT THE STUDY PROJECT

1. In which ways would you be able to uncover client expectations that have not been articulated explicitly?
2. Develop a quality plan for your project to form part of an integrated project management plan. Include quality management policies, standards, and specifications to meet metrics for meeting specifications/standards, training, and criteria for authorizing project phases, and discuss the use of specific tools and techniques for quality assurance and quality control.
3. Discuss how the quality plan is integrated with the schedule, budget, and risk management plan, and, if applicable, with the procurement plan.

4. Identify project budget items that aim to reduce the cost of external failures.
5. Draw a CE diagram, a causal loop diagram, a CRT, and a Pareto diagram to illustrate a project management problem that you have experienced in your study project.
6. Compile a list of "lessons learned," and indicate how these lessons could contribute to more successful future projects.

Case 9.1   Ceiling Panel Collapse in the Big Dig Project

(For more about the Big Dig Project—Boston's Central Artery/Tunnel Project, see Chapter 14, Example 14.4 and Case 14.3.)

Boston, July 11, 2006—four concrete panels weighing about 3 tons each fell from the ceiling of a Big Dig tunnel, crushing a woman in a car to death. The accident occurred in a 200-foot section that connects the Massachusetts Turnpike to the Ted Williams Tunnel. Said the Modern Continental Company, the contractor for that section of the project, "We are confident that our work fully complied with the plans and specifications provided by the Central Artery Tunnel Project. In addition, the work was inspected and approved by the project manager."[22]

The panels, installed in 1999, are held with metal trays secured to the tunnel ceiling with epoxy and bolts. The epoxy–bolt system is a tried-and-true method: holes are drilled into the concrete ceiling, cleaned, and filled with high-strength epoxy; a bolt is screwed into the hole; as the epoxy cures it bonds to the bolt. "That technique is used extensively," said an engineering professor at the Massachusetts Institute of Technology.[23] For work like the Big Dig's ceiling, he said, safety "redundancies" are added; that is, enough epoxy-and-bolt anchors that would hold the ceiling panels even if some failed. But in the connector tunnel, he contended, too few anchors were used. "They didn't have enough to carry the load. There was no room for error." He added, however, the evidence was preliminary, and such a conclusion would be premature.

Some of the bolts in the ceiling wreckage had very little epoxy, and three of them had none. State Attorney General Thomas Reilly's investigation is focusing on whether the epoxy used failed, or construction workers who installed the bolts misused or omitted the epoxy. An accident caused by improper installation or errors in mixing the epoxy, he said, would implicate the tunnel's design and designers. (Epoxy requires on-site mixing before use.) He added that some documents reflected a "substantial dispute" among engineers over the anchor system's adequacy to support the weight of the ceiling panels.

Seven years before the accident, Safety Officer John Keaveney wrote a memo to one of his superiors at contractor Modern Continental Construction Co. saying he could not "comprehend how this structure can withhold the test of time."[24] He said his superiors at Modern Continental and representatives from Big Dig project manager Bechtel/Parsons Brinckerhoff (B/PB) assured him the system had been tested and proven. Keaveney told the Boston Globe he began to worry about the ceiling panels after a third-grade class toured the Big Dig in 1999. While showing the class some concrete ceiling panels and pointing to bolts in the ceiling, a girl asked, "Will those things hold up the concrete?" "I said, 'Yes, it will hold,' but then I thought about it."

Some have argued that the investigation should look at the tunnel's design: Why were the concrete panels so heavy, weighing 2½ to 3 tons apiece? Why were they there at all? And why did the failure of a single steel hanger send 6 to 10 of the panels crashing down? Eyewitness report indicate the accident began with a loud snap as a steel hanger gave way, which set off a chain reaction that caused other hangers holding up a 40-foot steel bar to fail and send 12 tons of concrete smashing below. Were the bars under-designed to handle the weight?

Investigators are also looking at whether the use of the wrong epoxy may have played a role.[25] Invoices from 1999 show that at least one case of a quick-drying epoxy was used to secure ceiling bolts rather than the standard epoxy specified by the designers. The epoxy holds 25 percent less weight than standard epoxy.

Additional issues raised during the investigation include the following:[26]

- Design changes that resulted in the use of concrete ceiling panels in the connector tunnel which are heavier than panels used in the Ted Williams Tunnel
- The lack of steel supports in sections of the connector tunnel ceiling to which bolts holding the concrete panels could have been connected
- Possible tunnel damage caused by blast vibrations from nearby construction of an office tower
- Use of diamond-tipped drill bits, instead of carbide bits, in drilling holes for the bolts (epoxy may not hold as well in smoother holes drilled with diamond bits)
- Impact of cold weather during installation of the epoxy–bolt system.

B/PB, the project management contractor, said in a statement: "Determining the causes of this specific failure will require a thorough forensic analysis of design, methods, materials, procedures, and documentation." As investigators scrutinize the history of the $14 billion project, criticism is reviving that Massachusetts lacked adequate supervision of private contractors. B/PB was involved in both the design and construction efforts—an arrangement some say may have compromised oversight. "There was no one checking the checkers," said one US Representative. Wrote one blogger: "I wouldn't want to be the registered engineer whose signature is on the design. It will be his fault if the materials and workmanship are found not to be up to specifications. But who knows if it is his fault. This is a huge mess and the whole bunch of them, engineers, managers, inspectors, and testers, should be investigated."[27]

QUESTIONS

1. With 20–20 hindsight, draw a CE (fishbone, Ishikawa) diagram to illustrate possible causes and effects. Include the possible causes mentioned in the case. The diagram should have been developed before construction; therefore, also indicate other possible failure modes and other causes you can think of. How would the diagram (developed after the accident) be of value during litigation?
2. List the characteristics that should have been classified as critical.
3. Propose guidelines for a process to ensure that the epoxy would provide sufficient bonding to the concrete ceiling.
4. Explain the role that configuration management should have played in preventing the accident.
5. What role could modeling/prototyping, lab-

oratory tests, checklists, and training have played?
6. Explain how someone within B/PB would be accountable regardless of the findings of a forensic investigation. Would B/PB be off the hook if a subcontractor were found guilty?
7. What would the implications have been if the engineer who signed off on a specific design was an engineer-in-training instead of a registered engineer?
8. Comment on the relationship between project quality management and project risk management. How could risk management have prevented the accident? How does project quality management relate to project cost management?
9. Comment on the contribution that inspection and audits could have played.

Case 9.2 FIFA 2010 World Cup South Africa™[28]

Ten South African cities were selected for hosting the FIFA 2010 World Cup soccer games. In some cities existing soccer stadiums had to be upgraded, while in others new stadiums had to

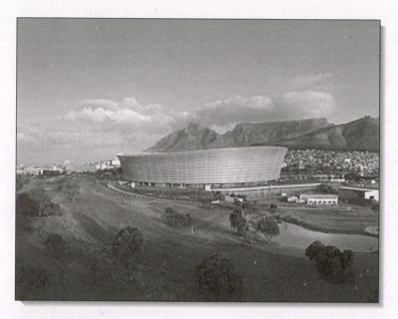

Figure 9.7
Cape Town Stadium.
Courtesy Murray & Roberts Holdings, Ltd.

be built at a cost of approximately R17b (approximately US$2.4b). A centerpiece stadium for the 2010 World Cup games is the newly constructed Cape Town Stadium, shown in Figure 9.7. The requirements for the once-off FIFA matches typically far exceeded what would be required by stadium owners after the games ended. For example, each stadium would normally make provision for about 200 journalists for an ordinary international match, but FIFA required 2,000 for the final game; normally a stadium would require about 10 broadcasting positions, but FIFA required 150. It therefore made sense to design facilities for normal use after the games, and to meet the temporary FIFA requirements by adding temporary items, the latter called the "Overlay." The Overlay, which would be removed after the event, included extra commentary positions, press desks, security equipment, hospitality tents, as well as numerous additional cables and other equipment. It was obviously easier to design accommodations for the Overlay in new "greenfield" stadiums than in existing stadiums that had to be upgraded.

The major stakeholders involved in the design and construction of the stadia are listed in Table 9.4. These stakeholders had to interface with each other and with additional role players needed for the Overlay, such as national security services and police, local transport organizations, and owners of land and buildings, including schools.

The FIFA publication, *Football Stadiums Handbook*, provides guidelines for planning and executing FIFA events, and is updated after each FIFA World Cup event. Members of the LOC made several visits to Europe to learn from the 2006 FIFA World Cup event held in Germany and the Euro 2008 event held in Austria and Switzerland. One LOC member commented that items that were on the "wish list" for the 2006 World Cup in Germany had become the norm for the 2010 World Cup.

The stadiums were constructed by companies appointed by the host cities, while Overlay contractors were appointed by the LOC. Some of the subcontracts for the Overlay were controlled by the Overlay contractor, while others, such as security, electric power, back-up electricity, water supply and waste water drainage, were controlled by others. While the Overlay contractors reported to the LOC, the host cities authorized them to take over spaces to construct the Overlay. The different parties, such as the LOC and their Overlay contractors, as well as host cities and their stadium contractors, worked in the same spaces at the same time, but with different responsibilities

Table 9.4 Main Stakeholders in FIFA 2010 and Their Roles

STAKEHOLDERS	ROLES
FIFA (International Federation of Association Football) (French: *Fédération Internationale de Football Association*)	Main customer
Host cities and their planners	Provide infrastructure, including match venues, training venues and roads
Stadium owners (in some cases the sporting bodies owned the stadiums, but most were owned by the host cities)	Customers with requirements regarding their properties
SA Government (Treasury and Department of Sport)	Financial guarantees
Task team appointed by the South African Government	Monitor and control finance on behalf of Government
South African Football Association (SAFA)	Arrange the World Cup on behalf of FIFA
Local Organizing Committee (LOC)	Arrange World Cup on behalf of SAFA; design, construct and finance the Overlay
LOC Technical Team (reporting to LOC Executive Committee and Board)	Inform host cities about FIFA and Government requirements and assist with interpretation of requirements Combine the technical guides from: • TV host broadcaster • Hospitality rights holder • Media rights holders • FIFA Marketing & Security • LOC constituent groups Prepare a Technical Guide to assist the host city planners on the requirements Monitor and report to the LOC Executive Committee and Board regarding: • Quality • Progress • Finance • FIFA Compliance
Stadium designers and construction companies	Design and construction of stadiums
Host city professionals	Design and construction of the precinct (surrounds) and the access roads
Overlay contractors (designers and suppliers), appointed by the LOC	Specifications and supply of Overlay items

and reporting structures. This posed a challenge for coordination, and caused some conflict.

Once a stadium was nearly completed, a process was followed where all the relevant stakeholders were required to attend an on-site inspection, with sign-off agreed by all of them. A series of such events was properly recorded by minutes and photographic recordings.

Reviews and audits on progress to ensure that all the stadiums and other spaces were FIFA compliant were mainly done by the LOC Technical Team. FIFA, LOC, and government constituent groups also regularly visited the host cities to inform, assess, and assist the host cities with FIFA compliance. These meetings were chaired by FIFA, though one member of the technical team later remarked: "This was a mistake—LOC should have taken control." In between these meetings, virtual tours were undertaken where the relevant stakeholders would assemble in Johannesburg and the host cities would present their progress through multimedia means, which included satellite link-up with the FIFA Headquarters in Zurich, Switzerland. This process ensured that all the host cities and their technical teams were fully aware of the requirements. It also afforded them the opportunity to discuss any concerns they had with the customers.

QUESTIONS

1. Given two sets of requirements, one for the FIFA games and the other for after the games, what would be an appropriate way to define "quality"?
2. List the quality management activities mentioned in the case.
3. (a) Comment on the reporting structures and responsibility for audits and reviews. (b) Who should have provided quality guarantees? (c) What planning processes and techniques would have been helpful regarding the roles of the various stakeholders?
4. Comment on the problem of people from different organizations working in the same space at the same time.

NOTES

1. Carruthers MC. *Principles of Management for Quality Projects.* London: International Thompson Press; 1999.
2. *Ibid.*
3. Yourdan E. *Rise and Resurrection of the American Programmer.* Upper Saddle River, NJ: Yourdan Press/Prentice Hall; 1998. pp. 157–181.
4. Crosby P. *Quality Is Free.* New York, NY: McGraw-Hill, 1979.
5. Bach J. The challenge of "good enough" software. *American Programmer* 8(10); 1995: 2–11.
6. Nicholas J. *Lean Production for Competitive Advantage: A Comprehensive Guide to Lean Methodologies and Management Practices.* Boca Raton, FL: CRC/Productivity Press; 2011.
7. See Mascitelli R. *The Lean Product Development Guidebook: Everything Your Design Team Needs to Improve Efficiency and Slash Time to Market.* Technology Perspectives, http://www.design-for-lean.com/; 2006 Lean Construction Institute. Homepage reads "We aim to extend to the construction industry the Lean production revolution started in manufacturing." http://www.leanconstruction.org/.
8. International Systems Organization. *ISO 9001 Quality Management Systems—Requirements.* Geneva: ISO; 2008.
9. Crosby P, *ibid.*
10. Kransdorff A. The role of the post-project analysis. *The Learning Organization* 3(1); 1996: 11–15.
11. The ISO/CD 10007 standard offers guidelines on configuration management systems: International Standards Organization, *ISO/CD 1007 Quality Management Systems—Guidelines for Configuration Management.* Geneva: ISO; 2003.
12. Gray M. *Angle of Attack: Harrison Storms and the Race to the Moon.* New York, NY: W.W. Norton; 1997. pp. 170–171.
13. East E, Kirby J, and Perez G. Improved design review through Web collaboration. *Journal of Management in Engineering* April; 2004: 51–55.
14. From Muirhead B and Simon W. *High Velocity Leadership: The Mars Pathfinder Approach to Faster, Better, Cheaper.* New York, NY: Harper Business; 1999. pp. 06–09, 178–179.
15. http://www.boeing.com/commercial/777family/pf/pf_computing.html, accessed August 2006.
16. Ishikawa K. *What Is Quality Control?* Englewood Cliffs, NJ: Prentice Hall; 1982.
17. Bamford D and Greatbanks R. The use of quality management tools and techniques: a study of application in everyday situations. *International Journal of Quality and Reliability Management* 22(4); 2005.
18. Juran J and Gryna F. *Juran's Quality Control Handbook*, 4th edn. New York, NY: McGraw-Hill; 1988.
19. Sherwood D. *Seeing the Forest for the Trees—A Manager's Guide to Applying Systems Thinking.* London: Nicholas Brealey Publishing; 2002; Sterman JD. *Business Dynamics: Systems Thinking and Modeling for a Complex World.* New York, NY: McGraw-Hill; 2000.

20. Steinkopf L. *Thinking for a Change—Putting the TOC Thinking Processes to Use.* New York, NY: St Lucie Press; 1999.
21. Goldratt E. *What Is This Thing Called Theory of Constraints and How Should It Be Implemented?* New York, NY: North River Press, Inc; 1990.
22. Belluck P and Zezima K. Accident in Boston's Big Dig Kills Woman in Car. *New York Times* July 12; 2006.
23. Bradley M. Bolt Failure at Big Dig: an anomaly? *The Christian Science Monitor* July 21; 2006.
24. Murphy S. Memo Warned of Ceiling Collapse: Safety Officer Feared Deaths in '99, Now Agonizes Over Tragedy. *Boston Globe* July 26; 2006.
25. Allen S and Murphy S. Big Dig Job May Have Used Wrong Epoxy. *Boston Globe* May 3; 2007.
26. Drake B. Investigators Probe Boston Tunnel Design. CENews.com; September 1, 2006, www.cenews.com/article.asp?id=1108 (accessed May 15, 2007).
27. Waters R. Physics forums, www.physicsforums.com/showthread.php?t=126374, russ_waters July 17; 2006 (accessed May 20, 2007).
28. Personal communication, Eugene van Vuuren. Member of the LOC Technical Team.

Chapter 10

Managing Risks in Projects

> Life "looks just a little more mathematical and regular than it is; its exactitude is obvious, but its inexactitude is hidden; its wildness lies in wait."
>
> —G. K. CHESTERTON[1]

> When our world was created, nobody remembered to include certainty
>
> —PETER BERNSTEIN[2]

*E*very project is risky, meaning there is a chance things won't turn out exactly as planned. Project outcomes result from many things, including some that are not predictable and over which project managers have little control. Risk level is associated with the certainty of outcomes. High-certainty outcomes have low risk; low-certainty outcomes have high risk. Certainty derives from knowledge and experience gained in prior projects, as well as from management's ability to mitigate project risks and respond to emerging problems.[3]

10.1 RISK CONCEPTS

Risk is a function of the uniqueness of a project and the experience of the project team. When activities are routine or have been performed many times before, managers can anticipate the range of potential outcomes and manipulate the system design and project plan to achieve the desired outcomes. However, when the work is unique or the team is inexperienced the potential outcomes are less certain, making it difficult to anticipate problems or know how to avoid them. Even routine projects have risks, because outcomes may be influenced by factors that are new and emerging, or beyond anyone's control.

The notion of project risk involves two concepts:

1. The *likelihood* that some problematical event will occur.
2. The *impact* of the event if it does occur.

Risk is a joint function of the two:

$$\text{Risk} = f\,(\text{likelihood, impact})$$

A project might be considered risky whenever at least one—either the likelihood or the impact—is large. For example, a project will be considered risky when the potential impact is human fatality or massive financial loss even when the likelihood is small. (Risk can also mean *opportunities*—e.g., the potential for additional rewards, savings, or benefits. Typically, however, risk identification is focused on the risk of failure.)

Many managers are accustomed to dealing with facts, figures, and hard numbers, so they find the concept of risk and the unknown hard to deal with. Faced with uncertainty, they prefer to ignore that there might be problems—though, of course, that doesn't make the problems go away.

Although risk cannot be eliminated, it can be reduced and plans readied in case things go wrong; this is the purpose of risk management. The process and elements of risk management are shown in Figure 10.1.

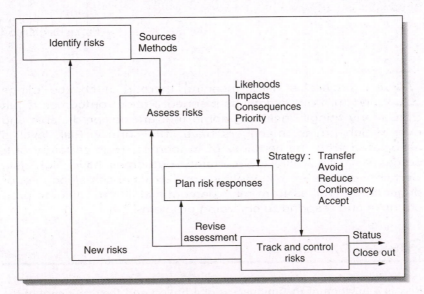

Figure 10.1
Risk management elements and process.

You can only manage things you are aware of. Thus, risk management begins with identifying the risks and predicting their consequences.

Risk in projects is sometimes referred to as the risk of *failure*, which implies that a project might fall short of schedule, budget, or technical performance goals by a significant margin.

Among ways to identify project risks, one is to proceed according to project chronology—that is, to look at the phases and stages in the life cycle (feasibility, contract negotiation, system concept, or definition, design, etc.) and identify the risks in each. Each phase presents unique hurdles and problems that could halt the project immediately or lead to later failure. In product development projects the risk of failure tends to be high in the early stages of preliminary design, but diminishes later. Some risks of failure are persistent, such as the loss of funding or management commitment.

Risk can also be identified by type of work or technical function, such as engineering risks associated with product reliability and maintainability, or production risks associated with the manufacturability of a product or availability of raw materials.

Risk identification starts in the conception phase, and focuses on those high risk factors that would make the project difficult or destined to fail. High risk typically stems from:

- Using an unusual approach
- Attempting to develop a system while furthering technology at the same time
- Developing and testing new equipment, systems, or procedures
- Operating in an unpredictable or variable environment.

Sources or causes of high risk must be studied and well understood before the project can be approved and funds committed. Risks identified in the conception phase are often broadly defined and subjectively assessed, though they might also be analyzed using the methods discussed later. When multiple, competing projects are under consideration, an assessment is performed to decide which of them, based upon trade-offs of the relative risks, benefits, and available funding, is best.[4] Comparing and selecting projects based upon criteria such as risk is discussed in Chapter 17.

Causes of Risk

Any uncertain factor that can influence the outcome of a project is a *risk cause* or *risk hazard*. Identifying risk causes involves learning as much as possible about what things could go wrong and the outcome for each, and it includes trying to identify things you don't already know—the "unknown unknowns."

Risk in projects can be classified as internal risks and external risks.

Internal Risks

Internal risks originate inside the project, and project managers and stakeholders usually have some measure of control over them. Three main categories of internal risks are market risk, assumptions risk, and technical risk.

Market risk is the risk of not fulfilling market needs or the requirements of particular customers. Sources of market risk include:

- Failure to completely or adequately define market or customer needs and requirements
- Failure to identify changing needs and requirements
- Failure to identify newly introduced products by competitors.

Market risk stems from the developer misreading the market environment. It can be reduced by working closely with the customer; thoroughly defining needs and requirements early in the project; closely monitoring trends and developments among markets, customers, and competitors; and updating requirements as needed throughout the project.

Assumptions risk is risk associated with the numerous implicit or explicit assumptions made in feasibility studies and project plans during project conception and definition. The risk of meeting time, cost, and technical requirements depends on the accuracy of many assumptions.

Technical risk is the risk of encountering technical problems with the end-item or project activities. (Sometimes these risks are listed in special categories—*schedule risks* being those that would cause delays, *cost risks* those that would lead to overruns, and so on.) Technical risk is high in projects that involve new and untried technical applications, but is low in projects that involve familiar activities done in customary ways.

One approach to expressing technical risk is to rate the project end-item or primary process as being high, medium, or low according to the following features.[5]

- *Maturity*: how experienced or knowledgeable the project team is in the project technology. An end-item or process that takes advantage of existing experience and knowledge is less risky than one that is innovative, somewhat untried, or cutting edge.

- *Complexity*: how many steps, elements, or components are in the product or process, and how tightly interrelated they are. An end-item or process with numerous, interrelated steps or components is riskier than one with few steps and simple relationships.

- *Quality*: how producible, reliable, and testable the end-item or process is. In general, an end-item or process that has been produced and is reliable and/or testable is less risky than one that has yet to be produced or has unknown reliability or testability.

- *Concurrency* or *Dependency*: The extent to which multiple activities in the project overlap or are dependent. Sequential activities with no overlap are less risky than activities with much overlap (e.g., the discrete-staged approach is less risky than fast-tracking).

External Risks

These originate from outside the project, and project managers often have limited or no control over them. External risk hazards include:

Market conditions	Customer needs and behavior
Competitors' actions	Supplier relations and business failures
Government regulations	Physical environment (weather, terrain)
Interest rates and exchange rates	Labor availability (strikes and walkouts)
Decisions by senior management or the customer regarding project priorities, staffing, or budgets	Material or labor resources (shortages)
	External control by customers or subcontractors over project work and resources
Subcontractor failure	

Any of these can affect the success of a project. Failure to identify or successfully react to them would be an internal risk.

Identification Techniques

Projects risks are identified in many ways; the principle methods are project analogy, checklists, WBS analysis, process flowcharts, project networks, cause–effect diagramming, brainstorming, and the Delphi technique.

Project Analogy

The *project analogy* method involves scrutinizing records, post-completion summary reports, and project team members' recollections from earlier analogous projects to identify risks in new, upcoming projects. The better the documentation (the more complete, accurate, and well-catalogued) of past projects and the better peoples' memories, the more useful these are as sources for identifying risks. The method requires more than just investigating past projects; it requires investigating projects that are similar in significant ways to the project for which risks are being assessed. *Knowledge management* methods, described in Chapter 16, promote learning from past projects that can help anticipate risks in new ones.

Checklist

Documentation from prior projects is also used to create risk *checklists*—lists of risk sources in projects. A checklist is originally created from the experiences from past projects, and is updated as new experience is gained from recent projects. Risk checklists can pertain to the project as a whole, or to specific phases, work packages, or tasks within the project.

To illustrate, the checklist in Table 10.1 shows the risk severity associated with three categories of risk sources: (1) status of implementation plan, (2) number of module interfaces, and (3) percentage of components that require testing. Suppose, for example, an upcoming project will use a standard plan, have eight module interfaces,

Table 10.1 Risk Checklist

RISK SOURCES	RISK LEVEL
Status of implementation plan	
1. No plan required	None
2. Standard plan, existing, complete	Low
3. Plan being prepared	Medium
4. Plan not started	High
Number of interfaces between modules	
1. Less than 5	None
2. 5–10	Low
3. 11–20	Medium
4. More than 20	High
Percent of system components requiring tests	
1. 0–1	None
2. 2–10	Low
3. 11–30	Medium
4. Over 30	High

and test 16 percent of the system components. According to the checklist, the project will be rated as low, low, and medium, respectively, for the three risk sources.

The more experience a company or managers gain with projects, the more they learn about the risks, and the more comprehensive they can make the checklists. As experience grows with completed projects, the checklists are expanded and updated. While a checklist cannot guarantee that all significant risk sources in a project will be identified, it does help ensure that the important known ones won't be overlooked.

A variant of the checklist is the *risk matrix*, a table wherein the columns are the project phases and the rows the sources of risks. The cells of the matrix indicate the presence, absence, or severity of a specified risk for the phase of the project.

A disadvantage of risk checklists is that people might look only the risks listed and not consider any not on the list. Checklists therefore need to be supplemented by other methods.

Work Breakdown Structure (WBS)

Risks can be identified through analysis of the WBS. Every work package is scrutinized for potential technical hurdles or problems with management, customers, suppliers, equipment, or resource availability. Processes or end-items within each work package are assessed for internal risks in terms of, for example, complexity, maturity, quality, and concurrency. The work package is also assessed for external risks—for example, relying on a subcontractor to manage the work package.

Process Flowchart

Project risks can also be identified from process *flowcharts*. A flowchart illustrates the steps, procedures, and flows between tasks and activities in a process. Examination of a flowchart can pinpoint potential trouble spots and areas of risk.

Project Networks and Convergence Points

Similarly, risks can be identified through scrutiny of the precedence relationships and concurrent or sequential scheduling of activities in *project networks* (Chapters 6 and 7). For example, risk sometimes increases at merge points in the project network. At these points, work performed by different teams comes together and must be integrated; sometimes only then do errors become evident, such as subsystems produced by two teams not matching up or functioning correctly. The risk of project delay from this so-called "merge-point bias" is discussed in Chapter 7.

Cause-and-Effect Diagram and Brainstorming

Risks can be identified from the collective experiences of project team members who participate in a *brainstorming* session to share opinions about possible risk sources in the project, and record them on a *cause-and-effect* (CE) *diagram* as shown in Figure 10.2. Brainstorming and CE diagrams are used in two ways: (1) Given an identified, potential outcome (*effect*), to identify the potential *causes* (sources); (2) Given a risk source (*cause*), to identify the outcomes that might ensue (*effects*). Figure 10.2 illustrates the first use: For the effect "completion delay," it shows the potential sources leading to a delay.

The diagram in Figure 10.2 is divided into the generic risk categories of software, hardware, and so on. (Other possible categories include poor time and cost estimates, design errors or omissions, requirements (scope) creep, and unavailability of resources.) Each category is broken down into more fundamental sources of risk. In Figure 10.2, for example, the category "staff" includes the risk of "staff shortage," which could be caused by the inability to hire and train additional staff. Analysis techniques related to CE are further discussed in Chapter 9.

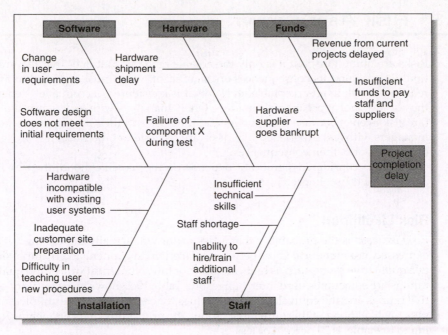

Figure 10.2
Cause-and-effect diagram.

To encourage original thinking and generation of the most comprehensive list of risks possible, risks should *not* be assessed while they are being identified. Any early mention that a risk is "unrealistic" or "impossible" might lead to some very important risks being discarded. Hence, no risks should be assessed until a comprehensive list of all identified risks has first been compiled.

Delphi Technique

The term *Delphi* refers to a group survey technique for combining the opinions of several people to develop a single judgment. Developed by the Rand Corporation in 1950, the technique comprises a series of structured questions and feedback reports. Each respondent is given a series questions (e.g., what are the five most significant risks in this project?), for which he writes his opinions and reasons. The responses of everyone surveyed are summarized in one report that is given to everyone. Seeing others' opinions, respondents have the opportunity to modify their own opinions. Because the written responses are anonymous, no one feels pressured to conform to others' opinions. If people change their opinions, they must explain the reasons why; if they don't, they must also explain why. The process continues until the group reaches a collective opinion. Studies have proven the technique to be an effective way of reaching consensus.[6]

Risk Symptoms and Triggers

As the sources and outcomes of each risk are identified, so are its *symptoms*, which are *visible indicators* or warning signs that the risk is materializing; these serve as a *trigger* to initiate counteractions or contingencies to mitigate or combat the risk. For example, for the risk "failure to meet technical requirements," a symptom might be "failure of component X during test"; should that symptom be observed, it would trigger the action "move to design plan B."

Risks are ubiquitous, but it is only the notable or significant ones that require attention. If a risk and its consequences are significant, ways must be found to avoid or reduce the risk to an acceptable level. What is considered "acceptable" depends on the *risk tolerance* of project stakeholders. Often, managers with experience avoid risks (are risk averse) because they understand the risks and their consequences, whereas managers with less experience take risks (are risk tolerant) because they are ignorant of the risks or of their consequences.

What is considered significant depends on the risk likelihood, the risk impact, and the risk consequence.

Risk Likelihood

Risk likelihood is the probability that a risk factor will actually materialize.[7] It can be expressed as a numerical value between 1.0 (certain to happen) and 0 (impossible), or as a qualitative rating such as high, medium, or low. Numerical values and qualitative ratings are sometimes used interchangeably. Table 10.2 shows an example of qualitative ratings and the equivalent percent values for each. When, for example, someone says the likelihood of this or that risk is low, the probability of its happening, according to the table, is 20 percent or less.

But Table 10.2 is an illustration only. The association between qualitative ratings and particular numerical values is subjective, and depends on the experience of the project team and the risk tolerance of stakeholders. For example, Table 10.2 might be for a project with high economic stakes, and therefore a numerical likelihood greater than 50 percent equates to "high risk." In a project with low economic stakes, "high risk" might equate to a numerical likelihood of 75 percent or more. Often, people have difficulty agreeing on the qualitative rating for a given numerical likelihood value and *vice versa*, even when they have the same information or experience; this is described below in Example 10.2.

Table 10.3 is a checklist for five potential sources of failure in computer systems projects and associated numerical likelihoods.[8] For example, looking at only the M_S column, the likelihood of failure for existing software is low, but for state-of-the-art software it is high. Again, the likelihood values are illustrative, and would be tailored to each project depending on the prior experience and opinion of stakeholders. A likelihood estimate based on the opinions of several individuals (assuming all have relevant experience) is usually more valid than one based on only a few.

When a project has multiple, independent risk sources (as is common), they can be combined into a single *composite likelihood factor*, or *CLF*. Using the sources listed in Table 10.3, the CLF can be computed as a weighted average:

Table 10.2 Risk Likelihood: Qualitative Ratings for Quantitative Values

QUALITATIVE	NUMERICAL
Low	0–0.20
Medium	0.21–0.50
High	0.51–1.00

Table 10.3 Sources of Failure and Likelihood*

Likelihood	M_H	M_S	C_H	C_S	D
0.1 (Low)	Existing	Existing	Simple design	Simple design	Independent
0.3 (Minor)	Minor redesign	Minor redesign	Minor complexity	Minor complexity	Schedule dependent on existing system
0.5 (Moderate)	Major change feasible	Major change feasible	Moderate complexity	Moderate	Performance dependent on existing system
0.7 (Significant)	Complex design; technology exists	New, but similar to existing software	Significant complexity	Significant complexity	Schedule dependent on new system
0.9 (High)	State of the art; some research done	State of the art; never done	Extreme complexity	Extreme complexity	Performance dependent on new system

* M_S, failure likelihood due to immaturity of software; C_S, failure likelihood due to complexity of software; M_H, failure likelihood due to immaturity of hardware; C_H, failure likelihood due to complexity of hardware; D, failure likelihood due to dependency on external factors.

Note: "failure" refers to not meeting technical goals.
Adapted from Roetzheim W. *Structured Computer Project Management*. Upper Saddle River, NJ: Prentice Hall; 1988: 23–26.

$$CLF = (W1)M_H + (W2)C_H + (W3)M_S + (W4)C_S + (W5)D \qquad (10.1)$$

where W1, W2, W3, W4, and W5 each have values 0 through 1.0 and together total 1.0.

Example 10.1: Computation of CLF

The ROSEBUD project involves development of hardware and software with characteristics as follows. The hardware is existing, and of minor complexity; the software is moderately complex and will be developed as a minor redesign of current software; and the performance of the overall system depends on how well it can be integrated into another, larger system. Thus, from Table 10.3, $M_H = 0.1$, $C_H = 0.3$, $M_S = 0.5$, $C_S = 0.3$, and $D = 0.5$. Assuming all sources are rated equally at 0.2, then

$$CLF = (0.2)0.1 + (0.2)0.3 + (0.2)0.5 + (0.2)0.3 + (0.2)0.5 = 0.34$$

The application of this CLF is discussed later.

Note that the computation in equation (10.1) assumes that the risk sources are *independent*. If they are not—if, for example, failure due to software complexity depends on failure due to hardware complexity—then the individual likelihoods cannot be summed. In such a situation, the sources would be subjectively combined into one source ("failure due to a combination of software and hardware complexity") and a single likelihood value based on judgment assigned.

One way to show the interdependency of risk factors is with an *influence diagram* (a variation of the causal-loop diagram described in Chapter 9). An example is Figure 10.3.[9] To construct the diagram, start with a list of previously identified risks (e.g., from Figure 10.2) and draw them as shown in Figure 10.3. Then look at each risk and ask whether it is influenced by, or has influence on, any of the other risks. If so, draw arrows between the related risks to indicate the direction of influence (e.g., S.1

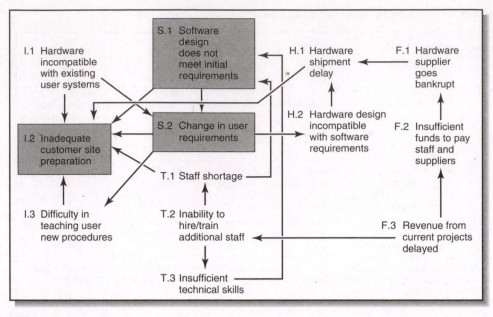

Figure 10.3
Influence diagram.

influences S.2 and I.2). To minimize confusion, keep the number of risks on the diagram small, about 15 or fewer.

Risks with the most connections are the most important. In Figure 10.3, risks I.2, S.1, and S.2 are each influenced by other risks, which would increase their failure likelihood.

Risk likelihood is also affected by the future: *ceteris paribus*, activities planned further in the future are more risky (have greater likelihood of failure) than those closer at hand.[10] This is because activities farther in the future have greater chances of being influenced by unknowns. After the project enters execution and moves toward completion, the likelihood of failure diminishes. But there is a trade-off: although risks diminish as the project progresses, the *stakes* in the project—the amount of human and financial capital sunk into it—increase, which means that the loss suffered from a failure later in the project will be much greater than the loss if suffered earlier. Risk does not disappear; it remains an important matter throughout the project.

Risk Impact

What would happen if a risk hazard materialized? The result would be a *risk impact*. A poorly marked highway intersection is a risk hazard; it poses the risk impact of a collision and injury or death. Risk impact in projects can be specified in terms of time, cost, performance, publicity, pollution, and so on. For example, the impact of insufficient resources might be failure to meet schedule or user requirements.

Risk impact can be expressed as a qualitative rating, such as high, medium, or low, based upon a manager's or expert's judgment about the impact. For example, a risk leading to a schedule delay of 1 month might be considered "medium impact," whereas a delay of 3 or more months might be deemed "high impact."

Risk impact also can be expressed as a numerical measure between 0 and 1.0, where 0 is "not serious" and 1.0 is "catastrophic." Again, the rating is subjective and

Table 10.4 Impact Values for Different Technical, Cost, and Time Situations

IMPACT VALUE	TECHNICAL IMPACT (TI)	COST IMPACT (CI)	SCHEDULE IMPACT (SI)
0.1 (Low)	Minimal impact	Within budget	Negligible impact; compensated by scheduled slack time
0.3 (Minor)	Small reduction in performance	1–10% cost increase	Minor slip (<1 month)
0.5 (Moderate)	Moderate reduction in performance	10–25% cost increase	Moderate slip (1–3 months)
0.7 (Significant)	Significant reduction in performance	25–50% cost increase	Significant slip (>1–3 months)
0.9 (High)	Technical goals might not be achievable	Cost increase in excess of 50%	Large schedule slip (unacceptable)

Adapted from Roetzheim W. *Structured Computer Project Management*. Upper Saddle River, NJ: Prentice Hall; 1988: 23–26.

depends upon judgment. Table 10.4, for example, represents judgments about the impacts associated with various technical, cost, and schedule situations, and suggested qualitative and numerical ratings associated with each of them.[11]

The values assigned to risk impacts are largely subjective—even when derived from empirical data.

Example 10.2: Estimating Risk Likelihood and Risk Impact in New Technologies

Risk assessment in new technologies is, well, difficult. The risk of a serious problem can stem from a chain of events (e.g., a machine malfunctions, a sensor does not detect it, an operator takes the wrong action), and to assign the probability of the risk requires identifying all the events in the chain, estimating the probability of each, and combining the probabilities together. Managers and designers can try to think of every event, but they can never be sure that they haven't missed some. When a project involves new technologies, the estimates are largely guesses. In 1974, MIT released a report stating that the likelihood of a reactor core meltdown is one every 17,000 years. According to the report, a meltdown in a particular plant would occur only after *many hundreds of years* of operation, yet less than 5 years later a reactor at Three Mile Island suffered a partial core meltdown and released radioactivity into the atmosphere.[12]

The space shuttle is another case: NASA originally put the risk of a catastrophic accident at 1 in 100,000, but after the Challenger disaster revised it to 1 in 200. With the additional loss of Columbia (the second loss in 113 missions), the actual risk became 1 in 56. The shuttles originally were design-rated for 100 missions, yet Columbia broke up during its 26th.[13] Few data points (5 operational shuttles and 113 missions over 20 years) in combination with incredible complexity make it impossible to accurately predict the risks for the shuttle system, yet for many projects the data available for estimating probabilities is even sparser.

Estimating impacts is equally difficult, and experts from different fields given identical facts often reach different conclusions. In one survey that rated the hazards of nuclear waste using a 17-point scale, biologists rated it 10.1, geologists 8.3, and physicists 7.3.[14] Risk assessment depends on culture and training, and is never completely rational; because of this, it should be based upon the opinions of many experts representing a range of disciplines.

Just as the likelihoods for multiple risks can be combined, so can the impacts from multiple risk sources. A composite impact factor (CIF) can be computed using weighted average,

$$CIF = (W1)TI + (W2)CI + (W3)SI \tag{10.2}$$

where W1, W2, and W3 have values 0 through 1.0, and together sum to 1.0. CIF will have values between 0.0 and 1.0, where 0 means "no impact" and 1.0 means "the most severe impact."

Example 10.3: Computation of CIF

A particular failure in the ROSEBUD project to meet certain technical goals is expected to minimally impact technical performance and be corrected within 2 months at a cost of 20 percent. Therefore, from Table 10.4:

TI=0.1, CI=0.5, SI=0.5

Suppose the most important criteria are technical performance, followed by the schedule, then cost, and the weights assigned to the criteria are 0.5, 0.3, and 0.2, respectively. Therefore, from equation (10.2):

CIF=(0.5)(0.1)+(0.3)(0.5)+(0.2)(0.5)=0.22

Equation (10.2) assumes that the risk impacts are independent. If they are not, equation (10.2) does not apply and the single value impacts must be treated jointly, an example being: "the impact of both a 20 percent increase in cost and a 3-month schedule slip is rated as 0.6."

Another way to express risk impact is in terms of what it would take to *recover* from, or compensate for, an undesirable impact. For example, suppose that using a new technology poses a risk that performance requirements will not be met. The plan is to try out the technology, but to abandon it and use a proven approach if early tests reveal poor performance. The risk impact would be the impact of switching technologies in terms of schedule delay and additional cost—e.g., 4 months and $300,000.

Risk impact should be assessed for the entire project, and articulated with the assumption that no response or preventive measures are taken. In the above instance, $300,000 is the anticipated expense under the assumption that nothing special will be done to avoid or prevent the failure of the new technology. This assessed impact will be used as a measure to evaluate the effectiveness of possible ways to reduce or prevent risk hazards, as discussed later.[15]

Risk Consequence

Earlier, the notion of risk was defined as being a function of risk likelihood *and* risk impact; the combined consideration of both is referred to as the *risk consequence* or risk exposure.

There are two ways to express risk consequence. One way sometimes suggested is to express it as a simple numerical rating with a value ranging between 0 and 1.0. In that case, the risk consequence rating, RCR, is

$$RCR = CLF + CIF - CLF(CIF) \tag{10.3}$$

where CLF and CIF are as previously defined in equations (10.1) and (10.2). The risk consequence derived from this equation measures the seriousness of the risk. Small values represent unimportant risks that might be ignored; large values represent important risks worth a serious look. In the previous examples, the assessed CLF was 0.34 (Example 10.1) and the CIF was 0.22 (Example 10.3). Thus, the risk consequence rating is

$$RCR = 0.34 + 0.22 - (0.34)(0.22) = 0.48$$

However, the approach using equation (10.3) is problematical. The factors CLF and CIF are fundamentally different entities, one representing a probability, the other the magnitude of an impact, and, like adding meters and grams, adding CLF and CIF doesn't make sense. Neither does the product (CLF)(CIF), which is supposed to represent the "intersection" of CLF and CIF; in reality the intersection would be empty, since CLF and CIF represent different entities incapable of intersecting.[16]

A second (more sensible and common) way to express risk consequence is as an *expected value*. Expected value can be interpreted as the average outcome if an event were repeated a large number of times (for example, 100). Computed this way,

$$\text{Risk consequence} = (\text{Impact}) \times (\text{Likelihood}) \qquad (10.4)$$

Example 10.4: Risk Consequence Using Expected Value

Suppose the likelihood associated with a risk is 0.40. Also, should this risk materialize, it would set the project back 4 months and increase the cost by an estimated $300,000. The expected risk consequences for time and cost are thus:

$$\text{Risk consequence time (RT)} = (4 \text{ months})(0.40) = 1.6 \text{ months} = 6.4 \text{ weeks}$$

$$\text{Risk consequence cost (RC)} = (\$300,000)(0.40) = \$12,000$$

The concept of "expected value" is further discussed in the Appendix to this chapter.

The magnitude of the consequences—whether high, medium, or low—as a function of the specified likelihood and impact values can be determined by plotting the values on a diagram such as Figure 10.4. Just as the likelihood and impact values are subjective, so is the positioning of the isobars demarcating regions of high, medium, and low risk consequence. Interesting to note is that this method is analogous to those used to assess projects, discussed in Chapter 17; a quick comparison of Figure 10.4 and Figure 17.5 reveals the similarity.

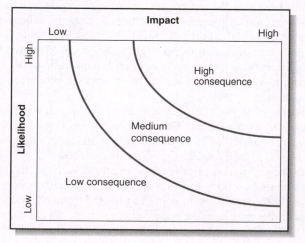

Figure 10.4
Risk consequence as a function of likelihood and impact.

The method is also similar to the Failure Mode and Effect Analysis (FMEA) technique discussed in Chapter 9. Both methods identify and analyze the consequences of risk, although FMEA is directed specifically at risks in technical systems.

PERT

The PERT and Monte-Carlo simulation methods discussed in Chapter 7 can be used to account for risk in project scheduling, and to estimate additional time needed to compensate for risks in meeting project deadlines.

The PERT method accounts for risk by using three time estimates for each project activity: a, m, and b (optimistic, most likely, and pessimistic times, respectively). Greater risk in an activity is reflected by a greater spread between a and b, and especially between m and b. For an activity with no perceived risk, a, m, and b would be identical; if risk hazards are identified, they are accounted for by raising the values of b and m or by moving b farther from m.

With PERT, recall, it is the expected time, not m, that is the basis for scheduled times, where the expected time is the mean of the Beta distribution

$$t_e = \frac{a + 4m + b}{6}$$

Thus, for a particular activity with given optimistic and most-likely values (a and m), using a larger value of b to account for greater risk will result in a larger value of t_e. This logically allows more time to complete the activity and compensate for any risks. In addition, however, the larger value of b also results in a larger time variance for the activity because

$$V = \left[\frac{b - a}{6} \right]^1$$

This larger V will result in a larger variance for the *project* completion time, which would spur the cautious project manager to add a time buffer (or schedule) reserve to the project schedule.

Risk Priority

Projects are subject to numerous risks, yet only a relatively few might be important enough to merit attention. Once the risk consequences for a project have been computed, they are listed on a *risk log* or *risk register*, and those with moderate to high consequences are given a second look. Project team members, managers, subcontractors, and customers review them and plan appropriate ways to respond to them. To better assess the risks, sometimes activities or work packages must be broken down further. For example, to better comprehend the consequences and magnitude of the risk of a staffing shortage, the risk must be defined in terms of the specific skill areas affected and the amount of the shortage.

To decide which risks to focus on, management might specify a level of expected risk consequence, and address only risks at that level or higher. For example, if the level were set at a consequence of 2 or more days of delay in the project, then only risks S1, F1, T1, T3, I1, I2, and I3 in Table 10.5 would be addressed.

One drawback with specifying risk priority using expected value is that very low likelihood risks are sometimes ignored even when they have potentially severe or catastrophic impact. Suppose, for example, the impact of a project failure is 1,000 fatalities. If the risk likelihood is infinitesimal, then the expected consequence will be very small (tiny likelihood of many fatalities), and hence the risk relegated to a low-priority.[17]

Table 10.5 Risk Likelihood, Risk Impact, and Expected Value Consequence

		LIKELIHOOD (%)	IMPACT: DAYS LATE	CONSEQUENCES
Software				
S1	Software design does not meet initial requirements	20	10	2
S2	Change in user requirements	30	5	1.5
Hardware				
H1	Hardware shipment delay	5	5	0.25
H2	Hardware design incompatible with software requirements	5	10	0.5
Funds				
F1	Hardware supplier goes bankrupt	5	40	2
F2	Insufficient funds to pay staff and suppliers	5	15	0.75
F3	Revenue from current projects delayed	30	5	1.5
Staff				
T1	Staff shortage	10	20	2
T2	Inability to hire/train additional staff	15	10	1.5
T3	Insufficient technical skills	10	30	3
Installation				
I1	Hardware incompatible with existing user systems	5	60	3
I2	Inadequate customer site preparation	20	10	2
I3	Difficulty in teaching user new procedures	20	20	4

In a complex system with a large number of relationships where joint failures in several of them would lead to system failure, it is common to ignore joint failures in the hope they will not occur or will be of insignificant consequence. Usually the likelihood of joint failure is very low. Very low, however, is not the same as impossible, and a failure with terrible impact should never be ignored, regardless of how little the expected value. For example, the chemical plant accident at Bhopal, India, has been attributed to over 30 separate causes, their joint probability being so small as to be beyond consideration. Yet they *all* did happen, causing an accident that resulted in between 1,800 and 10,000 deaths and 100,000–200,000 injuries.[18] Similarly, the nuclear meltdown at Chernobyl was the result of *six errors* in human action, any one of which, if absent, would have precluded the accident. Despite the minuscule likelihood, all six did happen, resulting in an accident that immediately caused several dozen deaths, several hundred hospitalizations, and 135,000 evacuations, plus, much later, an estimated 5,000 to 24,000 additional deaths from cancer in the former Soviet Union and many more throughout Europe and Asia.[19] The lesson: any risk with a severe impact should never be ignored, no matter how small the likelihood.

Risk response planning addresses the matter of how to *deal* with risk. In general, the ways of dealing with a risk are to transfer, avoid, reduce, accept, or contingency plan for it.

Transfer the Risk

Risk can be transferred between customers, contractors, and other parties using contractual incentives, warranties, penalties, or insurance.

Insurance

The customer or contractor purchases insurance to protect against a wide range of risks, including those associated with

- Property damage or personal injury suffered as a consequence of the project
- Damage to materials while in transit or in storage
- Breakdown or damage of equipment
- Theft of equipment and materials
- Sickness or injury of workers, managers, and staff
- Fluctuations in exchange rates (forward cover, see Chapter 18).

Subcontract Work

Risks arise from uncertainty about how to approach a problem or situation. One way to avoid such risk is to hire contractors that specialize in handling those problems or situations. For example, to minimize the financial risk associated with the capital cost of tooling and equipment for production of a large, complex system, a manufacturer might subcontract the production of the system's major components to suppliers familiar with those components. This relieves the manufacturer of the financial risk associated with the tooling and equipment to produce these components. But, as mentioned, transfer of one kind of risk often means inheriting another kind. For example, subcontracting work for the components means that the manufacturer must rely on outsiders, which increases the risks associated with quality control and scheduling. However, such risks often can be reduced through careful management of the subcontractors.

Contract Type

Risk can be transferred or allocated through the use of an appropriate contract type, as discussed in the Appendix to Chapter 3. When the statement of work is clear and involves little uncertainty, the contractor will readily accept a *fixed price* contract. An example would be the building of a wall according to a well-defined drawing and specifications, in which case the contractor perceives little risk. However when the scope of the work is unclear and the potential for change is great, the contractor is less likely to commit to a fixed price and take on the risk of an overrun. In such cases the contractor would find a *cost-plus* contract more appropriate, since it covers all expenses incurred during the project.

Whereas in a fixed price contract the contractor assumes most of the risk for cost overruns, in a fixed price with incentive fee contract the contractor accepts roughly 60 percent of the risk, and the customer 40 percent. In a cost plus incentive fee contract, the contractor assumes about 40 percent, the customer 60 percent. In a cost plus fixed fee (CPFF) contract, the customer assumes most or all of the risk of an overrun.

In large projects, a variety of contracts are used depending on the risk associated with individual work packages or deliverables. In the Chunnel project, the most uncertain part was tunneling under the English Channel; thus, that part of the work was contracted on a CPFF basis. The electrical and mechanical works for the tunnels and terminals were perceived as low risk, and done on a fixed price basis. Procurement of the rolling stock, perceived as slightly riskier, used a cost-plus-percentage-fee contract.[20]

Not all risks can be transferred. Even with a fixed price contract where ostensibly the contractor assumes the risk of overruns, the customer will nonetheless incur damages and hardship should the project fall behind schedule or the contractor declare bankruptcy. The project still must be completed, and someone has to pay for it. To avoid losses, a contractor might feel pressured to cut corners, which of course increases the risk to the customer of receiving a sub-par quality end-item. To lessen such risks, the contract should stipulate strict quality inspections and penalties.

Risk Responsibility

The individual or group responsible for each particular risk in a project should be specified. Risks may be transferred, but they can never be completely "offloaded." A warranty or guarantee specifies the time or place at which the risk is transferred from one party to another. For instance, when an item is procured and shipped from abroad, the risk of damage usually remains with the seller as long as the item is on the ship; as soon as it is hoisted over the rail of the ship the risk is transferred to the buyer.

A party willing to accept responsibility for high risk in a project will usually demand a high level of *authority* over the project. A customer agreeing to accept the risk of poor quality or cost overrun will almost certainly require a large measure of management control over aspects of the project that influence quality and cost. Parties willing to bear high risk will usually also insist on *compensation* to cover the risks. The CPFF contract illustrates this: the contractor's risk is covered by compensation for all expenses, but the customer's risk is covered by his management oversight of the contractor to prevent abuses.

Avoid Risk

Risk can be avoided by such measures as increasing supervision, eliminating risky activities, minimizing system complexity, altering end-item quality requirements, changing contractors, and incorporating redundancies. But attempts to avoid risk can entail the addition of innumerable management controls and monitoring systems, which tend to increase system complexity and, perversely, introduce new sources of risk. Risk avoidance attempts can also diminish payoff opportunities. Many risk factors can be avoided, but not all, especially in complex or leading edge projects. Projects for research and new product development are inherently risky, but offer potential for huge benefits later on. Because the size of the risk is often proportional to the potential payoff, rather than avoiding risk it is better to try to reduce risk to an acceptable level.

Reduce Risk

Among the ways to reduce the technical risk (its likelihood, impact, or both) are the following:[21]

- Employ the best technical team
- Base decisions on models and simulations of key technical parameters

- Use mature, computer-aided system engineering tools
- Use parallel development on high-risk tasks
- Provide the technical team with incentives for success
- Hire outside specialists for critical review and assessment of work
- Perform extensive tests and evaluations
- Minimize system complexity
- Use design margins.

The latter two points deserve further explanation. In general, system risk and uncertainty increase with system complexity: the more elements in a system and the more they are interconnected, the more likely it is that an element or interconnection will go wrong. Thus, minimizing complexity through reorganizing and modifying elements in product design and project tasks reduces the project risk. For example, by *decoupling activities* and subsystems—i.e., making them independent of one another—a failure of any one activity or subsystem will not spread to others.

Incorporating *design margins* into design goals is another way to reduce risk associated with meeting technical requirements.[22] A design margin is a quantified value that serves as a safety buffer held in reserve and allocated by management. In general, a design margin is incorporated into a requirement by setting the target design value to be *stiffer* or more rigorous than the design requirement. In particular:

$$\text{Target value} = \text{Requirement} + \text{Design margin}$$

By striving to meet a target value that is stiffer than the requirement, the risk of not meeting the requirement is reduced

Example 10.5: Design Margin Application for the Spaceship

The weight requirement for the spaceship navigation system is 90 lb. To allow for the difficulty of reaching the requirement (and the risk of not meeting it), the design margin is set at 10 percent, or 9 lb. Thus, the *target weight* for the navigation system becomes 81 lb.

A design margin is also applied to each subsystem or component within the system. If the navigation system is entirely composed of three major subsystems, A, B, and C, then the three together must weigh 81 pounds. Suppose C is an OTS item with a weight of 1 pound that is fixed and cannot be reduced, but A and B are being newly developed, and their design goals have been set at 50 pounds for A and 30 pounds for B. Suppose a 12 percent design margin is imposed on both subsystems; thus, the *target weights* for A and B are 50(1.0 − 0.12) = 44 pounds, and 30(1.0 − 0.12) = 26.4 lb, respectively.

Design margins provide managers and engineers with a way to address problems in an evolving design. Should the target value for one subsystem prove impossible to meet, then portions of the margin values from other subsystems or the overall system can be reallocated to the subsystem. Suppose subsystem B cannot possibly be designed to meet its 26.4 lb target, but subsystem A *can* be designed to meet *its* target; thus, the target for B can be increased by as much as 3.6 lb (its margin value) to 30 lb. If that value also proves impossible to meet, the target can be increased by another 6 lb (subsystem A's original margin value) to 36 lb. Even if that value cannot be met, the target can be increased again by as much as another 9 lb (the margin value for the entire system) to 45 lb. Even with these incremental additions to B's initial target value, the overall system would still meet the 90-lb weight requirement.

While design margins help reduce the risk of not meeting requirements, they encourage designers to exceed requirements—e.g., to design systems that weighs less than required. Of course, the margins must be carefully set so as to reduce the risks while not increasing the costs.

Design margins focus on risks associated with meeting technical requirements. Among ways to reduce risks associated with meeting *schedules* are the following:[23]

- Create a master project schedule and strive to adhere to it
- Schedule the most risky tasks as early as possible to allow time for failure recovery
- Maintain close focus on critical and near-critical activities
- Put the best workers on time-critical tasks
- Provide incentives for overtime work
- Shift high-risk activities in the project network from series to parallel
- Organize the project early, and staff it adequately
- Provide project and feeding buffers (contingency reserves), as discussed in Chapter 7.

To reduce the risk associated with meeting *budget or cost* targets:[24]

- Identify and monitor the key cost drivers
- Use low-cost design alternative reviews and assessments
- Verify system design and performance through modeling and assessment
- Maximize usage of proven technology and commercial off-the-shelf equipment
- Provide contingency reserves in project budgets
- Perform early breadboarding, prototyping, and testing on risky components.

The latter way is especially powerful for reducing risk. *Breadboards* and *prototypes* (i.e., test mock-ups and models)[25] enable ideas to be tested experimentally so designs can be corrected early in the project. This greatly reduces the need for later design changes, which can be costly.[26] The following illustrates other ways to reduce schedule and cost risks.

Example 10.6: Managing Schedule and Cost Risk at Vancouver Airport[27]

The expansion project at Vancouver International Airport involved constructing a new international terminal building (ITB) and a parallel runway. The schedule for the $355 million project called for full operation of the ITB less than 3.5 years after the project was approved, and opening of the new runway 5 months after that. The project team identified the following as major risk areas in meeting the tight budget and schedule constraints:

1. *Risk in Structural Steel Delivery and Erection.* Long procurement lead times from steel mills and difficulties in scheduling design, fabrication, and erection make big steel projects risky. Recognizing this, the project team awarded the structural steel contract very early in the project to allow ample time to design, procure, fabricate, and erect the 10,000 tons of steel required for the ITB. As a result, the ITB was completed on time.
2. *Material Handling Risk.* Millions of cubic meters (cum) of earth had to be moved, and over 4 million cum of sand were required for concrete runways and taxiways. The project team developed an advance plan to enable coordinated movement of earth from one locale to another, and used local sand in the concrete. This saved substantial time and money, enabling the runway to be completed a year ahead of schedule.
3. *Environmental Risk.* Excavations and transport of earth and sand by barges threatened the ecology of the Fraser River estuary. These risks were mitigated by advance planning and constantly identifying and handling problems as they arose through cooperative efforts of all stakeholders.

4. *Functionality Risk*. Because new technologies pose risk, the project team adopted a policy of using only proven (OTS) components and technology whenever possible. Consequently, all ITB systems were installed with few problems, and were operational according to schedule.

One additional way to reduce the risk of not meeting budgets, schedules, and technical performance is to do whatever is necessary to achieve the requirements, *but nothing more*.[28] The project team might be aware of many things that could be done beyond the stated requirements, but in most cases these will consume additional resources and add time and cost. Unless the customer approves the added time and cost, these things should be avoided.

Contingency Planning

Contingency planning implies anticipating whatever risks might arise, and then preparing a course of action to cope with them. The initial project plan is followed, yet throughout execution the risks are closely monitored. Should a risk materialize as indicated by an undesired outcome or trigger symptom, the contingency action is adopted. The contingency can be a *post hoc* remedial action to compensate for a risk impact, an action undertaken in parallel with the original plan, or a preventive action initiated by a trigger symptom to mitigate the risk impact. Multiple contingency plans can be developed based upon "what-if" scenarios for the multiple risks.

Accept Risk (Do Nothing)

Not all impacts are severe. If the cost of avoiding, reducing, or transferring the risk is estimated to exceed the benefits, then "do nothing" might be the best alternative. In Figure 10.4, the accept-risk strategy would be chosen for risks falling in the "low consequence" region (except when the impact is potentially catastrophic, which is off the chart). Sometimes nothing can be done to avoid, reduce, or transfer a risk, in which case the risk must be accepted, regardless of the consequence. Fortunately, such situations are rare.

Responding to a risk sometimes creates a new, *secondary risk* (see Example 11.1 in Chapter 11). When planning risk responses, the project management team should check for such risks before implementing the plan.

10.5 RISK TRACKING AND RESPONSE

Identified risks are documented, added to a list called a *risk log* or *risk register*, and rank-ordered with the greatest risk consequence first. For risks with the most serious consequences, mitigation plans are prepared and strategies adopted (transfer, reduce, avoid, or contingency); for those of little or no consequence, nothing is done (accept).

The project should be *continuously tracked* for symptoms of previously identified risks as well as newly emerging risks (not previously identified). Known risks may take a long time before they start to produce problems. Should a symptom reach the trigger point, a decision is made as to the course of action, which might be to institute a prepared plan or to organize a meeting to pick a solution. Sometimes the response is to do nothing; however, nothing should be a conscious choice, not an oversight, and be tracked afterward to ensure it was the right choice.

All risks deemed critical or important are tracked throughout the project or the phases to which they apply; to guarantee this, someone is assigned responsibility to track and monitor the symptoms of every important risk.

Altogether, the risk log, mitigation strategies, monitoring methods, people responsible, contingency plans, and schedule and budget reserves constitute the *project risk management plan*. The plan is continuously updated to account for changes in risk status (old risks avoided, downgraded, or upgraded; existing risks reassessed; new risks added). The project manager (and sometimes other managers and the customer) is alerted about emerging problems; ideally, the project culture embodies candor and honesty, and people readily notify the project manager whenever they detect a known risk materializing or a new one emerging.

10.6 PROJECT MANAGEMENT *Is* RISK MANAGEMENT

Risk management supplements and is a part of other project management practices such as requirements and work definition, scheduling, budgeting, configuration management, change control, and performance tracking and control. With all of these, managers identify and assess the risks so they can proactively reduce them or plan for the consequences. If, for example, a project must be completed in 9 months but is estimated to take closer to 12, management can take a multitude of steps to increase the likelihood of it finishing in 9.

Ideally, risk identification, assessment, and response planning is treated as a formal aspect of project planning, and the resulting risk management plan is integrated as part of the master project plan—alongside the quality management plan, change and configuration management plan, communications plan, procurement plan, schedule, budget, and so on. After the project is executed, risk tracking is incorporated as a measure in the project tracking and control process. If possible, many project team members and other stakeholders are involved in risk identification and response planning, and in subsequent risk tracking.

Of course, not all projects *need* comprehensive risk management. On small projects, a small, well paid and motivated staff can usually overcome difficulties associated with the risks, and if not the consequences are usually small anyway. In larger projects, however, where the stakes and risks of failure are high, risk management is especially important. These projects require awareness of and respect for all the significant risks—safety, legal, social, and political, as well as technical and financial.

Risk Management Principles

The following are general principles for managing risks:[29]

- Create a *risk management plan* that specifies ways to identify major project risks. The plan should specify the person(s) responsible for managing risks, as well as methods for allocating time and funds from the risk reserve.

- Create a *risk profile* for each risk that includes the risk likelihood, cost and schedule impact, and contingencies to be invoked. It should also specify the earliest visible symptoms (trigger events) that would indicate when the risk is materializing. In general, high-risk areas should have lots of eyes watching closely. Contingency plans should be updated to reflect project progress and emerging risks.

- Appoint a *risk officer* to the project; a person whose principal responsibility is the project's risk management. The risk officer should not be the same person as the project manager; he should *not* be a can-do person, but instead, to some extent, a devil's advocate identifying and tracking all the reasons why something might not work—even when everyone else believes it will.

- Include in the budget and schedule a calculated *risk reserve*—a buffer of money, time, and other resources to deal with risks should they materialize. The reserve is used at the project manager's discretion to cover risks not specified in the risk profile. It may include the RT or RC values (described later), or other amounts. It is usually not associated with a contingency plan, and its use might be constrained to particular applications or areas of risk. The project manager keeps the amounts held in the reserves strictly confidential (else the project will tend to consume whatever amount is available). But others should *not* know there is a reserve, else they will build in their own *secret* reserves.

- Establish *communication channels* (perhaps anonymous) within the project team to ensure that bad news gets to the project manager quickly. Ensure that risks are continually monitored, current risk status is assessed and communicated, and the risk management plan is updated.

- Specify procedures to ensure accurate and comprehensive documentation of proposals, detailed project plans, change requests, progress reports, and the post-completion summary report. In general, the better the documentation of past projects, the more information is available for planning future, similar projects and identifying possible risks.

- Document the profile and management plan for every identified risk. The template in Figure 10.5 illustrates this; it provides places to summarize everything known about the risk. Such a document should be retained in a binder or library, to be updated as necessary and until the risk is believed to no longer exist and is "closed out."

Expect the Unexpected

Having identified and analyzed myriad risk hazards and consequences, and prepared all kinds of controls and safeguards, people can be led to believe that everything that possibly could go wrong has been anticipated and covered—so when something *still* goes wrong, it catches them completely off guard. Although it is true that risk planning can cover many or most risks, it can never cover all of them. Thus, risk planning should be tempered with the concept of "non-planning," or Napoleon's approach, which is *to expect that something surely will go wrong* and to be ready to find ways to deal with it *as it emerges*. This is as important to coping with risk as is extensive planning and believing that all risks have been covered.[30]

Example 10.7: Managing Risks as They Arise—Development of the F117 Stealth Fighter[31]

An example of how to manage risk in R&D projects is the F117 Stealth Fighter program, aimed at developing a revolutionary new "low observable" (difficult to detect with radar) aircraft capable of high-precision attacks on enemy targets. The F117 involved high risk because many lessons had to be learned during the program, and significant challenges had to be overcome. But the program managers *expected* challenges throughout the program, from early design and test, through evaluation and final deployment. To handle the risks, numerous decisions were made on the spot between program managers for Lockheed (contractor) and the Air Force (customer). The program was set up for rapid deployment of resources to solve problems *as they arose*. Managers from the customer and the

Risk Profile and Management Plan			
Risk Number	Last Update	Originator	Risk Category
Project	Phase	Department	WBS Number
Likelihood	Impact	Consequence	Priority

Risk Assessment

Risk description

_____
_____
_____
_____
_____

Risk sources

_____
_____
_____
_____
_____

Risk assessment

_____
_____
_____
_____
_____

Strategy:	Risk Plan
☐ Accept ☐ Avoid ☐ Contingency ☐ Reduce ☐ Reserves ☐ Transfer	1. _____ 2. _____ 3. _____ 4. _____ 5. _____ 6. _____ 7. _____

Risk Tracking	
Member Responsible	Risk Officer
Measures/Symptoms	Comments
Trigger Event	Comments

Signoffs			
Cost Engineer	System Engineer	Quality Manager	Project Manager
Date:	Date:	Date:	Date:

Figure 10.5
Document for the profile and management plan of an identified risk.

contractor worked closely to minimize bureaucratic delay. Schedules were optimistic and based on assumptions that everything would work; however, everyone all through the management chain _knew the risks_ and the challenges to overcome, so problems never came as a surprise or threatened program support. This is a good example of _managing_ risk as opposed to _avoiding_ risk.

Risk Management Caveats

For all the good it can provide, risk management itself *creates* risks. Almost every philosophy, procedure, or prescription has caveats, and that is true of risk management as well. Misunderstanding or misapplication of concepts associated with risk management can stymie a project by fooling people into thinking they have nothing to worry about, which can actually leave them worse prepared for dealing with *emerging* problems they didn't anticipate.

Having created a risk management plan, managers might be emboldened to take risks they otherwise might not take. Much of the input to risk analysis is subjective; after all, risk likelihood is just that—it does not say what *will* happen. Data analysis and planning gives people a sense of having power over events, even when the events are chancy. Underestimating the risk likelihood or impact can make consequences seem insignificant, leading some people to venture into dangerous territory that common sense would disallow. For example, the security of seat belts and air bags encourages some drivers to take risks such as driving too close behind the next car or accelerating through yellow lights. The result is an *increased* likelihood of an accident.

Repeated experience and good documentation are vital ways to identify risks, but they cannot guarantee that all important risks will be identified. Same and similar outcomes that have occurred repeatedly in past projects eventually deplete people's capacity to imagine anything else happening. As a result, some risks become unthinkable. Even sophisticated computer models are worthless when it comes to dealing with the unthinkable, because a computer cannot be instructed to analyze events that have never occurred and are beyond human imagination. Experience provides a sample of all possibilities, not the entire population.

Managing risk does not mean eliminating it, although some managers don't know that. The prime symptom of "trying to eliminate risk" is micromanagement: excessive controls, unrealistic documentation requirements, and trivial demands for the authorization of everything. Projects inherently entail uncertainty and risk. Micromanagement is seldom appropriate, and for some projects it can be disastrous—particularly when the projects involve the new, untried, and untested. When management tries to eliminate risk, it stifles innovation and, say Aronstein and Piccirillo, "forces a company into a plodding, brute force approach to technology, which can be far more costly in the long run than a more adventurous approach where some programs fail but others make significant leaps forward." [32] The appropriate risk management strategy for most projects is to try to accommodate and mitigate risk, not to avoid or eliminate it.

10.7 Summary

Project risk management involves identifying the risks, assessing them, and planning and taking appropriate responses.

Identifying project risks starts in the project conception phase. Risks in projects stem from many sources, such as failure to define and satisfy customer needs or market requirements; technical problems arising in the work; weather, labor and supplier problems; competitors' actions; and changes imposed by outside parties. Such risk hazards are identified using a variety of methods, and draw from experience with past projects and scrutiny of planned projects.

Projects have innumerable risks, but only the important ones need be addressed. Importance depends on the likelihood, impact, and overall consequence of the risk.

Likelihood is the probability a risk will occur; impact is the effect of the risk and its potential influence on project outcomes. Risk consequence is a combination of both likelihood and impact, a way of expressing the two concepts as one. Measures of risk consequence are used to decide which risks should receive attention and which can be ignored. As a precaution, every risk with severe impact should be carefully considered, even when the likelihood is very small.

Risk response planning addresses the way identified risks will be handled. Some risks can be transferred to other parties or spread among many stakeholders or subcontractors. Some can be avoided and should be eliminated. On the other hand, high risk might be associated with high benefits, so trying to eliminate the risk can also reduce the payoff. Thus, better than trying to avoid risk is to try to reduce it to a manageable level. For areas of high risk, alternative contingency plans should be developed.

The principles for risk management include having a risk management plan that specifies the risks, their symptoms and back-up plans; a risk officer responsible for identifying and tracking the risks; and a budget and schedule reserve. The plan must specify the ways to monitor risks and emerging problems, and to communicate them to the project manager. Proper project documentation from past projects furnishes lessons learned, and forewarns managers about potential risks in upcoming projects. No amount of preparation can anticipate all risks; managers should expect the unexpected and be ready to deal with risks as they arise.

This and previous chapters have focused on aspects of project planning—work definition, scheduling, quality, budgeting, and risk. The next few chapters move into the project execution phase and methods for tracking and controlling project performance, creating and sharing information, and bringing the project to successful completion.

The Appendix to this chapter discusses common analytical methods for assessing risk consequences and deciding between alternative risk responses. These same methods are employed in project selection—the topic of Chapter 17.

APPENDIX: RISK ANALYSIS METHODS

Four common methods for risk analysis are expected value, decision trees, payoff tables, and simulation

Expected Value

Selection of the appropriate risk response sometimes depends on the risk consequences in terms of the expected value of costs and schedules.

In general, an expected value is the average or mean outcome of numerous repeated circumstances. For risk assessment, expected value represents the average outcome of a project if it were repeated many times, accounting for the possible occurrence of risk. Mathematically, it is the weighted average of all the possible outcomes, where the weights are the likelihoods of the possible outcomes; that is

$$\text{Expected value} = \sum[(\text{Outcomes}) \times (\text{Likelihoods})]$$

The consequence of risk on project duration is called the *risk time*, *RT*. It is the expected value of the estimated time to correct for the risk, computed as

$$RT = (\text{Corrective time}) \times (\text{Likelihood}) \tag{10.5}$$

The consequence of risk on project cost is called the *risk cost*, *RC*. It is the expected value of the estimated cost to correct for the risk, computed as

$$RC = (\text{Corrective cost}) \times (\text{Likelihood}) \qquad (10.6)$$

For example, suppose the baseline time estimate (BTE) for project completion is 26 weeks and the baseline cost estimate (BCE) is $71,000. Assume that the risk likelihood for the project as a whole is 0.3, and, should the risk materialize, it would delay the project by 5 weeks and increase the cost by $10,000. Because the probability of the risk materializing is 0.3, the probability of it *not* materializing is 0.7. If the risk does not materialize, no corrective measures will be necessary and the corrective time and cost will be nil. Hence if the risk does materialize:

$$RT = (5)(0.3) + (0)(0.7) = 1.5 \text{ weeks}$$

and

$$RC = (\$10,000)(0.3) + (0)(0.7) = \$3,000$$

These figures, RT and RC, are the *schedule reserve* and *project contingency* (budget reserve), respectively, mentioned in Chapters 7 and 8.

Accounting for the risk time, the *expected project completion time, ET,* is

$$ET = BTE + RT = 26 + 1.5 = 27.5 \text{ weeks}$$

and accounting for the risk cost, the *expected project completion cost, EC,* is

$$EC = BCE + RC = 71,000 + 3,000 = \$74,000$$

When the corrective time and cost cannot be estimated, then ET and EC are computed as

$$ET = BTE(1 + \text{likelihood}) = 26(1.3) = 33.8 \text{ weeks} \qquad (10.7)$$

$$EC = BCE (1 + \text{likelihood}) = \$71,000(1.3) = \$92,300 \qquad (10.8)$$

These examples account for risk factors that affect the project as a *whole*. Another way to determine risk consequence is to first disaggregate the project into work packages or phases and then, *for each*, estimate the risk likelihood and corrective time and cost. These individual estimates are then aggregated to determine ET and EC for the entire project. This approach tends to give more credible RT and RC estimates than do equations (10.5) through (10.8), because risks so pinpointed to individual tasks or phases can be more accurately assessed; similarly, the necessary corrective actions and associated time and costs for particular tasks are easier to identify.

Say a project has eight work packages; the following table lists cost information and EC for each, where EC is computed as

$$EC = BCE + [(\text{corrective cost}) \times (\text{likelihood})]$$

WBS ELEMENT	BCE	CORRECTIVE COST	LIKELIHOOD	EC
J	$10,000	$ 2,000	0.2	$10,400
M	8,000	1,000	0.3	8,300
V	16,000	4,000	0.1	16,400
Y	10,000	6,000	0.2	1,200
L	8.000	2,000	0.3	8.600
Q	9,000	2,000	0.1	9,200
W	5,000	1,000	0.3	5,300
X	5,000	1,500	0.3	5,750
Total		$71,000		$75,150

Therefore, the EC for the *project* is $75,150.

Now, for the same eight work-package project, the following table gives time information, where ET is computed as

$$ET = BTE + [(Corrective\ time) \times (Likelihood)]$$

WBS ELEMENT	BTE	CORRECTIVE TIME	LIKELIHOOD	ET
J	6	1	0.2	6.2
M	4	1	0.3	4.3
V	6	2	0.1	6.2
Y	8	3	0.2	8.6
L	2	1	0.3	2.3
Q	8	1	0.1	8.1
W	1	1	0.3	1.3
X	1	1	0.3	1.3

Suppose the project network is as shown in Figure 10.6. Not considering the risk time, the critical path would be J–M–V–Y–W–X, which gives a project BTE of 24 weeks. Accounting for risk consequences, the critical path does not change, but the duration increases to 27.9 weeks. This is the project ET.[33]

Although activities on critical and near-critical paths should be carefully monitored, in general *all* activities with high-risk consequences (high likelihood and/or high impact) should also be carefully monitored, even when not on the critical path.

Increasing the project schedule and budget to account for the expected risk time or risk cost is no guarantee of adequate protection against risk. Expected value is equivalent to the long-run average, which results from repeating something many times. Project activities are seldom repeated; even if they were, that would not preclude a bad outcome in a particular instance.

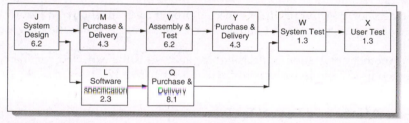

Figure 10.6
Project network, accounting for risk time.

Decision Trees[34]

A decision tree is a diagram wherein the tree "branches" represent different chance outcomes. It is used to assess which risk responses among alternatives yield the best-expected consequence.

One application of decision trees is to weigh the cost of potential project failure against the benefit of project success. Assume a project has a BCE of $200,000 and a failure likelihood of 0.25. If successful, the project will yield a net profit of $1,000,000.

The expected value concept can be used to compute the average value of the project. Assuming the project could be repeated many times, then it would lose $200,000 (BCE) 25 percent of the time and generate $1,000,000 profit the other 75 percent of the time. Thus:

$$Expected\ outcome = (-\$200,000)(0.25) + (\$1,000,000)(0.75) = \$700,000$$

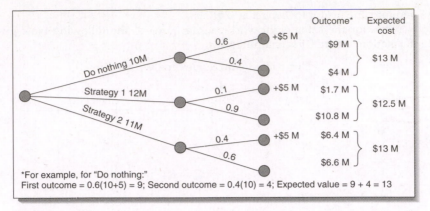

Figure 10.7
Decision tree.

This suggests that although there is potential to net $1,000,000, it is more reasonable to use $700,000 for the BCE. It also suggests that all project costs plus actions taken to reduce or eliminate the failure risk should not exceed $700,000.

Another application of decision trees is in deciding between alternative risk responses. Suppose a project has a BCE of $10 million, risk failure likelihood of 0.6, and risk impact of $5 million. Two strategies are being considered to reduce the risk likelihood (but not the risk impact):

Strategy 1 will cost $2 million and will reduce the failure likelihood to 0.1.
Strategy 2 will cost $1 million and will reduce the failure likelihood to 0.4.

The decision tree and resultant expected project costs are shown in Figure 10.7. The analysis suggests Strategy 1 should be adopted because it has the lowest expected cost.

Another application of decision tree analysis is the expected commercial value method used in project selection, discussed in Chapter 17.

Uncertainty and Payoff Tables

When there is no prior experience or historical data upon which to estimate the likelihood, then the expected-value risk consequence cannot be computed and other criteria must be used to assess courses of action in the face of risk. This situation is referred to as *uncertainty*, which implies no information is available about what might occur. To determine the best strategy under uncertainty, begin by identifying possible alternative paths the project could take in response to factors over which management has no control. These different paths are called *states of nature*. Consider different possible strategies or actions, and then indicate the likely outcome for each state of nature. The outcomes for different combinations of strategies and states of nature are represented in a *payoff table*.

For example, suppose the success of a project to develop Product X depends on market demand, which is known to be a function of particular performance features of the product. The development effort can be directed in any of three possible directions, referred to as Strategies A, B, and C, each of which will provide the product with different performance features. Assume also that a competing firm is developing a product that will have performance features similar to those under Strategy A.

Table 10.6 Payoff Table

	STATES OF NATURE		
STRATEGY	N_1	N_2	N_3
A	60	30	−20
B	60	50	60
C	90	70	40

When the product development effort ends, one of three future states of nature will exist: N1—no competing products enter the market for at least 6 months; N2—the competing product enters the market within 6 months of Product X; N3—the competing product is introduced before Product X. Suppose the likely profits in millions of dollars for the different combinations of strategies and states of nature are computed (shown in Table 10.6).

The question: Which strategy should be adopted? The answer: It depends! If project sponsors are optimistic, they will choose the strategy that maximizes the potential payoff. The maximum potential payoff in the table is $90 million, which happens for Strategy C and state of nature N1. Thus, optimistic project sponsors will adopt Strategy C. In general, the strategy choice that has the potential to yield the largest payoff is called the *maximax* decision criterion.

Now, if project sponsors are pessimistic, they will instead be interested in minimizing their potential losses, in which case they will use adopt the strategy that gives the best outcome under the worst possible conditions. For the three strategies A, B, and C, the worst-case payoff scenarios are −$20 million, $50 million, and $40 million, respectively. The best (least bad) of the three is $50 million, or Strategy B. In general the strategy that gives the best outcome out of several worst-case scenarios is called the *maximin* decision criterion.

Any choice of strategy other than the best one will cause the decision-maker to experience an opportunity loss or *regret*. This way of thinking suggests another criterion for choosing between strategies. the *minimax* decision criterion, which is the strategy that minimizes the *regret* of not having chosen the best strategy. Regret for a given state of nature is the difference in the outcomes between the best strategy and any other strategy. This is illustrated in a *regret table*, shown in Table 10.7. For example, given the payoffs in Table 10.6, for state of nature N1 the highest payoff is $90 million. Had Strategy C, the optimal strategy, been selected, the regret would have been zero, but had Strategies A or B been selected instead, the regrets would have been $30 million each (the difference between their outcomes, $60 million, and the optimum, $90

Table 10.7 Regret Table

	STATES OF NATURE		
STRATEGY	N_1	N_2	N_3
A	30	40	80
B	30	20	0
C	0	0	20

million). The regret amounts for states of nature N2 and N3 are determined in similar fashion.

To understand how to minimize regret, first look in the regret table at the largest regret for each strategy. The largest regrets are $80 million, $30 million, and $20 million for Strategies A, B, and C, respectively. Next, pick the smallest of these, $20 million, which occurs for Strategy C. Thus, Strategy C is the best choice in terms of minimizing regret.

Another strategy selection approach is to assume that every state of nature has the same likelihood of occurring. This is called the *maximum expected payoff* decision criterion. Referring back to the payoff table, Table 10.6, assume the likelihood of each state of nature is one-third, thus, the expected payoff for Strategy A given outcomes from the payoff table is

$$1/3(60) + 1/3(30) + 1/3(-20) = 23.33, \text{ or } \$23.33 \text{ million}$$

The expected payoffs for Strategies B and C, computed similarly, are $56.66 million and $66.66 million, respectively. Thus, Strategy C would be chosen as giving the maximum expected payoff. Notice in the previous examples that three of the four selection criteria point to Strategy C. This in itself might convince decision-makers that Strategy C is most appropriate.

Simulation

Application of simulation to project management, illustrated in Chapter 7, gives the probability distribution of outcomes, which can be used to determine the probability (or likelihood) of a particular outcome such as completion cost or time. In turn, this can be used to establish an appropriate target budget or completion date, or to prepare contingency plans. For instance, although the critical path in Chapter 7, Example 7.2, indicated the project would be completed in 147 days, the simulated completion time distribution (Figure 7.14) indicated that it would be 155 days, *on average*. Thus, at the *earliest*, the target completion should be set at 155 days, although the likelihood of *not meeting* that date would be 50 percent. Using the simulated probability distribution, a target completion date can be set such that the likelihood of not meeting it is more acceptable. Alternatively, given a prespecified date by which the project must be completed, simulation can be used to estimate the likelihood of failure and, hence, determine whether to prepare contingency plans or change the project requirements, activities, or network.

REVIEW QUESTIONS AND PROBLEMS

1. Should risks that have low likelihood be ignored? Explain.
2. How does a person's risk tolerance affect whether he rates a risk high, medium, or low?
3. What is meant by risk of failure?
4. What factors make a project high risk?
5. Discuss the difference between internal risk and external risk. List sources of risk in each of these categories.
6. Describe each of the following sources of technical risk: maturity, complexity, quality, and concurrency or dependency.
7. Briefly describe the following risk identification techniques: analogy, checklists, WBS analysis, process flowcharts, and brainstorming.
8. Describe a cause-and-effect diagram. Pick a problem (effect) of your own choice, and use a cause-and-effect diagram for illustration.

9. A project involves developing a system with state-of-the-art hardware and software, both complex, and where system performance depends on another, external system that is being developed concurrently. Based on Table 10.3, and assuming all risk factors are independent and equally weighted, what is the CLF for the project?

10. What is an influence diagram? How is it used to identify and analyze risk sources, and to assign priorities to those sources?

11. Tables 10.3 and 10.4 are for illustration purposes. Discuss the general applicability of these tables to rating risks in projects. Would *you* use these tables to assess the risk likelihood and impact in a project of your choice? Why, or why not?

12. Do equations (10.1), (10.2), and (10.3) present good ways for rating the overall likelihood, impact, and consequences of risk? Discuss pros and cons of using these equations.

13. Discuss briefly each of the following ways to handle risk: transfer risk, avoid risk, reduce risk, contingency plan, and accept risk.

14. Think of a project you are familiar with and problems it encountered. List some ways the problems could have been avoided, and explain each of them.

15. What is a design margin? How does its application reduce risk?

16. One requirement of a power-generating system states that it must provide 500 kWh minimum output. The system has three power-generating subsystems, X, Y, and Z. Constraints on physical size indicate that the output capacity of overall system will be split among the three subsystems in the approximate ratio of 5:3:2. A 3 percent design margin is applied to the system and the subsystems. Note, because the power requirement is stated as *minimum* output, the target output will be 3 percent *above* the requirement.
    a. What is the target requirement output for the overall system?
    b. What are the target requirement outputs for each of the subsystems? (Remember, subsystem margins are *in addition* to the system margin.)
    c. Suppose that, at best, Subsystem X can be designed to meet only 47 percent of the power output requirement for the overall system. Assuming that Subsystems Y and Z can be designed to meet their respective design targets, can the output requirement for the overall system also be met?

17. List and review the principles of risk management.

18. How does risk planning serve to increase risk-taking behavior?

19. Risk management includes being prepared for the unexpected. Explain.

20. Can risk be eliminated from projects? *Should* management try to eliminate it?

21. How and where are risk time and risk cost considerations used in project planning?

22. Where would criteria such as maximax, maximin, and minimax regret be used during the project life cycle to manage project risk?

23. Figure 10.8 is the network for the Largesse Hydro Project:

Figure 10.8
Largesse Hydro Project.

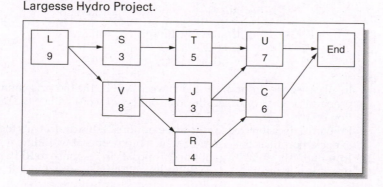

The table gives the baseline cost and time estimates (BCE and BTE), the cost and time estimates to correct for failure, and the likelihood of failure for each work package.

WBS Element	BCE	BTE (Week)	Corrective Cost	Corrective Time	Likelihood
L	$20,000	9	$4,000	2	0.2
V	16,000	8	4,000	2	0.3
T	32,000	5	8,000	2	0.1
U	20,000	7	12,000	3	0.2
S	16,000	3	4,000	1	0.3
J	18,000	3	4,000	1	0.1
R	10,000	4	4,000	3	0.3
C	15,000	6	5,000	2	0.3

a. Determine the risk time and risk cost for all the WBS elements of the project.

b. Consider the risk times on non-critical paths. Which activities and paths should be watched carefully as posing the highest risks?

c. What are the project expected cost (EC) and expected time (ET)?

24. Because of its geographical location, the Largesse Hydro project is threatened with weather-associated delays and costs. The likelihood of bad weather is estimated at 0.30 with a potential impact of delaying work by 10 weeks and increasing the cost by $20,000.

a. Ignoring the time and cost risks in Problem 23, what are the expected project completion time and completion cost considering the weather risk?

b. What is the estimated expected project completion time and cost considering the weather risk *and* the risks listed in Problem 23?

25. Softside Systems has a $100,000 fixed price contract for installation of a new application system. The project is expected to take 5 weeks and cost $50,000. Experience with similar projects suggests a 0.30 likelihood that the project will encounter problems that could delay it by as much as 3 weeks and increase the cost by $30,000. By increasing the project staff by 20 percent for an additional cost of $10,000, the likelihood of problems would be reduced to 0.10, and the delay and cost to 1 week and $8,000, respectively. Set up a decision tree to show whether Softside should increase the size of the project staff.

26. Corecast Contractors has been requested by a municipality to submit a proposal bid for a parking garage contract. In the past, the cost of preparing bids has been about 2 percent of the cost of the job. Corecast project manager Bradford Pitts is considering three possible bids: cost plus 10 percent, cost plus 20 percent, and cost plus 30 percent. Of course, increasing the "plus percent" increases the project price and decreases the likelihood of winning the job. Bradford estimates the likelihood of winning the job as follows:

	Bid Price	P(Win)	P(Lose)
P1	$C+0.1C=1.1C$	0.6	0.4
P2	$C+0.2C=1.2C$	0.4	0.6
P3	$C+0.3C=1.3C$	0.2	0.8

In all cases, the profit (if the bid is won) will be the bid price minus the proposal preparation cost, or $0.02C$; the loss (bid is not won) will be the proposal preparation cost.

Prepare a decision tree for the three options. If Bradford uses the maximum expected profit as the criterion, which bid proposal would he select?

27. Iron Butterfly Company submits proposals in response to RFPs and faces three possible outcomes: N1, Iron Butterfly gets a full contract; N2, it gets a partial

contract (job is shared with other contractors); N3, it gets no contract. The company is currently assessing three RFPs, coded P1, P2, and P3. For P3, the customer will pay a fixed amount for proposal preparation; for P1 and P2, Iron Butterfly must absorb the proposal preparation costs, which are expected to be high. Based upon project revenues and proposal preparation costs, the expected profits ($ thousands) are as shown:

	N1	N2	N3
P1	500	200	−300
P2	300	100	−100
P3	100	50	25

To which RFPs would Iron Butterfly respond using the three decision criteria?

28. Frank Wesley, project manager for the LOGON project, is concerned about the development time for the robotic transporter. Although the subcontractor, Creative Robotics, has promised a delivery time of 6 weeks, Frank knows that the actual delivery time will be a function of the number of other projects Creative Robotics is working on. As an incentive to speed up delivery of the transporter, Frank has three options:

S1: Do nothing
S2: Promise Creative Robotics a future contract with Iron Butterfly
S3: Threaten to never contract with Creative Robotics again.

He estimates the impact of these actions on delivery time would be as follows:

Payoffs:	Creative Robotics Workload		
Strategy	Slow	Average	Busy
S1	4	6	8
S2	3	4	7
S3	3	6	6

What strategy should Frank adopt based upon uncertainty criteria? Use criteria similar to the maximax, maximin, minimax regret, and maximum expected payoff, except note that the criteria must be adapted because here the goal is to *minimize* the payoff (time); this is in contrast to the usual case, which is to maximize the payoff.

QUESTIONS ABOUT THE STUDY PROJECT

1. What did managers and stakeholders believe were the major risks in the project?
2. In your own judgment, was this a risky project? Why or why not?
3. Was formal risk analysis performed? When was it done (in initiation, feasibility, etc.)?
4. Was a formal risk management plan created? Discuss the plan.
5. Was there a risk officer? Discuss her duties and role in the project.
6. How were risks identified?
7. How were risks dealt with (through risk transfer, acceptance, avoidance, reduction, etc.)?
8. Discuss the use of contingency plans and budget and schedule reserves to cover risks.
9. What risks materialized during the project, and how were they handled?

Case 10.1   The Sydney Opera House[35]

The Sydney Opera House (SOH) is a top tourist attraction and landmark for Sydney and all of Australia. It is a major arts center, although, owing to its design, it is not necessarily the best place to hear opera. The SOH is visually spectacular and a magnificent structure (Figure 10.9), but it was nightmare to design and build.

The original concept for the SOH was a sketch submitted by Danish architect, Jorn Utzon. Judges selected it from an open competition that ended with 233 entries from 11 countries. Though happy to win, Utzon was mildly shocked. The concept that had caught the judges' attention consisted only of simple sketches, with no plans or even perspective drawings. Utzon faced the challenge of converting the sketches into a design from which a structure could be built, but he had no prior experience in designing and constructing such a large building. Because there were no plans, detailed drawings, or estimates of needed materials, there was little on which to base cost estimates. No one knew how it would be built; some experts questioned that it could be built at all. (Interestingly, because the design was *so* very different, and unique, some people thought it would also be inexpensive to build.) The initial cost was estimated at $7 million, to be paid by the government through profits from a series of state-run lotteries.

Engineers reviewing the concept noted that the roof shells were much larger and wider than any shells ever built. Further, because they stuck up so high, they would act like sails in the strong winds blowing up the harbor. Thus, they would have to be carefully designed and constructed to prevent the building from blowing away!

Government managers worried that people scrutinizing the design might raise questions about potential problems and stall the project. They thus quickly moved ahead and divided the work into three main contracts: the foundation and building except the roof, the roof, and the interior and equipment.

As experts had warned, the SOH project became an engineering and financial debacle, lasting 15 years and costing $107 million ($100 million over the initial estimate). Hindsight is 20/20, yet from the beginning this should have been viewed as a risky project. Nonetheless, risks were downplayed or ignored, and little was done to mitigate or control them.

Figure 10.9
Sydney Opera House.
Photograph courtesy of Australian Information Service.

1. Identify the obvious risks.
2. What early actions should have been taken to reduce the risks?
3. Discuss some principles of risk management that were ignored.

Case 10.2   Infinity & Beyond, Inc.

Infinity & Beyond, Inc. produces high-tech fashion merchandise. The company's marketing department has identified a new product "concept" through discussions with three customer focus groups. The department is excited about the new concept and presents it to top management, who approves it for further study. Lisa Denney, senior director of new product development, is asked to create a plan and cost breakdown for the development, manufacture, and distribution of the product. Despite the enthusiasm of the marketing department, Lisa is unsure about the product's market potential and the company's ability to develop it at a reasonable cost. To her way of thinking, the market seems ill-defined, the product goals unclear, and the product and its production technology uncertain. Lisa asks her chief designer to create some product requirements and a rough design that would meet the requirements, and to propose how the product might be manufactured.

After a few weeks, the designer reports back with requirements that seem to satisfy the marketing concept. She tells Lisa that because of the newness of the technology and the complexity of the product design, the company does not have the experience to develop or even manufacture the product on its own. Lisa checks out several design/development firms, asking one, Margo-Spinner Works Company (MSW) to review the product concept. MSW assures Lisa that although the technology is new to them, it is well within their capability. Lisa reports this to top management, who tells her to go ahead with the development project.

Lisa sets a fixed price contract with MSW, and gives them primary responsibility for the development effort. MSW management had argued for a cost-plus contract, but when Lisa stipulated that the agreement had to be fixed price, MSW said okay, only under the condition that it be given *complete* control of the development work. Lisa feels uncomfortable with the proposition, but knows of no other design company qualified to do the work, so she agrees.

QUESTIONS

1. Discuss the major sources of risk in this project.
2. What do you think about Lisa's handling of the project so far? Would you have done anything differently?
3. Discuss what Lisa and other parties did that served to increase or decrease the risks.

Case 10.3   The Nelson Mandela Bridge[36]

Newtown, South Africa, is a suburb of Johannesburg that boasts a rich cultural heritage. As part of an attempt to help rejuvenate Newton, the Nelson Mandela Bridge was constructed to link it to important roads and centers of commerce in Johannesburg. Spanning 42 electrified railway lines, the bridge (Figure 10.10) has been acclaimed for its functionality and beauty.

Lack of space for the support pylons (towers) between the railway lines dictated that the

Figure 10.10
Nelson Mandela Bridge, Johannesburg.
Photograph courtesy of Jorge Jung, BKS (Pty) Ltd, Pretoria.

bridge design would have a long span. This resulted in a structure with the bridge deck supported by stay cables from pylons of unequal height. The pylons on the northern side are 48 meters high, and those in the southern side are 35 meters high.

The pylons are composite columns consisting of steel tubes that had to be filled with concrete after being hoisted into the vertical position. The decision was made to pump the concrete into the tubes through a port at the bottom of each tube. This had to be done in a single operation. Although the technology for casting concrete this way was not new, the columns were the highest in South Africa, and filling them would set a world record for bottom-up pumping of self-curing concrete.

The pump for the concrete was placed at ground level between the electrified railway lines, which exposed workers to the risks of being near continuous rail operations. The pumping method posed the risk of the stone and cement in the concrete mixture segregating in the pylon tubes before the concrete solidified, which would compromise

the strength of the concrete. Another risk was that the pump might fail and result in the concrete solidifying in an uncompleted pylon, rendering further pumping of concrete from the bottom impossible. Two contingencies were considered: an additional pump on standby, and completing the process by pouring concrete from the top of the pylon.

The concrete had to be transported by trucks to the site, which risked interrupting the concrete supply owing to traffic congestion in the city.

Despite working over a busy yard with trains running back and forth, no serious accident occurred at any time in the 420,000 man-hours project. The pump never failed, and construction finished on time. The stay cables—totaling 81,000 meters in length—were installed and the bridge deck lifted off temporary supports, all while the electrified railway lines beneath remained alive. Upon completion of the bridge, some felt that the costs incurred to reduce the risks had been excessive; others held that the risks were too high and not enough had been done to reduce them.

QUESTIONS

1. What methods would you have used to identify the risks? (Refer also to methods in Chapter 9.)
2. Using the table below discuss how the risks were addressed or how they *could* have been addressed. Include any additional risks you can think of.

Possible risk event	Plans to address risk				
	Accept	Avoid	Reduce	Transfer	Contingency Plans and/or Contingency Reserves
Failure to make an acceptable profit					
Not finishing the construction by Nelson Mandela's 85th birthday					
Interference with rail activities					
Geological structures necessitating expensive foundations					
The concrete mixture segregating when pumped into the columns					
A pump failure while concrete is being pumped					
Interrupted supply of concrete due to trucks transporting concrete delayed in traffic					

3. State whether the risks listed in the table above are internal or external.

4. Describe how you would determine the expected values of the risks listed in the table.

5. Compile a complete list of information that you would require in order to make an assessment of the risk of a pump failure.

6. What information do you think would have been available early in the project, and from where would you obtain it?

7. Draw a CE diagram showing different factors that could contribute to delaying the project.

8. Describe how risks are reduced over the lifespan of a project such as this one.

9. With reference to the concerns expressed upon completion of the construction, discuss the statement: "Risks always relate to the future. There is no such thing as a *past risk.*"

10. Discuss the difference between good decisions and good luck.

11. How could a manager protect himself against the risk of making a decision that might later have negative implications?

NOTES

1. Quoted in Bernstein P. *Against the Gods: The Remarkable Story of Risk.* New York, NY: John Wiley & Sons; 1996. p. 331.

2. *Ibid.*, pp. 207–208.

3. Asked once to define certainty, John Von Neumann, the principle theorist of mathematical models of uncertainty, answered with an example: To design a house so it is *certain* the living room floor never gives way, "calculate the weight of a grand piano with six men huddling over it to sing, triple the weight," then design the floor to hold it. That will guarantee certainty! Source: Bernstein, *Against the Gods*, p. 233.

4. See Argus R and Gunderson N. *Planning, Performing, and Controlling Projects.* Upper Saddle River, NJ: Prentice Hall; 1997. pp. 22–23.

5. Adapted from Michaels J. *Technical Risk Management.* Upper Saddle River, NJ: Prentice Hall; 1996. pp. 208–250.

6. Turoff M and Linstone H. (eds). *The Delphi Method: Techniques and Applications*, 2002. http://is.njit.edu/pubs/delphibook/

7. The term "likelihood" is sometimes distinguished from "probability." The latter refers to values based on frequency measures from historical data; the former to subjective

estimates or gut feel. If two of three previous attempts met with success the first time, then, *ceteris paribus*, the probability of success on the next try is 2/3 or 0.67. Even without numerical data, however, a person with experience can, upon reflection, come up with a similar estimate that "odds are two to one that it will succeed the first time." Although one estimate is objective and the other subjective, that does not imply one is better than the other. Objective frequency data will not necessarily give a reliable estimate because a multitude of factors can influence outcomes; a subjective estimate, in contrast, might be reliable because humans often can do a pretty good job of assimilating lots of factors.

8. Roetzheim W. *Structured Computer Project Management*. Upper Saddle River, NJ: Prentice Hall; 1988. pp. 23–26; further examples of risk factors and methods of likelihood quantification are given in Michaels, *Technical Risk Management*.

9. See Dingle J. *Project Management: Orientation for Decision Makers*. London: Arnold; 1997.

10. See Gilbreath R. *Winning at Project Management: What Works, What Fails, and Why*. New York, NY: John Wiley & Sons; 1986.

11. Roetzheim, *Structured Computer Project Management*, pp. 23–26.

12. Pool R. *Beyond Engineering: How Society Shapes Technology*. New York, NY: Oxford University Press; 1997. pp. 197–202

13. Kotulak R. Key differences seen in Columbia, Challenger disasters. *Chicago Tribune* Feb. 2; 2003. Section 1, p. 5.

14. Pool, *Beyond Engineering*, pp. 207–214.

15. Michaels, *Technical Risk Management*, p. 40.

16. Conrow E. *Effective Risk Management*. Reston, VA: American Institute of Aeronautics and Astronautics; 2000. pp. 135–140.

17. Statistics make it easy to depersonalize the consequences. For example, it is less distressing to state that there is a 0.005 likelihood of someone being killed than to say that 5 people out of 1,000 will be killed.

18. Mitroff I and Linstone H. *The Unbounded Mind*. New York, NY: Oxford; 1993. pp. 111–135.

19. *Ibid*.

20. Anbari F (ed.). *The Chunnel Project. Case Studies in Project Management*. Newtown Square, PA: Project Management Institute; 2005.

21. Eisner H. *Computer-Aided Systems Engineering*. Upper Saddle River, NJ: Prentice Hall; 1988. p. 335.

22. See Grady J. *System Requirements Analysis*. New York, NY: McGraw-Hill; 1993. pp. 106–111.

23. Eisner, *Computer-Aided Systems Engineering*, p. 336.

24. *Ibid*.

25. A breadboard is a working assembly of components. A prototype is an early working model of a complete system. Both are used to demonstrate, validate, or prove feasibility of a design concept.

26. Breadboards, prototypes, and modeling are discussed in Chapters 2 and 9.

27. Wakabayashi H and Cowan B. Vancouver International Airport expansion. *PM Network* 12(9); 1998. pp. 39–44.

28. Whitten N. Meet minimum requirements: anything more is too much. *PM Network* 12(9); 1998. p. 19.

29. DeMarco T. *The Deadline*. New York, NY: Dorset House; 1997. p. 83; Yourdan E. *Rise and Resurrection of the American Programmer*. Upper Saddle River, NJ: Prentice Hall; 1998. pp. 133–136.

30. Dorner D. *The Logic of Failure*. Reading, MA: Addison-Wesley; 1997. p. 163.

31. Aronstein D and Piccirillo A. *Have Blue and the F117A: Evolution of the Stealth Fighter*. Reston, VA: American Institute of Aeronautics and Astronautics; 1997. pp. 79–80.

32. *Ibid*., pp. 186–90.

33. For other approaches to risk time analysis, see Michaels, *Technical Risk Management*.

34. This section and the next address the more general topic of decision analysis, a broad topic that receives only cursory coverage here. A classic book on the subject is Luce RD and Raiffa H. *Games and Decisions*. New York, NY: John Wiley & Sons; 1957.

35. Adapted from Kharbanda O and Pinto J. *What Made Gertie Gallop: Learning from Project Failures*. New York, NY: Van Nostrand Reinhold; 1996. pp. 177–191.

36. Source: Kromhout F. Divisional Director, Bridges, BKS (Pty) Ltd, Pretoria.

Project Execution and Control

> *The rider must ride the horse, not be run away with.*

—DONALD WINNICOTT,
Playing and Reality

> *Prediction is very difficult, especially about the future.*

—NIELS BOHR

Upon completing Phase B, the definition phase, the project manager and team will have prepared a complete set of requirements and specifications and a comprehensive project plan with all the fine points for the most immediate stages of the project and a high-level outline for the remaining stages. The stages covered in the plan constitute Phase C, the *execution phase* of the project life cycle—what most outsiders see when they look at the project, and one of the topics of this chapter.

Given all the effort devoted to planning, scheduling, and budgeting in the definition phase, one might think that the resulting project plan will have accounted for everything to be done and every conceivable situation and problem. But no plan is ever complete or perfect, and, besides, rarely do things go entirely as planned. Keeping the project moving forward and on target, tracking progress, and overcoming obstacles is the purpose of *project control*, the other topic of the chapter.

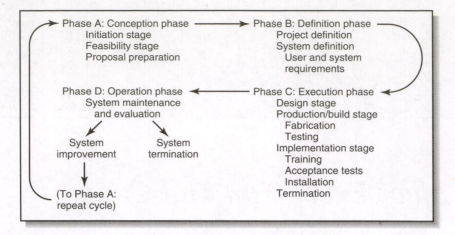

Figure 11.1
Phase and stages systems development life cycle (Phases A–C = Project life cycle).

11.1 PHASE C: EXECUTION

The execution phase typically includes the stages of *design*, *production/build*, and *implementation* (Figure 11.1), although in actuality the stages differ depending on the purpose of the project. For example, hardware development projects typically have the stages of design, development, and production; in construction projects the stages are design and build; and in consulting projects they are background research, report compilation, and presentation. Many companies have customized project methodologies with their own unique project phases and stages; these are discussed in Chapter 16. All projects that produce a physical end-item—a product, building, or system—also include an implementation stage, which is where the end-item is handed over to the user. This chapter will look at the stages of design and production/build. The stages of implementation and project closeout are covered in the next chapter.

11.2 DESIGN STAGE

In the design stage, system specifications are converted into documents such as plans, sketches, or drawings. The outputs of this stage are forms of pictorial representation—blueprints, flow charts, or schematic diagrams—or models showing the system components, dimensions, relationships, and overall configuration.[1]

During the design stage the system is broken into tiers of subsystems, components and parts. Various design possibilities for elements at each tier are reviewed for compatibility with each other and with elements at higher-level tiers, and for ability to meet specifications and system cost, schedule, and performance requirements. The breakdown into tiers and components uses block diagramming (Chapter 2), the requirements breakdown structure (RBS) (Chapter 3), and the work breakdown structure (Chapter 5).

The design process is composed of two interrelated activities. First is preparation of a *functional* design that shows the system components and their relationships. The purpose of this design activity is to determine the *logical*, functional elements of the system and how they should be interconnected to achieve the system's objectives. This is the thrust of the systems engineering process described in Chapter 2.

The second part of the design process is preparation of a *physical* design that shows what the actual system and its components will look like—their sizes, shapes, and relative positions. This design activity results in engineering, manufacturing, architectural, and other types of drawings and models. These drawings and models show details necessary for later fabrication, assembly, and maintenance of the system. This design activity sometimes reveals places where the functional design is impractical or infeasible because of assembly, maintenance, or appearance considerations, in which case the functional design must be redone.

Design often follows an evolutionary, trial-and-error process as illustrated in Figure 2.7 in Chapter 2 and Figure 4.6 in Chapter 4. A trial design is prepared, modeled, and then tested against system performance specifications. If it fails, the design is modified and retested. This design–build–test iteration is followed in virtually all projects to develop new systems.

When the system being designed is complex, the iteration occurs in many places throughout the system, and changes in one subsystem have a ripple effect on the others. One subsystem may require, for instance, a bigger motor, which robs space from another subsystem that then has to be moved to somewhere else, which displaces still another subsystem, and so on. Uncontrolled, the result is a never-ending redesign of the system. Thus, one responsibility of the project manager and systems engineer is to try to minimize the number of design iterations for each subsystem, and in each iteration to minimize the impact on other subsystems.

Example 11.1: Design Complexity in the Chunnel[2]

One of the mandated changes in requirements for the English Channel Tunnel (Chunnel) project was that trains running through it must be resistant to fire damage for at least 30 minutes; this would enable every train car to be capable of continuing along with a fire raging inside until it was out of the tunnel. But because the frame of a normal train car would deform from the heat and the train soon would become immobile, special metal alloys would have to be used that are unlike metals used in trains everywhere else in the world. This would make the trains heavier—2,400 tons instead of 1,600 tons—and would require heavier locomotives needing six axles instead of four. The locomotives would have to be specially designed, and because they needed more power, the tunnel's power system would have to be changed, too.

In many projects, the stages of design and production/build do not occur as discrete, sequential stages, but rather overlap. The building or constructing of a part of the system commences as soon as some of the detail design is completed, then building of another part begins when its detail design is completed, and so on. In other words, the system is built while it is still being designed—a practice referred to as *fast-tracking* or *design-build*. Fast-tracking is common in the construction industry: the foundation is being dug and steel being raised even though the roof and interior designs are not yet completed. The practice speeds up the work and can save up to a year on a major construction project, but it is also risky. Design problems often do not appear until the details have been worked out, but by then portions of the system or building will have been fabricated and might have to be rebuilt—increasing the costs and schedules. The usual sequential or "slow-tracking" method takes longer, but allows more time for design problems to surface and be resolved before construction begins.

Interaction Design[3]

Why is it that so many software-based products are difficult to use, designed to do things that people don't need, and filled with obscure or irrelevant features that most people don't want? Examples are software products, cell phones, and entertainment systems, all of which contain numerous features and functions that most people do not need and never learn to use. Yet in an effort to continuously "improve" the product, developers keep adding ever more features—a process that leads to "bloatware." Compare, for instance, all the things you presumably *could do* with word-processing and spreadsheet software with the few features that you actually use. The problem is not only that these products have too many features, but also that they inter-mix never-used features with often-used ones, making the whole product more difficult to use and understand. In the eyes of customers, they are too complex.

Complex systems have always been around, but in the past they were operated only by *trained* personnel. Farm and construction equipment, aircraft, trains, and electrical generators are complex, but they are designed for use by specially trained operators, not the average person. Commercial products (camera, car console, cell phone, etc.) are complex too, but amateurs, not skilled operators, use them.

System complexity and bloatware happen when product goals and user requirements are poorly defined, no one guides the design process to meet user requirements, and user–system interaction is not a key design issue. They also happen when design is *controlled* by engineers and programmers, people who are technically astute but tend to ignore "interaction design"—aspects of the design that address product functions and how they are presented to the user. Whenever a programmer includes a pet function in a product, or a marketing manager insists on another product feature, they are influencing the design; they are packing in features they want, ignoring the impact on the average end-user.

The project manager and systems engineer must retain control over the design process, and particularly over the interaction design. This starts with knowing the end-users and their wants, aptitudes, and skill levels, incorporating these into user requirements, and thereafter considering the end-user in every decision that will influence the function and operation of the product.

Controlling Design

Formal project reviews are scheduled at key milestones. Ideally, they are attended and headed by objective outside experts to ensure that the functional design satisfies requirements and the final design meets the users' personal tastes, needs, and budget.

During the design stage, changes to early designs might be necessary due to new technology, technical problems, or new requirements of the user. Since these inevitably require alterations to work activities, project management is responsible for monitoring the changes, determining their impacts on project plans, schedules, and budgets, and relaying the impacts to stakeholders for approval of changes. All of this is handled through a change control system, described later in the chapter.

Design changes tend to increase project costs, but, as shown in Figure 11.2, design costs typically are a small fraction of production costs. Consequently, prolonging this stage to get the design right the first time is usually far less costly than changing the design or fixing design-related problems later in the project. But the design stage cannot be allowed to continue indefinitely, and sometimes project management imposes a freeze date after which no discretionary design changes are allowed.

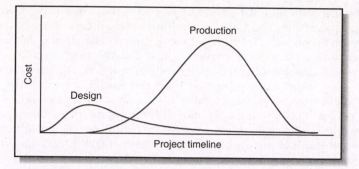

Figure 11.2
Relative costs for design and production.

Project management is also responsible for ensuring adequate documentation of design efforts. Documentation is necessary so everyone knows the design's features, configuration, strengths, and limitations; it is the precursor for planning for the subsequent system production, operation, and maintenance.

Planning for Production/Build and Later Stages

During the design stage, the project manager, who is always looking beyond the current stage, is already planning for the production stage. This plan will address all aspects of production—tools, equipment, and materials needed, assembly procedures, functional and integration tests, packaging, and so on—and will include a detailed production/build schedule. Because all the design documents (specs, drawings, etc.) might not be completed in time, production planning might have to be done in phases.

The overall plan for the production/build stage should account for systems, tasks, and resources that will be needed to *produce*, *operate*, and *maintain* the end-item system, and to *train* user personnel; these are project "side-items," so-called to distinguish them from the main contract end-item of the project. Side-items are no less important than the main end-item; in fact, without them it would be impossible to produce, operate, or maintain the end-item. Although side-items are usually developed and produced by subcontractors, the manager of the overall project is responsible for ensuring they have all been identified, that contractors are developing and producing them, and they will be ready for usage when the main end-item has been completed.

11.3   PRODUCTION/BUILD STAGE

Detailed designs in hand, the contractor is ready to begin production. For one-of-a-kind items, this means the system is ready to be built or constructed; for mass-produced items, it means the system is ready for manufacture. The main activities in this stage are system fabrication, testing, and planning for the next stages.

System Fabrication

System fabrication begins when sufficient design work has been completed. Components prepared by the contractor and its suppliers are assembled into the final end-item. As in earlier stages, the project manager monitors the work, coordinates efforts among departments, and tracks expenditures and progess against the project budget and master schedule. The principal management tasks during this stage are releasing work orders; monitoring, inspecting, and documenting progress; comparing planned versus actual results; and taking corrective action. The project manager and manufacturing or construction manager share responsibility for these.

During system fabrication, work quality is constantly being assessed. As with most tasks in the production/build stage, quality control is not, *per se*, the responsibility of the project manager; nonetheless, because the quality of the final system *is* the responsibility of the project manager, she must make sure that the managers involved in the production/build stage have implemented a quality plan (discussed in Chapter 9) to achieve the project's quality objectives.

System Testing

A variety of tests are performed to ensure that the system meets requirements. Tests fall into three groups: tests conducted by the *contractor* to make sure that the system design (1) meets system requirements, and (2) is being followed by the producer or builder; and (3) tests conducted by the *customer* to make sure the system meets user requirements and other contractual agreements.[4]

The first group of tests is aimed at verifying the design. If these tests should reveal inadequate performance because of faulty or poor design, then the design stage must be repeated; if they reveal problems because of faulty specifications, then the definition phase or parts of it also must be repeated. Since repeating steps is costly and time-consuming, the tests should be devised so as to catch problems as early as possible. Of course, even if the design is perfect, unless the builders follow it and do not cut corners on materials and procedures, the system will be inadequate; hence, the second group of tests is necessary to verify that the builders have correctly followed the design, and that the components and workmanship meet specifications. The final group of tests consists of verification tests, reviews, and audits conducted by the customer to ensure that user requirements have been met and that test documentation is complete and accurate. These tests often reveal design deficiencies not identified during the first group of tests. These tests, conducted by user personnel who will operate the system, may expose difficulties that designers and engineers in the project overlooked.

To minimize the need to redesign an entire system because of faulty components, testing should follow the sequence of components first, subsystems next, then the whole system last. Each part is tested to ensure it functions individually; parts are integrated into components and tested to ensure each component works; components are integrated into subsystems and tested to ensure each subsystem performs; finally, subsystems are integrated into the full system and tested to ensure that the system meets performance requirements.

Tests are performed against earlier developed system objectives, systems specifications, and user requirements. Sometimes, in addition, they are performed *in excess* of specifications for normal operating conditions to determine the actual capacity or point of failure of the system. In *stress tests*, an increasingly severe test load is applied to the system to determine its capability to handle heavier than probable conditions. In *fatigue tests* the system is loaded or submitted to repeated load cycles until it fails. This is done to determine the system's ultimate capacity. Contracts for development projects sometimes specify not only the design requirements and performance criteria, but also the types of tests to verify them. In other cases, the criteria and conditions for the tests are specified in the quality plan.

The project manager oversees preparation of test plans and schedules and includes them in the production/build plan. She ensures that the necessary resources are available to perform tests, and that test results are documented and filed for later reference.

Planning for Implementation

With phased project planning, details in the project plan are filled in as information becomes available; during each project stage, the detailed plan for the next stage is prepared. During production/build, a detailed plan is prepared for the next stage—implementation.

Implementation is the process of turning the system over to the user. The two prime activities in implementation are installing the system in the user's environment, and training the user to operate the system. The project manager must develop plans in advance so that the implementation stage can begin at or before completion of system fabrication. The plans must ensure that needed side-items will be available in time for user training, system installation, and operation. Planning for implementation starts early in the project, in the definition phase, but by the end of the production/build stage it must be substantially completed. The implementation strategy to replace the existing system with the new one should address:[5]

1. The approach to be used for converting from the old system to the new system
2. Sequencing and scheduling of implementation activities
3. Acceptance criteria for the new system
4. The approach to phasing out the old system and reassigning personnel.

An initial implementation plan might have been developed as part of the project master plan; now a more detailed plan is prepared with the participation of the customer to address the above points. As this plan is being prepared, the contractor accumulates materials to train the user in system operation and maintenance. For complex systems, these materials include manuals for procedures, system operation and repair, and servicing; testing manuals; training materials and simulators; manuals for training the trainers; and schematic drawings, special tools, and equipment for servicing and support. These are among the side-items mentioned previously.

Agreement must be reached with the customer about how and when the project can be closed out—that is, how and when the customer will consider the system acceptable and the project completed. Misunderstandings about this, such as "acceptance only after modification," can cause a project to drag on indefinitely; to prevent this, user requirements defined early in the project should include conditions or criteria for customer acceptance of the system. Further aspects of system implementation are discussed in Chapter 12.

11.4 THE CONTROL PROCESS

A major function of project management during the execution phase is to control the project. Author Daniel Roman defines the project control process as:

> Assessing actual against planned technical accomplishment, reviewing and verifying the validity of technical objectives, confirming the continued need for the project, timing it to coincide with operational requirements, overseeing resource expenditures, and comparing the anticipated value with the costs incurred.[6]

The control process can be compared to a home air-conditioning system:

1. The desired house temperature is set on the thermostat
2. The actual room temperature is measured by the thermostat, and the temperature variance determined (actual temperature minus desired temperature)
3. If the variance is positive, the thermostat turns on the air conditioner until the actual temperature coincides with the desired temperature (i.e., variance drops to zero).

Virtually every control process has similar steps, i.e.: (1) set the performance standards, (2) compare these standards with actual performance, and (3) take necessary corrective action. In projects there is a fourth step: report actions to all relevant stakeholders.

The first step, set *performance standards*, happens during the definition phase. These standards include user requirements, technical specifications, budgeted costs, schedules, and resource requirements set in the project plan.

The next step, compare the standards with *actual project performance*, happens during the execution phase. Budgets, schedules, and performance specifications are compared to actual expenditures, test results, work completed, and other measures of project performance.

The third step, take *corrective action*, happens whenever actual performance significantly differs from planned performance. Either the work is altered or expedited to achieve the planned results, or the plan is revised. If the original plan proves unrealistic, then the contractor must work with the customer to change the objectives and, accordingly, revise the requirements and modify the project plan.

The last step, *report changes to all relevant stakeholders*, is necessary to maintain trust and build a collaborative atmosphere among all stakeholders. There should be no surprises.

To keep the project aimed at requirements, schedules, and budgets, obviously there must initially be a plan! The precursor to project control is project definition; without clear and complete requirements and a good project plan, there can be no project control.

- Planning *sets the goals*; control *guides* the work toward those goals.
- Planning *allocates the resources*; control ensures effective *utilization* of those resources.
- Planning *anticipates problems*; control *corrects* the problems.
- Planning *motivates participants* to achieve goals; control *rewards* achievement of goals.

Project Monitoring

The purpose of *project monitoring* is to observe and track how well the project is doing, and to forecast how it will do in the future. Project monitoring involves collecting data, interpreting it, and reporting information.

The data collected must relate directly to project performance standards—i.e., to project plans, outputs, schedules, budgets, and requirements. Typical sources of data include materials purchasing invoices, worker time cards, change notices, test results, purchase and work orders, and expert opinion. A balance must be struck in the quantity and variety of data collected: too much data will be costly to collect and analyze, too little will not adequately capture the project status and will allow problems to go unchecked. The data must be analyzed, and the results reported quickly and frequently enough to enable managers to quickly spot deviations from the plan and take corrective action.[7]

How frequently should data be collected, assessed, and reported? A good rule of thumb is to assess work progress every week. For small projects, this ensures that even small work packages lasting only 2–3 weeks will be checked at least twice. For projects with work packages lasting several months, assessment every 2–3 weeks might be adequate. The goal is to check the work often enough so as to measure progress accurately, spot problems early, and foretell outcomes, yet not so often that it becomes burdensome. The frequency of assessing and reporting also depends on the people doing the work (competent and motivated people do not need to be monitored as often as less competent or less motivated people), and on the level of work monitored (e.g., less often at the program level and more often at the work package level).

Internal and External Project Control

Monitoring and regulating a project happens both internally and externally. *Internal control* refers to the contractor's procedures for monitoring work, reporting status, and taking action. *External control* refers to additional procedures imposed by the customer, including taking charge of project coordination and administrative functions. Military and government contracts, for example, impose external control by stipulating:[8]

- Frequent reports by the contractor on project-level schedules, cost, and technical performance
- Inspections of work by government program managers
- Inspection of the contractor's books and records by government auditors
- Strict terms imposed on the contractor on allowable project costs, pricing policies, etc.

External control can be a source of annoyance and aggravation to the contractor; since it involves managers overlooking managers, it adds to bureaucratic turmoil and administrative costs. Nonetheless, it is sometimes necessary to protect the customer's interests, especially in cost-plus projects. Ideally, the contractor and customer are able to work together to establish compatible plans, specifications, and methods for monitoring the work.

Traditional Cost Control

In non-project situations, work performance is measured with *variance analysis*, which compares the amount spent with the amount budgeted. For project control, simple cost variance analysis is inadequate.

Example 11.2: Cost Variance Analysis

Consider the following weekly status report for the work package "software development":

Budgeted cost for period=$12,000	Actual cost for period=$14,000	Period variance=$2,000
Cumulative budget to date=$25,000	Cumulative actual cost to date=$29,000	Cumulative variance=$4,000

The report indicates apparent overruns for both period and cumulative costs, with to-date cumulative costs running $4,000 over budget. But because we do not know how much work has been completed, it is impossible from this data to determine if the project is really over budget.

Suppose the $25,000 was the amount budgeted for completing 50 percent of software development. If 50 percent of the work had actually been completed (as intended), then the project would, in fact, be over budget, and something would have to be done to reduce or eliminate the $4,000 overrun. Now suppose only 30 percent of the work had been completed; in that case the project would be clearly over budget (and behind schedule too), and further cost overruns could be expected just to catch up. As a third possibility, suppose that 70 percent of the work had been completed, which is more than was scheduled, so the project would be ahead of schedule. In this case the project might not be over budget, because substantially more work had been completed than was planned for this date.

The point of the example is, to be able to assess project status, besides the cost variance you also need information about *work progress*—information such as percentage of work completed, milestones achieved, and so on, as discussed later.

Cost-Accounting Systems for Project Control

In the early 1960s, the US government developed a PERT-based scheduling and cost-accounting system called *PERT/Cost*.[9] The system became mandatory for all military and R&D contracts with the US Department of Defense and NASA (DOD/NASA). Any contractor wanting to work for DOD/NASA had to use the system and produce the necessary reports. The mandate increased usage of PERT/Cost, but also created resentment because many firms found the project-oriented system an expensive duplication of, or incompatible with, their existing functional-oriented accounting systems. Interestingly, many firms not working for DOD/NASA voluntarily adopted PERT/Cost with few complaints. PERT/Cost was an improvement over traditional cost-accounting techniques, and spurred the development of other even more sophisticated systems to track work and report progress and costs. It was the original network-based project cost accounting system (PCAS) mentioned in Chapter 8.

Today, most PCASs integrate information about work packages, budgets, and project schedules into a unified project control package. They permit the causes of cost and scheduling overruns to be pinpointed among numerous work packages or budgets. Two features common to many of these systems are use of *work packages* or *control accounts* as the basic data collection unit for project control, and the concept of *earned value* to measure project performance.

11.5 Work Packages and Control Accounts

Earlier chapters described the role of work packages and control accounts in project planning and budgeting; by no coincidence, they are also key elements of project control. Each control account consists of one or more work packages; each work package is considered a contract or agreement for a specific job, with a manager or supervisor, work descriptions, time-phased budget, work plan and schedule, resource requirements, and so on. Work packages and control accounts are also focal points for data collection, work progress evaluation, problem assessment, and corrective action.

Large projects may be composed of hundreds of work packages, making it potentially difficult to identify the ones causing a cost or schedule overrun. An advantage of a PCAS is that it can readily sort through all of the work packages to locate sources of problems. Although the individual work package remains the central element for control, a PCAS can consolidate and report information for *any* level of the project, from the individual control-account or work-package level up to the project level. Because higher-level accounts in the control-account structure are built up through the WBS and organizational hierarchies, variances in costs and schedules at any project level can be traced down through the structure to identify work packages causing the variances.

Work Authorization

A part of the control process is *work authorization* or start–stop control, which means that all work is started only after formal authorization and stopped only upon review and acceptance. This applies to all levels of a project, from the project level to the work package level. At the project level, authorization formally occurs upon the customer's, program manager's, and/or top management's acceptance of the project plan, which authorizes the project manager to execute the project. The project manager then authorizes the managers of subprojects to begin, who authorize managers and supervisors at the next level lower, and so on, as shown in Figure 11.3. The process is a continuation of the initiation and authorization process described in Chapter 3 and shown in Figure 3.8.

The same process also applies to authorizing the *phases* of a project: the customer and other stakeholders evaluate the plan for the next phase and, if they find the plan, the risks, and the *results* of the last phase acceptable, they authorize the project to proceed to the next phase (the "gating process" discussed in Chapter 16). Sometimes in contracted projects, if work during a phase is judged not up to expectation, the contractor is paid the amount owed at the end of the phase and the project is terminated.

On large projects, authorization is subdivided into the stages of *contract release*, *project release*, and *work order release* or *work requisition*. After the customer gives the okay and awards the contract, the contract administrator prepares a contract release document that specifies the contractual requirements and gives the project manager the go-ahead. The comptroller or project accountant then prepares a project release document, which authorizes project funding.

Work begins only upon receipt of a *work order* by the department or contractor responsible. The work order (or "engineering order," "shop order," or "test order," depending on the kind of work) specifies that the work package or activity is authorized to start. As the scheduled start date for the task draws near, the project manager or project office releases a work order or other authorization document, such as a

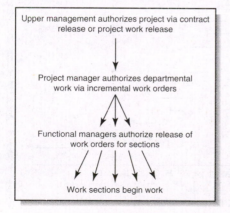

Figure 11.3
Project work authorization process.

purchase order or test request, as needed. For simple projects or simple activities, verbal authorization might suffice.

Collecting Cost, Schedule, and Work Progress Data

After work begins, data about *actual* costs and work progress on the work package are periodically collected and entered into the PCAS or project management information system, PMIS (discussed in Chapters 8 and 12). The PCAS generates performance reports periodically or as needed for each work package, department, and the entire project.

Assessing the impact of work progress on work schedules is the responsibility of the functional manager or team supervisor in charge of the work package. Each week, the supervisor tallies the labor hours for each task as indicated on time cards. She notes tasks completed and tasks still "open," and estimates the time still needed to complete open tasks. Progress is recorded on a Gantt chart showing completed (indicated by double lines) and open tasks. Figure 11.4 is an example showing the status of the LOGON project as of Week 20: work packages K, L, M, N, O, and Q are all open; the first three of them and Q are behind schedule.

How is work progress measured? Certainly costs and time elapsed are easy to measure. Unfortunately, neither says much about the actual progress made toward completing the project, so managers must rely on subjective measures. In a survey of conventional ways to measure ongoing project performance, Thompson identified the following.[10]

1. *Supervision*. Managers and supervisors assess progress by direct observation, asking questions, and reviewing written reports and project documentation.

Figure 11.4
Gantt chart showing work status as of Week 20.

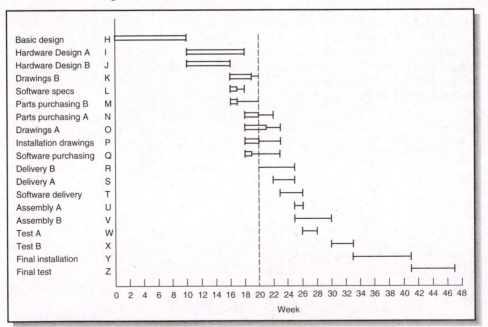

2. *Milestones achieved.* These are easily measured end-points of tasks, or transition points between tasks. Milestones represent achievement toward some desired level of performance, including, for example, completion of drawings, reports, design documents, or solution specific technical problems.

3. *Tests and demonstrations.* Described earlier, these can range from simple tests of system components to full-system and user acceptance tests. They are a good way of obtaining periodic, objective measures of technical progress at intermediate stages of the project.

4. *Design reviews.* Described earlier, these are meetings with managers and technical personnel to review the progress of a design or system against the plan.

5. *Outside experts.* The project manager or other stakeholder invites experts to serve on a panel. The panel assesses project status by observing work in progress, talking to project personnel, and reviewing documentation.

6. *Status of design documentation.* Experienced project managers can determine when a design is nearly finished by the "completeness" of documents such as drawings, schematics, functional diagrams, manuals, and test procedures.

7. *Resources utilized.* A request for or change in resources may reflect progress; for example, tasks nearing completion often require special testing or implementation facilities, personnel, and equipment.

8. *Telltale tasks.* Certain tasks such as concept design, requirements definition, feasibility analysis, and repeated testing usually happen early or midway in a project; their happening later in the project can signify a *lack* of progress.

9. *Benchmarking or analogy.* Certain tasks, or the entire project, may be compared to similar tasks or projects as a crude way to weigh relative progress.

10. *Changes, bugs, and rework.* Because, ordinarily, the number of changes, bugs, and so forth should decrease as the project nears completion, a sustained high number may indicate lack of progress. (This is called "issues tracking," and is discussed later.)

While measures like these are used to assess in-progress work and reveal emerging problems, still others are needed to *anticipate* problems; these are identified in the risk management plan (Chapter 10).

Any changes to estimates for budgets or schedules for remaining work are documented by the work package supervisor and submitted to the project manager for approval. Each week, the work package supervisor also tallies current expenses. Labor hours reported on time cards are converted into direct labor cost. The supervisor adds direct labor, material, and level-of-effort costs for completed and open tasks to the costs of work of prior periods, and then applies the overhead percentage rate to applicable direct charges. Late charges and outstanding costs (a frequent source of cost overruns) are also included.[11]

Each week a revised report is prepared showing costs of all work completed in prior periods plus work accomplished in the current period. This is reviewed, verified, and signed by the supervisor, and then forwarded to the project manager. Once work package information has been validated by the project manager it is entered into the PCAS, wherein costs to date for all work packages are accumulated and summary reports prepared. Periodically the project manager reviews the summary reports to reassess the project and prepare estimates of the work still needed and the cost to complete the project; these provide a forecast of the completion date and project cost at completion; this procedure is described later. Once a task or work package is completed, its budget is closed to prevent any additional, unauthorized billing.

Project control addresses five areas: scope, quality, schedule, cost, and procurement.

Scope Control

Projects have a natural tendency to grow over time because of changes and additions to the scope—a phenomenon called "scope creep." Changes or additions to the scope reflect changes in requirements and work definition, which are usually accompanied by increases in time and cost. The aim of scope control is to identify where requirements or work changes are occurring, ensure the changes are necessary and beneficial, restrain or delimit the changes wherever possible, and manage implementation of the changes. Because changes in scope directly impact schedules and costs, scope control is an important aspect of controlling schedules and costs. Scope control is implemented through the *change control system* and *configuration management*, described later.

Quality Control

Quality control is managing the work to achieve the desired requirements and specifications, and taking preventive measures to reduce or eliminate errors and mistakes in the work process.

Project quality control starts with the *quality management plan* described in Chapter 9. The quality plan states the necessary "quality conditions" for every work package; that is, prerequisites or stipulations about what must exist in each work package to ensure quality results. It also specifies the measures and procedures (tests, inspections, reviews, etc., as discussed earlier) to assess the conditions and progress toward meeting requirements. In technical projects, progress is tracked using a methodology called *technical performance measurement (TPM)*, discussed later.

Projects employ a variety of testing and inspection methods to eliminate defects and ensure that end-items satisfy requirements. The following illustrates an inspection approach appropriate for use in design engineering and software development projects.

Example 11.3: Team Inspection Process for Sofware Documents and Code[12]

The purpose of the team inspection process is to improve quality, shorten development time, and reduce costs by avoiding defects. The team meets in a group to review the requirements documents, design documents, and software code. The member roles during the meeting are as follows.

- *Moderator*: oversees the inspection procedure and records defects spotted in the document or code.
- *Reader*: reads the document or code, line by line.
- *Inspector(s)*: person who is the most knowledgeable about the document or code, has the most information, and is best able to detect errors.
- *Author*: creator of the document or code.

The author of the requirements document or code initiates the process by scheduling an inspection meeting. Every member of the inspection team is provided with a copy of the material to be inspected and all supporting documentation at least 2 days prior to the meeting.

Each inspection meeting lasts for about 2 hours, during which an average team can inspect 10–15 pages of text or 400 lines of code. Defects are documented, and the team decides whether it should meet again after the defects have been corrected. When the inspector signs off on the document or code, the process is considered complete and the material approved.

As part of a continuous improvement effort, the identified defects or mistakes can be entered into a database that, when referenced in other projects, reduces the chances of similar mistakes recurring.

To deal with quality problems that are both unique and repetitive, the project manager can appoint a *quality-improvement team*, which is a small group responsible for identifying and eliminating the sources of quality problems. On a small project, one cross-functional team might serve the function; on a large project, several specialized teams might be needed to address particular problems in certain phases or technical areas of the project.

Schedule Control

The intent of schedule control is to keep the project on schedule. Even when projects are carefully planned and estimated, they can fall behind for reasons beyond anyone's control—including, for example, necessary changes in project scope, weather problems, and material shortages. Other causes of schedule overruns discussed in Chapter 7 include multitasking, procrastination, and task time variability (the uncertainty about how long tasks will task).[13] Following are some guidelines for reducing schedule variability and schedule overruns.

Use Time Buffers

Described in Chapter 7, a time buffer is a schedule reserve, an amount of time included in the expected project duration to account for uncertainty. To implement a time buffer, the computed, expected finish date is increased by the buffer amount. If the late finish date is July 31 and the time buffer is 4 weeks, the target finish date is set for August 31.

Time buffers are an aspect of the critical chain methodology (CCPM), which prescribes locating them at the end of the critical chain for the entire project, and the ends of all subpaths feeding into the critical chain.[14] Once a project is underway, the amount of buffer "consumed" is tracked. Each time a task in the critical chain or a feeding chain is delayed, it "eats" into the time buffer. The more of the buffer consumed, the greater is the likelihood the buffer will be exhausted and the project will overrun the target finish date. Hence, the project should be managed so as to minimize consumption of the buffer.[15] Example 11.4 illustrates the process.

Example 11.4: Abbott Laboratories' Fever-Chart Tracking and Control[16]

Abbott Laboratories' Diagnostic Division (ADD) started using critical chain project management (CCPM) for some projects in 1999. Prior to that most projects were scheduled and tracked using the traditional critical path approach, and only about 20 percent were completed on time. Since using CCPM, about 80 percent have been completed on time.

The main tool for tracking and control in CCPM is the "fever chart," a graph that shows for a project the percentage of project buffer consumed versus the calendar time (Figure 11.5). Early on, a "healthy project" will have consumed little or none of its buffer. As the project progresses, however, the percentage of buffer consumed can be expected to increase, and the plot on the graph will rise diagonally. Monitoring the graph, the project manager is somewhat able to determine early in the project whether the project will be completed early, on time, or late; a sharp upward trend, for example, indicates that the project is stalled—little progress is being made on critical chain tasks. For a *healthy* project, the slope of the

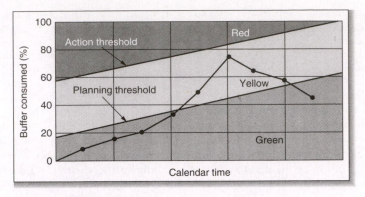

Figure 11.5
Chart of buffer consumed versus time.

line is shallow and a large part of the project buffer remains unconsumed by the end of the project. Completing a project with some buffer remaining is equivalent to the project being *completed ahead of target*. Thus, to complete the project early, the project must be managed so as to avoid consuming the project buffer; the more buffer remaining, the more the project is ahead of schedule.

The fever chart is divided into three regions, green, yellow, and red, to denote project status. Yellow indicates potential for the project to overrun its target date; red means strong potential to do so. Whenever a project falls into yellow or red, a flag is raised telling the project manager to seek out tasks in the project consuming the project buffer and causing the problem. A sharp upward line anywhere on the chart also indicates a problem—that little progress is being made on critical chain tasks. When a problematic task is identified, managers feed it more resources, decouple it from the critical chain, or employ other strategies. The fever chart is updated every week, and quick remedial action is taken whenever the plot veers out of the green zone.

The fever chart is but one way to manage time buffers.[17] The following explains another.

Example 11.5: Doling Out the Reserves: The Mars Pathfinder Project[18]

The goal of the Pathfinder project was to land on Mars a skateboard-sized, self-propelled, six-wheel rover that would move over the terrain and send back photos and scientific data (Figure 11.6). The project's budget reserve was $40 million, which represented 30 percent of the total budget (a large percentage, but common in risky technological projects), and its schedule reserve was 20 weeks, or about 13 percent of the project's 37-month design, build, and test schedule.

Once the project was underway, the question arose: How should the reserves be used? Use them too freely and too early and you have nothing left for later. Use them too stingily and you stifle progress, increase risk, and end up with leftover reserves that might have been put to good use. The guideline adopted was to set hard limits on the amount of the reserves available for use in each period of the project. For example, *none* of the schedule reserve was to be used (no slippage allowed) until the start of system assembly and test—at the halfway point in the project. But when problems arose, the guideline was to commit whatever budget reserves necessary to keep the project on schedule. (Time was a strategic issue, because the launch date had to coincide with the exact relative positioning of Earth and Mars.)

The project was a success. Pathfinder landed safely, and the little rover sent back thousands of pictures. The project established a new standard: it was able

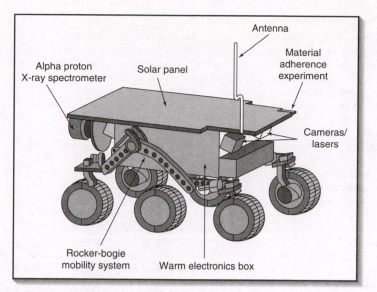

Figure 11.6
The Mars Pathfinder rover vehicle.

to design, build, and land a spacecraft in half the time and at one-twentieth the cost of previous Mars missions.

Fight Tendency to Multitask

As discussed in Chapter 7, it is important not to interrupt work on particular tasks or projects by interspersing it with work from other tasks or projects. Determining the priority of the tasks or projects and then working continuously on the high priority ones until they are completed reduces the total elapsed time to complete the work, and eliminates confusion about task or project priorities.

Frequently Report Activity Status

Tasks or work packages on the critical path or critical chain should be ready to start at the earliest possible time, but for that to happen the project team needs to know the status of each task's predecessors. Particularly in time-sensitive projects like Pathfinder, every activity should provide its successor activities with status reports on a daily basis, stating the expected days remaining to complete and the earliest date when successors should expect to begin work. The mandate is that *as soon as* immediate predecessors of a critical activity are completed, the group assigned to the next activity will begin work immediately, even if it has to stop doing something else. In CCPM, the resources or means that would enable work to begin early if needed is called a *resource buffer*.

Publicize Consequences of Schedule Delays, and Benefits of Early Finish

Everyone—team members, subcontractors, and suppliers—should know the consequences of a schedule overrun and the benefits of finishing early. The project contract might offer incentive payments for early completion, or the budget extra money for bonuses to workers and subcontractors who finish early. Other measures to keep projects on schedule are described next.

Microsoft meets product launch dates by utilizing visual freeze, internal target ship dates, and time buffers. A "visual freeze" is a halt imposed on the product that affects aspects of the product's visual appearance. The freeze date usually occurs at approximately the 40 percent mark of the schedule. Upon reaching that date, developers lock into the product its major features, and thereafter allow few (if any) changes in features such as menus, dialog boxes, and document windows. The freeze enables the user education group to prepare training and system documentation (side-items) in parallel with product final debugging and testing so the documentation will be ready at the time of product release.

Microsoft also sets "internal target dates" that pressure developers into deciding which product features absolutely must be included and which may be forgone. Without fixed dates, developers tend to keep adding product features and ignore the schedules. Given fixed ship dates, they must determine which features are minimally necessary to allow the product to be released on time.

To account for overlooked or poorly understood tasks, difficult bugs, and unforeseen changes in features, Microsoft also includes time buffers in project schedules. The buffers are used exclusively for uncertainties, not for routine or planned tasks. A buffer can range from 20 to 50 percent of the total schedule time. The project team strives to meet the internal ship date, which is the launch date announced to the public *minus* the time buffer.

Procurement Control[20]

The main contractor is responsible for the quality, schedule, and cost of all items procured for the project. Often, the project manager will visit and inspect the facilities of suppliers responsible for designing and producing these items to make sure they meet requirements. Once the project is underway, she monitors each supplier's progress by visiting the supplier's site and by requiring frequent status and, in the case of cost-type contracts, expense reports from the supplier. The project manager does whatever is necessary to prompt or assist suppliers when problems arise. For all major outsourced material, equipment, and components, contingency plans should be prepared, including possible contractual provision to transfer work to other suppliers if the original suppliers encounter serious or unrecoverable problems. These contingencies are addressed in the procurement plan and the project risk plan.

Cost Control

The purpose of cost control is to track variances in expenditures versus budgets, to eliminate unauthorized or inappropriate expenditures, and to minimize or contain cost changes. It identifies where and why variances have occurred, and when changes to cost baselines are necessary.

Cost control happens at both the work package level and the project level, using the cost account structure and PCAS, described earlier. Through the PCAS, actual expenditures are tallied, validated, accumulated, and compared to budgeted costs. Using the methods described next, the project manager periodically reviews actual and budgeted costs, assesses the work completed, and estimates the project's completion cost and completion date.

Cost and Schedule Analysis with Earned Value

The status of the project or any portion of it can be assessed with three variables: BCWS, ACWP, and BCWP. These are industry-standard acronyms, but to save ink and conform to the Project Management Institute (PMI), we will use the abbreviated terms PV, AC, and EV.

1. *PV* is the *planned value*—the sum cost of all work and apportioned effort scheduled to be completed within a given time period as specified in the *original budget*. For example, in Chapter 8, Table 8.5 and Figure 8.15 show the cumulative and weekly expenses for the LOGON project. These amounts represent PV. In Week 20, for example, to-date PV is $512,000 and weekly PV is $83,000. PV is also referred to as *BCWS*—the *budgeted cost of the work scheduled.*
2. *AC* (or *ACWP*) is the *actual cost of the work performed*—the actual expenditure as of a given time period.
3. *EV* is the *earned value* (also termed the *budgeted cost of the work performed*— BCWP)—the *value* of the work performed so far (fully and partially completed work packages) according to the *original budget*.[21] Thus,

   - EV for a completed work task is the same as the PV for that task.
   - EV for a partially completed work task is computed as the estimated *percent complete* for the task multiplied by the budget for the task. (Alternatively, it is computed as 50 percent of the task budget when the task is started, then the remaining 50 percent of the budget when the task is completed.)

The following example illustrates these concepts.

Example 11.7: EV versus PV in the Parmete Company

The Parmete Company has a $200,000 fixed cost contract to install 1,000 new parking meters. The contract calls for removing old parking meters from their stands and replacing them with new ones. The cost for this is $200 per meter.

Parmete estimates that 25 meters can be installed each day. At that rate (25 meters per day and a cost of $200 per meter), the project should take 40 working days to finish and have a final PV of $200,000. Also on that basis, the planned value of the work scheduled (PV) as of *any given day* can be determined by multiplying the number of working days completed as of that day by the cost of installing 25 meters ($200 times 25). For example, as of Day 18,

$$PV = 18 \text{ days} \times (25 \text{ meters}) \times (\$200) = \$90,000$$

That is to say, as of the 18th day of work on the project, the project schedule and budget say that $90,000 worth of work should have been done. Notice that PV is always associated with a specific date on the project schedule.

In contrast, the *earned value* (EV) for any given day represents the value if the work *actually* done in terms of the budget. In this project, EV is the number of meters *actually* installed to-date times the $200 budgeted for each meter. Suppose, for example, that as of the 18th day 400 meters had been installed; thus,

$$EV = (400 \text{ meters}) \times (\$200) = \$80,000$$

In other words, as of the 18th day, $80,000 worth of work has been performed. Now, given that $90,000 was the amount of work that was *supposed* to have been performed, the project is $10,000 worth of work *behind schedule*. Notice, the $10,000 does not represent a cost saving, but rather the value of work that

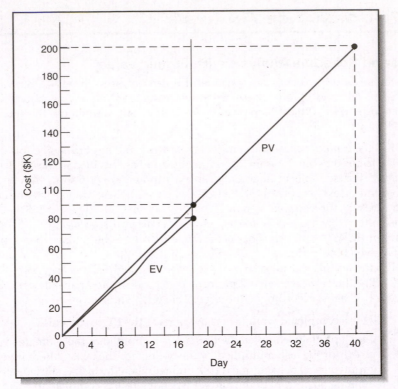

Figure 11.7
Graph of PV and EV.

should have been but has not been done. It represents 50 parking meters, or 2 days worth of work, meaning that as of the 18th day the project is 2 days behind schedule. (The 2 days is referred to as the time variance, or TV.) Thus, EV represents a translation of project cost into work progress. As of Day 18, this project has made only 16 days' worth of work progress. This is represented on the graph for PV and EV in Figure 11.7.

As stated, besides completed tasks, the EV must also reflect any tasks only partially completed (open tasks). For example, suppose that before quitting at the end of the 18th day the meter installer had just enough time to remove an old meter but not to put in a new one. Therefore, the work on that task was 50 percent completed. If this were the 401st meter, then EV would be the full cost for the first 400 meters plus 50 percent of the cost for the 401st:

$$EV = \$80,000 + (0.50)(\$200) = \$80,100$$

Thus, on Day 18 the EV is $80,100, which represents slightly more than 16 days [$80,100/(25×$200) = 16.02 days] of work completed; hence this project is slightly less than 2 days behind schedule.

The variables PV, AC, and EV can also be used to compute variances that reveal different aspects of a project's status. For example, assume for the LOGON project in week 20 that

$$PV = \$512,000$$
$$AC = \$530,000$$
$$EV = \$429,000.$$

Using these figures, three kinds of variances can be determined, as shown in Figure 11.8:

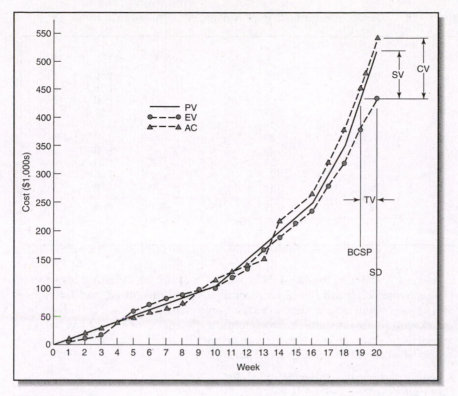

Figure 11.8
LOGON project status as of Week 20.

1. *Schedule variance*: SV = EV − PV = −$83,000
2. *Time variance*: TV = SD − BCSP [Note: SD is the "status date" (here, week 20); for BCSP (budgeted cost, scheduled performance), look on Figure 11.8 at EV for week 20, then see the week where PV equals this EV (about week 19)]; thus, TV = (20 − 19) = 1 week
3. *Cost variance*: CV = EV − AC = −$101,000.

A negative SV indicates that the project is behind schedule; a positive value suggests the project is ahead of schedule. Given that the SV as of Week 20 is −$83,000, the project is behind schedule. TV shows approximately how much the project is behind schedule—in this case about 1 week because only $429,000 worth of work has been completed (EV), which is roughly the value of work scheduled (PV) to have been completed about 1 week earlier.

The CV compares the earned value of work completed with actual costs: a negative CV indicates that the project is overspending for the work completed, while a positive figure indicates that it is underspending. The CV of −$101,000 indicates that LOGON is overspending.

Work Package Analysis and Performance Indices

Determining the status of the project requires information about the performances of all work packages. With information from the PCAS, charts similar to Figure 11.4 and Figure 11.8 can be prepared for every work package and control account.

Table 11.1 LOGON Performance Report Week 20 Cumulative to Date

ACTIVITY	PV	AC	EV	SV	CV	SPI	CPI
H*	100	100	100	0	0	1.00	1.00
I*	64	70	64	0	−6	1.00	0.91
J*	96	97	96	0	−1	1.00	0.99
K	16	12	14	−2	2	0.88	1.17
L	36	30	18	−18	−12	0.50	0.60
M	84	110	33	−51	−77	0.39	0.30
N	40	45	40	0	−5	1.00	0.89
O	20	28	24	4	−4	1.20	0.86
P	24	22	24	0	2	1.00	1.09
Q	32	16	16	−16	0	0.50	1.00
Project	512	530	429	−83	−101	0.84	0.81

*Completed.

Consider the status of the LOGON project as of Week 20. Referring back to Figure 11.4, activities H, I, and J have been completed and are closed, and activities K through Q are "open" and underway. This Gantt chart gives a general *overview* of work package and project status, but to determine the origins or sizes of any delays or overruns it is necessary to assess each work activity in detail; this is done by computing two *performance indices* for each work package:

1. Schedule performance index: SPI = EV/PV
2. Cost performance index: CPI = EV/AC.

Values of SPI and CPI greater than 1.0 indicate that work is ahead of schedule and under budget, respectively; values less than 1.0 indicate the opposite.

Table 11.1 shows performance information for all LOGON activities as of Week 20. The indices CPI and SPI show trouble spots and their relative magnitude: L, M, and Q have fallen the most behind schedule (they have the smallest SPIs), and L and M have the greatest cost overruns relative to their sizes (they have the smallest CPIs). The overall project is "somewhat" behind schedule and over cost (SPI = 0.84; CPI = 0.81).

Focusing on *only* the project level or *only* the work package level to assess project status can be misleading, and the project manager should scan both, back and forth. If she looks only at the project level, good performance of some activities may hide poor performance in others. If she focuses only on individual work packages, the cumulative effect from slightly poor performance in many activities can easily be overlooked. Even small cost overruns in many individual work packages can add up to a large overrun for the project.

The importance of examining variances at both project and work package levels is illustrated in the following example. The SV in Figure 11.8 (which is −$83,000) suggests that the project is behind schedule, and TV = −1 day. However, scrutinizing Figure 11.4 reveals that only one of the work packages behind schedule, Activity M, is on the critical path (see Chapter 6, Figure 6.8). Since Activity M appears to be about 3 weeks behind schedule (Figure 11.4), the project must also be 3 weeks behind schedule—*not* 1 week, as estimated by the project level SV.

The importance of monitoring performance at the work package level is further illustrated by an example from the ROSEBUD project. Figure 11.9 is the cost report for Work Package L for Month 2. (The numbers in the PV columns are derived from

Figure 11.9

Cost chart for ROSEBUD project as of Month 2.

Project ROSEBUD						**Date** Month 2				
Department Programming						**Work Package** L Software specifications				

Charge	Current Period					Cumulative to date				
	PV	EV	AC	SV	CV	PV	EV	AC	SV	CV

Direct labor
  Professional
  Associate
  Assistant										

Direct labor cost Labor overhead Other direct cost	6,050 4,538	4,840 3,630	6,050 5,445	−1,210 −908	−1,210 −1,815	6,050 4,538	4,840 3,630	6,050 5,445	−1,210 −908	−1,210 −1,815
Total direct cost General/administrative	10,588 1,059	8,470 847	11,495 1,150	−2,118 −212	−3,025 −303	10,588 1,059	8,470 847	11,495 1,150	−2,118 −212	−3,025 −303
Total costs	11,647	9,317	12,645	−2,330	−3,328	11,647	9,317	12,645	−2,330	−3,328

Note: EV is for 80 percent of work scheduled and labor overhead is increased
to 90 percent of labor cost.

SPI: EV/PV = 0.80   CPI EV/AC = 0.74

the Month 2 column in the budget plan in Figure 8.8, Chapter 8.) Current period and cumulative numbers are the same because Work Package L begins in Month 2.

The performance indices for ROSEBUD Work Package L are:

$$SPI = EV/PV = 0.80$$
$$CPI = EV/AC = 0.74$$

indicating both schedule and cost overruns as of Month 2. Suppose the project manager investigates the costs for Work Package L and finds the following:

First, although AC and PV for direct labor are equal, PV reflects the estimate that only 80 percent of work scheduled for the period was actually performed (EV = PV × SPI = 6,050 × 0.80 = 4,850). Second, although AC and PV for direct labor are equal, the AC and PV for labor overhead are different due to an increase in labor overhead rate from 75 percent to 90 percent during Month 2. Whereas PV would reflect the old rate (0.75 × 6,050 = 4,538), AC would reflect the new (0.9 × 6,050 = 5,445). The point? The fact that AC > PV in this case has no bearing on the actual work performance of the work package but stems from a change in overhead rates—something over which the project manager has no control.

Now look at Figure 11.10, the cost report for the same work package but for Month 3.

The performance indices for cumulative figures are

$$SPI = EV/PV = 1.00$$
$$CPI = EV/AC = 0.92$$

Notice first that direct labor AC and PV for the month are the same, but more work was performed than planned for the month (EV > PV). This made up for the work deficit in Month 2, with the result that the task was completed on schedule (indicated by SPI = 1.00). The work package has a negative CV, but that was caused by an increase in the labor overhead rate, budgeted at 75 percent but now at 90 percent.

In summary, of the numerous factors that affect project work progress and costs, some are beyond the project manager's control. To determine the sources of variances

Project ROSEBUD						Date Month 3				
Department Programming						Work Package L Software specifications				

Charge	Current Period					Cumulative to date				
	PV	EV	AC	SV	CV	PV	EV	AC	SV	CV

Direct labor
  Professional
  Associate
  Assistant										

Direct labour cost Labor overhead Other direct cost	5,000 3,750	6,050 4,538	5,000 4,500	1,050 788	1,050 38	11,050 8,288	11,050 8,288	11,050 9,945	0 0	0 1,657
Total direct cost General/administrative	8,750 875	10,588 1,059	9,500 950	1,838 184	1,088 108	19,338 193	19,338 193	20,995 2,100	0 0	1,657 166
Total costs	9,625	11,647	10,450	2,022	1,196	21,272	21,272	23,095	0	1,823

Note: EV is for 121 percent of work scheduled, but for cumulative it is 100 percent (made up for delay in Period 2). $1,823 CV reflects increase in overhead rate.

Figure 11.10
Cost chart for ROSEBUD project as of Month 3.

and places where action can or must be taken requires scrutiny of costs and performance at the work package level. Project level analysis is simply inadequate.

Monitoring Performance Indexes and Variances

Using project-level CPI and SPI, a project manager can get a quick "ballpark" estimate of the project's performance to date. Although the estimate can be somewhat inaccurate, it allows the manager to track broad trends in project performance. The plot of SPI against CPI in Figure 11.11 is an example. According to the plot, LOGON started out in the marginal and poor regions, briefly recovered, and then, disturbingly, drifted back to and *remained* in the poor region. If such were the case, the project manager would be talking to team leaders and functional managers to identify the detailed causes of the problems.

Seldom do actual and planned performance measures coincide; as a result, nonzero variances are more often the rule than the exception. This leads to the question: What amount of variance is acceptable before action should be taken?

For each level of the project organization—work package, departmental, and project—"acceptable" limits on variances should be set, as shown in Table 11.2. Only when a variance falls beyond the limit are corrective measures considered. Some variance limits are allowed to vary throughout the duration of the project; others are held constant. In research projects, for example, variance limits start out somewhat large

Table 11.2 Example of Variance Boundaries

Work Package A	Variances greater than $2,000
Work Package B	Variances greater than $18,000
Department C	Variances greater than $6,000
Department D	Variances greater than $38,000
Project	Variances greater than $55,000

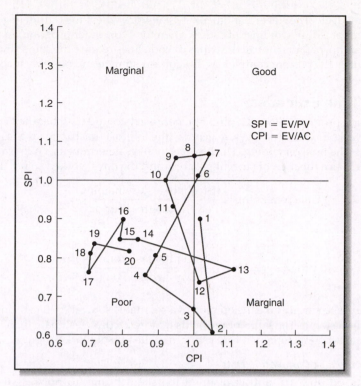

Figure 11.11
LOGON Project cost/schedule performance plotted for months 1 through 20.

early on, and are reduced as stages of the project are completed. This coincides with project uncertainty, which starts out large but diminishes as the project progresses.

Upper and lower variance limits are also set on parameters for technical performance. Lower limits are necessary to insure technical requirements are met, but upper limits are also necessary to prevent excessive or unnecessary development work. The limits are important for cost and schedule control, too. A project running ahead of schedule and under budget—an apparently desirable situation—might in fact be riddled with oversights, corner-cutting, and shoddy workmanship. Variance limits help identify places where work quality is in question.

Shortcomings of the Earned Value Method

Earned value information can be inaccurate and sometimes misleading, so it must be treated with caution. For example, a negative CV (overrun) can arise because of excessive overhead charges, which originate outside the project and have little bearing on its performance. Similarly, a positive CV (underrun) can occur simply because bills have yet to be paid. Whenever payments are made in periods other than when expenses are incurred or budgeted, the CV is skewed. This leads some companies to apply the method to some cost factors (e.g., labor-costs for their own employees) and not others (e.g., procured items requiring advance payment). In the end, individual cost sources should be scrutinized to identify the reasons for variances.

Also, the method relies on estimates of percent complete. Accurate estimates of percent complete are possible whenever work can be measured in uniform units (e.g., number of bricks laid, miles of asphalt laid, feet of weld run produced, number of fixtures installed, etc.); however, for other kinds of work where the output (e.g. drawings produced for a design or lines of code written for a computer program) cannot be measured in uniform units (not all drawings or code lines require the same amount of time to produce), the percent complete is difficult to estimate and possibly inaccurate.

Updating Time Estimates

Following each progress review, it might be necessary to update scheduled completion dates of tasks or work packages. In general, the forecast finish date for a task is the start date plus the time remaining. The *time remaining* is determined in two ways; one is to consider it as a function of current progress and the days worked so far; that is:

$$\text{Time remaining} = \frac{\text{Percent of task remaining}}{\text{Percent progress per day}}$$

where

$$\text{Percent progress per day} = \frac{\text{Percent of task completed so far}}{\text{Days worked on task so far}}$$

The other way is to simply take the opinion of a reputable source ("it'll take another 5 days to finish the job"). The latter often yields a more accurate estimate than the former, because it accounts for any recent changes in the rate of work progress.

Example 11.8: Revising the Task Completion Date

A task starts on July 10, and is planned to take 12 days to finish (weekends included). After 5 working days (end of July 14), the job leader estimates that the task is 20 percent complete. If the rate of progress stays the same, what is the forecast completion date of the task?

For 5 days of work, the estimated percent complete is 20 percent, so the work progress is 20 percent/5=4 percent per day. Thus, completing the remaining 80 percent of the task should take 0.80/0.04, or 20 working days, and the revised completion date would be August 3.

Now instead assume that the team leader believes that the remainder of the task will proceed much faster than 4 percent per day because of an accelerated work pace, and that, at most, 10 more working days will be required. If the team leader's estimate is considered more credible than the computation, the revised completion date would be July 24.

Technical Performance Measurement

Besides costs and schedules, project performance depends on how well the project is meeting technical requirements of the end-item. *Technical performance measurement* (TPM) is a method for tracking the history of a set of technical objectives or requirements over time. TPM's purpose is to provide (1) a best estimate of current technical performance or progress to date, and (2) an estimate of the technical performance at project completion. Both kinds of estimates are based upon results from modeling, simulation, or tests and demonstrations.[22]

To perform TPM, it is necessary first to specify the technical performance measures that are key indicators for the end-item system. These measures should be tied to customer requirements, and represent major performance drivers. A large-scale system might have a dozen or so high-level measures, in which case it is necessary to define the design parameters upon which each measure depends, and to set required values for these parameters. Examples of performance measures include:

Availability	Capacity	Size/space
Back-up utility	Response time	Reliability
Safety	Security	Power/thrust
Speed	Set-up time	Interface compatibility
Survivability	Durability	Interoperability
Maintainability	Range	Simplicity/complexity
Flexibility	Variance	Signal-to-noise ratio
Cycle time	Cost	Trip time
Efficiency	Utilization	Idle time
Output rate	Error/defect rate	Weight

Periodically during the project, performance is calculated or gauged and then compared to targets. Initially, measures are based upon estimates from computation, modeling, and simulations; later, measures are derived from test and demonstration results on actual hardware and software. Estimates and actual measures of the technical objective are plotted on a time-phased TPM chart that shows progress being made toward achieving the objective. If actual performance for one part of the system *exceeds* the target or objective by some margin, then that margin can be traded off against targets for other parts of the system where performance is lacking or at risk. This is illustrated next.

Example 11.9: TPM for Design Trade-Off Decisions

Example 5 in Chapter 10 discussed design margins. In the example, the design target weights for two components of a spacecraft navigation system were put at 44 pounds for Subsystem A and 26.4 pounds for Subsystem B. To cover the risk associated with meeting these targets, design margins were established for the two subsystems; these margins represent amounts by which the target values *could* be increased and still achieve system requirements.

The TPM chart in Figure 11.12 shows the design progress (actual versus target values) for the two subsystems. Managers and engineers use charts like this to assess progress toward design targets and to make design trade-off decisions. This chart shows current performance and design targets at three project milestones:

1. At the time of the *preliminary model demonstration*, the actual measured weights for both subsystems were too high, although Subsystem A was relatively much closer to its design target value than was Subsystem B.
2. By the time of the *pre-critical review*, Subsystem A had been improved and was close to meeting its design weight; however Subsystem B was still far away from its target. It was clear that Subsystem A would be able meet its design target of 44 pounds but Subsystem B would *not* be able to meet its target of 26.4 pounds. The decision was made to reduce Subsystem A's unused design margin by 3.6 pounds, and to increase Subsystem B's design target by that amount to 30 pounds.
3. As of the *critical design review*, Subsystem A had met its target value, but Subsystem B still lagged behind its own; further, it was anticipated that only limited additional improvement in B was possible. The decision was made to transfer 6 pounds more from Subsystem A's unused design margin to Subsystem B's target value, increasing it to 36 pounds. The dotted line for Subsystem B beyond the critical design review is the improvement still necessary to achieve Subsystem B's revised target value.

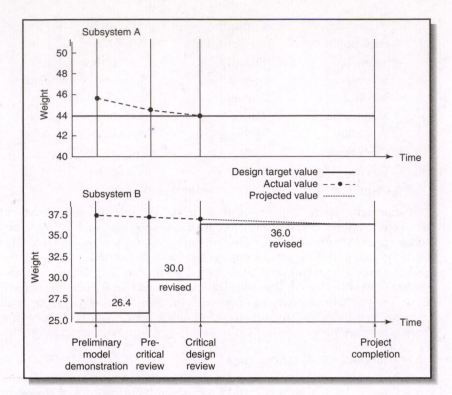

Figure 11.12
Time-phased TPM charts for subsystems A and B.

Issues Tracking[23]

Problems, concerns, or "issues" such as incomplete documentation, unending changes in designs and project plans, unresolved system bugs, and ongoing rework can build up and, if unresolved, stall the project. While every project encounters issues, in a healthy project they are dealt with expediently. When they are not, the backlog of issues grows and becomes increasingly difficult to handle. Figure 11.13 shows the

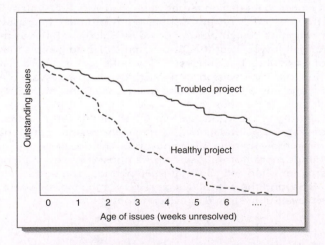

Figure 11.13
Number of outstanding (unresolved) issues versus age of issues.

number of outstanding issues at a particular time during a project, and how long they have gone unresolved. The slight decline in the top curve is for a troubled project; the outstanding issues are numerous, and some are many weeks old. The bottom curve is for a healthy project where issues are addressed and fixed rather quickly. Tracking issues like this is still another way to track project performance.

11.8 FORECASTING "TO COMPLETE" AND "AT COMPLETION"

As the project moves along, the project manager assesses not only what has been accomplished but also what remains to be done. Depending on the project's current status and direction, its expected final cost and completion date might be revised.

Estimate at Completion

Periodically the project manager prepares a *to-complete* forecast, which is an estimate of the time and cost needed to complete the project. This forecast plus the current status of the project provide an estimate of the date and cost of the project *at completion*. The following formulas provide estimates for the cost remaining to complete the project (the *to-complete* cost) and the estimated project final cost (the *at completion* cost):

$$\text{ETC (Estimated cost To Complete project)} = (\text{BAC} - \text{EV})/\text{CPI}$$

where BAC is the *Budgeted* cost At Completion for the project (= total PV at target completion).

$$\text{EAC (Estimated cost At Completion)} = \text{AC} + \text{ETC}$$

The following two examples illustrate.

Example 11.10: Forecasting ETC and EAC for ROSEBUD Project

Figure 11.14 shows the ROSEBUD project Gantt chart with percent complete for Week 13 and corresponding information about PV, EV, and AC. Based upon this information, how much will the project likely cost to complete, and how much will it cost at completion?

The value of the work completed so far (EV) is $268,081. The total budgeted amount for the project (BAC) is $344,205, hence the value of the work remaining is BAC – EV = $76,124.

The cost performance for the project so far is

$$\text{CPI} = \text{EV}/\text{AC} = 268{,}081/288{,}657 = 0.9287$$

Hence the project is receiving less than 93 cents value for each dollar spent. At that rate, the estimated to-complete cost

$$\text{ETC} = 76{,}124/0.9287 = \$81{,}968.$$

Since $288,657 has already been spent, the project cost at completion will be

$$\text{EAC} = \text{AC} + \text{ETC} = 288{,}657 + 81{,}968 = \$370{,}625.$$

This is an overrun of $370,625 – $344,205 = $26,420, or 7.7 percent.

Notice that according to EV, the project is slightly ahead of schedule (EV = 268,081) > (PV = 252,101). (More likely, however, the project is *behind* schedule because Activity V is on the critical path and is roughly 1 week behind schedule according to the Gantt chart.)

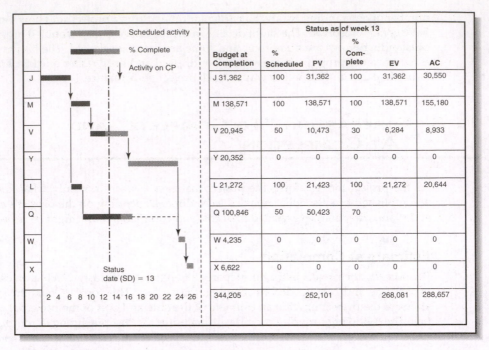

Figure 11.14
ROSEBUD project status as of Week 13.

The table in the figure, "Status as of week 13":

Budget at Completion	% Scheduled	PV	% Complete	EV	AC
J 31,362	100	31,362	100	31,362	30,550
M 138,571	100	138,571	100	138,571	155,180
V 20,945	50	10,473	30	6,284	8,933
Y 20,352	0	0	0	0	0
L 21,272	100	21,423	100	21,272	20,644
Q 100,846	50	50,423	70		
W 4,235	0	0	0	0	0
X 6,622	0	0	0	0	0
344,205		252,101		268,081	288,657

Example 11.11: Forecasting ETC and EAC for LOGON project

From discussion earlier in the chapter, for the LOGON project at Week 20:

$$CPI = 429,000/530,000 = 0.81, \text{ thus,}$$
$$ETC = (990,000 - 429,000)/0.81 = \$692,593, \text{ and}$$
$$EAC = 530,000 + 692,593 = \$1,222,593.$$

Lacking other information, the revised project completion date is estimated as shown in Figure 11.15 by extending the EV line, keeping it parallel to the PV line, until it reaches the level of BAC, $990,000. The *horizontal* distance between the PV line and the EV line at BAC ($990,000) is roughly the schedule overrun (negative time variance) for the project; on Figure 11.15 this is roughly 3 weeks, so the project will be completed in Week 50 instead of Week 47.

This revised completion date remains to be verified, because the actual delay will depend on whether the activities behind schedule are on the critical path. From an earlier discussion we know that since Activity M is on the critical path and is 3 weeks behind schedule, the LOGON project will also be 3 weeks behind.

As shown in Figure 11.15, another line, the "Forecast AC," can be drawn by extending the current AC line up to the level of EAC ($1,159,630) at the revised completion date of Week 50. This gives a running estimate of what the "actual" costs might be until project completion.

The forecast completion cost and date assume that conditions and resources will neither improve nor worsen. The LOGON project manager should question the validity of these assumptions in light of the project environment. Given the size of the current overrun ($101,000 as of Week 20), she should question the reasonableness of the forecasted completion cost of $1,159,530. Given that the project is less than half finished, is it likely that all remaining work can be completed for $692,593 without additional overruns? If the answer is no, the figure should be revised again according to best-guess estimates.

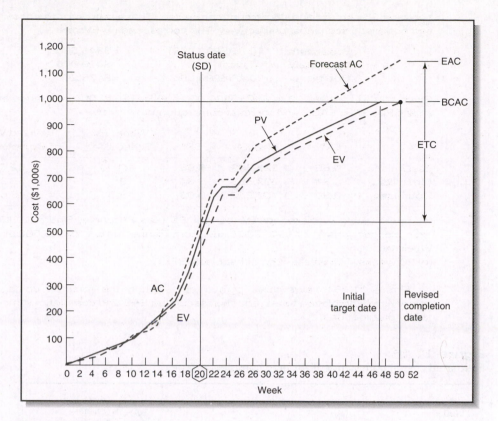

Figure 11.15
LOGON project status chart and forecast as of Week 20.

If the *schedule performance* does not improve, it is likely that the project will be completed later than the revised estimate of Week 50. As of Week 20, the EV is equivalent to the PV at Week 19. This means, in terms of budgeted cost, work remaining on the project might take

47 weeks (target date) – 19 weeks = 28 weeks.

However, given the current SPI = 0.84, it is possible the project has 28/0.84 = 33.3 weeks remaining. Since the project is now in Week 20, the revised completion date is 20 + 33.3 = Week 53.3.

Effect of Uncertainty

The EAC is based upon a single-value assessment of EV as of the SD. This assessment is usually based upon opinions about the percent complete, which means it is subject to uncertainty. If the EV is subject to uncertainty, then so is the EAC. A way to account for this uncertainty is to consider optimistic, pessimistic, and most likely values of EAC, as illustrated next.[24]

Example 11.12: Uncertainty in Forecast EAC and Completion Date

For the LOGON project, the EV as of Week 20 is $429,000. With the project budgeted at $990,000, this means the project is 43.3 percent completed. Suppose that an expert looks at the project and concludes that in actuality it is somewhere between 35 percent and 48 percent completed. These represent the pessimistic and optimistic scenarios, respectively. The corresponding EVs are:

Pessimistic	0.35($990,000)	=$346,500
Most likely	(given)	$429,000
Optimistic	0.48($990,000)	=$475,200

Given that as of Week 20 the AC=$530,000 and PV=$512,000, the range of possible CPIs, SPIs, EACs, and forecast completion dates are:

	CPI	EAC ($)	SPI	Week, PV Scheduled[a]	Revised Week of Completion[b]
Pessimistic	0.65	1,322,308	0.68	18	62.6
Most likely	0.81	1,222,593	0.84	19	53.3
Optimistic	0.90	1,102,222	0.93	19.5	49.6

(a) Approximate week where EV=current PV (see PV curve, Figure 11.15). For example, pessimistic EV=346,500 since, from Figure 11.15, PV=346,500 at about Week 18.
(b) 20 weeks+[47 weeks−(PV, scheduled)]/SPI.

Figure 11.16 shows three points representing the forecast costs (EAC) and revised completion times, and the associated EAC and completion-time probability distributions.

Figure 11.16
Estimated cost at completion (EAC) and completion times.

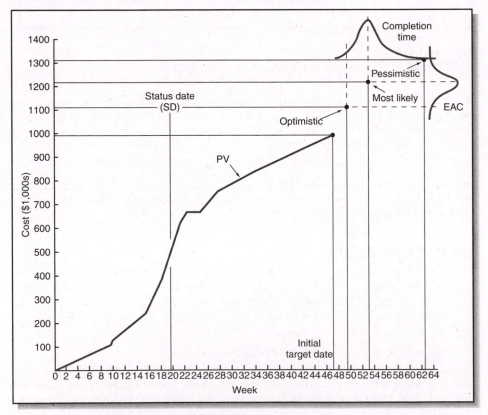

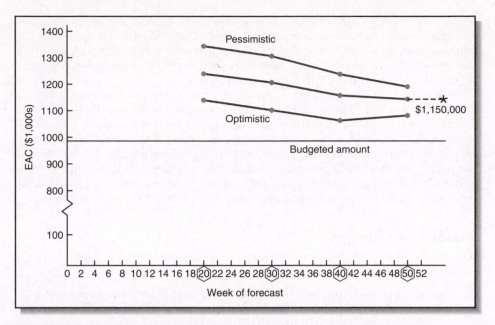

Figure 11.17
Plots of pessimistic, most likely, and optimistic EACs at four review periods.

The estimated completion times do not reflect which, if any, of the current behind-schedule activities are on the critical path; they reflect only the current rate at which the work is being done and assume that the pace of work is uniform everywhere in the project, on critical and non-critical activities alike.

The optimistic, most likely, and pessimistic measures for cost and time can be forecast at periodic intervals throughout the project. The forecasting procedure at Week 20 (Example 11.11) may be repeated at, say, Weeks 30, 40, and 50. Figure 11.17 shows plots of the three EAC forecasts at four times starting in Week 20. (Similarly, plots of periodic forecasts for optimistic, most likely, and pessimistic completion times can also be constructed.) The convergence of the pessimistic and optimistic forecasts in the figure suggests that the project is heading toward a most likely EAC of $1,150,000.

11.9   CONTROLLING CHANGES

No project goes entirely according to plan. Changes to the end-item system and project plan are inevitable because of planning oversights, new opportunities, or unforeseen events or problems. Such changes involve modifying the work, reorganizing or adding personnel, and trading off among time, cost, and performance. Alterations to specifications and sacrifices to technical performance are sometimes necessary to meet time and cost constraints.

The Impact of Changes

Generally, the larger and more complex the project, the greater the number of changes and the more that actual costs and schedules deviate from objectives. The fact is, changes are a chief cause of cost and schedule overruns, low worker morale, and poor relationships between contractors and clients. Each change has a ripple effect: in response to an emergent problem, elements of the end-item and project plan must be changed—but, in chain-reaction fashion, these then require changes to other elements of the end-item and project, which impact still others.

Because design changes to one component require redesign of other interrelated components, needed changes identified during system assembly and testing lead to rework, which increases project cost and duration. Changes made still later in the project, during construction and installation, are even more troublesome. Work is interrupted, torn down and redone, and materials are scrapped. Morale is affected, too: people see their work being dismantled, discarded, and redone, and everyone feels rushed and under pressure to get the project back on budget and schedule. In general, the further along the project, the more detrimental is the effect of changes.

Reasons for Changes

Harrison lists the following as typical kinds of changes sought or required during a project:[25]

1. Changes in project scope and specifications during the early stages of development. As a rule of thumb, the more uncertainty in the project, the more likely the scope and specifications will have to be altered later in the project.
2. Changes in design, necessary or discretionary, because of errors, omissions, unknowns, afterthoughts, or revised needs. Mistakes or omissions must of necessity be corrected or accommodated, but discretionary changes requested by clients should be questioned, especially when they alter the original, contractual scope of the project. Customers sometimes try to squeeze in changes beyond original specifications for the original price.
3. Changes mandated by government codes (health, safety, labor, environment), labor contracts, suppliers, the community, or other parties in the environment. There is usually no choice: the plan must be altered to incorporate these.
4. Changes that are believed to improve the rate of return of the project. Because estimating the rate of return is difficult, decisions of this nature should be referred to upper management.
5. Changes perceived to improve upon original requirements. Many people want to improve upon their work; although apparently desirable, these improvements can expand the project beyond its original scope and requirements.

Examples of the above changes include the following: (1) after the design is already completed, the payload requirement on a space probe is increased to allow for unanticipated but necessary hardware; (2) a buried cable is encountered during excavation and must be rerouted; (3) work is interrupted because of labor problems or municipal code violations; (4) the designed capacity of a refinery under construction is altered to increase the refinery's output rate; and (5) more features are added to an already acceptable software design (bloatware) to enhance the perceived marketability. Note that some changes are *discretionary*, i.e., they can be avoided (1, 4, and 5), while others are *de facto*, i.e., they just "happen" (2 and 3).

Change Control System and Configuration Management

Because of the adverse effect of changes on project costs and schedules, project managers usually try to resist changes. Disagreements between contractors, suppliers, project and functional managers, and customers over the necessity for changes and the impact of changes on project scope, cost, and schedule are common. Often such disagreements have to be resolved by upper management and result in renegotiated contracts.

One way to reduce the number of changes and their negative impact on project performance is to employ a formal *change control system*. Because changes are similar to other aspects of project work—i.e., they must be defined, scheduled, and budgeted—the process of drafting and implementing changes is similar to the project planning process. The change control system includes procedures to review all proposed design and work changes, weed out all but the necessary ones, and make sure that all related work is also reviewed, revised, and authorized. According to Harrison, the system should:[26]

1. Continually identify changes as they occur
2. Reveal the consequences of changes in terms of impact on project costs, project duration, and other tasks
3. Accept or reject proposed changes based upon analysis of impacts
4. Communicate changes to all parties concerned
5. Specify a policy for minimizing conflicts and resolving disputes
6. Ensure that changes are implemented
7. Report monthly a summary of all changes to date and their impact on the project.

The change control system is established early in the project, and thereafter managers use it to appraise the impact of proposed changes on estimates and plans, and to trace any differences between current performance and original estimates to the specific approved changes.

The change control system focuses on the project, but it is part of the broader process of controlling and integrating changes into the design, development, building, and operation of the end-item system, its subsystems, and components—the *configuration management* process mentioned in Chapter 9. Whenever an aspect of the design (e.g., a performance criterion) or element of the project plan (e.g., scope statement, schedule, or budget) is first approved, it is referred to as the *baseline*; subsequently, any time the baseline is altered to reflect approved changes, it is referred to as second baseline, third baseline, and so on.

The change control system includes strict procedures to control and minimize design and work changes; these include:[27]

- Requiring that original statements of work and work orders, with specific schedules and budgets, are clearly stated and *agreed to* by persons responsible.
- Close monitoring of work to ensure it is *meeting* (not exceeding) specifications.
- Careful screening of tasks for cost or schedule overruns (and potential changes in work scope), and quick action to correct problems.
- Requiring a pre-specified request and approval process of all discretionary changes.
- Requiring similar control procedures of all subcontractors and suppliers for all purchase orders, test requests, and so on.
- Assessing the impact of all changes on the end-item and project, and revising designs and plans to reflect the impact.
- *Freezing* the project against all non-essential changes at a predefined phase. The freeze prohibits additional changes to the design so that the next stage (procurement, fabrication, construction, or coding and testing) can begin. The freeze point must be set by management early in the project, and *project personnel constantly reminded of it.*

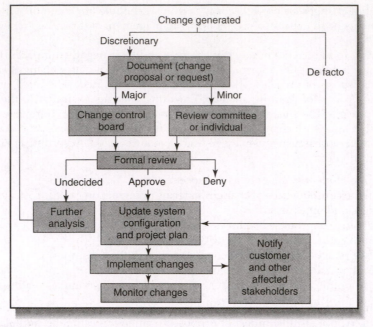

Figure 11.18
Change control process.

The process, summarized in Figure 11.18, ensures that all design and work changes are (1) documented as to their effect on work orders, budgets, schedules, and contractual prices; (2) formally reviewed; and (3) assessed and accepted or rejected. It accounts for both discretionary changes as well as *de facto* changes; the former are those subject to formal review and an approval or denial decision; the latter are those that are mandated or in fact have already occurred, and hence *must* be approved.

An essential part of the process is the change proposal or change request document (Figure 11.19), which provides the information and rationale for the proposed change. Any project team member or other stakeholder can request a change by submitting a change request. Everyone, regardless of role, title, or position, must follow the same change control procedures.

Often, a committee called a *change control board* oversees the process. In large projects, the change board consists of the project manager and managers from engineering, manufacturing, purchasing, contract administration, and the customer, and meets weekly to review change requests. The effects of proposed changes are estimated prior to the meeting, at which time the board decides which changes to reject and which to accept.

Any proposed or enacted change that impacts the time, cost, or nature of work of a single task and related tasks must be documented. Everyone involved in the project has the potential to recognize or originate changes, and everyone must be expected to bring them to the attention of the project manager.

11.10 CONTRACT ADMINISTRATION

Project control includes the ongoing comparison of project activities, changes, and accomplishments to the requirements stipulated in the contract. Ensuring that all

IRON *Butterfly Corp*			
Change request			Page ... of ...
Title:			
Project no.	Task no.	Revision no.	Date issued
Description of change			
Reason for change			
Documentation attached			
Originated by:	Date:		
Request logged by:	Date:		
Cost implications			
Schedule implications			
Implications on performance of deliverable(s)			
Other implications (risks & issues)			
Proposed plan for implementation			
Implications evaluated by:		Date:	
Recommendation			
Recommended by:		Date:	
Documentation attached			
Approved by:	Date:	Approved by:	Date:

Figure 11.19
Example of change request document.

commitments of the developer/contractor and the customer as specified in the contract are met is the function of *contract administration*.[28] Procurement management, discussed in Chapter 5, is an aspect of contract administration that deals specifically with managing deliverables and relations with vendors and subcontractors who provide contracted goods, work, and services.

An aspect of project control, but pertaining exclusively contracted work, contract administration includes authorizing work to begin; monitoring work with respect to budgets, schedules, and technical performance; ensuring quality; controlling changes; and sending and receiving payments for work completed. Contract administration ensures that change requests for contracted work are assessed against conditions as stated in the project contract, and that any necessary changes are made to the contract before proceeding with work. It also assures that all necessary approvals are secured before the contract is modified and changes implemented. The project manager administers all of this by using procedures and a system similar to those described for task authorization, performance tracking and reporting, and change control. When the contract incorporates customer-specified measures or requirements for project monitoring and reporting, the project control system must incorporate these measures into the usual performance tracking and progress reporting system.

The process must also ensure that customers are invoiced for services and materials as specified in the contract, and that subcontractors and suppliers are paid. For simple projects, billing and payment tracking is done through the contractor's accounts receivable system; for large, complex projects, it is handled through a dedicated billing and payments tracking system.

No matter how thorough and conscientious the project manager, or how sophisticated the project control system, problems still occur. Roman notes the following problematic situations:[29]

1. The control process focuses on only one factor, such as cost, and ignores others such as schedule and technical performance. This happens when control procedures are issued by one functional area, such as accounting or finance, and other areas are not involved. Forcing compliance to one factor usually results in excesses or slips in other areas. For example, overemphasis on costs can lead to schedule delays or shoddy workmanship.
2. Project team members resist or do not comply with control procedures, and they resent attempts to evaluate and control their work. Managers encourage noncompliance when they fail to exercise sanctions against people who defy the procedures.
3. Project team members do not report problems they are aware of. They may not understand the situation, or, if they do, may be hesitant to reveal it. The information they report may be fragmented and difficult to piece together.
4. The control system relies entirely on self-appraisal of work progress and quality. This causes people to act defensively and provide prejudiced information. Bias is one of the biggest obstacles to effective project control.
5. Managers act indifferently about controversial issues, believing that with time problems resolve themselves. This leads some workers to believe that management doesn't care—an attitude likely to spread throughout the project.
6. Managers overseeing several projects misrepresent charges so as to offset poor performance in one project by good performance in others (or, within a project, poor performance in one work package by good performance of another work package). The practice happens in organizations having multiple contracts with the same customer. While it may result in satisfying the overall requirements of all the contracts, it distorts historical data that might be used for planning and estimating future projects, and is unethical because it can result in mischarging a customer.
7. Reporting and control procedures are inadequate. For example, full reliance on subjective measures such as the earned value can suggest that more work was completed than actually was; similarly, a bad situation can be made to look good simply by altering accounting procedures.

To minimize these problems, management must actively support the control process, and everyone in the project must understand the relevancy of the process and how it benefits the project. The control process and performance measures must be impersonal, objective, and uniformly applied to all people, tasks, and suppliers.

11.12 SUMMARY

The execution phase includes the stages of *design*, *production/build*, and *implementation*. In the design stage the system concept is subdivided into tiers of subsystems, components, and parts, and for each of these designs, schematics, and models are created. The design stage has two interrelated activities: preparation of the *functional* design that shows the system components, and preparation of the *physical* design that shows what the system and its components will look like. Project management is responsible for coordinating design activities, and for controlling any changes to the design throughout the process.

In the production/build stage, the main activities are fabrication and testing. Components are assembled and the end-item system is produced and tested to ensure that requirements for the system and its components are met.

Throughout the execution phase, the project control process guides the work to keep the project moving toward scope, budget, schedule, and quality objectives. The focal point of the process is individual work packages and control accounts. Virtually all control activities—authorization, data collection, progress evaluation, problem assessment, and corrective action—occur at the work package/control account level. Because higher-level control accounts are built up through the WBS and organizational hierarchies, project cost and schedule variances can be traced through the control account structure to locate the sources of problems.

The control process begins with authorization; once authorized, work is continually tracked with reference to the project plan for conformance to scope, quality, schedules, and budgets. Key technical measures are monitored to gauge progress toward meeting technical objectives. Performance to date is reviewed using the concept of earned value, and estimates of project cost and completion date are revised.

Variances in costs and schedules are compared to pre-established limits. Whenever they move beyond acceptable limits or new opportunities or intractable problems arise, the work must be replanned and rescheduled. Such changes are inevitable, though every effort is made to minimize their impact on cost and schedule overruns. A formal change control system and configuration management ensures that changes are authorized, documented, and communicated.

The control process involves elements of contract administration and procurement management to ensure that contracted commitments with customers, suppliers, and subcontractors are met.

The next chapter concludes the subject of project control and covers the topics of project evaluation, reporting, and communication. It also covers the remainder of the project life cycle—system implementation and project closeout, and the last phase of the systems development cycle: Phase D, the operation phase.

Summary of Variables

PV = budgeted cost of work scheduled (BCWS)

AC = actual cost of work performed (ACWP)

EV = earned value = budgeted cost of work performed (BCWP)

SV = schedule variance = EV − PV

CV = cost variance = EV − AC

BAC = total budgeted cost of project

SPI = schedule performance index = EV/PV

CPI = cost performance index = EV/AC

ETC = forecast cost to complete = (BAC − EV)/CPI where BAC is the budgeted cost at completion

EAC = estimated cost of at completion = AC + ETC

BCSP (budget cost, scheduled performance) = date where PV is same as EV at the status date

TV = time variance

REVIEW QUESTIONS AND PROBLEMS

1. What is the practice of "fast-tracking" or "design/build?" What are the associated potential benefits and dangers?
2. What happens during the design stage? Who is involved? What do they do? What is the role of the project manager? How are design changes monitored and controlled?
3. What is the role of interaction design in product design and development?
4. What does the plan for production/build include?
5. What happens during the production or building stage? How is work planned and coordinated? Who oversees the work?
6. What is the distinction between the project end-item and project side-items? What role does the project manager have regarding each?
7. What is contract administration?
8. What are the three phases of the project control process?
9. Explain the differences between internal and external project controls.
10. How are overhead expenses allocated in work packages?
11. If a cost or schedule variance is noticed at the project level, how is it traced to the source of the variance?
12. Describe the process of work authorization. What does a work order usually include?
13. Describe the process of collecting data about the cost, schedule, and work accomplished.
14. Discuss different ways of measuring ongoing work progress.
15. Why is scope change control an important part of the project control process?
16. Discuss quality control as applied to projects.
17. What are the principal causes of project schedule overruns? Discuss at least four practices that may be used to reduce schedule variability and keep projects on schedule.
18. Explain PV, AC, and EV, and how they are used to determine the variances AV, SV, CV, and TV. Explain the meaning of these variances.
19. What does it signify if cost or schedule index figures are less than 1.00?
20. Explain TPM, its purpose, and how it is conducted.
21. Explain what is meant by ETC and how it is related to EAC.
22. Discuss reasons why the project manager frequently resists project changes.
23. What should a change control system guarantee? Describe procedures that minimize unnecessary changes.
24. What aspects of project control fall under contract administration?
25. What are some difficulties encountered when attempting project control?
26. Use the networks in Figure 11.20 to determine ES, LS, EF, and LF for all activities (number by activity is the duration in days). Apply the buffer concept to the critical path. For network (a), use a 3-week time buffer for the critical path, a 1-week time buffer for every path that connects to the critical path. For network (b), use a 4-week time buffer on the critical path, a 2-week buffer for every path that connects to the critical path.
27. In the LOGON project suppose the status of the project as of Week 22 is as follows (note usage of the longer acronyms; some project management software use these and not the shorter acronyms PV, AC, and EV).

$$BCWS = \$628,000$$
$$ACWP = \$640,000$$
$$BCWP = \$590,000$$

Answer the following questions:
a. What is the earned value of the project as of Week 22?
b. Compute SV and CV.

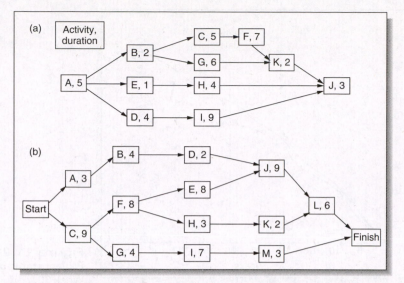

Figure 11.20
Two project networks.

c. Draw a status graph similar to Figure 11.15 and plot BCWS, ACWP, and BCWP. Show SV and CV. Determine TV from the graph.

d. Compute SPI and CPI. Has the project performance improved or worsened since Week 20?

e. Using BAC = $990,000, compute ETC and EAC. How does EAC compare to the Week 20 estimate of $1,222,593? From your status chart, determine the revised completion date. How does it compare to the revised date (Week 48–49) as of Week 20?

f. Are the results from part (e) consistent with the results from part (d) regarding improvement or deterioration of project performance since Week 20?

28. For a particular work package, the budgeted cost as of April 30 is $18,000. Suppose, as of April 30, the supervisor determines that only 80 percent of the scheduled work has been completed and the actual expense is $19,000. What is the BCWP? Compute SV, CV, SPI, and CPI for the work package.

29. Using the status chart in Figure 11.21:
    a. Estimate SV, CV, and TV, and compute SPI and CPI for Week 30. Interpret the results.
    b. Compute ETC and EAC. Estimate the revised completion date, and sketch the lines for forecast AC and forecast EV.

30. Assume for the following problems that work continues during weekends.
    a. A task is planned to start on April 30 and takes 20 days to complete. The actual start date is May 3. After 4 days of work, the supervisor estimates that the task is 25 percent completed. If the work rate stays the same, what is the forecast date of completion?
    b. Task C has two immediate predecessors, Tasks A and B. Task A is planned to take 5 days to complete; Task B is planned to take 10 days. The early start time for both tasks is August 1. The actual start dates for Tasks A and B are August 2 and August 1, respectively. At the end of August 4, Task A is assessed to be 20 percent completed and Task B 30 percent completed. What is the expected early start time for Task C?

31. Refer back to Problem 27. Assume the $590,000 indicated for Week 22 is the most likely EV. Given a BAC of $990,000, this represents 59.6 percent of the project completed. Suppose an expert assesses the LOGON project at that time, using

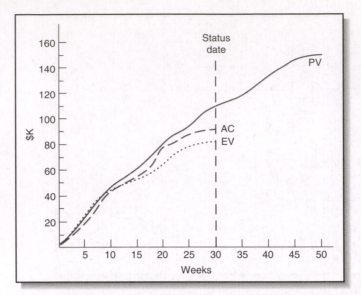

Figure 11.21
Project status as of Week 30.

various measures, and concludes that LOGON is between 50 percent and 65 percent completed. Let these represent pessimistic and optimistic scenarios. Compute the corresponding pessimistic, most likely and optimistic scenarios. Compute the corresponding pessimistic, most likely, and optimistic CPIs, SPIs, EACs, and forecast completion dates for the project.

32. Refer back to Problem 26 and Figure 11.20.
    a. For Network (a), suppose that after 7 weeks, activities A, B, and E have been completed, D is 50 percent completed, and C is 80 percent completed. What is the revised early completion date for the project?
    b. For Network (b), suppose after 25 weeks, activities A, B, C, F, E, G, and I have been completed, and D and H are ready to begin in Week 26. What is the revised early completion date for the project?

33. For the following questions, refer to Figure 11.22.
    As of Week 5, for the project:
    a. What is the planned value (PV)? Fill in the PV column.
    b. What is the earned value of the work completed (EV)? Fill in the EV column.
    c. What is actual cost of the project (AC)?
    d. What is the value of work remaining?
    e. What is the CPI?
    f. What is estimated cost to complete the project (ETC)?
    g. What is the forecasted cost at completion (EAC)?
    h. What is the estimated cost variance at completion, and the percent overrun or underrun?
    i. According to EV, is the project ahead or behind schedule?
    j. According the critical path, is the project ahead or behind schedule?

QUESTIONS ABOUT THE STUDY PROJECT

1. What kinds of external controls, if any, were imposed by the client on the project?
2. What kinds of internal controls were used? (For instance, work package control, cost account control, etc.) Describe.

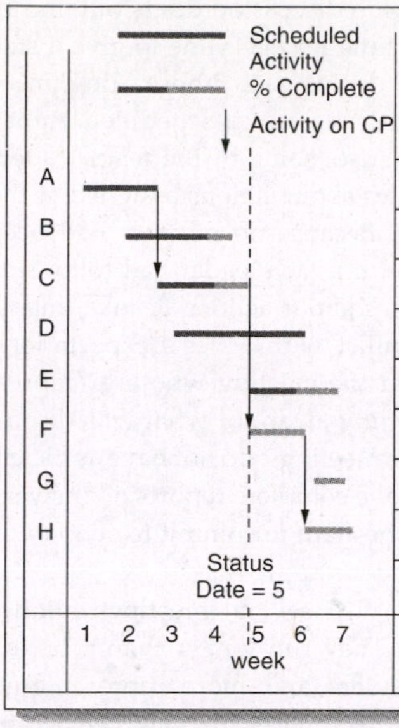

	Budget at completion	Project status as of Week 5					
		% Sche-duled	PV = BCWS	% Comp-lete	EV = BCWP	AC = ACWP	
A	A 200	100	0	100	200	240	
B	B 1000	100		70		900	
C	C 400	100		60		300	
D	D 1200	50		100		500	
E	E 800	0		50		440	
F	F 900	0		0		0	
G	G 300	0		0		0	
H	H 500	0		0		0	
	4300						

Figure 11.22
Project status as of Week 5.

3. Describe the project control process:
   How was work authorized to begin? Give examples of work authorization orders.
   How were data collected to monitor work? Explain the methods and procedures (time cards, invoices, etc.).
   How were the data tallied and summarized?
   How were the data validated?
4. Was the concept of earned value (budgeted cost of work performed) used?
5. How was project performance monitored? What performance and variance measures were used? Who did it? How often?
6. How were problems pinpointed and tracked?
7. Were the concepts of forecasting ETC and EAC used? If so, by whom? How often?
8. Were variance limits established for project cost and performance? What were they? How were they applied?
9. When cost, schedule, or performance problems occurred, what action did the project manager take? Give examples of problems and what the project manager did.
10. What changes to the product or project goal occurred during the project? Describe the change control process used. How were changes to the plan or system reviewed, authorized, and communicated? Show examples of change control documents.

Case 11.1   The Cybersonic Project

Miles Wilder, project manager for the Cybersonic project, considers himself a "project manager's project manager." He claims to know and use the principles of good project management, starting with having a good plan and then carefully tracking the project. He announces to his team leaders that status meetings will be held on alternating Mondays throughout the expected year-long project. All 18 project team leaders must attend and give a rundown of the tasks on which they are currently working.

All the team leaders show up for the first status meeting. Seven are currently managing work for the project and are scheduled to give reports; the other 11 are not yet working on the project (as specified by the project schedule) but attend because Miles wants them to stay informed about project progress. The meeting is scheduled for 3 hours, and the team leaders are to report on whatever they think is important. After almost 5 hours of reports by five of the leaders, Miles ends the meeting. Several major problems are reported that Miles tries to resolve at the meeting. Specific actions to resolve some of the problems are decided, and Miles schedules another meeting for the afternoon 2 days later to address the others and hear the remaining two reports. Some of the team leaders are miffed because they will have to change their schedules to attend this new meeting.

Miles arrives an hour late at the next meeting, which, after 3 hours, allows enough time to resolve the problems raised at the first meeting but not enough for the two leaders to give reports. Miles asks them if they are facing any major issues or problems with their tasks. When they respond "no," he lets them skip the reports but promises to start with them at the next meeting in 2 weeks. A few of the team leaders are assigned actions to address current problems. Some of the attendees feel the meeting was a waste of time.

Before the next meeting, a few of the team leaders inform Miles they cannot attend and will send representatives. This meeting becomes problematic for three reasons. First, several new problems about the project are raised and, again,

the ensuing discussion drags out and there is not enough time for everyone to give a status report. Second, during the 5-hour long meeting, only six team leaders of a scheduled eight give their reports. Also, some of the team leaders disagree with Miles about actions assigned at the previous meeting. Because no minutes had been taken at that meeting, each leader had followed his or her own notes about actions to take, many of which now conflict with Miles's expectations. Further, people at the meeting who are "representatives" are not fully aware of what was discussed at the previous meetings, do not have sufficient information to give complete reports or answer questions, and are hesitant to commit to action without their team leader's approval.

The next several meetings follow the same pattern. They run longer than scheduled. Fewer team leaders and more representatives attend. Some status reports are not given because of inadequate time. Attendees disagree over problems identified and actions to be taken. The project falls behind schedule because problems are not addressed adequately or quickly enough.

Miles feels that too much time has been wasted on resolving problems at the meetings, and that many of them should, instead, be resolved entirely by the team leaders. He instructs the leaders to work out solutions and changes on their own, and to report at status meetings only the results. This reduces the length of the meetings, but it creates other complications. Some of the team leaders take actions and make changes that ignore project dependencies and conflict with other team leaders' work tasks. Even though everyone is working overtime, the Cybersonic project falls further behind schedule.

QUESTIONS

1. Why is Miles's approach to tracking and controlling the Cybersonic project ineffective?

2. If you were in charge, what would you do?

Case 11.2   SA Gold Mine: Earned Value After a Scope Change[30]

The team at South African Gold Mine (SA) was tasked with sinking a 2000m deep ventilation shaft and excavating space for a station at the

bottom. The plan was to sink the shaft within 20 months at a cost of R65,000 (about US $10,000) per meter of shaft depth. For the station at the bot-

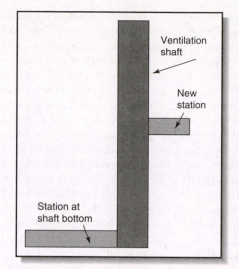

Figure 11.23
Mine shaft.

tom, 30,000 m³ of rock would have to be excavated within 3 months at a cost of R700 per cubic meter. The plan assumed a straight-line earned value over time.

After the work had begun, the scope of the project was changed to include excavation for a new station halfway down the shaft (Figure 11.23) with a volume of 20,000 m³. It was agreed that the additional work had to be done at the same excavation rate as the bottom station, but since removal of the rock required hoisting only 1,000 meters (as opposed to the 2,000 meters for the bottom station), the team agreed on the cost of R500 per cubic meter for the new station. Since working space and other resources available would limit the amount of work that could be done simultaneously, everyone agreed that the new station would delay the sinking of the shaft. After 13 months, the shaft had reached a depth of 1,400 meters below surface and excavation for the halfway station was completed. The actual cost at this time was R90 million, which was more than was budgeted for the period. This aggravated a cash-flow problem at that stage. The executive management requested an earned value report. Information on the relative amounts of time spent on excavating the new station and sinking the shaft was not available.

QUESTIONS

1. Calculate the CV, SV, TV, CPI, and SPI.
2. Prepare a graph to illustrate the initial plan for the work, including the excavation for the station at the shaft bottom, as well as the changed plan. Indicate the earned value and the actual cost after 13 months.
3. Regarding the cash-flow problem that was aggravated by the high rate of spending, discuss the desirability of performing projects faster than planned.

Case 11.3   *Project Change Control Process at Dynacom Company*[31]

At Dynacom Company, any change that potentially affects project scope is subject to a rigorous review and approval process. Anybody wanting to make a change must document and present it to the team lead. If the team lead agrees with the request, she enters the request into the company's change request software, which the project manager checks each day. The project manager then meets with the team lead and original requester to discuss the change's likely impact on the project. If they conclude the change is worthwhile, the project manager schedules a meeting with the entire team to discuss the need for the change, its impact on schedule and budget, and the risks. Sometimes a team approves changes immediately; other times it takes a few days or weeks of review. If the team approves the change, it sends a recommendation to the technical change management board (TCM) for a final decision. The TCM has no association with the project, and consists of upper managers and other project managers. If the TCM accepts the recommendation, the project manager makes the necessary changes to work schedules, budgets,

and other documents. Dynacom is a rather conservative company, and the process has served well in helping it to avoid risks associated with changes.

A drawback of the process is that it takes 3–5 weeks or more to decide on a change request. As a result, project managers sometimes implement changes *before* they are approved. For example, Karen, the manager of a project on a very tight schedule and running behind, needed to make changes that were on the critical path. She worried that if she waited for the changes to be approved, the project would fall so far behind that it might be cancelled. Intent on making the project a success and willing to break the rules to get it back on schedule, she made the changes immediately and assumed the TCM board would accept them, which it did.

QUESTIONS

1. What is your opinion of the change control process at Dynacom? What are the benefits and drawbacks?

2. What do you think about Karen bypassing the process to make changes?

NOTES

1. The design output is normally catalogued in a master record index or data pack that lists all drawings, material specifications, and process specifications (e.g., for heat treatment of materials, welding, etc.). One guide for specification practices is MIL-STD 490A.
2. Fetherston D. *The Chunnel*. New York, NY: Times Books; 1997. pp. 198–199.
3. Cooper A. *The Inmates are Running the Asylum: Why High-Tech Products Drive Us Crazy and How to Restore the Sanity*. Indianapolis, IN: Sams; 1999.
4. Where several copies of a system are produced, the first and second groups of tests are performed on a prototype. When the system is single-copy, the second group of tests takes place during construction, and the design is verified afterward.
5. Biggs C, Birks E, and Atkins W. *Managing the Systems Development Process*. Englewood Cliffs, NJ: Prentice-Hall; 1980. pp. 187–193.
6. Roman D. *Science, Technology, and Innovation: A Systems Approach*. Columbus, OH: Grid Publishing; 1980. p. 369.
7. The terms "variance" and "deviation" are used here interchangeably, although in some contracts variance refers to small changes

in the project plan for which compensation or correction is expected, whereas deviation refers to large changes that require a formal contractual response.
8. Roman, *Science, Technology, and Innovation*, p. 383.
9. *DOD & NASA Guide, PERT Cost Accounting System Design*. Washington, DC: US Government Printing Office; 1962.
10. Adapted from Thompson C. Intermediate performance measures in engineering projects. *Proceedings of the Portland International Conference on Management of Engineering and Technology*, Portland, OR, July 27–31, 1997. p. 392.
11. Archibald R. *Managing High-Technology Programs and Projects*. New York, NY: Wiley; 1976. p. 195.
12. Information for this application provided by Elisa Denney and Jennifer Brown.
13. Goldratt E. *The Critical Chain*. Great Barrington, MA: North River Press; 1997.
14. *Ibid*.
15. An approach to sizing time buffers is discussed in Hoel K and Taylor S. Quantifying buffers for project schedules. *Production and Inventory Management Journal* 40(2); 1999:

43–47. Control using percent buffer consumed is described in Leach L. *Critical Chain Project Management*, 2nd edn. Norwood, MA: Artech House, Inc.; 2005. pp. 117–120.

16. Interview with Doug Brandt, PMO Director, Abbott Diagnostics Division, May 2006.

17. Commercial software such as Sciforma by Sciforma Corporation supports fever charts and related ways to track buffer status.

18. From Muirhead B and Simon W. *High Velocity Leadership: the Mars Pathfinder Approach to Better, Faster, Cheaper*. New York, NY: HarperBusiness; 1999. pp. 40–42.

19. Cusumano M and Selby R. *Microsoft Secrets*. New York, NY: Free Press; 1995. pp. 204, 221, 256–257, 417.

20. Joy P. *Total Project Management: The Indian Context*. Delhi: Macmillan India; 1993. Chapter 11.

21. Ways to determine EV (BCWP) are explained in Pham TG. The elusive budgeted cost of work performed for research and development projects. *Project Management Quarterly* 16(1); 1985. 76–79; for the earned value approach, see Fleming Q and Koppleman J. *Earned Value Project Management*. Upper Darby, PA: Project Management Institute; 1996.

22. For examples of analytical models used for TPM, see Eisner H. *Computer-Aided Systems Engineering*. Upper Saddle River, NJ: Prentice Hall; 1988. pp. 297–326.

23. Adapted from Bennet B and Rea K. *Breakthrough Project Management*, 2nd edn. Oxford: Butterworth Heinemann; 2001. pp. 138–141.

24. Sigurdsen A. Method for verifying project cost performance. *Project Management Journal* 25(4); 1994: 26–31.

25. Harrison F. *Advanced Project Management*. Aldershot: Gower; 1981. pp. 242–244.

26. *Ibid.*, pp. 245–246.

27. *Ibid.*, p. 244; Archibald, *Managing High-Technology Programs and Projects*, pp. 187–90.

28. Hirsch W. *The Contracts Management Deskbook*, Revised edn. New York, NY: American Management Association; 1986. Chapter 6.

29. Adapted from Roman, *Science, Technology, and Innovation*, pp. 327–238, 391–395.

30. Source: Mr Joubert P of Anglo Platinum.

31. Case provided by Quane J, Kosin M, Heinlen L, Mahoney S, and Quantraro F. *Cyberdyne Project Planning Management (PPM) Investigation Report*. Graduate School of Business, Loyola University Chicago, May 2007.

Project Evaluation, Communication, Implementation, and Closeout

We look at it and we do not see it.

—LAO-TZU,
Sixth century BC

*An individual without information cannot take responsibility;
an individual who is given information cannot help but
take responsibility.*

—JAN CARLZON,
Riv Pyramidera!

*T*he previous chapter described how a project is tracked, assessed, and guided so that planned schedules, costs, and performance targets can be met. The project manager oversees the work, assesses progress, and issues instructions for corrective action; as information is received, she judges the project status and communicates directives and progress to workers, upper management, and the client. The first half of this chapter discusses the ways project information is used to evaluate and report project status, and the broader topics of project communication and information systems for project management.

The last stage in the project life cycle is implementation—the time when the project end-item is installed and turned over to the customer. The final duty of the project manager is to assist the customer in taking over the end-item system and to close out the project. The second half of this chapter describes system implementation, project closeout, and the project manager's role in each.

12.1 PROJECT EVALUATION

The purpose of project evaluation is to assess performance, reveal areas where the project deviates from goals, and uncover extant or potential problems so they can be corrected. Although it is certain that problems and deviations will occur, it is not known *a priori* where or when. Evaluation for the purpose of guiding the project is called *formative evaluation*; it addresses the questions "What is happening?" and "How is the project proceeding?" Evaluation for the purposes of appraising the project after it is completed and assessing the end-results is called *summary evaluation*; it addresses the questions "What happened?" and "What were the results?"

Project Formative Evaluation

Methods and Measures

A wide variety of methods, measures, and sources should be used to provide evaluative information, and these methods and measures should be specified in the project plan. As mentioned, using a variety of measures and sources increases the validity of the evaluation, particularly when they all lead to the same conclusion. The primary ways evaluative information is obtained and/or conveyed are written reports, oral reports, observation, and review meetings.

Written reports are the most common and expeditious way to review cost, schedule, and work performance information; however, they can hide or obscure information. Oral reports provide a quick way to gain information, although their accuracy depends on the interpretative and verbal skills and honesty of the presenter. Report accuracy, both oral and written, also depends on the number of channels through which the information passed to get to the writer or presenter; in general, the more channels, the less accurate the information. Project managers know this; as a consequence, they also try to walk around the project, talk to people, and make their own firsthand observations.[1]

Site Visits

Most project managers would never rely solely on second- or third-hand reports or remote sources (e.g., email) to track project progress. If they cannot always be at the project site, they make a point to visit it often—unannounced and uninvited. While at the site, they try to catch the team at lunch or on a break and speak to members informally. In this way, they demonstrate that they are actively involved in the project and care about the team. They build relations and learn what is happening.

Instead of inquiring about project "status," sometimes it is better to ask people about how life is going, what is going well or not so well, and what resources or support they need. Just because no one reports problems or complains does not mean everything is okay. Signs that problems might be brewing include team members being silent or not participating in meetings, avoiding discussions about the project, or giving conflicting reports about the project. The project manager watches people's facial expressions and body language. Rather than trying to talk to everyone, she concentrates on people whose tasks have traditionally been the most problematic. She tries to validate reported problems by getting at least two points of view.

Technology

The manager of a geographically dispersed project cannot be at every site—not a good situation, but it happens. In such cases she has to rely on technology—video- and audio-conferencing, websites, email, and telephone. Video-conferencing can be effective, but requires the appropriate technical facilities; audio-conferencing can be good too, but involves careful scheduling so as not to waste people's time. The Internet is effective for broadcasting plans, reports, documents and memos, but is passive and does not *require* that people see or respond to posted documents.

The best form of long-distance communication is frequent one-on-one *telephone* conversations. Over the telephone, the project manager can hear tone of voice, probe details, and obtain real-time feedback. But site managers, workers, and contractors are not always completely truthful, so the project manager also needs a trusted source at the site to *observe* work and report back progress.

Here is a good rule of thumb: the more sensitive the issue, the lower the technology to communicate it. For highly sensitive issues, it is worth traveling the distance to visit the site and meet face-to-face; for relatively sensitive issues, use telephone; for non-sensitive issues, email and fax are okay. Always follow up important discussions or commitments in writing.

12.2 PROJECT COMMUNICATION MANAGEMENT

The project master plan should include a communication plan. The communication plan addresses all forms of project communication—formal and informal, verbal and written. It includes a tentative schedule for all formal reviews and milestone meetings, and describes the meetings' formats, expected itineraries, advance preparations, presentation time limits, attendance policy, and who will lead. It also specifies important points of contact (who's who) among the customer, contractor, subcontractors and vendors, supporters, other interest groups.

The matrix in Figure 12.1 shows part of a communication plan that specifies the expected meetings and reports, and who will participate in each. This would be supplemented with details about the what, where, when, and how for each kind of meeting and report.

The communication plan should be distributed to everyone on the project team, and discussed before the project begins. So that everyone understands the required documentation and the content and format of each, the plan should include examples of good and bad documentation from previous projects. Many of these documents can be posted online.

Project Review Meetings

Review meetings are the most common and important way to communicate and assess project evaluative information. The main function of these meetings is to identify deviations from the project plan and quickly correct them. Participants at meetings discuss project progress, current and anticipated problems, and opportunities.

Role/type / Meeting/report	Status meeting (frequency)	Status meeting minutes (frequency)	Business feasibility	Information request	Technical feasibility	Business brief	Project plan (frequency)	Problems and issues (frequency)	Business study	Use case analysis	System architecture	Detailed technical design	Other
Client	X	X	X			X	X	X	X	X			
Relationship manager		X	X	X	X	X	X	X	X	X	X		
Business analyst	X	X	X			X	X	X	X	X	X		
Project manager	X	X	X	X	X	X	X	X	X	X	X		X
Client project team	X	X	X			X	X	X	X	X			
IT project team	X	X					X	X	X	X	X		X
Client director		X	X			X		X	X				X
IT director		X	X	X	X	X	X	X	X	X	X		
Project sponsor		X	X			X			X				
IT VP		X	X						X				
Architect	X	X	X	X	X	X	X	X	X	X	X		X
Security/audit	X	X	X		X			X	X	X	X		
Internet operations	X	X	X		X		X	X	X	X	X		X
Intranet operations	X	X	X		X		X	X	X				
Legal/corporations communication		X	X		X				X	X			
Other													

Figure 12.1
Sample communication plan.

Review meetings can be informal and convened as needed, or formal and scheduled at key project milestones. Most large projects require both.

Informal Reviews

Informal reviews are held frequently and regularly. Called "peer reviews," because they are attended by a group of peers, the meetings focus on project status, special problems, and emerging issues. Participation depends on the phase of the project and issues at hand; only those team members, customer representatives, functional or line managers, and project managers who need to be involved participate. Before the meetings, status reports and estimated time and cost-to-complete are updated. Attendees with assignments are expected to give presentations.

Because the reviews are intended to uncover problems and issues, bad news and problems are *expected* and openly confronted. The project manager acts as facilitator, and encourages honesty and candor. Finger pointing, passing blame, or smoothing over of conflict should be avoided; these behaviors waste time, discourage attendance, and negate the purpose of the meetings—to identify issues and agree on the course of action.

Stand-Up Meetings

A form of informal review is the "daily stand-up meeting." Intended primarily to update status, identify problems, and expedite solutions, the meeting is short (15 minutes) and to-the-point. Usually held at the start of every day, the team gives a quick run-through of yesterday's progress and today's next steps. (The occasional surprise attendance of a prominent person—e.g., a senior manager from the contractor or customer—adds zip and keeps everyone on their toes.) Problems that require more than a minute's reflection are deferred for a scheduled meeting.

Formal Reviews

Formal reviews are scheduled at milestones or critical project stages. Two common formal project reviews are the *preliminary review* and the *critical review*. These apply largely to design projects, and are discussed in Chapter 9. The preliminary design review assesses the functional design specifications' fit to the basic operational requirements; the critical design review assesses details of the design versus the preliminary design specifications. Sometimes the reviews serve as a precondition for continuing the project; the decision to continue or terminate the project at the end of a phase depends on the results of the review.

In every project, regardless of contractual obligations, the customer should assume some responsibility as project watchdog. The *project audit*, also discussed in Chapter 9, is a special formal review initiated by the customer to independently assess project progress. It can be conducted early in the project, during design or construction, or upon any significant change to the budget, schedule, or project goals. The audit scrutinizes the plans, schedules, budgets, constraints, communications, and overall management of the project. Its purpose is similar to that of the critical review: to verify project progress, identify constraints to progress, assess the effectiveness of the organization in doing its job, and advise possible solutions to problems.

Action Plan

Any problem surfaced in a review is noted on an action plan, and if the problem requires further investigation, someone is named responsible and another meeting is scheduled to address it. The action plan includes a statement of the problem, objectives for resolving the problem, the course of action, a target date, and person responsible (Figure 12.2). One of the first orders of business at each review meeting is to assess the status of items on the action plan. Always, the project manager (not a secretary or functionary) should lead the action plan review, take notes and, afterwards, summarize and distribute them. This reinforces the perception (and reality) that the leader is committed, involved, and in charge.

Another example of an action plan is a *problem failure report*. NASA, for instance, uses such a report for tracking problems and keeping focused on the most important ones. Each problem is assigned two weighted scores, one indicating its impact on mission success (e.g., 1 = negligible impact; 3 = mission catastrophic), the other indicating certainty about an identified problem cause and confidence in the proposed solution (e.g., 1 = known cause, known solution; 4 = unknown cause, unverified solution). Problems that average 2 or higher on the scores are potentially mission-threatening, and require the project manager's personal sign-off. On the Mars Pathfinder project mentioned in Chapters 9 and 11, over 800 of them were generated and subsequently evaluated.[2]

Project Meeting Room

Project meetings and conferences are often convened in a central meeting place or project office. The meeting room serves as a physical reminder of the project, and provides space for preparing, storing, and displaying project information. Gantt charts, networks, and cost charts showing planned and actual performance are displayed on the walls for easy reference. The room has a conference table, chairs, cabinets for project files, computers, a projector, and, sometimes, teleconferencing equipment.

Problem area	Objective	Actions	Who	When completed
1. Planning and scheduling	1. Establish backup support for each system.	1. (A) Discuss systems with analysts who support them; formulate plan for each system.	Project leaders and analysts	January 1
	2. Review all systems. Eliminate those not used; clean up others.	2. (A) Prepare questionnaire on system status.	Ron Gilmore	November 15
		2. (B) Complete questionnaires.	Analysts and programmers	December 1
		2. (C) Determine status and specific actions.	PL, analysts and programmers	January 31
	3. Provide information on purposes and uses of new project management system.	3. Prepare seminar on PMS and present to staff.	Joan Gibb	Before March 1

Figure 12.2
Sample action plan.

Formal Reports and Documents

Company management must be kept apprised of the status, progress, and performance of ongoing and upcoming projects. Problems affecting profits, schedules, or budgets, as well as recommended actions, need to be reported promptly. Stakeholders (the customer; professional, citizen, and activist groups; public agencies; stockholders; and others who have a genuine interest in the project) should also be kept up to date. Frequent, honest communication with stakeholders builds trust and avoids surprises.

Reports to Top Management and the PMO

The project manager and staff send reports to top management and the project management office (PMO) using information generated by the PCAS or PMIS. The reports include:[3]

1. A summary of project status
2. Red flag items where corrective action has been or should be taken
3. Accomplishments to date, schedule changes, and estimates for schedule and cost at completion
4. Current cost situation and cost performance
5. Manpower plan and limitations.

When several projects are simultaneously underway, the PMO compiles and provides to management monthly summaries showing their relative status. Each summary includes names of the customer and the project manager; monetary and labor investment; scheduled start and finish dates; possible risks, losses, and gains; and other information. The summaries enable management to assess the relative performance of the projects and their combined influence on the company, and the PMO to coordinate the plans, authorizations, and resource allocations for the projects. When projects are managed as a portfolio (Chapter 17), the summaries help management decide which projects to continue, which to allocate more or fewer resources to, and which to terminate.

Reports to Project, Program, and Functional Managers

On large projects, work package leaders send project and program managers monthly reports about the value of work completed, current and forecast costs, and updated schedules for completion (similar to Table 11.1 and Figure 11.15 in Chapter 11, aggregated up to second or third level). Each month the project manager sends the company financial manager or controller a report showing costs incurred, and the functional managers reports showing labor-hours and costs expended for work packages in their areas. The reports in Figures 8.8–8.12 in Chapter 8, modified to include actual expenditures, are representative.

Reports to Customers/Users

Each month the project manager should send the customer a report about work progress and the impacts of any changes on work scope, schedule, or cost. Although the contractor's marketing or customer relations director might be formally charged with communicating contract-related information to the customer, it is up to the project manager to make sure the customer is always kept well-informed. She must be available to answer customer questions and satisfy requests for project information. The customer should never be "surprised."

Informal Communication

Much communication in projects happens informally through the familiar *grapevine*. Certainly, such communication has drawbacks: it garbles messages, is neither thorough nor dependable, and does not guarantee that people who need information will ever get it. On balance, however, informal communication is largely beneficial and essential. It fulfills social and work needs, and conveys information more quickly and directly than formal systems. Some theorists posit that a vast network of informal communication is essential for any organization to perform well.

Managers cannot control informal communication, but there are ways they can influence it.[4] One is to *insist* on informality, remove status barriers, and inspire casual conversations between managers and workers. As examples, everyone at Walt Disney—from the president on down—wears a nametag; people at Hewlett Packard are urged to use first names; and the management philosophy at Delta Airline and Levi Strauss is "open door." MBWA (management by walking around), or getting managers out of the office and talking to people (instead of listening to presentations or reading emails), stimulates informal information exchange. The physical layout of the office is instrumental, too. Intermingling of desks for workers from interrelated functional areas, removing walls and partitions, "family groupings" of chairs and desks, and spot placement of lounges are ways to encourage informal communication.

Project management attempts to do what the informal organization sometimes does: allow people involved in a problem or decision to directly communicate and make decisions. One way or another, people affected by a problem talk about it and form ideas, although often the formal organization overlooks or stifles these ideas. Management should encourage informal communication processes that support or enhance its formal processes.

12.3 PROJECT MANAGEMENT INFORMATION SYSTEMS

The formal methods for planning and control described in this book do not require any more input data or information than is, or should be, available in any project. What they *do* require, in a word, is a framework—a *system*—for collecting, organizing, storing, processing, and disseminating that information. Such a framework or tool is the *PMIS—project management information system.*

PMIS Software

If you think about it, methods such as earned value analysis, forecasting, change control, and configuration management for large projects require processing and integrating a hefty amount of information. As computers are good at this, PMIS software has become an essential tool for project planning and control. In fact, without software it would be difficult to do much of the analysis necessary to plan and control large projects.

There are dozens of kinds of PMIS project software packages, but they vary greatly in capability, flexibility, and price.[5] Simpler PMIS software packages are limited in what they can do but are usually good at whatever that is; once simple software has been mastered, it is easy to upgrade to more sophisticated software.

Features of PMIS Software

Following is a rundown of the kinds of capabilities, outputs, functions, and features offered by various PMIS software packages. Important to note is that among the many available software packages, most do not have all of these capabilities; some perform only the most basic functions.

Scheduling and network planning

Virtually all project software performs project scheduling using network-based algorithms to compute early and late times, slack times, and the critical path. Among the capabilities to look for are the type of procedure (CPM, PERT, PDM, CCPM), the maximum number of allowable activities, the format for activities and events (some use a WBS scheme), and the quality and clarity of outputs (e.g., network, Gantt chart, tabular reports, or multiple types). All software allows calendar input of non-work periods such as weekends, holidays, and vacations.

Resource management

Most software performs resource loading, leveling, allocation, or multiple functions, but systems vary in analytical sophistication and quality of reports. Major considerations are the maximum number of resources permitted per activity or project; the kind of loading/scheduling techniques used (resource-limited, time-limited, or both); split scheduling (stopping and restarting activities); interchangeable usage of different resources; and rate of resource usage.[6]

Budgeting

Software packages vary greatly in the way they handle costs, and in their ability to generate budget and cost summary reports. In some, cost and expense information is not treated explicitly; in others, cost accounting is a major feature. The software for large projects should have a cost and budgeting module (like the PCAS described in Chapter 8) that is integrated with modules for planning, scheduling, procurement, and tracking.

Managing multiple projects and project portfolios

Many software systems allow data to be pooled from different projects for *multiproject* analysis, planning, and control. This is an important feature, since most project managers oversee multiple, simultaneous projects. With this feature, information from several concurrent projects can be combined to form a picture of the overall state of the organization. Some software provides a "dashboard" or overview of each project. By "clicking" on a particular project, managers can zoom in to view more detailed information about the project. They can readily distinguish which projects are performing as expected from those experiencing problems or overruns—an essential capability for project portfolio management (Chapter 17).

Cost control and performance analysis

To perform the control function, a system must be able to compare actual performance (actual costs and work completed) to planned and budgeted performance. Among the features to consider are the software's ability to compute and report cost and schedule variances, earned values, and performance indices, and to forecast by extrapolating past performance. The most sophisticated software systems "roll up" results and allow aggregation, analysis, and reporting at all levels of the WBS. Such systems also permit modification and updating of existing plans through input of actual start and finish dates and costs. Plus, they *integrate* schedule, budget, and resource information, and allow the project manager to ask "what if" questions under various scenarios while the project is underway. They allow the user to access, cross-reference, and report information from multiple sites or databases linked via web-based technology.

Reporting, graphics, and communication

Project software also varies in the number, kind, and quality of reports it produces. Some systems provide only tabular reports and schedules; others offer networks, resource histograms, various graphics, charts, and graphs, and provide customized forms and reports to fit a specific project management methodology.

Some PMIS software makes use of the Internet, which allows geographically dispersed team members easy access to project information and a common place to send and store information. Some automatically flags problems, such as excessive buffer consumption, illustrated by the fever chart in the previous chapter.

Interface, flexibility, and ease of use

Some software is compatible with and ties into existing databases for payroll, purchasing, inventory, ERP, cost-accounting, or other PMISs; some can be used with popular DBMS, modeling, and risk analysis systems.

Systems vary widely in their flexibility. Many perform a narrow set of functions; others allow the user to develop new applications or alter existing ones, depending on need. Among the applications sometimes available are change control, configuration management, responsibility matrixes, expenditure reports, cost and technical performance reports, and technical performance summaries. Many systems utilize Internet technology that allows easy access through a browser to a variety of business applications and databases.

Web-Enabled Project Management [7]

Web-enabled technology is well suited for situations where the project team and stakeholders are situated at different sites. Putting information on a project website or other network utilizing the Internet affords the benefits of immediate information availability, rapid and easy communication between workers, and information that is reliable and current because it is communicated in real time.

With web-browser integrated software, team members can report progress and retrieve assignments through their own individual Web pages. The manager can use information aggregated from scattered worksites to get an overview of the entire project.

In most cases, the necessary tools are already at hand. Web-enabled project software requires only one thing: access to a Web browser such as Internet Explorer, Netscape, or Mozilla. The costs for overhead, update, and maintenance of web-based communication are very low.

Intranets, Virtual Private Networks, and Security

The security of project information on a network is an important matter. Project websites may contain information that an organization does not want to share with outsiders, in which case the company should use an intranet, virtual private network, or password-controlled website.

An *intranet* is a private computer network that uses Internet standards and protocols to allow communication among people within an organization. It provides access to a common pool of information from computers within organizational walls. The intranet is owned by the organization it serves, and is accessible only by organizational members and other authorized parties. Access can be extended to trusted external organizations, partners, or clients through an extended network called an *extranet*.

Organizations take steps to keep unauthorized people out of their intranet systems by using firewalls and other mechanisms that either block unauthorized access or make internal information unreadable to unauthorized computers that gain access. A company can keep its stored information secure with the use of firewalls and *virtual private networks*, the latter of which offer access by authorized users to an organization's intranet from the Internet.

Group Productivity [8]

With an intranet, it is easy to access *group productivity software* and to store reports, profiles, calendars, and schedules. It is also easy for users to locate information in these documents using special *document-sharing tools*, such as newsgroups, chat rooms, and electronic whiteboards. These tools are especially useful for sharing pictorial information about product design requirements and descriptions.

One of the most common ways that project managers use intranets is for collecting information about time spent on projects. The information is retained in a project database and then processed by project management software to report and tally time spent and time still needed to complete the project.

E-mail is another important communication tool, although experienced project managers advise it is no substitute for face-to-face or telephone meetings. Other means for collectively sharing information on-line include *discussion forums* and *chat rooms*. Members of a discussion forum can view others' contributions and add comments. Chat rooms are similar to e-mail and discussion forums, but permit immediate response by participants to incoming messages.

It used to be that video- and audio-conferencing were the only ways for geographically dispersed teams to hold meetings. Today, video, voice, and data can be shared over the intranet or Internet at desktop locations. The information shared can be in the form of a spreadsheet, text document, presentation, graphic, photograph, engineering schematic, video file, or live streaming.

At Boeing, all designs are stored electronically and are kept current to reflect the most recent changes; they are available immediately to anyone who needs them. Notification of any change is sent via e-mail to everyone who needs to know. As long as team members have access to a computer and browser, they can participate in meetings. Engineers in Kansas having trouble assembling a mock-up can send video images to designers in Seattle who can *see* the mock-up, assess the problem, and offer suggestions; absent that technology, designers would have to *go* to Kansas.

PMIS in the Project Life Cycle

A computer-based PMIS can assist the project manager throughout all phases of the project life cycle. Figure 12.3 shows the range of managerial tasks and functions where a PMIS can help. Example 12.1 illustrates this use.

Figure 12.3
PMIS functions in the project life cycle.

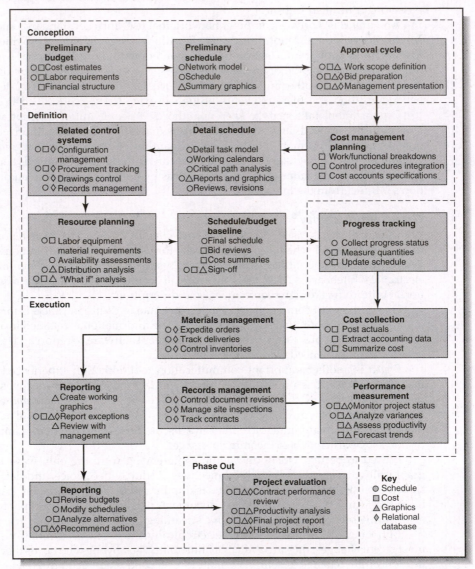

Sigma Associates, the architectural/engineering firm mentioned in Chapter 8, Example 8.7, uses a PMIS for most planning and control functions. So ubiquitous is Sigma's PMIS in its operations that employees think of it as a member of the team; they call it "Sally."

Once a project is approved, Sally's main function changes from planning assistance to monitoring and control. Sally's major use is to routinely compare original or current baseline plans with actual performance, raise warnings about discrepancies, and forecast date and cost at completion.

Each week, the system accumulates current costs and estimates of weekly time spent on each activity from all project participants. Non-labor expenses and client reimbursements are input through the company's general ledger system.

Biweekly project managers estimate the hours anticipated to complete each activity, which Sally converts into a percentage completed. The system multiplies budgeted labor hours by the percentage completed to determine the estimated labor hours needed to bring the activity to its current level of completion (a form of earned value). By comparing this estimate with actual labor expenditures from time cards, the project manager can determine whether the activity is moving at its budgeted pace. Sally makes actual-to-plan comparisons and reports discrepancies, which managers use to spot problems. Whenever project managers fail to make the biweekly estimates of anticipated hours, Sally prompts them about the missing estimate entries.

The comptroller uses Sally to forecast the timing and amounts of client billing and expected payments according to each client's payment history. Based on the percentage of work completed, the system computes an estimate of earned client fees. These fees are compared to actual labor costs, overhead costs, and non-labor expenses in a monthly profit/loss analysis. Sally generates monthly reports of net profit project-to-date and year-to-date, summarized by office, department, and project manager. It also combines net profit for all projects to give a picture of the company's financial health.

Sally also checks the discrepancies on time cards. Hours charged are compared with dates on the schedule; any card with discrepancies is withheld and a memo is sent to the employee. A summary report of rejected or uncorrected cards is sent each week to the comptroller. Sally is an example of a sophisticated, comprehensive PMIS.

Fitting the PMIS to the Project

Most PMI software is no match for the capabilities of Sally, but that's okay, since seldom are all such capabilities required. The purpose of a PMIS, in the words of Palla, is to "get the right information to the right person at the right time so the right decision can be made for the project."[9] Any PMIS able to do this is the right one. Firms often use more than one kind of PMI software—say, Microsoft Project for smaller projects and Primavera for large ones.

While a PMIS is essential for effective and efficient handling of the computational aspects of project management, its role should be seen in context: such systems do little to help the project manager identify key stakeholders, negotiate the project scope with them, decide on key subcontractors, or motivate the team. Too many novices, having attended a 2-day software seminar, leave with the impression that project management is little more than creating and using Gantt charts on a computer.

The final stage of the project execution phase is implementation—the stage where the end-item system or other deliverable is completed and turned over to the user for operation. Sometimes implementation happens in an instant; sometimes it takes months. Take a clock. If the clock is simple, you just plug it in and set it. If it is a digital clock with a radio, you might need to read the instructions first. If it is a nuclear clock, such as the one used by the US Bureau of Standards, you might need to attend a training program to learn how to operate it. If the clock is a replacement for an existing clock connected to a timing device that controls lighting and heating in a large skyscraper, you will need to develop a *strategy* for substituting the clock so as to minimize disruption and inconvenience to the people in the building. This section discusses issues associated with implementation.

User Training

The purpose of user training is to teach the user how to operate, maintain, and service the system. At one extreme, training is a simple instruction booklet; at the other, it is an extensive, ongoing program with a hefty annual budget. The first step is to determine the training requirements—the type and extent of training required. This will dictate the kind of materials needed (manuals, videos, simulators); personnel to be trained (existing or newly hired); techniques to be used (classroom, independent study, role plays); training schedule (everyone at once, in phases, or ongoing); and staffing (contractor, user, or subcontracted training personnel). Users should review and approve all training procedures and documents before training begins, and provide input afterward to improve the training. Often the user takes over training after the contractor's trainers have trained the user's trainers.

User training should address the issue of how the new system will fit into the user's environment. It should provide an overview of the system's objectives, scope, and operation, and how the system interfaces with the user organization. All new systems create fear, stress, and anxiety; one aim of training should also be to relieve or eliminate these.

User Acceptance Testing

User acceptance tests are among the last tests performed on the end-item. The results of these tests determine if the system warrants (1) acceptance as is, (2) acceptance pending modifications or adjustments, or (3) rejection.

User acceptance tests differ from tests conducted by the contractor during design and production, though the latter should anticipate and be rigorous enough to exceed the user's test requirements. Nonetheless, the contractor should be prepared for the possibility that aspects of the system might not pass some of the user tests.

Ideally, users perform acceptance tests with minimal assistance from the project team. In cases where the user cannot perform the tests, the project team must act as surrogate user and make every effort to test the system just as the user would. But lack of user participation in these tests is risky and can to lead to later long-term problems; therefore, even in the role of surrogate user-tester, the contractor must insist that the user be on hand to witness the tests.

System Installation and Conversion

During the system installation and conversion stage, equipment must be installed, tested, fine-tuned, and deemed operable to the fulfillment of requirements.

Virtually all new systems are, in a sense, designed to substitute other existing systems, so a major implementation issue is the strategy to be used for replacing the old system with the new—the process of *conversion*. Three possible strategies, illustrated in Figure 12.4, are:

Parallel installation: both new and old systems are operated in parallel until the new system is sufficiently proven

Pilot operation: the new system is operated in a limited capacity until proven, and then is phased in as the old system is phased out

Cold turkey (Big Bang): in one fell swoop, the new system is moved in and the old one is moved out.

Selecting a conversion strategy is no simple matter; it involves considerations of costs, risks, and logistics. For example, the first strategy seems safest: if the new system fails, the old one is still there. But it is also the most expensive, because two complete systems must be operated simultaneously and adequate staff must be on hand to operate both of them. With the second strategy, the costs and risks are low and staff can be trained in stages. The problem is, a pilot operation is not necessarily representative of full system operation. Often, only after the new system has been completely phased in (and the old one phased out) do critical problems become apparent. The last strategy is the fastest and potentially least costly, but it is also the most risky, and raises issues about when the staff will be trained to operate the new system, and what will happen if the new system fails.

Prior to installation, the project manager updates all schedules, gains approvals, and renews commitments from the contractor and customer teams. Implementation is

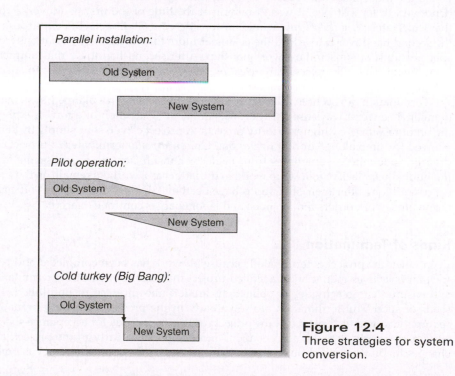

Figure 12.4
Three strategies for system conversion.

a high-stress stage for everyone, and the project team must be patient with users and sensitive to their questions, concerns, and fears.

After the new system has been installed, the contractor continues to monitor it and perform tests to ensure it was installed properly, operates as expected, and interfaces smoothly with other systems in the user environment.

12.5 PROJECT TERMINATION AND CLOSEOUT

By the time the end-item has been delivered and installed, many members of the project team will be eager to move on to something new. Managers eagerly shift emphasis to upcoming projects, and, as a result, might give the termination little attention. Yet, as common sense indicates, terminating a project is no less important than any other project activity. In fact, the method of termination can ultimately determine the project's success or failure.

Not only does the project as a whole have to be closed out; each phase of a project must also be formally closed. For example, at British Aerospace each end-of-phase is accompanied by a review meeting which is chaired by someone *not* from the function responsible for the phase; review for the marketing phase, for example, would be chaired by someone outside of Marketing.

At closeout, the product or deliverable is handed over to the customer. Sometimes contracts provide for a *first handover* at completion as well as a *second handover* after a *defects liability period* (also known as a retention period, guarantee period, or maintenance period). At first handover the customer should ensure that all *patent defects* (defects that can readily be detected by a qualified person) are identified and reported. After first handover the contractor is only liable for rectifying *latent defects*, which are those that could not be detected through a reasonable inspection at first handover. If, for instance, it wasn't raining at the time of the first handover, a roof that leaks later *when it does rain* would be considered a latent defect. The purpose of the second handover is to afford the customer more time to identify deviations from specifications, or substandard workmanship. After second handover the contractor is no longer liable for defects; any *retention fees* withheld by the customer to ensure compliance are paid to the contractor.

Termination can occur in a variety of ways, the best being in a planned, systematic manner. The worst ways are abrupt cancellation, slow attrition of effort, or siphoning off of resources by higher priority projects. A project can go sour simply by being allowed to "limp along" until it fizzles out. Unless *formally* terminated, a project can drag on indefinitely, sometimes from neglect or insufficient resources, sometimes intentionally for lack of follow-up work. In the latter case, workers remain on the project payroll long after their obligations have been met. Unless the project is officially terminated, work orders remain open and labor charges continue to accrue.

Kinds of Termination

Even when the project is terminated because all work has been completed and contractual objectives met, it takes a skilled project manager to orchestrate termination and ensure that no activities or obligations are left uncompleted or unfulfilled. The seeds of successful termination are sown early in the project. Because termination requires customer acceptance of the project results, the criteria for acceptance should have been clearly defined, agreed upon, and documented early in the project; any changes made after that should have been approved by the contractor and customer.

The reasons why some projects never reach successful completion are many. The project may be aborted when the financial or other losses from early termination are considered less than the losses expected from completing the project. The customer may simply change his mind and no longer want the project end-item.

Projects are also halted because of changing market conditions or technology, unsatisfactory technical performance, poor quality of materials or workmanship, violation of contract, or customer dissatisfaction with the contractor. Many of these reasons are the fault of the contractor, and could have been avoided had project management exercised better planning and control, respected the customer more, or acted in a more ethical manner. Such terminations leave the user with unmet requirements, and cast a pall over the contractor's technical competency and managerial ability.

Termination and Closeout Responsibilities

As with earlier stages of the project work, the project manager is responsible for planning, scheduling, monitoring, and controlling termination and closeout activities. The responsibilities listed by Archibald include the following.[10]

A. Planning, scheduling, and monitoring closeout activities:

- Obtain and approve termination plans from involved functional managers
- Prepare and coordinate termination plans and schedules
- Plan for transfer of project team members and resources to other projects
- Monitor completion of all contractual agreements
- Monitor the disposition of any surplus materials and project equipment.

B. Final closeout activities:

- Close out all work orders and contracts with subcontractors and completed work
- Notify all departments of project completion
- Close the project office and all facilities occupied by the project organization
- Close project books
- Ensure delivery of project files and records to the responsible managers.

C. Customer acceptance, obligation, and payment activities:

- Ensure delivery of end-items, side-items, and customer acceptance of items
- Notify the customer when all contractual obligations have been fulfilled
- Ensure that all documentation related to customer acceptance as required by contract has been completed
- Expedite any customer activities needed to complete the project
- Transmit formal payment and collection of payments
- Obtain from customer formal acknowledgment of completion of contractual obligations that release the contractor from further obligation (except warranties and guarantees).

Responsibility for group C, above, particularly for payment and contractual obligations, is shared with the contract administrator or others responsible for company–client negotiations and legal contracts. The final activity, obtaining the formal customer acknowledgment, may involve claims if the customer has failed to provide agreed-to data or support, or has requested items beyond contract specifications. In these cases, the contractor is entitled to compensation.

Before the project is considered closed, the customer reviews the results or end-item with the contractor to make sure everything is satisfactory. Items still open and in need of attention, and to which the contractor agrees, are recorded on a list, sometimes called a "punch list." The contractor then checks off the items on the list as they are rectified.

Example 12.2: Punch List for the Chunnel[11]

Five months before the scheduled completion date of the Chunnel, the punch list still contained a lot of items—over 22,000. Incredibly, by the day before scheduled handover of the Chunnel to its owner/operator, that number had been whittled down to only a hundred. The problem was, the contract allowed for *no* (zero) items on the punch list; any open items at the handover would void the agreement and stop payment. A simple solution would be to delay the handover until the remaining items were fixed, which was estimated to take only a week—but few things associated with the Chunnel were simple. Invitations for the handoff ceremony had already gone out, and preparations for the big gala celebration had been completed. Besides, a syndicate of some 200 banks located around the world had financed the project, and any proposed delay in the handover would require their approval.

What followed was a series of frenzied negotiations via telephone and fax that lasted throughout the night. By dawn, the bank syndicate had agreed to amend the contract. The gala sign-off ceremony went as planned, complete with fireworks, Champagne, a choral group, and a Dixieland jazz band. The ceremony—attended by executives and project managers from the Chunnel's 10 prime contractors plus 1,000 other guests—was a minor project in itself.

The importance of doing a good job at termination cannot be understated—and neither can the difficulty. In the rush to finish the project and the accompanying confusion, it is easy to overlook, mishandle, or botch the termination. The termination responsibilities listed previously should be systematically delegated and checked off as completed. Termination requires the same degree of attention as do other project management responsibilities.

Closing the Contract

Delivery, installation, and user acceptance of the main contract end-item (hardware, software, or service specified by the project contract) does not necessarily mean that the project is closed. Project completion can be delayed pending delivery of necessary, ancillary articles—*side-items*—or payment of compensation for failure to meet contractual agreements.

Side-Items

The installation, operation, maintenance, and monitoring of the contract end-item is often contingent upon the availability of numerous contract side-items, such as special tools, instruments, spare parts, reports, drawings, courses of instruction, and user operating and maintenance manuals. Side-items are usually provided by subcontractors, and can range from the simple and mundane to the complex and innovative. The former is exemplified by an operating manual for a network server, the latter by a high-fidelity computer simulator for training operators of a large chemical processing facility. Whether simple or complex, successful completion of side-items is important to successful completion of the project.

Side-items are deliverable contract items, and their cost may contribute a significant percentage of total project cost. Yet, perhaps because they are deemed "side" items, the time and effort required to develop and produce them is often underestimated, causing delay in implementing the end-item and closing the project.

Side-items should be included in all aspects of project planning and control. The project manager must make certain that the scope of side-item work is well understood, and qualified personnel or contractors are assigned to fulfill their requirements.[12] Side-items are part of the contracted work, not afterthoughts or project extensions. They must be given full consideration in the WBS, project schedule, and budget.

Handover and Negotiated Adjustments

In many high-cost projects, the contractor receives payment for only a portion of the total project cost—say, 80–90 percent—and the remainder is conditional upon the performance of the end-item, the contractor's compliance with contractual agreements, or the quality of the working relationship with the contractor.[13]

These final payment contingencies are considered post-acceptance issues because they occur after the customer has accepted the major end-item. If the delivered end-item is satisfactory yet does not perform up to the contracted specifications, if it is found defective after a trial period due to design or production inadequacies, or if it is delivered late, the contractor might have to pay a negotiated compensation to the user.

Contract sign-off might also be contingent upon how well the product functions after installation or delivery. In that case, beyond installation and initial operation at the customer's site, the project manager might also provide on-site user support, at no additional fee, until any operating deficiencies have been removed.

Sometimes the customer or contractor seeks to negotiate aspects of the contract price or completion date *after* the project is completed. The US government retains the right to negotiate overhead rates *after* it receives the final price on cost-plus contracts. Likewise, a contractor sometimes seeks to negotiate a revised completion date on the contract *after* the project is completed—usually because it overran the scheduled date and wants to salvage its reputation.

12.6 PROJECT SUMMARY EVALUATION

Among the final activities of the project team after project closeout is to perform a formal evaluation. This final *summary evaluation* gives project and company management the opportunity to learn from its successes and mistakes in the project. Without a summary review, there is a tendency to mentally suppress problems encountered and to understate the impact of errors or misjudgments. ("Things weren't really so bad, were they?") The project summary evaluation reviews and assesses the performance of the project team and the end-item system. Its purpose is to identify and assess what was done and what remains to be done—not to find fault or pass blame. Two forms of summary evaluation are the post-completion project review and the post-installation system review.

Post-Completion Project Review

The *post-completion project review* (perversely also called a *post mortem*) is a summary review and assessment of the *project* conducted by the contractor immediately after project closeout—early enough that project team members are still around, available to participate, and remember what happened. [14] It is an important task for which funds and time should be included in the project's budget and schedule. Post-completion reviews are one way companies try to continuously improve future projects through lessons learned from past projects—an opportunity that many companies forego.

The post-completion project review should review:

1. Initial project objectives in terms of technical performance, schedule, and cost; and the soundness of objectives in view of the problem the system should have resolved
2. Changes in objectives and reasons for changes, noting which changes were avoidable and which not
3. The activities and relationships of the project team throughout the project life cycle, including the effectiveness of project management; relationships among top management, the project team, the functional organization, and the customer; customer reactions and satisfaction
4. The involvement and performance of all stakeholders, including subcontractors and vendors, the client, and outside support groups
5. Expenditures, sources of costs, and profitability
6. Organizational benefits, project extensions, and marketable innovations
7. Areas of the project where performance was particularly good, noting reasons for success and identifying processes that worked well
8. Problems, mistakes, oversights, and areas of poor performance, and the causes
9. A list of lessons learned from the project, and recommendations for incorporating them into future projects.

The review happens in a half- or day-long meeting with representatives from *all* functional areas that substantially contributed to the project. To encourage openness and candor, the managers of these areas should *not* be at the meeting. An outside facilitator might be selected to guide the process to ensure the review is comprehensive and unbiased. At the meeting, participants independently list things that went right and wrong with the project; they then share their notes and create lists of lessons learned and recommendations for future projects. The completed lists are then formally presented to stakeholders, to others on the project team, and to project, functional, and senior managers.

The review seeks not to place blame, but to determine lessons that may be applied to future projects. Its results are documented in a *project summary report*, which becomes the authoritative document on the project. The report describes the project, its evolution, and the outcome. It describes the project plan, where it worked, and where it failed. Because projects affect different parties in different ways, the opinions and assessments of the customer, the project team, and upper management should be listed separately.

The project summary report becomes the reference for project-related questions that might arise later. Thoroughness and clarity are essential, since people who worked on the project usually will not be available later to answer questions. The report is retained in a project library, and its lessons learned and recommendations promoted in other projects, sometimes by the PMO. Post-completion reviews and summaries are ways to capture and reapply knowledge to future projects—tools for project *knowledge management*, discussed in Chapter 17.

Example 12.3: Microsoft Postmortems[15]

Product development projects at Microsoft often conclude with a written *post mortem* report that is circulated to team members, senior executives, and the directors of product development, coding, and testing, and to the highest levels of management, which for major projects includes the company president. A report can require as long as 6 months to prepare, and range from under 10 pages to over 100 pages in length. Its purpose is to describe what worked well in the project, what did not, and what could be done to improve future projects. Descriptive information is also included, such as *the size of the project team, duration of the project, aspects of the product* (size in thousand-lines-of-code [KLOC], languages and platform used), *quality issues* (number of bugs per KLOC, type and severity of bugs), *schedule performance* (actual versus planned dates), and the *development process* (tools used, interdependencies with other groups). Functional managers prepare the initial draft and then circulate it via e-mail to other team members for comment.

Post-Installation System Review

Some months after its delivery, the *operational end-item* or *system* should be evaluated to assess its performance in the user environment and under ongoing operational conditions. This *post-installation system review* focuses on the end-item system and serves a variety of purposes, such as providing operation and maintenance information for the system's designers, and revealing possible needed enhancements for the system's users. Based upon the original user requirements, the post-installation system review attempts to answer the questions: Now that the system is fully operational, is it doing what it was intended to do? Is the user getting the expected benefits from the system? What changes, if any, are necessary for the system to better fulfill user needs?

It is important that the evaluated system is *unaltered* from the one delivered. Frequently the user makes system modifications and improvements after installation; although there is nothing wrong with this *per se*, the system is physically or functionally changed from the one delivered or installed—a fact that must be considered when evaluating its performance.

During the course of the review, the evaluation team might discover elements of the system in need of repair or modification. Design flaws, operating problems, or necessary enhancements that could not have been foreseen earlier sometimes become obvious only after the system has been in routine operation.

Results of the review are summarized in a report that describes the system's performance compared to its objectives, any maintenance problems, and suggested possible enhancements. The post-installation system review and the project summary review are filed together and retained as references for planning future projects.

12.7 AFTER THE PROJECT—PHASE D: OPERATION

What happens after the conclusion of Phase C depends on whether the end-item or deliverable is a physical system or process that must be maintained and operated (e.g., a product, machine, or operating procedure), or a service for which no physical product remains (e.g., a rock concert, company relocation, corporate merger, or audit). When the former happens—the project develops and/or builds a physical system or product—the systems development cycle enters Phase D, Operation. The contractor can remain involved with the customer and the system in the operation phase in two ways: (1) by agreeing to maintain/repair the system, or (2) by initiating a new project to enhance or replace the system.

System Evaluation and Maintenance

The contractor may perform evaluation of the system either as part of the original contract agreement or by an additional agreement. The evaluation may occur as the last scheduled activity of the contractor in the form of a *post-installation review*, described earlier, or as an extended agreement to provide periodic review and/or service to the system on a continuing basis. The agreement can be a warranty arrangement whereby the contractor reviews and maintains the system for a pre-specified time period as part of the original contract, or it can be an "extended" arrangement that continues the contractor's involvement for a longer time period. The contractor may assign *system representatives* and technicians to the user site to perform preventive maintenance and system upgrades on a scheduled basis, or as requested by the user.

Enhancing or Replacing the System

When the customer wants to enhance or replace the originally contracted system, a new project emerges; from the original contractor's perspective, this is an *extension* to the original project.

There are two kinds of extensions: discretionary and essential. *Discretionary extensions* are requested by the customer or proposed by the contractor for the purpose of improving the operation, performance, or convenience of the original project end-item. The environment remains the same, but new and better ways now have appeared that can improve the system. The other kind, *essential extensions*, are compulsory; without them the system will cease to operate or will become obsolete. An end-item that is no longer adequate because of changes in the environment or design deficiencies *must* be enhanced or replaced.

The decision to expand, enhance, or replace a system marks the beginning of a new systems development cycle, one that is initiated with either a request from the user (e.g., an RFP) or proposal from the contractor. The extension itself becomes a project. Humankind engages in few dead-end projects; each spurs others, and the systems development cycle keeps rolling along—hence the term "cycle."

12.8 SUMMARY

Project formative evaluation relies on a variety of sources and measures for collecting and communicating information, including written and oral reports, site visits, one-on-one conversations, and informal and formal reviews. Informal reviews are held regularly and conducted by peer members of the project team. Formal reviews are special reviews or audits held at key stages or milestones in the project, and conducted by experienced outsiders and consultants. They provide independent assessments of overall project performance, suggestions or instructions for improving the project, and sometimes a decision about whether or not to continue the project. The kinds of reports and reviews and details about contents, formats, schedules, and participants are specified in the project communication plan.

In many projects, PMIS software is used to perform the planning and control functions. Most PMIS software does network scheduling, resource management, budgeting, tracking, cost control, and performance analysis. Many systems also utilize Web-based technology, which provides the benefits of ready accessibility at remote sites, ease of usage, and reliability and currency of information.

Implementation is the final stage of the execution phase when the end-item system or other deliverable is completed and turned over to the user. Among important tasks during implementation are user training, user tests of acceptance, and system installation and conversion. The contractor trains the user how to operate, maintain, and service the system, and develops a strategy for installing the system in the user's environment; three possible strategies are parallel, pilot, and cold turkey. The user performs his own set of tests to determine whether or not the installed end-item system is acceptable.

The project is terminated through a series of formal procedures. The project manager oversees termination activities and conducts the project closeout. Following project completion, a post-completion review (*post mortem*) is conducted to assess the effectiveness of the project organization. Additionally, after the main end-item system has been in operation, a post-installation system review is conducted to assess its performance and determine possible maintenance or enhancement needs. The documented results are combined with the summary report to provide a reference document for future project teams.

The preceding sections of the book have described how project managers, organizations, and teams plan, organize, and guide projects from start to finish; so far, though, not much has been said about the project managers, organizations, or teams *themselves*. The following section focuses on managers and teams; it addresses project *organizational behavior* and the topics of organization structure, leadership, teamwork, and conflict and stress, all which are crucial to effective management of projects.

REVIEW QUESTIONS AND PROBLEMS

1. Describe the difference between formative evaluation and summary evaluation in project management.
2. Why is it better to rely on a variety of information sources for evaluation than just a few? Give some examples of how several sources are used in project evaluation.
3. What are the advantages and disadvantages of the following sources of information: (a) charts and tables, (b) oral and written reports, (c) firsthand evaluation?
4. What is the purpose of internal peer reviews? When are they held? Who participates?
5. What is an action plan? What must it include?
6. What is a formal critical review? When is a formal review held, and what does it look at? Why do outsiders conduct it? Why would a customer or project supporter want a formal review?
7. What should be included in status reports to top management?
8. What reports should the project manager receive? How does the project manager use these reports?
9. What reports are sent to functional managers?
10. When and what kind of reports are sent to the customer? Why is reporting to customers so important?
11. What is the role of the PMIS in project management?
12. Discuss the applications and benefits of Web-based project management.
13. Discuss the uses of the PMIS throughout the phases of the project life cycle.
14. How is the system implemented? Describe the important considerations for turning the system over to the user.
15. Discuss user training and why it is sometimes included in the implementation stage.
16. How is the project end-item tested and checked out for approval?

17. Describe the different strategies for installing or converting over to the new system.
18. What are the reasons for project termination? How can termination for reasons other than achievement of project goals be avoided?
19. What is involved in planning and scheduling the project termination?
20. What is the role of the project manager and contract administrator in receiving customer acceptance of the work and final payment?
21. What are side items? Give examples not used in this book. How can they delay project completion?
22. What kinds of negotiated adjustments are made to the contract, post-acceptance? Why would a user or contractor want to specify the terms of a contract *after* the project is completed?
23. What is a punch list?
24. What is a project extension, and how do project extensions originate? How is a project extension managed?
25. What are the differences between the *post-completion project* (or *post mortem*) *review* and the *post-installation system review*? Describe each of these.
26. Describe what happens during the operation phase. What is the role of the systems development organization (contractor) in this phase?

QUESTIONS ABOUT THE STUDY PROJECT

1. How often and what kinds of review meetings were held in the project? Why were they held? Who attended them?
2. When and for what reason were special reviews held?
3. How was follow-up ensured on decisions made during review meetings?
4. Was there a project meeting room? How often and in what ways is it used?
5. Describe the kinds of project reports sent to top management, the customer, and project and functional managers. Who issued these reports?
6. Describe the PMIS used in the project you are studying. Was it the same one used for cost-accounting (PCAS) and scheduling? Does it combine scheduling, budgeting, authorization, and control, or were several different systems used?
7. What are the strong and weak points of the PMIS system? Does the system adequately satisfy the information requirements needed to plan and control the project? Does it employ web-based technology? What improvements would you suggest to the system?
8. Does the project manager encourage open, informal communication? If so, in what way?
9. How was the project terminated? Describe the activities of the project manager during the final stage of the project and the steps taken to close it out.
10. If the end-item is a building or other "constructed" item, how was it turned over to the user? Describe the testing, acceptance, training, and authorization process.
11. How was the contract closed out? Were there any side-items or negotiated adjustments to the contract?
12. Did any follow-up projects grow out of the project being investigated?
13. Describe the post-completion project (*post mortem*) review. Who prepared it? To whom was it sent, and how was it used? Where is it now? Show an example (or portion of one).
14. Was a post-installation system review conducted? When? By whom? What did they find? Did the client request the review or was it standard procedure?
15. What happens to the project team when the project is completed?
16. Does the contractor remain involved with the customer and end-item through an extended agreement?

Case 12.1   Status Report for the LOGON Project

The Logon Project began as scheduled in May 2010. In late September—after the project had been underway for 20 weeks—Midwest Parcel Distribution (MPD) Company, the customer, requested Frank Wesley, the project manager, to prepare a written summary status report about progress to date.

Review Appendices A, B, and C at the end of the book for background about the project; Appendix C has information on the budget and dates for scheduled milestones and deliverables. Prepare the report as if you were Frank. Note that the report is for MPD's top management, and should address issues of most importance to them: deliverables and other requirements, schedule, and budget, as noted in Appendix C. The report should also note any problems encountered to date, anticipated challenges, and recommended suggestions or changes to the plan.

Case 12.2   SLU Information Central Building

Construction of the new Information Central building at South Land University (SLU) is completed on time and on budget. Administrators at SLU and managers at Finley Construction Company, the building's prime contractor, are very pleased with the results. Besides meeting schedule and cost targets, the building and its equipment, including facilities and a variety of computer and technical gadgetry intended to augment learning, appear to have met all of the technical requirements. Much of the technology is leading edge, and some of it is being applied for the first time ever in a learning/teaching environment by SLU. By all accounts, the project is a success.

After reviewing and confirming that all of Finley's obligations for the project have been met, Jack Krackower, the project manager, meets with Sharon Holden, SLU's vice president of finance, and Ramat Ghan, SLU's vice president of facilities, to finalize details of project termination and payment. The meeting goes well, and ends with discussion of future projects at SLU and possible involvement of the Finley Construction Company. After the meeting Jack returns to his office, whereupon the director of Finley's PMO asks him if he plans to do a post-completion project review. "Nope," quipped Jack, "no need to. The project was a success and everything went just as planned."

A few months later, Sharon and Ramat give a final presentation on the project to SLU's president, reporting that it met all the technical and building requirements, the schedule, and the budget. In fact, they say, given the positive outcome of the project, some of the new technology in the building should be installed in other campus buildings and Finley hired to oversee it. "Not so fast," says the president. "I've heard reports that students and faculty find the new technology confusing, difficult to use, and maybe irrelevant. In fact, some rooms in the building are vacant for lack of use. Other rooms are crowded, but students go there to socialize or relax, not to take advantage of any sophisticated learning technologies. I don't know what the problem is—if it's with the technology or with way Finley handled it."

QUESTIONS

1. Comment on Jack's neglect to conduct a post-completion project review. Is a review unnecessary whenever a project is considered a success?

2. Is the project really a success? What kind of follow-up steps should Findley and SLU have done after the project was completed?

1. See Turner J and Muller R. Communication and cooperation on projects between the project owner as principle and the project manager as agent. *European Management Journal* 22(3); 2004: 327–336.

2. Muirhead B and Simon W. *High Velocity Leadership: The Mars Pathfinder Approach to Faster, Better, Cheaper*. New York, NY: Harper Business; 1999. p. 179.

3. Archibald R. *Managing High-Technology Programs and Projects*. New York: Wiley; 1976. p. 191.

4. Peters T and Waterman R. *In Search of Excellence*. New York, NY: Warner Communications; 1984. pp. 121–125.

5. First to run on a PC was Harvard Project Manager in 1983, followed soon by an explosion of products—well over 100. All but the strongest products have since disappeared.

6. Roman D. *Managing Projects: A Systems Approach*. New York, NY: Elsevier; 1986. pp. 181, 184; Suarez LF. Resource allocation: a comparative study. *Project Management Journal* 18(1); 1987: 68–71.

7. Portions of this section were prepared with the assistance of Elisa Denney.

8. Greer T. *Understanding Intranets*. Redmond, WA: Microsoft Press; 1998; see also Mead S. Project-specific intranets for construction team. *Project Management Journal* 28(3); 1997: 44–51.

9. Palla R. Introduction to micro-computer software tools for project management. *Project Management Journal* 18(3); 1987: 61–68.

10. See Archibald, *Managing High-Technology Programs and Projects*, pp. 235–236 and 264–270, for a complete checklist of closeout activities.

11. Fetherston D. *Chunnel*. New York. NY: Time Books; 1997. pp. 372–375.

12. Hajek V. *Managing Engineering Projects*, 3rd edn. New York, NY: McGraw-Hill; 1984. See pp. 233–240 for a good description of monitoring and support side items for both engineering hardware and computer software projects.

13. *Ibid.*, pp. 241–242.

14. Williams T. *Post-Project Reviews to Gain Effective Lessons Learned*. Newton Square, PA: Project Management Institute; 2007; Whitten N. *Managing Software Development Projects*, 2nd edn. New York, NY: John Wiley & Sons; 1995. pp. 343–357.

15. Cusumano M and Selby R. *Microsoft Secrets*. New York, NY: Free Press; 1995. pp. 331–334.

IV

Organization Behavior

*P*roject outcomes depend on the way individuals and groups are organized and interact. As human endeavors, projects are both influenced by and have influence on the behavior and well-being of the groups and individuals that belong to them.

The three chapters in this section focus on organizational and behavioral issues inherent to projects and the teams and individuals that comprise projects. They describe the ways that groups are organized and integrated, styles of leadership used by project managers, roles and responsibilities of members of the project team, and ways groups are managed to maximize teamwork and minimize the negative personal aspects of working in projects.

Chapter 13 covers topics discussed in the PMBOK guide under "Project Life Cycle and Organization." Chapters 14 and 15 address the PMBOK knowledge area of human resource management.

Chapter 13

Project Organization Structure and Integration

> *How can you expect to govern a country*
> *that has 246 kinds of cheese?*

—CHARLES DE GAULLE

*O*rganizations are systems of human and physical elements that interact to achieve goals. As with all of systems, they are partly described by their *structure*—the form of relationships that bond their elements. In all organizations, two kinds of structures coexist. One is the *formal* structure, the *published* one that describes normative superior–subordinate relationships, chains of command, and subdivisions and grouping of elements. The other is the *informal structure*, the unpublished one that describes relationships that *evolve* through the interactions of people. Whereas the formal organization prescribes how people are supposed to relate, the informal organization is how they actually do relate.

This chapter deals primarily with formal organization structures applicable to projects. There is no one best way to structure project organizations, but there are particular kinds of structures that enhance project performance. A project manager needs to understand these kinds of structures, and their relative advantages and disadvantages.

The chapter also deals with project integration, which is the way that individual functional groups, subunits, project phases, and work tasks are interlinked and coordinated to achieve project goals. The discussion covers various means of integration in projects, and the special case of integration in large-scale development projects.

13.1 FORMAL ORGANIZATION STRUCTURE

Concepts of organizational structure apply to all kinds of organizations (companies, institutions, agencies) as well as to their subunits (divisions, departments, projects, and teams). The formal organization structure is publicized in a chart such as the one for NASA in Figure 13.1; a quick glance reveals both organizational hierarchy and groupings for specialized tasks. Looking at the chart in Figure 13.1 one can see, for example:

1. The range of activities in which the organization is involved and the major subdivisions of the organization (exploration, space operations, science, aeronautics research)
2. The management hierarchy and reporting relationships (under "Mission," for example, directors at Ames, Goddard, and Jet Propulsion Laboratory all report to the administrator for science)
3. The type of work and responsibility of each subdivision (e.g., projects at research centers focus on specific disciplines or goals such as space exploration and space operations)
4. The official lines of authority and communication (the administrator is the highest authority, the deputy administrator the next highest, and so on; communication moves vertically along the lines from one box to the next).

Figure 13.1
NASA organization and program chart.

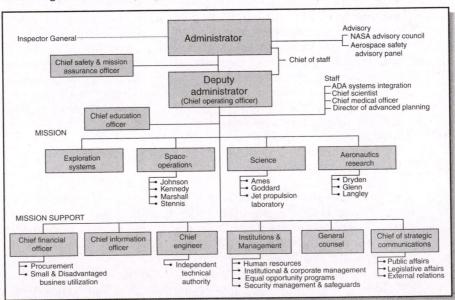

There are many things the chart does not show. For example, it does not show personal contacts whereby, for example, workers at Jet Propulsion Lab communicate directly with workers at Dryden via e-mail and telephone, not (as the chart implies) via the directors of these centers. Nonetheless, the chart is useful for its fundamental overview of the organization's departments and roles and the formal relationships among them.

13.2 ORGANIZATIONAL DESIGN BY DIFFERENTIATION AND INTEGRATION

There is no "best" kind of organization structure. The most appropriate structure depends on the organization's goals, type of work, and environment. Organization structures typically develop through a combination of planned and evolutionary responses to ongoing problems. Organizations create specialized roles and units, each with suitable expertise and resources needed to deal with certain classes of situations and problems. As they grow or the environment changes, new subdivisions and groupings are implemented to better handle new situations and emerging problems. For example, when a company increases its product lines, it may subdivide its manufacturing area into product-oriented divisions to better address problems specific to each of the lines. As a company expands its sales territory, it may subdivide its marketing force geographically to better handle problems of regional origin. This subdivision into specialized areas is called *differentiation*.

Obviously, the subunits of an organization do not act as independent entities but interact and support each other—at least in theory. The degree to which they interact, coordinate, and mutually adjust their actions to fulfill organizational goals is called *integration*.

Traditional Forms of Organization

How an organization is subdivided is referred to as the *basis* for differentiation. The six bases for differentiation are functional, geographic, product, customer, process, and project. We will start by looking at the first five forms of differentiation, and then focus on the project form.

Functional Differentiation

Functional differentiation is so called because it divides the organization into functional subunits such as marketing, finance, production, human resources, and research; the structure of the Iron Butterfly Company in Figure 13.2 is an example. Most of the integration between subunits is handled by rules, procedures, coordinated plans, and budgets. When discrepancies occur between subunits that cannot be handled by these measures, the managerial chain of command takes over, which means the managers of the subunits affected resolve them.

This form of organization works well in repetitive, stable environments, because there is little change and the rather low level of integration afforded by rules, procedures, and chain of command gets the job done. The functionally differentiated organization has a long history, including the Roman Army and the Catholic Church. It remains today the most prevalent form of organization.

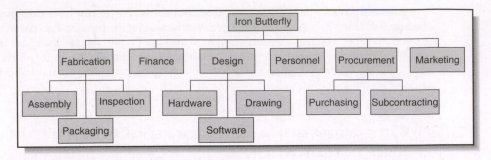

Figure 13.2
Functional differentiation in organization structure for Iron Butterfly Company.

Geographic Differentiation

Most organizations have more than one basis for differentiation. The Roman Army was also geographically differentiated; that is, it was structured according to region or location. Organizations subdivide according to region (e.g., Atlantic branch; European division; Far East command; etc.) to tailor themselves to the unique requirements of local customers, markets, suppliers, adversaries, and so on. Within each geographic subunit, functional differentiation is often retained. Regional subunits may operate relatively autonomously, and any necessary integration between them is achieved through standardized financial and reporting rules and procedures.

Product Differentiation

Firms that produce a variety of products use product-based differentiation. Corporations such as General Motors, General Foods, and General Electric are split into major subdivisions wherein each designs, manufactures, and markets its own product line. Within each subdivision is a functional, geographic, or other form of breakdown. As with geographically differentiated organizations, integration between product subdivisions tends to be limited to standardized financial and reporting rules and procedures.

Customer Differentiation

Organizations may also differentiate by customer type. For example, companies with large military sales often establish a separate division because federal requirements for proposals, contracting, and product specifications differ substantially from those for commercial customers. The level of integration between customer divisions depends on the degree of interdependency between their product lines; typically, however, integration is low.

Process Differentiation

The subunits of an organization can be differentiated based on a logical process or sequence of steps (e.g., design and development, then assembly, then inspection, etc.). This is illustrated for the fabrication department of Iron Butterfly Company, which has subunits for assembly, inspection, and packaging, shown in Figure 13.2. Subunits in this form of differentiation require a high level of integration because they are sequentially related, and problems in one area directly affect the others. Here, subunits are integrated through coordinated plans and schedules that span the subunits, and task forces and teams, discussed later.

Drawbacks of Traditional Forms of Organization

By their very design, traditional forms of organization can address only certain antici-pated, classifiable kinds of problems. As the environment changes and new kinds of problems arise, they react by further differentiating subunits and adding more rules, procedures, and levels of management. The price they pay for this is—in a word—bureaucracy, which translates into less flexibility and greater difficulty integrating the subunits.

Most traditional organization forms work on the assumption that problems or tasks can be neatly classified and resolved within specialized areas. Thus, the subunits tend to work independently and toward their own goals. When a problem arises that doesn't fit into any of the subunits, there may be no one to see that it gets resolved. Such problems fall through the cracks.

One way to handle unanticipated, unclassifiable problems is to redesign the organization whenever they arise. However, the process of redesigning organization structure to suit unique problems is slow and expensive, reflecting both the inertia of organizations as well as people's resistance to change. The alternative to redesign is to bump problems up the chain of command. This works as long as it is not done too often, because the chain of command can get quickly overwhelmed—the response to which is add more managers and subunits, which increases the size of the bureaucracy and makes the organization even less flexible than before. In short, traditional orga-nizations are not well suited for environments where there is high uncertainty and frequent change. Nonetheless, most projects are conducted within or use resources provided by organizations with a traditional form of structure.

13.3 REQUIREMENTS OF PROJECT ORGANIZATIONS

Project environments are characterized by complexity, change, and uncertainty. Projects typically require the resources and coordinated work effort of multiple people, subunits, and organizations. Each project is a new undertaking, somewhat unique, aimed at a new goal. Because of that, uncertainty and risk are inherent. Sub-units must pool their resources and be able to allocate and utilize them according to a coordinated plan. Changes, mistakes, or delays in one subunit have consequences for all others.

Organizations working in technologies such as software development, pharma-ceuticals, biomedicine, space exploration, product development, and even construc-tion routinely encounter the unexpected. As a result, they need to be adaptable to changing goals, customer needs, environmental demands, and resources, and able to deal with the uncertainty that accompanies these changes. They must be, in a word, *organic*, which means highly differentiated *and* highly integrated to accommodate a large variety of problems and situations, and to respond to them quickly. To achieve this, all project organizations have two properties:

- Subunits are integrated using horizontal relations
- Subunits are differentiated to suit the unique requirements of the project and the environment.

These properties are discussed next.

13.4 INTEGRATION OF SUBUNITS IN PROJECTS[1]

Traditional organizations are characterized by their "verticalness," or reliance upon up-and-down patterns of authority and communication. This makes them clumsy, slow, and ineffective in dealing with uncertain or quickly changing situations. In contrast, project organizations are characterized by their *horizontalness*, or use of direct communication between the parties involved in a problem. Horizontalness means cutting across lines of authority and moving decisions to the level of the parties affected.

All organizations have elements of horizontalness, mostly in the form of personal contacts, informal relationships, and friendships. These are particularly helpful for expediting communication and resolving problems between subunits. For example, whenever the assembly department in Figure 13.2 experiences a minor parts shortage, George, the assembly foreman, phones Helen in purchasing for a "rush order" favor. The call bypasses the formal structure (George and Helen's respective managers), and speeds up the ordering process.

A drawback with informal processes is that they do not ensure everyone who should be involved actually is. For example, Helen must charge all purchases to an account, but if George is not privy to the dollar amount in the account his informal requests might deplete the account before additional funds can be credited, which involves someone in the accounting area who is not aware of George's requests. Further, if George does not tell anyone about the parts shortages, then the reason for the problem—pilferage, defective parts, or under-ordering—will never be resolved. In short, informal processes are, in many regards, inadequate.

Project organizations improve upon informal processes by building horizontalness into the formal organization structure. They do this through the use of functions called *integrators*. Integrators greatly delimit the number of decisions referred up the chain of command, and facilitate communication between subunits working together on a common task. Integrators bypass traditional lines of authority and speed up communication, but they also ensure that everyone affected by a problem is involved and has the necessary information.

Several kinds of integrators are used in projects. They are listed below in order of increasing authority, need, and cost; in the list, the latter kinds take on all the authority and responsibility of the former.[2]

Liaison role
Task forces and teams
Project expeditors and coordinators
Pure project managers
Matrix managers
Integrating contractors.

13.5 LIAISON ROLES, TASK FORCES, AND TEAMS

The *liaison role* is held by a specialized person or group that links two or more departments. In Figure 13.3, the dotted line represents the liaison role of "inventory controller." This person performs duties in the assembly department, but also notifies purchasing of impending shortages and keeps track of orders placed. The role relieves

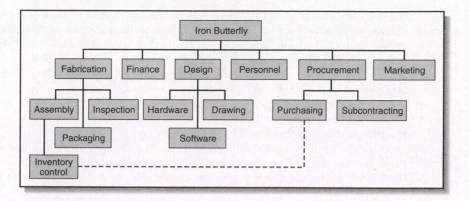

Figure 13.3
Liaison role linking Assembly and Purchasing departments.

the assembly foreman of the responsibility, and, by legitimizing the process, ensures that orders get placed and are funded and documented.

However, the liaison role is not always effective. Though the inventory controller in the example expedites parts ordering, the reason for part shortages goes unresolved. To unravel the problem it is necessary to involve people from other areas of the company. This is where the next kind of integrative role, an *interdisciplinary task force* or *team*, comes into play.

A *task force* is a temporary group with representatives from several areas that meet to solve a problem. When such a group is formed and actively begins addressing the problem, it is, in fact, conducting a project. For example, when a shortage occurs, the assembly foreman might call together liaison people from the areas of inspection, finance, and purchasing. The task force meets as often as needed to solve the problem, and then it disbands. The most effective task forces have 10 members or less and a team leader or coordinator, and are short-lived.[3]

Both the leader and members are selected by (and the leader reports directly to) the person responsible for the project—a functional manager, vice president, or CEO. Leaders are responsible for expediting and coordinating efforts, and may have authority to direct tasks and to contract out work. Usually, though, they have little formal authority over team members, who often must divide time between the task force and their "usual" work. The variety of projects undertaken by task forces is unlimited, and includes special purpose assignments such as:

Reorganizations
Mergers, acquisitions, or divestitures
Special studies, surveys, or evaluations
Major audits
Efficiency, modernization, and cost reduction efforts
Geographic or marketing expansions
Relocation of facilities or change in facility layout
Management and organization development programs
New equipment or procedures installation.

Members of a task force must have information relevant to the group task, plus the authority to make commitments for their functional areas. Lacking information, the group's decisions will be faulty; lacking authority, the group will not be able to act on its decisions.

For problems that are novel but need *continuous* attention, *permanent teams* are formed. These teams have the same characteristics as task forces, except that they convene periodically on a regular basis. For example, if the products that Iron Butterfly Company produces each require repeated design changes throughout the year, then representatives from design, fabrication, procurement, and other areas must meet on a regular basis. Only through repeated face-to-face association is the team able to coordinate decisions regarding design changes in response to changing markets and competition. Members work on the team either part-time or full-time.

Most projects have several kinds of teams; some convene during a single phase of the project life cycle, others for the full duration. One example of the latter in development projects is the *change board* discussed in Chapter 11—a multifunctional team that meets frequently to discuss and approve design changes. Another is the design-build team, described later.

Sometimes it is difficult to find people with the requisite knowledge, authority, and inclination to serve on multifunctional tasks forces and teams. People develop attitudes and goals oriented toward their specialization, and although this helps them be effective in their own area of work, it delimits their ability to interact with people from other areas. For cross-functional projects, the team-building methods described in Chapter 15 help break down barriers and forge bonds between project team members.

13.6 Project Expeditors and Coordinators

The simplest kind of project organization is a single, small group of people, a task force or team formed on a full- or part-time basis to perform an assignment. Such a group can exist inside one functional area or span across multiple functional areas.

Projects Within One Functional Area

It makes sense that a project which affects only one functional area should be located in that area. For example, a project to survey customer attitudes about a new product would ordinarily be placed entirely within the marketing department because all the necessary resources and expertise are there. The team does everything—it prepares the survey instrument, obtains mailing lists, distributes the survey, and processes the results. A project team like this is managed by a *project expeditor*[4]—someone selected by the manager of the area wherein the project lies. The expeditor coordinates decisions, creates and monitors schedules, makes suggestions, and keeps the manager apprised. The expeditor, however, typically has no formal authority over team members, and so must rely on persuasion, personal knowledge, and information about the project to influence team members. A single-function project organization is shown in Figure 13.4. In a large organization, it would not be uncommon for over a 100 such projects to be conducted within functional departments throughout the organization.

Multifunctional Project Teams

An example of a project that might use a *multifunctional team* is one for the development of an enterprise resource planning (ERP) system. ERP is a company-wide system that ties together information about forecasting, order entry, purchasing, and inventory. The team, which might be called the "ERP Task Force," would include representatives

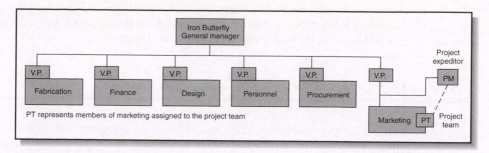

Figure 13.4
Project expeditor within a single functional area.

from all the departments that must provide inputs to the system or would utilize its outputs, such as accounting, inventory control, purchasing, manufacturing, engineering, and IT. Sometimes representatives from suppliers and customers are also on this team. The team is responsible for defining the system requirements, and overseeing the development and installation of the system. Multifunctional teams such as this are typically formed for projects that are large but do not require the resources to merit a complete reorganization.

A common place to see multifunctional teams is in product development. By using closely knit teams of engineers, designers, manufacturers, assemblers, marketers, lawyers, suppliers, dealers, and customers, phases of the systems development cycle usually done sequentially can be done simultaneously. This approach, called concurrent engineering, eliminates cross-functional barriers and can result in higher quality and lower cost. Concurrent engineering is discussed in Chapter 4, and later in this chapter.

The multifunctional project team may be located either in the functional area most responsible for the project or at a higher-level position, such as reporting to the general manager as shown in Figure 13.5. The latter arrangement imputes greater importance to the project. The person managing such a project is designated the project *coordinator*. Though this person has no line authority over team members, he does have authority to make and execute decisions about project budgets, schedules, and work

Figure 13.5
Multifunctional project team.

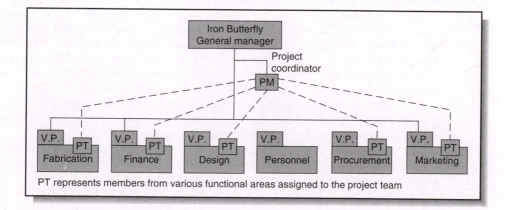

performance. Besides the high-level position of reporting to the general manager, the coordinator's influence, like that of the expeditor, originates in his knowledge of the project and being at the center of everything that is happening.

13.7   PURE PROJECT ORGANIZATIONS

Projects that entail much complexity, major resource commitments, and high stakes require a *pure project* or *projectized* form of organization. A pure project is a separate organization, similar to its own company, created especially for and singularly devoted to achievement of the project goal. Whatever is needed to accomplish project goals— all necessary human and physical resources—is incorporated into the pure project organization. These organizations are able to respond to the changing demands of the environment, the customer, and the parent organization. Often, within the pure project there are liaisons, task forces, and teams.

Heading the pure object organization is the *pure project manager*. Unlike a coordinator or expeditor, the pure project manager has formal authority over all people and physical resources assigned to the project, and, thus, maximum control. The project manager can bring in resources from internal functional areas as well as contract out with external subcontractors and suppliers. The pure project manager is involved in the project from start to finish: during proposal preparation, she requests and reconciles plans from functional areas and prepares preliminary budget and schedule estimates; after acceptance, she hires personnel; during project execution, she allocates resources and approves changes to requirements and the project plan. When personnel must be "borrowed" from functional areas, she negotiates to obtain them.

When resources are not internally available, the project manager heads selection of and negotiations with subcontractors. She oversees their work and coordinates it with other projects. The project managers in the Delamir Roofing, disaster recovery, and NASA examples in Chapter 1 are pure project managers.

Pure Project Variations

Three common variations of the pure project structure are the *project center*, the *partial project*, and the *stand-alone project*.

In the *project center*, the structure of the parent organization remains the same except for the addition of a separate "project arm" and project manager. This form is shown in Figure 13.6 for the Iron Butterfly Company and two of its pure-project arms, LOGON and SPECTOR. (Of course, unlike people, organizations can have any number of project arms.) Resources and personnel are borrowed from functional and staff areas for as long as needed. General Motors used a project center when it chose 1,200 key people from various divisions for the task of downsizing vehicle size in all of its automotive lines. The project center developed suggestions, turned them over to the automotive divisions for implementation, and then disbanded. In another corporation, a project center was used to oversee the relocation of its corporate offices. Having a project center dedicated full-time to the tricky problems of relocation allowed the rest of the organization to continue work as usual.

In a *partial project*, the functions critical to the project (such as construction or engineering) are assigned to the project manager while other, support-oriented functions (such as procurement and accounting) remain within functional areas of the parent organization. In Figure 13.6, for example, the LOGON project manager might

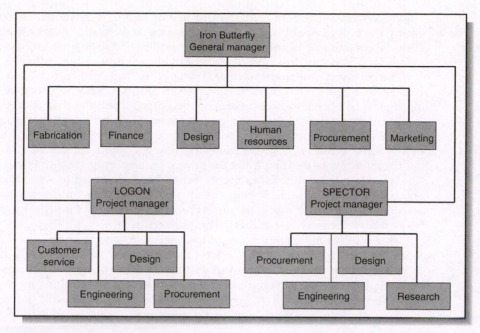

Figure 13.6
Pure projects as an "arms" to the functional organization.

have full control over design and fabrication, yet receive functional support from the areas of finance, human resources, and marketing. The manager of a partial project has direct control over all major project tasks, but receives assistance from areas in the parent company over which he does not have control.

The *stand-alone project* is an entire organization created especially for the purpose of accomplishing the project. It is typically used for large-scale government public works, or development and installation projects that involve one or more prime contractors, dozens of subcontractors, and numerous supporting organizations, suppliers, and consultants. The International Space Station development program, Quebec's LaGrande hydroelectric complex, the English Channel Tunnel, China's Three Gorges Dam, and Boston's Big Dig are examples. When these projects are completed, an operating function remains but the rest of the organization is dissolved. Stand-alone projects are discussed later in this chapter in sections 13.11 and 13.13, on integration in large-scale projects and concurrent engineering, respectively.

Disadvantages

The chief disadvantage of the pure project organization is its *cost*. Because each pure project is a completely or partially independent organization, it must be fully or substantially staffed. Each project becomes a self-contained empire, and there is often little sharing or cross-utilization of resources with other projects. Companies conducting multiple pure projects may incur considerable duplication of effort and facilities, and high overhead.

To ensure that resources will be available when needed, pure project organizations must begin acquiring them in advance of the project. One of the authors was among numerous engineers hired in anticipation of a large government contract to ensure the project would be able to begin as soon as the contract was signed. However, the contract was never awarded, and everyone had to be transferred elsewhere or laid off. The payroll loss alone amounted to hundreds of man-months.

In most organizations, the functional manager is the driving force behind workers further developing their technical competencies. Most functional managers encourage their professional workers to expand their capabilities, and they back it up with raises and promotions. But in a pure project organization there might be no functional managers, and hence no one to emphasize competency development. The usual tactic of the project manager is, lacking suitable in-house technical competency, to contract out the work. While this might suit the project's needs, it represents a missed opportunity for the organization to develop its own in-house expertise. Further, those workers that do have considerable competency often resign after completing what they consider the interesting part of the project because they cannot foresee what they'll be doing next in the project—or what the next project will be.

This suggests still another cost: outplacement. Whenever there is no follow-up work, the pure project organization faces the problem of what to do with its workforce when the project ends. Personnel who have worked on long-term projects often become so specialized that they cannot be placed in projects requiring more generalized or up-to-date skills.

Pure project organizations are strictly temporary; as the project draws to a close, uncertainty about the fate of the team grows, and morale and enthusiasm decline. A project manager may become so preoccupied with generating new contracts or finding jobs for himself and his team that he becomes neglectful of his closeout responsibilities for the current project.

13.8 MATRIX ORGANIZATIONS

Although the pure project form often provides the only way to do a large-scale, one-time project, its disadvantages make it impractical for many businesses that *continually* operate on a project basis. Examples of such businesses include architecture and construction, where every building, bridge, or highway is a project; product development, where every product concept, design, manufacture, and promotion is a project; IT, where every hardware and software installation is a project; law and accounting, where every case and audit is a project; and aerospace, where every new aircraft and space system is a project. Most of these projects are too large, too complex, and have too much at stake to be handled by task forces. In addition, most of these businesses are involved in many projects at a time; they are *multi-project* organizations. They need the capability to create large project groups quickly without the personnel and cost disadvantages associated with pure project organizations.

To achieve this capability, a new form of organization evolved. First adopted in the aerospace industry by such firms as Boeing and Lockheed-Martin, it is called the *matrix*. This organization, illustrated in Figure 13.7, is a grid-like structure of authority and reporting relationships created by the overlay of a project organization on a traditional, functional organization.[5] This overlay gives the matrix four unique capabilities.

First, the functional part provides the pool of technical expertise and physical resources needed by projects. Each project manager creates a project team by negotiating with functional managers and then "borrowing" the expertise and physical resources needed for her project. Each project is composed of workers who are on

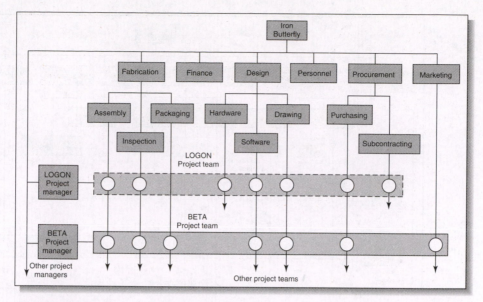

Figure 13.7
Matrix form of project organization.

loan to work on the team during the course of the project. This sharing of the same workforce across several projects reduces duplication of effort.

Second, while in their "functional homes," workers associate with colleagues in their fields of specialization; this not only keeps them current in their profession or trade, but also makes them more assignable to new projects. Each functional area has, at a given time, many individuals working on different projects, sharing ideas, and exchanging points of view. This makes all of them more effective in their respective projects.

Third, when individual assignments are fulfilled or the project is completed, workers return to their functional homes for new assignments. This eliminates anxiety and reduces fluctuations in work-force levels and worker morale.

Finally, while managers of functional areas provide resources and technical support to each project, one person, the project manager (or *matrix manager*), oversees the resources and unifies and integrates their efforts to achieve project goals.

The matrix structure shares the virtue with pure-project organizations of having dedicated resources and a project manager to give the project visibility, but within the matrix structure the project manager's range of authority can vary. The Project Management Institute distinguishes matrix organizations as "strong," "weak," or "balanced." In a strong matrix organization, project managers have authority and control over project funds and other resources, and devote most or all of their time to managing each project. In a weak matrix, the managers are actually coordinators or expeditors who, as explained before, are not quite full-fledged project managers and must fit the role into other, usually non-project, work. They oversee projects, but have little authority, no budget responsibility, and no ability to command resources on their own. In the balanced matrix, the managers are full-fledged project managers, but their level of authority and control over budgets and resources is less than in a strong matrix.

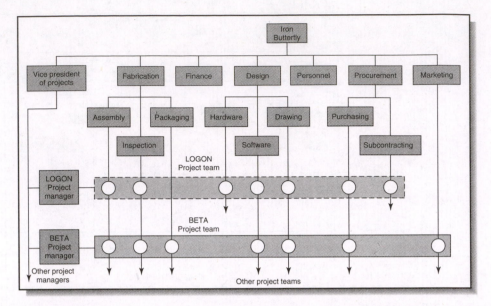

Figure 13.8
Location of the vice president of projects in a matrix organization.

In strong-matrix, multi-project matrix organizations, prioritizing and balancing resources shared by the different projects is the responsibility of the *manager of projects* or the *PMO director*, shown as the "vice president of projects" in Figure 13.8. The manager of projects attends to the requirements of current and upcoming projects, resolves resource conflicts between projects, and relieves top management of project operations responsibility. The PMO is discussed later.

Problems with Matrix Organizations

The main benefit of the matrix organization—its combined vertical–horizontal structure—is at the same time the root cause of its problems.[6] The matrix is not just a structure, but a whole different way of doing things. Most organizations are accustomed to hierarchical decision-making and vertical information flow. With its emphasis on horizontal relations, lateral information flow, and decentralized decision-making, the matrix is clearly contrary. It superimposes a horizontal team system on a vertical functional system, and companies that adopt the structure must add horizontal information processing systems to existing vertical accounting and command systems. It can be done, but tends to be somewhat difficult and expensive.

In human terms, the drawback of the matrix is that it induces conflict. Theoretically, the matrix promotes coordinated decision-making among functional areas, and enables trade-off decisions to be made for the benefit of the project. It assumes, however, that a balance of power exists between functional and project managers. Often, though, authority in the matrix is unclear, and functional and project managers jockey to control one another. In multi-project organizations functional managers control project resources, so conflict arises over which project gets priority and which project managers get the best resources.

The matrix structure attempts to be the better of two worlds—functional and projectized. The main problem with the matrix is rooted in something few people like to admit—power struggles and fear: functional managers fear that project managers (who are sometimes perceived as having the more interesting and challenging work) might take control over "their" resources and reduce their role to a mere "support/staff" function. They become even more worried when the vice president of projects controls project funding and threatens to outsource work normally provided by the functional areas. Project managers get frustrated, too, because, unlike functional managers, they have little or control over worker incentives such as promotions, salaries, or bonuses. There are no easy solutions to these problems, but as a start everyone must understand their roles: the project manager should say *what* has to be done, and the functional managers should say *how* it must be done (and, to a large extent, *who* within the function should do it).

Here is another problem: each project worker in the matrix has two bosses—a functional manager and a project-matrix manager. This violates a major principle of management: a single chain of command. The project manager directs the worker on a project, but the functional manager evaluates the worker's performance. The inevitable result is role conflict and confusion: to whom should the worker give allegiance, the project manager *or* the functional manager?

For managers and workers to avoid conflict and confusion in the matrix, everyone must have a common reference. For this to happen, organizations must establish clear priorities. Boeing, for example, which has used the matrix successfully for years, sets priorities day-to-day: people operate *either* in a project team *or* in a functional area, and they put priority on whichever area they are in.[7] The matrix can lead to still other dilemmas, explained below.

Example 13.1: Two-Hat Problem

The matrix structure requires *a lot* of managers, yet in many organizations managers are scarce. One solution is for managers to wear two hats—one as project manager, the other as functional manager. While wearing the functional hat, the manager allocates resources to different projects; the problem is, while wearing the project hat it is hard to convince other project managers that he hasn't grabbed the best resources for the projects that *he* is managing. Also, to people from his department who are working on his projects, the "project hat" is invisible. All they see is that "functional hat," ever mindful of the fact that he controls their wages and promotions; as a result, they *always* give his projects priority over others they are working on.

Any attempt to adopt a matrix structure must be accompanied by both attitudinal and cultural changes, which are difficult to achieve. In many companies, conflicts over priorities and resource allocation are eliminated or reduced by the PMO, which sets the priorities and assigns resources. Even with a PMO, however, anxiety and conflict remain common maladies of the matrix structure.

13.9 SELECTING AN ORGANIZATION FORM FOR PROJECTS

Although project managers are seldom involved in designing the organization structure of the projects they lead, they can offer suggestions to the managers who do. It is impossible to state which organization form is always best, but general criteria help

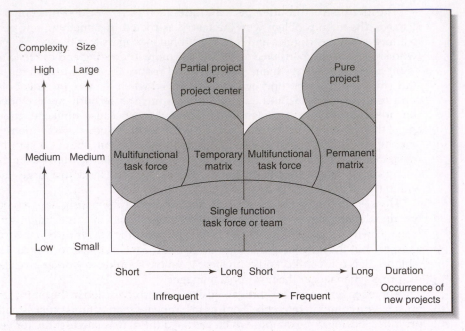

Figure 13.9
Some criteria for selecting the appropriate project organizational form.

specify which form is most appropriate for a given project. Figure 13.9 shows the approximate applicability of different project organization forms, based upon four criteria:

1. Frequency of new projects (how often, or to what degree the parent company is involved in project-related activity)
2. Duration of projects (how long a typical project lasts)
3. Size of projects (level of human, capital, or other resources in relation to other activities of the company)
4. Complexity of relationships (number of functional areas involved in the project and degree of interdependency).

Matrix and pure project forms are applicable to projects of medium and higher complexity, and of medium or larger size. These kinds of projects require large amounts of resources and information, and need project managers and integrators with strong authority. In particular, the matrix works best where a variety of different projects are going on at once and all can share functional resources on a part-time basis. In contrast, when there is less variety between projects, when specialists must be devoted full-time, and when complete project authority is desired, then the pure project form is better. Both forms are applicable where projects are the organization's "way of life."

For smaller projects involving several functional areas, task forces and cross-functional teams are more appropriate. Part-time task forces managed by expediters can effectively handle short-term projects involving one or a few functional areas. When several areas are involved, a multifunctional task force led by a coordinator who reports to the general manager is more suitable. Projects of longer duration, but small in scope, are best handled by full-time project teams with coordinators. When the team size needed to accomplish the task becomes large and the interrelationships complex, then a temporary matrix or partial project should be set up. Teams, task forces, and project centers are appropriate when the existing structure and work flow of the organization cannot be disrupted.

In selecting a project form, consider the relative importance of the following criteria: the stake of the project, the degree of technological uncertainty, the criticalness of time and cost goals, and the uniqueness of the project.[8] For example, task forces and teams are generally appropriate when the project task involves high certainty and little risk, and when time and cost are not major factors. When the risk and uncertainty is great, when time and cost goals are critical, or when there is much at stake, matrix and pure project forms better afford the obligatory high level of integration and control. When a project differs greatly from the normal business of the firm, it should use a partial or full pure project form.

These considerations all relate to the project itself, which, in fact, is sometimes less important than the attributes and experiences of the parent company. For example, matrix and pure project forms are seldom used in small organizations, which usually don't have sufficient resources and managers to commit. Top management's attitudes about the appropriate level of responsibility and authority for the project manager also matter. The most important factor is the company's experience with projects and management's perception of which project forms work best. Firms with little project experience avoid the matrix because it is difficult to adopt. Faced with a complex project, they adopt a partial or project center approach.

Most organizations are involved in a variety of projects and use a variety of different project forms—whatever best suits each project. In a given organization much or most of the work might be done by matrix teams, but a few high-visibility projects will be set up as pure projects. Meantime, within functional departments, innumerable small, single-function projects are being conducted, and scattered elsewhere are project task forces. Within a given project, a *composite* structure might be created— i.e., a structure that combines features of a functional, matrix, and pure-project form, depending on the scope and kinds of work in the project. At Microsoft Corporation, for example, the organization structure of development projects mirrors the products they produce.

Example 13.2: Product Development Organization at Microsoft[9]

A software product-development project at Microsoft might involve 300 to 400 people, including specialists in product specification, development, testing, user education, and planning. Program managers and developers divide the product into "features," where each feature is a relatively independent building block that will be apparent to customers (e.g., printing, adding a column of numbers, or interfacing with a particular brand of hardware). They then divide the project organization into development teams where each concentrates on one or more of these features. In essence, the project is divided into small, feature-driven projects that mirror the structure of the overall product. This feature-driven organization enables product functionality to be increased simply by adding more development teams: the more features desired in the product, the more teams are assigned to the project.

Each team consists of three to eight developers, one of whom is the "lead." The lead reports to the project's development manager, who has a broad view of the product and interconnections among its features. A recent version of Excel had 10 feature teams; 8 working on the basic Excel product, 1 on a graph product, and 1 on a query tool product. Paired with the feature development teams are parallel teams responsible for feature testing and user education.

Chapter 13   Project Organization Structure and Integration   479

Each feature team has considerable autonomy, though it must follow rules so its work stays coordinated with that of the other teams. Each team is expected to "build" and have checked a certain amount of code each day. This forces the teams to synchronize their work at the pace of the overall project.

Microsoft's philosophy for organizing projects is that a product tends to mirror the organization that created it. A big, slow organization will create a big, slow software product. A small, nimble group in which everyone gets along well will produce pieces of code that work together well, which is why Microsoft uses small, flexible teams.

13.10 PROJECT OFFICE AND PMO

The term *project office* has dual meaning: it refers first to a support staff group that reports to the project manager, and second to a physical place where the project team meets. Our discussion here will focus on the *project staff*.

The purpose of the project office is to *coordinate* work efforts and advise the different functional areas and subcontractors on *what* they should do (but not *how* they should actually do it). The office is responsible for planning, directing, and controlling project activities, and for linking the project teams, users, and top management. When projects are small and procedures are well established, the office might consist of just one person: the project manager. When the office must coordinate multiple projects, the staff is larger and comprises what is called the *office of projects* or, more commonly, the *project management office*. The PMO is a *support office* that develops project management policy and methodology, offers training, and provides various services to project managers, as described in Chapter 16.

Functions of the Project Office

The functions and composition of the project office depend on the authority of the project manager, and the size, importance, and goal of the project. The project office shown in Figure 13.10 is for a large-scale engineering development effort. Among the functions shown is planning and control. During project concept and definition, this function prepares the WBS, schedules, and budgets. During execution, it monitors work, forecasts trends, updates schedules and budgets, and distributes reports to functional, upper-level, and customer management.

Also shown are functions for systems engineering and configuration management, both headed by the project engineer. The systems engineering function oversees systems analysis, requirements definition, and end-item specifications (discussed in the Appendix to Chapter 2), and furnishes inputs for planning and control. Configuration management (discussed in Chapters 9 and 11) defines the initial product configuration, and controls changes in product and system requirements and project plans. As shown, the project office also handles contracting and financial control.

Integration of the functions within a project is achieved by structuring the project office to mirror the functional areas it must integrate.[10] This happens by including in the office a representative from each functional area working in the project (in Figure 13.10, purchasing, accounting, etc.). Although each representative is a specialist in a functional discipline, while in the project office his primary role is to integrate that discipline with the others. As a result, through *coordinating and integrating the functional representatives* in the project office, the work of the functional

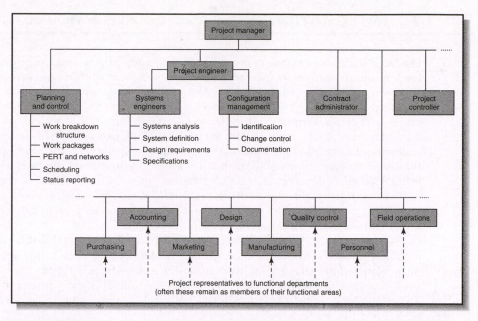

Figure 13.10
Project office for a large development project.

areas in the project is coordinated and integrated. Usually members of the project staff are co-located in the same physical office, where they can intermingle and meet face-to-face. In smaller projects, the size of the project office can be reduced by allowing some or most of the functional representatives to remain in their functional areas.

Office of Projects, PMO, and the Program Office

Multi-project organizations also have an *office of projects* (not to be confused with the project office), program office, or *PMO*. This was shown in Figure 13.8 as the "vice president of projects." In pure project organizations, the office is located at a level between senior management and project managers (in Figure 13.6, it would be located below the general manager and on the line connected to the LOGON and SPECTOR projects). When projects are small, the office of projects substitutes for individual project offices and handles proposals, contracting, scheduling, cost control, and report preparation for every project. When projects are large or overlap, the office of projects or PMO is used *in addition* to project offices, and coordinates the combined requirements of all the projects.[11]

When projects are part of a program, *a program office* is set up to ensure that the projects supplement one another and "add up" to overall program goals. The program office handles interfaces external to each project, maintains user enthusiasm and support, keeps project managers informed of potential problems, and handles interfaces and integration between projects. The NASA program office described in Chapter 1 is an example. When programs are very large, the integration work of the program office is supplemented by outside "integration contractors," discussed next.

In a large-scale project (LSP) or *mega project*, numerous parties—sponsors, prime contractors, subcontractors, consultants, and suppliers—contribute to one effort. Figure 13.11 shows the principal contributors and relationships in an LSP. Relationships are complex, and lines of authority connecting the parties are often weak (sometimes based entirely on contracts and purchase orders). If Figure 13.11 appears somewhat confusing, well, that simply reflects the fact that relationships in LSPs *are* sometimes confusing. Examples of LSPs include space systems (e.g., the International Space Station), construction projects (Canada's LaGrande hydroelectric venture, Holland's Delta flood control project, the English Channel Tunnel, China's Three Gorges Dam), as well as company relocations (involving the client, movers, construction companies, recruiters, consultants, and suppliers) and corporate mergers (dual sets of clients, consultants, and attorneys).

Notice in Figure 13.11 the direct relationships, both horizontal and hierarchical, among different contributors' managers, as well as between their functional areas. Such relationships between, for instance, design groups from the sponsor and its contractors and subcontractors help speed up decision-making and tighten integration. The relationships between contributors are facilitated by project managers, coordinators, expeditors, liaisons, and task forces.

Figure 13.11
Integration relationships in a large-scale project.

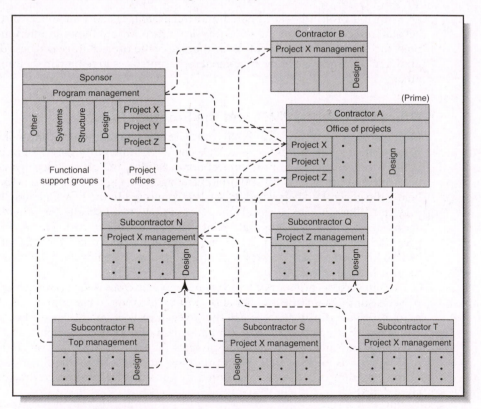

Most LSPs are devoted to development and/or construction of complex systems. The total effort is subdivided among a number of contributors, each responsible for a specific subsystem or component that must be integrated with others to form the overall system. Figure 13.12, for example, shows the major components in the International Space Station. The figure is simplified, and does not show major elements of the program such as launch vehicles to place the components into Earth orbit, support systems, and the numerous organizations that work to develop, produce, and integrate the components (prime contractors, subcontractors, and suppliers).

Oversight and Integration Contractors

In public works and government projects, integration is usually the responsibility of the sponsoring agency. Sometimes, however, the engineering and management tasks are quite difficult or extensive, and outside help is required.

Among the first LSPs to experience the integration problems inherent to large systems were weapons system development projects during World War II.[12] For instance, within the Army Air Corps separate offices purchased the components that made up a system such as a bomber, and these components—airframe, engines, and electronics—were then furnished to and assembled by the airframe manufacturer. As systems grew more complex, this approach no longer worked. Sometimes the subsystem interfaces were different, so plugs and fasteners would not fit, or the sizes of the components were different than planned and the entire system had to be redesigned to accommodate them. To overcome these difficulties, the military formed technical

Figure 13.12
Major components in the hardware and assembly of the International Space Station. Diagram courtesy of NASA.

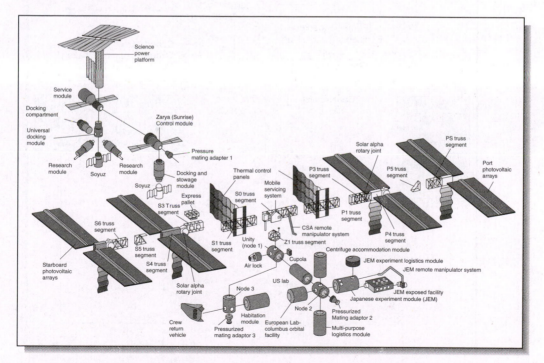

groups to coordinate subsystem interfaces, but this resulted in massive red tape and only worsened matters, as illustrated by Livingston:[13]

> A contractor wished to change the clock in an airplane cockpit from a one-day to an eight-day mechanism. It wrote a request and gave it to the military representative, who forwarded it to the military technical group. The tech group reviewed the request and asked the contractor for more details about the change. The contractor revised the request and resent it to the group. The group approved the request and sent it to the change committee. The committee reviewed and accepted the change, and then sent authorization back to the representative, who forwarded it to the contractor. All in all, this simple change request took *three months* to approve.

Today the process is expedited by giving integration responsibility to a single "oversight" body, usually the *lead* or *prime* contractor (the "prime")—a role similar to that of a wedding consultant or general contractor, but on a larger scale. The project sponsor is still responsible for contracting with *associate* contractors (subsystem manufacturers), making major decisions, and resolving conflicts between the prime and associates. The associates become subcontractors ("subs") to the prime contractor, take orders from the prime, and are subject to its surveillance and approval. Figure 13.13 shows the relationships among the sponsor, prime, and subs for a large urban transit project.[14]

Sometimes the prime is conferred with greater responsibility, such as assisting the sponsor in selecting associates, pricing of subsystems, and allocating project funds. This

Figure 13.13
Management and authority relationships in a large construction project.

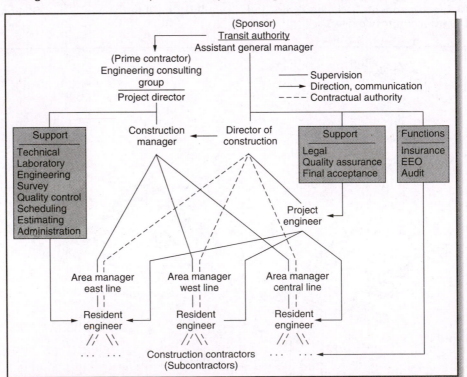

situation poses a problem when the prime and the subs are competitors, since, understandably, subs are hesitant to divulge innovative design concepts or subsystem details, even though the prime needs to know those things to integrate the overall system.

Sometimes even the largest prime contractors aren't big enough. At such times they form teams and submit joint proposals where one company serves as leader and takes on responsibility for systems engineering and management of the others. This appeals to small and medium-sized firms that ordinarily would not have the resources to contract independently. With this approach, however, unless the lead company is strong there could be serious interface problems. But no team is likely to have all the best ideas, and the sponsor may require the lead firm to open up development of subsystems to competitors and, if necessary, change the members of the team.

When the prime contractor lacks the capability to perform all the integrating work, a separate consulting firm or *integration contractor* is engaged entirely to provide integration and engineering advice.[15] These contractors, which sometimes employ thousands of workers, are able to quickly pull together all the necessary resources. The problem is that they often operate in the same business as the contractors they are responsible for integrating, which puts them in the awkward position of managing their competitors and being able to learn their secrets.

Example 13.3: Corporate Merger — Large-Scale Non-Technical Project[16]

Special integration management is necessary not only in technical projects, but also in any *large*, *complex* project. When one of the US's largest pharmaceutical companies acquired one of Europe's largest for $6.9 billion, an acquisition that involved 10,000 people, 18 manufacturing locations, and 30 international affiliates, it engaged a well-known global consulting firm to oversee the integration effort. The consulting firm established a program management office and a global acquisition integration management (AIM) team with 18 full-time director-level individuals from the US corporation. The purpose of the AIM team was to plan, manage, and execute the integration across all divisions and functional areas of the corporation. This team went on to create other teams, eventually numbering 24 and including more than 500 people from both corporations. The consulting firm composed the teams, structured the work of the teams, participated in their major decisions, watched over critical path activities, and consulted with the European company's managers and functional teams. By hiring the consulting firm as integration contractor, the project benefited from the best practices and lesson learned through the consultant's many years of merger and acquisition experience—experience that the two pharmaceutical giants lacked. The project structure, consisting of the consulting firm, AIM team, and the other teams, was a pure-project organization devoted entirely to the corporate merger.

13.12 INTEGRATION IN SYSTEMS DEVELOPMENT PROJECTS

Project integration can be conceptualized in two ways: integration of the *functional areas* of the project organization, and integration of the *phases* of the project. The former, which has been the subject of the chapter thus far, is called *horizontal integration*; the latter is called *vertical integration* (Figure 13.14). The two ways are interrelated because integration of the project phases also usually requires integration of the functional areas working within the phases.

Large-scale projects in product development and software development require the integrated efforts of many functional units throughout the stages of conception,

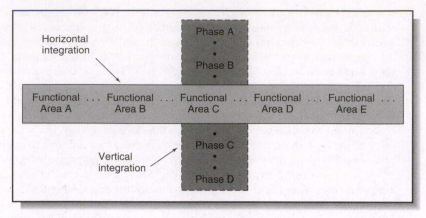

Figure 13.14
Horizontal and vertical integration in systems development projects.

definition, design, testing, production, and installation. Achieving the necessary high-level integration can be difficult, and does not always happen.

Non-integrated Systems Development

In a traditional development project, a different functional group is responsible for each phase. For example, the marketing group specifies the initial concept and user requirements, then the design group defines the technical specifications and creates the system design, then the manufacturing groups determine how it will make the product, and so on. Even when a project manager oversees the process, work at each phase remains largely centered in one functional area and minimally involves the other areas. At each stage of the project a new functional area takes over, "inheriting" and being forced to accommodate the output of previous phases. As a result, the design group must create a product design that conforms to the requirements it inherited from marketing; in turn, the manufacturing group must develop a production process that conforms to the design it inherited from the design group. The process, illustrated in Figure 13.15, involves little interaction and knowledge-sharing between participating groups.

Since different functional areas make decisions regarding definition, design, and production independently, the decisions are often incomplete or incorrect because they do not address the needs or requirements of other parties and functional areas involved in the project. The result is, for example, that the marketing group specifies a requirement that is not really necessary, but that the design group inherits and must incorporate into the product design; the manufacturing group inherits the design, which it discovers will be very difficult or costly for it to produce. Each functional group entering the process must struggle to accommodate commitments made by earlier groups. When it encounters a prior commitment to a decision (about a requirement, design, procedure, etc.) that is difficult or impossible for it to implement, it must request a modification from the other groups. This back-and-forth exchange between groups results in numerous *change requests*, each with detrimental consequences for the schedule, budget, and end-item quality. The problem is lack of horizontal and vertical integration—a failure of groups involved early in the process to address the complete life cycle of the system and the needs of functional areas and stakeholders that will later inherit and have to live with the consequences of their decisions.

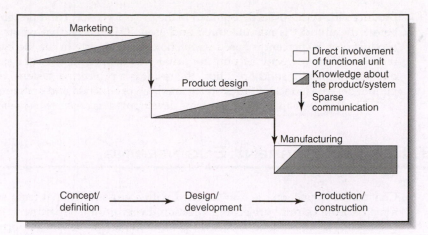

Figure 13.15
Traditional interaction between functional areas during phases of systems development.
Adapted from Wheelwright S and Clark K. *Revolutionizing Product Development*. New York, NY: Free Press; 1992. p. 178.

Impact on Life Cycle Costs

The integration of functional teams in system development has a major impact on *life cycle costs*, which, as described in Chapter 8, include all costs of materials, production, distribution, and operation of the end-item for as long as the product is produced and used. The fact is, most of this cost is predetermined by decisions made very early in the systems development cycle. As Figure 13.16 shows, about 80 percent of a

Figure 13.16
Percent of product life cycle cost set during stages of the systems development life cycle.

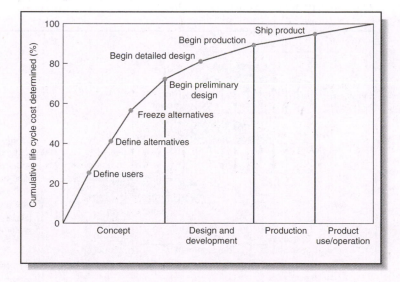

product's life cycle cost is determined in the project's concept and design stages, well before the product is manufactured and used. This means that whatever the total product cost, 80 percent is based upon choices made early in the life cycle.[17] Unless these decisions correctly account for what will happen in the later stages of production, installation, and operation, the result is a protracted systems development period, delayed launch of the product, and high production and operating costs.

The integrated approach to systems development is *concurrent engineering*.

13.13 CONCURRENT ENGINEERING

Concurrent engineering is implemented with a cross-functional team structured as a matrix team or pure-project organization. Every group, department, or contractor responsible for or influenced by some piece of the project has the opportunity to participate in the project early on, and to contribute to key decisions. The parties participate in decisions long before they actually begin to design, produce, test, or operate the system (Figure 13.17). Horizontal integration and vertical integration are achieved in one fell swoop.

In concurrent engineering, decisions about design, development, production, and operation overlap; this greatly reduces the time between concept formulation and product launch. For example, the process of making dies for stamping automobile body-panels, which is expensive and time-consuming, does not usually occur until near product launch. With concurrent engineering, however, the dies are designed and produced soon after the body panel has been designed, which happens months before launch and allows ample time to work out bugs in the dies and make changes if needed. Concurrent design of the panels and dies like this can reduce the production preparation time for a new automobile by more than a year.

Figure 13.17
Concurrent interactions between functional areas during phases of systems development.
Adapted from Wheelwright S and Clark K. *Revolutionizing Product Development.* New York, NY: Free Press; 1992. p. 178.

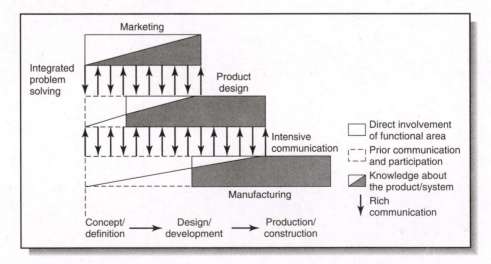

Concurrent engineering also improves trade-offs between product features and production capabilities. Working together, product and process designers can discover subtle changes to product design features that would be transparent to the customer but that take advantage of existing production capabilities. The result: lower production costs from fewer production bugs and rework, and fewer customer usage problems and warranty claims.

Team Organization

A concurrent engineering team is organized to encourage maximal communication between members and maximal control over design decisions. This is achieved as follows:[18]

- *Autonomy.* Members of a concurrent engineering team are relieved of unrelated obligations and expected to fully commit to the development effort.

- *Full-time, full-duration.* Ideally, team members are involved in *all* decisions throughout the *entire* systems development process. That's what "concurrent" means.

- *Co-location.* Team members work in close proximity and share one office, which encourages frequent, spontaneous informal chats. Periodic formal weekly meetings are largely replaced with continual informal meetings.

- *Small size.* The team is small enough to allow open communication and encourage team commitment, yet large enough to represent all the affected functional areas, customers, and key suppliers. About 6 team members is optimal, although as many as 10–20 can be effective. If the size exceeds 20, smaller sub-teams are formed and coordinated by an inter-team steering group.

- *Team of doers.* Although each member of the team is a specialist in some area (design engineering, manufacturing, marketing, purchasing, etc.), everyone is expected to take on a wide range of responsibilities and obligations. They must be "can do" folks, willing to visit customers and suppliers, work on design, and do modeling, assembly work, and anything else that needs to be done.

Concurrent engineering is more than just organizing people into a team. It is taking people normally involved in only one step of the system development process and engaging them in the other phases and stages. Product designers wander the factory to see how their designs are manufactured and what features of the design make it hard or easy to produce. At the same time, production engineers and assembly workers talk to designers to learn why a design feature is important and has to be retained. General Motors requires that its designers spend a full day every 3 months assembling the portion of the car they had helped design.

There are other ways in which organizations organize teams to achieve vertical and horizontal integration in the systems development cycle. Example 13.4 describes two.

Example 13.4: Systems Development at Motorola and Lockheed-Martin[19]

Motorola's systems development cycle includes the phases of product definition, contract development, product development, and program wrap-up. The process emphasizes integration of functions to develop innovative next-generation products and effective resource utilization for speedy product development. Projects are conducted by a core cross-functional team responsible for most of the development decisions and detailed design work, as well as for specifying resource requirements and setting performance targets. Functional units provide support to the core team.

The core team approach is used where speed is critical, such as projects that aim to create systems with entirely new product architectures, or in markets that quickly change. An example is the Motorola core team that developed a new personal communication device. The team consisted of a project manager and eight members from industrial engineering, robotics, process engineering, procurement, product design, manufacturing, human resources, and accounting/ finance, plus a member from Hewlett Packard, the vendor for a crucial component in the system. The team worked in a glass-enclosed office located in the middle of a manufacturing facility. This encouraged others to "look in" on the team and offer suggestions. The team created the work plan for the project; senior management approved the plan, and then delegated the team with responsibility for performing the bulk of the project. The project was completed in 18 months (half the usual time for a project of that size), met the cost objective (which was much lower than normal), and yielded a product of high quality and reliability.

Lockheed-Martin's advanced development division, called "Skunk Works," has a reputation for developing radical designs and breakthrough aircraft and space vehicles.[20] The term "Skunk Works" is trademarked by Lockheed, but in common usage refers to an autonomous project team working on advanced technology that can achieve results more quickly and at a lower cost than traditional development projects. For each development effort, the Skunk Works team handpicks the project manager and cross-functional team. Unlike the core teams at Motorola, which rely on functional teams for resources and support, each Skunk Works team is fully autonomous and controls virtually all of the resources it needs. The team is similar to a separate business unit: it works on its own and has authority to requisition resources and subcontract work. Emphasis in Skunk Works teams is on technical excellence and speed. Although projects tend to broadly follow the familiar phases of conception, definition, and so on, the team is free to create procedures and standards that best suit a project's goals. Members of the team are selected for high competency, broad skills, strong commitment, and ability to think on their feet. They are co-located, usually at an isolated site to increase motivation and teamwork and to maintain secrecy. Aside from budgets and general procedures, the team gets minimal direction from senior management. Since its inception in World War II, the Skunk Works has become a model for creating highly innovative, leading edge aircraft and space vehicles quickly and on-budget.

An example is the F117 Stealth fighter mentioned in Chapter 10.[21] The Air Force specified rapid development of a relatively low-cost production aircraft that would be difficult to spot on radar (stealth). The Skunk Works team created a design that was radical and used new materials but minimized costs by using an engine, computers, flight controls, and other parts from pre-existing aircraft. The project was completed in record time—only 31 months. The cost for research, development, and production of 59 airplanes was $6.6 billion, considered low at the time when other aircraft programs were running $1 billion over budget. Efficiency and low cost were partly attributed to the small size of the development team (a few hundred people in the design phase), thus minimizing red tape and maximizing communication and project control.

Heavyweight Teams

The Motorola teams described in Example 13.4 are what Wheelwright and Clark call "heavyweight" teams.[22] These are the systems development project-equivalent to the pure project organizations described before. The project managers are heavyweights because they are minimally on the same level as functional managers, giving them organizational clout to exert strong influence over everyone involved in the development effort. The Lockheed-Martin Skunk Works teams are fully autonomous and even "heavier," in that they control all the resources necessary to get the job done. Of course, being autonomous, the team can only blame itself if the project fails.

Both cross-functional core teams and autonomous teams provide for strong emphasis on the project goal, discipline in coping with complexity, and consistency between design details. In the teams, customer requirements are defined, brought into focus, and translated into terms everyone on the team can understand. Elements of the development process and details of the system are handled in a coherent fashion, minimizing inconsistencies and changes later on.

One disadvantage of heavyweight teams is that individual components or elements of the end-item or system might not reach the same level of technical excellence as they would if they had received attention from a traditional functional area. Although a cross-functional team might design a component that meets requirements and integrates with the entire system, the component might contain flaws that only a functional team of specialists could have prevented. A way around that problem is to involve specialists in design reviews, mentioned in Chapters 9 and 12.

13.14 SUMMARY

Structure is the way organizations attempt to achieve goals and respond to problems in the environment. Two key features of structure are differentiation and integration; the former is the way organizations subdivide into specialized subunits, the latter is how they link the subunits to coordinate actions. Organizations traditionally differentiate subunits along functional, geographic, customer, and process lines. They integrate subunits with rules and procedures, coordinated plans, and chain of command. These kinds of differentiation and integration are effective when the environment is stable and tasks are certain, but ineffective when there is frequent change, high complexity, and task uncertainty—the case with most projects.

Project's organizations are structured to uniquely suit each project's goals and environment. They are formed to include all the functions needed, and to integrate the functions through formal management roles that emphasize horizontal relations. When a project goal involves just one specialty, the project team is comprised of staff from one functional area. When it requires multiple functions, the team is comprised of members drawn from all the functional subunits involved or impacted by the project; this form of organization, called a task force or cross-functional team, is managed by a project expeditor or coordinator. Expeditors and coordinators direct project work, but lack authority to command resources or strongly influence the behavior of team members.

For projects that have much at stake and require sizeable resource commitment, the appropriate form of organization is the pure project (projectized). This form gives the project goal highest priority, and the project manager authority to command and control whatever resources are needed, although it tends to be costly in terms of start-up and shut down.

The matrix organization form creates project teams by sharing members and resources from across functional subunits. It is effective for a creating a continuous stream of project teams; however, it can be difficult to implement, and induces organizational conflict.

Many companies use a variety of forms—the matrix and pure project for large projects, cross-functional teams and task forces for smaller ones. Most project organizations are hybrids; they combine the task force, pure project, and matrix forms.[23]

In a large project, the project manager is often assisted by specialists and functional representatives in the project office. This office handles project contracting, planning, scheduling, and control, but its major role is integrating functional units. In a large-scale project that involves multiple organizations, integration of all the organizations' efforts is sometimes taken on by the project sponsor. When a project is large and technically complex, responsibility is usually handled by the prime contractor or a special integration contractor. In companies that must coordinate the efforts of multiple projects, oversight and integration of the projects is handled by the office of projects, PMO, or program office.

Project integration involves coordinating not only the efforts of multiple units (horizontal integration) but also the phases of the project (vertical integration). In system development projects, both kinds of integration are achieved through concurrent engineering, which in practice combines representatives from all parties affected by the end-item system and the project into a single cross-functional team. The team is formed early in the project, and has the resources and authority to make decisions that affect not only the project but also the full life cycle of the end-item product or system.

REVIEW QUESTIONS AND PROBLEMS

1. What do the terms "differentiation" and "integration" mean?
2. What are the traditional forms of differentiation? List some companies that presently use each.
3. List the various forms of integration. Give examples of each. Which of these are "lateral" forms of integration?
4. What are the advantages of functional organizations? What are the disadvantages?
5. What distinguishes project forms from other forms of organization?
6. Describe the responsibility and authority for each of the following:
   Project expeditor
   Project coordinator
   Project leader in a pure project
   Project leader in a matrix.
7. Describe the applications, advantages, and disadvantages for each of the following:
   Project task force
   Project team
   Pure project and project center
   Matrix.
8. Give some examples of organizations where each of these project forms has been used.
9. What is the project office? Describe its purpose. Who is in the project office? How should members be selected for the project office?
10. What is meant by the informal organization? Give some examples. How does it help or hinder the formal organization? How can its beneficial aspects be influenced by the project manager?
11. Describe the role of the prime contractor and integration contractor in large projects.
12. One form of integration contractor is the wedding consultant; another is the consultant who organizes high school reunions. For each of these
    • List the various groups, organizations, and individual parties that are involved and must be integrated.
    • Describe the relationship among these parties and how the consultant coordinates their efforts, both prior to and during the wedding or reunion.

13. What parties should or might be included in a concurrent engineering team? What are the contributions of each? How does their inclusion in the team improve (a) the systems development process and (b) the resulting final product?
14. What do you think are some of the major difficulties in changing from a traditional non-integrated development approach to a concurrent engineering approach?

QUESTIONS ABOUT THE STUDY PROJECT

1. In your project, how is the parent organization organized—for example, functionally or geographically? Show the organization chart, its overall breakdown, and relationships.
2. How does your project fit into the organization chart of the parent organization?
3. What form of project structure is used in your project? Show the project organization chart; indicate the key roles and the authority and communication links between them.
4. How was the project structure developed? Has it "evolved" during the project? Who designs or has influence on the project structure? What role did the project manager have in its design? Is the design similar to those used in other, similar projects in the organization?
5. Critique the project design. Is it appropriate for the project goal, the parent organization, and the environment?
6. Is there a project office? Is there also an office of projects or a program office? In each case:
   (a) Describe the office and how it is used
   (b) Describe the members of the project or program office staff—representatives, specialists, and so forth.
   What is the purpose of the project office staff? Describe the various tasks and functions handled by the project office. What is the members' participation in the project office (full-time, as needed, etc.)? What is the reporting relationship between the project manager and members of the project office?
7. How does the project manager integrate functional areas?
8. Are there prime and associate contractors involved? If so, what is the function of the company you are studying (prime contractor, subcontractor, or supplier), and how does it fit into the structure of all the organizations contributing to the project? If applicable, discuss the involvement of integration contractors or team leader contractors.
9. Did the project use a concurrent engineering team? If so, discuss how this concept was applied and tailored to fit the project.

Case 13.1 Organization for the LOGON Project

The Iron Butterfly Company is a medium-sized engineering and manufacturing firm specializing in warehousing and materials handling systems. The company purchases most of the subsystems and components for its products, and then assembles them to satisfy customer requirements.

Every IBC system is made to customer specification, and most of the firm's work is in system design, assembly, installation, and checkout. The firm's 250 employees are roughly divided equally among five divisions: engineering, design, fabrication, customer service, and marketing. Recently, competition has forced the firm to expand into computerized warehousing systems despite its rather limited experience and expertise in that field.

The company has been awarded a large contract for a robotic system for placement, storage, retrieval, and routing of shipping containers for truck and rail by the Midwest Parcel Distribution Company. This system, called the Logistical Online System, LOGON, is to be developed and installed at Midwest's main distribution center in Chicago. The contract is for a fixed price of $14.5 million, which includes design, fabrication, and installation at the center. IBC was awarded the contract because it was the lowest bid, and because it has an outstanding record for quality and customer service. A clause in the contract imposes a penalty of $1,000 daily for failure to meet the specified delivery date.

At various times throughout the estimated 47-week project, personnel from the functional divisions of design, fabrication, procurement, and customer service will be involved, most on a full-time basis for between 4 and 18 weeks. In the past, the company has set up *ad hoc* project management teams comprising a project coordinator and members selected from functional areas. These teams are then responsible for planning, scheduling, and budgeting the actual work to be done by the functional departments. Members of the teams serve primarily as liaisons to the functional areas, and work part-time on the teams.

The LOGON contract differs from other IBC systems, both in its usage of neural network software and real-time operation via remote terminals, and in its size. Although the company has some prior experience with real-time warehousing systems, the technology involved is still developing. Iron Butterfly has recently hired people with the background needed for the project. In addition, it has signed contracts with CRC and CreativeRobotics to provide the computer and robotics hardware, and assistance with system design, installation, and checkout.

The LOGON contract is among the largest IBC has ever undertaken. At present, the company is in the middle of two other projects that absorb roughly three-fourths of its labor capacity; is winding down on a third that involves only the customer service division; and has two outstanding proposals for small projects under review.

QUESTION

Discuss how you would organize the LOGON project if you were the president of Iron Butterfly. Discuss the alternatives available for the LOGON project and the relative advantages and disadvantages of each. What assumptions must be made?

Case 13.2   *Pinhole Camera and Optics, Inc.: Why Do We Need a Project Manager?*

Beverly is the newly appointed vice president of strategy for Pinhole Camera and Optics, Inc. (motto: "See the World through a Pinhole"), a medium-sized, privately owned manufacturing firm. Until recently, the 14-year-old company had experienced rapid growth through developing new products and optical manufacturing processes. Beverly believes that the company's market position has slipped because Pinhole has been unable to react quickly enough to changing market requirements and increasing competition. The company is divided into the traditional functional departments of research, marketing, sales, production, and so on. New product development projects are managed by handing off responsibility between managers of the departments. Beverly believes this is the greatest contributor to Pinhole's inability to identify and respond to market opportunities, and she would like to create a new position, manager of new products, for the purpose of integrating departments during product development projects. This position would be the project manager of new product development.

The owner of the company, Ovid Pinoli, disagrees. He contends that the managers of the functional departments, most of whom have been with the company since its start, are excellent managers, really know their business, and usually are able to work together. He feels there is no need to create the position, although he wonders where such a person would come from. Mr. Pinoli instead suggests that for each new project one of the current department managers should be picked to coordinate the efforts of all the departments. The manager would be selected from the department that has the biggest role in the project—in other words, according to whether the project primarily involves research, marketing, or production.

Beverly is convinced that Mr Pinoli's idea won't improve the situation. She decides to prepare a formal written report that will address the pros and cons of Mr Pinoli's suggestions and persuade him that the new position of manager of new products must be filled by someone other than a functional department manager. She also wants to describe how Pinhole's new development projects could be better organized and staffed.

QUESTION

If you were Beverly, why would you disagree with Mr Pinoli's suggestion that the existing departmental managers serve as project managers? What would you say in the report to argue for the position of manager of new products?

NOTES

1. Detailed discussion of the organization structure, coordination, and integrating mechanisms in high technology environments is given by Galbraith J. Environmental and technological determinants of organizational design. In Lorsch JW and Lawrence PR (eds), *Studies in Organization Design*. Homewood, IL: Irwin-Dorsey; 1970. pp. 113–139.
2. See Galbraith J. *Designing Complex Organizations*. Reading, MA: Addison-Wesley; 1973.
3. Peters T and Waterman R. *In Search of Excellence*. New York, NY: Warner Communications; 1984. p. 127–130.
4. See Davis K. The role of project management in scientific manufacturing. *IEEE Transactions of Engineering Management* 9(3); 1962: 109–113.
5. A discussion of the matrix organization, its applications and implementation is given by Davis S and Lawrence P. *Matrix*. Reading, MA: Addison-Wesley; 1977.
6. McCann J and Galbraith J. Interdepartmental relations. In Nystrom P and Starbuck W (eds), *Handbook of Organizational Design II*, No. 61. New York, NY: Oxford University Press; 1981.
7. Peters and Waterman, *In Search of Excellence*, pp. 307–308.
8. See Thomas R, Keating J, and Bluedorn A. Authority structures for project management. *Journal of Construction Engineering and Management* 1983; 109(4): 406–422.
9. Cusumano M and Selby R. *Microsoft Secrets*. New York, NY: Free Press; 1995. pp. 74, 235–236, 248–249.
10. Burns J. Effective management of programs. In: Lorsch JW and Lawrence PR (eds), *Studies in Organizational Design*. Homewood, IL: Irwin-Dorsey; 1970. pp. 140–152.
11. Archibald R. Multiproject management. *Managing High-Technology Programs and Projects*. New York, NY: John Wiley & Sons; 1976. Ch. 4.
12. This discussion is based on Livingston J. Weapons system contracting. *Harvard Business Review* July–August; 1959: 83–92.
13. *Ibid.*, p. 85.
14. Adapted from Lammie J and Shah D. Construction management: MARTA in retrospect. *Journal of Construction Engineering and Management* 110(4); 1984: 459–475.
15. For a complete discussion of integration contractors, see Sayles L and Chandler M. *Managing Large Systems: Organizations for the Future*. New York, NY: Harper & Row; 1971. pp. 253–271.
16. Arndt D, Clampett L, Fedder W, Foxx K, Lorenz C, Ward N, and Worthington J. Analysis of the role of the AIM team in the

integration of Knoll Pharmaceuticals into Abbott Laboratories. Loyola University Chicago; July 13, 2002.

17. Smith P and Reinertsen D. *Developing Products in Half the Time*. New York, NY: Van Nostrand Reinhold; 1991. pp. 224–225.

18. Adapted from Nicholas J. Concurrent engineering: overcoming obstacles to teamwork. *Production and Inventory Management Journal* 35(3); 1994: 18–22.

19. Portions adapted from from Wheelwright S and Clark K. *Revolutionizing Product Development*. New York, NY: Free Press; 1992. pp. 159–162, 200–203.

20. Its SR-71, a high-performance reconnaissance aircraft, was developed in the 1960s, but still holds the world's speed record three decades

later. See Rich B and Janos L. *Skunk Works*. Boston, MA: Little, Brown, & Company; 1994.

21. See Aronstein D and Piccirillo A. *Have Blue and the F-117A: Evolution of the "Stealth Fighter."* Reston, VA: American Institute of Aeronautics and Astronautics; 1997; Stroud M. How the F-117A flew on budget, on time. *Investor's Daily* February 1; 1991.

22. Wheelwright and Clark, *Revolutionizing Product Development*, pp. 194–196, 202–212.

23. A thorough review of strengths and weaknesses of different project forms is in Bannerman P. Risk implications of software project organization structures. 20th Australian Software Engineering Conference, IEEE Computer Society, April 14–17, 2009, Gold Coast, Australia.

Chapter 14

Project Roles, Responsibility, and Authority

> *All the world's a stage,*
> *And all the men and women merely players.*

—DONALD WINNICOTT,
Playing and Reality

When an organization undertakes a project, it forms a pure project team, matrix team, or task force, but unless it is a pure project most people on the team are "borrowed." Project management "gets work done through outsiders"[1]—people from various technical, functional, and professional groups scattered throughout the parent company and outside subcontractors. As Sayles and Chandler describe, project management

> . . . is dealing laterally, but not in the informal-group, informal-organization sense. It requires a capacity on the part of the manager to put together an organizational mechanism within which timely and relevant decisions are likely to be reached [as well as] a conceptual scheme for "working" interfaces . . . [It is a] dynamic, interactive, iterative, and intellectually challenging concept of the managerial role.[2]

Part of being a project manager is the ability to influence people without giving orders or making decisions in the same way as other managers. Most project managers have a great deal of responsibility but not much formal authority, so they need a different skill set and leadership style than traditional managers.

Project Manager's Role

Without the project manager there would be no such thing as project management. The project manager is the glue holding the project together, and the mover and shaker spurring it on. To be a project manager, a person must wear different hats, often at the same time; they include the hats of integrator, communicator, decision-maker, motivator, evangelist, and entrepreneur.

The importance of integration in project work was emphasized earlier. As the central figure in the project, the project manager's prime role is to *integrate everything and everybody* to accomplish project goals. The project manager has been called the organizational "metronome," the person who keeps the project's diverse elements responsive to a single, central beat.[3]

The project manager is the *communication hub*, the end of the funnel for most reports, requests, memoranda, and complaints. She accepts inputs from more sources and directs information to more receivers than anyone else in the project. Between sources and receivers, she refines, summarizes, and translates information to make sure that all significant stakeholders are well-informed about policies, objectives, requirements, plans, progress, and changes.

Being the communication hub, the project manager is also the central *decision-maker* for allocating resources, setting project scope and direction, and balancing schedule, cost, and performance criteria. Even when lacking authority to make high-level decisions, she is often well-situated to influence the decisions and actions of others who do have authority.

The prime motivational factor in any diverse group is strong commitment to a central goal. In a project organization, it is the project manager who provides *direction* and builds commitment to the goal. The successful project manager is able to foster enthusiasm, team spirit, confidence, and drive the team toward excellence, even when the work becomes stressful and frustrating.

You could say the project manager is a sort of *evangelist* who builds faith in the project, its value, and workability. During the conceptual phase, she is often the only person who sees the big picture. Whether or not it gets funded often depends on her ability to gain the endorsement of influential stakeholders.

The project manager is like an *entrepreneur* too, driven to procure the funds, facilities, and people needed to get the project off the ground and keep it flying. She must win over reluctant stakeholders who question supporting or assigning resources to the project. After the work is underway, she must continue to champion the project and might find herself fighting for its very existence. In the end, whether the project succeeds or fails, the project manager is ultimately held accountable.

Example 14.1: Gutzon Borglum: Project Manager and Sculptor[4]

If you are familiar with the carvings pictured in Figure 14.1, then you know the handiwork of Gutzon Borglum. More than 2 million people a year visit Mount Rushmore National Memorial. Most of them who hear the name Gutzon Borglum think that it was he who *sculpted* the faces; of course, he *was* the sculptor, though not of the actual faces on the mountain. The contract for the project specified that the memorial was "to be carved . . . by . . . and/or under the direction of Gutzon Borglum," and that Borglum was to enjoy "full, final, and complete freedom of authority in the execution of the monument's design." He did carve the faces, but on a miniature model one-twelfth the size of the ones on the mountain to serve as a guide for workers who actually sculpted the monument. Much of

Figure 14.1
Gutzon Borglum's most famous work attracts millions of visitors a year.
Photograph courtesy of John Nicholas.

this "sculpting" consisted of removing huge quantities of granite using dynamite, heavy drills, and pneumatic jackhammers.

Projects of such grandiose size are never the work of just one person; however, in the case of Mount Rushmore, if anyone should get credit it would have to be Gutzon Borglum. Although many others contributed to the project in important ways, it was Borglum's tireless efforts that yielded much of the project funding, and his genius and stubborn dedication that made it happen. He picked the site; he wrote letters and spoke personally to businessmen, wealthy industrialists, senators, congressman, and US presidents; he determined that the faces would be of Washington, Jefferson, Roosevelt, and Lincoln; he hired and directed the work crew; he created the innovative means for transferring the design from the model to the mountain; and, *in addition to that*, he attended to myriad details, from designing the scaffolding, work platforms, tramway, hoists, and grounds buildings to orchestrating the pageants for the initial dedication and final unveiling ceremonies. Meantime, he also kept trying to revive his Stone Mountain project in Georgia, which he had started years earlier but not finished. People wondered when he ever rested, or if he ever slept. Of course, he was by no means perfect; he did not always have project problems under control, and his efforts were criticized for being unorganized, especially in the early years. When the project began in 1927, Borglum wasn't completely sure what the monument was going to look like. At the time, however, all that mattered to South Dakotans was that it would bring recognition to their obscure state, and to Borglum that it was a chance at artistic immortality.

People familiar with Borglum were impressed with his artistic talent, but they were even more impressed with his "capacity for affection, wrath, generosity, stinginess, nobility, pettiness, charm, and sheer obnoxiousness."[5] He was short on modesty and humility, and long on "mulish stubbornness." He thought big, dreamed big, talked big, and was not afraid to tackle any undertaking. His enthusiasm was contagious.

The project work crew consisted of 22 men. Most of the carving they did using 80-pound drills and jackhammers while dangling on the side of a cliff. They sat in harnesses designed by Borglum that were lowered down the mountain face with hand winches. Imagine their feelings, as described by biographer Rex Smith:

> You do your drilling while hanging on the side of a stone wall . . . From where you sit you can look down upon mountains and plains that stretch farther than the eye can see. Surrounded by these vast spaces, suspended against a stone cliff, you feel dwarfed and insignificant . . . and uneasy.[6]

Borglum was a stickler for safety, so despite the dangers there were few accidents and no fatalities throughout 14 years of work. Borglum was never chummy with his crew, but he cared and looked out for them, and in return they were loyal to him and to each other.

Seeing the monument today, we realize that its construction must have posed great challenges, but that, obviously, those challenges were overcome. Borglum, however, was never sure they would be overcome. Although he had selected the mountain, he knew there was the risk that it might contain some disastrous hidden flaws—cracks or bad rock—that could not be worked around. In fact, besides funding, it was the shape of the mountain and its deep fissures that determined that the number of presidential busts had to be just four. Time and again obstacles arose, funds ran out, and the project had to be stopped—but Borglum and other believers persevered so that the project would again be revived. In the end, the carving was abandoned and the monument left uncompleted because the nation was about to become embroiled in World War II and would no longer support the effort. Just months before the project was canceled, Borglum died. He had been the project's prominent driving force, and you have to ask: had he lived, how much more of the monument would he have completed? Borglum was a sculptor, but when it came to turning a mountain into a monument, he was the ultimate project manager.

Job Responsibilities

The project manager's principal responsibility is to deliver the project end-item within budget and on time, in accordance with technical specifications, and, when specified, in fulfillment of profit objectives. Other, specific responsibilities vary depending on the project manager's capabilities, the stage of the project, the size and nature of the project, and the responsibilities delegated by upper management. Delegated responsibility ranges at the low end from the rather limited influence of a project expeditor up to the highly centralized, almost autocratic control of a pure project manager.

Though responsibilities vary, they usually include:[7]

- Planning project activities, tasks, and end results, which includes creating the work breakdown structure, schedule, and budget, and coordinating tasks and allocating resources
- Selecting and organizing the project team
- Interfacing with and influencing stakeholders
- Negotiating with and integrating functional managers, contractors, users, and top management
- Maintaining contact with the customer

- Monitoring project status
- Communicating project status to stakeholders
- Identifying technical and functional problems
- Solving problems directly or knowing where to find help
- Dealing with crises and resolving conflicts
- Recommending termination or redirection of efforts when objectives cannot be achieved.

Spanning all of these is the umbrella responsibility for integration, coordination, and direction of all project elements and life cycle stages.

Most managers of medium and large-sized projects report in a line capacity to a senior-level executive. They are expected to monitor and narrate the technical and financial status of the project and to report current and anticipated errors, problems, or overruns.

Domain Competency and Orientation

Project managers work at the *interfaces* between top management, the customer, and technologists or contractors, so they must have managerial ability, technical competency, and other broad qualifications. They must feel as much at home in the office talking with executives and customers about policies, schedules, and budgets as in the plant, the shop, or on-site talking to specialists and supervisors about technical issues.

Broad background is also essential. The more differentiated the functional areas, the more prone they are to conflict. To effectively integrate multiple, diverse functional areas, the project manager needs to understand each of the areas—their jargon, techniques, and procedures—and their contributions to the project. Referred to as *domain competency*, the project manager must have a good understanding of all areas of the project. Another way of saying this is that the project manager's competency must cover the full scope of the project; she should be familiar with all areas within the project scope statement, and at the first or second level of the work breakdown structure (WBS). Although most project managers cannot be expert in every area of the project, they must be sufficiently familiar with the areas to intelligently ponder ideas offered by specialists and to evaluate and make appropriate, balanced decisions. Along the same lines, to deal effectively with top management and the customer, they must be familiar with the workings and businesses of the parent and customer organizations. In technical projects the project manager sometimes relies on the project engineer for technical assistance; this is discussed later.

Managers cannot know everything. When they are responsible for areas about which they are ignorant, they admit it and seek input and advice from people they trust. As a rule of thumb, a project manager never tries to bluff; doing so risks losing credibility with stakeholders.

Studies indicate that the most effective project managers have goals, time, and interpersonal orientations intermediate to the functional units they integrate. In other words, they take a balanced outlook.[8] For instance, to integrate the efforts of a production department and a research department, the project manager's time perspective should be intermediate between production's short-term, weekly outlook and research's long-term, futuristic outlook.

Regarding the relative importance of technical ability versus managerial competency, that depends on the project. In R&D projects, project management requires greater technical competency because of the technical nature of problems and the technical orientation of the project team. In product development and non-technical projects, however, project management requires greater managerial ability because of the involvement of multiple, diverse functional areas. In general, project managers must be sufficiently technical to be able to understand the problems, but not so technical as to neglect their managerial role. There is no substitute for strong managerial competency in the role of the project manager.

14.2 PROJECT MANAGEMENT AUTHORITY

Authority refers to a manager's power to command others to act or not to act. There are different kinds of authority; the most familiar is that conferred by the organization and written in the manager's job description, called *legal authority*. Given legal authority, people in higher organizational positions are viewed as having the "right" to control the actions of people below them. Associated with legal authority is *reward power*, the power to evaluate and reward subordinates.

Another kind of authority, *charismatic authority*, stems from the power one gains by personal characteristics such as charm, personality, and appearance. People both in and outside the formal organization can increase their authority by being charismatic.

Traditional Authority

Management theory says that authority is always greater at higher levels in the organization, and is delegated downward from one level to the next. This is presumed to be how it ought to be, because managers at higher levels are assumed to know more and, therefore, to be able to make decisions, delegate responsibility, and "command" workers at lower levels. This point has been challenged on the grounds that managers, particularly in technology-based organizations, cannot possibly know everything needed to make complex decisions. They often lack technical expertise and so, increasingly, must rely upon subordinate specialists for advice. Even managers who are technically skilled cannot always manage alone; they rely upon staff groups for personnel and budgetary assistance. Especially in projects, this aspect of "participatory management" (described in the next chapter) has become commonplace.

Influence

It is important to distinguish between legal authority and the *ability to influence*. Managers with legal authority influence subordinates by giving orders and controlling salaries and promotions. Generally, however, the most effective managers are able to influence others *without* "ordering" them or making issue of their superior–subordinate relationship (this is especially true when subordinates are well-educated or highly experienced). In fact, managers who rely solely on legal authority are often relatively ineffective. Effective managers tend to rely instead on two other sources of influence: *knowledge* and *personality*.[9] The first source, called *expert power*, refers to a special level of knowledge or competency. Others believe that the person possesses knowledge and information that is important and that they themselves do not have. Simply, the expert power holder is viewed as being right because he knows more, and others readily defer to his requests.

The other, called *referent power*, derives from rapport, personal attraction, friendship, alliances, and reciprocal favors. The subordinate in some way identifies with the power holder and defers to his requests.

Given expert power and referent power, a person can influence others irrespective of the formal hierarchy and legal authority. These forms of power can even subtly reverse the authority relationship. A subordinate may exert considerable influence over a superior if the superior comes to rely upon the subordinate for information or advice, or if a bond of trust, respect, or affection develops between them. Everyone has seen this, and history is replete with examples of people of "lower" social or organizational stature controlling people of higher stature: Alexandria was Queen of Russia; Rasputin was a lowly priest.

Authority in Projects

Functional managers tend to rely on different forms of influence—knowledge, expertise, persuasion, and personal relationships; when these fail, however, they are able to fall back on their legal authority. But project managers are not able to do this. Except in the case of the pure project manager, the typical project manager *lacks any form of legal authority*.

Unlike traditional organizations where influence and authority flow vertically, in projects influence and authority flow horizontally and diagonally. The project manager exists *outside* the traditional hierarchy. The role is temporary, superimposed on the existing structure, and so is not afforded the leverage inherent to a hierarchical position. Project managers work across functional and organizational lines, and, except for members of the project office, have no subordinates reporting to them in a direct line capacity. The issue is further complicated in matrix organizations wherein project managers must share authority with functional managers.

Thus, despite the considerable degree of responsibility they carry, most project managers lack a comparable level of formal authority. Instead they have *project authority*, meaning they can make decisions about project objectives, policies, schedules, and budgets, but cannot give orders to back up those decisions.

The disparity between high formal responsibility and low formal authority has been referred to as the *authority gap*.[10] The gap implies that project managers must strive to develop other forms of influence in the absence of legal authority. "How to make friends and influence people" is not an academic issue for project managers.

Project Manager's Authority

Most project managers handle the authority gap in similar ways: having no legal authority, their only recourse is to rely on influence derived from expert power and referent power. They have to do this also because, usually, no matter the project, they depend on others to get the job done. Numerous decisions must be made, many of which they have neither the time nor the expertise for. Even in the rare case of a project manager having legal authority, she seldom uses it because unilateral decisions and orders are inconsistent with the need for reciprocity and trade-offs in projects. Project managers know that not all information needs to be channeled through them, and they encourage direct informal contact between the individuals involved.

Project managers also gain influence through networks of alliances and informal connections they build with other managers. The strength and breadth of these networks increase with the project manager's perceived competency, reputation from prior project accomplishments, and charisma. The final feature, charisma, refers to the project manager's personal appeal—something about the project manager's demeanor, behavior, or personality that people *like*. Why should this matter? Well, project stakeholders are more likely to associate with, assist, or comply with requests from a project manager if they like her then if they do not; it's as simple as that. If the

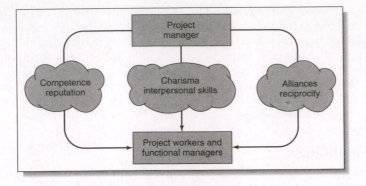

Figure 14.2
Project manager's sources of influence.

project gets into trouble, a project manager that people like will have many friends to call upon for help.

In summary, project managers tend to rely upon knowledge, experience, personal relationships, and personality to influence others (Figure 14.2). To build expert-based power, they must be perceived as technically and administratively competent. To build referent-based power, they must develop effective interpersonal, persuasion, and negotiation skills. The ways that different project managers employ these sources of influence is illustrated in Example 14.2.

Example 14.2: Effective Project Managers, Contrast in Styles[11]

Two examples of how different project managers uniquely influence people are Kelly Johnson and Ben Rich, both former head managers of the advanced projects division of Lockheed-Martin Company, the "Skunk Works" mentioned in Chapter 13.

Kelly Johnson was a living legend, not only at the company but also in the whole aerospace industry. With the help of a highly cohesive team of engineers and shop workers, he created over 40 airplanes, including the fastest, highest-flying ones in the world. Yet he was strictly business, without humor, hot tempered, and reputed to "eat young engineers for between-meal snacks." He made people with whom he had dealings sweat—whether bureaucrats or engineers—particularly excuse-makers and faultfinders, so he had as many detractors as friends. Nonetheless, when the company needed someone to head up the most difficult and challenging projects, management repeatedly selected Kelly. Why? Beneath the bad temper and somewhat unkempt appearance was an unquestioned, sure-fire genius. He knew everything, it seemed, and his ability to make accurate, on-the-spot deductions was amazing. For a new engine inlet, Kelly simply glanced at the initial design and pronounced it wrong, being about 20 percent too big. His engineers worked a full day to re-compute the design only to discover that, sure enough, the engine inlet was 18 percent too big. In another instance, he looked at a design and said "the load here is 6.3 psi." After an hour of complicated calculations, his people measured it as 6.2 psi. When he retired, Kelly Johnson was recognized as the pre-eminent aerodynamicist of his time.

Kelly chose as his successor Ben Rich. Ben was the first to acknowledge that he didn't possess Kelly's genius and, therefore, would rely on his teams for most decisions. His first move was to loosen the reins and allow the teams latitude to make most calls on their own. Ben was decisive in telling a team what he wanted, but he then let the members decide which methods to apply. He stuck to schmoozing and cheerleading through an endless supply of one-liners. As one employee said, "Whereas Kelly ruled by his bad temper, Ben ruled by his bad jokes." Ben believed in using a non-threatening approach. Whereas he didn't shirk from scolding deserving individuals, he preferred complimenting people and boosting morale. According to a colleague, he was the perfect manager—there to make the tough calls, defend and protect his project teams, obtain more money and new projects, and convince the government and senior management of the value of his teams' work.

Johnson and Rich led using different styles, yet both have been acknowledged by the industry as exemplary project managers. Kelly Johnson accomplished great things, despite his temperament, and most engineers considered it an honor to have worked with him. Competency and reputation were his strengths; people tolerated his personality. Ben Rich, no technical slouch, acknowledged that he had a few smarter people working for him. Unlike Kelly, however, he had charisma and many personal friends, and with that he too was able to accomplish great things at the Skunk Works.

The Balance of Power

In most cases project managers and functional managers share authority, although in the high-performing projects that authority is clearly differentiated.[12] Project managers have power to procure critical resources, coordinate work efforts, and mediate conflicts; in contrast, functional managers have power to decide the technology to be used and to resolve technical problems.

Although project managers rarely have any form of reward power, it is usually beneficial that workers *perceive* them as having some reward power. In general, project personnel tend to listen to managers who they perceive as having influence over their salaries and promotions.

14.3 SELECTING THE PROJECT MANAGER

Qualifications of successful project managers fall into four categories: personal characteristics, interpersonal skills, general business skills, and technical skills.

Personal Characteristics

Archibald lists the following as essential personal characteristics for a project manager:[13]

- Flexible and adaptable
- Preference for initiative and leadership
- Confidence, persuasiveness, verbal fluency
- Effective communicator and integrator
- Able to balance technical solutions with time, cost, and human factors
- Well-organized and disciplined
- A generalist rather than a specialist.

These characteristics make sense, given the project environment and the responsibilities and restrictions placed on the project manager role. Obviously, project managers must be able to work in situations where there are constant deadlines, great uncertainty, start-ups and closeouts, and constant changes in goals, tasks, people, and relationships. At the same time, they must be able to gain the respect, trust, and confidence of those they associate with.

Interpersonal Skills

A project manager needs strong behavioral and interpersonal skills; in particular, she must be able to "actively listen" and "read people."[14] Active listening means that the project manager asks questions for clarification and paraphrases to make sure she understands what people are saying. In particular, the project manager knows how to:

- Ask leading questions
- Remain quiet and give the other person sufficient time to talk
- Reflect on the person's answer and check for correctness
- Reflect on the person's emotions.

The acronym for active listening is LEAR: Listen, Explore, Acknowledge, Respond.

The project manager must be sensitive to project stakeholders' attitudes. Many specialists in the project team will disdain anything non-technical, and resent schedule and budgetary constraints. The project manager must be able to convince them why these matter.

The project manager must also be able to build trust, promote team spirit, and reward cooperation—often through the only forms of reward she can give: praise and credit. She must understand the personalities, attitudes, and strengths of her team members and know how to utilize their talents even when they do not measure up to her standards. The project manager must be sensitive to human frailties, needs and greed, and able to resolve conflict, manage stress, and coach and counsel team members. It seems like a tall order, but good project managers can do all of that.

General Business Skills

The project manager is, after all, a *manager* and so must also have general business knowledge and skills that include:

- Understanding of the organization and the business
- Understanding of management–marketing, accounting, contracting, purchasing, personal administration, and the concept of profitability
- The ability to translate business requirements into project and system requirements
- A strong, active, continuous interest in teaching, training, and developing subordinates.

Most project managers have cost responsibility, so they must understand the concepts of cost estimating, budgeting, cash flow, overheads, incentives, and cost sharing. They are involved in contract agreements, so they must be informed about contract terms and implications. They are responsible for the phasing and scheduling of work to meet delivery dates, so they must be familiar with the work tasks, processes, and resources necessary to execute the project. And they are responsible for enforcing schedules, so must be knowledgeable about tools and techniques for planning, tracking, and control.

Technical Skills

To be able to make informed decisions, project managers must have a strong grasp of the technical aspects of the project. As mentioned, their "domain competency" must span the full scope of the project. In non- or low-technology environments, grasp can be developed through experience and informal training. In high-technology projects, qualifications are more rigorous and usually require a career molded in the technology environment and a degree in science or engineering.[15]

Although project managers seldom do technical analysis, they must be qualified to integrate concepts from different fields and make technical judgments. Many technically qualified people are not very good at integrating concepts from different specialties because most training in engineering and technology emphasizes analysis and ignores integration.[16] The project manager must be able to understand and speak the language of all the specialists on the team, regardless of their specialty; this is the minimal requirement for communicating with and integrating the work of the specialists.

Selection and Recruiting

The project manager for a given project is selected from among the ranks of product and functional managers, functional specialists, and experienced project managers. The last source is the best, though often not feasible. It might be difficult to find an experienced project manager who has the right mix of qualifications and whose current project ends just as the new one is beginning. As a result, when an experienced project manager is needed he is often recruited from the outside; this is readily observable in the Sunday job listings of major metropolitan newspapers (Figure 14.3 shows a sample). The downside of bringing in an outsider is that it will take time for him to make friends, build alliances, and learn organizational policies. On the plus side, he is likely better suited to objectively take on the task (without political influence), and will not have any enemies—at least initially.

The project manager can also be selected from among functional managers, although functional managers sometimes have difficulty shifting to a project perspective. The new role requires adjusting from managing one area exclusively, to overseeing and integrating the work of many areas. Unless the manager has abundant well-rounded experience, everyone will likely perceive him as just another functional manager.

Project managers are also "created" by promoting non-managerial specialists (engineers, scientists, system analysts, product designer, etc.), although the problem with this is the same as with putting any non-manager into a managerial role: he must first learn how to manage. Someone being a good engineer or auditor is no assurance he will be a good project manager. Besides that, the specialist must learn how to remove himself from his area of specialty and become a generalist. Ideally, the project management assignment will not conflict with existing lines of authority. It is a bad idea, for example, to promote a functional specialist into a project management role that would give him authority over his former boss.

Training

Project management skills cannot be learned quickly, so organizations devote substantial time and expense to preparing individuals to become project managers. Some sponsor internal training programs that focus on the special requirements of their organizations; others use external seminars and university programs. Recent years have seen a rapid proliferation in both kinds of programs, as well as the rise of training oriented toward professional certification, such as the PMI's Project Management

Figure 14.3
Advertisements for project management positions.

Professional, or PMP. Often, a project support office or PMO assists with this training and professional development.

Still, there is no substitute for experience. Many organizations allow promising people who aspire to become project managers the benefit of on-the-job training.[17] As part of their career path, they rotate assignments throughout all areas of the organization. This gives them the domain competency to be able to manage projects that involve those areas. Technical specialists also work full- or part-time as assistants to experienced project managers. While this gives them exposure to management, it also tests their aptitude and talent for being managers. Valued specialists with little managerial aptitude or ability should be given other career opportunities commensurate with their skills and interests.

Example 14.3: On-the-Job Training of Project Managers[18]

Microsoft Corporation's approach to preparing project managers (who they term "program managers") is typical. There is neither an official training program for program managers, nor guidelines that spell out job requirements.

Program managers at Microsoft learn the job primarily by "doing" it. Microsoft carefully selects and mentors the right people, then expects them to learn on the job. For about 90 percent of program managers, training happens by pairing a new program manager with an experienced, successful program manager; the other 10 percent receive formal training that includes a 3-week training session. Microsoft occasionally holds videotaped luncheons where managers present their experiences. The videotapes then may be circulated.

Moving into the Role

Project management responsibilities range from few and mundane on simple projects, to extensive and challenging on complex projects. Regardless of the qualifications of the person in the project manager role, the burden of that role is eased when the project manager:[19]

- Understands what has to be done
- Understands his authority and its limits
- Understands his relationship with others in the project
- Knows the specific results that constitute a job well done
- Knows when and what he is able to do exceptionally well, and when and where he falls short
- Is aware of what can and should be done to correct a bad situation
- Believes that his superiors have an interest and believe in him
- Believes that his superiors are eager for him to succeed.

That the project manager knows or understands these is partly the responsibility of senior management. Sometimes, however, the project manager must seek, request, or demand these from management.

14.4 WAYS OF FILLING THE PROJECT MANAGEMENT ROLE

Organizations use various titles for the role of project manager, including "project director," "project leader," and "task force chairman." The titles "task force coordinator," "project supervisor," and "project engineer" also are used, though these usually imply more focused roles with less responsibility than other forms. The most effective project management role occurs when one person becomes involved during proposal preparation and stays on until project completion. When it is impossible to find someone available and competent enough to manage the project, the role is filled in other ways. For example, the role may be assigned to the general manager or plant manager, though these managers usually have neither the necessary time to devote to a project nor the flexibility to shift roles. Alternatively, the role may be assigned temporarily to a functional manager. Here, the manager must divide her time between the project and her department, and both may suffer. Also, these combination functional–project managers may have trouble gaining cooperation from other functional managers when they are seen as competitors for resources. This "two-hat" role has other problems, described in Chapter 13.

In long-term projects, responsibility may pass from one functional manager to the next as the project progresses. In that situation, however, there is no one to guarantee managerial or technical continuity from one stage to the next. The managers of later stages are forced to inherit problems created by managers of earlier stages.

Sometimes project management responsibilities are divided among two or more people. This happens in construction projects where the architect is responsible for technical matters while the so-called project manager handles administrative "paperwork." Two managers tend to complicate issues of coordination, communication, and authority because both share responsibility. Further, when the project manager becomes subservient to the architect, his ability to manage the project is compromised. A similar split is common in the motion picture industry. The movie *producer* manages the resources, schedules, and budgets (in essence, the project manager), while the *director* oversees technical-artistic matters. Only occasionally are they the same person. Because the shooting of a motion picture is an artistic pursuit, directors need flexibility in budgets and shooting schedules, but costs matter too, and the producer faces the question of "at what price creativity?" It comes as no surprise that the two do not always have a happy relationship.[20] Nonetheless, the movie industry holds the role of project manager in high regard. When an Academy Award is given for "Best Picture," it is awarded to the picture's producer—the person who manages resources, budgets, and schedules.

Some projects, especially large ones in the public sector, require exceptional presentation, negotiation, and political skills to deal with broad constituencies and powerful public- and private-interest groups. In such cases it is also common to see two people heading up a project—one to deal with the technical side, the other with stakeholders.

Ideally, there is but one project manager; all others on the project also serving in a managerial or administrative capacity (engineers, architects, directors, etc.) report to her.

Although ideally the person filling the project management role is dedicated full-time to managing the project, it is common for managers to oversee multiple projects. This is acceptable as long as the manager can adequately fulfill his responsibilities to all of them. In fact, managing multiple projects can be advantageous because it puts the project manager in a position to resolve resource and priority conflicts and to negotiate resources among all the projects he oversees.

14.5 ROLES IN THE PROJECT TEAM

Early in a project the project manager and functional managers divide the overall project into work packages. This division determines skill requirements and serves as the basis for personnel selection and subcontracting. Those in functional support areas, contractors, and the project office who will contribute to the project become part of the *project team*. This section describes roles of members of the team.

Members Serving in the Project Office

Chapter 13 described the purpose of the project office and its placement within the organization. An example is the project office for a large engineering-development

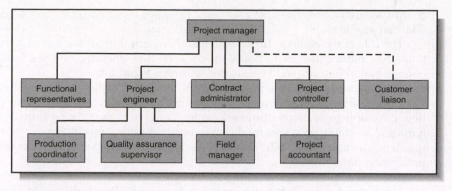

Figure 14.4
Members of the project office.

project shown in Figure 14.4. This section describes the roles of members of the project office.

The *project engineer* (also known as the systems engineer or systems designer) shoulders responsibility for coordinating technological areas and assuring integrated design of the project end-item. When several functional areas or subcontractors are involved, the project engineer:[21]

1. Oversees product or system design and development
2. Translates performance requirements into design requirements
3. Coordinates and directs the work of the functional areas and subcontractors
4. Plans, monitors, evaluates, and documents progress in the design and testing of all subsystems and the overall system
5. Oversees configuration management and everything related to controlling system changes.

The title "project engineer" sometimes denotes a person having full project manager responsibilities, although commonly it refers to the more limited role described here.

The *contract administrator*[22] is responsible for project legal aspects, such as authorization to begin work and subcontracting with outside firms. The administrator is involved in preparing proposals, defining and negotiating contracts, integrating contract requirements into project plans, ensuring the project fulfills contractual obligations, and monitoring and communicating to the customer changes to project scope. During closeout, he notifies the customer of fulfilled obligations, documents customer acceptance of the end-item, and initiates formal requests for payment. He is also responsible for collecting and storing RFPs, correspondence, legal documents, contract modifications, bills, payment vouchers, and other documents.

The *project controller*[23] works with functional managers to define tasks on the WBS and to identify individuals responsible for controlling tasks. She maintains work package files and cost summaries, releases approved work authorization documents, monitors work progress, evaluates schedule and cost progress, and revises estimates of time and cost to complete the project. She also prepares revisions to budgets, schedules, and work authorizations, drafts progress reports to users and management, and closes control accounts upon completion.

The *project accountant* provides accounting support to the project. He establishes procedures for using the PMIS, assists in identifying tasks to be controlled, establishes control accounts, prepares cost estimates, validates reported costs, and investigates financial problems.

The role of the *customer liaison* is to maintain amicable contractor–customer relations. She participates in technical discussions and ongoing reviews (within the bounds of the contract) and helps expedite contract changes.

The *production coordinator* plans and coordinates production aspects of the project. His responsibilities include reviewing engineering documents released to production; developing requirements for equipment and parts; monitoring procurement of parts and assembly processes for the end-item; monitoring production costs; scheduling all production related activities; and serving as the project manager's liaison to the production department.

The *field* or *site manager* oversees construction, installation, testing, and handing over of the project end-item to the customer. Responsibilities include scheduling field operations, monitoring field operations costs, and supervising field personnel.

The *quality assurance supervisor* establishes and administers quality assurance procedures. His responsibilities encompass raising quality awareness and instituting means for improving work methods and producing zero defects.

The project office also has *representatives* from participating functional departments and subcontractors. These people work with the project manager and each other to coordinate the activities of their functional areas with the overall project. Whenever they must meet often with the project manager or others in the office, or when their services are required continuously and for an extended period they physically work in and charge their time to the project office. They return to their functional departments as soon as their work has ended.

The number of staff in the project office should be as small as is practical. This keeps the office flexible, minimizes personnel costs and assignment problems, and makes it easier for the project manager to manage. Members of the office staff contribute full- or part-time as needed, and might be physically located in different places.

Functional Managers

Often the glamour of work sits on the project side, and functional managers may perceive their roles as mundane. But if earlier discussions have led you to believe that functional managers are somehow subservient to the project manager, be advised that that is rarely the case. Functional and project managers depend on one another to achieve project goals. Functional managers are responsible for maintaining technical competency in their disciplines, and for staffing and executing project tasks *within their functional areas*. They work with the project manager to define the tasks and plan, schedule, and budget the tasks.

Personnel in matrix organizations shift from one project to another, and their only permanent "home" is their functional department. The manager of the department is responsible not only for the hiring, performance reviews, and compensation of the people in his area, but also for their career development. Unlike project managers who tend to solicit "human resources" solely in terms of what is best for their projects, a functional manager is more likely to look out for the interests of the people being solicited.

In most project organizations, functional managers retain much the same authority and responsibility as in non-project environments. Nevertheless, some functional managers believe that the project manager role undercuts their authority, and that they could handle the project better if it were exclusively within their domain. Project managers who try to establish empires or undermine the authority of functional managers will have difficulty obtaining support when they need it.

Before a project begins, the responsibilities and contributions to technical content for each functional manager should be delineated and clearly defined.[24] This will ensure a continued strong technical base for all projects, and alleviate much potential animosity between functional and project managers.

Project Functional Leaders and Work Package Supervisors

In large projects, each functional manager selects a *project functional leader* to serve as liaison between the project manager and the functional manager. This person prepares his department's portion of the project plan and supervises project work performed by the department.

In still larger projects, the work of a given department is divided into multiple work packages, and responsibility for each is delegated to a *work package supervisor*. The supervisor prepares the plan for the work package and supervises the work.

14.6 ROLES OUTSIDE THE PROJECT TEAM

This section discusses some of the roles of individuals and groups beyond the project team who influence or control the management, resources, and outcomes of a project (Figure 14.5).

The Manager of Projects or PMO Director

The *manager of projects* (also called the PMO director, vice president of projects, director of projects, or program manager) is positioned in the hierarchy at the same level as functional managers (refer to Figure 13.8 in Chapter 13). This manager oversees multiple projects, and:[25]

- Directs and evaluates all the project managers
- Ensures that projects are consistent with the resource limitations and strategic objectives of the organization

Figure 14.5
Roles outside the project team.

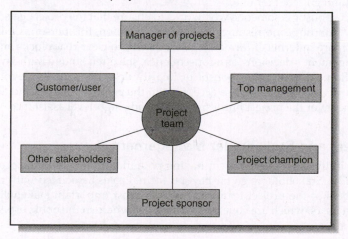

- Works with functional heads to allocate resources and resolve priority conflicts between projects
- Assists in development of project management policies, and planning and control techniques and systems
- Ensures consistency among projects and that any changes to the project cost, schedule, and performance objectives are integrated with those of other projects.

Chapter 16 describes the role of the PMO in more detail.

Top Management

Top management makes all major project selection decisions. It approves the project feasibility study, selects the project manager, and authorizes project start-up. Ultimately, top management is responsible for the quality of the organization's project management. Directly or through the PMO, top management:[26]

- Defines the project manager's responsibility and authority relative to other managers
- Defines the scope and limitations on the project manager's responsibilities
- Establishes policies for resolving project conflicts and setting priorities
- Specifies criteria for evaluating the project manager's performance
- Supports the project management methodology.

Project managers are able to exercise authority only as granted by the manager of projects and as stated in the organization's charter. In situations involving critical negotiations or irresolvable conflicts, top management may pre-empt the authority of the project manager.

Project Supporters: Champion and Sponsor

Every project needs the support of two key outsiders: the *project champion* and the *project sponsor*. The champion is someone who firmly believes in the project and is willing to argue in favor of it, both at its inception and thereafter. The champion must have "clout" and be the sort of person able to convince stakeholders about the value or benefits of the project. Often, the champion is the project's most visible spokesperson. If the project does not have a champion, the project manager might have to put on his evangelist hat and go scout for one.

The project sponsor is someone who works to ensure that the project gets the necessary priority, funding, and resources. Like the champion, this person is influential too, although more in terms of formal, legal authority to clear roadblocks and influence top management's decisions; as a consequence, she often holds a high-level management position. Although the sponsor ordinarily does not actually devote much time to the project, she is nonetheless accessible to the project manager and available to help out whenever the project hits a snag and needs high-level assistance.

Stakeholders and Stakeholder Management

Any group or individual affected by or having potential influence on the project is a *project stakeholder*. Stakeholders go far beyond formal roles associated with the project and members of the project team. Among the most important stakeholders are customers and users, which are covered in depth elsewhere in the book, especially in Chapters 2–4.

Some stakeholders support the project and want it to succeed; others resist it and seek to delay or kill it. The latter include managers of areas that compete with the project for resources, environmental or political interest groups or lobbies, and anyone who perceives the project as detrimental to their own or society's interests. Most stakeholders are not aware of and don't care about other stakeholders. From the very start, the project manager should make it his business to learn who the important stakeholders are. In essence, he should prepare a big list of the stakeholders—all individuals, organizations, and groups influenced by or able to influence the project—and determine any relationships among them. This is part of *stakeholder management*, which includes identifying key stakeholders and their interests, needs, and attitudes regarding the project, and preparing strategies to accommodate them, entice or enhance their support, or mitigate their opposition. The table provides a simple rule of thumb for dealing with stakeholders.

	Stakeholders with Low Influence	Stakeholders with High Influence
Stakeholders with high interest in project	Keep in mind	Focus on these
Stakeholders with low interest in project	Possibly ignore	Keep in mind

Example 14.4: The Big Dig[27]

Boston's Central Artery/Tunnel Project (CAT)—known locally as the Big Dig—is a good example of a complex project that must accommodate the interests of many stakeholders, including federal, state, and local governments, contractors, and numerous interest groups (Figure 14.6).[28]

Figure 14.6
Map of key stakeholders in the Big Dig project prior to 1992.

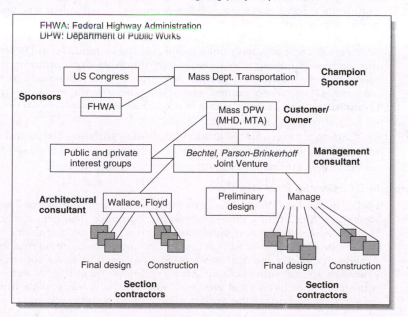

The central artery portion of the project replaced the elevated interstate highway that ran through downtown Boston with a tunnel. The elevated highway (derisively called the "green snake") was an eyesore that separated Boston's North End and waterfront from the rest of downtown. Besides replacing the central artery, the CAT project included a tunnel under Boston Harbor to Logan Airport, and new bridges across the Charles River to Cambridge—a total of 160 miles of lanes over 3.7 miles of tunnels, 2.3 miles of bridges, and 1.5 miles of surface streets. Celebrated as "the largest, most complex highway project ever undertaken in the US," its original price tag was $5 billion; present estimates put the price at four times that amount.

Project supporters faced daunting problems. The Massachusetts congressional delegation had to shepherd through the US Congress bills that would provide most of the funding; this required taking into account the interests of—and making promises to—a large host of *ad hoc* congressional allies. With funding authorization from the Federal Highway Administration (FHWA), supporters turned to the issue of who should oversee the project: the Massachusetts Bay Area Transportation Authority (BATA) or the Massachusetts Department of Public Works (DPW). Although BATA had a better construction management reputation, DPW was given the job on the rationale that BATA is a transit, not a highway, agency. To manage the project, DPW hired the experienced contractor team of Bechtel/Parson Brinkerhoff, a joint venture formed by two of the world's largest consulting and management engineering firms—Bechtel Civil division of Bechtel Corporation, and Parsons Brinkerhoff Quade & Douglas. The two (called *Joint Venture*) had partnered before as contractors for the San Francisco BART Project, and Bechtel had worked on the English Channel Tunnel and the Disney-MGM theme park in Florida.

To manage the project, CAT was broken down into the phases of conceptual design, preliminary design, final design, and construction. Joint Venture created the preliminary design, but hired contractors for final design and construction. The project initially consisted of 56 design and 132 construction work packages, each with a prime contractor. Managing the contractors responsible for the artery and tunnel design packages required especially close coordination, since these packages produced contiguous road and tunnel sections that had to dovetail. The Joint Venture team coordinated everything from the CAT "control center," where contractors pored over data about progress, graphics of the interface connections, critical paths, and schedules.

In accordance with the law, Joint Venture placed a draft of the project in public libraries and provided public hearings. These resulted in DPW and Joint Venture engineers having to negotiate with hundreds of neighborhood, church, business, and environmental groups, developers, and individuals to mitigate countless issues regarding community and environmental impacts. These ultimately contributed to large escalations in project scope, costs, and schedules.

Getting a project off the ground involves negotiating hoops and hurdles held by many stakeholders. The project manager is always mindful of those stakeholders, and works to gain and retain their support in ways big and small.

Example 14.5: McCormick Place West[29]

McCormick Place West is part of a major multi-year, multi-phase project to expand Chicago's McCormick Place convention complex. The group of companies that teamed up to design and build the structure (another "joint venture") engaged in a number of programs to build relations with nearby residents and businesses. Project managers and staff visited local high schools to educate students about practices and careers in construction, engineering, and architecture. They offered a program that hires local workers, teaches them trade skills through hands-on experience, and offers the opportunity to become union certified; about 20 people a year have become certified in this way. The contractor donated old computers to local schools and cars for their shop classes. Copying a popular reality TV series, the company remodeled the home of a local needy family. These and other charitable programs benefited the local community and helped the contractor to substantially gain the community's support.

14.7 SUMMARY

Project managers work at the project–functional-user interface, integrating project elements to achieve time, cost, and performance objectives. They have ultimate responsibility for the success of the projects, yet in most cases work outside the traditional hierarchy and have little formal authority. To influence decisions and behavior, they tend to rely on negotiations, alliances, favors, and reciprocal agreements. Their strongest source of influence is the respect they gain through skillful and competent administration, technical competency, or charisma.

Successful project managers are perceived as both technically and administratively competent. They have business as well as domain competency—broad knowledge encompassing the full scope of the project. They also have strong behavioral and communication skills, and are able to function effectively in uncertain, changing conditions.

The role of project manager is best filled by one person who is involved in the project from start to finish. Sharing or rotating the role among several people is usually less effective, although sometimes necessary to meet technical, administration, and political considerations.

Project managers get work done through a team composed of people from various functional and support groups scattered throughout the parent company, and from outside subcontractors. The project office provides administrative assistance and services. Functional managers contribute to the technical content of the project, and share responsibility for developing tasks, plans, schedules, and budgets for work required of their areas. They maintain the technical base from which projects draw.

Top management, the manager of projects or PMO director, and the project champion and project sponsor all play key roles in the project. Top management establishes the policies, responsibilities, and authority relationships through which project management is conducted. The manager of projects or PMO director ensures that projects are consistent with organization goals and receive the necessary resources. The champion rallies support for the project and convinces others of its virtues, benefits, or value. The sponsor supports the project and has the organizational clout to get the project the necessary priority and resources. Numerous other stakeholders support or resist the project and can have a big impact on its success or failure.

People find project work challenging, rewarding, and exhilarating, but without question they often also find it taxing and stressful. Maximizing the chances of project success—and minimizing human casualties along the way—requires special skills for dealing with groups and individuals. These are covered in the next chapter.

REVIEW QUESTIONS AND PROBLEMS

1. What is the project manager's primary role?
2. What is meant by "the project manager is an evangelist and entrepreneur?"
3. Describe the responsibilities of a project manager. In what ways are budgeting, scheduling, and controlling considered as integration and coordination responsibilities?

4. Discuss the relative need for both technical and managerial competence in project management.
5. Why is a broad background essential for the project manager? What *is* a broad background?
6. What is legal authority? How does it differ from charismatic authority?
7. Describe how and in what ways people in organizations, regardless of hierarchical position, influence others.
8. How does the authority of the typical project manager differ from authority of other managers?
9. What is meant by the "authority gap?"
10. What is the most common source of influence used by project manages? How does the project manager use this influence to induce functional managers to assign personnel to the project?
11. List the ideal qualifications—personal, behavioral, technical—for project managers. How do they differ from the qualifications for functional managers? How do these vary depending on the project?
12. Discuss the considerations in selecting a project manager from among each of the following groups: experienced project managers, functional managers, functional specialists.
13. Discuss the pros and cons of the various ways of filling the role of project manager (e.g., part-time, multiple project managers for one project, one manager for multiple projects, etc.).
14. How are project managers trained on the job? What are the advantages and drawbacks of relying upon on-the-job training as a source for project managers?
15. Describe the responsibilities of key members of the project office for a large-scale project.
16. Describe the responsibilities of the manager of projects.
17. Describe the project-related responsibilities of top management.
18. Describe the responsibilities of the functional manager, the project leader, and the work-package supervisor in project management and their interfaces with one another.
19. Who is the project champion, who is the project sponsor, and who are the stakeholders? What influence do they have on a project?

QUESTIONS ABOUT THE STUDY PROJECT

1. In your project, what is the formal title given to the role of project manager?
2. Where in the organization structure is the project manager? Show this on an organization chart.
3. Describe in one sentence the overall role for the project manager of your project. Now, list his or her *specific* responsibilities.
4. In your opinion, is the so-called project manager the *real* project manager, or is someone else controlling the project? If the latter, what effect does this have on the project manager's ability to influence the project?
5. Would you describe the project manager's orientation as being more technical or more managerial? Explain.
6. Describe the project manager's professional background. Has it helped or hindered his or her ability to be a project manager? (You might pose this question to the project manager.)
7. Describe the project manager's authority. How much legal authority does the project manager have? Is the project manager's authority specified in the organization charter?
8. How big would you say is the project manager's authority gap? Explain. Does the project manager have any complaints about it?

9. From where does this organization get its project managers? Does it have a procedure or seminars for training and selecting project managers? Where did the manager of your project come from?
10. How does this project manager fill the role: part- or full-time, shared or rotated with other managers, manager of several projects at once? Explain. Does the project manager have enough time to do an effective job? Would another way of filling the position be more effective?
11. Is there a project office? If not, how are the responsibilities (e.g., for contract administration) handled? If so, who is in the project office (a project engineer, contract administrator, field representative, etc.)? Are they on loan, full-time, or part-time? Describe their responsibilities.
12. What functional managers are involved in this project? Describe their responsibilities in the project, decisions they make unilaterally, and decisions they share with the project manager.
13. Is there a manager of projects? A project champion? A sponsor? Describe their responsibilities and influence on the project.
14. What has been the role of top management in your project? What, in general, is the involvement of top management in projects in this organization?

Case 14.1   The LOGON Project

Top management of the Iron Butterfly Company (IBC) has decided to adopt a project-management form of organization for the LOGON project. As a consultant to top management, you have been given two tasks to help implement this. First, you must develop a project management policy statement and a project manager job description. Your policy statement should define the project manager's role with respect to other functional managers, as well as clarify the role of functional managers in the project. Your job description must define the specific responsibilities and legal authority of the project manager. You should consider the reactions of functional managers to the policy statement and job description, and how best to get their "buy in." How can you give the project manager sufficient authority to manage the LOGON project without usurping the authority of other managers who must give their support? You should also suggest to top management what forms of evaluation can be used as incentives for team members to work together toward project goals. Remember, the functional departments are also currently involved in their own work and work in other project activities.

Your second task is to specify and document the qualifications for the position of LOGON project manager. After considering the nature of the project (technical scope, risks, complexity, etc.) as described in Case 13.1 in Chapter 13, prepare a list of qualifications—general background and experience, personality characteristics, managerial, technical, and interpersonal skills—for screening candidates and making the final selection. IBC has some employees who have worked as project coordinators and expediters, but no one with experience as a pure project or matrix manager. Consider the assumptions and pros and cons of selecting a functional manager or technical specialist from inside IBC, or an experienced project manager from an outside the company. A contract has been signed, and LOGON is to begin in 4 months.

Case 14.2   Selecting a Project Manager at Nuwave Products Company

Nuwave Products Company is a medium-sized manufacturer of small motors and motor parts. Nuwave recently contracted with a software consulting firm, Noware, Inc., to design software for a new manufacturing process to be installed at some time in the near future. The software design is part of a much larger project that also involves procurement and installation of new manufacturing equipment, a new production process, and retraining of workers. The new production process will involve "lean production" concepts that are very different from Nuwave's current process and will engage workers in improvement efforts and require no less than a cultural change among Nuwave's supervisors and line workers. The new software will integrate information from the sales, finance, and manufacturing departments with information from suppliers to create production schedules for Nuwave's automated lines.

Ordinarily, the manufacturing department assigns a project manager to projects that involve new processes. However, no one in the department has had experience with a project of this scope,

the new software and equipment, or with lean production concepts and cultural change. Some Nuwave managers think that besides designing the software, Noware should oversee the entire project—the "lean transition," equipment installation, and worker training. In contrast, the manufacturing department manager thinks that one of his senior engineers, Roberta Withers, should handle the project. She has a thorough knowledge of Nuwave's current manufacturing process, and is considered the department's expert in mechanical systems. Ms Withers is a degreed mechanical engineer, and has been with Nuwave manufacturing department for 6 years. She knows nothing about lean production or computer integrated manufacturing systems, but her boss thinks the project would be a good opportunity for her to learn.

QUESTIONS

1. Assume that you must act on the information available in the case. If it was your choice, who would you select to manage the project: Noware, Roberta, or someone else? Explain.

2. If you could get more information before making a choice, what would you want to know?

Case 14.3 Stakeholders in Boston's Big Dig[30]

(Refer to Example 14.4.)

Before the Massachusetts congressional delegation could seek federal funding for the Big Dig project, it first had to poll constituents about sensitive transportation issues. Then-Speaker of the House Philip "Tip" O'Neal wanted to know where his supporters—voters of East Boston—stood. When first told about the project, he said, "We're not building any tunnel." He changed his mind when supporters predicted that "the trade unions are going to be marching on you [if you veto the tunnel]" and assured him that in East Boston "no homes would be lost." The delegation then faced formidable opposition from the Reagan Administration and Federal Highway Administration, both of which initially argued that the project was ineligible for federal funding.

An early responsibility of Joint Venture/ DPW was to prepare an environmental impact statement, the draft of which consisted of several thick volumes. Part I described impacts in 17 cat-

egories, including "transportation," "air quality," "noise and vibration," "economic aspects," "visual characteristics," "historic resources," "water quality," "wetlands and waterways," and "vegetation and wildlife." Under "economic characteristics," it described commercial and industrial activity, tourism, and employment patterns in the affected areas. According to the report, the project would not displace any residences, but would relocate 134 businesses with 4,100 employees.

At the first public hearing 175 persons spoke, including some from the EPA and the Sierra Club, and 99 provided written commentary. The magnitude and complexity of the project is reflected in a sampling of the public interest groups represented: the 1000 Friends of Massachusetts, American Automobile Association, Archdiocese of Boston/Can-Do Alliance, Beacon Hill Civic Association, Bikes Not Bombs, Boston Building Trades Association, Boston Society of Architects, Charles River Watershed Association, Conservation Law

Foundation of New England, and Haymarket Pushcart Association. Project officials quickly dispelled public concern about large-scale displacement of businesses and neighborhoods.

The Massachusetts Secretary of the Environment issued a certificate of approval, allowing construction to proceed only after certain mitigation measures had been implemented to ease environmental impacts. The certificate recommended planning for utilization of the 27 new acres of downtown Boston that would be created by the removal of the elevated Central Artery, and urged formulating "creative strategies" for integrating the new highway system with mass transit, limiting downtown parking, and reserving highway lanes for high-occupancy vehicles.

Beyond environmental matters, the project had to respond to issues raised by hundreds of groups, businesses, and agencies. Project officials put the number of early mitigation commitments at 1,100, and the added cost to the project at $2.8 billion. The commitments addressed state and federal requirements, as well as construction impacts, including $450 million for temporary lanes, curbs, and sidewalks that would enable businesses to continue during construction, and $230 million for the City of Cambridge to build a park along the Charles River.

QUESTIONS

1. From information provided here and in Example 14.4, create a list of stakeholders for the project. Revise Figure 14.6 to include them and show possible or likely links between them. For each stakeholder, state its likely interests in the project and in what ways it could influence the conduct of the project and its tunnels, roadways, bridges, etc.

2. Considering the technical aspects of the project (building tunnels, roadways, and bridges; demolishing the old roadway structure and replacing it with parks) and the political, economic, environmental, and social impacts (and the stakeholders with interests in each), what characteristics (skills, background, competencies) would you expect of the "ideal" manager or managers overseeing a project of this scope and magnitude?

NOTES

1. Sayles L and Chandler M. *Managing Large Systems: Organizations for the Future.* New York, NY: Harper & Row; 1971. p. 204.
2. *Ibid.,* p. 212.
3. *Ibid.,* p. 204.
4. Portions adapted from Smith RA. *The Carving of Mount Rushmore.* New York, NY: Abbeville Press; 1985.
5. *Ibid.,* pp. 17–18.
6. *Ibid.,* p. 164.
7. Archibald R. *Managing High-Technology Programs and Projects.* New York, NY: Wiley; 1976. p. 35; Atkins W. Selecting a project manager. *Journal of Systems Management* October; 1980: 34; and Roman D. *Managing Projects: A Systems Approach.* New York, NY: Elsevier; 1986. p. 419.
8. Lawrence P and Lorsch J. *Organization and Environment: Managing Differentiation and Integration.* Boston, MA: Graduate School of Business, Harvard University; 1967. Ch. III.
9. These bases of interpersonal power were first described by French JPR and Raven B. *The Bases of Social Power.* Reprinted in Cartwright D and Zander A (eds), *Group Dynamics,* 3rd edn. New York, NY: Harper & Row; 1968. pp. 259–269.
10. Hodgetts R. Leadership techniques in the project organization. *Academy of Management Journal* 11; 1968: 211–219.
11. Rich B and Janos L. *Skunk Works.* Boston, MA: Little, Brown & Co; 1994.
12. Katz R and Allen TJ. Project performance and the locus of influence in the R&D matrix. *Academy of Management Journal* 28(1); 1985: 67–87.
13. Archibald, *Managing High-Technology Programs,* p. 55.
14. Adams JR, Barndt SE, and Martin MD. *Managing by Project Management.* Dayton, OH: Universal Technology; 1979. p. 137.
15. Gaddis PO. The project manager. *Harvard Business Review* May–June; 1959: 89–97.
16. *Ibid.,* p. 95.
17. Roman, *Managing Projects,* pp. 439–440.
18. Cusumano M and Selby R. *Microsoft Secrets.* New York, NY: Free Press; 1995. pp. 105–106.

19. Kerzner H. *Project Management: A Systems Approach to Planning, Scheduling, and Controlling*, 10th ed. New York, NY: Wiley; 2009. p. 148.

20. An example is the movie *Heaven's Gate*, where the director was allowed virtually to dominate the movie's producers. Originally scheduled for completion in 6 months at a cost of $7.5 million, the production was released a year late and $28 million *over* budget. The movie was a box office flop, and helped clinch the demise of United Artists, which had to underwrite the expense. From Bach S. *Final Cut*. New York, NY: William Morrow; 1985.

21. Responsibilities for project engineers in development projects are described in Chase W. *Management of Systems Engineering*. New York, NY: Wiley-Interscience; 1974. pp. 25–29.

22. According to Archibald, *Managing High-Technology Programs*, pp. 124–128, 199.

23. *Ibid.*, pp. 128–131.

24. Katz and Allen, *Project Performance and the Locus of Influence*, pp. 83–84.

25. Cleland D and King W. *Systems Analysis and Project Management*, 3rd edn. New York, NY: McGraw-Hill; 1983. p. 358.

26. *Ibid.*, pp. 362–363.

27. Hughes T. *Rescuing Prometheus*. New York, NY: Vintage Books; 1998. Ch V (this book provides interesting historical perspectives on the Big Dig and other large, complex projects); Luberoff D, Altshuler A, and Baxter C. *Mega-Project: A Political History of Boston's Multibillion Dollar Artery/Tunnel Project*. Cambridge, MA: Taubman Center, John F. Kennedy School, Harvard University; 1993. http://www.bigdig.com/:http://lfmsdm.mit.edu/news_articles/sdm_business_trip_fall03/sdm_business_trip_fall03.html .

28. Figure 14.6 shows stakeholders prior to 1992. After that, B/PB-Joint Venture accountability shifted from the Massachusetts DPW to the Massachusetts Highway Department, and after 1997 to the Massachusetts Turnpike Authority (MTA). In 1998, key personnel from B/PB and MTA formed an "integrated project office" with the purpose of combining the expertise of the management consultant (B/PB) with the longer-term dedication and specialized experience of the owner (MTA). Source: *Completing the "Big Dig": Managing the Final Stages of Boston's Central Artery/Tunnel Project*. Washington, DC: National Academies Press, 2003. Ch. 5. http://books.nap.edu/openbook.php?record_id=10629&page=31; accessed May 8, 2007.

29. Klinger A, Belmonte D, Chou E, Phares C, Volman N, and Pina R. *The McCormick Place West Expansion Project*. Loyola University Chicago Report; February 2005.

30. Source: Hughes T. *Rescuing Prometheus*. New York, NY: Vintage Books; 1998.

Managing Participation, Teamwork, and Conflict

Eh! je suis leur chef, il fallait bien les suivre.
[Ah well! I am their leader, I really ought to follow them.]

—ALEXANDRE AUGUSTE LEDRU-ROLLIN

Teambuilding. We don't need that!
I'll skip this chapter.

—ANONYMOUS PROJECT MANAGER

*D*uring the manned landings on the moon, a study was conducted of NASA project management by researcher Richard Chapman.[1] This was during NASA's heyday—a period marked by extraordinary achievements and a time when NASA was upheld as exemplar of a large agency that worked, and worked well. It is interesting and instructive to begin this chapter with a few of Chapman's comments about the project managers of that era:

[In addition to technical competency and management capacity] all agree that the project manager must have the ability . . . to build a cohesive project team.

(p. 93)

523

Those project managers who [developed the most closely-knit project teams emphasized] decentralized decision making [and] technical problem-solving at the level where both the problem and most experience reside. [They encouraged project members] to feel a sense of responsibility for problem-solving at their respective levels, within the assigned guidelines . . .

(p. 83)

Most project staffs believe that they receive generous support and attention from the project manager. Most also acknowledge that the project manager is vigorous and fair in bestowing recognition on team members and in rewarding them to the best of his capability.

(p. 82)

In another study of NASA, E. H. Kloman compared the performance of two large projects, Lunar Orbiter and Surveyor. Lunar Orbiter was a success, and fulfilled objectives within time and resource limits; Surveyor was less successful, and experienced cost and schedule overruns. The study characterized Lunar Orbiter's customer/contractor organizations as tightly knit *cohesive* units, with good *teamwork* and mutual *respect* and *trust* for their project counterparts. In contrast, teamwork in Surveyor was characterized as "slow and fitful" to grow and "spurred by a sense of anxiety and concern."[2] Kloman concluded:

What emerges perhaps most forcefully from a broad retrospective view is the importance of the human aspects of organization and management. Both projects demonstrated the critical nature of human skills, interpersonal relations, compatibility between individual managers, and teamwork.

(p. 39)

These remarks are the crux of this chapter: behavioral issues such as decentralized decision-making, interpersonal skills, and teamwork are important in project management. Unfortunately, they are often overlooked in project practice and given short shrift in project management education, possibly because inexperienced managers and specialists in the "hard" disciplines (technicians, engineers, and businesspeople) see them as "soft" issues of little consequence. But in reality these are not soft issues. They are hard as nails, and can profoundly impact project performance and success.

This chapter discusses issues broached by the two studies cited: leadership, participative decision-making, teamwork, conflict resolution, and the related matter of emotional stress in work.

15.1 LEADERSHIP IN PROJECT MANAGEMENT

Leadership Style

Chapter 13 described a variety of organizational forms for different purposes and types of work. Likewise, there are a variety of suitable leadership styles depending on the situation. Leadership is the ability to influence the behavior of others to accomplish what is desired; *leadership style* is the way in which a leader achieves that influence.

Leadership style can be categorized between the two extremes of *task-oriented* and *relations-oriented*. Task-oriented managers show higher concern for the goal and the work, and tend to behave in a more autocratic fashion. Relations-oriented managers show greater concern for people, and tend to exercise a more democratic leadership style.

Numerous studies have attempted to discern the most effective leadership style. Most conclude that no one leadership style is best for all situations. Effective style depends upon characteristics of the leader, the followers, the leader's interpersonal relationship with followers, and the nature and environment of the task. This perspective is called the *contingency* or *situational approach* to leadership. These approaches suggest that the leader should use the style that best fits the work situation, and try not to apply the same style to all employees and situations. Brief mention will be made of two of these approaches—those of Fred Fiedler and Hersey and Blanchard.

Contingency and Situational Approaches

According to Fiedler,[3] the three variables that most affect a leader's influence are whether (1) the work group accepts or rejects the leader, (2) the task is relatively routine or complex, and (3) the leader has high or low formal authority. Although the project manager might encounter any of these situations, commonly (as described in previous chapters):

- The project manager gets along with team members and is respected for his ability and expertise
- The task is relatively complex and requires a good deal of judgment or creativity
- The project manager has relatively low formal authority.

Fiedler's research indicates that under these conditions a *relations-oriented* style is the most effective. The most prominent behavior in this style is the leader's positive emotional ties with and concern for his subordinates.

Hersey and Blanchard[4] use a model called *situational leadership* that weighs the interplay of three variables: (1) the amount of direction and guidance a leader gives (task behavior); (2) the amount of socio-emotional support he gives (relations behavior); and (3) the readiness of followers to perform the task (maturity). The last variable, "maturity," has two aspects: the person's *skill or ability* to do something, and the person's *motivation or willingness* to do it. According to the model, the most effective leader behavior depends upon the maturity level of the followers. Project managers seldom manage laborers or even shop-floor people. Usually they deal with technical specialists, managers, professionals, tradespeople, and other highly trained people. Thus, they tend to work with people who are either (1) able but perhaps unwilling to do what the manager wants, or (2) both able and willing to do what he wants. For Group (1) the model recommends a *participative* style—i.e., a style that emphasizes facilitating, supporting, and communicating with followers. Managers and followers share in decision-making. For Group (2), the model recommends a delegating style as more effective. The manager identifies the problem or goal and delegates the followers the responsibility to carry out the task. Followers are permitted to solve the problem and determine what to do, and how and where to do it.

In their research on managing scientific and technical personnel, Hersey and Blanchard found that people with high-level education and experience responded well to participating and delegating management, and did *not* respond well to detailed directions and close supervision.[5]

Of course, this is not to say that project managers never face workers who are unwilling to follow instructions or will not take initiative. In cases where delegation or diplomacy fails, a project manager with legal authority may need to cajole, give orders, and even fire people.

Project Circumstances

Effective leadership style also depends on project circumstances, especially the length and intensity of the project. For example, a more directive style may be appropriate when there is less time to complete the work; in other words, the work *pace* sometimes constrains the available leadership options, and the intensity of the work serves as the incentive. People generally find it difficult to build trust when a job must be completed in only a few days, especially when the job involves subcontractors with which no more than an arms-length association exists or when the workforce is transient and unfamiliar. In such situations, the project manager may need to be more directive and assertive.[6] As in other regards, the project manager must be adaptable—able to wear different leadership-style hats and change them quickly.

15.2   PARTICIPATIVE MANAGEMENT

The models of Fiedler and of Hersey and Blanchard both offer similar conclusions about project situations: the most effective leadership style for project managers is a relations-oriented style—supportive, facilitative, and encouraging. This does not mean that project managers must never give orders or tell people what to do, but that in *most* project situations a high relations style works best, even when combined with high task behavior.

This conclusion is further supported by research in large aerospace projects that the most effective leadership style is *participative management*. Managers in those projects seldom give orders to the individuals they must influence, partly because most of these individuals are not subordinate to the project manager, partly because giving orders induces a "no, I won't do it" reaction, and partly because the subordinates are, after all, the experts. They use participative management because they *must* share decision-making with specialists and other managers. Although project managers have a good purview of the total system, they are farther removed from problems than the specialists and often do not know the answers to technical questions.[7]

Motivation

Project work can be stimulating, satisfying, and provide a great sense of achievement. Combined with constant pressure to meet project goals, these are natural motivators. Elements inherent to project management—contractual agreements, work breakdown structures, responsibility matrixes, and work package orders—are also motivators. They provide clear goals that, when combined with financial and career rewards, motivate people in the same way as the management-by-objective approach.

But project work includes de-motivators as well. Too much pressure leads to stress, tension, and conflict. On large jobs, individuals can lose sight of the end-item, become alienated, and feel threatened. One advantage of participative decision-making is that it helps diminish potential de-motivators and garners workers' commitment to project decisions.

Participative project managers do not relinquish responsibility; they delegate it. Even when they have legal authority, they involve others by, for example, acquainting them with problems, consulting them for their opinions, and giving frequent feedback. Knowledgeable workers are allowed to help prepare project plans and budgets. Through such participation they gain an appreciation for how their work fits in. They feel more closely associated with the project, and dedicated to its success. As stated earlier, however, people and situations vary, and the project manager must determine for each individual worker how much responsibility she can handle and how much she needs to be monitored and directed.

Management Development

Most project managers are supportive, involve others in decision-making, and avoid dogmatic or impatient behavior. Especially in projects with high potential for conflict, they work at developing trusting personal relationships; they do this by investing considerable emotional energy in their work, being open with people, and working to build trust. This is especially true in international projects, as discussed in Chapter 18.

But simply telling project managers they need to develop a participative, high-relations, high task-oriented style is not enough. Especially in matrix organizations, unless a project manager receives support in adjusting styles, she might not be able to do it; left alone, old patterns of behavior remain or new ones develop naturally that can destroy trust and cooperation.[8] A planned process of interpersonal skills training and team-building is often necessary to enable managers to make the transition.

In the words of Bennis and Nanus, the most effective leaders are able to "align" the energies of people and groups behind the goal. They lead by "pulling rather than by pushing; by inspiring rather than by ordering"; and by creating achievable, challenging expectations and rewarding progress rather than by manipulating.[9] The ample evidence, both anecdotal and empirical, is that effective project managers are strong leaders who utilize participative management.

15.3 TEAMS IN PROJECT MANAGEMENT

All project organizations are comprised of groups. As Figure 15.1 illustrates, in a large project some of these groups comprise people from within one organization (the

Figure 15.1
Groups comprising the project team.

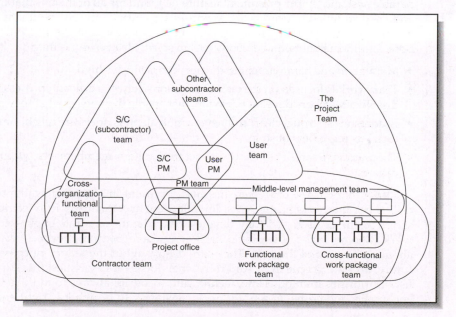

project office, mid-level managers, and functional and multifunctional work package teams), while others comprise multiple organizations (cross-organizational project management, functional groups, and so on). In many of these groups membership overlaps and people serve dual roles that link the groups together.

The term *project team* as used here refers to any particular group working in the project, or to all groups in combination. The difference between a group and a team is that the former is simply a collection of people, whereas the latter is a collection working toward a common goal. Thus, virtually all work accomplished in a project, whether mental or physical labor, is the product of teams. To be successful, a project needs *teamwork*.

The Trouble with Teams

Failures in projects often can be traced to the inability of a team to make the right decisions or perform the right tasks. These failures often stem from the maladies that teams suffer: internal conflict; time wasted on irrelevant issues; and decisions made haphazardly. Team members often are more concerned with getting the task *done* than with doing it *right*. Many teams never know what their *purpose* is, so they never know when, or if, they have achieved it.

In projects with multiple teams, each might have a different orientation and goals. The teams might be physically isolated and maintain separate offices, creating and reinforcing separating boundaries that lead to "us versus them" attitudes. These make for a portentous project environment and bode ill for project success.

High-Performing Teams

In contrast, successful projects are the result of the efforts of *effective* teams—those that succeed in achieving whatever they have set out to do. In an effective team, individuals and groups work together as a single cohesive unit.

What makes a team effective? Peter Vaill has studied a large number of highly effective teams, teams that "perform at levels of excellence far beyond those of comparable systems."[10] The prominent feature he found for all of them is that they know and are committed to team goals. Members are never confused about why the team exists or what their individual roles are. Leaders inculcate belief in the team's purpose, eliminate doubts, and embody a team spirit. He also found that:

- Motivation and commitment to the purpose is always high.

- Teamwork is focused on the task. Distinctions between task and process functions dissolve. Members develop behaviors that enable them to do what they must.

- Leadership is strong, clear, and never ambivalent. Leaders are reliable and predictable, regardless of style.

- The team views itself as clearly distinct from others; members feel "we are different."

Vaill found three characteristics *always* present in high-performing teams. He calls them *time, feeling,* and *focus*. First, leaders and members fully commit themselves to the project, and they devote extraordinary amounts of time to it. They work at home, in the office, in taxicabs—anywhere. Second, they feel very strongly about attainment of the goal. They care deeply about the team's purpose, history, future, and the people in it. And third, they focus on key issues; they have a clear list of priorities in mind. Time, feeling, and focus are always found together. Vaill encourages would-be leaders to "Seek constantly to do what is right and what is needed in the system (focus). Do it in terms of your energy (time). Put your whole psyche into it (feeling)."[11]

Successful project organizations are high-performing teams. For project managers, Vaill's findings underscore the importance of clear definition of project objectives, clarification of the roles and tasks of team members, strong commitment to achieving objectives, and a "project spirit" that bonds everyone together.

Example 15.1: Time, Feeling, and Focus in Project Management: Renovating the Statue of Liberty

The renovation of the Statue of Liberty is a good example of the kind of commitment and effort required to successfully manage a large-scale project.[12] Over 25 firms submitted proposals for the task of leading the team of 500 engineers, architects, artisans, and craftsmen who would do the renovation. Selected for the job was the small construction management firm of Lehrer/McGovern, Inc.

Hofer describes the firm's partners: Lehrer is soft-spoken and generally conservative in appearance; McGovern clean-shaves his head, has a handlebar mustache, and wears cowboy boots. Despite differences in appearance, the two share similar goals and broad experience as civil engineers and construction managers.[13]

Did they devote a lot of time to the project? To coordinate the more than 50 businesses doing the job, Lehrer and McGovern worked as many as 16 hours each day. They handled everything from helping architects and craftsmen implement plans, to making arrangements with subcontractors and ensuring that materials were ordered and delivered on time.

Did they instill feeling for the project? Said Lehrer, "this project is a labor of love. The spirit and pride of hundreds of men and women involved bring out the best of us as Americans."[14] They expected and they inspired feelings like that from everyone else, too. They only hired people who had "the same commitment and dedication as we do, who are aggressive and ambitious and understand that virtually nothing is impossible."[15] Before beginning this job, they gave each subcontractor a lecture that nothing be allowed to damage the "crown jewel of the United States."

Did they maintain focus? Their major emphasis was on top-quality work. The two partners believed that management's close and personal involvement was crucial to quality, so they made frequent visits to the site and personally supervised or handled thousands of details.

Obviously this was an exceptional project; it was highly publicized and faced considerable political pressure. But many projects bomb, despite high pressure and publicity. In this case, management's time, feeling, and focus helped the project succeed.

Effective Project Teams

Project work requires close collaboration, and people in project teams must rely on and accept one another's judgment. Managers must share information and consult with each other to make decisions, and team members must support each other. Every person and group must be committed to the project objectives, not just their own.

One way to increase collaboration and common commitment is to locate everyone in the project team in the same office quarters. Presumably, frequent daily contact will make individuals more likely to identify with the team and its goals.

However, even if co-locating team members were possible, close proximity alone will not guarantee an effective, cohesive team. Vaill's findings show that effective teams are clear about their purpose, committed to it, know their individual roles, and understand how to work together as a team. In many projects, though, especially where people have not previously worked together, team members don't know the team's goals or their own responsibilities, and they never learn to work together. A purpose of team-building is to ensure that doesn't happen.

15.4   THE TEAM-BUILDING APPROACH[16]

In a study of two NASA research centers, 36 project managers were asked to rank the most important functions of their job. The function of collecting, organizing, directing, and motivating the *project team* and supporting groups was ranked as either first or second in importance by all the managers.[17] In another study involving 32 research and product development projects, *group cohesiveness* was identified as the *single most important factor* in achieving project goals.[18]

Effective groups do not just happen. Like any other purposeful system, every team and organization must be developed. This is the purpose of *team-building*, a procedure whereby a team formally ponders how it should work or has been working, with the purpose of improving its functioning. Team-building considers issues such as decision-making, problem-solving, team objectives, internal conflict, and communication. These are called *group process issues*, referring to processes or methods by which the team gets things done. Ordinarily these are responsibilities of the team leader, though many leaders ignore them. Effective groups recognize and monitor these issues, regardless of the leader. Using the team-building approach, a group explores whatever process issues its members consider important and then *plans* for how it will address these issues and perform its work.

When It Is Needed

The need for team-building depends on the team members and the nature of the task. Generally, the more varied the backgrounds and responsibilities of team members, the greater the need. For example, members of multidisciplinary teams have different work backgrounds and different outlooks on planning and doing work; some members take a wider perspective, others are detail people. Team-building can help both types accept their differences and define common goals.

Projects involving innovation, new technology, high risks, and tight schedules typically place teams under heavy stress. Some stress will motivate a team, but after a point it becomes detrimental. Team-building can help the team to deal with the stress, to disclose and resolve problems as they occur, before they escalate and interfere with team performance.

Aspects of Team-Building Efforts

The purpose of team-building is to improve group problem-solving and group work efforts. To this end, the approach strives to achieve norms such as:

1. Effective communication among members
2. Effective resolution of group process problems
3. Techniques for constructively using conflict
4. Greater collaboration and creativity among team members
5. A more trusting, supportive atmosphere within the group
6. Clarification of the team's purpose and the role of each member

Three features common to any team-building effort are that:

- It is carefully planned and facilitated, often by a consultant or professional staff person from human relations or the PMO
- A consultant collects data about the team's process functioning in advance, then helps the team "work through" the data during a diagnostic/problem-solving workshop
- The team makes provisions for later self-evaluation and follow-up.

Following are examples of team-building as applied to three situations: an experienced work team, a new team, and multiple teams that must work together.

15.5   IMPROVING ONGOING WORK TEAMS

First consider how team-building is applied to an existing team within a functional department or project. Such teams include cross-functional management teams, design-build teams, and teams of managers representing the client, contractor, and several subcontractors. Typical problems of these teams include inability to reach agreement, lack of innovative ideas, too much conflict, or complacency of team members.

Initially, a human relations consultant or other person with facilitation skills is called in by the project manager or manager of projects to facilitate the effort. Her function is to help the group solve its own problems by drawing attention to the *way* the group's behavior is affecting its decision quality and work performance.

The consultant collects data from members using personal interviews or questionnaires. She then summarizes the data, but keeps the sources of individual comments anonymous. This summary will later be presented to the team so that members may discuss and analyze the team's problems.

The consultant first shares the results with the team leader (project manager, functional leader, or work package supervisor) and coaches him on how to prepare for the upcoming workshop. The consultant remains impartial: the *entire team* is her client.

A workshop is convened for members to review and analyze the group's problems. This workshop differs from ordinary staff meetings in many ways. It convenes at an off-site location away from interruptions, it can last up to several days, and it includes all team members. The atmosphere is open and candid, without the usual superior–subordinate restrictions. Usually the workshop is facilitated by the consultant, who may alternate the role with the group leader, depending on the agenda.

The workshop specifics vary. One common format is this:[19]

1. The workshop begins with a discussion of the agenda. Team members describe what they would like and do not want to happen.
2. The consultant posts a summary of the information collected on the wall for easy reference. Discussion may be necessary to make sure everyone understands the issues. The consultant may also post anonymous quotes from the interviews, for example:

   "Our meetings are always dominated by the same two or three people."
   "Our way of getting things done is slow and unorganized."
   "I have no voice in decisions that affect my functional group."
   "Even though the team leader asks for our opinions, I know she ignores them."
   "This group works a lot of overtime because there is no scheme for how we should fit new tasks into our existing workload."

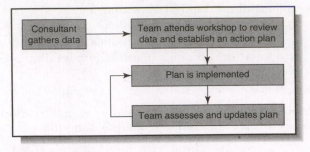

Figure 15.2
The team-building process.

"There is nothing to distinguish the roles of engineers and researchers in this project."

3. The team sets priorities for the problems it wants to resolve within the time constraint of the workshop.
4. The group works to resolve the priority issues. In the meantime
   a. The consultant monitors the session and points out dysfunctional group behavior, encouraging members to express their feelings, confronting behaviors that lead to defensiveness or distrust, and reinforcing effective behavior.
   b. The group periodically critiques itself. After working through a problem, the group pauses to evaluate what helped or hindered the process.
   c. The group prepares a formal action plan with solutions, target dates, and people responsible. The plan may include "operating guidelines" specifying *how* the group will function. (Typical guidelines are described in the next section.)

One of the authors has worked with project teams where problems ranging from technical issues to interpersonal conflict were resolved in team-building workshops.[20]

To ensure that action steps are implemented, the workshop always includes follow-up sessions. These take place formally at 2- to 3-month intervals, or less formally during regular meetings. The team takes stock of its functioning, what improvements it has made, and what still is needed. The group itself takes over the consultant's role. Whenever new problems emerge, the process is repeated. The full cycle is summarized in Figure 15.2.

Two conditions are necessary for team-building to succeed. First is management's *support*. The team leader and upper managers must face the issues uncovered and assist in (or provide resources for) working toward solutions. Second, team members must *want* to resolve the group's problems. They must be open and honest in providing information, willing to share in the responsibility for having caused problems, and willing to work toward solutions.

15.6 BUILDING NEW TEAMS

With small variation, team-building can be applied to *new* project teams. The new team might be a concurrent engineering team, a work-package team, or a management or design team with representatives from the client and contractor. The purpose of team-building in this context is for a new team to develop a plan for working together and build good working relationships. New teams have the advantage of not having established bad habits and poor working relationships.

The first task of a newly formed team is to reach agreement on the team's purpose, how it will achieve its purpose, and the roles of its members. It then asks itself: How can we effectively work together in a manner that will allow us to accomplish our purpose and leave us feeling good about it and one another?

A team-building workshop led by a facilitator is convened to help members become acquainted, reach agreement on objectives, and decide how they will function as a team. In *Team Building: Issues and Alternatives*, William Dyer describes several workshop agendas. The following is one possible application to new project teams.[21]

Step 1: Develop a priority level

Sometimes members of a team differ widely in the priority they place on the project goal or work tasks. Especially in *ad hoc* teams or task forces with part-time members, some members give the project high priority, others low. One way of acknowledging these differences is for each member to indicate, on a scale of 0 to 10, the priority of the project compared to her other work. Another way is to ask each one to indicate the amount of daily or weekly time she can devote to the project. The information then is tallied and posted on a chart similar to Figure 15.3. The team members discuss their commitments to the project, and which people are willing to accept more responsibilities than others. People who so desire can explain their position on the chart. This discussion helps reduce the potential resentment of some members committing to more work or less work than others.

Step 2: Share expectations

Each person is asked to think about the following questions: (1) What would this team be like if everything worked ideally? (2) What would it be like if everything went wrong? (3) In general, what kinds of problems occur in work groups? (4) What actions do you think need to be taken to develop an effective team? Each person's responses are shared verbally and then posted. Concerns and answers are discussed. Differences that surface will be worked through later, in Step 4.

Step 3: Clarify purpose and objectives

The team discusses and records its purpose and objectives. Sometimes this is straightforward, as for a work-package team where the objectives have already has been set; other times the group will have to define its own objectives. Either way, the purpose and objectives should be clearly defined and accepted by all members; they are the standard against which all plans and actions will be measured. The group then develops sub-objectives so that members may be given specific assignments. The team objectives should complement and conform to the user and system objectives and requirements as defined in the SOW or Charter (described in Chapters 3–5). In fact, a session like this can be used to create the SOW or charter.

Figure 15.3
Priority ranking for 10 team members.

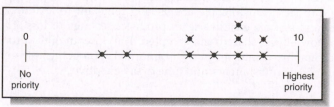

Step 4: Formulating operating guidelines

Commonly, group dysfunction arises over different expectations about work roles, job assignments, and how the group ought to work. The team can avoid problems by establishing guidelines that address the following topics.

1. *How will the team make decisions*—by dictate of the leader, by vote, by consensus, or by other means? Who should be involved in making decisions? Not everyone need always be involved, because some decisions will require input from only two or three members. In most cases, the best-informed people should make decisions. Total group decision-making should be done as often as necessary, but as little as possible.[22]
2. *How will the team resolve differences among members and subgroups?* Disagreements waste a lot of time, so guidelines should address the kinds of conflicts likely to arise and options for resolving them—consensus, vote, or calling in a mediator.
3. *How will work be assigned?* The team should specify which activities will be handled by the whole group and which by subgroups or individuals. Tasks may be divided according to expertise, position of authority, or personal preference. If several people want to do a task, how should they be chosen—by skill, experience, or volunteering?
4. *How will the team ensure that work is completed?* One person falling behind can delay the work of others. The team must ensure that assignments and completion dates are clear, and that corrective action is taken when efforts lag or are out of control. How will the team handle slackers?
5. *How will the team ensure open discussion?* The team must ensure that members are able to openly discuss issues so that ideas are not ignored or suppressed and personal problems do not block team effectiveness. People less inclined to speak up because of personality, language, or culture must be as engaged in the process as everyone else (sometimes by pointedly calling on them and requiring their input).
6. *How frequently and where will the team meet?* What do members expect about attendance?
7. *How will the team evaluate its performance and make changes?* There should be procedures for periodic review and evaluation of the team, and opportunity for the team to change some of its guidelines.

Teams also might discuss roles and responsibilities of group members and points of ambiguity, overlap, and conflict. Some teams appoint one member each meeting to the role of making sure the team conforms to its guidelines.

New teams do not have to wait for problems to arise before they take action; they can prevent potential problems. Through team-building, members develop the common expectations necessary to build trust and mutual commitment.

Disbanding Teams

Successful teams generate close ties and strong relationships, but when projects end, so do their teams. People are usually reluctant to abandon relationships, and the disbanding of a cohesive team produces feelings of loss. These feelings should be acknowledged, shared, and accepted. The closeout of the project may be followed by a ceremony– a banquet, party, or informal get-together—to give the team recognition for its accomplishments, and time to say goodbye.

15.7   INTERGROUP PROBLEM-SOLVING

Intergroup problem-solving (IGPS) is a technique for improving working relationships among several teams that must work together. It confronts issues such as communicating or withholding information, competition against or collaboration between teams, or coordinating joint efforts. Following is a general design for an IGPS intervention.[23]

The two or more groups meet together in a 1-day session, where they do the following:

1. Each group separately compiles four lists: (1) what they believe are the responsibilities of the *other* group; (2) how they feel about the other group, including its strengths and weaknesses; (3) what the group thinks are its own responsibilities; and (4) what the group anticipates the other group thinks about them (strengths and weaknesses).
2. The groups meet together to share their lists. The only discussion allowed is to clarify points of disagreement, and to prioritize the issues that need to be resolved.
3. The groups separate, this time to discuss what they learned from each other's lists and to prioritize the issues that need to be resolved.
4. Finally, the groups meet together again to discuss differences and develop a plan to resolve them.

A few weeks later, at a follow-up session, they meet to determine how well their plan is working. The result is usually a much-improved understanding of each group's expectations about the other(s), and a more effective working relationship.

IGPS is applied whenever groups interface or must work together. Examples are project and customer teams, and project teams from different organizations and functional areas. Without IGPS, groups often try to optimize their *own goals*, and overall project or program goals suffer. One group does not understand the requirements of another group or share its expectations about what they should do. IGPS is useful whenever there are interdependencies, deadlines, or situations that induce intergroup conflict and stress.

Participants in an intergroup session are likely to have a "gee whiz" experience. Through IGPS, each group may find that their expectations are very different from (and often conflicting with) the expectations of other groups. This realization is a first and necessary step to aligning expectations and planning ways to resolve differences.

One caveat is that groups should *not* be brought together for IGPS until they have first resolved any *internal* problems. A group that does not have its own internal affairs in order should team-build itself before it tries to resolve its relationship problems with other groups.

15.8   ORIGINS OF CONFLICT

In all organizations, differences in objectives, opinions, and values lead to conflict. Project organizations are no exception and, if anything, are predisposed to conflict. Conflict arises between customers and contractors, project staff and functional groups, and different contractors and departments. It occurs between people on the same team, different teams in the same organization, and teams in different organizations. Some conflict is natural; too much is destructive.

Between User and Contractor

Seeds of conflict between the customer and the contractor are sown early in a project during contract negotiations. People representing the two parties are usually less concerned with developing trust than with driving a hard bargain for their own best interests. The customer wants to minimize cost, the contractor to maximize profit. One's gain is the other's loss. In the extreme, each side strives for an agreement that provides an "out" in case it cannot keep its part of the bargain; each tries to make the other side responsible in case of failure. In technology-based firms, the non-technical, "legal types" who negotiate contracts may try to enlarge their prestige by using legalistic frameworks that try to cover all eventualities.[24] Says one manager:

> You start with science and engineering, but the project, once it's decided on, has to be costed. You have to select contractors and get budgets approved. Then you turn to the contractors working with you and write contracts that say you don't trust them. What starts as a fine scientific dream ends up being a mass of slippery eels.[25]

After negotiations are completed, the contract itself becomes a source of conflict. In cost-plus agreements there is little incentive for the contractor to control expenses, and the customer must closely supervise and question everything. Such scrutiny is a constant irritant to the contractor. In fixed price contracts, costs may have to be periodically renegotiated and revised upward. This is also a source of conflict. Any contract that is poorly specified in terms of cost, schedule, or performance is likely to have multiple interpretations and lead to disagreements.

Within the Project Organization

Functionalism is based upon and promotes differences in ideas and objectives. This is good for functional departments because it makes them better at what they do, but bad for projects because the functional areas are somewhat self-serving. High-level interdependency in projects between functional areas increases the amount of contact between them and, at the same time, the chances of conflict. The different areas have different ideas, goals, and solutions for similar problems—differences that sometimes must be resolved without the benefit of a common superior.

In addition, the needs of functional areas are often incompatible with the needs of the project. Functional areas often request changes to the project plan that the project manager must sometimes refuse. The project manager might have to compromise the high technical standards of the research and engineering departments with project time and cost considerations. Even when project managers defer to the technical judgment of specialists, they sometimes disagree over the means of implementation.

Work priorities, schedules, and resource allocations also lead to conflict. The priorities of functional areas working in multiple projects might conflict with priorities of project managers.

In matrix organizations, functional managers sometimes see project managers as impinging on their territory, and they resent having to share planning and control with them. They might refuse to release certain personnel to projects, or try to retain authority over the personnel they do release. Workers with dual reporting relationships are often confused about priorities and loyalties.

Moreover, given that projects are temporary, goal-driven systems, project workers are under constant pressure to meet time and cost objectives. People are ordinarily reluctant to accept change, yet in projects change is the norm. Administrative procedures, group interfaces, project scope, and resource allocations are constantly changing. Expansions and contractions in the labor force make it difficult to establish obligations and reporting relationships that will last.

Finally, projects inherit feuds that have nothing to do with them. Regardless of the setting, clashes arise from differences in attitudes, personal goals, and individual traits, and from people trying to advance their careers. These create a history of antagonisms that set the stage for conflict well before a project begins.

The Project Life Cycle

Thamhain and Wilemon[26] investigated sources of conflict in a study that involved 100 project managers. They determined that the three greatest sources of conflict are schedules, project priorities, and the workforce—all areas over which project managers generally have only limited control. Other sources of conflict identified are technical opinions and performance trade-offs, administrative and organizational issues, interpersonal differences, and costs. Costs are a relatively minor cause of conflict, the authors surmise, not because costs are unimportant but because they are difficult to control and usually dealt with incrementally over a project's life.

They also found that the sources of conflict change from one phase to the next, as summarized in Figure 15.4.

During project conception, the most significant sources of conflict are priorities, administrative procedures, schedules, and labor. Disputes between project and functional areas arise over the relative importance of the project compared to other activities, the amount of control the project manager should have, the personnel to be assigned, and scheduling the project into existing workloads.

During project definition, the chief source of conflict remains priorities, followed by schedules, procedures, and technical issues. Priority conflicts carry over from the previous phase, but new disputes arise over the enforcement of schedules and functional departments' efforts to meet technical requirements.

During the execution phase, friction arises over schedule slippages, technical problems, and labor issues. Deadlines may become difficult to meet because of accumulating schedule slippages. Efforts aimed at system integration, technical performance of subsystems, quality control, and reliability also encounter problems. Manpower requirements grow to a maximum and strain the available pool of workers.

Figure 15.4
Major sources of conflict during the project life cycle.
Adapted with permission from Thamhain H and Wilemon C.
Conflict management in project life cycles. *Sloan Management Review* Spring; 1975: 31–50.

Start ———————	Project life cycle ———————		→ Finish
Project conception	*Project definition*	*Project execution*	*Project closeout*
Priorities	Priorities	Schedules	Schedules
Procedures	Schedules	Technical	Personality
Schedules	Procedures	Manpower	Manpower
Manpower	Technical	Priorities	Priorities

During closeout, schedules remain the biggest source of conflict as accumulated slippages make it difficult to meet the target completion date. Pressures to meet objectives and anxiety over future projects increase tensions and personality-related conflicts. The phasing in of new projects and the absorption of personnel back into functional areas create further conflicts.

15.9 CONSEQUENCES OF CONFLICT

Conflict is inevitable in human endeavors, and is not always detrimental. Properly managed, a certain amount of conflict:[27]

1. Compels people to search for new approaches
2. Causes persistent problems to surface and be dealt with
3. Forces people to clarify their views
4. Stimulates interest and creativity
5. Gives people the opportunity to test their capacities.

In fact, it is unhealthy when there is no conflict. Called *groupthink*, lack of conflict is a sign of over-conformity. It causes dullness and sameness, and results in poor or mediocre judgment. In contrast, conflict over differences in opinion stimulates discussion and can enhance problem-solving. In project groups charged with exploring new ideas or solving complex problems, some conflict is essential.

Conflict between groups that are in competition is beneficial because it increases group cohesion, spirit, loyalty, and the intensity of competition. However, conflict between teams that *should be* cooperating can be devastating. Each group develops an "us versus them" attitude, and selfishly strives to achieve its own objectives. Left uncontrolled and unresolved, destructive conflict spirals upward and creates hostility. Within a project, destructive conflict fosters lack of respect and trust, and destroys communication between groups and individuals. Ideas, opinions, or suggestions of others are rejected or discredited. Project spirit breaks down, and the project organization splinters apart.

Example 15.2: Conflict in Product Development Team[28]

Microsoft forms small teams around products, and then allows them to organize and work as they wish. They hire very bright, aggressive people right out of school, then push them hard to get the most and best out of them.

As author Fred Moody describes, each product team consists of designers whose assignment is to try to add features to the product; developers whose partial role is to resist the features for the sake of meeting deadlines; and a program manager whose role is to mediate and render verdicts. Besides having different assignments and goals, there is a big chasm between developers and designers in terms of temperament, interests, and styles. Developers often feel it is impossible to make the designers understand even the simplest elements of a programming problem. Designers might spend weeks on some aspect of a product, only to be rudely told by a developer that it will be impossible to implement. Designers are from the arts; developers from math and science. Designers tend to be female, vegetarians, talkative, and live in lofts; developers tend to be male, eat fast food, and talk little except to say "Not true." The way they deal with conflict also differs. Developers are given to bursts of mischievous play and will pepper a designer's door with shots from a Nerf-ball gun. Designers merely complain to their supervisor.

This adversarial relationship levies a toll on the team, the product, the customers, and the company. Moody quotes the lead developer on one project, who said,

"I've never been through anything like this. This was the project from hell. We made the same mistakes before, and now we're making them again. Every project is like this. We keep saying that we learn from our mistakes, but we keep going through the same [expletive] over and over again."

15.10 MANAGING CONFLICT[29]

How do project managers deal with conflicts? In general there are five ways:

1. Withdraw or retreat from the disagreement
2. Smooth over or de-emphasize the importance of the disagreement (pretend it does not exist)
3. Force the issue by exerting power
4. Compromise or bargain to bring at least some degree of satisfaction to all parties
5. Confront the conflict directly; work through the disagreement with problem-solving.

All of these are at times appropriate. In a heated argument, it may be best to withdraw until emotions have calmed down, or to de-emphasize the disagreement before it gets distorted out of proportion. But neither of these resolves the problem, which will likely arise again. The project manager might force the issue by using authority; this gets the action done, but risks creating hostility. As discussed earlier, if authority must be used, it is better that it is based upon knowledge or expertise. To bargain or compromise, both sides must be willing to give up something to get something, and, ultimately, they may feel they lost more than they gained. Of the five approaches, the only one that works at resolving the underlying issues is *confrontation*.[30]

Confrontation

Confrontation involves identifying potential or existing problems, then facing up to them. At the organization level, this happens by all areas involved in the project agreeing on project objectives, plans, labor requirements, and priorities. It requires careful monitoring of schedules, close contact between project groups, and prompt resolution of technical problems.[31]

At the individual level, a project manager confronts conflicts by raising questions and challenges such as[32]

How do you know this redesign will solve the problem? Prove it to me.
What have you done to correct the malfunctions that showed up on the test we agreed to?
How do you expect to catch up on lost time when you haven't scheduled overtime?

Questions like these demonstrate that the project manager is vitally interested and alert, and that everything is subject to question. It is a crucial part of effective project management.

However, there is a catch: the very *process* of being confrontational is itself a source of conflict, but at the *interpersonal* level. Frequently, what begins as a conflict of schedules, priorities, or technical matters degenerates into a conflict over power and "personalities."

Successful confrontation assumes a lot about the individuals and groups involved. It assumes that they are willing to reveal why they favor a given course of action, and that they are open to and not hostile toward differing opinions. It assumes that they are all working toward a common goal and are willing to abandon one position in favor of another.

The simple fact is, many groups and managers are highly critical of others' opinions. Faced with differences, they tend to operate emotionally, not analytically. For individuals to use confrontation as a way to resolve conflict, they must first be able to manage their emotions.

15.11 TEAM METHODS FOR RESOLVING CONFLICT

Confrontation assumes that parties can discuss issues frankly, and level with one another. One way the project manager can make confrontation work is with team-building. As discussed earlier, team-building helps members develop attitudes more accepting of differences, and leads to greater openness and trust. It attacks conflict directly by engaging members in problem-solving. The following team methods focus on conflict stemming from work roles and group interaction.

Role Clarification Technique[33]

Conflict in projects often arises because people have mixed expectations about work plans, roles, and responsibilities. In particular, disagreements arise because:

- The project is new and people are not clear about what they are supposed to do and what others expect of them
- Changes in projects and work reassignments have made it unclear how individuals in the team should interact
- People get requests they do not understand, or hear about things on the grapevine that they think they should already know
- Everyone thinks someone else is handling a situation that, really, no one is
- People do not understand what their group or other groups are doing.

The *role clarification technique (RCT)* is a systematic procedure to help resolve these sources of conflict. As the title "role clarification" suggests, the goal is that everyone understands their own and others' major responsibilities and duties, and that everyone knows what others expect of them.[34]

RCT is similar to team-building. It includes data collection, a day-long meeting, and a consultant who serves as facilitator. When incorporated as part of team-building for a new team, it allows the project manager and team to negotiate team member roles. It is especially useful in cases where responsibilities are somewhat ambiguous.

The technique as applied to an existing team begins with each person answering a questionnaire prior to a meeting:[35]

1. What does the organization expect of you in your job?
2. What do you actually do in your job?
3. What should others know about your job that would help them?
4. What do you need to know about others' jobs that would help you?
5. What difficulties do you experience with others?
6. What changes in the organization or activities would improve the group's work?

For a new team, the questions would be modified to reflect job expectations and anticipated problems.

At the start of the group meeting, ground rules are announced: people must be candid, give honest responses, and express their concerns, and everyone must agree to decisions. The meeting begins with each person reading the answers to the first three questions. As each person reads, others are given the chance to respond. It is important that each person hears how others see her job and what they expect of her.

Each person then reads the answer to Question 4 and hears responses from the people she identified. Issues in Question 5 that have not already been resolved are addressed next. Throughout the process, the emphasis is on solving problems, not placing blame. The group then discusses Question 6 and tries to reach consensus about needed changes.[36]

Intergroup Conflict Resolution[37]

When two or more groups conflict because of mixed expectations, a procedure similar to intergroup problem-solving (IGPS) can be used. The procedure begins with each group preparing a list of what they would like the other groups to start doing, stop doing, and continue doing in order to improve relations. As a variation, the groups might also guess what the others think about them and want from them. Guesses are often accurate and facilitate reaching an agreement.

The groups share their lists in a meeting, and negotiate an agreement stating what each will do in return for equitable changes on the part of the other. The focus is on finding solutions, not fault. A facilitator oversees the meeting and the negotiation. To increase the groups' commitment, the agreements are put in writing.

Another approach is for Team A to select a subgroup of members to represent it. Names in the subgroup are given to Team B, which selects three or four members from the list. Team B also prepares a list of names and gives it to Team A. This creates a mixed team with representatives that both sides agree to. The mixed team tries to resolve problems between the teams. It can interview people in other teams, invite a facilitator, and so on. The mixed team prepares a list of actions, people to be responsible, a time frame, and ways to prevent problems from recurring. This approach is easy to implement without a consultant, and requires less involvement from members than the first method, but it also tends to have less impact.

There are several preconditions for these procedures to be effective in resolving conflict. The conflicting parties must agree that they have problems, that the problems should be solved, that they both have a responsibility to work on them, and that they need to come together to solve them. Often it is easier to get people to deal with conflict if they realize that the purpose is not to get them to like each other but to understand and be able to work with each other.

15.12 EMOTIONAL STRESS[38]

There are numerous downsides to working in projects. Long hours, tight schedules, high risks, and high stakes take a toll on social and family relationships, and on individual mental and physical health. Projects achieve great things, but they also instigate ulcers, divorce, mental breakdowns, and heart attacks. One of the major problems associated with working in projects—and a contributor to personal, family, and organizational difficulties—is emotional stress. It is a problem that affects the performance and health of project workers and that, at one time or another, every project manager faces.

Factors Influencing Stress

How much emotional stress a person experiences, and whether that experience is positive or negative, depends upon the fit between two factors: the demands or threats of the environment, and the adaptive capabilities of the person. In other words, work-related stress depends upon a person's perception of the demands or opportunities of the job and his self-perceived abilities, self-confidence, and motivation to perform. A manager faced with impending failure to meet a deadline might experience stress if he feels the deadline must be met at all costs, but no stress if he simply accepts that meeting the deadline is impossible. Stress is a reaction to prolonged internal and environmental conditions that overtax a person's adaptive capabilities. To feel distress (negative stress), an individual's capabilities must be overtaxed. Even when a person has the ability to handle a situation, he will still feel distressed if he lacks self-confidence or cannot make a decision.

Stress in Projects

Among numerous causes of distress in projects are rapid pace, a transient work force, anxiety over discrepancies between performance and goals, and impending failure to meet cost, schedule, or contract requirements. In construction, for example, in the words of Bryman and colleagues:

> [The project manager] is in the front line controlling the labor force; he's answerable to the client, to his organization at a high level; he's responsible for millions of pounds [or $] worth of work . . . In a very fragile environment he is at the mercy of the weather, material deliveries, problems with labor, and problems with getting information.[39]

We will restrict discussion about stress in projects to three main causes: work overload, role conflict, and interpersonal relations.

Work overload is experienced in two ways. One is simply having too much work or doing too many things at once, with time pressures, long hours, and no let-up. The other is taking on work that exceeds one's ability and knowledge. Overload can be self-induced by an individual's need to achieve, or it can be imposed by the responsibilities of the job. Job-induced work overload is prevalent during crash efforts to recover lost ground, and when projects are rushed toward completion. When overload is in balance with abilities, it is positive and motivating. When it exceeds ability, it is distressful. A related problem, *work underload*, occurs when there is too little work, or the work is beneath a person's ability. Project workers suffer from underload whenever there is a long hiatus between projects.

Role conflict happens, for instance, when a person reports to a functional manager *and* a project manager, and the two managers impose contradictory or incompatible demands. It also happens when a person has multiple roles with incompatible requirements. For example, a project manager may find that being a good administrator requires doing things that conflict with his values as a professional engineer. *Role ambiguity* results from inadequate or confusing information about what a person needs to do to fulfill his job, or about the consequences of not meeting requirements of the job. The person knows neither where he stands nor what to do next.

Role conflict and role ambiguity are common in projects because workers must interact with and satisfy the expectations of many people. Project managers in particular might find their work frustrating and stressful because the authority they need to carry out project responsibilities is often inadequate.

Stress also develops from the demands and pressures of *interpersonal relations*. A boss who is self-centered and dictatorial causes his workers stress. Irritable, abrasive, or condescending personalities are hard to work with; they make others feel unimportant and provoke anxiety.

In short, the typical project is a haven of environmental stressors; stress is inevitable.

15.13   Stress Management

Most people accept distress as the price of success. However, although stress is inevitable, *distress* (negative stress) is not. Project managers should be able to anticipate which work demands are most stressful, and try to ameliorate the negative effects.

In general, means for reducing negative stress at work are aimed either at changing the organizational conditions that cause stress or at helping people to cope better with stress. Because stress results from the interaction of people with their environment, both are necessary. Organizational means are aimed at task, role, physical, and interpersonal stressors; individual means are aimed at people's ability to manage and respond to stressful demands. We will focus on organizational means—methods applied by managers to reduce the stress in projects.[40]

Set Reasonable Plans and Schedules

One way to reduce stress is preplanning and scheduling projects so as to allow for reasonable work hours and time off. Well-conceived plans and schedules prepared in advance help balance the workload; they tell workers what is expected and when, and help avoid ambiguous expectations, work overload, and the "crunch" that precedes milestones and project closeout.

Modify Work Demands through Participation

The distressful influence of some kinds of leadership styles is well known. Dictatorial, self-centered leaders (the too-bossy boss) cause frustration and annoyance; the opposite kind, the do-nothing, under-stimulating boss is just as bad. In contrast, there is supporting research that the least stressful style of leadership is participative.[41] Allowing workers decision latitude and autonomy commensurate with work demands and their ability is one way to reduce stressful project demands. Participative leaders set goals and define task limits, but allow workers considerable flexibility as to how the goals and limits will be achieved.

Social Support

One way to reduce stress arising from work roles and relationships is to increase *social support* within project teams. Social support is the assistance one gets through interpersonal relationships. Generally, people are better able to cope when they feel others care about and are willing to help them.[42] Social support at work comes in the form of listening and caring, fairly appraising performance, and giving advice, information, and direct assistance in a task.

Vital sources of social support are family, close friends, and a supportive boss, co-workers, and subordinates. Social support from managers and co-workers does not necessarily alter the stressor, but it does help people to cope better. Supportive managers act as barriers against destructive stress, and their subordinates are less likely to suffer harmful consequences than those with unsupportive managers.[43] Co-worker social support is equally important, though often the groups' supportiveness correlates with the amount of support modeled by the leader. Caught between the conflicting expectations of a functional manager and project manager, a person with supportive co-workers will be better able to deal with the conflict.

How do people become supportive? Simply telling someone to be supportive does not work. Even when managers try to be supportive by giving advice, they often leave the distressed person worse off. Giving physical assistance is easy, but giving true emotional support is difficult and subtler. Empathic listening, understanding, and real concern are essential parts of support often missing in naive efforts to help. Thus, usually, it is necessary to provide training in social support skills and then reinforce and reward the usage of these skills. Unfortunately, as with many other behavioral aspects of management, empathy and sensitivity are considered "soft" issues and are devalued as "non-productive."

15.14   SUMMARY

According to contingency theories of leadership, the most effective leadership style in the majority of project situations is relations-oriented and participative; this is because project managers must rely upon the opinions of members of the project team and others.

A significant factor affecting project performance is team cohesiveness and teamwork. Teamwork must be developed and nurtured. Especially when a project comprises team members from different backgrounds or exposes members to high stress, groups need help in developing effective teamwork. Team-building methods are applicable to a variety of situations, such as for resolving problems in an experienced team, building teamwork in a new group, or resolving issues and building teamwork between two or more groups. With slight variation, these methods can be adapted to bring customers, subcontractors, and suppliers together at the start of a project.

Conflict is inevitable in organizations, and, properly managed, beneficial. The primary sources of conflict in projects are schedules, costs, priorities, manpower levels, technical opinions, administrative issues, and interpersonal conflicts, which vary in relative importance depending on the stages of the project life cycle. Conflict is generally best dealt with through confrontation—i.e., examining the issues and attempting to resolve the conflict at its source. Confrontation presumes, however, that people will be open, honest, and willing to work together to resolve the conflict. Lacking these conditions or poorly handled, confrontation can lead to hostility and personality conflicts.

Conflict often occurs because of a violation of expectations between parties. Role clarification and intergroup conflict resolution are two techniques for resolving conflict through parties sharing, clarifying, and reaching mutual agreement on expectations.

Stress in projects is inevitable. Stress induces energy, increases vitality, and helps people deal with the demands of work. However, stress from too few or too many work demands can be debilitating. In projects, the main sources of stress are demanding goals and schedules, work tasks, roles, and social relations. Advance planning of workloads and deadlines can help reduce many of the technical sources of stress. Participative management and social support help workers cope with stress; the former gives workers latitude in meeting requirements, the latter shows workers that others care about them and are willing to assist or provide support.

REVIEW QUESTIONS AND PROBLEMS

1. Explain the difference between task-oriented and relations-oriented leadership styles.
2. Describe the contingency approach to leadership. According to this approach, what is the best way to lead?
3. Discuss the differences between the leadership models of Fiedler and Hersey-Blanchard. What do these models say about leadership in the situations faced by project managers?
4. How is participative management useful for motivating and gaining commitment?
5. Why is teamwork important in projects? Isn't it enough that individual workers are highly skilled and motivated?
6. What characteristics are common to Vaill's high-performing systems?
7. What is meant by group process issues? What kinds of issues do they include?
8. What is the purpose of team-building? Where is team-building needed?
9. Outline the steps in a team-building session for a group that has been working together. Outline the steps for building a new project team.
10. Outline the steps in the IGPS process.
11. What conditions of management and the team members are necessary for team-building interventions to succeed?
12. Describe some situations that you know of where team-building could be used.
13. What do you think are the reasons why team-building is not used more often? What barriers are there to applying team-building?
14. What are the sources of conflict between the user and the contractor? How do contracts lead to conflict?
15. What are the sources of conflict between parties in the project organization?
16. Describe how the sources of conflict vary with the phases of the project life cycle.
17. What are the negative consequences of conflict in projects?
18. Explain why some conflict is natural and beneficial.
19. Describe five ways of dealing with conflict.
20. Explain how the project manager uses confrontation to resolve conflict.
21. What conditions must exist for confrontation to be successful?
22. Describe the role clarification technique. What sources of conflict does it resolve?
23. Describe intergroup problem-solving. What sources of conflict does it resolve?
24. Describe each of these major sources of stress in project environment: project goals and schedules, work overload, role conflict and ambiguity, and social/interpersonal relations. Describe your work experiences with these sources of stress.
25. Describe the means by which (a) participative management and (b) role clarification help to reduce work stress.
26. What is "social support?" What are the sources of social support? How does social support reduce job stress?
27. What are some ways of improving social support among project team members?

1. How would you characterize the leadership style of the project manager in your project? Is it authoritarian, *laissez faire* (do nothing), or participative? Is the project manager task-oriented, relations-oriented, or both?
2. What kind of people must the project manager influence? Given the theories of this chapter, is the project manager's leadership style appropriate? Despite the theories, does the style used by the project manager seem to be effective?
3. What do you think are the primary work motivators for people in this project? Discuss the relative importance of salary, career potential, incentives, and participation in decision-making.
4. Describe the different groups (management teams, project office, functional groups) that comprise the project team in this project.
5. What mechanisms are used to link these teams—for example, coordinators, frequent meetings, or close proximity of workers?
6. What kinds of formal and informal activities are used to increase the cohesiveness of the project team? Can any of these be termed team-building?
7. What steps are taken to resolve problems involving multiple groups?
8. How would you characterize the level of teamwork in this project?
9. Ask the project manager if he or she knows about formal team-building and intergroup problem-solving procedures like those described in this book.
10. At the end of this (or other projects), what does the organization do to disband a team? Are there any procedures for giving recognition or dealing with members' feelings about disbanding?
11. How prevalent is conflict, and what effect does it have on individual and project performance?
12. How does the project manager resolve conflict? Is confrontation used?
13. Are any formal procedures used, such as RCT or IGPS, to resolve conflicts?
14. Emotional stress is a personal issue, and most people are hesitant to speak about it other than on a general level. Still, you might ask the project manager or other team members about stresses they personally feel or perceive in the project.
15. Is this a high-stress or low-stress project? Explain. If high stress, is it taken for granted that that is the way it must be or do people feel steps could be taken to reduce the stress?
16. Does the project manager try to help team members deal with job stress? Explain.

Case 15.1 Wilma Keith

Wilma Keith had worked for over 20 years as a successful project manager, but even with that background she found the Wiseteam Project frustrating and overwhelming. Soon after being assigned to the project she met with Cappun Queeg, vice president of communications. "Wilma," he said, "the long and short of it is that the Wiseteam Project *must* be completed and operational within 6 months." She had already estimated the project would take about a year and protested. Queeg became annoyed and told her "Just do it!" Wilma scoured the company for the best people she could

find, settling on four young technical analysts from different departments. None of them was people-oriented or very good at communicating; technically, however, they were the best. Upon reviewing the project requirements, they all agreed: it would take a year—at least. When Wilma reported back to Queeg, he said, simply, "If you don't finish this in 6 months, you're fired. That's a promise!"

So Wilma set the team to work. Everyone knew Queeg's deadline. At one point he dropped by to say that if they didn't succeed they would *all* be fired. This unnerved the analysts, but Wilma promised them that if anyone were to be fired, it would be her, not them. She also promised that she would handle all dealings with Queeg, buffer them from his abuse, and take responsibility for any delays or problems. The team warmed to Wilma and set out to work—on average 6 days a week, 15–20 hours a day. Wilma never left them; if they were working, so was she. She started bringing brownies—lots of brownies—acting like a "den mother," and treating the team like they were family. Indeed, given the long hours, the team seldom saw their real families and Wilma's maternal care seemed to fill a void.

Several months into the project, Queeg stormed in and asked Wilma why she had requested help from two outside consultants. She said despite the unbearably long work hours, the team was still behind and needed additional resources to meet the deadline. Queeg fumed that he was not about to hire any consultants. Wilma looked him straight in the eyes. "You don't, and I quit!" Queeg knew she was serious. "Alright," he said, "but that's all you'll get." The team was amazed: Wilma had stood up to the vice president. This bonded them even more and united them against the common "enemy."

The intense pressure, long hours, strong competency of the team, and Wilma's nurturing worked: the team finished the project 2 weeks early and under budget—even with the expense of the two consultants. But ultimately the project was a failure because the Wiseteam system that Queeg had demanded did not provide any new benefits to its users. Queeg had never talked to the users; Wiseteam was his own "pet" project. A year later, he was gone from the company.

QUESTIONS

1. What do you think about Wilma's leadership style? What aspects of her style motivated the team? Would you say Wilma's style is more task-oriented or relations-oriented?
2. What aspects of Wilma's style do you think are typical of good project managers?
3. This was a stressful project. What did Wilma do that helped the team manage stress?
4. Is this case realistic? Are unrealistic demands like this actually put on project managers?

Case 15.2 Mars Climate Orbiter Spacecraft[44]

NASA designed the Mars Climate Orbiter spacecraft to collect data about Mars' atmospheric conditions and serve as a data relay station. Instruments aboard the Orbiter would provide detailed information about the temperature, dust, water vapor, and carbon dioxide in Mars' atmosphere for approximately 2 Earth years. The Orbiter would also provide a relay point for data transmissions to and from spacecraft on the surface of Mars for up to 5 years.

Nine months after launch, the Orbiter arrived in the vicinity of Mars and fired its main engine to go into orbit around the planet. Everything looked normal as it passed behind Mars as seen from the Earth. After that, however, the Orbiter was never heard from again; presumably it had crashed into the planet. Paraphrasing project manager Richard Cook:

We had planned to approach the planet at an altitude of about 150 kilometers, but upon review of data leading up to the arrival, we saw indications that the approach altitude was much lower, about 60 kilometers. We believe the minimum survivable altitude for the spacecraft would have been 85 kilometers.

Later, an internal peer review attributed the $280 million mission loss to an error in the information passed between the two teams responsible for the Orbiter's operations: the spacecraft team in Colorado, and the mission navigation team in California. In communicating back and forth, one team had used imperial units (feet, pounds), the other had used metric units (meters, grams). Without knowing it, the two teams were using different measurement systems for information critical for maneuvering the spacecraft into proper Mars orbit.

QUESTIONS

1. How could such a mistake have occurred between the two teams?
2. What does the mistake suggest about the degree of interaction and coordination between the teams?
3. How might this problem have been prevented?

NOTES

1. Chapman R. *Project Management in NASA: The System and the Men.* Washington, DC: NASA SP-324, NTIS No. N75-15692; 1973. The project team Chapman refers to is the project office staff, which numbered from a few members on small matrix projects to 70 in large pure project organizations.
2. Kloman E. *Unmanned Space Project Management.* Washington, DC: NASA SP-4102; 1972: 23.
3. Fiedler F. *A Theory of Leadership Effectiveness.* New York, NY: McGraw-Hill; 1967.
4. Hersey P and Blanchard K. *Management of Organization Behavior: Utilizing Human Resources,* 4th edn. Upper Saddle River, NJ: Prentice Hall; 1982. pp. 150–173.
5. Hersey P and Blanchard K. Managing research and development personnel: an application of leadership theory. *Research Management* September; 1969.
6. Bryman A, Bresnan M, Beardsworth A, Ford J, and Keil E. The concept of the temporary system: the case of the construction project. *Research in the Sociology and Psychology of Organizations* 5; 1987: 253–283.
7. Sayles L and Chandler M. *Managing Large Systems: Organizations for the Future.* New York, NY: Harper & Row; 1971. p. 219.
8. For a discussion of the interpersonal and leadership requirements for the matrix, see Davis SM and Lawrence PR. *Matrix.* Reading, MA: Addison-Wesley; 1977. pp. 108–109.
9. Bennis W and Nanus B. *Leadership: Strategies for Taking Charge.* New York, NY: Harper & Row; 1985. pp. 224–225.
10. Vaill P. The purposing of high-performing systems. *Organizational Dynamics.* Autumn; 1982: 23–39.
11. *Ibid.*, p. 38.
12. This discussion is largely based on Hofer W. Lady Liberty's business army. *Nation's Business* July; 1983: 18–28; see also Hall A. Liberty lifts her lamp once more. *National Geographic* July; 1986: 2–19.
13. Hofer, Lady Liberty's business army, pp. 18–28.
14. *Ibid.*, p. 28.
15. *Ibid.*, p. 21.
16. Nicholas J. Developing effective teams for system design and implementation. *Production and Inventory Management* Third Quarter; 1980: 37–47; and Nicholas J. Organization development in systems management. *Journal of Systems Management* 30(11); 1979: 24–30. Much of the following discussion is derived from these sources.
17. See Chapman, *Project Management in NASA,* pp. 59–62. The other functions of project management were defined to be project planning, information and control, and consultation.
18. Keller R. Predictors of the performance of project groups in R&D organizations. *Academy of Management Journal* 29(4); 1986: 715–726.
19. See, for example, Dyer W. *Team Building: Current Issues and New Alternatives,* 3rd edn. Reading MA: Addison-Wesley; 1995; Nicholas, Organization development in systems management, pp. 24–30; Reilly A and Jones J. Team building. In Pfeiffer J and Jones J (eds), *Annual Handbook of Group Facilitators.* LaJolla, CA: University Associates; 1974.
20. Nicholas, Organization development in systems management.
21. This discussion is largely based on Dyer, *Team Building.*
22. Davis and Lawrence, *Matrix,* p. 134.
23. Blake R, Shepard H, and Mouton J. *Managing Intergroup Conflicts in Industry.* Houston, TX: Gulf Publishing; 1965.
24. Sayles and Chandler, *Managing Large Systems,* pp. 277–278.
25. *Ibid.*, p. 278.
26. Thamhain H and Wilemon D. Conflict management in project life cycles. *Sloan Management Review* Spring; 1975: 31–50; and Thamhain H and Wilemon D. Diagnosing conflict determinants in project management. *IEEE Transactions of Engineering Management* 22; 1975.
27. Schmidt W. Conflict: a powerful process for (good or bad) change. *Management Review* 63; 1974: 5.
28. Moody F. *I Sing the Body Electronic.* New York, NY: Viking; 1995. pp. 110–115.

29. This section focuses on managing conflict from a group level perspective. For an individual level perspective, see Robert M. *Managing Conflict from the Inside Out*. Austin, TX: Learning Concepts; 1982.

30. It is not only the best approach, it is also the one most favored by project managers (followed by compromise, then smoothing, then forcing and withdrawal). See Thamhain and Wilemon, Conflict management in project life cycles, pp. 42–44.

31. *Ibid.*, pp. 46–47.

32. Sayles and Chandler, *Managing Large Systems*, p. 216.

33. This discussion is based upon Dyer, *Team Building*, pp. 109–116.

34. *Ibid.*, p. 111.

35. *Ibid.*, p. 112.

36. *Ibid.*, pp. 113–114.

37. *Ibid.*, pp. 116–117, 135.

38. Portions of this section are adapted from Huse E and Cummings T. *Organization Development and Change*, 3rd edn. St Paul, MN: West; 1985. Ch. 12; Quick J and Quick J. *Organizational Stress and Preventive Management*.

New York, NY: McGraw-Hill; 1984; and Williams J. *Human Behavior in Organizations*, 2nd edn. Cincinnati, OH: South-Western; 1982. Ch. 9.

39. Bryman A, Bresnen M, Beardsworth AD, Ford J and Keil ET. The concept of the temporary system: the case of the construction project. *Research in the Sociology and Psychology of Organizations* 5; 1987: 253–283.

40. Portions of this section are adapted from Huse and Cummings, *Organization Development and Change*; Quick and Quick, *Organizational Stress and Preventive Management*; Williams, *Human Behavior in Organizations*; House JS, *Work Stress and Social Support*. Reading, MA: Addison-Wesley; 1981; and Warshaw LJ. *Managing Stress*. Reading, MA: Addison-Wesley; 1982.

41. See research cited in Quick and Quick, *Organizational Stress and Preventive Management*, p. 170.

42. House, *Work Stress and Social Support*, pp. 22–26, 30–38.

43. *Ibid.*, pp. 98, 99.

44. NASA website, December 1999.

Part V

Project Management in the Corporate Context

*B*eyond skilled project leaders and good project management tools and methods, what else does an organization need to enhance its project success? One part of the answer is that the organization must support its managers and encourage and enable them to apply project management best practices; the other part is that the organization must take on projects that are viable and beneficial to the organization; i.e., it must select projects that meet sound criteria based upon organizational objectives and available resources. These are the topics of Chapter 16 and Chapter 17.

In today's growing globalization of industries, businesses, and technology, a topic of increasing importance is international project management—the subject of Chapter 18. International project management involves most everything else covered in this book (although from an international perspective), so the chapter serves as a fitting summary and review of project management.

Chapter **16**

The Management of Project Management

> *If you can't describe what you are doing as a process,*
> *you don't know what you're doing.*
>
> —W. Edwards Deming

> *He attacked everything in life with a mix of extraordinary*
> *genius and naïve incompetence, and it was often*
> *difficult to tell which was which.*
>
> —Douglas Adams

*T*he topics in this chapter address an organization's policies and practices regarding the management of *all* of its projects. In most cases, such policies and practices stem from senior management decisions about what is necessary or desirable to manage projects, and what the organization, as a whole, must do to improve project execution and outcomes. Project managers can only do so much. Beyond that requires measures the *organization* must take to enhance the likelihood of project success; these measures relate to project management methodology, project management maturity, knowledge management, and the project management office (PMO).

Project management methodology is a framework and process mandated or recommended by an organization for the management of its projects. It often includes many of the topics of this book, though organized in whatever way suits the organization. It provides a structure so that all projects are managed and performed in a standardized, disciplined, and systematic manner, using practices that increase the likelihood of projects meeting requirements of the organization and the customer. The methodology is created or adopted by the organization so as to uniquely fit its business requirements, procedures, and culture, and the size, scope, technology, and nature of its projects.

Although some methodologies prescribe the technical tasks of the project, our focus is on those that emphasize the *management* of projects.

Why Methodology?

By encouraging or requiring conformance to a prescribed project management methodology, an organization helps assure that all of its projects will be conducted and managed in a consistent manner. Lacking a methodology, individual project managers will use their own management practices and styles—some good, some not so good. Every project is managed differently, even those managed by the same person.

The aim of the methodology is to ensure that recognized "good" and "best" project management practices are applied across all projects, and to elevate the management practices of all project managers to those of the best in the organization. The methodology provides a common way to do things and a common terminology. When everyone does things in similar ways, communication and learning about those ways are enhanced.

Of course, for the organization and managers to benefit from the methodology, they must accept and practice it. Managers accustomed to a structured, documented approach to project management will readily adopt the methodology, but those not accustomed might find it burdensome.

What Does the Methodology Mandate?

The methodology specifies the stages of the life cycle for the organization's projects, and the particular roles and management tasks of project managers and stakeholders during each stage. For instance, it specifies who is responsible for initiating, proposing, and reviewing and selecting projects. It specifies the roles and responsibilities within the project review board (discussed in Chapter 17) and the PMO (discussed later in this chapter). The methodology also spells out the individuals who must sign-off on budgets and schedules, and approve performance results at project gates.

Phases and Gates

Most projects are conducted in stepwise fashion. The project management methodology defines the phases or stages of the project—that projects are divided into, for example, the stages of initiation, feasibility, definition, development, and launch—and then states what should happen in each. Often, at the start of each stage is a "gate," so-called because at that point the preceding phase, imminent phase, and the rest of the project are assessed and a decision is made to move on, hold, or cancel the project. The number of stages and gates depends on the methodology; the minimum is usually 4 or 5. Motorola has 16 stages and 5 gates for its Cellular Systems Group. The gates represent decision points for, say, approval of project initiation, systems requirements, system validation, and system launch. Decisions at each gate are based on specific criteria.

The gating process is common in organizations that conduct concurrent internal projects in, for example, product development, IT, or infrastructure and process improvement, and where the projects "compete" for product or market goals and resources. It is one way of culling weaker, less promising projects so that scarce resources are available for the stronger, more promising projects. The process also helps reduce risk for large, stand-alone projects. Application of the gating process in project selection and portfolio management is described in Chapter 17.

Relationship with Project Life Cycle

Figure 16.1 illustrates a project management methodology for a seven-stage project life cycle (Initiation through Maintenance). In general, the methodology should conform to the technical and business practices of the organization; for example, in the methodology in Figure 16.1, stages 4 and 5 must be able to accommodate whatever development methodology the organization employs, such as waterfall, spiral, iterative, or Scrum.

Elements of the Methodology

The content of the project management methodology has been the subject of most of this book. In fact, one way to create a methodology is to look at the topics and methods in project management books, determine which of them are applicable to the organization's projects, and then arrange them into a framework that follows the project life cycle.

However, the actual content and details of the methodology—its tasks and requirements—depend on the scope and scale of the organization's projects. For large, complex, risky projects, the methodology would specify detailed tasks and methods for analysis, definition, planning, monitoring, control, and closeout. For small, no-risk projects, a somewhat simplistic methodology is more appropriate. Choices about

Figure 16.1
Project life cycle phases versus project management methodology.

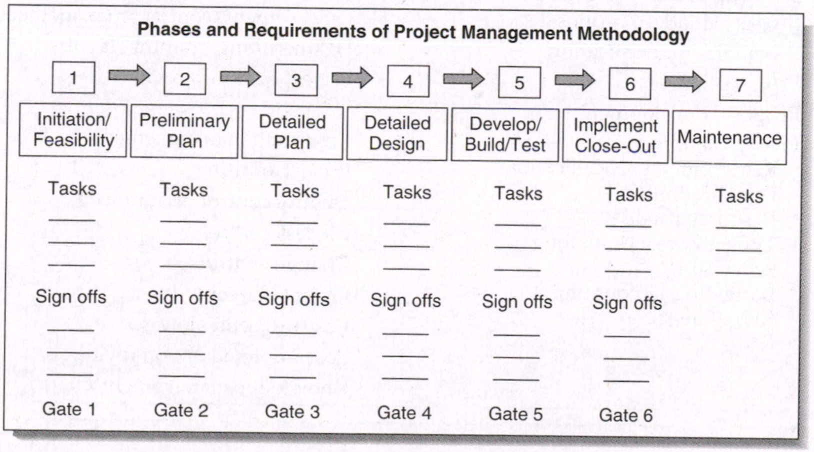

which aspects of the methodology might be bypassed and which must be followed in a given project should be stated in the methodology, and not left to the discretion of the project manager.

A typical methodology defines the phases or stages of the project life cycle and for each phase the tasks and deliverables, and stakeholders and their responsibilities.

Project Life Cycle

This book has used the phases of conception, definition, and execution, each with a series of stages; in general, however, a particular project may be defined in terms of any number of phases or stages. The methodology defines the nominal phases or stages in terms of whatever best represents the "natural" progression of the organization's projects, from initiation to execution and closeout. The methodology can also identify what happens before and after the project (the methodology in Figure 16.1 includes the post-project stage of Maintenance).

Required Tasks and Deliverables

For each phase or stage, the methodology specifies project management tasks and deliverables such as documents, plans, reports, and performance metrics. As an example, *Phase 1: Initiation/Feasibility* of the methodology in Figure 16.1 might specify the following tasks and deliverables:

- Assemble team and identify stakeholders
- Prepare project charter
- Prepare a preliminary task list
- Perform risk analysis and prepare key-risk list
- Develop a requirements list
- Prepare funding request
- Prepare resource plan, timeline, spending plan
- Prepare project proposal.

The methodology will include tasks and deliverables that cover virtually all of the topics covered in this book, such as those in Table 16.1.

Table 16.1 Project Management Tasks and Deliverables

Project initiation/proposal	Procurement/contract management
Stakeholder identification	HR recruiting, training, layoffs
Project selection	Project tracking/review
Proposal development	Data entry
Project planning	Reporting to management
Requirements/specifications	Project auditing
Work definition	Quality control/assurance
Resource needds	Process control
Time and cost estimating	Change control
Scheduling	Project closeout
Budgeting/accounting	Post-project review
Risk analysis	Post-implementation review
	Knowledge management

Who is Responsible—Sign-Offs and Approvals

As shown in Figure 16.1, the methodology might include gates at which the project must be approved before it can proceed. The methodology would specify the persons who have sign-off authority, and the roles of particular stakeholders such as the client, sponsor, champion, and project manager.

The methodology for a large corporation is shown in Figure 16.2. Interesting in its details, it exemplifies the scope and depth of tasks, deliverables, and responsibilities denoted in a comprehensive project management methodology.

One Size Fits All?

Most methodologies are somewhat flexible. They specify project management requirements at a high level for a generic kind of project, but allow for inclusion of other requirements, depending on the unique features of each project. When all projects in an organization tend to be the same in terms of scope, size, and complexity, then one methodology might be suitable for all of them.

Figure 16.2
Comprehensive six-stage project management methodology.

Project Approval	Customer Requirements	Solution Analysis/ Recommendation	Detailed Design	Attain the Solution	Solution Implementation
Preliminary Plan	**Preliminary Plan**	**Detailed Plan**	**Working Plan**	**Working Plan**	**Working Plan**
Project initiation form	Updated project initiation form	Updated project initiation form	Updated project initiation form	Updated project initiation form	Updated project initiation form
Preliminary task list	Preliminary task list	Preliminary task list	Detailed task list	Detailed task list	Detailed task list
Risk analysis	Risk analysis	Risk analysis	Risk analysis	Risk analysis	Risk analysis
Issue log	Issue log	Issue log	Issue log	Issue log	Issue log
Prelim customer business unit analysis	Scope management	Scope management	Scope management	Scope management	Scope management
	Prelim customer business unit analysis	Prelim customer business unit analysis	Final customer business unit analysis	Final customer business unit analysis	Final customer business unit analysis
Deliverables			Benefits realization plan	Benefits realization plan	Testing plan/QA
Project initiation form	**Deliverables**	**Deliverables**	Implementation plan	Implementation plan	Implementation plan
• general business case	Process definition	Conceptual design	Conversion plan	Conversion plan	Conversion plan
• project description	Business function requirements	Solution evaluation	Training plan	Training plan	Training plan
• project timeline		Feasibility/proof of concept	Resource plan	Resource plan	Resource plan
• project spending plan	• business model	Customer sign-off document	Procurement plan	Procurement plan	Procurement plan
• assumptions	• work process flows	Contingency plan	Documentation plan	Procurement plan	Documentation plan
• dependencies	Define target population	Fit analysis	Operations/support plan	Documentation plan	Operations/support plan
• potential risks	Current and proposed states	• architecture		Operations/support plan	Benefits realization plan
• project team	Outputs/inputs	• functionality	**Deliverables**		
• governance team	Budget cap	• skills	Business impact plan	**Deliverables**	**Deliverables**
• requirements for next phase	Business rules	• training	• detailed work flow	QA/user test documentation	Closure document
• ROI	Policy changes		• organization impact	Implementation checklist	Final communication
• sign-offs	Metrics		• business process	Change management	Shut-down old systems
Resource plan	Security		• reengineering		Hand-off to operations
High-level requirements	Regulatory		• operations impact		Project post-completion review
Change control process	Environmental		• resource plan		Schedule benefits review
Communication strategy	Interfacing		QA/user test plan		
	Recovery requirements		Back-out plan		
			Security		
	Phase Review: Governance Team	**Phase Review: Governance Team**	**Phase Review: Governance Team**	**Phase Review: Governance Team**	**Phase Review: Governance Team**
Sign-offs	**Sign-offs**	**Sign-offs**	**Sign-offs**	**Sign-offs**	**Sign-offs**
Project sponsor	Project sponsor	Project sponsor	Project sponsor	Project sponsor	Project sponsor
Project champion	Project champion	Project champion	Project champion	Project champion	Project champion
Project manager	Project manager	Project manager	Project manager	Project manager	Project manager
Governance team	Governance team	Governance team	Governance team	Governance team	Governance team
Customer business unit manager		Customer business unit manager	Customer business unit manager		

To accommodate projects of different size and complexity, the methodology can be "scalable." It might come in, say, three or four versions, the particular one to be applied depending on the capital resources, labor hours, duration, number of work packages and contractors, and risk of the project. One problem with multiple methodologies, however, is deciding which one is appropriate for a given project. The decision is usually based upon factors of the project, such as novelty, complexity, technology, and pace.[2]

Most organizations have one basic—perhaps scalable—methodology because all of their projects tend to be similar. Some organizations, however, such as oil and gas companies that are involved in several different categories of projects (product development, exploration, construction of refineries and pipelines, applied research, marketing) have multiple, different methodologies. One methodology would be applied to, say, projects in search of new oil sources, another for projects to construct new refineries or ocean-drilling platforms. The technical stages, tasks, and even life cycles of these projects differ, and call for somewhat different project management methodologies.

Creating the Methodology

Two ways an organization develops a methodology are (1) to create it from scratch, or (2) to adopt it from elsewhere. In the first way, a small group of the organization's best project managers meet with the purpose of creating a methodology that incorporates methods they all use or recognize as good and believe should be adopted for use in every project. In the second way, managers look at methodologies created by other organizations and that represent industry standards, and adopt portions of the ones they find most suitable. Examples of industry "standard" project management methodologies are Prince2 (meaning PRojects IN Controlled Environments), widely used in the UK, and PMBOK (Project Management Body of Knowledge), published by PMI in the US. Both standards include processes, tools, and techniques that can be incorporated into a methodology. Various companies have developed their own somewhat unique methodologies, some which can be found online. Many of these methodologies are similar in terms of scope and details, and are a good source for ideas.

When an organization adopts an industry standard or another organization's methodology, it uses that standard or methodology as a baseline from which to create a methodology precisely tailored to its own projects and business practices. Ideally the tailoring is done by a group of the organization's best project managers (not by senior managers or outside consultants); this helps ensure that the methodology is appropriate for the organization's projects and resources, and will be accepted by its project managers.

Evolving, Continually Improving Methodology

A project management methodology is not a static thing. Like all frameworks or systems, it is subject to change and improvement based upon experience and a changing environment. A methodology should be periodically reviewed to incorporate changes in projects, technology, and business practices. As new steps and requirements are added, others are pruned to prevent the methodology from becoming unwieldy. Of course, ability to improve the methodology depends on how much the organization is able to learn from its past projects; this subject is covered later.

Perhaps the essential desideratum for any methodology is that the payoff from using it exceeds the effort in creating and maintaining it. The methodology must not become yet more red tape, forcing managers to attend to paperwork rather than managing projects. It should be the means to an end, not an end in itself—i.e., "Let's just fill in these forms so we can carry on with the job."

16.2 PROJECT MANAGEMENT MATURITY AND MATURITY MODELS

How good are we really? How well do we measure up to our competitors? In which areas should we improve? These are questions that competitive companies continually ask themselves about their capabilities and competencies. An organization's capability or competency regarding project management is referred to as its "maturity."

Maturity Continuum

Just as people mature physically and mentally, organizations mature in project management. Typical maturity levels are shown in Figure 16.3.

The process of increasing an organization's maturity in project management begins when one person or a few people start to understand the principles of good project management and to practice these principles on their own. Of course, for the organization to further develop its capability *many* people must practice the principles. For that to happen requires awareness at the executive level as to the importance of project management, and a willingness to support steps that will spread the principles of good project management throughout the company. These steps include documenting lessons learned from every project for the benefit of other projects, and developing a common language of project management terms to be used everywhere in the company. A company with projects across the globe might create a glossary of terms in multiple languages. Naturally, moving to higher-level maturity also requires

Figure 16.3
Levels of project management maturity/competency

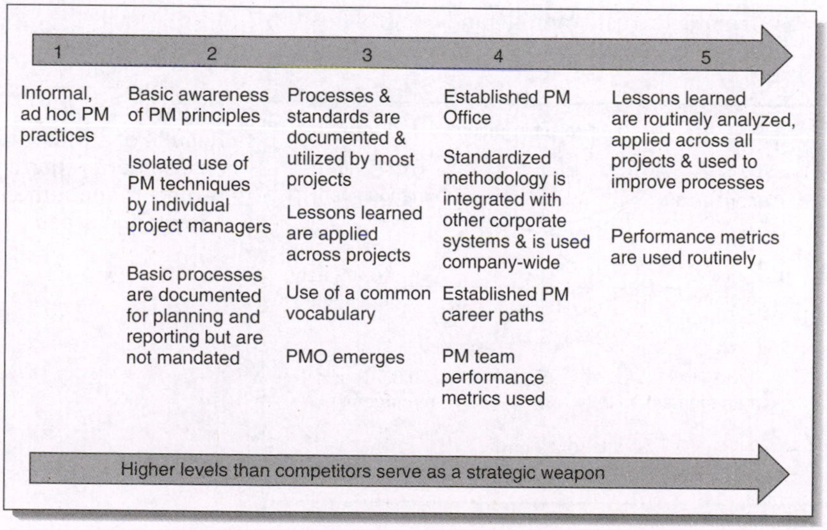

1	2	3	4	5
Informal, ad hoc PM practices	Basic awareness of PM principles	Processes & standards are documented & utilized by most projects	Established PM Office	Lessons learned are routinely analyzed, applied across all projects & used to improve processes
	Isolated use of PM techniques by individual project managers	Lessons learned are applied across projects	Standardized methodology is integrated with other corporate systems & is used company-wide	
	Basic processes are documented for planning and reporting but are not mandated	Use of a common vocabulary	Established PM career paths	Performance metrics are used routinely
		PMO emerges	PM team performance metrics used	

Higher levels than competitors serve as a strategic weapon

that the organization develops a project management methodology. Ultimately, the organization is in the position to benchmark its project management capabilities against project organizations that are industry leaders.[3]

Maturity Models

An organization's project management maturity is gauged according to so-called "maturity models"; currently there are more than 30 of these models,[4] although none has achieved acceptance worldwide.[5] Maturity models fall into three general categories:[6]

- Technical Delivery Process Models
- Project Management Process Models
- Total Organization Models.

Technical Delivery Process Models originated in the Total Quality Management movement of the 1980s, when companies started to measure their quality management capabilities. An example is the Capability Maturity Model (CMM), developed by the Software Engineering Institute of Carnegie-Mellon University during the 1980s and 1990s in response to a US Department of Defense request for ways to identify competent software contractors. The model, which emphasizes documentation of processes, similar to ISO quality standards, assesses project management practices against standard criteria, and has five levels of maturity.

The next category, Project Management Process Models, generally focuses on knowledge areas.[7] Many of these models are based on the nine knowledge areas in the *Guide to the Project Management Body of Knowledge (PMBOK)*[8] of the Project Management Institute (PMI). The level of maturity achieved in each knowledge area is determined by an assessment of standardized criteria during an audit. Figure 16.4 shows the results of such an audit and the assessed maturity levels for eight knowledge areas.

These process models commonly specify five possible levels of maturity, comparable to the levels in Figure 16.3:[9]

- *Ad hoc*—no formal procedures or plans
- Individual Project Planning
- Systematic Project Planning and Control

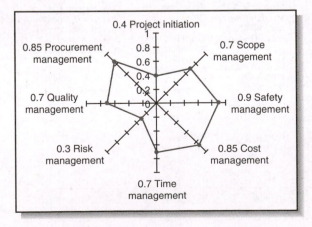

Figure 16.4
Results of a maturity assessment regarding project management knowledge areas.

- Integrated Multi-project and Formal Planning and Control
- Continuous PM Improvement.

Following the development of CMM, the PMI sponsored research at the University of California Berkeley and George Washington University that produced the Organizational Project Management Maturity Model (OPM3).[10] This is an example of a Total Organizational Model, so-called because it takes into account the entire organization and the way it manages projects, programs, and portfolios of projects.

How Good Should We Be?

It would be incorrect to presume that an organization should strive for the highest-level maturity in all aspects of project management as prescribed by these models. Different companies have different needs that each requires different levels of maturity. For example, whereas a company doing research with limited internal funding needs strong capability in project selection, a construction contractor with ample capacity to accept whatever work comes along does not. Likewise, a company that develops nuclear reactors needs high maturity in environmental protection and safety practices, but a company that develops computer games might get by with low maturity in those areas. One study of project management maturity in product development found that use of standardized tools and project management processes increases project success up to a point, beyond which it can reduce success—i.e., conformity to industry standards can only take you so far.[11] No single maturity model adequately gauges project success across all industries and types of projects. Each organization must identify which areas of competency are important, and avoid wasting resources to achieve high maturity in areas that are not important or are irrelevant.

Benefits and Shortcomings of Maturity Models[12]

Achieving a high rating according to a standard maturity model gives a company bragging rights. In a proposal, for example, a company can point out the high-level maturity it has achieved for a recognized model.

By their very nature, however, maturity models emphasize formal processes and procedures, and focus only on explicit knowledge, which is knowledge that can be documented. A weakness of all the models is that they ignore the importance of tacit knowledge, which is knowledge that cannot be easily written or described. Leadership, communication, teamwork, and the knowledge and skills held by project managers and team members also play a big role in project success; being tacit, however, this knowledge is not accounted for by the maturity models.[13]

Project Maturity and Project Success

Studies indicate that about two-thirds of all organizations rate at levels 1 or 2 on the 5-level maturity scale. Companies in petrochemical and defense industries are relatively more mature; those in insurance, financial and health services, pharmaceutical R&D, and telecommunications are less mature.[14]

Does achieving higher maturity according to the models automatically confer greater project success? The empirical evidence is paltry, but the answer is, "not necessarily." Project success depends on many things, including aspects of the project environment, the team, and the project manager, none of which the maturity models account for. According to one study, senior managers see little association between maturity level and project performance;[15] the few studies that do claim a correlation between maturity and project success lack a theoretical basis and, not surprisingly, were conducted by consultants, not researchers.[16] As to the question of whether maturity offers a competitive advantage, the answer is also mixed. The models measure only explicit knowledge—that which can be standardized and documented, and hence copied or adopted by other companies. An organization that mimics standard practices and ignores developing its own unique strengths can never become better than its competitors.[17]

16.3 KNOWLEDGE MANAGEMENT IN PROJECT MANAGEMENT

One potential pitfall in project management is to treat each project as if it were completely unique and ignore the lessons of other projects. Solutions to problems are invented . . . and reinvented. Mistakes in projects are repeated . . . and repeated again. Why does that happen? As the saying goes, "Fool me once, shame on you. Fool me twice, shame on me!" As an example, consider a project that is thought to be truly unique. The project manager must ponder what to expect and how to proceed. He must start with a clean slate and, he presumes, there is no one in the organization to help because—after all—the project is unique. But in most organizations rarely can it be said that there is no one who can help. Almost always there is someone, *somewhere*, with experience and knowledge that is relevant to the project. If only the project manager knew whom that someone is!

Authors O'Dell and Grayson describe the problem in their book *If Only We Knew What We Know*.[18] In many organizations critical knowledge is wasted; the knowledge exists, but people don't know it exists or how to gain access to it. Often the waste occurs because the organization has no formal process for capturing and disseminating knowledge, a process called *knowledge management*. In a project organization, a knowledge management process would help ensure that in every project people learn something, and that whatever they learn will be available to others who could use it. Knowledge management can provide project managers with the knowledge they need, even in cases where they themselves don't know they need it!

Organizational Forgetting

According to the classic learning curve, knowledge accumulates with experience: the more of something you do, the more you learn about it and the better you get—at least up to a point. The same principle holds for organizational knowledge, but sometimes with a twist: initially the organization gains knowledge through experience—learning more as it does more—but after a while it reaches a plateau or starts to regress, knowing less even as it continues to do more. This "organizational forgetting" happens when knowledgeable workers leave the organization, new processes and technologies render old ones obsolete, procedures are not documented, or records and documents get discarded or lost.[19] Since project teams disband after each project, it is easy for them and the organization to miss opportunities to learn from their experiences, forget what they learned, and not apply learning from one project to the next.

Capturing Knowledge

Knowledge is information put to use. Everything experienced in projects, intentional or not, is a source of information, but to learn from those experiences managers and teams must think about what happened, what they did, and the outcome. They must reflect on each experience and draw conclusions; otherwise they will not learn or will quickly forget.

One way to learn from a project is to conduct a *post-completion project review* or *post mortem*. During the review the team carefully looks at what it did and what it might learn from that. The team reflects on significant events, successes, and failures, and the actions that led to them. This is discussed under continuous improvement and project closeout in Chapters 9 and 12.

Sometimes a post-completion review is not enough; it happens at the end of the project, and by that time memories of events have faded, recollections of details have dimmed, and information has been lost. Therefore, especially in long projects, besides the post-completion review *multiple mid-stream* reviews should be held at key milestones and after notable events. Unlike status reviews that measure progress and identify problems, the purpose of these reviews is to reflect on actions taken and to learn from experience.

Common Knowledge and Knowledge Transfer[20]

Nancy Dixon defines *organizational common knowledge* as knowledge available and readily accessible to everyone in the organization. It is "how to" knowledge gained through the experiences of the company, largely *unique* to the company, and generally not available to the public. Because it is gained from the experiences of the company's workers and not known to outsiders, it is potentially what sets organizations apart. It cannot be measured by maturity models, yet is perhaps the most important kind of knowledge for helping an organization move beyond the competition.

But for organizational knowledge to become "common" it must be captured, retained, and shared through a mechanism called *knowledge transfer*. Knowledge transfer can happen broadly throughout the organization, or directly between individuals.

Documentation and Databases

Among ways to transfer knowledge about projects are to document knowledge gained from post-completion and mid-stream reviews, and to incorporate that knowledge into the project management methodology, and in checklists such as "lessons learned," "risks and pitfalls," and "best practices." Documented knowledge is also transferred via project report libraries, training seminars, and online knowledge databases. These sources provide information for, among other things, "analogy" estimating for project proposals.

Example 16.1: Preparing a Proposal: Using Databases and Peer Advice

Jacque, an engineering consultant, has received an RFP from a client to provide consultation for a new process. The client wants an answer soon. Jacque accesses the company knowledge database to see what his company has done concerning the process, what it is doing now, and the leading practices of the industry. He also reviews online abstracts and articles to learn more about the process, and then checks the company competency tracking system for names of consultants in the company who are familiar with the process. One name pops out, Leslee, someone he had met earlier at a network meeting. Jacque's company, a large technology consulting firm, holds frequent gatherings for the special purpose of people meeting each other and sharing project experiences. Jacque arranges a phone conference with Leslee. Before the conference, Leslee checks the company database for background about Jacque's client. During the phone conference, Leslee and Jacque create a draft of the proposal and work out the details. Barely a week after receiving the request, Jacque sends the completed proposal to the client.

Databases play a useful role in knowledge management, but their creation and upkeep is a subject on its own and is beyond the scope of this book. Suffice it to say a knowledge database requires substantial effort, and is ideally managed by a team of knowledge experts who know how to make it useful and user friendly. Ernst & Young, for instance, retains a database of outstanding proposals, presentations, and plans arranged into topical areas called "Powerpacks."[21] Powerpacks are managed by a team of experts; each contains only the best-written and most informative reports on a topic, presented in a standardized form and targeted to specific user groups.

One problem with knowledge in a database is that it is *latent*: it exists but is useful only when the database is accessed. A person needing information has to initiate the transfer process—and to know where to look in the database and what questions to ask.

In some companies, potentially useful knowledge is actually *imposed* on the persons who need or could use it. A project support group (PSG) or PMO keeps track of information that might be of interest to others, and forwards it. If, for example, a project has done an outstanding job at reducing material costs, the support group will write about the project and send a brief report to managers in other projects who might be interested. Through documenting and distributing reports on "best practices," the PSG is helping to build the organization's common knowledge base.

Tacit Knowledge and Personal Interaction

But some kinds of knowledge cannot be abridged into brief, standardized reports, and hence cannot be transferred via a document or database. In Example 16.1, Jacque used databases but also relied on Leslee for advice. Such one-on-one interaction and peer advice is a form of knowledge transfer that Jacque's firm encourages through companywide meetings at which people make acquaintances they might one day call upon.

Such personal interaction is necessary for transferring *tacit knowledge*—i.e., knowledge that is difficult to put into written words or even pictures; that exists only in people's heads and is sometimes hard to articulate. (For example, although you might easily recognize a person's face, you might not be able to verbalize the person's facial features that enable you to do that.) Much of the knowledge required to manage and conduct a project is tacit, which means it cannot be adequately retained or transferred via databases, documents, reports, or checklists.

After-Action Reviews

For teams that remain largely intact from one project to the next, after-action reviews (AAR) enable them to learn and develop a continually growing storehouse of knowledge. The concept is derived from troop teams in the US Army that use AARs to debrief and learn from the consequences of their actions immediately following an event.[22] In industry, an AAR is a brief meeting, held daily or immediately after an event, where a team looks at what actions it took, what happened, what was supposed to happen, and what accounted for the difference. Not really a "meeting" but rather an aspect of the way the team performs its work, an AAR is quick, to the point, and takes as little as 20 minutes. Everyone involved in the action participates, and one member facilitates. The rule is to be candid and tell the truth without fear of recrimination. AARs are most effective for projects that have specific, clear goals, and where the team has established clear measures by which to assess the impact of its actions toward reaching goals.[23]

Information generated in an AAR is mostly held confidential, which encourages candor and reduces fears of the team or individuals getting a bad reputation or being punished. Teams wanting to learn must feel free to try out different actions—some that might not work—and to openly admit mistakes. Knowledge captured and shared in an AAR remains within the team, unless the team later decides to share it with outsiders.

Peer Consultation and Project Resource Groups

AARs apply to intact teams doing somewhat repetitive projects. What about newly formed teams just starting out and where many things about the project are new to them—the technology, geographic location, culture, and so on? Likely the knowledge they need exists somewhere in the organization, but the challenge is to connect the people who have the knowledge (providers) with those who need it (receivers), and then to personally *interact* one-on-one.

Why personally interact? Because when people seek assistance through personal interaction amazing things happen, like *questions and solutions occurring between them that neither the providers nor receivers would have thought of beforehand.* Perhaps you have experienced this: you ask someone for advice, which leads them to ask you a probing question, which leads you to ask a question back, and so on. Often the result of this back-and-forth questioning is new knowledge—exploring paths that neither you nor the other person anticipated. The knowledge provider comes to see the situation in a new light, draws parallels, and comes up with insight and new ideas. The question is: How does the organization bring knowledge providers and receivers together so this can happen?

Example 16.2: Peer Consultation

A team of spacecraft engineers is preparing a proposal to bid on a communications satellite. The team has reviewed the requirements of the customer, a telecommunications corporation, and prepared a preliminary design, but because of the large risk and investment is not able to decide on certain features of the satellite's configuration. For advice, the team leader contacts 11 people at other company divisions who he knows either personally or via the grapevine. Six respond that they are willing to help out—four from divisions in California and Texas, and two working for NASA at JPL and headquarters. The leader arranges for this team of "peer consultants" to meet with her team for 1 day in California. At the meeting, the satellite team presents data it has collected and posts diagrams and charts on the walls. The peer consultant team questions the satellite team about the implications of the data, and the combined group develops criteria for deciding the final configuration. The satellite team leaves the room briefly while the consultation team reviews everything and prepares recommendations. When the satellite team returns, the consultation team summarizes its conclusions. A final decision about the configuration is not reached at the meeting; however, the satellite team has learned much about the issues it must still address to make a decision.

The formal knowledge-sharing process in Example 16.2 works like this: any project manager needing assistance can request it from peers anywhere in the company, and the peers' travel expenses and time off to serve as consultants will be covered by the company. The process emphasizes questioning, analysis, and feedback, *not* decisions. The knowledge receivers listen to the providers, but still make the decisions on their own.[24]

Some companies use a "locator system" that provides names, addresses, phone numbers, and other pertinent information of people worldwide working in specific knowledge areas. While some companies rely solely on peers to provide knowledge, others supplement that with project consultants.

Example 16.3: Project Support Group[25]

A large pharmaceutical corporation has a project support group (PSG) that includes 10 consultants available on request to provide expert support to any project manager who requests it. The PSG is a profit center that charges the company units of the project managers it assists. The PSG also sponsors semi-annual forums where project managers gather to share experiences. Available to the PSG are the part-time services of over 50 managers throughout the corporation experienced in project planning and execution.

The benefit of the PSG is illustrated in the story of Trevor, a typical project manager. Around the time his project was nearing completion, Trevor attended a forum. Feeling confident that his project had been a big success, he was surprised to learn about two other projects similar to his that had recently been completed. One had developed a process that, had he known about it, would have shaved 3 months off his project; the other had made mistakes similar to ones made in Trevor's project, and had he known about those he could have saved $50,000. In other words, the cost of Trevor not knowing what other managers at his company already knew was 3 months and $50,000!

For his next project Trevor contacted the PSG, who assigned Jiang to work with him. Although Trevor's department had to pay for Jiang's services, Trevor felt the advice he would receive could substantially benefit his $250 million project. The PSG provided a database listing current projects with state-of-the-art practices, which Jiang and Trevor used to develop the project plan. Throughout the 2-year project, Jiang contributed ideas, project management tools, benchmarking goals, and a peer process review; he was always available on call for mentoring and coaching.

Although project managers in the company use knowledge databases, the most important knowledge they gain is from consultants who are able to devote the time to understand each project well enough to draw upon their tacit knowledge for insight and suggestions. The consultants are "living databases" who travel from project to project, tailoring their knowledge to the needs of each. The consultants' broad experience enables them to look at each project from a new perspective, make new associations, and sometimes develop ideas not previously considered.

Knowledge transfer from personal interaction works best when the process is formalized. In other words, requests for assistance should be viewed as a legitimate business process, not as asking for favors. In formalized processes such as peer consultation or PSG, people freely ask for help without feeling intrusive. Everyone is encouraged or required to take advantage of the process—not just those who are inclined to anyway. Knowledge is power, which is another reason to formalize the process. In some organizations, knowledgeable but power-hungry people sometimes resist requests for assistance and avoid sharing what they know.

Discussion

Companies with the best knowledge management practices utilize a variety of methods that account for both tacit knowledge and explicit knowledge. For instance, spacecraft designers at Hughes Space & Communication Company are able to save on development costs by "reusing" previous designs wherever possible. So they do not "reinvent" anything, they rely on the "Knowledge Highway"—a process that includes an intranet, a database of lessons learned and best practices compiled by an editorial team, and pointers to experts.[26] Microsoft encourages informal, cross-group sharing of information though regular lunch meetings. Each month, for 2 hours, managers from Word, Excel, and MS Project meet to talk about their work, problems, and thoughts. They are encouraged to meet informally with or give presentations to other managers company-wide and worldwide.[27]

Who has ultimate responsibility for knowledge management? Although the project manager has responsibility for capturing knowledge in each project and sharing it with his peers, responsibility for organizational "common knowledge" must fall to the higher-level managers or organizational units that oversee projects. In many cases, the responsibility resides in a PSG or knowledge management team. Often this team is a part of the PMO.

16.4 PROJECT MANAGEMENT OFFICE[28]

Think for a moment about everything required of the project manager as described in this book, and you soon realize that being a project manager is a lot of work! Much of that work involves collecting and processing data, and preparing documents, reports, plans, budgets, and presentations. The workload imposed on the project manager can be overwhelming, and sometimes there is not enough time in a day to do it all.

Example 16.4: Bay Area Medical Center

Gaurav and several other project managers from the Bay Area Medical Group attended a series of seminars on project management. At the end of the series everyone agreed on the value of the tools learned, and they returned to their jobs with every intention of putting them into practice at BAMG. Months later, the reality was that Gaurav and his colleagues had used little of what they had learned and that almost nothing had changed about the way they managed projects. Gaurav had started to create a WBS and Gantt chart for one of his bigger projects, but gave up; already working long hours, he had scant time remaining to put into them. Besides, he thought, his organization offered neither support nor recognition for any effort to use these or other common project management tools.

BAMG is no different from many organizations: they send project managers to seminars to learn new and better ways, but then do nothing to encourage or support usage of those ways. The tools learned fall by the wayside, and nothing changes.

Countering this in many other organizations is the *project management office* or *PMO* (also called the *project support office*)—a department or unit whose purpose is to assist and support project managers, allocate project resources, and, in general, facilitate good project management practice. The PMO establishes and maintains the project management methodology, instigates initiatives that will increase its project management maturity, and oversees project knowledge management. It also plays an important role in integrated multi-project planning and control of project portfolios—topics of Chapter 17. A PMO adds structure to the practice of project management, but also provides project managers with support so they are not overwhelmed and can adapt to that structure.

PMO Leadership

Senior managers often do not realize the importance of project management; they see it as a role or job, not as a profession. To them projects are discrete occurrences that

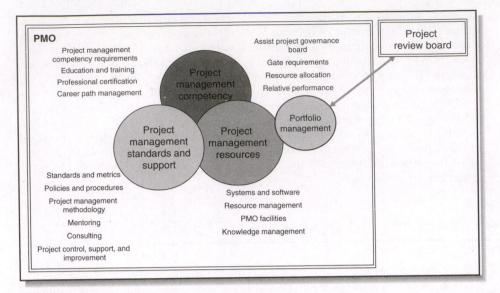

Figure 16.5
Major functions and responsibilities of the PMO.

have little in common. They allow project managers to work independently, treat every project as unique, and give little authority to the role of project manager. One challenge of the PMO is to impress on senior managers the importance of the project management role, and of everyone adhering to a prescribed project management methodology. To gain the attention of senior managers, the PMO should be staffed with some of the organization's most experienced and respected project managers.

The PMO can take many forms. Usually it is a permanent staff that helps guide projects in all or certain departments of the organization, although sometimes it is created to serve a single large project and disbands after the project is completed. Some PMOs are client-centered and some are department-centered; for example, serving managers and projects working for a certain client, or for departments such as IT, research, or product-development—units where the work is largely project-based.

What exactly does a PMO do? The foci and activities of a PMO, shown in Figure 16.5, are described in the following sections, in each case starting with the basic activities of virtually all PMOs and ending with those of only rather mature project organizations.

1. Project Management Standards

Project management methodology. Methodology is the organization's prescribed way to manage a project; if it is the "law," then the PMO is the "law-maker," "law promoter," and "law enforcer." Often the PMO originates and maintains the methodology, and is responsible for its implementation, update, and improvement.

Project management policies, procedures, standards, and metrics. Application of the methodology usually involves policies, procedures, standards, and metrics. One example of a policy is the requirement that managers of all projects of a certain size must conform to the methodology. Should the methodology include the task "Create the Project Plan," it will also specify details about what constitutes the "plan" as well as procedures for creating it (e.g., define scope, create WBS, estimate resources, time, and cost, etc.). The PMO sets the policies and defines the procedures.

Ideally, the PMO also provides project managers with support and assistance regarding whatever policies, procedures, or requirements it suggests or mandates. So that the policies and procedures are readily do-able and not overly burdensome, the PMO offers support in many ways, such as providing easy-to-use standard forms, worksheets, templates, and checklists, and clerical and data collection and data entry support.

2. Project Resources and Project Management Support

Resource management. A common problem in project-based organizations is that individual projects simply do not have the adequate resources. This happens when projects are approved and initiated without considering the resources they need versus the resources available. As a result, resources are shifted from one project to another, and some projects are delayed or deferred so that others can be started or finished on time.

A role of the PMO is to maintain a record of project resources, such as the number of full-time employees in each job title or skill grade category. The record includes, for each resource, the number allocated to current projects and the number available for assignment to new projects. This allows the organization to determine for each new project whether sufficient resources will be available when needed, additional resources must be acquired, or the project should be postponed or cancelled.

In many organizations, the selection and relative priority of projects is determined by a Project Review Board (PRB). The PMO provides information about resources so the PRB can determine the feasibility of undertaking each new project and allocate resources to projects with the highest priority. Details of this are covered in the next chapter.

Project management software and communication technology. In most project-based companies, all the project managers use the same project management software. Often, this software is integrated with other software for procurement, human resources, and finance, and includes Internet/intranet and telecommunication applications. In essence, the project software comprises an "enterprise project management system" that is part of the company's ERP system. Often it is the PMO that is responsible for its procurement, installation, and upgrade, as well as training managers and staff in its usage and applications. For software that requires periodic data entry for time- and cost-estimating, planning, and tracking, the PMO often provides clerical and data-entry support.

Project facilities. Projects located at stand-alone sites (construction projects) or away from the home organization (including overseas projects), or that are multifunctional or multi-organizational, need a physical project office—a central place for the project staff to meet and work. The PMO arranges for the project office and related facilities such as meeting rooms for conferences and forums. For overseas projects, it might also arrange for travel, lodging, and other needs of the project staff.

Mentoring, consulting, and knowledge management. As discussed earlier, the staff of some PMOs includes technical subject-matter experts and experienced project managers on call to provide advice and consultation. Some PMO staffers serve as mentors to project managers, and offer assistance or guidance throughout the project or with particular problems. The PMO also schedules and facilitates team-building sessions, status meetings, and post-completion reviews, and provides consultants/facilitators for the sessions.

The PMO is the center of project knowledge management, not only by virtue of its consulting and mentoring services but also by sponsoring and organizing forums, professional gatherings, and discussion groups where project managers meet and share experiences and lessons learned. It promotes organizational common knowledge by incorporating documented best practices into the organization's project management methodology.

3. Project Manager Competency

The PMO oversees most matters pertaining to the skills and abilities of the organization's project managers. Specifically, it:

- Determines skill and competency requirements for project managers
- Assists in hiring new project managers
- Arranges for project managers to attend training courses and seminars
- Prepares career paths for project managers and offers career-path coaching
- Helps managers in preparing for certification (PMP, CPM, APM, CAPM, RegPM)
- Assists in the assessment and promotion of project managers
- Works to enhance the organization's project management maturity
- Offers training in project management methodology and tools, and leadership and communication skills.

4. Liaison with Project Review Board

The PMO shares with the PRB responsibilities for project management that rest above the individual project managers. As mentioned, the function of the PRB is to manage the organization's projects collectively as a portfolio—to select and prioritize projects according to their relative importance and contributions to organizational goals (a topic covered in Chapter 17). For now, suffice it to say that the PRB is charged with oversight of all significant projects, including deciding which to fund, which to defer, and which to kill. The PMO serves as advisor to the PRB, and ensures that the PRB has the information necessary to make these decisions. As each project moves through the gating process the PRB assesses its performance, in part based on information from website-posted project "dashboards" that compare the project's performance to that of other projects in terms of a few key metrics. The PMO makes sure that projects arriving at a gate have met the documentation and other gating requirements, and posts information about the projects for the PRB to review. In fact, it could be said that the ability of the PRB to make effective decisions rests largely on the PMO's ability to provide it with accurate and timely project information. The PMO director sits on the PRB, and assists with project selection and prioritization decisions.

Evolution of the PMO

Creating a PMO is a project in its own right, and should be managed as such. Sometimes PMOs are established all at once and with the aid of outside consultants, but often they are created more slowly and internally. They start out with a small staff and limited purpose, instigated by one or a few veteran project managers who recognize the need for a standardized approach to project management. Most commonly this happens in either the IT or product development (PD) department, where the work is project-based and resources are shared. Among project managers in IT and PD, there are some who recognize the need for a uniform "better way" to manage all projects in the area. It is often these managers who spark the creation of the PMO.

With the support from a departmental or division manager to champion the concept, the group creates a project management methodology. It also develops the procedures, standards, forms, and templates needed to make the methodology workable, and begins to offer training to project managers in how to use them. Initially the PMO might consist of one person—the PMO "director," who (not coincidentally) is often the same person who conceived the PMO and helped create the methodology. The position might be part time, and while promoting the methodology and training managers, the director is managing projects too.

Eventually the director's position and the size of the PMO staff expand as their responsibilities increase to include counseling, consulting, refining the methodology, creating templates and tools, and providing clerical and technical support. Typically the PMO oversees projects exclusively in the area of the organization wherein the PMO emerged, such as PD or IT.

If all goes well, the department with the PMO will start to see improved project performance; noticing this, senior management will direct other departments in the company to also use the project management methodology. At this point the role of the PMO expands. Starting with training and assisting project managers throughout the company in the application of the methodology, the PMO might broaden the methodology or assist in developing alternative methodologies to better account for the diversity of projects in other areas of the company. The expanded role includes knowledge management—organizing forums and seminars, accumulating lessons learned, and creating project checklists, knowledge databases, and competency lists. The PMO might also be requested to establish a gating process. The PRB, if the organization has one, begins relying on the PMO to provide information and participate in selecting and prioritizing projects.

Eventually the PMO might become a full-fledged department wherein project managers are "based" and from which they are assigned to projects throughout the company. The PMO director is elevated to executive-level status, and the staff enlarged to include project management consultants, technical consultants, trainers, and knowledge specialists to provide project-related support everywhere in the organization.

PMO Morphing

In response to this section, some readers might react "That's not like the PMO in *my* organization!" In fact, project managers sometimes view the PMO as being little more than top management's "project police" center, whose main purpose is to keep an eye on projects, post red, yellow, or green tickets on the project dashboard, and enforce top-management mandated practices and requirements, viewed by many as largely bureaucratic red tape. PMOs like that are PMOs in name only, and are contrary to the originally intended spirit of the PMO, which is to facilitate better management of projects—and enable project managers to do their jobs better.

16.5 SUMMARY

The topics of this chapter—project management methodology, maturity, knowledge management, and the PMO—lie largely or wholly beyond the project manager's responsibility and capability, yet are critical or at least relevant to project success.

The project management methodology provides a framework and set of structured tasks, tools, and techniques to conceive, define, plan, schedule, budget, track, control, and closeout projects. It is the means by which all projects in an organization are managed and performed in a standardized, disciplined, and systematic manner, using recognized best practices. The methodology defines the phases or stages of the project and what should happen during each, including the roles and tasks of the project manager and of other project stakeholders. The breadth and details of the methodology are based upon the scope, scale, and risk of the projects to which it is applied.

Project management maturity refers to an organization's capability or competency in managing projects, including the extent to which it employs a methodology and formalized methods for planning and control, multi-project integration, and continuous improvement. A high rating on a maturity model indicates that an organization has achieved a high level of standardization in its project management practices and processes.

Because projects are unique and temporary, it is easy for individuals and organizations to miss opportunities to learn from project experience, forget what they learned, or not apply learning to other projects. A formal knowledge management process is necessary to learn from project experience, and to retain what was learned and share it with others. Ways of learning from projects include mid-stream or post-completion reviews, and after-action reviews. Ways to retain and transfer knowledge from projects include checklists, databases, and other forms of documentation; these ways are suitable for retaining explicit knowledge—i.e., knowledge that can be easily documented in words or diagrams. For knowledge that is difficult to express in words or pictures (i.e., tacit knowledge), knowledge access and transfer can only happen via personal interaction, peer consultation, project resources support groups, or expert knowledge consultants.

The PMO is a unit or department devoted to improving the practice of project management and providing support to project managers. The PMO establishes and maintains the methodology, instigates initiatives to increase the organization's project management maturity, and manages project knowledge. It develops standards and procedures, and manages resources for projects. The PMO provides training, consulting, and mentoring, and assists in integrated multi-project planning and control, and portfolio management. A PMO adds structure to the practice of project management, but ideally also supports and assists project managers so they are able to adapt to that structure.

REVIEW QUESTIONS AND PROBLEMS

1. What are the benefits of a project management methodology? What are the disadvantages of an organization not having one?
2. What does the project management methodology specify? Describe the key features and topics addressed by the methodology. Discuss the kinds of tasks and deliverables covered in the methodology.
3. Where does the methodology originate? Who creates and promotes it?
4. What is the purpose of project gates? Describe how the gating process fits in with the project management methodology.
5. Why might an organization have more than one methodology? What is a potential problem with having more than one?
6. Discuss the meaning of the term "project management maturity."
7. What do project management maturity process models measure or assess?

8. List five levels of project management maturity.
9. Name the benefits of an organization being highly rated on a project management maturity model.
10. What aspects critical to effective project management do the maturity models ignore?
11. In a sentence, what is the purpose of knowledge management in project management?
12. Describe some ways of capturing project knowledge.
13. What is the difference between tacit knowledge and explicit knowledge?
14. Name some difficulties associated with retaining and sharing (transferring) tacit knowledge.
15. What kind of knowledge can be retained in a database?
16. What kind of knowledge cannot be retained in a database? Where is that knowledge to be found?
17. What is an after-action review? How does it differ from a post-completion review?
18. How is peer consultation used in knowledge sharing?
19. What responsibility does the project manager have for project knowledge management?
20. What is the overall purpose of the project management office (PMO)?
21. What is the role of the PMO with respect to each of the following:
    a. Project management methodology
    b. Project management policy, procedures, and standards
    c. Project resource management
    d. Project software and communications technology
    e. Mentoring, consulting, and knowledge management
    f. Project manager competency
    g. Project review board (or governance board or project steering committee).
22. How does a typical PMO get started and grow? Describe the role of project managers in initiating and managing the PMO.

QUESTIONS ABOUT THE STUDY PROJECT

1. Did the project follow an established, formal methodology? If so, describe the methodology. In your opinion, did it help or hinder the project? What is the opinion of the project manager and project staff as to the effectiveness of the methodology? Where did the methodology originate, and how was it created?
2. If no formal methodology existed, did the project manager have her own, informal methodology? If so, what was it? Was it effective?
3. What is your opinion about the project management maturity of this organization? Would you say the organization is mature or somewhat immature?
4. Was anything done to capture knowledge in this project? Were any measures taken to retain this knowledge for application and transfer to other projects?
5. Of the many knowledge management methods described in this chapter, which were practiced in this project? Which of the methods does the project organization practice? How is knowledge shared in the organization?
6. Does the organization have a PMO? If so, what are its functions? How was the role of the PMO visible in this project? In your opinion, did the PMO help or hinder the project manager? Explain.

Case 16.1   Maxim Corporation America (MCA)

Maxim Corporation is a leading provider of risk management services, insurance brokerage, and specialty insurance underwriting. With an employee base of over 50,000 people at 600 offices in more than 100 countries, the corporation has a broad view of the insurance industry and can leverage its expertise across hundreds of disciplines worldwide.

IT OPERATIONS AND PMO

The IT Operations department for the US division is located at Maxim Corporation America corporate headquarters. Previously the department had over 1,200 employees and was responsible for 80 percent of all MCA IT projects (the other 20 percent going to consultants); it handled three kinds of projects: strategic, infrastructure, and client applications.

In 2009, the department established a PMO to oversee infrastructure projects. The office consisted of a director, support staff, and 10 project managers. The director reported to the Chief Technology Officer (CTO), who reported to the Global Chief Information Officer (CIO). The PMO's primary role was assigning managers to infrastructure projects and tracking the projects. At any given time, about 30 infrastructure projects were underway and many more were under consideration.

PM METHODOLOGY

One of the PMO director's first tasks was to develop a project management methodology, which he did with the assistance of his most experienced project managers. The methodology, called the Project Management Framework (PMF), specifies prescribed project phases, documentation, and gates, and covers all aspects of the project life cycle, from project initiation to completion sign-off and *post mortem* review. It is thought to be one of the best in the business: it is rigorous, but not bureaucratically cumbersome.

PMO SERVICES

The PMO enforced the methodology but assisted project managers in its usage through training and coaching. Besides this, the PMO conducted courses on topics such as project communication and leadership skills. It also convened meetings for the project managers to discuss current projects, and sponsored special seminars. It created templates and forms to reflect the lessons learned from completed projects, and arranged for experienced project managers to coach and mentor other project managers who sought assistance.

PORTFOLIO MANAGEMENT

An additional role of the PMO was to assist the Project Review Board in the selection of proposed projects and assessment of underway projects. The PRB is a committee of 10–12 managers that includes the Global CIO, CTO, director of the PMO, VP of Finance, and senior managers with budget responsibility for proposed and current projects. The PMO insured that documentation for each project as specified in the PMF was completed and signatures obtained prior to each gate. It also assessed the relative performance of projects, which enabled the PRB to decide which to approve, hold, or kill at gates.

REASSESSMENT OF IT OPERATIONS

As part of a larger study of MCA in late 2010, consultants recommended that all IT infrastructure operations be outsourced, a move that could save MCA $30–50 million annually. MCA responded rapidly, and by June 2011 had outsourced all of its IT infrastructure operations to CorCom, a large IT contractor. CorCom had a reputation for operational discipline, solid project management, and good reporting. It had an internal PMO to oversee projects, including those it had taken over from MCA. Of the 600 people in IT Operations at MCA originally working on infrastructure projects, CorCom hired 480.

IT PMO TODAY

The director of the PMO at MCA was retained, but his unit reduced to four project managers and one support specialist. These managers mostly oversee tasks associated with the outsourcing and the initiation and feasibility of IT projects. The education role of the PMO has been diminished and the breadth of its course offerings greatly reduced. The PMO conducts courses to familiarize CorCom staff with the MCA PMF, but it no longer provides mentoring and coaching services.

One problem observed since outsourcing IT infrastructure is that CorCom does not become involved in a project until after it has been defined. Whereas in the past MCA project managers were involved during project conception and requirements definition, CorCom project managers are not involved until after project approval and definition. The stance of CorCom managers is, "Tell us exactly what you want and we'll deliver it." This contrasts to the old way of "Let us help you define your needs and requirements, and suggest the best alternatives." CorCom project managers have no say in defining the requirements they must meet. The concern of some units at MCA is that this lack of early user–developer interaction precludes thorough identification of customer needs. But it is too early to tell if this concern is more than just a perception.

FUTURE OF THE PMO

The director is convinced about the continued importance of the IT PMO. He has scheduled a meeting with the Global CIO to discuss the PMO's future.

QUESTIONS

1. Does the IT PMO at MCA have a future? What, if any, role can it retain?
2. How does the PMO director's role compare to the VP of projects or PMO director as discussed in Chapters 13 and 14?

Case 16.2 Motorola's M-Gate Methodology and the RAZR Project[29]

Motorola employs the following 16-stage project methodology called M-Gate:

M15 Idea Concept	M7 Contract Book
M14 Concept Accept	M6 Design Readiness
M13 Solution Select	M5 System Test Readiness
M12 Portfolio Accept	M4 Ready for Field Test
M11 Solution Lock	M3 Ready for Controlled Intro
M10 Project Initiation	M2 Volume Deployment
M9 System Requirements Baseline	M1 Retirement Plan Approved
M8 System Requirements Allocated	M0 End of Life

The methodology corresponds roughly to a five-phase product life cycle:

M15 M14 M13	M12 M11	M10 M9 M8 M7 M6	M5 M4 M3	M2 M1 M0
Business Case	Portfolio Planning	Project Definition	Implementation	Launch to Closeout

Each stage specifies entrance and exit criteria, management and task requirements, and key participants and stakeholders. The process includes five "go/no-go" gates at which a product's viability must be proved in order for the project to survive.

The M-Gate methodology emphasizes product quality and customer needs, but it was created before the era of ubiquitous cell phones. It produced some well-known successes—but at the snail's pace of one every 3–4 years. The stages and gates reduce risk and increase quality, but they tend to discourage radical new ideas and hold up product launch—big drawbacks in the crazy, fiercely competitive handheld phone market.

In fact, the lengthy process initially killed the RAZR concept that was to become Motorola's hottest phone in a decade. It imposed cumbersome iterations of market research and mandated requirements that conflicted with RAZR's design goals. Motorola's marketing research showed phone sizes increasing, but RAZR aimed for the opposite—to be the thinnest possible (razor thin). As a rule, product designers were required to incorporate whatever features its wireless company customers desired, though for RAZR they thought it better to exclude customers in the interests of secrecy. Only through the persistence of a dedicated cadre of engineers was the project approved. Thanks to high-placed supporters, management allowed RAZR the freedom to operate in a "Skunk Works" fashion—as a small tight-knit team, working in top secrecy and largely by its own rules.

For the RAZR project, stages M15 and M14 were supplanted with a process better suited for break-the-mold products. In terms of the funnel selection method described in Chapter 17 (Figure 17.2b), the process starts with selected and prioritized product concepts streaming from the narrow end of the funnel. The concepts then go through five stages:

Stage 1: Prepare a short technical proposal for each product concept
Stage 2: Categorize the proposals
Stage 3: Develop a resource plan to convert each concept into a prototype
Stage 4: Build a prototype to demonstrate the concept to managers and product groups; kill the poorly-received concepts
Stage 5: Transfer surviving concepts to the portfolio planning team for entry into a multi-year product portfolio (enter M-Gate process at stage M12).

As soon as the RAZR phone was launched it became an immediate hit, selling more than 110 million units in 4 years and boosting Motorola to second in the cell-phone market after Nokia. In 2008, *PC World* ranked the RAZR as #12 in *The 50 Greatest Gadgets of the Past 50 Years*.

QUESTIONS

1. Why was it necessary for the RAZR team to work outside of the M-Gate methodology? In what situations might it be necessary to work around or modify the existing project management methodology?

2. What are the potential drawbacks of allowing projects to deviate from the methodology?

Case 16.3   Tecknokrat Company

Tecknokrat Company is a software consulting firm founded in 1977. The firm has 18 project managers, many who started with the company as systems analysts and developers.

Tecknokrat has a good reputation in terms of quality products and services, but has recently seen its business and profits fall because many of its projects are completed late and over budget. To reverse the trend the firm hired Drago Kovacic, an experienced project manager who had been PMO director of IT at a bank. Drago's mandate is to assist project managers so as to improve project schedule and budget performance.

In his first 2 weeks at Tecknokrat, Drago interviewed the project managers and observed them in practice. He noted the following:

- They all have their own way of doing things. There are no prescriptions about how to manage projects.
- Although they all work in the same office, there is practically no interaction among them. No one knows much about what the others are doing.
- Some of the managers seem antagonistic toward each other.
- They seem almost to be competing with each other.
- There is no mentoring. The attitude among old-timers is: whatever I know I had to learn through experience; new-timers have to do that too.

Digging further, he discovered some curious company policies:

- At year-end, the "best" project managers in terms of meeting schedules and budgets get awards: the best gets $20,000, the second best gets $10,000, the third best gets $5,000. Every year for as long as anybody can remember, the same four or five people have won the awards; all of them have been with the company over 20 years.

- The company uses education as an incentive. For each project that exceeds goals or receives high praise from the customer, the manager can attend a local business seminar of his choice. The incentive tends to go to a small group of managers that, not coincidentally, includes the same managers who get the year-end dollar awards.

The ostensible purpose of the awards and incentives is to spur managers to do a better job in terms of meeting project goals.

QUESTIONS

1. Based on Drago's observations, what do you think are the main issues in Tecknokrat's project management?
2. What do you think about the awards and incentives? Why haven't they had the desired effect?
3. What should Drago do? What difficulties is he likely to encounter?

NOTES

1. Information in this section obtained from interviews with project managers and PMO directors at 11 organizations: Doug Brandt (Abbott Laboratories); Jacki Koehler (ABN-Amro); Ruta Kulbis (Accenture); Holly Wells (Aon); Carson Neally, Jim Yeck, Robert Wunderlick, and Jeff Roberts (Argonne National Laboratory); Douglas Gilman, Joe Wolke, and Eileen Will (Chicago Board of Trade): Martin Wills (Information Resources, Inc.); Cynthia Reyes (Nicor); Thomas Foley (Sears Roebuck); Gurran Gopal (Tellabs); and Carol Bobbe (TransUnion).
2. Shenhar A and Dvir D. *Reinventing Project Management: The Diamond Approach to Successful Growth and Innovation.* Boston, MA: Harvard Business School Press; 2007.
3. Common language, processes, methodology, and benchmarking and continuous improvement are the five levels of maturity defined by Kerzner H, in *Strategic Planning for Project Management using a Project Management Maturity Model.* New York, NY: Wiley; 2001.
4. Cooke-Davies T. Project management maturity models: does it make sense to adopt one? *Project Manager Today* May; 2002.
5. Jugdev K and Thomas J. Project management maturity models: the silver bullets of competitive advantage? *Project Management Journal* 33(4); 2002: 4–14.
6. Cooke-Davies T, Schlichter J, and Bredillet C. Beyond the PMBOK Guide. *Proceedings of the 32nd Annual Project Management Institute, 2001 Seminars & Symposium.* Newtown Square, PA: Project Management Institute.
7. Jugdev K and Thomas J. Project management maturity models: the silver bullets of competitive advantage?
8. *A Guide to The Project Management Body Of Knowledge* (PMBOK Guides), 4th edn. Newtown Square, PA: Project Management Institute; November 2008.
9. Kwak Y and Ibbs C. *Project Management Process Maturity (PM)2 Model (the Berkeley PM Model).* www.ce.berkeley.edu/~ibbs/yhk-wak/ pmmatrutiy.htmel; see also Crawford J. *Project Management Maturity Model—Providing a Proven Path to Project Management Excellence.* New York, NY: Marcel Dekker, Inc.; 2002.
10. Ibbs C and Kwak Y. Assessing project management maturity. *Project Management Journal* 31(1); 2000: 32–43; PMI. *Organizational Project Management Model.* Newtown Square, PA: Project Management Institute; 2003.
11. Milosevich D and Patanakul P. Standardized project management may increase development project success. *International Journal of Project Management* 23; 2005: 181–192.
12. Pennypacker J and Grant K. Project management maturity: an industry benchmark. *Project Management Journal* 34(1); 2003: 4–11; Jugdev K and Thomas J. Project management maturity models: the silver bullets of competitive advantage?
13. Skulmoski G. Project maturity and cost interface. *Cost Engineering* 43(6); 2001: 11–18;

Andersen E and Jessen S. Project maturity in organizations. *International Journal of Project Management* 21; 2003: 457–461.

14. Cooke-Davies T and Arzymanow A. The maturity of project management in different industries: an investigation into variations between project management models. *Project Management* 21; 2003: 471–478; Pennypacker and Grant. Project management maturity: an industry benchmark; Crawford LH. Senior management perceptions of project management competence. *International Journal of Project Management* 23; 2005: 7–16.

15. Crawford LH. Senior management perceptions of project management competence.

16. For example, see Jugdev and Thomas, Project management maturity models: the silver bullets of competitive advantage? An example of an industry study is in Nietro Rodriguez A and Evrard D. *A First Global Survey on the Current State of Project Management Maturity in Organizations Across the World*. Price Waterhouse Cooper; 2004.

17. Jugdev and Thomas. Project management maturity models: the silver bullets of competitive advantage?

18. O'Dell C and Jackson Grayson C. *If Only We Knew What We Know*. New York, NY: Free Press; 1998.

19. See Argote L. *Organizational Learning: Creating, Retaining, and Transferring Knowledge*. Boston, MA: Kluwer Academic Publishers; 1999.

20. Dixon N. *Common Knowledge: How Companies Thrive by Sharing What They Know*. Boston, MA: Harvard Business School Press; 2000.

21. Ernst & Young. *Knowledge Management*. http://www.ey.com/global/content.nsf/ Middle_East/Knowledge_Management_-_ Tools, downloaded April 13, 2007.

22. USDA. *A Leader's Guide to After Action Review* (TC 25–20). US Department of the Army; 1993.

23. Dixon. *Common Knowledge*, pp. 77–79, 81–82.

24. Ernst & Young. *Knowledge Management*; National Library for Health, Knowledge Management Specialists Library, *Peer Assist*. http://www.library.nhs.uk/knowledgemanagement/ViewResource.aspx?resID=125167, downloaded April 14, 2007.

25. Other examples provided by *Ibid.*, pp. 103–104, and Welch N. *Peer Assist Overview*. http://003cce4.netsolhost.com/PeerAssit.htm, accessed April 12, 2007.

26. O'Dell and Grayson. *If Only We Knew What We Know*, pp. 51–52.

27. Cusumano MA and Selby RW. *Microsoft Secrets*. New York, NY: Free Press; 1995. p. 243.

28. Sources: see Note 1.

29. Case derived from McQuellon R, Pini L, Benedicata M, Mjavanadze D, Madura S, Grzybowski M, and Velasco M. *Razr Project*. Graduate School of Business, Loyola University Chicago, February 2007; Lashinsky A. RAZR's edge: how a team of engineers and designers defied Motorola's own rules to create a cell phone that revived the company. *Fortune* June 1, 2006; Koerner B. *Motorola Insider Blame Game: Engineers Shoved Designers Aside*. Gizmodo website, http://gizmodo.com/5038839/motorola-insider-blame-game-engineers-shoved-designers-aside, accessed August 24, 2010.

17

Project Selection and Portfolio Management

> *Lilies that fester smell far worse then weeds.*

—SHAKESPEARE, SONNETS

> *Errors, like straws, upon the surface flow;*
> *he who would search for pearls must dive below.*

—JOHN DRYDEN

Projects are the means by which an organization pursues and achieves its strategic objectives, so doing the *right* projects is crucial for business success. If the organization proclaims it wants to "be the low-cost leader," "expand market share in Europe," "develop state-of-the-art technologies," or "preserve the natural environment," then you would expect that many or most of its projects would be directed at or incorporate those objectives.

However, often that is not the case. In many companies, projects have little or nothing to do with strategic objectives. Instead, they represent narrow, short-term interests, easily seized opportunities, or the pet agendas of a few people. The hobbyhorses of senior executives, they get "sacred cow" status despite questionable benefits, and hog resources from and squeeze out projects with more obvious business value.

A study of 35 predominantly North American firms revealed relatively little overall spending on projects that contributed directed to company goals and strategies.[1] In general, project resources were spread thinly because the companies had too many projects and no systematic way to prioritize them. Most projects were "low-hanging fruit"—relatively easy to do, but offering little in the form of business potential. Projects such as these waste resources and deprive a company of superior project opportunities.

17.1   PROJECT PORTFOLIO MANAGEMENT

A project portfolio is a group of projects or programs in an organization or business unit that aim at strategic objectives, share resources, and compete for funding. Any organization that funds, manages, and allocates resources to more than one project has a project portfolio—even though managers may not know what it looks like or how to manage it.[2] In a formal *project portfolio management process*:

- Project proposals are assessed for benefits and strategic contributions, costs, and risks
- Based on conscientious decisions, projects are authorized, put on the "back burner," or disposed of
- Scarce resources are allocated so as to ensure that approved priority projects get adequate funding and support
- Projects as a whole are "balanced" in terms of high vs low risk, large vs small size, long-term vs short-term focus, etc.—whatever balance is deemed best
- Projects are tracked, compared, and managed collectively; decisions about each project are based upon their benefits and required resources compared to other projects.

The most rudimentary form of portfolio management is to simply know and keep track of projects underway and projects under consideration. The organization has two lists: one for "active" projects, the other for "potential" projects. Simple as it might appear, creating and maintaining such lists in a company where there is no culture of portfolio management is not a trivial step. Functional managers are accustomed to starting projects without registering them anywhere. From an organization-wide perspective, there is no accounting of projects.

Academics, consultants, and software firms have proposed many approaches for managing a project portfolio. The breadth of the subject fills books; hence, treatment in this chapter is limited to a survey of the most common methods.

Process for Successful Projects[3]

Successful projects depend upon two things: doing the *right projects* and doing those *projects right.* The two happen as a multi-tiered process that spans the organization and involves senior managers, business unit managers, and project managers.

- *Strategic management: focus the organization.* Senior managers articulate the vision and mission of the organization, define strategic initiatives, set the budget, and allocate resources to business units. Examples of contrasting strategic initiatives are to be the low-cost or technology leader, to be innovative or imitative, or to pursue mass or niche markets.

- *Portfolio management: choose the right projects.* Business unit managers develop strategies, goals, and initiatives that are consistent with the corporate mission. These become the basis for setting specific criteria, which they use for selecting projects from proposals generated internally or from among customers.

- *Gating methodology: nurture or get rid of projects.* Business unit managers assess each project as it moves through gates. They compare project performance to gating criteria and make decisions: important but struggling projects are allocated more resources; poorly performing or mediocre projects are put on hold or cancelled.

- *Project management: do the projects right.* Project managers manage and guide projects using sound principles and practices of project management.

Project Review Board

Responsibility for project selection and portfolio management rests with the *Project Review Board* or *PRB* (also known as the Portfolio Management Team, Project Governance Board, Project Steering Committee, or Project Council). Membership in the PRB typically includes a project portfolio manager, chief financial officer (CFO), chief risk manager (CRO), chief human resource officer (CHRO), project management office (PMO) director, and chief technical officer (CTO—from IT, engineering, or product development, depending on the organization). For each proposed project, the CFO weighs the costs and financial benefits; the CRO assesses the risks; the CHRO assesses the human resource requirements; the CTO assesses the technical benefits and difficulties, and the PMO director assures that documentation necessary to make selection and gating decisions is complete.[4] The portfolio manager typically chairs the PRB and has final approval over project additions or deletions in the portfolio.

For research and engineering projects the PRB will include a group of technically competent "peer reviewers" who independently appraise and rate each proposal according to its scientific and/or technical merit, the competency or capability of the proposal originator, likelihood of success, and so on. If the reviewers all assign low scores to a proposal then the project is rejected. If all assign high scores then the project is approved, given that others on the PRB also approve it and funds are available. If funding is tight, few projects are approved, regardless of high scores. If funding is abundant, even mediocre rated projects might be approved.[5]

17.2 FRAMEWORK FOR PROJECT SELECTION AND PORTFOLIO MANAGEMENT

When an organization has excess capacity it readily takes on all the projects it can get. But when it does not—when its resources (talented people, finances, technological capacity) are constrained—then logically it pursues only those that contribute the most to its objectives. In organizations where most projects are generated internally, the portfolio management process is used to evaluate proposals and approve projects; in those where projects are generated externally, the process is used to determine which RFPs it should respond to.

Since projects differ with regard to resource requirements, risk, cost, and strategic value, choosing the right projects for the portfolio can be a complex problem. Most projects represent investments, and many of the methods used in project portfolio management derive from general principles of investment management. Just as an investment portfolio can reduce monetary risk by, say, investing in multiple currencies (pound, euro, yen, or dollar), a project portfolio can reduce risk by spreading projects across multiple business sectors. Managers use the logic and techniques of project selection and portfolio management to decide in which, among alternative markets, business partners, and technologies, to invest.

Selection Process

An organization that routinely faces project selection decisions should have a prescribed means for assessing and comparing project proposals. It should also have a set of *measurable* criteria that reflects its strategic goals and initiatives, as well as a process for evaluating and selecting projects in terms of those criteria. This process and its relation to other aspects of portfolio management are shown in Figure 17.1. In Phase I, each project is independently evaluated and screened; in Phase II, all projects are considered together and a subset is approved.[6]

Phase I

Phase I includes a *prescreening stage* to quickly eliminate project proposals that are clearly deficient. For a project to pass this stage, it must be justified in terms of either survival or growth.[7] Survival projects are necessary for the health and continued

Figure 17.1
Project analysis, selection, and portfolio management methodology.
Adapted from Archer N and Ghasemzadeh F. An integrated framework for project portfolio selection. *International Journal of Project Management* 17(4); 1999: 207–216.

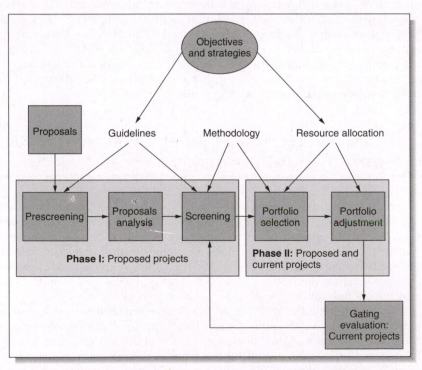

viability of the organization. Growth projects, though not necessary, expand or take advantage of opportunities for the organization. The requirements for a project to pass this stage include, for example, project justification (survival or growth) in a feasibility study, a champion and sponsor who support the project, and *documented* expected benefits. Projects lacking justification or sufficient information upon which to make a decision are eliminated. Sometimes a simple checklist is employed and each proposal is rated as excellent, good, etc., on a small number of criteria. The ratings are converted to a numerical score, and proposals falling below a "threshold" score are automatically cut.

Project proposals that pass prescreening are subjected to formal analysis using quantitative and qualitative models and scoring methods. The analysis might rate or value the proposal using diverse criteria such as "link to strategic objectives," "financial value" (e.g., rate of return, cost/benefit), or "compliance to constraints" (e.g., financial, human resources, or technology/architecture). To be considered for Phase II and possible funding, a proposal must exceed a minimum cut-off value or score. This is the purpose of *screening*—to assess and eliminate projects that do not meet minimum requirements for expected benefits, risk, or other specific criteria.[8]

Phase I restricts the pool of projects entering Phase II to those that are the "right" projects, and generates information for portfolio selection decisions in Phase II. To discourage proposals for projects that are frivolous or clearly sub par, RFPs and project initiation procedures should clearly specify the minimal acceptance criteria.

Phase II

Portfolio selection involves reviewing screened proposed projects and existing projects together and determining which of them in combination constitute the "best" portfolio. Projects are compared in terms of scores from the analysis or, for existing projects, measures of their current status and performance. Common decision criteria are set so that all projects, proposed and existing, can be compared against each other.

Phase II is not a single event but a continuing process. Projects underway are evaluated within the *gating process* for expected benefits, performance, and costs. Those in trouble and not meeting minimal requirements are terminated outright. The remaining ones are pooled with new projects, and all are rank-ordered for reconsideration about continued, reduced, or increased support, or cancellation. Rank-ordering helps ensure that limited resources and funding go to the high-priority projects. Because of changes in objectives, opportunities (new strategies develop, new RFPs or proposals arrive), and resources, the portfolio will need periodic changing: some newly proposed projects will be added; some current projects will be accelerated, delayed, or cancelled.

Funnel and Filter

The purpose of the analysis and selection process is not to discourage projects but to make sure only the "right" projects are pursued. Whether they internally develop new products or processes or work under contract, companies rely on projects for survival and growth; ideally, however, they have the option of *choosing* projects from a number of proposals, RFPs, and initiation requests. Hence, the selection process can be likened to a *funnel* into which project proposals and concepts flow, and a *filter* that allows only the best to proceed. As illustrated in Figure 17.2, the trick is to design the process so the funnel mouth is wide enough to take in lots of ideas, but the filter fine enough to screen out bad proposals yet provide a constant flow of high-quality projects.[9]

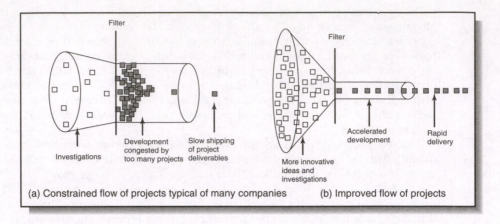

(a) Constrained flow of projects typical of many companies   (b) Improved flow of projects

Figure 17.2
Project selection process viewed as a funnel and filter.
Adapted from Wheelwright S and Clark K. *Revolutionizing Product Development*,
New York, NY: Free Press; 1992.

17.3   METHODS FOR INDIVIDUAL PROJECT ANALYSIS

Screening and selection decisions are based upon results from analysis of individual projects. Every analysis method incorporates assumptions, some that later might prove to be wrong, and for this reason the assumptions should always be explicitly stated and the analysis work documented. Among many popular methods for analysis, the most common are financial models and scoring models.

Financial Models

Financial models measure project proposals in terms of economic or financial criteria such as net present value (NPV), internal rate of return (IRR), return on original investment (ROI), payback period, and so on. One common method is the expected commercial value (ECV), which is an application of decision-tree analysis described in the Appendix to Chapter 10. The ECV model as illustrated in Figure 17.3 considers the costs, earnings, and likelihood of success of the development and launch phases for a product.[10] Suppose for a proposed product the development cost is $10M, launch cost is $1.5M, and NPV for the future stream of earnings is $50 M. If the probabilities for success are 80 percent in development and 60 percent in the market, then

$$ECV = [(\$50)0.6 - \$1.5M]\,0.80 - \$10M = \$12.8M$$

Using this criterion, the higher the ECV, the more preferred the project.

Another financial model is the benefit–cost ratio (B/C), which weighs the benefits of a project against the costs. A simple example is

$$\frac{B}{C} = \frac{\text{Estimated revenues} \times \text{Probability of success}}{\text{Estimated cost}}$$

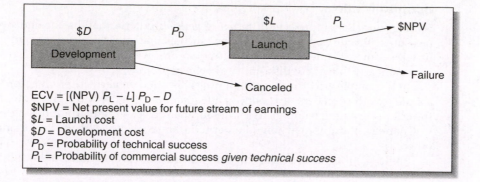

$$ECV = [(NPV)\ P_L - L]\ P_D - D$$
NPV = Net present value for future stream of earnings
L = Launch cost
D = Development cost
P_D = Probability of technical success
P_L = Probability of commercial success *given technical success*

Figure 17.3
Model for computing expected commercial value, ECV.
Adapted from Cooper R, Edgett S, and Kleinschmidt E. Portfolio management
in new product development: lessons from leaders, phase I. In Dye L and
Pennypacker J (eds), *Project Portfolio Management*. West Chester, PA: Center
for Business Practices; 1999. pp. 97–116.

Values in the numerator and denominator are all expressed in the same form, as either annualized or present worth amounts. For example, if estimated annual revenue is $100,000, estimated annual cost of the project is $25,000, and probability of success is 50 percent, the resulting ratio is 2.0. Thus, for each dollar spent on the project, 2 dollars in benefit would be expected back in return. B/C can also be computed when benefits are expressed in terms of cost reduction.[11] For instance, in the ratio

$$\frac{B}{C} = \frac{\text{Worth of benefits}}{\text{Capital recovery cost} + (\text{Operating cost} + \text{Maintenance cost})}$$

the "worth" can be cost savings. Suppose, for example, renovation of a plant and installation of new equipment is expected to provide present worth savings of $6M for a present worth cost (facility renovation, equipment installation, and annual operating and maintenance expenses) of $3M. The B/C ratio for the project is 2.0.

Of course, computing an accurate ratio depends on having assigned accurate values to *all* significant, relevant costs and benefits, including "hidden" or external ones such as impacts on society, the economy, and the environment.[12] Although hidden costs and benefits can be difficult to identify and measure, often they exceed by far the more obvious costs and benefits. In the renovation example, suppose after the project is begun the factory electrical system is found to be out-of-code and must be replaced, and portions of the flooring are determined to be unsound and must be reinforced; or suppose the environmental regulations are changed and require installation of equipment that will clean up smoke and liquids discharged from the factory. Not anticipating these costs, the B/C ratio would be erroneous and misleading.

The main weakness of B/C, ECV, and all financial models is total reliance on *estimates* for costs, cost savings, future streams of earnings, probabilities, etc.; lack of data for estimating these values during project conception; and project supporters' tendency to understate costs and overstate benefits. Another weakness is sole emphasis on financial and economic criteria, and neglect of other criteria equally or potentially more important.

Scoring Models

Scoring models rate projects in terms of *multiple* criteria that, besides quantifiable measures, include non-quantifiable ones such as market risk, customer enthusiasm, fit with company mission and goals, and so on—whatever criteria are considered important and thought to discriminate between projects.

In the simplest scoring models, a project is rated on each criterion according to a scale (say, 5 = excellent, 4 = good, 3 = adequate, 2 = poor, 1 = bad). The scores for all the criteria are summed to yield a score for the project. Weighted ratings (described in Chapter 3) are used when some criteria are considered more important than others.

Table 17.1 illustrates a rating method that includes probabilities and weights. The first column is the scoring criteria, and the next five columns ("Very Good" through "Very Poor") are *the expected probability* that the project will fit the criteria. For example, the probability that the long-range outlook for the project will be "Very Good" is 80 percent, and will be "Good" is 20 percent. The way these probabilities are obtained depends on the information available to the scoring team, and can range from gut-feel to sophisticated quantitative analysis. The score in the table for "Risk level acceptability," for example, can be opinion-based or derived from analysis of risk impacts and probabilities, as explained in Chapter 10. As with all project analyses, the more data available and the more experienced the scoring team, the more accurate the estimates.

Numbers in the Expected Rating column in Table 17.1 are calculated as the sum of the probabilities times the score. The Expected Rating for long-range outlook for the product, for instance, is $0.8(4) + 0.2(3) = 3.8$.

The next column, Weight, reflects the relative importance of the criteria (for example, a criterion weighted 10 is considered twice as important as one weighted 5); sometimes the weights are set to total to 100, as shown. The next column, Weighted Expected Score, is the Weight multiplied by the Expected Rating. For the long-range outlook of the product, the Weighted Expected Score is $3.8 \times 10 = 38$.

At the bottom of Table 17.1 is the Total Weighted Expected Score (sum over all criteria): 336.8 out of a possible maximum 400. This score is used to screen the proposal in Phase I, or rank-order it with other projects in Phase II.

One limitation of scoring methods is that they ignore the resources needed to implement projects. Big projects tend to be more attention-grabbing and score higher than smaller projects, but they also consume more resources and shut out other projects—even those important to survival or growth. This limitation can be offset by simultaneously considering both a project's required funds or resources and its score or rating, as in the cost-effectiveness method, described later.

17.4 METHODS FOR COMPARING AND SELECTING PROJECTS

After proposed projects have been analyzed, scored, and screened in Phase I, the next step, in Phase II, is to compare the surviving ones with current projects and determine which of them in combination constitute the best portfolio. As a result of this step, some new projects will be added to the portfolio and some current projects will be dropped.

In their review of project portfolios in product development, Cooper and colleagues found that companies tend to use project selection approaches aimed at some combination of the following goals:[13]

Table 17.1 Project Weighted Scoring Model

Criteria		Very good 4	Good 3	Fair 2	Poor 1	Very poor 0	Expected rating	Weight	Weighted expected score
Long-range outlook	1. Product	0.8	0.2				3.8	10	38
	2. Market	1.0					4.0	10	40
Meets objectives	1. ECV	0.8	0.2				3.8	5	19
	2. ROI		1.0				3.0	6	18.0
	3. Image		0.6	0.4			2.6	4	10.4
Fits strategy	Phase 1	0.8	0.2				3.8	10	38
	Phase 2				1.0		1.0	5	5
	Phase 3	0.6	0.2	0.2			3.4	5	17
Goal contribution	Goal A	0.2	0.8				3.2	10	32
	Goal B	1.0					4.0	5	20
	Goal C		0.2	0.2	0.6		1.6	4	6.4
Risk level acceptability		0.7	0.3				3.7	10	37
Competitive advantage		0.9	0.1				3.9	8	31.2
Compatibility with other systems		0.2	0.7	0.1			3.1	8	24.8
Total								100	336.8/400

Adapted from Cleland D. In *Project Management: Strategic Design and Implementation*, 3rd edn. New York, NY: McGraw-Hill, 1999; reprinted in Dye L and Pennypacker J (eds). *Project Portfolio Management*. West Chester, PA: Center for Business Practices; 1999. pp. 3–22.

- Maximizing the value or utility of the portfolio
- Achieving balance in the portfolio
- Fitting the portfolio to the organization's objectives and strategic initiatives.

Value or Utility

Value or utility methods select projects with the highest "value" or usefulness as determined from financial models or scoring methods.

Single-Criterion Methods

Projects can be rank-ordered according to a single value or utility measure (e.g., B/C ratio, ECV from model in Figure 17.3, score from Table 17.1, etc.), and the highest-ranked ones are selected subject to resource availability. A minimum-value threshold can be applied for screening projects, such as rejecting any proposal having a B/C ratio of less than 1.5 or a score of less than 50 percent maximum (200/400 in Table 17.1).

Beyond our scope are other value methods, including mathematical programming techniques that select the combination of projects which maximizes the portfolio value subject to project dependencies, limited resources, and other constraints. An advantage of some of these methods is that they allow *sensitivity analysis* for a *range* of conditions (e.g., what happens if expected revenues drop 20 percent, costs rise 30 percent, and the exchange rate increases 10 percent?).[14]

The main drawback of single-criterion methods is their reliance on just one value to rank-order projects; this can be risky because underlying estimates of costs, benefits, probabilities, etc., are usually fraught with inaccuracies. Also, the methods tend to be laden with assumptions that, if incorrect or overlooked, can lead to erroneous conclusions. Rank-ordering of projects according to B/C, for instance, assumes that all the projects are of comparable size in terms of expected costs and benefits. Project A with a B/C of 3.0 would be ranked ahead of Project B with a B/C of 2.0 even if Project B had a benefit of $2 million and Project A had a benefit of only $200,000.

Multiple-Criteria Methods

There are many ways to value a project, and a project valued high in one way might be valued very poor in another. The way to account for this is with scoring methods that use several value criteria.[15] For example, in Table 17.2 each project is rated for three criteria: Fit with Corporate Strategy (subjective rating 0–4; 0 is poor fit, 4 is perfect fit), Reward (ECV, computed from financial model), and Risk (subjective rating 0–4; 0 is no risk, 4 is high risk). Project scores for each criterion are compared and the projects ranked. For example, in Table 17.2 Project Adrastea is ranked 5 for Strategic

Table 17.2 Multiple Criteria Rank-Ordered List

Project	Strategic Fit	Reward (ECV)	Risk	Ranking Score
Project Metis	4 (1)	2.3 (7)	3 (3)	3.67 (5)
Project Adrastea	0 (5)	3.5 (4)	4 (4)	4.33 (7)
Project Thebe	2 (3)	3.1 (5)	4 (4)	4.0 (6)
Project 10	3 (2)	2.6 (6)	2 (2)	3.33 (4)
Project Europa	1 (4)	6.4 (1)	4 (4)	3.0 (3)
Project Ganymede	3 (2)	4.6 (3)	3 (3)	2.67 (2)
Project Callisto	4 (1)	5.3 (2)	2 (2)	1.67 (1)

Fit because it scored lowest, 0 (note, some projects are ranked the same because their scores are tied); it is rated 4 for ECV because it has the fourth largest ECV value; and it is ranked 4 for Risk because it has the highest risk (tied with Projects Thebe and Europa). The Ranking Score column is computed as the average of the three rankings; for Project Adrastea it is $(5+4+4)/3 = 4.33$, which places the project seventh and last.

The advantage of this approach is that it accounts for multiple criteria simultaneously, and allows for additional criteria to be added if desired. It assures that "good" projects (in terms of the financial or scoring criteria used) are retained as candidates for selection. A limitation of this and all value methods is that they alone do not guarantee a portfolio that is "balanced" or is aligned with organizational objectives and strategies.

Portfolio Balance[16]

Wise investors avoid taking on too much risk. Rather than putting all their eggs into one basket, they diversify and strike a balance between investments that are high-gain but high-risk and ones that are low-gain but low-risk. Despite enticing opportunities for large profits or other rewards, few real estate developers, pharmaceutical companies, software developers, or others put all their resources into projects, markets, or products where outcomes are highly uncertain. They seek a balance between projects that are gambles and projects that are safe bets.

A way to display this balance is with a "bubble chart" that maps projects onto two axes. In Figure 17.4 each "bubble" represents a project; the x-axis represents the project reward or expected benefits, the y-axis the likelihood of project success. The reward axis can be an interval scale (e.g., values for ECV, NPV, etc.) or ordinal scale (e.g., high, low); similarly, the likelihood axis can be interval (0–100 probability) or ordinal (e.g., low, high).

The sizes of the bubbles in Figure 17.4 correspond to the relative sizes of the projects based on, say, funding or resources. Given fixed funding or resources for all the projects, the combined areas of the bubbles must remain constant (e.g., if a project is added or increased in size, then the others must be decreased in size).

In product development organizations, the four quadrants in the chart are labeled according to the kinds of projects one typically finds—pearls, oysters, bread and butter, and white elephants.

"Pearls" are the projects that every company wants—high likelihood of success and high reward. In reality, companies are strapped with many projects in the other quadrants as well. "Oysters" have lower success likelihood because of technical or other difficulties, but are worth pursuing because of the high potential reward. The aim is to find pearls in the oysters; most oysters do not contain pearls, but you don't know that until you have tried them all.

"Bread and butter" projects are often the most common: rewards are low to moderate, but the success rate is high, usually because of easy implementation. Too many bread and butter projects, however, detract resources from the pearls and oysters and reduce opportunities for future business.

"White elephants" are projects with low likelihood of success *and* low payoff. You have to wonder why a company would retain any projects in this category. The fact is, people often feel that once having spent money and effort on a project, they should continue. It sometimes takes courage to cull a white elephant from the project portfolio, especially when the project was the idea of an influential manager.

Figure 17.5 shows another kind of bubble chart wherein the size and shape of each bubble reflects the range of uncertainty about the likelihood of project success and the reward. The larger or longer the bubble, the greater the uncertainty.[17]

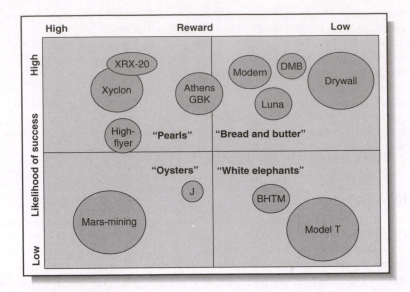

Figure 17.4
Bubble chart for project likelihood of success and reward, and project size.
Adapted from Cooper R, Edgett S, and Kleinschmidt E. Portfolio management in new product development: lessons from leaders, phase I. In Dye L and Pennypacker J (eds), *Project Portfolio Management*. West Chester, PA: Center for Business Practices; 1999. pp. 97–116.

Like other assessment methods, the drawback of bubble charts is that they rely on estimates or guesses of likelihoods, rewards, cost, etc. And although they show the distribution of projects across two axes, they do not indicate the project rank-order or priority by other criteria (e.g., which is better, "High-flyer," "Drywall" or "Mars-mining"?) or how projects *should* be distributed across the axes. Nonetheless, assuming the project selection team has in mind the balance it wants, the charts can be used to decide which projects to analyze more carefully and which to ignore. Conceptually, at least, every organization has a "threshold" line, shown in Figure 17.5, above which projects are accepted and below which they are rejected.

Strategic Fit

Another way to select projects is by how well they fit organizational goals and strategies. Starting with the organization's mission, strategic initiatives, and objectives, top management decides on the "kinds" or categories of projects that best fit them.

Projects are typically categorized or grouped according to:[18]

- Strategic goals (e.g., defending the product base, growing the base, diversifying products, etc.)
- Product lines (product A, B, C, etc.)
- Project type (R&D, capital improvement, process improvement, etc.)

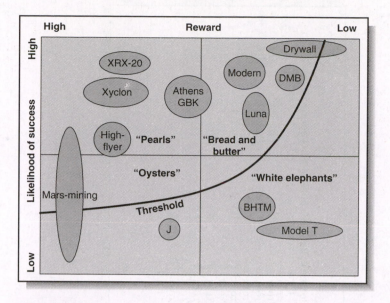

Figure 17.5
Bubble chart for likelihood of success and reward, and uncertainty range.
Adapted from Cooper R, Edgett S, and Kleinschmidt E. Portfolio manage-
ment in new product development: lessons from leaders, phase I. In Dye
L and Pennypacker J (eds), *Project Portfolio Management*. West Chester,
PA: Center for Business Practices; 1999. pp. 97–116.

- Geography (Toronto, California, Indonesia, Central America, etc.).
- Business unit (marketing, manufacturing, product development, etc.).

Examples of categories are the five headings in Table 17.3. Associated with each
category is an allocated funding amount ($12.5M, $8.5M, $10M, etc.); this is the total
budget available to projects in that category.

In small companies, these categories would be consolidated into one portfolio
and managed by a single portfolio group; they might constitute a program and be
overseen by a program manager. In large companies, however, *each category* would be
a *separate portfolio* managed by its own project review board (PRB). In the latter case,
the process starts by top management dividing all projects and proposals in the organization.

Companies routinely undertake more projects than they can handle. For example,
in Table 17.3 the totals at the bottom of the columns indicate that projects in all but
the second category require funding in excess of the allocated funding. To decide
which projects to select, the PRB creates a rank-ordered list of projects (using methods described earlier), and, starting at the top, approves projects until funds run out.
Supposing the projects in Table 17.3 have been rank-ordered, the underlined projects
are the cutoff projects. In the last category, for instance, Project S is the cutoff, and
Projects A1 and E1 will not be supported.

An approved project is admitted to the portfolio and enters a queue. However,
the ultimate execution of the project depends on availability of key resources.

Table 17.3 Projects Rank-Ordered by Category

PROJECTS RANK-ORDERED WITHIN CATEGORIES

Asian Operations $12.5M		European Operations $8.5M		OEM Product Line Development $10M		Domestic Product Line Development $8M		Process Improvement $7.2M	
Project E	3.2	Project B	0.2	Project A	3.4	Project D	2.2	Project C	2.2
Project G	1.4	Project F	2.2	Project H	0.8	Project J	1.2	Project I	0.8
Project O	0.6	Project N	0.4	Project L	1.7	Project M	0.1	Project K	1.2
Project Q	3.7	Project P	1.5	Project R	3.1**	Project T	1.3	Project S	2.7**
Project W	2.3**	Project U	1.3	Project CI	1.6	Project V	0.2	Project AI	0.7
Project BI	1.8	Project X	0.6	Project GI	1.1	Project Y	0.8	Project EI	1.2
Total	13.0*	Project FI	1.9**	Total	11.7*	Project Z	1.2**	Total	8.8*
		Total	8.1			Project DI	2.2		
						Project HI	0.2		
						Total	9.4*		

* Required funding exceeds allocation.
** Cutoff project.

Someone, somewhere (perhaps the PMO) is keeping track of deployment of key limited resources. Only when the needed resources become available can the project be scheduled to begin.

Deciding on the categories and appropriate funding for each is the responsibility of top management. These decisions presumably are based upon consideration of organization mission, strategies, and objectives, although sometimes the allocation is debatable. The mission of NASA, for instance, is to support research and development in aeronautics, manned spaceflight, and unmanned space exploration, although currently the overwhelming share of NASA funding goes to manned spaceflight programs, which leaves little remaining for unmanned space exploration, and even less for aeronautics research. This has led critics to charge that NASA's skewed funding allocation and project portfolio does not support the agency's full range of purported objectives.

Cost–Benefit Grids

A method well suited for prioritizing and selecting projects according to several criteria is Buss's cost–benefit grid.[19] Suppose two important criteria are financial benefits and project cost. The PRB reviews each project proposal and rates the project's financial benefits as high, medium, or low, and its cost as high, medium, or low. This outcome can be displayed on a three-by-three grid. When several projects are rated in this way, the result looks like Grid A in Figure 17.6, which shows the ratings for 12 projects.

After reviewing the grid and reaching agreement on the relative positioning of the displayed projects, the team repeats the procedure for additional criteria such as

Figure 17.6
Buss's cost–benefit grids, ratings for 12 projects.

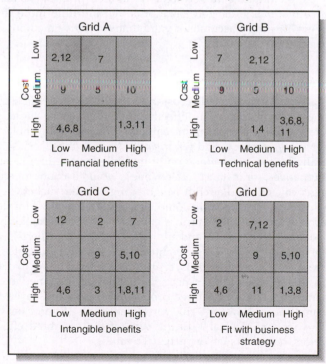

technical benefits, intangible benefits, fit with company business strategy, and so on, and plots the results on other grids (Figure 17.6).

How are intangible benefits assessed? First, the team agrees on the intangible benefits it wants to consider, such as company image, customer satisfaction, strategic fit, and so on. Teams having members with different perspectives—i.e., some members see projects in terms of financial return and others see them in terms of technical capabilities or strategic benefits—can usually better identify intangibles than teams where everyone thinks alike. Given the list of intangibles, the team chooses a scoring method. If, for example, each intangible benefit is scored on a scale of 1–5 and there are six benefits, each project's total score for intangibles will range from 30 (score of 5 on all six benefits) to 0. To locate a project in the grid, scores are converted into simple categories—for example, greater than 20 is High, less than 11 is Low, and in between is Medium.[20]

From the completed grids, the team creates a rank-ordered list. Projects in the right cells would be listed at the top; those in the upper left at the bottom. But besides location in the grids, rank-ordering also depends on organizational priorities. In Figure 17.6, projects 1, 3, 5, 8, 10, and 11 appear in the right cells in three of the grids, yet if the organization's top priority is financial return, then projects 5 and 8 will be ranked lower—and might even be rejected. Final ranking will also depend on each project's size and the funding and resources available, as described earlier.

The main advantage of the grid method is clear exposition of the comparative benefits of projects as determined by the collective judgment of the team. For this (and all team assessment and selection methods), the team ideally is composed of members representing a broad range of perspectives (technical, product/market, financial, environmental, social, etc.).[21]

Although this approach might seem to rely too much on subjective judgment and too little on formal analysis, there is nothing to prevent the team from using formal analysis methods and quantitative models to arrive at their ratings. (As mentioned, though, quantitative methods often rely on inputs that are little more than mere guesses, making them little more accurate or valid than subjective methods—despite creating false perceptions to the contrary.)

Cost-Effectiveness Analysis[22]

Cost-effectiveness analysis is similar to the cost–benefit grid method, but uses numerical values for cost and benefits. The term "effectiveness" refers to the degree to which a project is expected to fulfill project requirements; it is interchangeable with the terms *benefit*, *value*, *utility*, *efficiency*, and *performance*. As with those terms, assessing effectiveness typically involves consideration of multiple factors. In assessing commercial aircraft alternatives, for instance, effectiveness would account for some combination of passenger capacity and aircraft weight, range, speed, fuel efficiency, and maintainability, which are interrelated in complex ways. One method for deriving a single measure incorporating multiple factors is to rate the factors subjectively (but using results from quantitative analysis and advice from technical experts), weigh the ratings, and add them up—similar to the weighted scoring model illustrated in Table 17.1. The factors chosen for the analysis must represent significant ways to distinguish the projects, and in all other important respects the projects are assumed identical.

The example in Table 17.4 shows three proposed projects and seven factors.[23] Each project is scored for each factor 0–100 for effectiveness (E) and for weighted effectiveness (WE = weight × E). Total WE, the sum of the weighted effectiveness across all seven factors, represents the project effectiveness.

Table 17.4 Cost-Effectiveness Data Analysis

FACTORS	W(WEIGHT %)	PROJECT A E	PROJECT A WE	PROJECT B E	PROJECT B WE	PROJECT C E	PROJECT C WE
Speed	10	95	9.5	80	8	85	8.5
Range	15	70	10.5	80	12	75	11.25
Efficiency	20	75	15	75	15	85	17
Comfort	15	70	10.5	85	12.75	85	12.75
Capacity	20	70	14	90	18	95	19
Loaded mass	15	90	.13.5	60	9	70	10.5
Maintainability	5	75	3.75	85	4.25	80	4
Total WE			76.75		79		83
Cost			$ 1.9 B		$2.0B		$3.0 B

The method does not rank the projects, but does suggest which ones should be dropped from consideration, and allows trade-off analysis of the projects remaining. For example, Figure 17.7 shows the three projects from Table 17.4 and five other projects. Projects *j*, *h*, and *m* (in the shaded area) fall below the minimal effectiveness threshold of 75 percent, and should be dropped from consideration. The line connecting the uppermost points (*j*, *A*, *n*, *C*)—called the "efficient frontier"—represents the *maximum effectiveness* attainable for a given cost (or minimum cost for a given level of effectiveness). Projects below this line (projects *B* and *k*) are inferior to at least one other project in terms of both cost and effectiveness, and can also be dropped. Hence only projects *A*, *n*, and *C* are worthy of further consideration.

A maximum effectiveness line with a positive slope indicates that increasing project cost is justified by increasing effectiveness. But the *degree* of slope matters too:

Figure 17.7
Effectiveness versus development cost for eight projects.

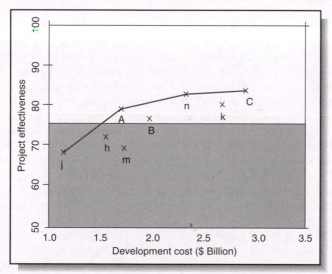

Project *C* is only slightly more effective than Project *n* but costs a lot more, suggesting that it is probably not worth pursuing.

Project selection involves imperfect information about project costs and benefits. While the models in this chapter provide "objective" ways to sort through the maze of facts, figures, and issues associated with project selection, rarely are final decisions ever based solely upon them. They all entail assumptions and subjectivity that allow human instincts, emotions, and ulterior motives to influence project selection.

17.5 PERIODIC PROJECT REVIEW AND ASSESSMENT

Portfolio management includes both selection of new projects and periodic review of current projects. The PRB must decide when to start each newly approved project—immediately or later—and whether the resources for each current project should be sustained, increased, or decreased. Projects exceeding deadlines or expected costs, not meeting requirements, or no longer suited to changing company objectives or the environment must be reconsidered. Underperforming or no longer necessary projects are cancelled to make way for essential or more promising projects. A sign of an effective portfolio management process is that periodically some projects get cancelled.

17.6 INTEGRATING THE GATING PROCESS WITH PORTFOLIO MANAGEMENT[24]

Gating augments portfolio management, but the two processes are very different. In the gating process a project is reviewed at certain milestones or stages, and at each stage a decision is made about what to do with it. The decision happens for the individual project by comparing its progress to the plan, requirements, and expectations; it does not consider other projects or the project's impact on organizational resources or objectives.

In contrast, portfolio management looks at all projects in the portfolio and compares them in terms of benefits, costs, and resources. Because of the time and difficulty involved, this might happen only three or four times a year—maybe less. Since companies are usually involved in many projects and proposals at any given time, each arriving at a decision gate at a different time, it is not feasible to compare all of the projects in the portfolio every time one of them reaches a gate.

Moreover, the two processes tend to use different decision criteria: whereas gating typically permits a project to continue as long as it conforms to plans and pre-set expectations, portfolio management allows it to continue only if it compares favorably to other projects. In addition, the two processes usually involve different people: in the gating process decisions are made by middle-level managers and customers; in portfolio management they are made by the PRB.

Nonetheless, ideally the two processes and teams assist each other. Gating managers weed out marginal projects so the portfolio will not include underperforming projects, and the PRB weeds out projects that do not contribute to company objectives. Further, the PRB assists managers in the gating process by sharing its rank-ordered listings and noting any changes in company strategy and objectives. Gating managers consider this information and sometimes kill projects that ultimately would have been killed by the PRB anyway.

Portfolio management refers to the process of choosing and managing those projects that best achieve organizational objectives subject to resource constraints. It is a good example of the systems approach wherein the focus is on integrating the elements of a system to best accomplish overall system objectives. Portfolio management in combination with strategic management, the gating process, and project management helps assure that the organization does the right projects, and does those projects right.

Project selection and portfolio management happen through a multi-stage process that includes prescreening, analysis, and screening of new-project proposals, and then ranking, selecting, and ongoing review of current projects. Although top management establishes the high-level criteria for project selection decisions, actual project selection and portfolio management rests with the project review board. The PRB prioritizes projects and decides which to approve, delay, deny, or cancel.

This chapter has reviewed a variety of methods for rating, screening, and comparing projects in terms of benefits, costs, risk, resource requirements, and strategic objectives. Yet although they cover a wide range of decision criteria, the methods do not account for everything. Project dependency is an example: when Project B depends on the completion of Project A, then approval of Project A might depend on the importance of Project B, and, of course, approval of Project B will depend on whether Project A has been has approved.[25] A separate but related matter is selecting parallel projects, such as multiple new-technology product development projects to increase the likelihood that at least one will achieve a technological breakthrough.

Given a variety of methods to analyze, rate, and select projects, the question is: which is best? In practice, no one method stands head and shoulders above the rest. But it is not necessary to choose just one method; in fact, the methods described can be used in combination, and they should be. For example, projects first divided according to strategic categories can then be judged by the benefit–cost grid method; the best of these can then be ranked and selected subject to available resources. Or, projects prioritized and tentatively approved using financial, scoring, or cost-effectiveness approaches can then be checked for portfolio balance on bubble charts, and then judged again with the grid method. Using multiple selection methods helps assure that the projects selected are the "right" ones.

REVIEW QUESTIONS AND PROBLEMS

1. What are the three or four main features of project portfolio management?
2. What is project portfolio? How do project portfolios differ from programs?
3. Is it poor practice to do the easiest projects first ("pick the low hanging fruit")?
4. Compare the following; for each state the focus and how it relates to projects:
   - Strategic management
   - Portfolio management
   - Gating methodology.
5. What is the responsibility of the project review board? Who typically are members of the PRB?
6. "Some projects you simply have to do. You have no choice." Give examples of different types of cases where you have no choice.
7. Do "obligatory projects" (see previous question) necessarily have high priority?
8. What is the purpose of *prescreening* in the project selection process? How does it differ from project *screening*?

9. Explain portfolio selection. What kinds of projects does it consider—current, proposed, or both?
10. How would spare capacity influence project selection decisions? What should you do with spare capacity?
11. Projects W, X, Y, and Z are each being screened according to four criteria: Potential Return on Investment, Lack of Technological Risk, Environmental "Friendliness," and Service to Community:
    - Project W: Return, high; Risk, medium; Environment, medium; Service, low
    - Project X: Return, medium; Risk, high; Environment, medium; Service, low
    - Project Y: Return, medium; Risk, medium; Environment, high; Service, high
    - Project Z: Return, medium; Risk, medium; Environment, high; Service, low.

    Create a scheme for screening the projects, assuming equal weight for all criteria. Which project comes out best; which worst?
12. For the above four projects, assign scores of high=3, medium=2, and low=1. Assume the criteria are weighted: Potential Return on Investment=0.3, Lack of Technological Risk=0.3, Environmental "Friendliness"=0.3, and Service to Community=0.1. Now which projects come out best and worst?
13. Compare the ECV and B/C methods for evaluating projects.
14. What is the expected commercial value (ECV) of a project involving the launch of a new product with an estimated development cost of $15M, launch cost of $0.8M and an NPV for the future stream of earnings of $45M if the probabilities for success are 70 percent in development and 50 percent in the market?
15. A project has three phases, concept, development, and launch, that are expected to cost $5M, $15M, and $4M, respectively. The likelihoods of success for the three phases are 0.5, 0.8, and 0.7, respectively. If the estimated NPV of future earnings is $90M, what is the ECV for the project?
    [Answer: $11.1 M.]
16. In the previous example, what else must be considered if the stream of earning were in euros instead of dollars?
17. In Problem 15, suppose the likelihood of project success is $0.5 \times 0.8 \times 0.7 = 0.28$.
    - What is the B/C ratio for the project?
    - Which measure makes the project look more attractive, ECV or B/C? In your opinion, does the project merit approval?
18. Project A and Project B both have the same overall cost of $4M. Project A's likelihood of success is 95 percent, B's chances are 50 percent. Project A is expected to generate $11M but will incur $5M maintenance in costs. Project B is expected to generate revenue of $8M and also to provide increased efficiencies that would save $5M in expenses. Applying the B/C ratio, which project would you recommend?
19. What advantage do scoring models have over financial models in terms of assessing the value or utility of projects?
20. What are the drawbacks of (a) financial models; (b) scoring models?
21. What are the three main approaches to comparing and selecting projects?
22. What is the drawback of ranking projects using single-criterion methods?
23. Repeat the example in Table 17.2, but besides Fit, Reward, and Risk include a fourth criterion: Public Image of Project (4=high, 0=none). Assume the projects are rated as follows on Public Image (numbers in parentheses are ranking on list):

Project	Public Image
Project Metis	0 (5)
Project Adrastea	1 (4)
Project Thebe	4 (1)
Project 10	3 (2)
Project Europa	4 (1)
Project Ganymede	2 (3)
Project Callisto	3 (2)

Include this ranking with the rankings for Strategic Fit, Reward, and Risk; recompute the Ranking Scores for the projects based on all four criteria.

24. Draw a bubble chart for Risk versus Reward similar to Figure 17.4 for the projects in Table 17.2. Assume ECV <3 is "Low" and ECV >6 is "High." For risk, 1 is "Low" and 4 is "High." Use the Public Image ratings (not rankings) from Problem 23 to "size" the projects on the chart: i.e., 4 is the largest project, 3 is smaller, etc., and 0 is a dot. Based on the bubble chart, which projects are pearls? Which are white elephants? Which are bread and butter?

25. Top management has decided to reallocate funds among the five categories of projects listed in Table 17.3 as follows: $13M, $8M, $7.5M, $10M, and $7.8M, respectively. What are the cut-off projects in each of the five categories?

26. Explain how cost–benefit grids can be used to rank-order projects.

27. Discuss similarities and differences between bubble charts and cost–benefit grids.

28. Suppose project D is added to the projects in Table 17.4 and has been rated for effectiveness as follows:

Project D

Factors	E
Speed	80
Range	90
Efficiency	95
Comfort	85
Capacity	95
Loaded mass	90
Maintainability	80
Cost	$2.5 B

Compute the total weighted effectiveness using the weights in Table 17.4. How does Project D compare to the others in Figure 17.7?

29. Once a project has been approved and admitted to the project portfolio, how is it monitored thereafter? Under what circumstances might it be cancelled?

30. Describe the differences between the gating process and the portfolio management process. What are the difficulties in integrating the two processes? How might the difficulties be overcome so that portfolio projects can also be gated projects?

QUESTIONS ABOUT THE STUDY PROJECT

1. Does the organization have a portfolio management process? If so, describe the key steps in the process, and the managers and others who participate in the process. In your opinion, is the process effective? What are its strengths and weaknesses?

2. Does the organization have a project review board (governance board, project steering committee, etc.)? Describe the board, its role, membership, meetings, etc.

3. Describe the organization's project analysis and selection process. What kind of analysis and selection models and methods are used?

4. How are projects compared and rank-ordered? Are techniques described in this chapter used? Who makes approval and funding decisions?

5. If the organization has a gating process, describe the gates, the assessment criteria at each, and who participates. In your opinion, is the process effective?

6. If the organization has both portfolio management and gating processes, discuss the relationship between the two and the manner in which they are integrated.

7. If the organization has a PMO, discuss the PMO's role in portfolio management and the gating process.

Note: Case 3.3 and Case 16.3 are also appropriate for this chapter.

Case 17.1   Consolidated Energy Company

Consolidated Energy (CE) is a public utility company that generates and distributes electricity throughout a large portion of the US. The company is involved in all kinds of projects, including construction of new electrical generating and transmission equipment and facilities, upgrade and repair of existing equipment and facilities, information technology for customer service, and energy research projects. Much of this project work is contracted out, although CE units handle about half of it with internal expertise in construction, equipment upgrade and maintenance, information technology, and research. The company has construction units and equipment specialists in five cities, information technology specialists in three cities, and research units in two cities. The research units work on projects initiated by the corporate office, but the construction, equipment upgrade and maintenance, and IT units work on projects initiated by the five regional offices. Each of the units is assigned to one or two regions, so whenever a regional office identifies a project, that project is automatically handled by the construction, IT, or equipment unit pre-assigned to its region.

Decisions about projects are made at both regional and corporate levels: projects costing more than $20M are handled at the corporate level; otherwise they are handled regionally. Whenever a regional office funds a project, it first decides if the IT, equipment, or construction unit for its region can handle the job; if so it assigns the job to them, otherwise it contracts the work out using the RFP/proposal process. A corporate PRB makes decisions for projects that exceed $20M. When the PRB approves a project, it awards the job either to the internal unit assigned to the region that requested the project, or to a contractor via the RFP/proposal process.

Recently, a member of the corporate PRB had a brainstorm: why not use the RFP/proposal process for *all* projects, including ones that might be done internally? When a regional office identifies a potential project, instead of giving the project automatically to the pre-assigned internal unit, it would send an RFP to *all* of the company's IT, construction, or equipment units. The unit with the best proposal would get the job, regardless of its location. Some members of the board balked at the suggestion, saying it would put units with the same expertise in competition with each other. Others argued that it did not make sense for, say, a construction unit to take on a project beyond its region, because transporting equipment and moving work crews to distant project sites would increase project costs. The member with the suggestion countered that such arguments were pointless, because competition among the units would encourage higher quality work and reduce overall corporate costs.

QUESTIONS

What do you think of this idea? What are the pros and cons?

NOTES

1. Cooper R, Edgett S, and Kleinschmidt E. Portfolio management in new product development: lessons from leaders, phase II. *Research Technology Management* Nov–Dec; 1997: 43–52, reprinted in Dye L and Pennypacker J (eds). *Project Portfolio Management*. West Chester, PA: Center for Business Practices; 1999. pp. 27–33.

2. Sommer R. Portfolio management for projects: a new paradigm 1998. *Proceedings of the Annual Project Management Institute Seminars & Symposiums*. Newtown Square, PA: Project Management Institute; reprinted in Dye and Pennypacker J, *Project Portfolio Management*, pp. 55–59.

3. This section adopted from Cooper *et al.* Portfolio management in new product development: lessons from leaders, phase II: 34–35; and Bridges D. Project portfolio management: ideas and practices. In Dye L and

Pennypacker J, *Project Portfolio Management*, pp. 97–116.

4. Levine H. Project portfolio management: a song without words? *PM Network* July; 1999.

5. Frame JD. *The New Project Management*. San Francisco, CA: Jossey-Bass Publishers; 1994. p. 190.

6. Archer N and Ghasemzadeh F. An integrated framework for project portfolio selection. *International Journal of Project Management* 17(4); 1999: 207–216.

7. Sommer, Portfolio management for projects: a new paradigm; and Bridges, Project portfolio management: ideas and practices.

8. Bridges, Project portfolio management: ideas and practices.

9. The project selection process as a funnel is described in Wheelwright S and Clark K. *Revolutionizing Product Development*. New York, NY: Free Press; 1992.

10. Method described in Cooper *et al.*, Portfolio management in new product development: lessons from leaders, phase I: 16–19; reprinted in Dye and Pennypacker, *Project Portfolio Management*, pp. 97–116.

11. Shtub A, Bard JF, and Globerson S. *Project Management: Processes, Methodologies, and Economics*, 2nd edn. Englewood Cliffs, NJ: Prentice Hall; 2005. pp. 182–183.

12. *Ibid.*, 186–7

13. Cooper *et al.*, Portfolio management in new product development: lessons from leaders, phase I.

14. Mathematical programming optimization approaches for project selection are described in the literature in operations research. For an example, see Dickinson M, Thornton A, and Graves S. Technology portfolio management: optimizing interdependent projects over multiple time periods. *IEEE Transactions of Engineering Management* 48(4); 2001: 518–527.

15. Method described in Cooper *et al.* Portfolio management in new product development:

16. *Ibid.* Bubble charts are easily created with commercial software (Google the term "bubble chart" for examples of methods and products).

17. Cooper *et al.*, Portfolio management in new product development: lessons from leaders, phase I.

18. Method described in Cooper *et al.*, Portfolio management in new product development: lessons from leaders, phase II.

19. Frame, *The New Project Management*, pp. 181–185; Buss M. How to rank computer projects. *Harvard Business Review* Jan–Feb; 1983.

20. Buss, *ibid.*

21. Frame, *The New Project Management*, p. 185.

22. Overview of method as presented in Shtub *et al.*, *Project Management: Engineering, Technology, and Implementation*, pp. 127–130.

23. This example, like others in this chapter, is a much-simplified illustration. Assessing options for development of large-scale systems such as aircraft involves engineering studies to assess alternative configurations and design details, as well as economic analysis of development, purchasing, and operating costs, and projections of unit sales, etc. See, for example, Jenkinson L, Simpkin P, and Rhodes D. *Civil Aircraft Design*. London: Arnold; 1999.

24. This section adapted from Cooper *et al.*, Portfolio management in new product development: lessons from leaders, phase II; and Nelson B, Gill B, and Spring S. Building on the stage/gate: an enterprise-wide architecture for new product development. *Proceedings of the Project Management Institute 28th Annual Seminars and Symposium*, Chicago, IL, pp. 67–72.

25. Dependent projects are handled with a "dependency matrix." See Dickinson *et al.*, Technology portfolio management: optimizing interdependent projects over multiple time periods.

Chapter 18

International Project Management

> You can know the name of a bird in all the languages of the world, but when you're finished, you'll know absolutely nothing whatever about the bird ... So let's look at the bird and see what it's doing—that's what counts. I learned very early the difference between knowing the name of something and knowing something.
>
> —RICHARD FEYNMAN

Consider three recent projects:

1. General Electric divided the development project for a new cardiac monitoring device between two teams, one in Milwaukee, one in Bangalore. The hardware development work was done by the US team, the software work by the Indian team. The project required continual back-and-forth exchange of people, equipment, software, and information. The manager coordinating the project was based in Milwaukee, but made frequent trips to Bangalore.
2. Bechtel, a US corporation with divisions around the world, oversaw the construction of a complete industrial city in Saudi Arabia. As prime contractor, it managed and coordinated on-site work, materials, and major systems provided by subcontractors from Europe, the US, and Saudi Arabia. The project manager, an employee of Bechtel-UK, stayed on site during most of the project, but traveled globally to meet with Bechtel's senior managers and contractor associates.[1]

3. Boeing Commercial Airplane Division is the principal designer, systems integrator, and final assembler for the 787 commercial aircraft, but virtually all of the design and manufacture for the plane's major components and subsystems—wings, fuselage sections, engines, and instrumentation—is done by contract suppliers in Japan, Canada, Spain, Italy, and the US. Oversight and integration of suppliers and other Boeing divisions contributing to the program is run from Boeing's program management office in Washington State.

The obvious commonality among these projects is that they are all "international" or "global" in scope. Unlike single-country, domestic projects, where most or all stakeholders and physical project work are confined to one country, stakeholders in these projects are in different countries, and project teams and work sites are cross-national and cross-cultural.

18.1 INTERNATIONAL PROJECTS

International projects have become ubiquitous as more companies establish divisions, seek customers, and outsource work to suppliers and contractors in different countries. Thanks in large part to lower costs and increased capacity of global air and sea transportation, enhanced communication technologies fueled by the Internet, and emerging business and technological capabilities in nations such as China and India, companies seek out and execute projects everywhere.

While such projects are enticing because of the benefits and opportunities that come with operating on an international scale, they are at the same time vulnerable to considerable risk. Regardless of its scope or end-item, a project that is "global," "international," or "overseas" automatically inherits more issues and greater risk than one that is not. And regardless of the issues and problems that face the manager of a domestic, one-country project, the manager in an international project automatically faces an "extra layer" of issues. That extra layer touches almost everything about management—leadership, interpersonal relations, stakeholder identification and involvement, communication, planning, work definition, estimating, risk management, and work tracking and control. Language, communication, local customs, transportation, and infrastructure—all that might cause little or no concern in a home-country project—become potential showstoppers in an international project.

18.2 PROBLEMS MANAGING INTERNATIONAL PROJECTS[2]

Each new international project poses a new set of unknowns. To illustrate, think of an international project as analogous to a play with actors, scripts, sets, and props. Actors are the project stakeholders and social networks, scripts are the social institutions that guide and constrain peoples' behavior, the set is the project's natural environment, and props are the project technologies. Just as the actors, scripts, sets, and props differ in every play, so do the stakeholders, institutions, natural environment, and technologies differ in every international project. These differences expose the project manager to potential mistakes and oversights in organizing, planning, and running the project.

Table 18.1 lists important issues and unknowns in an international project, most concerned with aspects of the project's locality. Some of these issues are "explicit" (somewhat easy to identify and account for in project plans and estimates); others are "tacit" (more difficult to pinpoint and address). The less a project manager knows about the locality of the project—the host country and its people—the harder he must work to make sense out of these issues and adapt to them. (Hereafter, "host" refers to the place where the project is executed; "home" to the native country of the contractor, developer, or project manager.) Ignorance about the unknowns makes it difficult for managers to anticipate problems, set priorities, and act appropriately. It is why international projects often have trouble meeting schedule, budget, or requirements commitments.

18.3 LOCAL INSTITUTIONS AND CULTURE

Stakeholders in international projects comprise diverse languages and cultures that influence communication, attitudes, behavior, work practices, decision patterns, and, ultimately, project performance. Additionally, they are guided or restricted by regional or national laws, regulations, and rules.

Language
When project stakeholders speak different languages, conversations and shared documents about project scope, requirements, schedules, budgets, and contracts must be

Table 18.1 Unknowns in an International Project*

1. Local institutions and culture

   a) Language (explicit)
   b) Norms, social customs, attitudes, traditions (tacit)
   c) Laws, rules, rights, sanctions (explicit)

2. Local stakeholders—laborers, managers, consultants, suppliers (tacit)

   a) Skill, experience, motivation
   b) Reputation, honesty, integrity
   c) Who knows who; who has knowledge, resources, and connections

3. Local natural environment (explicit)

   a) Site environment—soil, ground slope, vegetation
   b) Regional environment—climate-weather, geography, seismic activity

4. Local technology (explicit)

   a) Infrastructure—roads, buildings, communication
   b) Available tools and systems—GPS, equipment, hardware, software, materials

* Note: "Local" refers to people and factors situated *at* the location or region of the project, or that become activated in the local context, including international NGOs, associations, and other organizations that play a role in "promulgating environmental, technological, occupational, and legal" rules and regulations to the local level.
Adapted from Orr R. *Strategies to Succeed in Foreign Environments*. Collaboratory for Research on Global Projects, Stanford University, presented at the CIB W92 International Symposium Construction Procurement—The Impact of Cultural Differences and Systems on Construction Performance, Las Vegas, Feb 8–10, 2005, 3. http://crgp.stanford.edu/publications/conference_papers/RyanVegas.pdf, downloaded April 10, 2007.

translated. The challenge is that every translation faithfully reflects the content and intention of the original message.

Even projects wherein ostensibly everyone uses the same language face difficulties. For example, the same English words when used in America, the UK, South Africa, Australia, and India may have different meanings; add to that slang, vernacular, idiomatic terms, and poor diction, and what happens is the message gets "lost in translation." For example, "tell the English to walk on the pavement and they will walk on what the Americans call the sidewalk; tell the Americans to walk on the pavement, they will walk down the middle of what the English call the tarmac."[3] US managers often say it is more difficult to communicate with British subjects than with French.

The best practice in international communication is to *always* use the simplest, most clear and concise wording and phrasing. Before sending out important messages and documents, ask several people to interpret them. Napoleon did something like this: before issuing military orders he always had a corporal read them, reasoning that if someone of such low rank could understand them, then certainly so would his officers.[4]

Often locals will claim to understand English when in fact their grasp of it is poor at best. When they pepper their responses with "yes, yes, yes," it is a sure bet they don't understand what's being said. When giving verbal directives, always follow it up in writing.

Managers sometimes create a project glossary of terms that at times can be extensive and even include pictures. For the 1960s project to develop the Anglo-French Concorde supersonic airplane, a special French–English project dictionary was created.

Formality

Whereas business associates in North America tend to address one another—subordinates, immediate superiors, and even senior managers—by first name, almost everywhere else in the world they use some variant of sir, mister, or madam. Such formality extends to the way people introduce themselves, communicate ideas, make commitments, and give and receive business cards. The workplace itself may be subject to a code of behavior that discourages kidding around and other forms of informality. Formality pertains to documents, too: in most countries proposals and contracts are commonly faxed, emailed, or verbally communicated; in international projects, however, such practices pose questions regarding the country where agreements are made or contracts concluded, and, hence, whose contract law and court of law should prevail.

Gift Giving

Many companies and countries permit gift giving and taking as suitable ways to show gratitude and respect, but many others prohibit it. Only certain gifts are considered acceptable, and discretion is necessary to avoid violating local laws or etiquette customs.

Attitudes about Age

Many cultures associate wisdom with age. Older people automatically garner greater respect, and seldom can a younger manager command the same level of attention, reverence, or credibility as an older manager, regardless of experience. Managers in senior positions are always older (and usually male), and they tend not to deal with or even listen to anyone much younger than they are. In meetings, older managers do most of the speaking, and younger managers never contradict them—even when they disagree.

Social Behavior

In Middle- and Far-Eastern countries, most relationship-building and much formal business happens after-hours at social gatherings. Proper conduct at such gatherings is dictated by local norms, although in general any sign of inebriation, fraternizing with business associates, careless or too-casual dress, or sharing of personal details about family or friends is considered inappropriate. Behavior that would be considered suitable or even expected elsewhere—like bringing a spouse to a gathering or talking to another's spouse—can be cause for embarrassment, and damaging to a business relationship.

Of course, offensive behavior and dress should always be avoided, although what is considered offensive varies by country. In the Middle East a woman's head should be covered in public, and men and women are not supposed to greet each other by shaking hands. People in Rome tend to be more nicely dressed and courteous than, say, in US cities, and a tourist from the US who would not draw any attention at home might come across as somewhat slovenly and crass in Rome. When working in Rome (or Beijing or Mumbai), a good rule of thumb is to try to adopt some of the local customs of dress and behavior (assuming they do not violate a personal or universal code of ethics).

Food and Drink

Newly arriving expatriates often will scan local menus looking for familiar items—not knowing that the foods listed won't be the same as back home. (Home-based or well-known franchises are more reliable and sometimes provide welcome familiarity.) Meat portions in Europe and Asia tend to be small—miniscule by US standards. Meat and martinis might not be on the menu, or on any menu anywhere in the country, and even to ask about them is utterly inappropriate. The rule of thumb concerning food and drink—but applicable to everything about local customs—is to be respectful, polite, and accepting, even when the items or customs do not suit your taste or predisposition.

Attitudes about Time

In some Western countries, punctuality is everything. Time is viewed as a limited resource, and being on time assures it is never wasted. People who dither or are late are considered rude and inconsiderate of others' time! But in the Middle and Far East and most of Africa the concept of time is viewed differently: more important than doing things punctually is to make sure they are done right. If it takes time to prepare a plan, and then revise the plan and revise it again, so be it, even if the schedule slips. A Western manager accustomed to filling every minute with work will be annoyed by the many "time-wasting" gatherings organized by his Asian or Middle-Eastern business associates; they, in turn, will be insulted by *his* angst to get on with business, and will question his motives and loyalty to them.

Holidays, Weekends, Vacations

Every country has its own non-work holidays. The US has 7 national public holidays; most European countries have 10, but Germany has 16. A project that involves participants from, say, 4 countries, each with 5 national holidays could conceivably face 20 days of holiday downtime. Ramadan and Chinese New Year are major holidays that affect the schedules of many projects. Even when different counties share the same holidays, exact dates may differ. In the US the Christmas holiday runs December 23 through January 2, but in Russia and some Eastern European counties it is between December 31 and January 8—sometimes later. In the Southern Hemisphere, where summer holidays are in December, project work is sometimes halted for most of the month. The "weekend" in many parts of the world is Saturday and Sunday, but in the Middle East it is Thursday and Friday. While these differences create problems for some projects, they offer solutions to others by enabling work to continue at different places around the world 7 days a week.

Vacation time-off also varies by country and region. While in the US 2 or 3 weeks' vacation is standard, Australian law prescribes 4 weeks, as does the European Union—usually the whole month of August. Some countries mandate by law 6 weeks' vacation, plus another 6 weeks for sick leave.

Labor Time

What constitutes a "usual" work day and work week also varies. French law mandates and enforces a 35-hour work week that cannot be exceeded, and Chinese law specifies a five 8-hour day work week. Labor laws are not always enforced, but no project manager in any country should gamble on violating them.

Social norms also matter. If the local culture dictates that the "work day" is between 6 am and 2 pm, the manager of a 9-to-5 project will probably see his local workforce falling asleep around 3 pm.

Layoffs

Although it is common in the USA to terminate employees when a project ends and there is no follow-up work, in some countries such termination is not automatic, especially for workers who have served 12 continuous months on the project. What is a manager to do with these employees? In many European countries labor laws determine who an employer can lay off and how the employer must go about it. According to David Pringle of *CareerJournalEurope* on Expatica.com, German employers must base layoff decisions on social criteria that sometimes force them "to retain staff that is older, have large families, and might find it very difficult to get new jobs."[5] Companies in France often must "give detailed reports on the progress of staff-cutting programs to state authorities."

Laws, Contracts, Rights

The law in effect for a project is the law of the host country, not of the home country of the developer or contractor—although US contractors working overseas must confusingly also comply with US law, and the trick is to not violate laws in either country.

In countries like China some rules are not always enforced, and local contractors and customers might tell you just to ignore them (of course, risking the possibility that at any time the rules *could* be enforced).[6] A safe practice is to verify whatever the locals say about the law and never do anything illegal.

Because of differences in language, formalities, terminology, regulations, and laws, international contacts take longer to finalize than domestic contracts. Getting the wording and terminology right on contracts is extremely important, and even the littlest details (like initialing changes and pages) matter.[7] The project manager should be involved in contract negotiations from the beginning and—this is essential—have access in the host country to his own legal counsel or sound legal advice.

To minimize confusion about contract terminology, the International Chamber of Commerce has created a list of International Commercial Terms, or "Incoterms," described in its website as "standard trade definitions most commonly used in international sales contracts . . . [and] at the heart of world trade." Usage of Incoterms in contracts helps clarify expectations and "goes a long way to providing the legal certainty upon which mutual confidence between business partners must be based."[8]

The contractor must be sure to include stipulations and actions in the contract to protect its intellectual rights, and be prepared to take action should it discover that its ideas, products, or technology are being pirated.

Litigation, Payment, Meeting Contract Terms

Contracts should be designed to avoid legal disputes, which in the international arena can be a nightmare—messy, slow, expensive, and sometimes corrupt. They should specify that any legal disputes would be litigated in a neutral country—i.e., neither the host nor the contractor's home country. US contractors often specify England.

The contract should provide stipulations to assure that the customer will receive its deliverables and the contractor its payment. This would seem customary even in single-country, domestic projects, yet because of the extreme difficulties of litigation in international projects the stipulations must be such as to remove even the slightest chance of problems. The contract might impose severe penalties for failure to meet schedules or requirements, and offer strong incentives to exceed them (such incentives assume that the contractor is in the position to perform work to meet requirements—which is not always the case in developing countries).

To protect the contractor, the contract might specify a large first payment followed by payments upon meeting frequent time-phased targets. Payments are often delayed, not by the customer but because international funds transfer typically requires approval by an agency of the host country, which can take 60 days. Sometimes payments to foreigners must be made via tax agents, further complicating the payment process.

Ordinarily, contractors should never perform work for unsecured payment after project completion. In many countries, including China, the system for managing credit and receivables is not very good, and customer creditworthiness is difficult to ascertain.

Politics

National and local political stability, and the government's position regarding the project, are potential risk factors. Radical political reform, overthrow of the government, local military intervention, and labor strikes are clearly situations that could threaten a project. While phenomena such as labor strikes are seldom experienced in countries such as the US, they are common in some other countries. However, such events rarely materialize on short notice and without early warning signs. A contractor working on an international project must have reliable people in the host region to monitor these signs and keep project management informed.

It should be obvious from this section that international projects are fraught with problems absent in single-nation projects. The following example illustrates a few more problems—plus what happens when cross-cultural teams don't try to integrate.

Example 18.1: The Chunnel Project[9]

The initial construction phase of the 32-mile (51km) Channel Tunnel between Britain and France was managed almost as two separate projects—one starting from Britain, the other from France, both racing to see which would reach the halfway mark first. Competition, it was felt, would speed things up. But the teams represented two cultures, and the competition only aggravated their differences and exacerbated problems.

For starters, ideally contracts are written in one language and governed by one legal system, but in the Chunnel project there were *two* contracts, one each in English and French, and neither had precedence over the other. Although the contracts were purportedly based on principles common to the two legal systems, legal approaches to health, safety, trade unions, and taxation differed significantly, and a panel appointed to resolve disputes often faced the situation of having to make very tough decisions.

The two countries also differ with regard to standards concerning, for example, train engines and cars, railway width, voltages, and signaling systems, although clearly in every case there would have to be only one. It was decided that where a difference existed between the standards of the two countries, the higher should prevail—though it was not always obvious which standard was the higher (for example, in the way to pour concrete).

Decisions by a democratic government can require substantial deliberation, but decisions by *two* democratic governments require even more deliberation. Simply deciding whether to increase door width from 600mm to 700mm took 9 months.

18.4   LOCAL STAKEHOLDERS

Contractors[10]

Project teams operating in foreign countries are often required to hire local contractors. Although subcontracting to local contractors can reduce costs for labor and relocation, it can increase costs for training and supervision. Sometimes lower labor cost equates to lower productivity, which translates into needing more workers, thus erasing any potential savings (many countries like India, however, have low labor costs yet productivity as high as in Western nations). A local contractor who is familiar with local customs and bureaucracy can sometimes cut through red tape and avoid hassles that would stymie a contractor from the outside.

Selecting a local contractor requires considerations beyond the usual criteria of skill, experience, resources, and financial stability. One is the likely quality of the local contractor's communications as determined by language and culture. Another is the contractor's familiarity with common business practices. Practices taken for granted in most countries (e.g., RFPs, proposals, SOWs, change controls, and status reporting) may be unfamiliar to a local contractor and a challenge for it to adopt. Also important is the contractor's ethical reputation ("ethical" as defined according to US standards, not local standards). Although perhaps difficult to undertake, a due diligence review of the contractor's business history, reputation for honesty, and political connections is nonetheless a necessity.

Customers and Supporters

Good relations with customers and supporters is always important, but even more so in international projects. In general, whereas Westerners tend to first set contractual agreements and then build relationships, Easterners build relationships first and then reach agreements. Regardless of the professional track record of the project manager and his company, local stakeholders (business associates, subcontractors, vendors, and potential customers) are apt to withhold agreement, collaboration, or support until they feel they know the project manager personally. Building personal relationships and trust with business colleagues and associates is fundamental to the business process.

Example 18.2: How to Ruin a Business Relationship[11]

Negotiations between a firm in India and a US company to finalize the contract on a promising project began with a series of informal meetings. The American project manager sensed that his Indian customers were needlessly dragging their feet, so he tried to urge them along. But the more aggressive he became, the more the Indians doubted his motives and the less they trusted him. As is their custom, they had planned to delay serious talks until after becoming acquainted with the American—a trust-building process that was supposed to happen during a few days of after-hour dinners and social gatherings. But the project manager was expecting serious talks to begin immediately upon his arrival and conclude after no more than a few days. Because the negotiations were in English and most of the project work was to be done in the US by a US team, and only later to be transferred to the customer's site in India, the project manager hadn't bothered to become familiar with Indian social customs. No agreement was reached, and the manager returned home without a contract.

Managers and Laborers[12]

Beyond building relations with business associates and customers, the project manager must also gain buy-in from local managers and workers. This is done not by the project manager telling them how important the project is to his company or home office (which locals do not care about), but by pointing out the project's benefits to the local population. The more the project manager can show how the project improves employment, services, availability of products, or infrastructure for the locality or region, the more the local stakeholders are likely to commit to the project.

18.5 GEO-NATIONAL ISSUES

International projects are subject to many issues that originate from the simple fact that the stakeholders are in different nations or geographic regions.

Exchange Risk and Currency

Swings in the economy can alter exchange rates and relative currency values, and significantly affect project costs, revenues, and profits. To protect the value of its contracted work, a contractor should require payment in terms of its home currency (e.g., US dollars for an American contractor), although it must be said that virtually all international contracts are concluded in US dollars. A customer is likely to agree to this for short-duration projects, though not necessarily for longer projects because of the greater risk of significant changes in exchange rates. Of course, the matter is moot unless the host government grants the customer the legal right to pay for the project in foreign currency.

Example 18.3: Impact of Change in the Currency Exchange Rate

A French contractor agrees to do a project in France for an American customer. The contractor estimates the project will cost €900,000 and, so as to earn a nice profit, prices the project at €1,000,000. To accommodate the customer, the contract price is set in dollars. At the time of contract signing the exchange rate is $1.3 per euro; hence the price specified on the contract is US $1,300,000.

Many months later the project is completed and, as predicted, the work ends up costing €900,000. The customer pays the agreed price of $1,300,000, but the exchange rate has changed and is now $1.4 per euro. That being the case, the payment equates to $1,300,000/1.40 =€928,571. Instead of making €100,000 profit, the contractor made only €(928,571 – 900,000)=€28,571. An alternative way of looking at this is to say that the increase in the $/€ rate led to a decrease in the euro value of the payment. A still different way is to say that the increased rate led to an increase in the dollar expense of the project (from €900,000(1.3)=$1,170,000 to €900,000(1.4)=$1,260,000). Whichever way you choose to look at it, the contractor received much less profit than expected.

One way to reduce exchange risk is to lock into the contract today's price for a payment that will not occur until the future. Called *hedging* of expected foreign currency transactions, this protects the future cash flow against negative currency fluctuations and eliminates some of the uncertainty of doing business abroad. The locked-in forward price reflects the difference in interest rates between the customer's and contractor's countries.[13] Another way to reduce the risk is for both parties to agree upon and specify the exchange rate in the contract. The amount of payment is thereby determined by the rate set in the contract, not the rate at the time of payment. A third and the most common way to reduce exchange risk is to "*forward cover*," or transfer the risk of an unfavorable change in currency value to an insurance company.

Offsets[14]

A foreign contractor on a large government-funded project is often subject to requirements concerning spending in the host country called an "offset" or *counter trade*. The offset might require the contractor to spend a percentage of project cost on local labor, locally supplied materials or products, local airlines and transportation services, and local subcontractors. Offsets like these that are tied directly to project activities are called "direct offsets." Another form, called "indirect offsets," requires the contractor to contribute to non-project endeavors such as business enterprises or improvements to roads, communications, or other national infrastructure. The purpose of the offset is to reduce the net amount of payments going outside the country. The value of the offset can range from a few percent to more than the full cost of the project. Sometimes the trick is for the contractor to satisfy the offset requirement, yet still make a profit.

Offset requirements are specified in the RFP, and sometimes a contractor wins the job based primarily on the offset plan as described in the proposal. In essence, the offset is the deal-clincher, exceeding in importance the principle work of the project.

Export/Import Restrictions

The export/import of certain US technology, software, and hardware is regulated by government agencies such as the US Departments of Commerce, State, and Agriculture. Early in the project, systems designers and project planners should try to identify items that are essential for the project but are restricted or prohibited from import/export; these items will have to be substituted with non-restricted alternatives.

Time Zones[15]

Project stakeholders located in different time zones around the globe might have no overlapping normal business hours, and it might take days for messages between them to be read or responded to. Avoiding communication delays is largely a matter of planning, such as scheduling work hours in different time zones so they overlap by a minimum of 2–3 hours, and assuring 24-hour accessibility of the project manager and other key participants via cell-phone messaging and email during critical stages of the project.

18.6 PROJECT MANAGER

Typical problems in an international project include the following:[16]

- A member of the project team does not have a valid passport
- Team members need travel visas
- A coworker needs health tests and inoculations before heading to the project site
- Someone on the team gets sick or injured at the project site
- Someone gets arrested for a local traffic violation.

At times like these, the first place people go is to the project manager, expecting he will be able to handle the predicament personally or know where to get help. Of course, while dealing with issues such as these the project manager must also continue to deal with project-related problems both on site and back home.

Self-Sufficiency

In unfamiliar surroundings, faced with unique challenges and often without support from nearby associates and family, the project manager must be adaptable to the local environment and able to resolve problematic situations that would perplex or immobilize a lesser person. A sense of humor helps, as does prior work experience in international projects.

Sensitivity and Acceptance

The project manager must understand local norms and customs, and be able to develop trusting relationships with business associates, supporters, and customers in the host country. The local staff, contractors, and laborers might not know what to expect from or how to deal with foreign managers; to gain their acceptance and respect, the project manager must be able show respect for and acceptance of their culture. Sometimes he does this in subtle ways, like emulating aspects of their social customs, eating local popular foods, or wearing forms of local dress.

Every Culture a New Experience

Each project in a new country or region requires new learning and familiarization, and experiences from one culture or country cannot be generalized to others. For example, although local laborers might *appear* to be unmotivated or lacking in creativity, the reality might be that they simply do not know what they are supposed to do; they might just need careful instruction and explanation. The project manager must seek out whatever sources of motivation are effective. Sometimes it is a simple matter of modifying the workday hours to conform to local biological clocks!

Nor should it be assumed that because a process or method has succeeded in one country that it will be workable in another, or that local laborers and suppliers will automatically accept the process or method. Making assumptions without considering the local sentiments and attitudes can lead to resentment and resistance among the local staff.

On Hand, Fully Engaged, Fully in Charge

The project manager must be in the middle of everything, ideally managing the project not from a remote office but at the project site. He is always or frequently there to see what is happening, and to discuss problems with local managers, staff, and workers. He is fully committed to the project, and willing to remain at the work site until the project is completed and the customer has signed-off.

People on the project team witness the project manager making decisions that affect the project and them personally. The project manager must be in constant touch with his team and available to assist them when they need help—not only with project decisions, but also with documents, currency, housing, or medical assistance; in this way he earns their gratitude, respect, and commitment.

Local Project Manager

In cases where the project manager cannot be on site, then day-to-day responsibility for the project should be delegated to someone who workers see as visibly engaged and fully in charge—a *local project manager*. Thus, each subproject in a global project will have two project managers: the global project manager who plans and coordinates from the home office and travels among sites, and the local project manager who is responsible for on-site, detailed planning and day-to-day management. The local manager reports to the global manager; the responsibilities and authority of the two are clearly delineated and understood by everyone on the project.

At time of hiring, the local project manager should be informed about expectations, responsibilities, and performance targets, and then reminded again periodically. Hiring and training a good local project manager is not easy, so when a problem arises the manager should be given every opportunity to work it out. If the problem is serious and thought to be getting worse, the global project manager should "parachute in" a trusted person to assess the situation and offer assistance. Only when the situation is deemed hopeless should the local project manager be replaced.

18.7 LOCAL REPRESENTATIVE[17]

Every international project needs someone at the project site or host country to keep the project manager informed about local matters, mediate with local laborers, unions, and government officials, and help resolve cultural and regulatory issues. This person—the *local representative*—works beside the project manager and is responsible for:

- Representing the project manager and company to the customer, and *vice versa*
- Keeping the project sold to customers and supporters
- Arranging for in-country services such as hotel and car reservations, local communications, interpreters, office staff and space

- Arranging meetings with government officials, attaches, and consulates
- Educating the customer about home-country government requirements concerning, for example, the transfer of technology and technical knowledge
- Helping arrange local housing for project personnel
- Assisting in locating in-country subcontractors
- Keeping the project manager informed about in-country politics and economy.

Qualifications of the local rep include thorough knowledge of the project—its mission, scope, technology, management, and team members—and of the contractor company—its officers, products, and services. If the contractor is doing several projects in the host country, the local rep should be familiar with all of them.

The local rep must have a good working knowledge of the culture and social customs of the host country, and, in some cases, fluency in the local language. It is not necessary that he is a native of the host country, but it is necessary that he is sensitive to and comfortable with local customs and culture. Also, the local rep must be committed to the project and not eager to race off as it nears completion.

When the project has a local project manager, ideally that person also fills the role of the local rep. If, however, the local project manager is not familiar with local culture, customs, and stakeholders, then he too should have a local rep.

One way to obtain a local rep is by partnering with a local company for a portion of the project work. In effect, the partner becomes the local rep. Qualifications of the partner combine those described in section 18.4 with capability to perform the contracted work, ability to communicate, and ethical reputation.

18.8 TOP MANAGEMENT, STEERING COMMITTEES, AND PMO

Practically everything about an international project is more difficult and takes longer than a home project. Sustained backing and support from top management is crucial, yet when the project is far away, running into problems and taking too long, it is easy for managers back home to get distracted and lose interest. To avoid that, top management should create committees to guide the project and assign the PMO a role to help manage it.

Steering Committees[18]

The steering committee (or review board) for an international project includes senior managers and sponsors from both company headquarters and the host country/region of the project. For a global project comprised of multiple project sites, the manager in charge of the overall project (i.e., the global project manager) also sits on this committee. The role of this "executive" or "global" steering committee is to establish a governance framework to coordinate and fund the project. If the project comprises subprojects at multiple sites around the globe, the committee also sets global goals and coordinates work and resources among the subprojects.

Each project should also have a second, "local," steering committee. This committee is comprised of local sponsors and managers and, for a global project comprised of multiple project sites, the local project manager. This committee plans and executes details of the project, and handles problems originating at the project site or host country. Serious issues that it cannot resolve are forwarded to the executive committee.

Role of the PMO[19]

In addition to the PMO functions described in Chapter 16, the PMO for an international project does the following:

- Assists senior management in assessing and selecting international projects
- Collects lessons learned from international projects, and incorporates them into templates, checklists, and training sessions
- Follows up on issues and problems identified by management that require coordination among multiple international projects
- Manages files and a library of documentation for international projects
- Identifies project managers for international projects
- Provides support and mentoring for project managers overseas
- Schedules forums for managers of international projects to share experiences
- Provides training and education about language, culture, protocol, norms, laws, etc., pertaining to each international project.

In general, project personnel going overseas should be well informed about the project and know what to expect. After they arrive, they should not have to worry about what to do, where to go or stay, or who to see—worries that can only detract from their ability to work on the project. The PMO and executive steering committee share responsibility for these matters; they arrange for training and coaching, travel and living arrangements, the local project rep, and numerous other matters, big and small.

18.9 Team- and Relationship-Building

The project manager kicks off the international project with a team-building session for key members from the project team, including local managers and staff. The purpose of the session is to develop a common purpose and shared expectations, identify likely or possible problems, and develop project guidelines to avoid problems. The guidelines address familiar matters such as collaboration, conflict management, and role assignments, but also problems unique to international projects, such as coordination across multiple countries and time zones, and cross-cultural language and social factors that could hamper communication and decision-making.[20] A useful exercise is for each participant to express how much he assumes people from other cultures are willing to adapt to his culture, and how much he is willing to adapt to others' cultures—a variation of the role clarification technique described in Chapter 15.

The contractor should also hold a similar session with each local subcontractor to discuss issues that might arise and prepare a plan to prevent or mitigate them. At the session, they determine which tasks they will do individually and which together. Ideally, a large portion of the work packages (20–30 percent) will be performed jointly by team members from both the host and the home countries. This will encourage local workers to take ownership in the project yet allow the contractor to retain control over the work.

Beyond building relationships with local members of the project team, the project manager must develop relationships with key stakeholders in the host country. If the project becomes embroiled in problems, having strong personal ties with local and national vendors and officials—government, trade, labor—will come in handy, especially if the problems are serious. To this end, the project manager should make time to attend social events in the host country for newly arriving staff, and to celebrate local holidays and cultural events.

18.10 PROJECT DEFINITION

An international project cannot be approached in the same way as a domestic project. Potential issues in the project associated with culture, country, laws, people, and politics must first be identified.

Where to Start

How do project managers learn the important issues they need to be aware of in each international project? Some common ways are:[21]

- *Look at examples of similar projects* done in the country by your company or others and try to learn what they did. Seek out project managers who have experience in the host country or region and ask for advice.
- *Hire a credible consultant or freelance expatriate* to provide guidance and serve as a cultural intermediary with local stakeholders. Seek those with project experience in the host region who have developed a social network of important local connections.
- *Ask trusted guides, professionals, or international advisory groups* for advice about local politics, norms, customs, business practices, and economic environment. Although they might not be familiar with the business or technology of a particular project, they will know about local labor, resources, and laws.
- *Attend formal training programs* devoted to coping with foreign stakeholders, institutions, and environment.
- *Start with a small pilot project* in the country to allow time to become familiar with the culture and laws before committing to larger, more risky projects.
- *Create a culture risk management team* to identify potential cross-cultural and cross-national issues and steps to reduce or avoid them. The membership of this team should mirror the national and ethnic groups of the project stakeholders.

Customer Requirements

Most projects begin when the customer provides a list of needs and wants to the contractor, which the latter then expands upon and converts it into a list of technical requirements. In a multi-language project the process is more complicated, because the customer's list of technical requirements has to be summarized and translated into the contractor's language, and the contractor's list has to be translated back into the customer's language for approval. This back-and-forth process can be lengthy and frustrating, and, typically, Western managers are eager to get through it as soon as possible. But managers from non-Western cultures may take a different stance, preferring to hold off on defining the details, and to build relationships and establish areas of agreement first. The attitude is, not to worry, disagreements over details are inevitable, but they will be worked out. This process of trust-building and establishing areas of agreement is critical to the project; it must be handled by the project manager and cannot be delegated to others in business development, sales, or marketing, as happens in domestic projects.

Scope and SOW in Global Projects[22]

For a project that has global reach and consists of subprojects at multiple international locations, a global steering committee prepares the scope statement, SOW, and a preliminary plan specifying the countries or regions of the subprojects. The plan identifies goals, strategies, targets, costs, etc., for each country and subproject, although only in the form of estimates, proposals, or suggestions.

The local project manager, local sponsor, and local steering committee for each subproject then review the preliminary plan and expand it into greater detail, accounting for what they know about the region and site. They also make suggestions to the global committee about the subproject's purpose, goals, benefits, and costs. The process is repeated for every subproject, and results in the information illustrated in Table 18.2.

Because of differences in culture, norms, and languages, subprojects that start out with almost identical purpose, scope, and SOW often end up varying substantially. To accommodate differences in purposes, goals, strategies, etc. (Table 18.2, rows 1–8), the global steering committee must adjust the scope and SOW (rows 9 and 10) for each subproject. In the course of back-and-forth iterations between the global and local steering committees, the scopes and SOWs of the subprojects and the global project (row 11) are mutually adjusted and made compatible.

The intended outcomes of the process are that:[23]

1. Local project managers and teams are brought into and become committed to their subprojects
2. Each local sponsor agrees to the goals and scope of the subproject and promises his support
3. The scope, goals, and SOW of the subprojects conform to local customs, regulations, and laws
4. Stakeholders at the global level and local level are in agreement
5. Goals, scope, and SOW of the subprojects align with those of the global project.

Table 18.2 Impacts of Country Differences on Global and Local Scope and SOW

	SUBPROJECT IN COUNTRY A	SUBPROJECT IN COUNTRY B	SUBPROJECT IN COUNTRY C
1. Purposes			
2. Goals			
3. Strategies			
4. Cost			
5. Schedule			
6. Benefits			
7. Issues			
8. Risks			
9. Scope			
10. SOW			
11. Goals, Scope and SOW of global project			

Adapted from Lientz B and Rea K. *International Project Management*. Amsterdam: Academic Press; 2003. Ch. 2.

Work Definition and WBS[24]

Work definition must account for the many additional factors that distinguish an international project from a domestic project. One approach is to start with a generic WBS template for the technical part of the project, and then expand it to include international factors. The starting template lays out the first-level breakdown of activities or end-items, general areas of work and resources needed, and so on, and in fact might not look much different than a one-country, domestic project.

Each first-level activity is assigned to the project team member who will be responsible for managing it (presumably the person who knows the most about it). This person, who might include the local project manager, subdivides the activity into detailed task definitions with estimates for resources, time, and cost.

Thus far, the work-definition process is not much different than for a domestic project. In an international project, however, as activities are broken down into greater detail, relevant local and international matters begin to surface. It is at the lower levels of the WBS that an international project becomes truly unique. Although a generic kind of project repeated in each of several countries might look the same in terms of high-level technical activities, subprojects in different countries look quite different at lower work levels owing to differences in culture, institutions, geography, infrastructure, and so on. Local or international issues identified in each work package (e.g., Table 18.3) must be addressed by detailed tasks within work packages or by additional work packages.

How does the project team know what unique issues and factors need to be addressed in an international project? Besides discovering issues through the traditional WBS process, the team can create a separate cross-cultural/cross-national WBS devoted entirely to international issues (Figure 18.1). This special WBS can be created by a special "culture risk team" whose sole purpose is to identify and deal with cultural/international issues. At the first-level breakdown of this WBS the work packages might consist of the following tasks:[25]

1. Identify important international and local issues and factors in the project
2. Assess risks associated with these issues and prepare plans to address them
3. Provide support for overseas personnel on the project

Table 18.3 Issues in International Projects

- Team members speak different languages
- Expatriate team members need vaccinations, passports visas, etc.
- Expatriate team members need local room, board, transportation
- Local team members lack knowledge and skills about project work
- Local communication infrastructure is poor
- Project leader lacks prior international experience
- Expatriate team members lack knowledge about the local culture and host country
- Local team members are unfamiliar with business practices of the contractor
- Work status might be difficult to determine
- Project will at times require people from the home office with critical skills
- Local transportation infrastructure is poor
- The business needs of the local office differ from those of the home office
- Project will depend on vendors who do not have strong presence in the country
- Business processes in the host country differ from those in the home country
- Technology or material require export licenses and import approvals
- Project or task start-up is dependent on success of another project or task
- Team members might be pulled off project due to other higher-priority needs

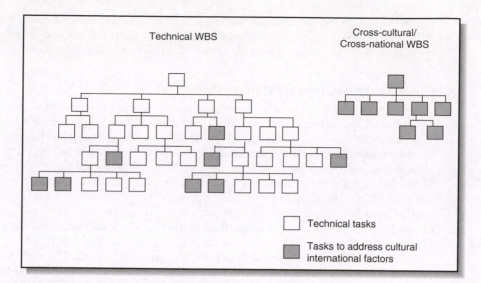

Figure 18.1
WBSs for an international project.

4. Provide team-building and relationship-building support
5. Manage knowledge obtained for this and other international projects.

As Figure 18.1 illustrates, the two WBSs can be used to identify work packages wherein international issues reside, and to address and resolve the issues. This dual-pronged approach helps assure that no important issues are overlooked; any redundancies that appear in both WBSs are simply consolidated.

One way to keep track of the detailed tasks and work packages in a global project is with a summary matrix, shown in Table 18.4. The matrix reveals which tasks are

Table 18.4   Summary Matrix of Tasks versus Subprojects

TASKS	SUBPROJECT IN COUNTRY A	SUBPROJECT IN COUNTRY B	SUBPROJECT IN COUNTRY C
TECHNICAL TASKS			
Survey		X	X
Site development		X	X
Site construction		X	X
System implementation	X	X	X
System test	X	X	X
Training	X	X	
TASKS ADDRESSING LOCAL ISSUES			
Labor		X	X
Subcontractors		X	X
Permits	X		X
Customs	X		X
Time zone	X	X	
Language	X		X

Approach adapted from Seward J. *Managing a Global Project*, pp. 3–4. ETP. The Structure Programme & Project Management Company. Downloaded September 9, 2005 from http://www.etpint.com/globalproject.htm.

unique to certain subprojects and countries, and which are common among many or all. It also suggests places where knowledge gained from one subproject might be used in another, and helps ensure that important tasks or issues are not overlooked.

Work Packages and Responsibilities

Tracking technical tasks in an international project can be difficult. Since, in general, smaller work packages are easier to track and control than larger ones, the technical WBS should ultimately be subdivided into small packages of short duration and measurable outcomes. Early in the definition process, however, a detailed breakdown for all activities will be neither possible nor—because of the many unknowns—desirable. Nonetheless, after the project gets underway and the picture of pending activities becomes clearer and the unknowns fade, the work can be defined in greater detail. As with phased project planning for other aspects of the project, the WBS and plan are continually reviewed, and the immediate, upcoming work packages are subdivided into detailed, short-duration tasks (ideally, no more than 2 weeks each).

While the WBS is being created, so is the responsibility matrix. The matrix should show the responsibilities of all individuals and groups working on or supporting the project—customer, subcontractors, and other supporting stakeholders, both at home and at the project site/host country.

Resources, Schedule, and Budget[26]

Any estimates for resources, time, and cost based upon experience in the home country must be revised when applied to overseas projects. Planned resources must account for differences in equipment and labor productivity levels, and schedules and budgets must be adjusted for the additional time and costs for communication (fax, phone, courier, translators), travel (air fares, car rentals, taxi and limo fares), and arrangements for conferences and local services. The budget must include fees and costs for insurance, licenses, governmental reviews, local housing, overseas work salary incentives, automobile, daycare, schooling, security, and medical care. Expenses and lead times for obtaining passports and visas, and for transporting managers, workers, and replacements in accordance with the project schedule, must also be accounted for.

In addition to those factors already mentioned, others adding to time and cost in international projects include shipping preparation, transport between countries, clearing port-of-entry customs, and transportation in the host country. Time for customs inspection and clearance depends on the item shipped and local politics. Transport time in the host country depends on the quality of roads, and on available airport, harbor, trucking and other local services. If the only available transport to or from the project site departs only once a week, missing it by a minute could result in a week's delay. Any material or equipment to be brought in from the US but deemed as "transfer of technology" must first be approved by the Department of State, which can take months. Fluctuating exchange rates should also be anticipated—for example, by forecasting the impact of, say, a change of ±10 percent in the euro on the project estimated cost at completion. All of these extra activities make international projects, *ceteris paribus*, more costly, lengthy, and risky than domestic projects.

Example 18.4: Added Time and Cost of an International Project

A contractor working on an overseas project encountered bad weather that fouled the equipment and stopped the project. Back home, the contractor simply would have brought in other equipment more appropriate for the weather. That equipment, however, was not available in the host country, and had to be imported. Problems associated with international transport of the equipment (export licensing, shipping schedules), local transport (local roads and hauling services), and local bureaucracy (customs inspection, and import regulations on equipment) substantially added to the project's time, cost, and risk. A solution that would have been relatively straightforward in a domestic project became a lengthy, costly, and risky proposition in the overseas project.

The skills and work ethic of local professionals and laborers must also be factored into time estimates and schedules. Owing to language differences, the productivity of a local engineer might be considered equivalent to only half that of, say, an American engineer, and would be compensated for by extending the project's engineering work schedule. On the other hand, if lower labor costs of local engineers would allow hiring several of them to replace one American, then extending the project schedule might not be necessary. However, such trade-offs are rarely easy to determine in advance.

Example 18.5: Productivity in International Projects

One of the authors has worked with several American, Canadian, and German engineers in projects in South Africa. Despite their professional competency, in all cases these engineers needed significant time before they became as productive as the local engineers, due to many factors—including time to "settle in," lack of personal networks, lack of knowledge about local companies and processes, poor understanding of the cultural environment, and communication problems. Such factors put expatriate engineers at a handicap and reduced their productivity, at least initially, and restricted them to working on tasks below their full potential. In the South African projects the expatriate engineers were given only technical assignments, whereas local engineers with similar qualifications and experience were also given assignments with management responsibility.

Training

Often, much advance preparation goes into training and coaching expatriate managers and staff in the culture, traditions, and regulations of the host country. Typically overlooked but sometimes as important is to train the local managers and staff in the culture, common business practices, and technical procedures of the contractor and the home country. Cultural adjustment is a two-way street. For training of locals the strategy and setting must be carefully designed, since in some cultures the Western mode of classroom lecture–discussion is not very effective.

18.11   PROJECT MONITORING

Tracking and Updating the Plan[27]

The project manager should make certain that every local subcontractor understands his expectations and procedures about communication and progress reporting. He should require that the local project manager and team leaders submit task updates on a weekly basis; in an international project this is simplified by posting the project plan and updates on the Internet. Assuming that technical work packages have been defined to be of relatively short duration—no longer than 2 or 3 weeks—the project manager will then be able to easily discern whether work has been completed, is on schedule, or is behind.

When a local subcontractor starts to fall behind or miss requirements, the project manager must step in to take a more direct role in managing the subcontractor's work; if that is not possible, he must assign a local person to assist the subcontractor. International litigation can be a big hassle, so it is always better first to try to coach a subcontractor into getting back on track rather than to resort to legal action.

The project manager who cannot be on site will rely heavily on telephone and teleconferencing to communicate with locals. Good practice is to precede all verbal communication with written communication so local workers will know what to expect and can be prepared, and then to follow up with written directives or action plans. This will help reduce misunderstandings among parties—common in international projects.

Site Visits

The project manager of an international project must make his presence known; if he cannot always be on-site, then he should make frequent visits—unannounced. Nowhere is the value of site visits and visibility more important than in international projects.

18.12 COMMUNICATION

Communication Plan[28]

As in any project, the project manager should prepare a communication plan. In addition to the usual contents described in Chapter 12, the communication plan for an international project must address difficulties arising from differences in languages and time zones. It should specify important contact persons (who's who) in the host country, home country, and elsewhere. It is important to ensure that everyone—domestic and foreign project staff and subcontractors—understands the required reports and written communication, and the content and format of each. Foreign contractors and local project staff might not be familiar with "common" project documents and have to be taught why they are important and how they will be used.

A common "working language" should be adopted for all or specific portions of the project. Those not familiar with the working language should be given accelerated language lessons; everyone using the common language should be reminded to speak slowly and use simple terms and no slang. The project newsletter should be published in multiple versions for the different languages of the key stakeholders on the project.

Meetings

The communication plan should include a tentative schedule for all formal reviews and milestone meetings, and describe the format of meetings, expected content, advance preparations, time limits on presentations, attendance policy, and who will lead. Since formal meetings in international projects can be difficult to schedule, require time-consuming preparation, and expose people to cultural gaffes or imbroglios, it is best to restrict them to as few as possible. The project manager should meet with local customers or officials before formal meetings to report any major problems. No one should be shocked by what they hear in a meeting.

The primary method for status tracking and identifying problems should be one-on-one communication and frequent *informal* meetings, convened as needed, the time and place determined by urgency and purpose—for example, alternate weeks if everything is okay, more often if not, and at the location experiencing the problems or issues. Attendance should be restricted to those who can contribute to the meeting or would benefit from being there. As with domestic projects, the project manager should be the person who takes notes, writes them up, and distributes them.

18.13   RISKS AND CONTINGENCIES

An international project is, almost by definition, fraught with risk; often, these risks are subtle or hidden and can be exposed only by looking at the project from the perspectives of the different cultures and countries of the project stakeholders. Any standing risk policies of the contractor or customer (described Chapter 10) should be applied in a consistent manner across all projects in all countries. In other words, the risk tolerance upon which the policy is based should remain constant, no matter the project or country.

As discussed in Chapter 10, risk analysis begins during project conception and definition by imagining different scenarios about what could go wrong. Project risk is associated with level of uncertainly: the less certain you are about something, the greater the risk. In an international project, much of the uncertainty relates to ignorance about local and international culture, customs, language, institutions, infrastructure, and stakeholders. The more you know about these matters, the better you can identify and mitigate the risks. Thus, learning is an important strategy for reducing risks in international projects.

Another strategy, however, is to decrease the amount of learning necessary to deal with local regulations, laws, and resources. This is done in the following ways:[29]

- *Outsource activities that are heavily restricted by local regulations.* Purchasing land, obtaining permits, hiring locals, and moving materials through customs are risky because they require knowledge about local laws and customs. By outsourcing these activities to knowledgeable subcontractors, the burden of responsibility (and much of the risk) is shifted to the subcontractors.

- *Perform technology intensive work at home.* Rather than dealing with the uncertainties of local labor, materials, and infrastructure, do most of the work on major hardware and software components at home and then transport them abroad to the site for simple assembly and installation.

- *Sign contracts under international law or third-country law.* Rather than learn the intricacies of local laws and depend on local lawyers, finalize all contract agreements according to international law or in a neutral country where the laws are more familiar. This practice is mandatory in countries where local laws are unclear or enforcement is unpredictable.

Most companies employ a mix of the above—they learn about and deal with some aspects of the host country and culture themselves, but avoid having to learn about and deal with others. The mix depends on the kind of project. In general, the more a project requires the contractor to be "imbedded" in a foreign country, the more the contractor must learn about the country, its laws, and culture. Contractors such as Fluor and Bechtel performing large construction projects must be heavily imbedded in the local environment because the projects take years, have large scope, and rely somewhat on local resources. Hence, the firms must learn about the country or region of the project, which they do by hiring local contractors, local laborers, and expatriates who thoroughly know the language and the country. They also methodically manage all knowledge gained about the host country. At the same time, they reduce their need to learn about *everything* by utilizing prefabricated components from home wherever possible, outsourcing to local suppliers and contractors, and hiring local representatives to deal with local stakeholders and freelance expatriates to manage technology and contracts.

But, of course, the on-site project manager of an international project is always "imbedded" in the host country—even when the contractor (his employer) is not. Although much about the local environment might not matter to his firm, knowing the local ways and protocols does matter to the manager, who has to live and work in the host country for as long as the project takes. Of all the ways to reduce the risks in an international project, perhaps the overall best is to learn and adapt to the local customs, laws, infrastructure, and social norms, and to build trusting relationships with leaders, subcontractors, laborers, and officials in the host country.

18.14 SUMMARY

A project that is international automatically inherits more issues and greater risk than a project that is not. These issues touch most everything about project management—leadership, interpersonal relations, stakeholder involvement, communication, planning, estimating, risk management, and tracking and control.

The project manager must be able to work with local subcontractors, suppliers, customers, business associates, and officials. Often these stakeholders withhold effort, collaboration, or support until they feel they know the project manager personally. Thus, gaining personal familiarity and building relationships is a fundamental aspect of managing international projects. Besides "domain competency" over technical aspects of the project, the project manager must possess the qualities of self-sufficiency, adaptability in unfamiliar environments, and readiness and ability to understand and respect local culture and customs.

When the project manager cannot always be on site, he should appoint a local project manager to handle detailed planning and daily management. In addition, the project should have a permanent "local representative" to update the project manager on local matters, mediate with local stakeholders, and help resolve any local issues.

Each global project should have an executive steering committee to oversee governance and funding, and to set goals and coordinate work and resources among subprojects at different sites. It should also have a local steering committee for each subproject to plan and execute the details and handle local problems.

Definition and planning for an international project requires identifying the many issues and unknowns associated with culture, country, laws, people, etc., and accounting for them in project plans, schedules, and budgets. Managers, representatives, consultants, and others familiar with the local environment must be consulted and involved in preparing detailed plans. The project might have two WBSs—one for technical aspects of the project, another for cultural or international aspects. Almost everything takes more effort, time, and cost, and this must be factored into tasks, schedules, and budgets.

The project manager must give firm direction—explaining to local managers and subcontractors the project goals, and his expectations for communication and progress reporting. Ideally he is on-site; if not, he makes frequent visits, unannounced. The project plan should describe the required forms of communication, identify points of contact, and include a schedule for formal review meetings.

Many of the risks in international projects stem from ignorance about local and international customs and conditions; thus, one of the best ways to reduce risk is to learn about local customs, laws, infrastructure, and social norms, and to build trusting relationships with local stakeholders.

REVIEW QUESTIONS AND PROBLEMS

1. Consider the analogy of an international project to a play. In international projects, who are the actors, what are the scripts, what are the sets, and what are the props?
2. What are the four main categories of "unknowns" in an international project?
3. In the above list, which unknowns are implicit and which are explicit? Why are implicit unknowns potentially more problematic for the project manager?
4. Consider two countries you are familiar with. Compare and contrast them in terms of the following: language, formality, gift giving, attitudes about age and about time, social behavior, food and drink, holidays and time off, and customary labor time.
5. Why might worker layoffs following the project cause legal problems for the contractor or employer?
6. For an overseas project, whose laws prevail—those of the host country or those of the home country?
7. What are "Incoterms"?
8. What difficulties are associated with contracts in international projects? What steps should be taken to avoid legal problems, and to deal with them should they arise?
9. How can the project manager know in advance of impending political or labor/union problems in the host country?
10. What are the potential benefits of hiring local contractors in an international project? What are the potential drawbacks and difficulties?
11. Describe the role of informal gatherings and social events in building trust in international projects.
12. Describe some ways that the contractor can protect against rising costs or falling prices as a result of fluctuating exchange rates.
13. What is an "offset"? Compare indirect and direct offsets.
14. Name some forms of export/import restrictions. In what ways can export/import restrictions impact an international project?
15. A project involves team members in New York and Rome. Discuss how you would accommodate the 6-hour time difference between the countries to encourage maximal communication and coordination between the teams.
16. In global projects that include subprojects at multiple sites, who is responsible for day-to-day oversight of each subproject at each site?
17. Can it be assumed that a technology or process that proved successful in a project in one country or culture will automatically be successful in an identical project in another country or culture?
18. In an international project, who should be trained in the cultures, traditions, and regulations of the home or host country—the managers and staff who will be going to the host country to work on the project, or the local managers and subcontractors in the host country who will be working on the project for a contractor that is based overseas?
19. What are the responsibilities and qualifications of the local representative?
20. What is the role of the project steering committee (or governance committee or review board), and who is on the committee? What is the difference between the global and local steering committees?
21. What is the role of the PMO in an international project?

22. What are ways to build teamwork and encourage cooperation between members of the project team from the home and host countries?
23. What are ways to build good relations with local stakeholders? With local vendors and officials? Why are these relations so important?
24. How can the project manager learn about the host country and about potential risks related to culture and environment in the project?
25. What are the unique issues in defining the scope and SOW for an international project?
26. Discuss the process of developing the scope and SOW for the subprojects in a multi-site, multinational global project.
27. Describe the WBS for identifying the unique issues of an international project. How is the technical WBS similar to or different from a technical WBS for a single-country, domestic project?
28. Name some of the issues the WBS in an international project might have to address.
29. Describe the purpose and content of the summary matrix in Table 18.4.
30. Comment on the size of work packages in an international project. How are work packages tracked and controlled?
31. List some of the many factors that must be accounted for in estimating project resources, time, and cost, and in establishing budgets and schedules for an international project.
32. What special issues should the communication plan for an international project address?
33. What strategies are used for handling risks in international projects?

QUESTIONS ABOUT THE STUDY PROJECT

If your investigation project was a global or international project, or involved customers and/or contractors overseas, consider the following questions.

1. Describe what the contractor and or project manager did for this project that differed from typical preparations for a domestic project.
2. Discuss aspects of the country, culture, language, and social behavior of the host country that posed challenges to the project manager.
3. How did the project manager and staff learn about the culture, country, and traditions of the host country? In your opinion, were they knowledgeable and well-prepared to work with stakeholders in the host and other countries?
4. What difficulties did the project encounter that stemmed from the international nature of the project? Could these difficulties have been avoided through better planning?
5. Discuss the following, as appropriate: the role of a local project manager; the role of the steering committee; the role of the PMO.
6. How did the project manager identify special issues related to the international nature of the project and account for them in planning the project?
7. What adjustments did the project manager make to estimated resources, time, and cost to account for differences countries supplying labor and materials to the project?
8. What strategies, if any, did the contractor and project manager employ to identify and reduce risks in the project?

Case 18.1 Mozal Project—International Investment in an Undeveloped Country[30]

Mozal is a $1.4 billion project launched in 1998 to construct a 250,000 tons per annum (tpa) aluminium smelter in Mozambique (Figure 18.2). At first glance, the idea of such a project seemed preposterous. To build such a large, modern, state-of-the-art production facility would require stable supplies of raw materials and labor, and international financing, but Mozambique was one of the world's poorest nations with an infrastructure in ruins after two decades of civil war. Yet the project was a success, completed months ahead of schedule and well under budget. It is worthwhile seeing how that happened.

Figure 18.2
Mozal aluminum smelter.

MOZAMBIQUE

Mozal's primary promoting and controlling shareholder was Gencor, a large South African mining firm (later a part of BHP Billiton) that had recently completed the world's largest (500,000 tpa) Hillside smelter in Richards Bay, Republic of South Africa (RSA). In 1995 Gencor sent a multinational team of South African, Canadian, and French specialists from the Hillside project to search for the site for another smelter.

The team chose to focus on Mozambique for several reasons (Figure 18.3). Its capital, Maputo, offered a suitable (though run-down) harbor for importing alumina and exporting aluminium, plus abundant low-cost (though largely unskilled) labor. Also, the South African power utility Eskom saw an opportunity to extend its power grid into Mozambique. The grid would provide Swaziland with reliable power, and might later be the conduit to supply hydropower from the Zambesi River in Mozambique to the RSA.

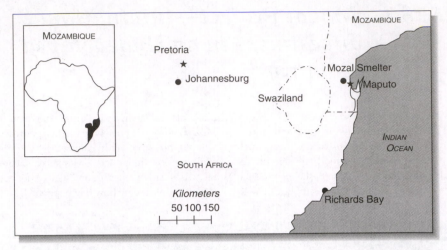

Figure 18.3
Mozal Smelter and surroundings.

Mozambique's government was especially receptive to Mozal, since the project would provide impetus to its industrialization policy and opportunity to modernize its investment procedures. Mozal would become the first enterprise to qualify as an enterprise in the Industrial Free Zone, giving its supporters important tax and duty exemptions. In addition, since Mozambique is an Asian-Pacific-Caribbean country under the Lome Agreement, aluminium produced there would enter the European Union duty free. After a visit to the Hillside smelter, Mozambique's prime minister championed the project and facilitated the regulatory and bureaucratic changes necessary for it to proceed.

The site chosen for the smelter lay in an undeveloped area 17 km from the harbor. To clinch the project Gencor agreed to finance all related infrastructure work, including developing the harbor facilities, against repayment over time through taxes and harbor revenue offsets. Key members of the Mozal team relocated to Mozambique; this enabled them to build relationships with stakeholders throughout government and the community.

FINANCING

Another sponsoring shareholder for the project was the Industrial Development Corporation (IDC), a development bank of the RSA government created to seek investment opportunities that promote economic stability. IDC agreed to provide low-cost financing and export credit, and guarantees to South African manufacturers and contractors. The International Finance Corporation (IFC), a member of the World Bank Group that promotes sustainable investment in developing countries, also agreed to provide financing after being convinced that the project was commercially viable, environmentally sound, and offered important benefits to the local economy. All major cash inputs and outputs were set in US dollars to minimize currency exposure.

RISK MITIGATION AND GO-AHEAD

The project's production costs were anticipated to be in the bottom 5 percent of industry capacity, and the commercial case supporting the project surpassed Gencor's investment criteria. The only major risk in the project was Mozambique. In May 1997, the governments of Mozambique and the RSA signed an agreement pledging to honor and protect cross-border investments. After private discussions with influential interest groups in Mozambique, the IDC and IFC decided to seek an influential international shareholder to share in the risk. In 1997, Mitsubishi Corporation, the $78 billion Japanese conglomerate, signed on, and in May 1998 the project was given the go-ahead at a ceremony in London.

CONSTRUCTION

Construction at the Mozambique site provided major management challenges. The locals speak

Portuguese, but the expatriate managers, supervisors, and computer software used English. Some basic engineering work was done in Canada and France; some specialized equipment was designed and manufactured in Japan and France. Most of the planning, coordination, detailed design, and preparation of material took place in the RSA.

Road and rail links connected Mozal to Richards Bay, RSA, where material and equipment arrived from overseas for transport to the project site. At one stage of the project it became clear that Mozambique agents were having trouble processing the 60–80 trucks of equipment and materials crossing the border daily. But the project director had built good relationships with key stakeholders, including Mozambique's president, and convinced them to allow the Mozal team to assist in managing the border post.

The project employed many experienced workers from the Hillside project, though thousands more unskilled workers had to be hired. Schools were set up near the project to train them in construction, and increase awareness of safety and the risks of HIV infection. To combat malaria the area surrounding the site had to be continually sprayed, and full-time on-site clinics were set up that would eventually handle over 6,000 cases. For residents displaced by the project, new farming land was allocated and cultivated, and a development trust established to provide for local schooling and other community needs. Before contractors could access parts of the site and service corridors, land mines laid during the civil war had to be cleared. In the latter stages of construction, the placing of cross-country power supply lines and, consequently, commissioning of the smelter were threatened by major country-wide cyclonic floods. Heavy-lift helicopters were needed to fly in large pylons prefabricated offsite, and to string power cable.

One goal of the project was to maximize local content. An estimated $75M was spent in the local economy. At peak construction, 70 percent of the 9,000 people employed at the site were Mozambicans.

QUESTIONS

1. Summarize the issues and factors that posed risks to the Mozal project. Which of these arose from the international nature of the project?
2. What actions led to successful completion of the project despite the risks?
3. The team began searching for a suitable site in 1995 but the project was not launched until 1998. Discuss the kinds of work required during the pre-project phase of a high-risk international project such as Mozal, and the importance of that work.
4. Discuss the social responsibilities relating to projects in developing countries such as Mozambique.

STUDY ASSIGNMENTS

1. You are the newly appointed director for the proposed Mozal project. The feasibility study is complete, and you now must convince the international sponsors, shareholders, and lenders to commit to the project. Develop a presentation to a special board of stakeholders asking for the go-ahead to commit $1.4 billion to the project; address their expectations and how you will deal with the perceived risks.
2. The project has received the go-ahead, and you now face the reality of mobilizing your team and starting work in a foreign country. What special project challenges can you expect to face, and how will you go about laying the foundations for success?
3. What do you see as the criteria for evaluating the success of this international project?

Case 18.2　Spirit Electronics' Puerto Rico Office[31]

Spirit Electronics Company, a US firm, is building an office branch in Puerto Rico. Susan Marcie of Weller & Waxhall, a construction management consulting firm, is managing the project. This is Susan's first non-US project. She visited the project site and met with the person who would be her local project representative. In preparing the budget, she sought bids from vendors in the US and Puerto Rico. Bids received from US firms seemed extremely high (possibly due to the perceived risk of working outside the US); this, plus the fact that labor laws in Puerto Rico require certain jobs to be performed by local vendors, led Susan to select mostly Puerto Rican vendors.

Spirit wanted the project completed within 30 weeks. Since cost bids from the vendors were slow to arrive, Susan prepared the budget using her firm's cost estimating spreadsheet and standardized costs. Spirit's budget review process takes 4 weeks, and, she thought, the quicker the budget is approved, the sooner the project can begin. The project budget for $690,457 was approved.

As project planning progressed, issues arose from the project being in Puerto Rico:

- Permits are required from both city and state (the US requires only city permits)

- Labor insurance is required at 5 percent construction cost (not required in US)

- City taxes for construction work are unusually high

- Furniture costs are high (much higher than in the US)

- Security costs are high due to the risk of theft (higher than in the US)

- Work shut down due to a state holiday (December 22 through January 15).

These plus other smaller issues raised the estimated cost to $1,250,998. Spirit threatened to cancel, but Susan was able to negotiate with vendors and reduce the cost to $987,655, to which Spirit agreed.

Susan knew that in overseas projects extra time must be included in the schedule to account for unknowns. She proposed delaying the target completion by 8 weeks, but Spirit objected. She was able to create a schedule to meet the original target by paying the government $20,000 to rush the permits.

As the project progressed, Susan had to respond to several other high-risk issues:

- Long lead times for custom-made fixtures (6–8 weeks). Susan asked contractors to estimate and order the needed fixtures at the earliest possible date.

- Millwork for cabinets and shelving, which usually must be done on-site after walls are completed and exact room dimensions known. To avoid this, the building design was changed so millwork could be premade.

- Long lead times on permits (3–16 weeks). She submitted drawings and permit applications far in advance, showing dates when permits would be needed.

- Disorganized furniture installation vendors. Susan made the vendors create a plan (from which she estimated 8 weeks completion time) and then held them to it.

- Local labor pool dichotomy—extremely high-cost (five times more expensive than in US but reliable and able to meet expectations) or extremely low-cost (uncertain ability to do quality, on-time work). In most cases, Susan hired the first.

- Added cost and time for imported materials due to import tax and shipping costs, and 6 weeks for government inspections. To avoid delays, Susan arranged for local storage space and shipping of materials far in advance of need.

- Language differences between locals and US members of the project team (site superintendent, IT personnel, some carpenters and laborers). For tasks requiring coordination between local and US members, Susan extended the duration times.

QUESTIONS

1. In managing the project, how did Susan explicitly address the fact that it was an "overseas" project?

2. How might Susan have pre-identified the issues that ultimately required her to redo the budget? How might she have anticipated other issues that emerged later?

Notes

1. *Jubail City-2: SR 200bn Industrial Hub in the Making, Zawya.* http://www.zawya.com/story.cfm/sidZAWYA20050321123628, downloaded June 12, 2006.

2. Adapted from Orr R. *Strategies to Succeed in Foreign Environments.* Collaboratory for Research on Global Projects, Stanford University, presented at the CIB W92 International Symposium Construction Procurement—The Impact of Cultural Differences and Systems on Construction Performance, Las Vegas, February 8–10, 2005. http://crgp.stanford.edu/publications/conference_papers/RyanVegas.pdf, downloaded April 10, 2007.

3. Turner J. *Handbook of Project-Based Management.* New York, NY: McGraw-Hill; 1998. p. 483.

4. Murphy O. *International Project Management.* Mason, OH: Thompson; 2005. p. 23.

5. Pringle D. Finding ways around rigid labour laws. *CareerJournalEurope.* http://www.expatica.com/actual/article.asp?subchannel_id=157&story_id=10562, accessed May 8, 2006,

6. www.buyusa.com/pittsburgh/advice-forchina.html, accessed March 10, 2006.

7. Murphy, *International Project Management,* p. 36.

8. International Chamber of Commerce, Policy and Business Practices, Incoterms 2000. http://www.iccwbo.org/policy/law/id315/index.html, accessed April 11, 2007.

9. Lemley J. Managing the Channel Tunnel—lessons learned. *Tunneling and Underground Space Technology* 10(2); 1995: 9–11. http://www.ita-aites.org/applications/30th/PDF/TUST_95_v10_n1_5–29.pdf, downloaded December 2, 2007; Anbari FT (ed.), *Case Studies in Project Management, The Chunnel Project.* Newtown Square, PA: Project Management Institute.

10. Murphy, *International Project Management,* p. 63.

11. Adapted from Mathew M. *Doing Business in India: A Cultural Perspective.* www.stylusinc.com/business/india/cultural_tips.htm, downloaded September 25, 2006.

12. Lientz B and Rea K. *International Project Management.* Amsterdam: Academic Press; 2003. p. 161.

13. *Foreign Exchange.* TD Commercial Banking. www.tdcommercialbanking.com/foreignx/products/forward.jsp, accessed March 10, 2006,

14. Murphy, *International Project Management,* p. 63.

15. Seward J. *Managing a Global Project,* pp. 3–4. ETP. The Structure Programme & Project Management Company. Downloaded September 9, 2005 from http://www.etpint.com/globalproject.htm.

16. Lientz and Rea, *International Project Management,* p. 49

17. Murphy, *International Project Management,* pp. 65–66.

18. Lientz and Rea, *International Project Management,* pp. 44–45.

19. *Ibid.,* p. 56

20. *Ibid.,* pp. 71–72.

21. Orr, *Strategies to Succeed in Foreign Environments,* p. 5.

22. Similar approaches are discussed by Seward, in *Managing a Global Project,* and Lientz and Rea in *International Project Management,* Ch. 2.

23. Derived from Seward, *Managing a Global Project.*

24. Lientz and Rea, *International Project Management,* pp. 81–95.

25. Grove C, Hallawell W, and Smith C. *A Parallel WBS for International Projects.* Professional Knowledge Centre, Grovewell LCC; 1999. www.grovewell.com/pub-project-wbs.html, downloaded January 25, 2006.

26. These and other considerations are discussed in Murphy, *International Project Management;* see especially pp. 72–73, 88, 91–94, 178.

27. Lientz and Rea, *International Project Management,* pp. 124–128.

28. *Ibid.,* pp. 155–170.

29. Orr, *Strategies to Succeed in Foreign Environments*, pp. 6–7.

30. Personal communication, Rob A. Barbour, former chairman, Mozal.

31. Case adapted from Carta K, Cisek A, Cho L, Farr B, Hobbs M, and Kim C. *Sprint Powered Workplace*. Graduate School of Business, Loyola University Chicago, February 2007.

Appendix A

RFP from Midwest Parcel Distribution Company

*T*he following is the RFP for the LOGON system sent by Midwest Parcel Distribution Company (MPD) to contractors perceived as most capable of meeting the requirements. (Only partial entries are shown to minimize the length of the example. Reference to "Appendix" is for a hypothetical appendix attached to the RFP, not to appendices of this book.)

INTRODUCTION

You have been selected by MPD as potentially capable of meeting our requirements for a new system. You are invited to present a proposal to supply the hardware, software, and support services for the system described in this request for proposal

SECTION 1: BACKGROUND

MPD seeks to award a contract for the design, fabrication, installation, test, and checkout of a transport, storage, and database system for the automatic placement, storage, and retrieval (PSR) of standardized shipping containers. The system, called the Logistical Online system (LOGON), will be installed at MPD's Chicago distribution facility . . . [*Additional discussion of current environment at the Chicago distribution facility, projected future needs, and purpose and objectives of the LOGON system*].

Section 2: Statement of Work

The contractor shall be responsible for furnishing expertise, labor, material, tools, supervision, and services for the complete design, development, installation, check-out, and related services for full operational capability for the LOGON system. All necessary testing of systems and subsystems designed and installed by the contractor, as well as of current facilities to ensure compatibility with the new system and with local, state, and federal requirements, will be performed by the contractor.

The LOGON system must meet performance requirements, be compatible with existing structural and utility limitations of the facility, and be compliant with packaging and logistical standards and codes, all as specified in Section 6: Technical Information . . . [*Additional discussion of the services, equipment, and material to be provided by the contractor, and a list of specific end-items*].

Exclusions

Removal of existing PSR equipment will be performed under separate contract and is the responsibility of MPD. Removal will be completed in time for the new system to be installed . . . [*Discussion of services, equipment, and material provided by MPD or other contractors and for which the contractor is NOT responsible*].

Scheduled Delivery Date

LOGON system is to be fully operational on or before April 30, 2011. All necessary hardware, software, and support services necessary for full system operation will be supplied and/or completed by April 30, 2011. Site installation will initiate no later than November 30, 2010.

Subcontractors

Contractor shall submit with the proposal a list of subcontractors and work to be assigned to each. Subcontractors shall be subject to MPD approval prior to placement of a contract.

Cost and Contract

Price of contract will not exceed $15 million. Contract will be fixed price with a penalty charge of $10,000 per day for failure to meet the operational completion date of April 30, 2011.

Section 3: Proposal Content and Format

Proposal will include the following sections and conform to the instructions as follows.

Proposal Table of Contents
1. Cover sheet (use Form I provided in Appendix)
2. Executive summary
3. Statement of work

(a) Background statement of need

(b) Technical approach and distinguishing features

(c) Project plan and schedule (use Forms II to V provided in Appendix)

4. Budget and price (use Form VI provided in Appendix)
5. Project organization and management plan
6. Prior experience and key personnel
7. Attachments

(a) Signed statement of confidentiality (use Form VII in Appendix)

(b) MPD supplied confidential information

(c) Letters of commitment for work contracted to third parties.

Specific Instructions

[*Details about the purpose, specific content, specific format, and approximate length for each of the sections listed above.*]

SECTION 4:   PROPOSAL SUBMITTAL

Submittal

Contractor will submit two (2) copies of the completed proposal along with all MPD confidential information to:

Lynn Joffrey
Administrative Assistant
Midwest Parcel Distribution Company
13257 N. Wavelength Avenue
Chicago, IL 60699, USA
(773) 773–7733

Deadline

Proposal must be received at MPD by 5 p.m. August 15, 2009.

SECTION 5:   SELECTION DATE AND CRITERIA

Selection and Award Date

September 5, 2009.

Selection Criteria

Completed proposals received by the deadline will be evaluated by the following criteria:

1. Technical ability:
   (a) Ability of system to meet performance requirements within limitations of existing facility, standards, and codes.

    (b) User friendliness of the system with respect to operation, reliability, and maintenance.

    (c) Use of state-of-the-art technology to ensure system remains current into the next decade.

    (d) System support services during contract period and available afterward.

2. Contractor's bid price.

3. Contractor experience and qualifications.

4. Project management and project plan.

SECTION 6: TECHNICAL INFORMATION

Confidentiality

The attached technical data and any additional requested drawings, specifications, requirements, and addenda shall be treated as confidential and the property of MPD. Information provided in this RFP or requested from MPD will not be duplicated beyond that necessary to prepare the proposal. The original and all duplicates will be returned with the proposal. (See Form VII, Appendix.)

[*Attached to the RFP are Appendices containing forms, agreements, and supporting technical data, standards, and performance requirements necessary for preparing and submitting a proposal.*]

Supporting Technical Data

1. Technical data attached in Appendix C to this RFP:

    (a) Technical performance requirements and standards for LOGON system

    (b) Facility structural and utility specifications

    (c) Facility floor plan

2. For clarification and additional information, contact:

    Mr. Ed Demerest
    Project Director, Facilities
    Midwest Parcel Distribution Company
    13257 N. Wavelength Avenue
    Chicago, IL 60699, USA
    (773) 773–7733

Appendix  B

Proposal for Logistical Online System Project

Submitted to Midwest Parcel Distribution Company from Iron Butterfly Company

---

1 COVER SHEET

Form I: Cover Sheet

1. **Project Name:** Logistical Online System Project (LOGON) for the Midwest Parcel Distribution Company, Chicago distribution center

2. **Ref. Job No.** 904–01

3. **Contractor:** Iron Butterfly Corporation, Goose Rocks, Maine

4. **Name and Address of Contact:** Frank Wesley, Project Manager, Iron Butterfly Corporation, Robotics Applications Division, 150 Seaview Lane, Goose Rocks, Maine 715–332–9132, fwesley@ibuttc.com

5. **Proposal Contents Check-off**

---

1. Cover Sheet	
2. Executive Summary	X
3. Statement of Work	
A. Background Statement of Need	X
B. Technical Approach and Distinguishing Features	X
C. Project Plan and Schedule (Forms II to V from RFP)	
(II. Work packages, III. Deliverables, IV. Work Schedule, V. Subcontractors)	X

4. Budget and Price (Project Price: $14,413,905)
   A. Budget and Price (Form VI from RFP)   X
   B. Variations, Changes, Contingencies   X
   C. Billing and Payments   X
5. Project Organization and Management Plan   X
6. Qualifications and Key Personnel
   A. Company and Prior Projects   X
   B. Résumés of Project Manager and Project Engineer   X
7. Attachments (provide as specified in the RFP or as necessary to
   substantiate assertions in the proposal)   X

2   EXECUTIVE SUMMARY

Iron Butterfly Corporation of Goose Rocks, ME, is submitting this proposal for the design and installation of the LOGON system at Midwest Parcel Distribution Company's Chicago distribution center. Our proposed system integrates robotic and neural network technology to streamline parcel transport and storage, and will complement MPD's existing distribution information processing system.

The *proposed system utilizes robotic transporters* on ceiling-mounted tracks to place and retrieve stored parcels. The *system will utilize neural network technology*, and because of that it will actually learn where to place and retrieve parcels and gain in efficiency over time.

The significant benefits of the proposed system are:

- It can *readily accommodate the expected 20% increase in volume* anticipated by MPD.
- It can *be operated for about 10% less* than the annual operating cost of the current system.
- It can be *readily implemented in the existing facility* with no structural changes to the building and only minor changes to the electrical utilities.
- It is *easily expandable* in case the current facility is extended into the adjacent vacant lot.
- It can be *designed, installed, and made fully operational within 1 year* of contract.
- Conversion can be done in three 2-month phases, each on only one-third of the facility. Hence, throughout the 6-month conversion the *current facility will be able to operate at more than 60% capacity*.
- The *system hardware and software is durable and easy to maintain* as demonstrated by many 1,000s of hours operational usage of current systems by Iron Butterfly Company (IBC) customers.

IBC's partner in this project, Creative Robotics Company of Newton, MA, will design and build the robotic transporters. CRC is an *industry leader in robotic technology* and has developed robots for NASA as well as the robotic transporters for all of IBC's installed robotic transporter systems.

IBC has 35 years' experience in the project management of the design and implementation of large warehousing transporter and storage systems. We have chosen highly experienced professionals as the project manager and the project engineer to oversee the LOGON project administration and technology. They will work closely with MPD to assure that the installed system satisfies the MPD needs identified in the RFP and feasibility study and as emerge during the project.

Our price for the system is *$14,413,905*; we will hold this price fixed for the next 120 days. Iron Butterfly and Creative Robotics are fully committed to this project and guarantee its benefits. We invite you to contact us for more information and a formal presentation at your convenience.

3 STATEMENT OF WORK

A. Background Statement of Need

We recognize that MPD Company seeks a parcel storage, transport system, and tracking system to replace the current system at its main distribution facility system in Chicago. The existing system is operating at capacity; the new system must be able to accommodate an expected 20% increase in parcel shipments over the next 10 years. Further, we recognize that the existing system utilizes a process that has become antiquated. MPD's objectives for the new system are to accommodate the expected growth, substantially improve the speed of parcel handling, increase utilization of existing storage facility space, enhance record-keeping, and reduce the costs of labor, insurance, and shrinkage. The new system, to be called LOGON, will fully automate the process for placement, storage, and retrieval (PSR) of standardized shipping containers. MPD seeks a contractor to design, fabricate, and install the system, which is to include all hardware and software for transport and storage of parcels, and the associated processing and storage of information for inventory and parcel tracking and control. This will be accomplished with the deliverables listed in Form III, as described in Section B.

We also recognize that removal of existing PSR equipment will be performed under a separate contract. During system installation MPD will arrange for alternate storage at other sites.

B. Technical Approach and Distinguishing Features

Based upon analysis of information provided to us by Mr Ed Demerest about MPD's Tulsa facility, which is considered a model facility, and data included in the RFP package, we conclude that the best approach for meeting MPD's needs and objectives is a system that uses an overhead conveyor track, robot transporter units, racks with standard size shipping containers and storage buckets, and a computer database for automatic placement and retrieval of parcels and record-keeping. The new system will be derived from a combination of advances in robotic technology, as well as application of existing technology. Our company has 35 years' experience in design and installation of parcel handling and associated information systems, including eight installed robotic systems for companies in North America and Europe. (Experience is explained in Section 6, Qualifications and Key Personnel.) While using advanced technology, the proposed system will incorporate features of MPD existing systems to avoid duplication of effort and provide a fully operational system in less than 12 months from start.

The proposed systems work like this:

Upon a parcel's arrival at the distribution center receiving dock, it is placed into one of three standard-sized parcel "buckets." The buckets are electronically coded as to item and shipping destination. This code is relayed to a master database from any of four terminal workstations located at the dock. The workstations are connected via a DEM-LAN network to a CRC Model 4000 server. The Model 4000 has 128-gigabyte storage plus backup for retaining information about parcel description, status, location, and destination. The system tracks available, remaining storage space, and, if need be, reallocates buckets for optimal space utilization. Allocation for space utilization relies on neural network technology, which enables the system to "learn" and improve its reallocations over time. The CRC 4000 will also provide reports about system status and performance as requested by management.

Parcel buckets are attached to a robot transporter mounted on an overhead track-conveyor system. The robot carries the bucket to à "suitable" vacant storage slot within a shipping container located on a rack. The computer determines which container has a vacant slot of sufficient size and containing parcels destined for the same or nearby destination as parcels in the transporter's bucket. The robot transporter then conveys the bucket to the appropriate shipping container and unloads it into the vacant slot. Shipping containers are stacked three high in seven rows of racks. The facility storage capacity is 400 shipping containers, each with 150 cubic feet storage capacity.

When a truck headed to a specific destination is to be loaded, the destination is keyed in at the dock terminal workstation and the database system identifies all containers with buckets with parcels going to the same or nearby destinations. The system routes the robot transporters to the appropriate containers for retrieval of the buckets. The system has four robot transporters that operate independently and simultaneously. The transporters retrieve the buckets and transport them to the loading dock for placement of parcels into departing truck. The longest specified retrieval time is 8 minutes.

Based upon structural tests performed at our request by M&M Engineering Corp., the ceiling structure of MPD's Chicago facility was deemed capable of supporting additional loads of up to 600 pounds per square inch. The proposed system would add at most 325 pounds per square inch, including parcel weight; hence it can be installed to the existing ceiling frame without additional reinforcement. Structural tests performed by M&M on walls and floors also indicate sufficient strength to support the system with a safety factor of 2.1. The system can be connected to the existing main electrical harness.

[*Discussion continues about features of the robotic system and neural network software, including the benefits and advantages over alternative designs.*]

C. Project Plan and Schedule (Forms II to V from RFP)

Form II: Work Packages

1. Perform functional design of overall system.
2. Prepare detailed design specifications for subcontractors of robotic transporter, conveyor track, storage rack systems, and shipping and parcel containers.
3. Prepare specifications for the software system and for DEM-LAN and CRC4000 system interface.
4. Prepare detailed assembly drawings for robotic transporter units, conveyor track system, and storage rack system.
5. Prepare plan for system installation and test at the site.
6. Fabricate robotic transporter units, conveyor track, and rack support subassemblies at IBC facility.
7. Perform preliminary functionality tests on robotic transporter units.
8. Perform structural and functional tests of conveyor track and storage rack systems.
9. Perform installation of all subsystems at MPD Chicago facility site.
10. Perform checkout of subsystems and final checkout of overall system at MPD facility site.
11. Codes and Standards [*List of requirements and standards for local, state, and federal agencies, and measures for compliance*]

Form III: Deliverables

Hardware Group A

7 storage racks $10' \times 15' \times 6'$
   Installed at site with final structural and functional checkout
400 shipping containers installed at site
1,000 size D43A parcel buckets
600 size D25B parcel buckets
600 size D12C parcel buckets
Overhead track-conveyor system (1567 feet non-contiguous linear section, 18
   crossover points, distribution uniform balance, weld supported at 6 inch
   intervals), installed at site
Final structural, functional checkout

Hardware Group B

4 robot transporter units (each 300 pounds maximum load capacity compatible with
   three-size parcel buckets, 380 Mh, retrieval at farthest point 8 minutes), installed
   at site
Four unit functional checkout
Integration checkout, Groups A and B

Software Group

DEM-LAN network, four CRC2950 workstation terminals and CRC4000 server,
   operating system software (CRC)
Vista-Robotic software (Creative Robotics)
Triad warehousing system; Mobius transaction processing (CRC)

Support

Two copies, system operation/maintenance manuals
Robot transporter/CRC4000 integration
User training to competency
Final system checkout, user

Form IV: Work Schedule

1. Commence basic design	May 2010
2. Basic design review	July 2010
3. Process/Track Design approval	September 2010
4. Computer system specs review	October 2010
5. Hardware Groups A and B received	December 2010
6. Begin installation at site	January 2011
7. Finish installation of complete system 1/2	March 2011
8. Final user approval	May 2011

Form V: Subcontractors

1. Creative Robotics, Inc., Newton, MA, will supply the robot transporters and necessary software.
2. Steel Enterprises, Inc., West Arroyo, OH, will supply the parts for the overhead track-conveyor system and storage racks.
3. United Plastics Co., Provo, UT, will supply the shipping containers and parcel buckets.
4. CompuResearch Corp., Toronto, Ont., will supply terminal workstations, DEM-LAN network, and CRC4000 computer; will provide neural network software, support, and installation of software and related hardware.

4 BUDGET AND PRICE

A. Budget and Price (Form VI from RFP)

Task	Labor Cost	O/H @0.25	Material Cost	S/C	G/A @0.10	Total
Project coordination	800,000	20,000	20,000		12,000	852,000
Project design and development	260,000	65,000	51,000		143,000	519,000
Basic hardware	684,000	171,000	54,100		90,910	1,000,010
Hardware design and drawings	1,165,200	291,300	143,400		160,000	1,759,900
Software specs	150,400	37,600	23,300	116,000	32,730	360,030
Parts purchase	10,320	2,490	600	1,477,500	149,100	1,640,010
Drawings	703,000	175,750	121,200	0	100,000	1,099,950
Software purchase	6,080	1,520	2,000	2,550,000	72,720	2,632,320
Assembly	562,800	140,700	151,000	0	85,450	939,950
Test	343,000	85,750	117,000	0	54,580	600,330
Final installation and test	997,600	249,400	133,500	165,000	154,550	1,700,050
Totals	5,682,400	1,240,510	817,100	4,308,500	1,055,040	13,103,550
Price		Profit	10%	1,310,355		14,413,905

B. Variations, Changes, Contingencies
[*List conditions under which costs will change: change in the scope of work, cost of steel-fabricated materials, work stoppages for labor disputes, etc.*]

C. Billing and Payments
[*Proposes the method for billing and payment.*]

5 PROJECT ORGANIZATION AND MANAGEMENT PLAN

Our company knows project management and has the experience, skills, procedures, and software to successfully perform this project. The project manager, Mr Wesley, will be responsible for managing project work, including all client contact work, reporting of progress, adherence to contractual commitments regarding schedule and technical performance, and monitoring of budgetary expenditures (see Section 6, Qualifications and Key Personnel). The project engineer, Julia Melissa, will be responsible for specification definition and ensuring the system meets technical requirements. She will supervise preparation of design requirements and drawings, and ensure fulfilment of system technical requirements at the site. Ms Melissa has worked at IBC for 7 years and on IBC's three most recent robotic projects. The fabrication manager, Ira Block, will be responsible for managing materials procurement and assembly and related work at the IBC plant, and coordinate assembly operations and give approval for assemblies prior to shipment to the MPD site. Mr Block has worked with IBC for 9 years.

Within 1 month of contract signing the project manager will prepare a preliminary project master plan for MPD to review. Thereafter he will prepare progress reports for presentation at monthly meetings with MPD staff. Written documentation will be provided in advance to MPD. The meetings will review expenditures to date, progress on work, and milestones and deliverables attained, all tracked by IBC's IRIS project management planning, tracking, and control system. Other formal meetings include a mid-project review meeting and a project summary meeting; plus others as requested by MPD or IBC.

[*Additional sections address reporting and communication structure and risk mitigation.*]

6 QUALIFICATIONS AND KEY PERSONNEL

A. Company and Prior Projects
Iron Butterfly Corporation has been in the business of designing and installing custom warehousing systems for 35 years. Among our customers are Nalco, Firebrand, Kraft, Abbott Laboratories, Cardinal Health, Swiss Guard, and Boeing. Our company has been ISO 9000 certified since 1996; we have also been certified as a Category A supplier for Grego Systems and a Class IIA supplier for Boeing's Commercial Aircraft Division. [*Author's note: this is a hypothetical example.*] In 2005 we received the Genie Design Award from IAWA. In 1998 we teamed with Creative Robotics Company to design the first fully automated robotic warehousing system, and in 2001 we installed the first operational system at the 300,000 sq. ft AIKEN distribution center in Hamilton, Ont. In 2002 we installed a similar system for Genteco Distributors at their 400,000

sq. ft packaging center in Everett, WA. The robotics devices are designed by CRC president and MIT professor Dr Sanjeev Rayu. [*Include a few sentences about Creative Robotics' experience, projects, and achievements.*]

So far we have installed a total of eight of these systems for satisfied customers.

[*Additional paragraphs provide details of these systems: size and applications, cost of projects, names of customers, and information for contacting these customers.*]

B. Résumés of Project Manager and Project Engineer

[*Attach one-page résumé each for project manager and project engineer showing experience on related projects and relevant background—degrees, memberships, and certifications. Also include half-page résumés for one or two other key people in the project.*]

7   ATTACHMENTS

[*This section provides attachments as specified in the RFP or as necessary to substantiate assertions in the proposal, for example*:]

A. Signed statement of confidentiality (use Form VII in RFP)
B. MPD supplied confidential information
C. Technical data and analysis to support the proposed system
D. Letters of commitment for work contracted to third parties.

Appendix C

Project Master Plan for Logistical Online System Project

CONTENTS

Attachments

Item 1.   Robot transporter
Item 2.   MPD site layout
Item 3.   Storage rack assembly
Item 4.   LOGON organization chart
Item 5.   Responsibilities
Item 6.   Principal subtasks
Item 7.   Project schedule
Item 8.   LOGON project cost estimate

Iron Butterfly, Corp.

Elegant design. Built to last.

To: SEE DISTRIBUTION   Ref. Job No.: 904–01

From: Frank Wesley, Project Manager   Date: 1-3-10

Subject: Logistical Online System Project

Project Summary Plan

The Project Summary Plan for the Logistical Online System Project for the Midwest Parcel Distribution Company's Chicago distribution center has been modified to include your suggestions and approved by everyone in distribution. Copies of this document are herewith sent for use in the performance of contract requirements.

FW:es
Enclosure

Distribution:

    Julia Melissa, Project Engineer
    Sam Block, Fabrication Manager
    Noah Errs, Quality Control Supervisor
    Larry Fine, Software Manager
    Sharry Hyman, Design Manager
    Brian Jennings, Assembly Supervisor
    Frank Nichol, Site Operations Manager
    Emily Nichol, Assembly Supervisor
    Robert Powers, Drawing Supervisor
    Burton Vance, Purchasing Manager

Logistical Online System Project Summary Plan

I MANAGEMENT SUMMARY

On September 5, 2009, the Midwest Parcel Distribution (MPD) Company awarded the Iron Butterfly Company (IBC) the contract for the Logistical Online (LOGON) System to be installed at MPD's Chicago distribution facility.

The project consists of designing, fabricating, and installing a parcel transport, storage, and database system, for automatic placement, storage, and retrieval of standardized shipping containers. The system uses an overhead conveyor track system, conveyor-robot transporter units, and a computerized database for automatic placement and retrieval of parcels and record keeping.

Iron Butterfly is the prime contractor, and is responsible for the design of hardware and software, fabrication of component parts, system installation, and checkout. The major subcontractors are Creative Robotics, Inc. (CRI), Steel Enterprises, Inc. (SEI), United Plastics Co. (UPC), and CompuResearch Corp. (CRC). Iron Butterfly will provide overall project management between CRI, SEI, and UPC Corp. and related contract administration. The project manager is Mr Frank Wesley, and the project engineer is Ms Julia Melissa.

The project will commence with basic design on or before May 17, 2010 and final system approval by MPD Co. will happen on or before May 2, 2011. The principle subtasks are shown in Item 7.

The price of the contract is $14,520,000, fixed fee with limited escalation, based on a target final approval date of May 2, 2011. Total expenses, tabulated in Item 8, for labor, overhead, materials, subcontracting, and general/administrative are $13,140,270. The agreement provides for an escalation clause tied to inflation indices for material expenses for the steel conveyor track and rack support systems. A penalty of $10,000 a day will be imposed on IBC for target completion overruns. Contingency arrangements in the agreement allow for reconsideration of the penalty in event of disruption of work for labor dispute with management.

II PROJECT DESCRIPTION

On September 5, 2009, IBC was awarded the contract for the LOGON System Project. The award followed a 4-month competitive bidding review by the MPD Company of New York. The system is to be installed at MPD Co.'s main Chicago distribution facility.

The project consists of designing, fabricating, and installing a parcel transport, storage, and database system (LOGON) for placement, storage, and retrieval of standardized shipping containers. The system will substantially improve the speed of parcel handling, increase the utilization of storage facility space, enhance record keeping, and reduce labor costs at the facility. Anticipated ancillary benefits include reduced insurance premium and shrinkage costs.

The system uses an overhead conveyor track system, conveyor-robot transporter units, racks with standard size shipping containers and storage buckets, and a computerized database for automatic placement and retrieval of parcels and record-keeping. The system works as follows:

Upon a parcel's arrival at the distribution center receiving dock, it is placed into one of three standard-sized parcel "buckets" that are electronically coded as to parcel item and shipping destination. This code is relayed to a master database from any of four terminal work stations. The work stations are connected via a DEM-LAN network to a CRC Model 4000 server with 128 gigabytes storage with back-up to retain information about parcel description, status, storage location, and destination. The system keeps track of available storage space, and reallocates buckets for optimal space utilization; upon request it provides reports about system status and performance.

The parcel buckets are attached to a robot transporter mounted on an overhead track-conveyor system (Item 1). The transporter carries the bucket to a "suitable" vacant storage slot within a shipping container located on a rack in the facility. The computer determines which shipping container has a vacant slot of sufficient size and containing parcels going to the same or nearby destination as parcels in the transporter's parcel bucket. The transporter then conveys the bucket to the appropriate shipping container and unloads it into the vacant slot. Shipping containers are stacked three high in seven rows of racks (Items 2 and 3). The facility holds 400 containers, each with 150 cu. ft. of storage capacity.

When a truck going to a specific destination is to be loaded, the destination is keyed in at the dock terminal workstation so the database system can identify all shipping containers with parcels going to the same or nearby destinations. The system then routes the robot transporters to the appropriate shipping containers for retrieval of parcel buckets. The system has four robot transporters that operate independently

Item 1
Robot transporter.

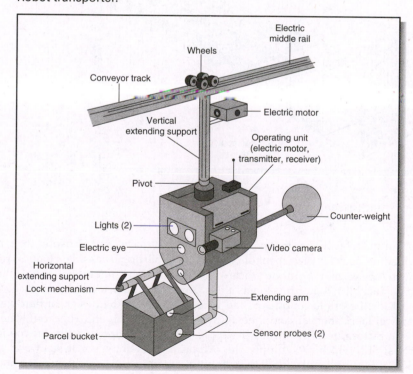

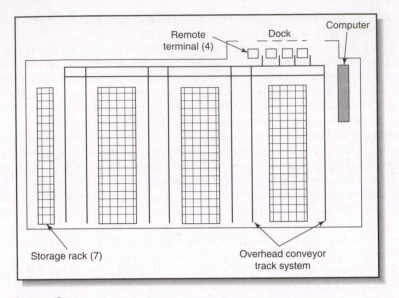

Item 2
MPD site layout.

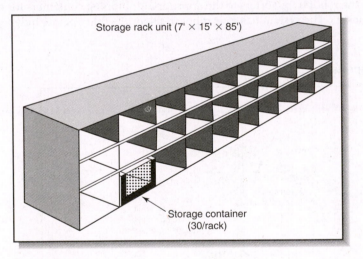

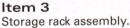

Item 3
Storage rack assembly.

and simultaneously. The transporters retrieve the buckets and transport them back to the loading dock for placement of parcels into departing trucks. The longest retrieval time in the system is 8 minutes. The system will employ neural network technology that will enable it to improve on its ability to place and retrieve containers.

IBC is the prime contractor, and is responsible for the design of hardware and software, fabrication of components, system installation, and checkout. The major subcontractors are CRI, which will supply the major components for the robot transporters; SEI, which will supply the overhead track-conveyor system and storage racks; UPC, which will supply the shipping containers and parcel buckets; and CRC,

Appendix C   Project Master Plan for Logistical Online System Project

which will supply the terminal workstations, DEM-LAN network, neural network software, CRC4000 computer, as well as software development support and installation of computer hardware.

Structural tests performed by M&M Engineering Corp. indicate that the present ceiling structure of the facility can support additional loads of up to 600 pounds per square inch. The LOGON system would add a maximum of 325 pounds per square inch, including parcel weight, and thus can be installed directly to the existing ceiling frame without additional reinforcement. Structural tests performed on walls and floors also indicate sufficient strength to support the system with 2.1 safety factor.

During system installation, MPD has arranged for alternate, temporary storage at another facility and rerouting of most parcel traffic to its other sites.

Design information about MPD's Tulsa facility will be utilized to try to initially move the project to an advanced stage. Remaining design work will use as much as possible of work that has been done already, without compromising confidentiality of clients, on previous, similar projects.

III ORGANIZATION ADMINISTRATION

III.1 Project Administration

Correspondence on project matters will be between the project manager for IBC and the project director for MPD. Project personnel may correspond directly with the client or subcontractors for information, but must provide the project manager and project director with copies of memos and conversations.

The account number assigned to the LOGON project is 901–0000. Work packages and tasks will be assigned subaccount numbers at the time when work package instructions and schedules are authorized. A single invoice for the project accounts as a whole is acceptable for billing at monthly intervals.

III.2 Project Organization and Responsibility

The organization of IBC for the performance of the LOGON project is shown in Item 4. Administrative and managerial responsibilities are summarized in Item 5.

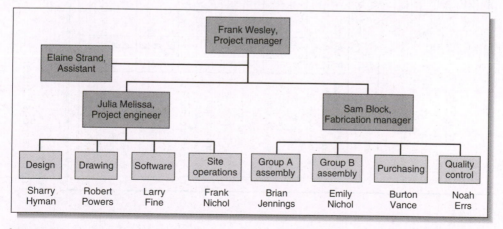

Item 4
LOGON organization chart.

Responsibility code

P Primary responsibility
S Secondary responsibility
N Must be notified
A Must give approval

Persons responsible → Project manager → Project engineer / Site operations / Fabrication manager

Project task or Activity	Design S.E.H.	R.L.Q.	P.J.	D.V.R.	Drawing R.L.P.	O.E.M.	P.V.P.R.	D.M.N.	R.L.	Software L.S.F.	L.L.L.	J.R.S.	D.V.O.	F.W.N.	Site oper. J.M.M.N.	L.Q.T.	A.U.A.	D.A.R.	S.O.B.	Assembly A E.N.	G.G.F.	R.T.T.	B.V.L.	B.J.	T.T.Y.	Assembly B H.R.D.	B.V.-Purchasing	F.W.	J.M.
Project coordination																			S									P	S
Project development	A	A	P	S															N								N	A	P
Project design	A	P	S											A					N									N	A
H Basic design	A				A	S	P			A	P	S	S																
I Hardware design A						A	P	S		N																		N	N
J Hardware design B						A	P	S	N	N																			
K Drawings B										A	P	S	S																
L Software specs										A	P	S	S																
M Parts purchase B																												N	N
N Parts purchase A						A	P							N				A	A										
O Drawings A								S	P									N	N										
P Installation drawings								S							A			A	N	A	P	S	S	A	S	P	P	N	N
Q Software purchase														N													P	N	N
U Assembly A															A	P				A	P	S	S	A	S			N	N
V Assembly B														N												A	P	N	N
W Test A														N	A	P	S	A	N					A	S			N	N
X Test B														A				A	A	P						P	P	N	N
Y Final installation														A	A	P	S	A	A	P				P		P		N	N
Z Final test																	S		A					P		P	P	N	N

Item 5
Project responsibilities.

652

The project manager, Mr Wesley, is responsible for all client contact, reporting of progress, adherence to contractual commitments regarding schedule and technical performance, and monitoring of budgetary expenditures. He and his staff will report directly to Mr Ed Demerest, vice president and project director for MPD Co.

The project engineer, Ms Melissa, is responsible for establishing specifications and system delivery to meet technical requirements. She will supervise the preparation of design requirements and drawings, estimate quantities, check drawings and calculations, and ensure that system technical requirements are fulfilled at the site.

The fabrication manager, Mr Block, is responsible for managing procurement, assembly, and related work at the IBC plant. He will ensure that delivered parts from subcontractors meets requirements, coordinate assembly of robotic transporters, track conveyor, and storage rack subsystems, and sign off final approval for assemblies prior to shipment to the site.

III.3 Subcontractor Administration

Key personnel at the four primary subcontractors CRI, SEI, UPC, and CRC are:

Bill Plante	Project coordinator, CRI
Terry Hemmart	Manager, manufacturing, SEI
Delbert Dillert	Customer representation, UPC
Lynn Duthbart	Systems engineering representative, CRC
Elmer Hyman	Customer representative, CRC

Changes to the respective agreements requested by a subcontractor or by IBC will be acted upon by the IBC project manager, Mr Wesley, upon receipt of a written proposal from the subcontractor.

Correspondence to subcontractors concerning technical matters will be directed to the previously named first four parties or their substitutes. Software specifications-related work with CRC will be coordinated by the CRC customer representative. Project telephone conversations between IBC and subcontractors shall be noted in handwritten memos and copies sent to the IBC project engineer.

Progress reports shall be prepared by the CRI project coordinator, the SEI manufacturing manager, the UPC customer representative, and the CRC systems engineering representative for presentation at weekly meetings to be held at IBC's Chicago office for the duration of scheduled involvement. Other meetings may require attendance by other individuals as required by the subcontractors or requested by the project manager. The following meetings are included in the respective subcontractor agreements.

CRI	5 meetings
SEI	3 meetings
UPC	2 meetings
CRC	5 meetings (software development)
CRC	8 meetings (site system integration)

The subcontractors will provide information and perform services on the project as follows:

1. CRI will perform all work associated with procurement, manufacturing, and component functional tests of parts and subassemblies according to specifications, plans, and drawings provided by IBC. Parts and components for four robotic transporters will be delivered to IBC per the criteria and dates specified in the agreement.

2. SEI will perform all work associated with procurement, manufacturing, and functional tests of parts and subassemblies per specifications, plans, and drawings provided by IBC. Parts and components for the complete overhead conveyor track system and seven storage racks will be delivered to IBC per criteria and dates specified in the agreement.

3. UPC will perform all work associated with procurement, manufacturing, and component functional tests of parts and subassemblies per specifications provided by IBC. Plastic containers and parcel buckets will be delivered to the MPD Chicago distribution facility in quantities and according to dates specified in the agreement. One plastic container and one each of three-size parcel buckets will be delivered to the IBC facility for tests per the agreement.

4. CRC will perform all work associated with development, programming, and tests of LOGON system robotic transporter control and neural networking software and system database per specifications provided by IBC. Software will be delivered to the IBC facility per the agreement.

5. CRC will transport, install, and perform component and integration tests for checkout of four terminal work stations, DEM-LAN network, CRC4000 server, NN software, back-up system, and peripheral hardware per criteria and dates specified in the agreement.

IBC will provide overall project management of CRI, SEI, and UPC and related contract administration, and legal, accounting, insurance, auditing, and counselling services as may be required.

III.4 Client Interface

Key personnel associated with the project for MPD Company are:

Ed Demerest	Project director, Chicago
Lynn Joffrey	Administrative assistant, Chicago
Cecil Party	Financial manager, Chicago
Mary Marquart	Operations manager, New York

Changes or modifications to the agreement requested either by MPD or by IBC will be acted upon by the operations manager upon receipt of a written proposal from IBC.

Correspondence with MPD will be directed to the project director. Project telephone conversations between IBC and outside parties shall be noted in handwritten memos and copies sent to Ms Joffrey.

Progress reports shall be prepared by Mr Wesley, IBC project manager, for presentation at monthly meetings to be held at MPD Co.'s Chicago office. Other meetings may require attendance by other individuals as required by MPD or requested by Mr Wesley. Mr Wesley shall also convene a mid-project review and a project summary at the MPD New York office. Fifteen meetings are included in the agreement. MPD Co. will provide information and perform services on the project as follows:

1. Perform all elements of work associated with vacating the site prior to the date in the agreement for commencing of system installation.

2. Provide surveys, design criteria, drawings, and preliminary plans prepared under previous agreements or received through requests for proposals for the LOGON system.
3. Provide design criteria, drawings, and plans prepared for the automated parcel storage and retrieval system at MPD Co.'s Tulsa facility.
4. Obtain all internal, municipal, state, and federal approvals as may be necessary to complete the project.
5. Provide overall project management between MPD, IBC, and CRC Corp., and legal, accounting, insurance, auditing, and consulting services as may be required by the project.

The contract administrator is the operations manager. Changes or modifications to the agreement with MPD, requested either by MPD or IBC, shall be subject to a written proposal by IBC to MPD's contract administrator through IBC's project manager.

The financial manager is responsible for approvals of monthly expense summaries provided by INC and monthly payment to IBC. MPD is responsible for securing necessary support from electrical and telephone utilities for system hook-up, and for making available to IBC all criteria, drawings and studies prepared for the Chicago site facility and the Tulsa facility automated system.

III.5 Manpower and Training

No additional manpower requirements beyond current staffing levels are envisioned to perform services for this project. Five personnel from IBC's design group have been enrolled in and will have completed a robotics seminar before the project begins.

III.6 User Training

Two systems operations manuals and 16 hours of technical assistance will be provided. Thereafter, ongoing operator training will be the responsibility of MPD.

IV TECHNICAL SECTION

IV.1 Statement of Work and Scope

The major tasks to be performed are the design, fabrication, installation, and checkout of the LOGON system for the Chicago distribution center of MPD Co. The work will be executed in accordance with the conditions set forth in the specifications in IBC's proposal and confirmed in the agreement.

Subtasks required to perform the major tasks are shown in Item 6 (letters below refer to task designations on Item 6):

1. Perform basic design of overall system (H).
2. Prepare detailed design specifications for robotic transporter, conveyor track, storage rack systems, and shipping and parcel containers to be sent to CRC, SEI, and UPC (J, I, M, N).
3. Prepare specifications for the software and DEM-LAN and CRC 4000 system interface (L).

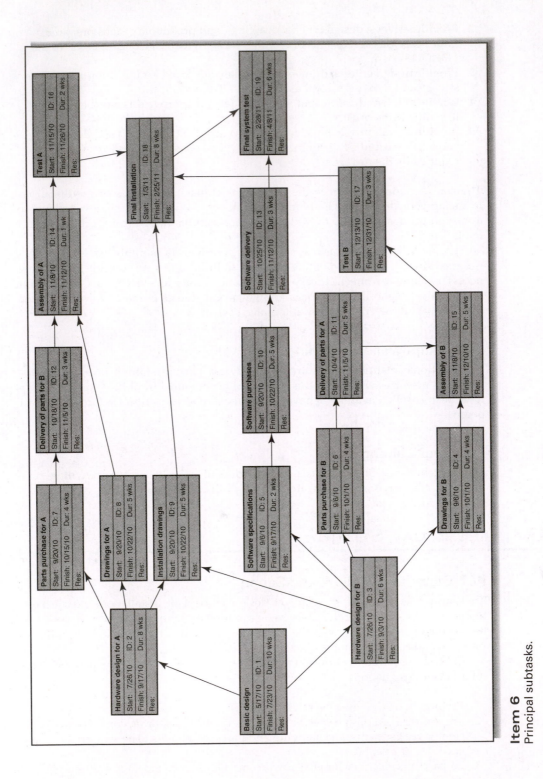

Item 6
Principal subtasks.

4. Prepare detailed assembly drawings for robotic transporter units, conveyor track system, and storage rack system (O, K).
5. Prepare drawings and a master plan for system installation and test (P).
6. Fabricate robotic transporter units, conveyor track, and rack support subassemblies at IBC facility (U, V).
7. Perform functionality tests on transporter units at IBC facility (X).
8. Perform structural and functional tests of conveyor track and rack systems at IBC facility (W).
9. Perform installation of all subsystems at MPD Chicago facility site (Y).
10. Perform subsystems checkout and overall system final checkout at MPD site (Z).

IV.2 Schedule and Calendar

The project will commence with basic design on or before May 11, 2010; installation at the site will begin on or before January 10, 2011; and final system approval by MPD Co. will be on or before May 2, 2011. The schedule for significant aspects of the project is in Item 7. The indicated milestones are:

1.	Commence basic design	May 11, 2010
2.	Basic design review	July 26, 2010
3.	Transporter and conveyor design review	September 6, 2010
4.	Computer system specs review	September 20, 2010
5.	Hardware group A and B review	November 29, 2010
6.	Begin installation at site	January 10, 2011
7.	Final user approval	May 2, 2011

Starting dates for activities that are dependent on results of reviews will be adjusted to allow for significant changes in the length of predecessor activities, although no adjustments are anticipated.

Work package instructions and a detailed schedule for basic design have been distributed. Subsequent schedule and work package information will be distributed and discussed at review meetings.

The schedule of contract deliverables is given in Section IV.9.

Item 7
Project schedule.

ID	Task Name	Duration	Start	Finish	Predecessors
1	Basic design	10 wks	Mon 5/17/10	Fri 7/23/10	
2	Hardware design for A	8 wks	Mon 7/26/10	Fri 9/17/10	1
3	Hardware design for B	6 wks	Mon 7/26/10	Fri 9/3/10	1
4	Drawings for B	4 wks	Mon 9/6/10	Fri 10/1/10	3
5	Software specifications	2 wks	Mon 9/6/10	Fri 9/17/10	3
6	Parts purchase for B	4 wks	Mon 9/6/10	Fri 10/1/10	3
7	Parts purchase for A	4 wks	Mon 9/20/10	Fri 10/15/10	2
8	Drawings for A	5 wks	Mon 9/20/10	Fri 10/22/10	2
9	Installation drawings	5 wks	Mon 9/20/10	Fri 10/22/10	2,3
10	Software purchases	5 wks	Mon 9/20/10	Fri 10/22/10	5
11	Delivery of parts for A	5 wks	Mon 10/4/10	Fri 11/5/10	6
12	Delivery of parts for B	3 wks	Mon 10/18/10	Fri 11/5/10	7
13	Software delivery	3 wks	Mon 10/25/10	Fri 11/12/10	10
14	Assembly of A	1 wk	Mon 11/8/10	Fri 11/12/10	8,12
15	Assembly of B	5 wks	Mon 11/8/10	Fri 12/10/10	4,11
16	Test A	2 wks	Mon 11/15/10	Fri 11/26/10	14
17	Test B	3 wks	Mon 12/13/10	Fri 12/31/10	15
18	Final installation	8 wks	Mon 1/3/11	Fri 2/25/11	9,16,17
19	Final system test	6 wks	Mon 2/28/11	Fri 4/8/11	13,18

IV.3 Budget and Cost

The price of the contract is $14,520,000, fixed fee with limited escalation, based on a target final approval date of May 2, 2011. Expenses and fees will be billed and are payable monthly as incurred. The agreement provides for an escalation clause tied to inflation indices for material expenses for the steel conveyor track and rack support systems. A penalty of $10,000 a day will be imposed on IBC for target completion overruns. Contingency arrangements in the agreement allow for reconsideration of the penalty in event of disruption of work for labor disputes.

Principal tasks, subtasks, man-hours, and dollars to perform them have been estimated. Total expenses, as tabulated in Item 8, for labor, overhead, materials, subcontracting, and general/administrative are $13,140,270.

Item 8
LOGON project cost estimate.

LOGON Project Cost Estimate (in Dollars)

Task	Labor Time	Labor rate	Labor cost	O/H @ 0.25	Materials	S/C	G/A @ 0.1	Total
Project	5,000	112	560,000	140,000				
coordination	5,000	48	240,000	60,000				
		Total	800,000	200,000	20,000		102,000	1,122,000
Project	1,000	112	112,000	28,000				
development	1,000	80	80,000	20,000				
		Total	192,000	48,000	45,000		28,500	313,500
System	125	112	14,000	3,500				
design	375	96	36,000	9,000				
	375	48	18,000	4,500				
		Total	68,000	17,000	6,000	1,550,000	164,100	1,805,100
H Basic	750	120	90,000	22,500				
hardware	4,000	96	384,000	96,000				
	3,500	60	210,000	52,500				
		Total	684,000	171,000	54,100		90,910	1,000,010
I Hardware	450	104	46,800	11,700				
design A	2,750	96	264,000	66,000				
	2,250	60	135,000	33,750				
		Total	445,800	111,450	24,500		58,175	639,925
J Hardware	625	104	65,000	16,250				
design B	3,375	96	324,000	81,000				
	3,250	80	260,000	65,000				
		Total	649,000	162,250	61,500		87,275	960,025
K Drawings B	400	104	41,600	10,400				
	400	72	28,800	7,200				
		Total	70,400	17,600	57,400		14,540	159,940
L Software	400	112	44,800	11,200				
specs	600	96	57,600	14,400				
	600	80	48,000	12,000				
		Total	150,400	37,600	23,300	116,000	32,730	360,030

Item 8
(continued)

Task	Labor Time	Labor rate	Labor cost	O/H @ 0.25	Materials	S/C	G/A @ 0.1	Total
M Parts	5	112	560	140				
purchase B	40	96	3,840	960				
		Total	4,400	1,100	250	758,000	76,375	840,125
N Parts	10	112	1,120	280				
purchase A	50	96	4,800	1,200				
		Total	5,920	1,480	350	719,500	72,725	799,975
O Drawings A	1,625	104	169,000	42,250				
	1,750	72	126,000	31,500				
		Total	295,000	73,750	85,800		45,455	500,005
P Installation	1,125	112	126,000	31,500				
drawings	1,500	104	156,000	39,000				
	1,750	72	126,000	31,500				
		Total	408,000	102,000	35,400		54,540	599,940
Q Software	20	112	2,240	560				
purchase	40	96	3,840	960				
		Total	6,080	1,520	1,600	717,500	72,670	799,370
U Assembly A	25	112	2,800	700				
	250	96	24,000	6,000				
	300	80	24,000	6,000				
		Total	50,800	12,700	64,000		12,750	140,250
V Assembly B	250	112	28,000	7,000				
	2,750	96	264,000	66,000				
	2,750	80	220,000	55,000				
		Total	512,000	128,000	87,000		72,700	799,700
W Test A	50	104	5,200	1,300				
	750	96	72,000	18,000				
	750	80	60,000	15,000				
		Total	137,200	34,300	47,000		21,850	240,350
X Test B	75	104	7,800	1,950				
	1,125	96	108,000	27,000				
	1,125	80	90,000	22,500				
		Total	205,800	51,450	70,000		32,725	359,975
Y Final	800	112	89,600	22,400				
installation	3,000	96	288,000	72,000				
	2,250	88	198,000	49,500				
		Total	575,600	143,900	121,000	105,000	94,550	1,040,050
Z Final test	500	112	56,000	14,000				
	2,500	96	240,000	60,000				
	1,500	84	126,000	31,500				
		Total	422,000	105,500	12,500	60,000	60,000	660,000
Totals			5,682,400	1,420,600	816,700	4,026,000	1,194,570	13,140,270

Expenditures of direct labor are under immediate control of department heads in design, fabrication, procurement, and customer service departments because they assign personnel to the project.

The project manager is responsible for man-hour and direct expenses, and will receive biweekly accounting of time and money expenditures.

IV.4 Information Requirements

Most of the information required by IBC to perform under the terms of the agreement has been supplied by MPD Co. A limited amount of site information will be obtained from additional required surveys performed by IBC. MPD will assist in survey work to expedite the project.

IV.5 Documentation and Maintenance

Functional managers will send biweekly expense and progress reports to the project manager. The project manager will send monthly project summary reports to functional managers and to other managers and supervisors listed in distribution.

Cost, performance, and progress documentation will be maintained and reported through the company project cost accounting system.

The project manager will prepare a final summary report for IBC and MPD company archives.

The project manager is responsible for maintenance of all project files. All copies of project documents sent outside IBC will leave only under his direction.

IV.6 Work Review

Internal review of work produced in each of the design, fabrication, procurement, and customer service divisions is a responsibility of the division head for each of the functional disciplines.

IV.7 Applicable Codes and Standards

Track conveyors, storage racks and supporting structures, electrical harnesses, and radio transmitters are to be designed to the applicable standards of AATOP, ASMER, OSHA, the Illinois Building Requirements Board, and the City of Chicago.

IV.8 Variations, Changes, Contingencies

The agreement with MPD defines the conditions for considering a change in compensation or penalties due to a change in the scope of work or cost of steel-fabricated materials, or unanticipated stoppage of work for labor dispute. It describes the procedure whereby authorization for such a change may be obtained from MPD.

The agreement, Paragraph 9.2, under prime compensation, states:

"Whenever there is a major change in the scope, character, or complexity of the work, or if extra work is required, or if there is an increase in the expense to the CONTRACTOR for steel-fabricated materials as negotiated in the agreement with the responsible SUBCONTRACTORS, or if there is a stoppage of work resulting from a labor dispute with management, the CONTRACTOR shall, upon request of the CLIENT, submit a cost estimate of CONSULTANT services and expenses for the change, whether it shall involve an increase or a decrease in the Lump Sum. The CLIENT shall request such an estimate using the form provided herein (Attachment F). Changes for reasons of labor dispute with management will be reviewed and determined according to the conditions specified (Attachment G)."

During system installation and tests, MPD has made arrangements to reroute 70% of its Chicago parcel business to other centers. The remainder will be stored at an alternate facility near Chicago. In the event of a schedule overrun, the reroute plan will remain in effect. MPD requires 30 days notice of anticipated schedule overrun to extend the agreement with the alternate Chicago storage facility.

IV.9 Contract Deliverables

All items are to be assembled, installed, and in operation at the site in accordance with technical specifications in the agreement.

Subcontractors will transport components and parts to the IBC plant per this schedule:

Item	Date
Parts and components for robot transporters from CRI	November 1, 2010
Parts and components for overhead conveyor track and storage rack systems from SEI	November 4, 2010
One shipping container and one each of three-size parcel buckets from UPC	November 10, 2010
Robotic transporter system control software from CRC	October 25, 2010

Following are the items identified in the agreement as deliverable to MPD:

Item	Date
Hardware (Group A):	
7 storage racks, 10′ × 15′ × 6′	
Installed at site	November 15, 2010
Final structural, functional checkout	November 29, 2010
Delivered 400 shipping containers installed at site	December 6, 2010
Delivered 1,000 size D43A parcel buckets	December 13, 2010
Delivered 600 size D25B parcel buckets	December 13, 2010
Delivered 600 size D12C parcel buckets	December 13, 2010
Overhead track-conveyor system (1567′ non-contiguous linear section, 18 crossover points, weld supported at 6″ intervals)	
Installed at site	November 1, 2010
Final structural, functional checkout	November 8, 2010
Hardware (Group B):	
4 robot transporter units (each 300 pounds. maximum load capacity compatible with three-size parcel buckets, 380 Mh, retrieval at farthest point 8 minutes)	
Installed at site	November 8, 2010
Four unit functional checkout	November 10, 2010
Integration checkout, groups A and B	January 3, 2011

Software Group:

Submission of software specifications to CRC	September 19, 2010
(Installation of DEM-LAN network, four CRC2950 workstation terminals, and CRC4000 server, all performed by CRC)	February 7, 2011
(Software-integration checkout, performed by CRC)	March 7, 2011

Final checkout:

Two copies, system operation/maintenance manuals	March 7, 2011
Robot transporter/CRC4000 integration	April 4, 2011
Benchmark systems test, with parcels	April 8, 2011
User training	April 11–12, 2006
Final system checkout, user	Latest, May 2, 2006

INDEX

Note: Page references in *italics* refer to Figures and Tables

663

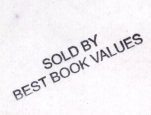